D1565987

A History and Ethnography of the Beothuk

The Beothuk, the aboriginal inhabitants of Newfoundland, were hunters, gatherers, and fishers who moved seasonally between the coast and the interior. With the influx of European settlements and fisheries in the 1700s the Beothuk found their territory increasingly reduced and conflict between the two groups escalated. The Beothuk declined steadily in numbers and by the early 1800s they had ceased to exist as a viable cultural group. Shanawdithit, the last of her people, died in 1829.

Following their extinction, the Beothuk came to be viewed as a people whose origins, history, and fate were shrouded in mystery. In recent years this view has been widely questioned and a new interest in this native group has emerged. On a quest to sort fact from fiction, Ingeborg Marshall, a leading expert on the Beothuk, has produced an elegant, comprehensive, and scholarly review of the history and culture of the Beothuk that incorporates an unmatched amount of new archival material with up-to-date archaeological data.

Part I documents the history of the Beothuk from the first European encounter in the 1500s to their demise. Marshall focuses on relations between Beothuk and English through the centuries and the reasons for change in Beothuk distribution and population size. She provides a highly readable and lucid account of the increasing competition between Beothuk and English for resources on the coast, the interferences of English trappers with Beothuk hunting activities, and the hostilities that resulted. She examines the conciliatory attempts of private citizens and naval officers to meet with the Beothuk, the taking of Beothuk captives, and factors, such as disease and starvation, that contributed to the decline of the population. Relations with Inuit, Montagnais, and Micmac are also discussed.

Part II is a comprehensive review of Beothuk culture. Each chapter focuses on an ethnographic theme, such as size and distribution of the Beothuk population, aspects of social organization, food consumption and subsistence economies, tools and ustensils, hunting and fishing techniques, appearance and clothing, dwellings, canoes and other means of transportation, burial practices, and fighting methods, as well as the Beothuk world view and language.

INGEBORG MARSHALL is an honorary research associate with the Institute of Social and Economic Research, Memorial University of Newfoundland.

Miniature portrait of "A female Red Indian of Nfld. 'Mary March' painted by W. Gosse at St John's Nfld. July '41 fm an original by Lady Hamilton May 1821 [1819]," which probably portrays Shanawdithit.

A History and Ethnography of the Beothuk

INGEBORG MARSHALL

McGill-Queen's University Press
Montreal & Kingston • London • Buffalo

ISBN 0-7735-1390-6

Legal deposit second quarter 1996
Bibliothèque nationale du Québec

Printed in Canada on acid-free paper
Reprinted 1997

This book has been published with the help of a grant from the Social Science Federation of Canada, using funds provided by the Social Sciences and Humanities Research Council of Canada.

McGill-Queen's University Press is grateful to the Canada Council for support of its publishing program.

Publication of this project was assisted jointly by the Government of Canada and the Province of Newfoundland through the Canada/Newfoundland Cooperation Agreement on Cultural Industries, and by the Association for Canadian Studies through funds made available by the Department of Canadian Heritage.

Canadian Cataloguing in Publication Data

Marshall, Ingeborg, 1929–
A history and ethnography of the Beothuk
Includes bibliographical references and index.
ISBN 0-7735-1390-6
1. Beothuk Indians – History. 2. Ethnology – Newfoundland.
I. Title
E99.B4M37 1996 971.8′004979 C96-900349-8

This book was typeset by Typo Litho Composition Inc. in 10/12 Times.

Contents

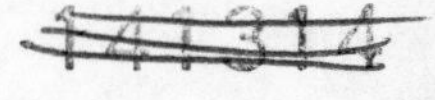

APPENDICES

PART TWO ETHNOGRAPHY

Tables, Maps, Graphs, and Sketches

TABLES

MAPS, GRAPHS, AND SKETCHES

Plates

Acknowledgments

The research for this book has been supported by a grant from the Social Sciences and Humanities Research Council of Canada and the Urgent Ethnology Division, National Museum of Civilization, Ottawa; also by grants from the Dean of Graduate Studies Fund, the Vice-President's Fund, and the Institute of Social and Economic Research (ISER), Memorial University of Newfoundland. Financial assistance for the writing and publication has been granted by the Association for Canadian Studies through funds made available by the Department of Canadian Heritage, by the Social Science Federation of Canada, using funds provided by the Social Sciences and Humanities Research Council of Canada, and by the Government of Canada and the Province of Newfoundland through the Canada/Newfoundland Cooperation Agreement on Cultural Industries. I am grateful to these agencies for their financial contributions.

A comprehensive study of this nature inevitably draws on the work of many scholars and writers from a variety of disciplines, and I wish to acknowledge my debt to all those who have, over the years, created the extensive knowledge base on which I have built. I have also benefited from the assistance and expertise of a large number of colleagues and friends without whose support this study could not have been completed.

More than any other people Marianne P. Stopp and W.H. Marshall deserve credit and sincere gratitude. Marianne Stopp has been an invaluable source of inspiration and encouragement and has reviewed, commented on, and edited several drafts of each chapter. W.H. Marshall has made himself available for discussions and has edited every section of the book.

I am also much indebted to Philip J. Cercone, executive director and chief editor at McGill-Queen's University Press, for taking on the publication of this work and for his support, to Joan McGilvray for orchestrating the publication process, and to Claire Gigantes for her skilful and sensitive editing, to Heather Ebbs for her extensive index, and to the typesetters for their excellent work. I also wish to thank the readers of McGill-Queen's University Press and of the

Grant in Aid of Publication Programme of the Canadian Federation for the Humanities for their helpful comments.

I wish to express profound gratitude to the late David Howley and to Consie Howley, St John's, for having graciously encouraged my work, and to the Howley family for having granted access to the papers of James Patrick Howley, author of *The Beothucks or Red Indians* (1915), and permission to publish selected items. I wish to thank John Cartwright, Johannesburg, South Africa, and his mother, the late Patricia Cartwright, for their generous hospitality and for allowing me to examine and copy some of the Cartwright family papers. My thanks are extended to Mrs L.H. Baxter, Westbury, UK, a member of the David Buchan family, for information on the Buchans, to Bodil Larsen for putting me in touch with Mrs Baxter, and to Regina O'Keefe, Manuels, for information on Shanawdidthit and W.E. Cormack. Special thanks are due to Don Locke, Grand Falls, who made his collection available to me and took me to Beothuk sites on the Exploits River, and to Marg Locke, who kindly provided hospitality.

I extend sincere thanks to the late F.A. Aldrich, Kirsten Alnaes, Selma Barkham, the late Hedi Brueckner, Elaine Harp, and Elmer Harp, Jr, and to Leslie Harris, for their assistance and support; to Richard E. Buehler for checking the bibliography, Gillian Cell for providing me with her transcript of Henry Crout's letter and permission to publish, Maxine Frecker for checking out Shanawdithit's family tree, John Hewson for reviewing the chapter on Beothuk language, Scott James for sharing his experience of building Beothuk-type canoes, William J. Kirwin for drawing my attention to the article "Sketches of savage life" by John McGregor, Charles A. Martijn for reviewing the chapters on relations between Beothuk and Micmac, Inuit, and Montagnais, Thomas Nemec for his advice and continued support, Ralph Pastore and James A. Tuck for giving me access to unpublished archaeological information and for reviewing the chapter on prehistory; to Helen Peters for her editorial work on the manuscript, Françoy Raynauld for generously making his research material available, K.B. Roberts for his advice, Peter Scott for information on flora and fauna, Lloyd Seaward for information on the performance of the Beothuk-type bark canoe he built, Adrian Tanner for reviewing the chapter on the Beothuk world view, Edward Thompkins for sharing his research material with me, and Ruth Holmes Whitehead for reviewing and commenting on specific chapters and supplying me with comparative material. I am also grateful to Robin Bartlett, Richard H. Ellis, Olaf Janzen, Peggy Hogan, Sonja Jerkic, Alan Macpherson, Alfred, Christopher, and Mary-Anne Marshall, Thomas Price, Hans Rollmann, the late Senator Frederick Rowe, D.W.S. Ryan, Cathy and John Sheldon, and other colleagues and friends for their assistance; and to Shane Mahoney and E. Mercer for information on caribou behaviour and on terrestial mammals, Bruce Atkinson on groundfish, John Chardine on seabirds, Gerry Ennis on shellfish, Gary Stenson on seals, Rex Porter on salmonids, John Lien on whales, and Oscar Forsay for figures on furs obtained between 1975 and 1984.

Archaeological work that I have drawn on is credited in the notes and in the bibliography. I appreciate that I was able to use the surveys and field notes of Helen Devereux, University of Toronto. Discussions and correspondence with graduates from Memorial University whose research has contributed to our knowledge of the prehistory and history of the Beothuk were also helpful: among them, Reginald Auger, Shaun Austin, Paul Carignan, Janet E. Chute, William Gilbert, Raymond J. LeBlanc, Laurie MacLean, Gerald Penney, Ken Reynolds, Doug Robbins, and Anna Sawicki.

I am also indebted to the curators, librarians, and archivists in institutions in St John's and elsewhere whose assistance has been invaluable. Particular thanks are due to the following: Memorial University of Newfoundland, Queen Elizabeth II Library, the Centre for Newfoundland Studies (CNS): Anne Hart, head, Joan Ritcey, librarian; CNS Archive: the late Nancy Grenville and Bert Riggs, archivists; Maritime History Archive (MHA): Heather Wareham and Roberta Thomas, archivists; Historic Resources Division of the Department of Tourism, Culture and Recreation: Martha Drake, provincial archaeologist; Newfoundland Museum: Kevin McAleese, curator of archaeology and ethnography, Susan Maunder, registrar, and John Maunder, curator of natural history; Provincial Archives of Newfoundland and Labrador (PANL): David Davis, provincial archivist, and archivists John Murphy, Photograph and Map Division, Howard Brown, Manuscript Division, Shelley Smith, Government Records, R. Calvin Best, Reference and Researcher Services; Provincial Reference and Resource Library (PRRL): Charles Cameron, division head, Joan Grandy, archivist; Methodist Archive, St John's: Burnham Gill, archivist; Mary March Museum, Grand Falls: Clifford Evans, director; National Archives of Canada, Ottawa (NAC): Patricia Kennedy, senior specialist in the State and Military Archive Program, Manuscript Division; Edward Dahl, early cartography specialist; Canadian Museum of Civilization, Hull: David L. Keenlyside, Atlantic Provinces archaeologist, and J. Garth Taylor, Central Algonkian ethnologist; also Kitty Bishop-Glover, Annette Clark, Louise Eastabrooks, Geneviève Eustache, Helen Montminy, and Rachel Perkins; McCord Museum, Montreal: Conrad Graham, curator; National Maritime Museum, Greenwich, UK: N.E. Upham, curator of models; National Museums of Scotland, Edinburgh, UK: Dale Idiens, curator of ethnography, and Maureen Barrie, curator; Museum of Mankind, London, UK: J.C.H. King, keeper; Völkerkundliches Museum, Vienna: Christian Feest, director. I also gratefully acknowledge assistance from countless unnamed staff members in institutions in Canada, the US, Britain, Germany, and Norway.

Credit is due to John Bourne and Patricia Adams, Photographic Service, and Eugene Ryan and John Crowell, Health Science Information Media Service, both at Memorial University of Newfoundland, for excellent photographic work; to Gary McManus, Cartographic Laboratory, Memorial University, for producing maps; and to Brian Payton and Cliff George for creating graphics.

Finally, I gratefully acknowledge the following for permission to publish maps, drawings, photographs, and paintings.

Public Record Office, Kew, UK: Lieut. David Buchan, "Sketch of the River Exploits as explor'd in Jan. and March 1811 Newfoundland," MPG.589, CO 194/50; Shanawdithit's drawing of a profile of a person, CO 194/68 f.250.

The British Library, London, UK: "Capt. David Buchan's Track into the Interior of Newfoundland undertaken in the month of January 1820 to open a communication with the Native Indians," 2 maps, MSS 51222, Add. 57703 f.1 and f.2,

The British Museum, London, UK: Photographs of birchbark meat dish, neg. CC6975; mug-shaped birchbark container, neg. CC6976; coat fringe, no.2583, neg.K 50762; netting tool from Beasley collection, neg.mm 028323.

The Archbishop of Canterbury and the Trustees of Lambeth Palace Library, London, UK: John Guy's sketch "The picture of the Savages canoa," MS NO. 250, f.412.

United Society for the Propagation of the Gospel, London, UK: Portrait of "Shanawdithit," engraving by W. Dickes, from *The Mission Field*, 1856.

Trustees of the National Museums of Scotland, Edinburgh, UK: Photographs of birchbark dish, UC 305, neg.10241; oval bark dish, UC 306, neg.10242; folded bark dish, UC 307, neg.10243; birchbark canoe replica, neg.0418.

National Maritime Museum, London, UK: Photographs of a birchbark canoe replica made by Shanawdithit, negs. C-5514 A, B-6075.

Ethnographic Museum of the University of Oslo, Norway: Photograph by Anne Christine Eek, Beothuk harpoon head, neg. EM 462.

The Honourable Michael Willoughby and the Department of Manuscripts, University of Nottingham, UK: [Transcript of] a letter from Henry Crout to Sir Percival Willoughby, 1613, MS Mi X 24.

Newfoundland Museum, St John's: Photographs of projectiles made from iron and harpoon head with metal blade; a wooden bowl; gaming pieces; combs; strings of discoidal beads; carved bone pendants; necklace of bone pendants and an animal tooth; four bark dishes; wooden figurine; two moccasins; two birchbark canoe replicas; Shanawdithit's sketch 6; figures on back of Shanawdithit's sketch 10; William Gosse's miniature portrait of "a female Red Indian," 1841.

Provincial Archives of Newfoundland and Labrador, Cartographic Section: John Cartwright, "A Sketch of the River Exploits the East End of Lieutenants Lake ... 1768," MG 100, Cartwright Collection.

Government of Newfoundland, Department of Tourism, Culture and Recreation, Canadian Museum of Civilization, Hull, and Helen Devereux, University of Toronto: Two drawings of the Beothuk site at Indian Point, Red Indian Lake, from Devereux MS 743, 1970:ii, and Fig. 5.

National Archives of Canada, Ottawa, Cartographic and Architectural Archives Division: John Cartwright, "A Sketch of the River Exploits and the East End of Lieutenants Lake in Newfoundland," NMC 27; John Cartwright, "A Map of the Island of Newfoundland," NMC 14033; Picture Division: Miniature portrait of Mary March [Demasduit], painted by Lady Hamilton in 1819, neg.C 87698.

Canadian Museum of Civilization, Hull: Photograph of carved bone pendants, sketch of end profile of canoe replica from Marshall, 1985.

Gillian Cell, Williamsburg, Virginia: Transcript of a letter from Henry Crout to Sir Percival Willoughby, 1613.

The late David Howley, St John's: Sketch of the interior of a room, presumed to have been drawn by Shanawdithit; J.P. Howley's map (1880s) of Beothuk caribou enclosures on Lloyd's River; J.P. Howley's photograph of a Beothuk figurine.

Raymond J. LeBlanc: "Plan of pentagonal house at the Wigwam Brook site," from 1973 Fig. 10.

Dennis Minty, St John's: Photograph of a full-sized Beothuk-type birchbark canoe.

Regina O'Keefe, Manuels: Photograph of braid of Shanawdithit's hair and of paper cuttings ("watch glasses") made by Shanawdithit.

Ralph Pastore, St John's: Photographs of the Boyd's Cove site and of Little Passage Indian tools from Inspector Island.

Gerald Penney, St John's: Photographs of the Brighton Tickle Island site, Triton Island, and of cave burial, Launch I, Long Island.

Ned Pratt, St John's: Photograph of native stone quarry in Bonavista Bay.

Anna Sawicki, Charlottetown: Photograph of bone needle from a beach burial near Musgrave Harbour.

Marianne Stopp, St John's: Photograph of burial site on Phillip's Island off Western Indian Island.

Ruth Holmes Whitehead, Halifax: Drawings of legging used as burial shroud and of two moccasins from child's burial, Big Island, Pilley's Tickle.

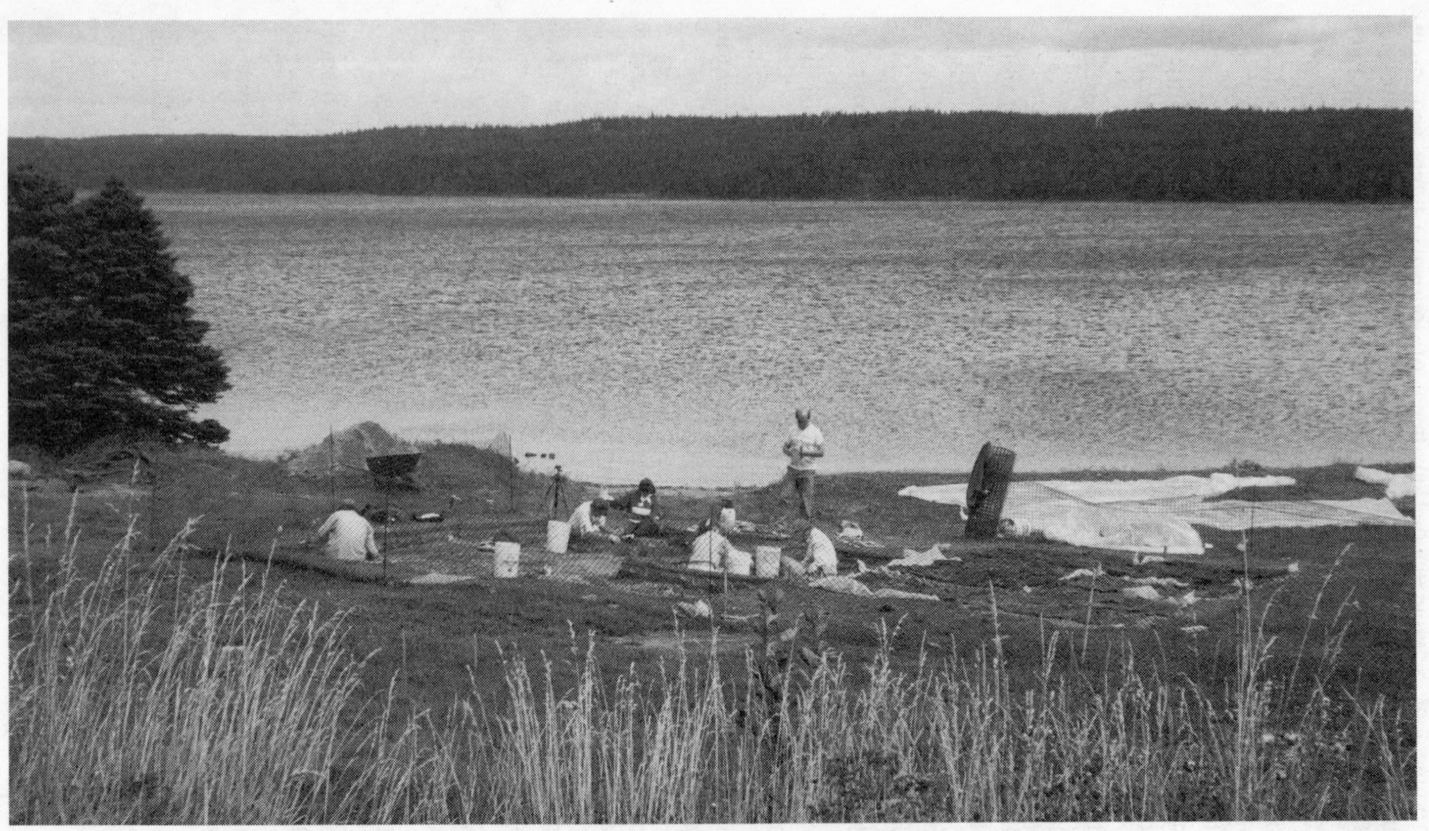

Plate 2.1 Excavation by William Gilbert and Ken Reynolds at Russel Point site, Dildo Pond, where John Guy found Beothuk dwellings.

Plate 9.1 John W. Hayward's Reproduction from Description of the painting of Beothuk and English trading, original painted by Miss Cuoran, 1808 (Howley 1915)

Plate 12.1 Miniature portrait of Mary March (Demasduit), painted by Lady Hamilton in 1819. (National Archives of Canada, neg.c87698)

A History and Ethnography of the Beothuk

Introduction

The Beothuk were the aboriginal inhabitants of Newfoundland at the time of the island's discovery by Europeans in 1497. They were hunters, gatherers, and fishers who moved seasonally in order to harvest coastal and inland resources. In spring and summer they lived on the coast, pursued marine mammals and seabirds, and caught salmon and other seafood; in fall and winter they moved to small camps or to settlements in the wooded interior, where they hunted caribou and other fur-bearing animals.

As an island population the Beothuk lived on the periphery of conflicts among continental native groups, and there is no evidence that they were involved in intertribal strife in Labrador or in the St Lawrence region. From the mid-sixteenth century onwards Beothuk became the target of attacks by Inuit parties from Labrador who crossed the Strait of Belle Isle to trade with the French. The Inuit fought from their watercraft and were said to have been formidable enemies. By the 1760s interaction had ceased.

Early in the sixteenth century, fishing fleets from England, Portugal, France, and Spain began to frequent the Newfoundland coast for the summer season to fish for cod. Their contacts with the native population were rarely recorded; the few meetings that have been described were hostile. In the seventeenth century, fishermen and planters from England settled on the Avalon Peninsula in southeastern Newfoundland, while French fishermen built stations along the south coast and up the Northern Peninsula. In the wake of the French, Micmac from Cape Breton Island, who may already have been visiting Newfoundland for the purpose of hunting and trapping, relocated to southern Newfoundland. Large groups of Montagnais from Labrador came to hunt and trap on the north and west coasts. Although the English and French occasionally encountered Beothuk, trade contacts were rare and no formalized exchange of goods or ideas took place. Throughout their coexistence with Europeans and other native populations in Newfoundland, the Beothuk remained relatively isolated and continued with many of their aboriginal traditions.

Archaeological evidence has shown that, before the arrival of Europeans, the prehistoric ancestors of the Beothuk ranged throughout the island. By the mid-

1700s, due to encroachment into their territory from all sides, the majority of Beothuk retreated to secluded harbours and islands in Notre Dame Bay, and to the watershed of the Exploits River and Red Indian Lake. The continued expansion of hunting and trapping activities into this region by the English and their opening of salmon stations in river mouths led to strife and acts of violence by Beothuk and English alike. Isolated incidents developed into an increasingly vicious cycle of retaliation. In these conflicts the Beothuk were outnumbered and, without guns, were unable to defend important food resources. Starvation, harassment by Europeans and by other native groups, and diseases brought from Europe contributed to a steady population decline.

At the end of the eighteenth century several private citizens, naval officers, and governors submitted proposals to British authorities to improve the situation of the Beothuk and to put an end to hostilities by English settlers. Decades passed before such plans were considered. Eventually, in the early 1800s, naval parties were sent to make contact with the Beothuk, but to no avail. Although captives were taken to be used as mediators, plans to return them to their people with messages of goodwill never materialized. Measures taken to appease the Beothuk were either ineffective or came too late to prevent the extinction of the tribe. Stragglers may have led a sequestered existence for a few more years, but the Beothuk as a viable cultural unit had ceased to exist by the late 1820s.

It is the demise of the Beothuk – at once the most distressing aspect of their history and the most complex – that has rooted itself most deeply in public consciousness. Oral traditions of violent interaction between Beothuk and English settlers that formerly flourished in the northern bays were later replaced by stories in which the Beothuk were characterised as mild and inoffensive forest dwellers who had been cruelly extirpated by Newfoundlanders. But the facts were elusive and lack of information led to the idea that the Beothuk were a people whose origin, history, and fate were shrouded in mystery.[1] In the last few decades the basis for these traditions has been widely questioned and a new interest in the Beothuk has emerged, inspiring scholarly investigations as well a poetry and fiction, the latter frequently centring around questions of blame and guilt.[2]

In order to sort fact from fiction I began a search for reliable documentation. This started in a small way but gradually became more engrossing and wider in scope, until I decided to make it as comprehensive as possible, not only reviewing known material but also searching museums, archives, and libraries in North America and Europe to discover new information (see Appendix 5). Collections in private hands and private papers in possession of families whose forebears had been closely connected with the Beothuk were also targeted. Although I often found myself at a dead end, the search nevertheless brought to light a substantial amount of new information. Studies for a master's degree in Anthropology/Archaeology at Memorial University offered ample opportunity for examining Beothuk artifacts and for assessing reports and theses on Beothuk culture and on archaeological investigations. I also made a point of visiting every known Beothuk campsite and burial place and went on field surveys with the purpose of discovering Beothuk remains. The collection of data has taken close to twenty years but all avenues of enquiry have borne fruit. In the course of my research and writing I integrated the new documentation with previously known material and analyzed, sorted, and interpreted all accumulated data.

The source material that I have collected can be divided into four major categories, each contributing specific information while at the same time presenting its own problems: 1) Beothuk artifacts; 2) information solicited from Beothuk captives; 3) archaeological data from site reports, carbon-date files, theses, and published papers; and 4) unpublished and published contemporary reports, notes, correspondence, log books, maps, and newspaper accounts.

1) Artifacts that were produced by the Beothuk are an important component of the source material. However, few items made of perishable raw materials such as skin, bone, and bark still exist; known collections contain mostly stone and iron tools that represent only a fraction of the Beothuk's material culture. To compensate for this limitation, every effort has been made to locate and examine all existing artifacts and to extract additional information on Beothuk material culture from contemporary records. Since the artifacts that have been preserved were almost exclusively found on excavated campsites or in burial places, and since their usage has not been observed, the purpose of some of them had to be deduced. Such deductions, often done in comparison with the usage of similar objects by other native groups, give clues but may fall short of providing an understanding of the full significance the objects held for the Beothuk.

2) Another category of first-hand evidence is information obtained from Beothuk captives. The chief informant was the Beothuk woman Shanawdithit, captured in 1823, who was questioned by William E. Cormack, founder of the "Boeothick Institution." In his enquiries Cormack appears to have focused on the decline of the Beothuk tribe and on Beothuk interactions with the English; in a series of drawings, Shanawdithit has depicted several encounters of this sort. However, since they were done at Cormack's request it is possible that Shanawdithit presented an expurgated version of what she knew. She also produced drawings of Beothuk artifacts that Cormack annotated; some of the items are not adequately explained. Cormack never published this information, though some of his notes were published anonymously in an 1836 article in Britain. Certain clues indicate that the author was Cormack's friend John McGregor, with whom Cormack stayed after he left Newfoundland in 1829. For example, the authors refers in a footnote to his book *British America* (1832), in which he had discussed a specific topic at length.[3] The section "Shaa-naan-dithit ... the last of the Boeothics" in the 1836 article contains information on Shanawdithit's personal history and on belief-related practices of her people; it also makes reference to Mr Cormack, who "gleaned whatever she recollected relative to her tribe." Cormack seems to have left these notes with McGregor;

hence their absence from the Cormack material that found its way back to Newfoundland, probably through the efforts of the Honourable Joseph Noad, Surveyor General of Newfoundland. In a lecture he gave on the Beothuk in the early 1850s, Noad included information that could only have come from Cormack's notes. These notes later became available to J.P. Howley, who published all information that was directly relevant to Beothuk history and culture as well as ten of Shanawdithit's drawings in his classic work *The Beothucks or Red Indians* (1915). The drawings are now in the collection of the Newfoundland Museum; the Cormack papers are in private hands; some of the notes published by Howley are missing. The information gathered by Cormack and published by McGregor and Howley is considered to be as reliable as one can hope for under the circumstances and is accepted in this book as an authentic primary source.

There are also some lists of Beothuk words obtained from the Beothuk women Shanawdithit and Demasduit, and from the child Oubee. The words appear to have been solicited by pointing to an object or activity and then writing down the Beothuk term. Since the recorders were unfamiliar with the Beothuk sound system and since the captives could easily have misunderstood which word was sought, these vocabularies contain many inconsistencies. They also lack verb forms and grammatical and structural information; even the most skilful linguistic analysis cannot fully compensate for the limitations of the material and for the inadequate recording.

3) Archaeological surveys and excavations, largely undertaken in the last three decades, have provided information on Beothuk origin and an approximate time frame for their presence in many areas of Newfoundland. They have also disclosed some tangible evidence for the size of the Beothuk population as a whole, and for the size and distribution of bands. In addition, artifacts and site investigations have enabled archaeologists to infer details of subsistence economies and burial practices, and to obtain insights into techniques used in the manufacture of tools and the construction of houses. However, many archaeological data are unpublished and hard to gain access to, and it is sometimes difficult to draw conclusions from raw data such as field notes on archaeological investigations.

4) Contemporary reports, correspondence, maps, notes, and newspaper accounts constitute the bulk of the source material. The most important publication of source material and an indispensible tool for the Beothuk scholar is J.P. Howley's *The Beothucks or Red Indians*. The book was first published in 1915 by Cambridge University Press and was reprinted in facsimile editions in 1974 and 1980; it is currently out of print. Howley not only assembled contemporary accounts but also collected Beothuk artifacts, which he preserved in the Geological Museum in St John's, recorded traditional stories about the Beothuk that circulated among residents in northern Newfoundland, and corresponded with linguists and other scholars to bring Beothuk material to their attention. Howley found and published some of William E. Cormack's papers, which included information obtained from the Beothuk Shanawdithit and eleven of her

drawings. Howley's work will remain a classic in the field. Indeed, his compilation has often been thought to represent all the information there is, which has discouraged researchers from looking for further documentation. However, Howley made no attempt to interpret the material or place it within an historical context; nor did he piece together the ethnographic information that is buried in the documents to elucidate Beothuk culture. In addition, he was unable to confirm the written evidence with archaeological data, since most investigations of this nature did not begin until the 1960s.

One comprehensive source of information that Howley tapped is the correspondence between Newfoundland governors and the Board of Trade, the secretary of state, and other officials in the Colonial Office in Britain. The private papers of some of these high-ranking British officials also contain pertinent material, as do the papers of naval officers or private persons who were particularly interested in the Beothuk, such as the earl of Liverpool, president of the Council for Trade and Plantations (1786–1804) and later secretary of state for the colonies, and those of Lieut. John Cartwright, an officer in the Royal Navy. Admiralty papers and ships' logs are apt to provide only small details; contemporary manuscript maps, while inaccurate geographically, include instructive features. Some nineteenth-century newspaper articles have also been informative.

The majority of archival documents used in this study were consulted in the original, even if they had been published. This verification covered the texts of most of the records reproduced in J.P. Howley's work.

Among a host of familiar problems with documentary evidence, particularly in the case of sixteenth-century accounts, is the difficulty of locating an event geographically since few of the early records include geographic information or maps. Similarly, it is not always possible to identify a specific native group when a generalized term such as "savages" or "naturells of the country" is used; these terms could refer to Beothuk as well as to Inuit or other native people. Also, the time lag between the occurrence of an event and its subsequent recording often results in inaccuracy. A number of records are incomplete, selective, or distorted and allowances have to be made for these defects. For this reason every attempt has been made to obtain confirmatory evidence for important points and to take into consideration the context in which a report was written and the reliability of the writer.

In theory, after establishing the validity of a set of documents, the historian proceeds to develop an interpretation of the past that is logical and consistent with all evidence.[4] However, a major problem with the interpretation of Beothuk history is that most of the available material consists of records kept by Europeans who not only consistently presented a one-sided picture but tended to be ethnocentric because they considered the value system and way of life of native populations to be inferior to their own. With rare exceptions, not even the more enlightened and well meaning perceived native people as their equals. Europeans also rarely acknowledged that the Beothuk had been deprived of territory and resources without justification or compensation and therefore had good reason to be suspicious, hostile, and revengeful. Although some observers deplored the atrocities that were perpetrated against the native population, they generally ignored the fact that hunting expeditions and the setting up of salmon stations by the English amounted to "stealing the Beothuk's livelihood." The Beothuk's appropriation of settlers' tools or gear has consistently been labelled pilfering or stealing; yet to the Beothuk it may have been a courageous act of retaliation. Not until 1828 was a Beothuk, the captive Shanawdithit, questioned about her people in the context of European encroachment and about guiding principles and values within her culture. As a result the Beothuk voice is nearly absent from the records. This substantial imbalance in the documentation has prevented a proper evaluation of the majority of the (English) records against evidence from the Beothuk. To compensate, quotation marks and other devides have been used to remind the reader of the ethnocentricity inherent in accounts by the English and of the need to see these accounts in the context of attitudes about native people that were prevalent at that time. But such devices can do little more than reduce bias in the interpretation; they cannot replace the missing Beothuk voice.

Despite the limitations and shortcomings of the available information, the history and ethnography of the Beothuk as presented here is an authentic record of events involving the Beothuk and an up-to-date review of their cultural traits and practices. Part of the value of the work lies in the incorporation of a hitherto unmatched amount of archival material with the lastest archaeological data.

Part One of the book presents a history of the Beothuk from the time they were first encountered by Europeqans in the 1500s to their demise in the late 1820s. The focus of this chronological account is the relation between Beothuk and English through the centuries and causes of change in Beothuk distribution and population size. The narrative covers the increasing competition between Beothuk and English for resources on the coast, the interference of English trappers with Beothuk hunting activities in the interior, and the resulting hostilities, particularly in the late eighteenth century. Also discussed are conciliatory attempts by private citizens and naval officers to meet with Beothuk, the taking of Beothuk captives, attitudes of the clergy towards the native people, and the various factors touched upon here that contributed to the decline of the Beothuk population. The Micmac's parallel encroachment on Beothuk territory and the increasingly hostile relations between the two are also addressed, as are Beothuk relations with Inuit and Montagnais.

Although the records from different disciplines have been integrated chronologically, specific topics are discussed separately to present a comprehensive picture of each theme; this has inevitably resulted in some overlap. Because of the meagre documentation, reconstruction of events between the sixteenth and early eighteenth centuries is sketchier and more speculative than the account of events in the late eighteenth and early nineteenth centuries, where the records are more extensive. A certain amount of commentary and interpretation is included in the text, but there is much room for further analysis. However, since the aim of this study was to bring together and present as much basic data as could be gathered, such elaborations are left to future studies.

After positioning the Beothuk among the prehistoric inhabitants of, and visitors to, Newfoundland, Part Two presents a review of Beothuk practices and cultural traits. Each chapter focuses on an ethnographic theme such as distribution, subsistence economies, transportation, and language. The advantage of this approach is that each chapter constitutes a complete survey of what is known about a particular aspect of Beothuk culture and can therefore be consulted independently. Since direct input from Beothuk is limited, the topics in this section are confined to those for which reasonably reliable information is available. In discussing cultural traits I have drawn on comparable practices of other native groups so as to place the Beothuk in the North American aboriginal context. Comparisons were also made to identify cultural traits that may have been unique to the Beothuk. It has been my aim to collect as much ethnographic material as possible from primary sources, artifacts, and archaeological investigations, and to integrate and present this material in a systematic and focused manner. Analysis of cultural dynamics and theoretical discussions are considered to be beyond the scope of this work. The two parts of the book, although independent, complement each other. In order to obtain the most complete information possible on any given topic a reader may need to refer to both.

The book is illustrated with modern and contemporary maps, portraits of Beothuk women, and photographs of Beothuk artifacts, burial places, and campsites. The latter not only show the different types of location that Beothuk chose for camps and for the disposal of their dead but also convey an impression of the environment in which they lived. Illustrations of Beothuk artifacts such as a coat fringe, canoe replicas, bone tools, and decorated birchbark containers demonstrate the type of objects that have been preserved. From the collections of stone and iron tools and of carved bone pendants – altogether more than four hundred bone carvings in various stages of preservation have been collected – only representative samples are included. Of particular importance and interest is the set of maps and drawings by the captive Shanawdithit, which is reproduced *in toto* (nine of them are copies from Howley's monograph); it is the only record of its kind.

PART ONE

History

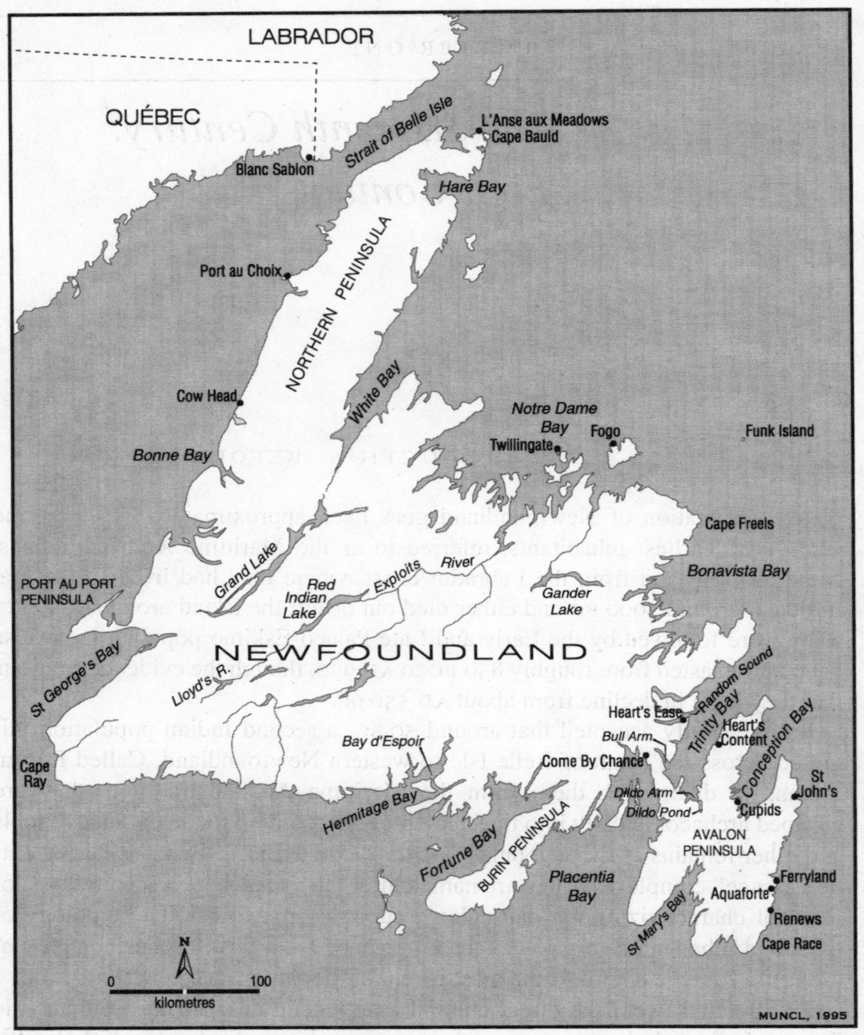

Fig 1.1 Map of Newfoundland

CHAPTER ONE

The Sixteenth Century: First Contact

INTRODUCTION: BEFORE CONTACT

Native occupation of Newfoundland goes back approximately five thousand years. The earliest inhabitants, referred to as the Maritime Archaic Indians, came to the island from the Labrador coast, where they had lived for several millenia, around 3000 BC and either died out or left the island around 1050 BC. They were followed by the Early and Late Palaeo-Eskimo populations, whose occupation lasted from roughly 850 BC to AD 950, though the evidence suggests that they were in decline from about AD 550 on.

It is generally accepted that around 50 BC, a second Indian population migrated across the Strait of Belle Isle to western Newfoundland. Called Recent Indians to distinguish them from the Maritime Archaic tradition, they are grouped archaeologically into three complexes according to the distinctive tools and other remains of these populations: the "Cow Head," "Beaches," and "Little Passage" complexes. They are named after the sites where a specific type of material characterizing the particular group was first found. The typology of tools and other indicators places the emergence from the Beaches complex of the Little Passage complex, the most recent of the three, at ca. AD 1100-1200.

The Beothuk were the direct cultural and genetic descendants of the Little Passage Indians. Indeed, they were the same population; for purposes of classification, however, Beothuk denotes the historic phase of this people – that is, the period coinciding with the written history, beginning around AD 1500, of Newfoundland and its inhabitants. There is no sharp ethnohistorical line between the prehistoric Little Passage Indians and their historic descendants. While we are not certain of their geographic distribution (see chapter 16), Beothuk congregated at campsites established by the Little Passage Indians, whose remains have been excavated in all major bays and along the Exploits River and at Red Indian Lake. Their subsistence economy was marine based, supplemented by inland hunting, though some Beothuk bands developed an interior orientation in pursuit of migrating caribou. The stone tools used by Beothuk and Little Passage Indians are almost identical, though they were modified in size and shape over time. With the introduction of iron, the Beothuk produced fewer stone tools and by the mid-eighteenth century were making most of their tools from iron implements.

A fuller account of the prehistoric habitation of Newfoundland, from Maritime Archaic Indians to the Beothuk, can be found in Part Two (chapter 16). But at the time Newfoundland was discovered by Europeans around AD 1500, the Beothuk are believed to have been the only permanent residents on the island. Other native groups may have travelled now and then to certain areas in Newfoundland to exploit resources. Micmac, for example, may have visited the south coast to trap or fish, and Montagnais may intermittently have hunted on the Northern Peninsula. To date, however, there is no evidence of persistent prehistoric residence in Newfoundland of Micmac or Montagnais. Thus, when the Europeans made their first approaches in the sixteenth century, the Beothuk would have had the island more or less to themselves.

THE HISTORIC PERIOD: EARLY RECORDS OF NATIVE PEOPLE IN NEWFOUNDLAND

Information on encounters between Europeans and native people in Newfoundland in the sixteenth century is exceedingly sparse and what data are available may not be reliable. Either there was little contact or the relevant records are no longer extant. Most references to native populations are found in printed accounts of explorations, but because these accounts were often published long after the event, they are liable to contain errors or to incorporate extraneous information from unidentified sources. When reviewed critically, few provide more than a general idea of the appearance and subsistence of northeastern Indians. European observers were often biased towards their own cultural concepts and tended to describe the natives' appearance rather than cultural features by which one ethnic group could be differentiated from another. In addition, even careful navigators were not always able to state the precise location at which they met native people so that places named in documents are rarely fully authenticated.

Sixteenth-century information on the distribution of native people on the island does suggest, however, that they occupied the south coast west of Cape Race, the east and north-east coast between Cape Race and the Strait of Belle Isle, and the west coast of the country, particularly St Georges Bay.

In this chapter the documents that claim to pertain to Newfoundland Indians are scrutinized with regard to their content as well as their authenticity, so as to establish how far they can be considered valid observations of Beothuk.

THE CABOTS AND CÔRTE REAL

On his first exploratory trip to the New World in 1497, John Cabot is believed to have reached Newfoundland.[1] Though Cabot did not make contact with native people he found signs of human habitation close to the shore: snares, a needle for making nets, and felled trees.[2] His second voyage in 1498 is poorly documented. While some records suggest that he brought native people back to England and presented them to King Henry VII, the natives who were introduced at court may actually have been captured in 1501 by Bristol merchants.[3] Cabot's son, Sebastian, returned to the New World in 1508–09 and brought home with him "sundry people" and many other things from the country called "Bacallaos."[4] Yet descriptions of these people by Peter Martyr (1530) and in the inscription on Cabot's World Map (1544), being of such a late date, may incorporate information collected by other explorers in different locations, particularly by Côrte Real.

According to the accounts the captured natives resembled their European captors, although their complexion was generally darker. They used body paint, their language was unintelligible to the Europeans, and their demeanour was that of "brute beasts."[5] However, it has also been said that when the three Indians who were brought to England exchanged their fur robes for the apparel of Englishmen they could no longer be recognized as "savages." In their home environment, the native people were said to hunt and fish, using bows and arrows, spears, darts, slings, and wooden clubs. They also gathered plant foods. Their houses were made of timber and covered with the skins of fish (seal) and beasts.[6] They were said to go naked in summer and to clothe themselves in winter with furs. They prayed to the sun, moon, and other idols, had silver and copper bracelets, and a store of "latten" (a metal of yellow colour).[7] Some of them were said to have consumed human flesh but to have concealed this activity from their chief.

While the appearance and practices of these people are consistent with what we know about Beothuk, the recorded information is equally applicable to other northeastern Indians and is simply too general to identify a specific ethnic group.

Three years after John Cabot had returned from his second voyage, the Portuguese explorer Gaspar de Côrte Real passed through the Strait of Belle Isle from south to north. He landed, in 1501, on either the Newfoundland or the Labrador side of the strait and found the land well populated. Though the native people had neither gold nor precious stones, commodities that he had hoped to find, they were healthy and strong and considered to be fit for every kind of labour. Rather than leaving the land empty handed, Côrte Real captured fifty men and women and brought them back to Portugal.

Information on these captives has been preserved in letters written by Alberto Cantino and Pietro Pasqualigo, who were present when one of Côrte Real's ships returned. Cantino actually went to see them though he was not able to communicate with them.[8] Additional information is given in the chronicle of Côrte Real's voyage by Damiano Gois, published in 1566.[9] Both Cantino and Pasqualigo thought that the captives looked tanned and resembled Gypsies but otherwise did not substantially differ from the Portuguese. They were tall or of middle stature, they had long black hair and well-proportioned limbs and bodies, and their faces were "punctured" – possibly tattooed. They were of a gentle disposition and given to laughter. The garments of the natives consisted of loincloths and furs that were draped over their shoulders. The hairy side was worn outward in summer and reversed in winter. Lacking iron, they had knives and arrow points of stone and spears made of burnt pieces of wood. A piece of metal from a broken sword and two silver rings in their possession were thought to indicate that they had traded with other Europeans. Beyond the practice of divination and a close heterosexual association resembling European marriage, their social organization and religious beliefs were thought to be "poorly developed" or nonexistent.

The native people described in these letters would have been northeastern Indians rather than Inuit, who wore tailored clothing and did not drape furs over their shoulders as the Indians did. However, lack of reference to other specific traits prevents further identification of their ethnic origin.

OTHER EARLY SIXTEENTH-CENTURY SOURCES

Of the many English fishing vessels that spent a summer in Newfoundland waters, one is recorded to have brought back from "Terra Nova" a bow made of red wood (or of wood painted red) and two red arrows. This record is dated 1503.[10] In 1508–09, a French fishing crew captured seven native people in a birchbark canoe on the ocean east of Newfoundland and took them to Rouen. Three accounts of natives captured at sea may refer to this one incident, or they may refer to two different events. The accounts were published by Eusebius in 1518, Bembo in 1551, and Crignon in 1556.[11] According to the first two, the natives had coarse black hair and facial markings but no facial hair. Their loincloths and garments were made of bear, deer (caribou), or seal skins, and their hunting tools consisted of bows strung with roots or sinews, and of arrows fitted with stone or bone points. They ate broiled meat and drank water. Their captors were unable to communicate with them and were of the opinion that they had neither money nor religion.

Since these seven individuals were travelling in a birchbark canoe east of Newfoundland, though rather far out to sea, it is possible that they were Newfoundland Beothuk. Facial decorations or tattoos, already noted by Côrte Real, seem to have been applied by many northeastern Indians and may also have been customary among sixteenth-century Beothuk, though later records do not mention this feature.[12]

Bembo's report differs in that the seven natives who were travelling in a birchbark boat were picked up not far from England. They had scar-like marks and wore garments made from skins of different spotted fish (seal) and "diadems of painted straw with seven ear-like objects woven into them." They also consumed raw meat and drank blood. Six of them died shortly after their arrival in France, but a surviving boy was brought to the king. This account is ambiguous because the spotted-fish (sealskin) clothing and the eating of raw meat would suggest Inuit and the birchbark canoe would point to Indians, while the exotic head dress cannot be traced to any specific group.

A brief account of the inhabitants of Newfoundland recorded by John Rastell around 1519 claims that they worshipped the sun, lived in small caves or wooden shelters rather than houses, and dressed in animal skins. They were not familiar with iron but used copper, which they found on the surface of the ground.[13] Since Rastell does not describe more distinctive features, it is assumed his information was derived from Newfoundland fishermen or from reports by earlier explorers. Its authenticity cannot be verified.

The explorer Giovanni da Verazzano came to Newfoundland in 1524 but did not meet any Beothuk.[14] Verazzano traded with what were probably Cape Breton Island Indians as well as other Indians farther south. His experience with the former is of interest in this context because occasionally Cape Breton Indians have been likened to Newfoundland Beothuk.[15] Verazzano considered the Cape Breton Indians to be crude and barbarous. In exchange for his goods they accepted only knives, fish hooks, and sharp metals, and to scorn his men they laughingly showed them their buttocks. When a party of his men ignored the Indian's objections and disembarked to explore the country, the Indians shot at them. In Verazzano's opinion, they compared poorly with the native people farther south who had most civil customs, and who had led his ship to safe anchorage and been generous to the point of giving away all they had.

Another party that passed the Newfoundland shores in the 1520s but probably did not contact Beothuk was that of the Spaniard Estavao Gomes.[16] Gomes first investigated the Penobscot River in Maine and then sailed northward as far as Cape Race, Newfoundland. Before returning home, he captured fifty-eight Indians. A messenger who heard about Gomes's landing in Coruna, Spain, spread the news that Gomes had brought cloves (*clavos*) instead of slaves (*esclavos*), which caused much laughter once the mistake was discovered. Some authors have assumed that Gomes had captured the Indians in Newfoundland, but, taking all available information into account, they most likely were taken at the Penobscot River.[17]

The capture and enslavement of native people was the likeliest cause of hostile reactions from Indians towards fishing crews and other visitors. For example, in 1527 the crew of the English ship *Mary Guildford* encountered hostility after entering the coastal waters either of Newfoundland or of Labrador. Of the two records that refer to this incident, one claims that their pilot died. Navigational clues suggest that this occurred well north of Newfoundland. The second document states that their pilot was killed by Indians when a small party went ashore in a boat to find a suitable landing place.[18] Since it does not pinpoint the position of the ship at that time, there is only a slender chance that the hostile natives were Beothuk.

JACQUES CARTIER AT BLANC SABLON

While exploring the Strait of Belle Isle and the Gulf of St Lawrence in 1534, Cartier met Indians on the Labrador coast near Blanc Sablon.[19] They were well-built "savage folk" who painted their bodies with tan colours. Their garments were made of furs. The women wrapped the furs more tightly around themselves than did the men and used belts. These Indians wore their hair twisted up on top of the head, secured by a nail and decorated with feathers. They had come in birchbark canoes "from warmer countries" to fish, hunt seal, and collect other foodstuffs.

From the area of Blanc Sablon Cartier proceeded southward along the west coast of Newfoundland, but he did not make contact with Indians there. If he had seen any native people in Newfoundland on earlier voyages, we have no record of it.[20]

The tribal identity of the Indians encountered near Blanc Sablon is still a matter of controversy. Howley thought they were Beothuk because the Beothuk, it was said, had travelled to southern Labrador, used birchbark canoes, and painted their bodies with ochre.[21] But these characteristics were not exclusively those of the Beothuk. Birchbark canoes were a common means of transportation among Indians, and body paint was applied by many northeastern tribes.[22] Rogers and Leacock believe that Cartier met Montagnais/Naskapi, who lived in the vicinity of Blanc Sablon and habitually came to the coast.[23] Hoffman argues that the Indians described by Cartier would have been Iroquois.[24] Their Iroquoian identity is also favoured by Martijn, who quotes the statements of two Basque eyewitnesses as evidence.[25] The first statement comes from the Basque Lefant, who had met and traded for furs with Indians in the Gulf of St Lawrence in 1537. He said that they understood French, English, and the language spoken in Gascon. These linguistic skills, indicating previous contacts with several European nations, do not fit with what we know of the Beothuk but could have been acquired by Montagnais as well as Iroquois.[26] The second statement was made by the Basque shipowner Odelica in 1542. Indians who had come on board his vessel in the Strait of Belle Isle and had eaten and traded with his men claimed that one of their group was chief in "Canada" and that they had killed more than thirty-five of Cartier's men. This information would point to Iroquois, who were hostile to the French.[27] In addition to these accounts, a potsherd from an Iroquoian-style vessel, found on the Basque site at Red Bay in a sixteenth-century stratum, was until recently considered to be further evidence.[28] However, neutron-activation analysis by Chapdelaine and Kennedy has since shown that the sherd came from a vessel that could have been made by a northern Algonquian group but not the Beothuk, who did not produce pottery.[29]

The different arguments and conflicting evidence indicate that the present state of knowledge is inadequate for identifying the tribal affiliation of the Indians described by Cartier beyond a shadow of doubt. What can be extrapolated from the records is that Labrador's southern shore was probably exploited by a number of native groups who visited specific locations at different times.

ACCOUNTS BY HOARE, CRIGNON, AND ALPHONSE

Encouraged by reports of amicable contact with Indians, a Master Hoare from England organized a voyage of discovery for a party of gentlemen who "wanted to see the strange things of the world."[30] Their ship left Gravesend in April 1536 and after two months at sea arrived at Cape Breton. From there it sailed to Penguin Island, which is believed to have been Funk Island, at fifty degrees latitude and proceeded to the Newfoundland shore, probably Bonavista Bay.[31] When "savages" approached the ship, everybody on board wanted to "take a view of the naturall people of the country" and the crew launched a boat to capture them. The Indians, presumably Beothuk, fled. At their camp on shore, the crew found a side of bear roasting on a wooden spit, a decorated leather boot, and a winter mitten.[32]

In 1529, on a voyage half way around the world, the brothers Jean and Raoul Parmentier from Dieppe visited the Strait of Belle Isle. This journey was recorded in an "Account of a voyage conducted in 1529 to the New World ...," which is attributed to Crignon, an experienced sea captain also from Dieppe, who is thought to have taken part in the voyage.[33] Crignon's description of Indians in Newfoundland appears to be based on several sources, probably interspersed with information collected by himself. He states that the coast between Cape Race and Cape Breton, that is, the Newfoundland south coast, was well populated by cruel and austere people with whom it was impossible to trade or to converse.[34] They were tall and dressed in skins of seal and other animals tied together. They painted themselves with a dark brown substance, marked their faces with lines by applying fire, and gathered the long hair on their heads like a horse's tail. Their weapons consisted of bows and arrows tipped with stone or fishbone. The east coast of Newfoundland, running north from Cape Race to the Strait of Belle Isle, was less-densely populated. The people who lived there were smaller and friendlier.

Crignon's contention that the native people on the south coast were taller and less friendly than those who lived on the east coast has introduced the idea that two different populations lived on the island. Hoffman believed that the south coast was inhabited by Indians and the east coast by Inuit. Another author suggested that the Indians on the south coast could have been Micmac and those on the east coast Beothuk.[35] Neither of these interpretations is supported by archaeological or historic evidence (see Part Two). Inuit remains on the Newfoundland east and north-east coast predate the sixteenth century, and there are no archaeological or historical records of an extensive Micmac presence in southern Newfoundland before 1600. A likelier explanation would be that the behaviour of the Indians differed. Those on the south coast, including Placentia

Bay, were extensively disturbed by the fishery on the Grand Banks and may have become hostile within a relatively short time. In the eastern bays, Beothuk appear initially to have been less affected by European fishing crews and remained approachable into the early 1600s.[36]

Describing the subsistence of the inhabitants during the fishing season from spring through the summer, Crignon recorded that they hunted mainly seal and porpoise for oil and caught seabirds on islands: "Numerous excellent cod fisheries along this coast, [are prosecuted]… only by the French and Bretons *since the natives do not fish for them*" (emphasis added).[37] Crignon's is the only account that expressly states that the Indians in Newfoundland did not fish for cod. He said that they lived in bark-covered huts and houses during the summer; with the approach of winter, they returned with their catch in birchbark boats to "warmer countries but we know not where." Since Crignon's reference to warmer countries and his description of the Indians' hairstyle are almost identical to those in Cartier's earlier report, it is possible that he copied this information from Cartier.[38]

Generally, by the 1540s a negative image of the Beothuk had been formed. Jean Alphonse de Saintonge, who accompanied Jean-François de la Rocque de Roberval on his voyage to northeastern Canada in 1542–43, described the Newfoundland Indians as "evil folk" who lived on fish, meat from wild beasts, and the fruits of trees and "have no more God than the beasts."[39] They were large people with a dark complexion similar to the inhabitants of Cape Breton Island, in contrast to the people on the St Lawrence who were "of our size." He also reported that the Newfoundland Indians were called Tabios, a term that is unidentifiable. Since Alphonse appears to have been familiar with Newfoundland, which had, he said, the best harbours of all the places he had visited, his account should be given some weight.

DESCRIPTIONS BY JEHAN MALLART AND ANDRÉ THEVET

Around 1545–47 Jehan Mallart, a Dutchman, commented that the natives in Newfoundland were tall men with fine bodies who lived on fruit, fish, and uncooked meat. He also claimed that they had dogs.[40] Since we have no idea how Mallart collected this information, and since the Beothuk cooked their food and have not otherwise been associated with dogs, it is doubtful whether Mallart's tale is authentic.

It is worth noting that the Europeans who actually saw Beothuk or had occasional contact with them would in most cases have been local fishermen, rather than the explorers or navigators who committed descriptions of native people to paper. More often than not, the latter appear to have picked up snippets of information that circulated among fishing crews, but they did not investigate native populations themselves. As a result, much of what has been recorded is likely to be hearsay and bound to contain inaccuracies, misunderstandings, or embellishments.

A case in point is André Thevet's description of Newfoundland's inhabitants. Thevet wrote that he gathered his material from a Spanish captain and a French fisherman, and he evidently also used other sources.[41] According to Thevet, Newfoundland was sparsely inhabited by "inhuman" and "intractable" people who dressed in skins of large animals and sealskins. Those who lived on the coast subsisted mainly on fish but also caught porpoise and dogfish and collected lobsters, mussels, and oysters. They ate seal meat and drank reddish oil, which they rendered from seal fat. To prevent polar bears from attacking their houses, the natives made pits covered with leaves or branches (presumably traps). They practised common ownership and lived by the law of nature. Those who lived far from the sea gathered the fruits of the land but had no agriculture.

Thevet also informs us that Newfoundland natives did not engage in warfare unless they were attacked. They defended themselves in the manner of the "Canadians" (St Lawrence Indians) who lived close to Cartier's fort in Quebec. Their weapons were bows and arrows and they incited their warriors to do battle by beating circular drums. These drums were made of stretched skin, had deer bone "fleusters" (knuckles) to produce the sound, and were similar to those of the Canadians.[42] Their leader dressed in fine skins and feathers and was carried on the shoulders of two powerful men ahead of the fighters, "so that all will recognize him and will be prompt in obeying him." After a victory the leader was honoured, and the war party returned with banners and branches decorated with feathers.[43] These natives collected the facial skins and hair of their enemies and stretched them on circular frames.

In a later manuscript Thevet repeated some of this information but added that the religion of the people in Newfoundland was comparable to that of the "Canadians," that they used red and blue colouring substances on their skin, imposed strong justice, and formerly had been cannibals. They were also said to have caught good salmon in the Bay of Chaleur.[44]

Much of what Thevet wrote had been recorded in earlier sources, while other details such as the existence of common ownership, the enactment of justice, and war practices including the use of drums were new. According to the historian Biggar, Thevet was unfamiliar with the local situation and was not scrupulous in differentiating between information from a variety of geographic areas occupied by different ethnic groups. Though some of his colourful description is compatible with what we know about the Beothuk, the Indians of his accounts do not emerge as people whose cultural traits clearly identify them as Beothuk.

MEETINGS AND TRADE BETWEEN SIXTEENTH-CENTURY FISHING CREWS AND NEWFOUNDLAND INDIANS

While early sixteenth-century records of the Newfoundland fishery are sketchy, one can nevertheless conclude that a modest fishing trade had been established by 1530. It involved British, French, Portuguese, and Spanish ships as well as

French and Spanish Basques, all competing for productive fishing grounds with no consideration for the aboriginal inhabitants. The northerly route from Europe to the Strait of Belle Isle was already well known before Cartier explored the Gulf of St Lawrence in 1534, as was Funk Island, which became a regular landing place *en route*.[45] The British generally operated along the east coast of Newfoundland, the French on the south and west coasts as well as to the north of the British. The Portuguese fished between Cape Race and Bonavista Bay.[46] Basque codfishers frequented the southern shore of the Avalon and Burin peninsulas and later also fished in the Strait of Belle Isle.[47] Each group guarded its fishing grounds and landing places; no area was set aside for the Beothuk.

The fleets usually arrived in Newfoundland in or before May and continued fishing at least until October. Their various methods for curing cod determined the length of time spent ashore and, by implication, the extent to which Beothuk would have been affected by their presence. One method of curing fish was to split and lightly salt it and then dry the fish in the open air until it was sufficiently dehydrated to avoid deterioration during storage and transportation. This process required proximity to shore where suitable structures known as fish flakes could be erected. They were often reused for several seasons and may have been targets for pilfering by Beothuk. A second method, necessary when frequent fog or rain prevented the drying process, was that of heavily salting the fish on board so that it could be transported home without spoiling. This method involved less time on shore but required considerable amounts of salt, which was available cheaply to the Portuguese and French but not to the British. It was therefore the British who would have spent more time on shore than the Portuguese and the French.

Even though the success of the fishery fluctuated, overall it grew into a significant trade.[48] Barkham has estimated that between 1530 and 1550 up to fifty fishing vessels worked in Newfoundland waters every year.[49] With crews of roughly twenty-five men each, this would have brought an annual transient population of about 1,250 people to the island. In the second half of the century the yearly visitors are likely to have numbered several thousand, given that the fishery had by then grown considerably and that larger vessels were being employed.[50] In the absence of documentation, we are left to speculate on how the Beothuk adapted to the increasing presence of fishing crews in Newfoundland waters and on shore during the summer months, when they too depended upon resources harvested along Newfoundland's coasts. One thing that emerges from the records, or perhaps one should say from the lack of records, is that Beothuk seemed reluctant to communicate with Europeans and withdrew from the places they frequented.

Considering the large profits reaped in the fur trade elsewhere on the Atlantic coast, it is not unreasonable to assume that ships that came into Newfoundland waters would have expected comparable trade opportunities with the indigenous population of the island. But while Beothuk were occasionally referred to in the early 1500s, between the 1550s and 1580s no trade ventures with, or even sightings of, Beothuk are recorded. It has therefore been concluded that the Beothuk deliberately avoided meetings and disappeared from beaches that were easily accessible to European ships.

SIR HUMPHREY GILBERT'S EXPEDITION AND AN EYEWITNESS ACCOUNT FROM 1594

Under the circumstances, it is not surprising that Sir Humphrey Gilbert, on his visit to Newfoundland in 1583, was unable to make contact with Beothuk.[51] Ignorant of the situation, he had brought with him musicians, Morris dancers, and petty haberdashery to entice the Beothuk and engage them in barter, but to no avail. Gilbert perished with his ship in a storm on his journey back to England; the voyage was recorded by Edward Hayes, the only surviving commander of this ill-fated expedition. With regard to the native population Hayes commented: "In the south parts we found no inhabitants which by all likelihood have abandoned those coasts, the same being so much frequented by Christians. But in the North are savages altogether harmlesse."[52]

The claim that the south coast had been abandoned by the Beothuk was at best misleading. Their continued presence in Placentia Bay, while it may have been reduced, is attested to by the fact that native people, believed to be Beothuk, cut the mooring ropes of boats of an English fishing vessel in the bay in 1594. And in 1612 John Guy recorded the presence of a Beothuk camp close to the Come by Chance River in Placentia Bay where Beothuk from Trinity Bay harvested salmon.[53] They probably also came to hunt harbour seal, since large aggregates of this species are known to have assembled on the islands of the bay.

With regard to the harmless Indians in the north, Captain Hayes would not have met any himself; for we have no evidence that Gilbert's party contacted native people further north *en route* to St John's from Funk Island. Most likely they were the Indians who assisted Basques in the whaling industry on the Labrador coast, mentioned in the 1570s by the shipowner Parkhurst and subsequently by Captain Whitbourne. Although Whitbourne believed that they were Indians from Newfoundland, the evidence at our disposal suggests that they were Montagnais.[54]

The cutting of mooring ropes in Placentia Bay in 1594 was experienced by the crew of the English vessel *Grace* from Bristol.[55] They had first anchored in St George's Bay, where they saw two Basque shipwrecks and several native houses. These dwellings were made of fir trees set in a circle and covered with bark. The occupants of the camp had all fled, but judging by footprints left in the sand, the group was estimated to have numbered about forty to fifty people. Upon examining the camp, the crew found caribou meat roasting on wooden spits, a bark dish filled with caribou fat, and cormorants plucked and "ready to be dressed." Although *Grace* fished for ten days in the vicinity, her crew did not make contact with the occupants of the camp. It has been suggested that they had come to this bay to loot the wrecks and that they could have been either Beothuk or Micmac.[56] Circumstantial evidence favours the idea that the elusive Indians were Beothuk. Firstly, they fled from Europeans, which was the usual reaction of the Beothuk; secondly, Whitbourne reported that the Newfoundland "sauages" (the Beothuk) lived in the "West parts of the Countrey … seldome frequented by the English," where Basque and French ships were fishing for whale and cod.[57] Another piece of supporting evidence is a Micmac tradition that Micmac first settled close to and later took over a Beothuk encampment at St Georges Bay.[58] The archaeological record of the area would support this sequence of events.[59]

The ship *Grace* later moved on to Placentia Bay, into the harbour of "Pesmark." Pesmark, said to be ten leagues (55.6 kilometres) into Placentia Bay, may be today's Presque, a sheltered harbour on the Burin Peninsula west of Merasheen Island.[60] The men built stages there and successfully fished for cod until one night natives cut the ropes of their two pinnaces and the ship's boat.[61] The pinnaces were retrieved, but the captain elected to depart for fear of "a shrewder turne of the Savages."

CHAPTER TWO

The Seventeenth Century: Colonization, Trade, and Encroachment

ENGLISH PLANS TO COLONIZE

By the 1580s it was thought that the fishery, by then profitable and important for the British economy, could be improved and stabilized by establishing settlements in Newfoundland. Such outposts would permit English dominance over the best fishing grounds and at the same time constitute a base from which the search for a northwest passage to the Orient could be pursued.

One of the promoters of settlement, Anthony Parkhurst, accompanied his fishing ships several times between 1575 and 1578 to investigate Newfoundland's resources.[1] In his report Parkhurst made no mention of native inhabitants, probably because he explored only those areas on the Avalon Peninsula (Conception Bay and the coast south of St John's) where the English fishery had long been concentrated and where native people were no longer evident. Captain Whitbourne, who made his first journey to Trinity Bay in 1579, believed that the "naturall Inhabitants of the Country," of which there were few, lived altogether to the north and west in an area that was rarely frequented by the English.[2] He claimed that the most suitable locations for settlement were on the Avalon Peninsula, which had not previously been occupied by native people and was not part of their tribal lands. While we now know that this assertion was erroneous, it would at the time have reassured prospective settlers that natives would not interfere with English communities.[3]

One reason for colonization that was widely publicized by its promoters was the need to convert the natives to Christianity. Eloquent arguments aroused compassion for the "poor infidels captivated by the devil" and conjured up a vision of multitudes of heathens to be saved.[4] This prospect justified the venture morally and secured the support of the churches. Since British sovereignty over land occupied and exploited by native people was not legally sanctioned, those pushing for colonization claimed their rights to the country by virtue of ancient English connections with the island, bolstered by the assertion that settlement would be for the good of the "savages."[5] Sir George Peckham, for instance, took great pains to present a convincing case that the "savages" who lived in sinfulness and practised idolatry were actually thirsting for Christianity. It was therefore the duty of the English to help them towards this end. Once the "savages" had agreed to a truce, the English could give them presents of small value such as glass beads, bells, and bracelets and could undertake to defend them against their enemies. Eventually, so Peckham enthused, they could be educated and taught mechanical occupations, liberal arts, and sciences. In return for these benefits the English should be permitted to enjoy large areas of their land. However, if the natives did not yield to these means, if they used violence to repel the Christians or withheld the rights to their land for which the English so "painfully and lawfully adventured themselves hither," then it would be considered no breach of equity for the Christians to defend themselves, to pursue the natives, and to avenge themselves with force. Peckham concluded that the value of the gift of Christianity exceeded by far the earthly riches that settlers would be able to gather, and that the benefit to the native people would be greater by far than the inconvenience of sharing their land and resources.[6]

Richard Eburne, vicar of a parish church in Somerset, carefully considered the moral and practical implications of settlement in the New World in his 1624 treatise *A Plain Pathway to Plantations*.[7] Eburne believed Newfoundland to be for the most part devoid of inhabitants and therefore suitable for English settlement.[8] In contrast to Peckham's ideas concerning native lands, Eburne was opposed to the occupation of countries by invasion. He considered it morally wrong as well as unlawful for one nation to destroy another in order to seize its land. By the time Eburne argued his case, the North American Indians were no longer an unknown people. Trade relations had been established in several regions and enough was known about Indian practices and their way of life to indicate that they could be astute and useful allies. However, like Peckham and others, Eburne assumed that Christians were superior to the native inhabitants.

Other arguments in favour of settlement were based on the idea that the native people represented an untapped market for European goods. Selling and bartering English merchandise such as cloth, knives, fish hooks, copper kettles, beads, and mirrors would stimulate industry, cure the lagging economy in the home country, and be a source of new profits, though some proponents of this idea agonized over the prospect that Indians might not be able to pay for the desired goods.[9] The possibility of trade relations nevertheless had a great appeal.

In order to be better informed of the Indians' needs and customs, Peckham and others organized a voyage of reconnaissance to North America, including Newfoundland, in 1582 or 1583. The captain of this voyage was to collect and record extensive information about the native people, their stature, apparel, and foods, the size of the population of each country, the way they armed and ordered themselves in war, their friends and enemies, and the languages they spoke.[10] Unfortunately this expedition, which could have provided much valuable information, did not take place. It was probably cancelled when Sir Humphrey Gilbert failed to return from his voyage to Newfoundland in 1583. In the event, Virginia was chosen as the most promising location for settlement and the colonization of Newfoundland was delayed for several decades.

Eventually, in 1610, a group of London and Bristol merchants founded the Newfoundland Company, the first of several enterprises with the aim of initiating settlement in Newfoundland. In their original petition to the Privy Council for a Newfoundland charter, the merchants stated that colonists would be free from molestation by the "savages" as none had been seen in any part of the country where Englishmen fished.[11] This notion was repeated in the royal charter and may have been a fair assessment of the situation at the time.[12] Since members of the Council for the Plantation of Newfoundland were clearly anxious to avoid complications, they instructed the colonists not to meddle with the native population. If any native was to appear at the plantation, he should be treated with kindness but neither detained nor allowed to see the house and provisions.[13] The council members seem to have feared that a view of European goods might precipitate attacks and plundering by the native people. As it was, the Indians consistently avoided settlements and it was the colonists and fishing crews who could not resist plundering the Indians' clothes, gear, or stores when they chanced upon their camps.

In 1610, John Guy, one of the founding members of the company, was appointed governor of the colony in Newfoundland. Accompanied by thirty-nine colonists, he sailed for Newfoundland in the same year. Guy chose Cupids in Conception Bay as the site of the first officially sanctioned settlement on the island. In his original plans for the colony, Guy had placed no emphasis on profits from a fur trade with the native population, believing that animal husbandry and fishing would provide the necessary income.[14] However, establishing the settlement proved to be costlier than he had anticipated, and, anxious to make it self-sufficient, Guy reconsidered. Presumably, he was influenced in his decision by the news that the French farther north made extensive profits in the fur trade.[15]

At the beginning of the seventeenth century, the fur trade was one of the few meaningful links between Europeans and native people and had become an important feature in their relations. During his exploration in 1534, Cartier found that if the natives had no surplus pelts, they traded the clothes off their backs until "nothing was left to them but their naked bodies."[16] While some native groups had certainly been unprepared for barter, many others on the Atlantic seaboard soon adapted to the Europeans' quest for furs. Small beginnings quickly grew into a profitable trade, particularly for the French. The possibility of reaping great profits became as strong an incentive for Europeans to foster good relations with Indians as the desire of many Indians to obtain European goods, particularly metal tools. French and English traders who were engaged in such exchanges would pass along the coast and stop when native people showed a willingness to barter. One of the traders was Stephen Bellanger, who completed several successful trading voyages to Acadia before 1583.[17] Basque fishermen and whalers who visited the Atlantic coast further to the north were routinely equipped with axes and other goods in case an opportunity to trade presented itself.[18] Nonetheless, barter with natives remained a secondary source of income for them. The French Basque Martizan Aristega, who came to "Terre Neuf" (a term designating Newfoundland as well as the Strait of Belle Isle and the Gulf of St Lawrence) in 1597 to fish, procure whale oil, and trade for furs, trucked forty buckskins, forty beaver, and twenty martin pelts for tobacco. Since it is doubtful whether the Beothuk were interested in tobacco (there is no record of their using it), Aristega most likely effected his trade with mainland tribes.[19]

In Newfoundland no regular trade developed, although the main ingredients – an abundance of fur-bearing animals and Indians skilled at procuring them – were present.[20] No sixteenth-century record positively attests to trade for furs with native people in Newfoundland, though some documents mention trade goods being taken by shipowners or crew in anticipation of barter. The Spaniard Juan de Agramonte, for instance, on his voyage in 1511, brought merchandise for barter in Newfoundland and granted his sailors permission to carry goods for trade in their personal chests. Whether such barter came about is not recorded.[21] What is recorded is that by the end of the sixteenth century trade for fur on the mainland coast, particulary by French traders, had become extensive, much to the alarm and envy of the English.[22]

JOHN GUY MEETS WITH BEOTHUK

Since John Guy thought trade in beaver and other furs might be a likely source of additional income, he dispatched exploring parties overland to Trinity Bay to contact Indians who were said to live there – fourteen of their houses had been seen thirteen kilometres across from Heart's Content. Neither of the two parties that made the attempt reached the intended destination.[23] These failures convinced Guy that reconnaissance trips to Trinity Bay would have to be made by sea. Accordingly, he set off with eighteen men from the colony in two boats, a barque of twelve tons and a shallop of about five tons. He planned to investigate harbours and potential resources such as scurvy grass and iron ore and to assess opportunities for trading. Guy recorded details of this voyage in "A journall of the voiadge of discoverie made in a barke builte in Newfoundland called the Indeavour, begunne the 7 of october 1612, & ended the 25th. of November following."[24] Henry Crout, who was one of the party, described the events in letters to Sir Percival Willoughby, for whom he acted as agent. He generally corroborated what Guy had recorded but occasionally gave additional information.[25]

Having heard that Indians lived south of Heart's Content, the party sailed to the lower reaches of Trinity Bay, making their first stop at Mount Eagle Bay (Hopeall), the harbour to which the party that had gone overland had cut a trail.[26] From there they proceeded to Dildo Arm, where they found a deserted camp in a spacious harbour (Dildo South).[27] Savage Harbour, the name they gave to the campsite, was thought to be no more than two days' journey by land from Cupids. About half an hour's walk inland on a well-trodden path brought the colonists to a large lake (Dildo Pond) where an Indian canoe was drawing close to an island on which a fire had been lit. Smoke on the lakeshore led them to the site of three dwellings, two of which had recently been used (Plate 2.1).[28] Guy left "bisket," "brasslets," points, and amber beads in exchange for a piece of beaver meat and two or three children's moccasins.[29]

The party then turned towards the western shore of Trinity Bay, but contrary winds made progress difficult and at times the shallop, propelled by oars, was sent ahead or had to pull the barque. Guy's and Crout's descriptions of their route sometimes diverge and researchers do not always agree on the places where the party anchored.[30] On 31 October they entered a broad sound, probably Collier Bay, and later sailed into Bull Arm where they put into two fine harbours.[31] The first would have been Stock Cove, where they saw nine houses that had not been used for some time, and the second, Great Mosquito Cove.[32] The party continued to the bottom of the sound, where Guy recorded "eighte or nine savage housen in severall places, and a way cut into the woodes, w[hi]ch being prosequted, yt was fownd to lead directlie to a harborough in the bay of Placentia distant onlie two miles w w[hi]ch harbour in Placentia bay is now called Passage harbour. A river came unto yt from the NNE."[33] The men who pursued the Indians' path to its outcome in Placentia Bay found various artifacts and traces of Indians who were apparently in the habit of carrying their canoes overland to the bay.[34] Crout remarked on the ample supply of salmon in the river (Come By Chance) and noted a place where the natives had tanned a bearskin. In the camp in Trinity Bay, the colonists found a new canoe drawn up on shore and Guy, who was otherwise careful not to interfere with the Indians' property, carried it off with the intent of sending it to England.[35]

Continuing with the exploration, Guy hoisted a white flag to signal his peaceful intentions. In time Indians lit a fire further down the shore and then approached the colonists in two canoes, beckoning for them to come ashore. When both the barque and the shallop advanced, the Indians began to leave, whereupon Guy waved his white flag and had the barque come to anchor. The shallop first landed Master Whittington (the commander of the ship);[36] eventually five others joined him, including Guy and Crout; the Indian party, which had to ford a river to reach them, consisted of eight men, though it is not clear whether all of them disembarked or whether some held the two canoes in readiness. The ritual of meeting and exchanging gifts included oration and the shaking of a white wolfskin by one of the Indians, followed by prolonged dancing, leaping, and singing, in which the colonists participated, all holding hands, and by the Indians striking their own and their guests' chests.[37] The two parties then shared a meal. Guy contributed bread, butter, raisins, aquavitae, and beer; the Indians brought smoked or dried caribou meat and a root. When one of the Beothuk blew into the aquavitae bottle, "it made a sound, which they fell all into laughture at."[38] After the white wolfskin and the colonists' white flag had been exchanged, the Indians indicated that the colonists should repair for the night.

In his journal Guy described the Indians as follows: "They are of a reasonable stature, of ane ordinarie middle sise; they goe bareheaded, wearing theire haire somewhat long, but rounded, they have noe beards. Behind they have a great locke of haire platted with feathers, like a hawke's lure w[i]th a feather in yt standing uprighte by the crowne of the head, & a small locke platted before … their faces something flat & broad, red w[i]th okir, as all theire apparell is, & the rest of their bodie. They are braod breasted, & bould, & stand very uprighte."[39] Each man wore a short fur gown, the furry side turned inwards, with sleeves and a collar of beaverskin. One of the Indians, who "seemed to have some com[m]and over the reste," wore shoes of caribou and sealskin as well as mittens. To salute, he pulled the mittens off and kissed the top of his fingers.[40]

Guy sketched a "Savages canoa" in his journal and described the craft as being made "in the forme of a new moon, stem & stern alike … In the middle the canoa is higher a great deale than in the bow & quarter."[41] The canoe was six metres (twenty feet) long and had a keel and timbers made of thin pieces of fir. It was covered with birchbark sewn together with quartered roots, and it carried four persons. The accuracy of Guy's sketch and description was confirmed in 1768 by Cartwright, who gave a detailed account of Beothuk canoe construction and made a drawing of the same canoe type.[42] Other native artifacts seen by Guy and Crout were oars and paddles, round dwellings made of poles and covered with caribou skins or sail, a square house with a small roof, a "holberte," "long staffes as pikes," a wooden "target" [shield], an arrow, bark "coffins" [boxes], little bowls, several leather "chains" [thongs] with periwinkle shells, and arrows without points.[43]

Although Guy did not record in his diary an agreement with the Indians to meet them again in the following year, Crout, in a letter to Willoughby, mentioned Guy's intent to return to Trinity Bay. In 1639 David Kirke, who acquired a land grant for Ferryland, also claimed that Guy had planned another meeting.[44] This may well have been the case, because Guy set his men to work building a house that was to serve as a shelter and trading post on future visits. The structure was probably erected on McKay Island, locally known as Frenchman's Island.[45] When Bull Arm began to freeze over, Guy's party hastened to leave for Cupids. On passing the place where they had met the Indians, they noted that the "tilt," made from an old canvas sail, was still standing.[46] Close by, a dozen poles from which goods were suspended were pitched into the ground, apparently for silent barter. Used in the absence of the trading partners, this was a mode of exchange with which Guy's party was not familiar. Crout thought at first that the pelts had been hung up to dry.[47] There were about a dozen furs, mostly beaver, but also a fox, a sable, and a birdskin, a few shell chains, an old boat sail, and an old mitten.

It is not clear whether this mode of exchange was an aboriginal Beothuk custom or had been introduced to them by Europeans. In North America, a form of silent barter was recorded in 1568 by David Ingram, who travelled from the Bay of Mexico to within fifty leagues (ca. 250 kilometres) of Cape Breton. The principle in this trade, so he explained, was to leave goods on the ground and retire until the trading party had matched the value of these items with their own wares.[48] The procedure of placing goods on the ground to be inspected, with sellers remaining at a distance, was also recorded by the cartographer Carolus from Eskimo in the Strait of Davis, and by men from Frobisher's expedition who traded with the Central Eskimo in Cumberland Sound in 1577. There too greeting took the form of leaping, dancing, and calling.[49]

Guy eventually fathomed this concept of barter, but because he was "not furnished with fit things for to trucke," he took only four skins and left in payment a hatchet, a knife, four needles (threaded), and a pair of scissors.[50] Since Guy had specifically come to Trinity Bay to meet Indians, it is puzzling that he was so poorly equipped with trade goods.

Having completed the transaction, the colonists sailed homeward. In one of the harbours, probably Mosquito Cove, they found the discarded staff from Guy's flag of truce, so they called the place Flagstaff Harbour.[51] Guy and Crout both thought that the natives with whom they had traded might have come across from Dildo Pond, because they had seen no signs of recent habitation in any other place. Crout also claimed to have recognized the old sail at the trading place as having previously covered one of the Indians' lakeside houses.[52]

Initially, Guy's encounter with Indians in Trinity Bay seems to have been the looked-for breakthrough, yet trade had been negligible and there is no evidence that he ordered trade items from England or attempted barter on another occasion.[53] Guy's journal, preserved in the Lambeth Palace Library in London, is the first undisputed eyewitness account of contact between Englishmen and Beothuk. Their identification as Beothuk rather than Micmac or another native people is based on their extensive use of ochre as body paint, the half-moon shape of their canoe, and their continued presence in the area into the second half of the seventeenth century.

While archaeologists have not been able to locate the Beothuk camp recorded by Guy in the area of Sunnyside, three places mentioned in his journal were excavated in the 1980s. One site is at Russel Point on Dildo Pond where Guy had seen three houses. It has yielded a large number of Little Passage/Beothuk stone tools as well as residue of bone and has been interpreted as a caribou killing site.[54] Another site is on Frenchman's (or McKay) Island, where Guy's party built a trading post, and the third is at Stock Cove in the entrance of Bull Arm. The Frenchman's Island site yielded stone tools of Maritime Archaic Indian, Early and Late Palaeo-Eskimo, and Little Passage Indian origin as well as European remains, among them glass, earthenware, nails, and several hundred pipestem pieces from around 1650. The Stock Cove site, which is considerably larger, also contained Maritime Archaic Indian, Early and Late Palaeo-Eskimo, and Little Passage Indian stone tools, showing that over several millennia native people repeatedly chose this cove as a location from which to procure food.[55] Although no historic Beothuk remains were identified during excavation – house pits may have been eliminated through growth of vegetation, and bone or iron tools could have disintegrated due to the acidity of the soil – some of the Little Passage-type stone tools from this site may have belonged to Beothuk.

HENRY CROUT RETURNS TO TRINITY BAY

In a letter written after the expedition in 1612, Crout mentioned that John Guy had intended to "retorne this spring into trynity againe [to investigate] every crooke, [and to have some] parle agayne with the sollvagges."[56] As a first measure Guy sent ten men provided with food for fifteen to twenty days in January or February 1613 "to find out the salvages in solvage [Trinity] bay."[57] He hoped not only to establish contact with the Beothuk but also to learn about their way of life in winter, their methods of procuring food, and their way of avoiding scurvy, which had become the most frequent cause of disablement and death among the colonists. The overland expedition did not meet with success. After two days of tramping through high snows the men became discouraged and returned to Cupids. This was Guy's last attempt at contacting Beothuk. Having become disenchanted with the colonizing venture, he left Newfoundland permanently in March 1613.

Crout remained for another summer in the colony. He firmly believed that a friendly meeting with the Indians could lead to profitable trade and in July 1613 arranged for a small party to return to Trinity Bay.[58] *En route* to Savage Harbour in Dildo Arm they noted an Indian habitation on a small, pleasant island, possibly Hopeall Island, but by the time the party came ashore the occupants had fled.[59] Crout's men wanted to capture them, though it is difficult to imagine what advantage they would have gained had they succeeded in doing so. Had Crout not been firm in refusing to give them permission, the attempt could well have led to injury and unwelcome retaliation. In contrast to other colonists, Crout had sufficient foresight to avoid possible conflict and considered it important that they neither interfere with the native population – his men had also wanted to take their canoe – nor "take any of them by force." Reputedly the natives were "bentt to revenge," and Crout feared that any interference would jeopardize peaceful relations and trade and thereby cause great losses to the Newfoundland Company.[60]

After leaving the island, the party pressed on to look for the Indians who had camped by the freshwater lake (Dildo Pond) the previous fall. Apparently they expected to meet them at Dildo South, but the campsite there was deserted.[61] Crout thought that the Indians had gone to collect eggs and birds for winter provisions, as they were often seen to do on the islands between Heart's Ease and English Harbour, which were known to be the breeding ground of innumerable sea fowl.[62] Without revisiting the previous year's trading place in Bull Arm, Crout turned back. His failure to look for Beothuk where he had seen them before strongly suggests that Guy had arranged to meet Beothuk at Dildo South. On his homeward journey Crout stopped again at the small island. The Indians had gone but they had left morsels of broiled meat by the fireplace, in exchange for which Crout left cheese and "bisket."[63] About a league (5.5 km) farther down the coast, Crout noted a fire that he recognized as a signal for trade. According to their custom the Indians had suspended skins on poles as if it were "a markett place." A few of them were dodging back and forth in the forest, and Crout would have liked to speak with them but was unable to entice them to come any closer.[64] To ensure their satisfaction, he exchanged the skins for items twice their value and then returned home without further delay.

Based on their personal experiences neither Guy nor Crout considered the Beothuk dangerous. If any of their men were to meet Beothuk in the forest, as could happen on overland expeditions, there would be no cause for alarm.[65] This opinion was later shared by Sir Arthur Aston, one-time governor of Calvert's colony at Ferryland, who surmised that the few natives who inhabited Newfoundland were of a gentle disposition and neither caused harm to strangers nor destroyed stages or boats left unattended over winter.[66] Captain Whitbourne, who had lived in Newfoundland for many years, confirmed that the natives did not "hurt or burne any thing" belonging to the English.[67] With regard to trade, Henry Crout believed that a fur trade could be developed, provided the Indians were approached in a suitably circumspect and inoffensive manner. He enquired about the type of "commodities" that were best suited for exchange and, in his correspondence with Sir Percival Willoughby, painted a rosy picture of potential profits that might accrue. The plot of land that the company had allocated to Willoughby as his personal property was situated in Trinity Bay close to where the Indians lived and therefore in the most convenient location for trade, since whoever was to "first break the ice" with them might become a trade partner.[68]

Crout was confident that he himself would be able to win the Indians' trust and become as familiar with them as the French were with Canadian Indians, whom they traded with extensively.[69] In his opinion the best way to create good relations would be to have a few of the Indians live with the English while a few Englishmen should be left in their place, as the French had done in Canada. Crout's confidence in the feasibility of such an exchange in Newfoundland suggests that he felt the Beothuk could be trusted. Indeed, he knew a person who had stayed with them for five years and could speak their language very well.[70] Presumably, Crout believed this man would be a suitable go-between to assist in making arrangements for an exchange. Regrettably, he elaborated neither on the circumstances under which the man had joined the Beothuk nor on what his experiences with them had been. The thought that an English or French man had actually lived with Beothuk and then returned to his countrymen to tell the tale is tantalizing in the absence of any other record of this or a similar incident. One may speculate whether the purpose of the man's sojourn with Beothuk was to escape enslavement by the pirate Peter Easton. Richard Holworthy, one of

Guy's colonists, reported in 1612 that Easton had taken men and food from many ships on the Newfoundland coast, and that some of the French, whom he treated with particular cruelty, had "fled into the woods" to avoid being taken prisoner.[71] If the person who lived with Beothuk had been a member of a French fishing crew, Crout might have found it difficult to recruit him for an excursion of English colonists to the Beothuk in Trinity Bay.

Despite Crout's enthusiasm and plans to become a trade partner of the Indians, befriending the elusive Beothuk turned out to be more difficult than expected. With the passage of time, trade as a goal may also have become less attractive as several of the colonists began to procure their own furs. By the time Crout left the colony later in the year (1613), no progress had been made towards establishing trade.[72]

While the colonists regretted the absence of trade relations, the Beothuk may well have been satisfied with their encounters with Guy's and Crout's parties. In exchange for presents or furs they had received a linen cap, two hand towels, three knives, a small piece of brass, a shirt, two table napkins, gloves, twelve points (nails or spikes), a hatchet, a knife, four needles (threaded), and scissors. Guy had also left three or four amber beads, points, bracelets, and biscuit in one of the lakeside wigwams. Crout had placed cheese and biscuit in the wigwam on the small island, in addition to the trade goods he left in exchange for furs.

Other European objects in possession of the Beothuk, referred to in Guy's journal and Crout's letters, were several old sails (one was used to cover a wigwam), three brass or copper kettles, a fishing reel, a splitting knife, a French basket, "Fishermans hookes," fishing line and lead, a caulking iron, flint stones, a goatskin and a lambskin, a buckle, and "Fishermans coopers."[73] Some of these items may have been picked up at deserted fishing camps or stages, others would have been acquired through barter.[74] Since the position of Beothuk camps was generally known, summer fishing crews or passing traders may occasionally have exchanged goods with them, as Guy and Crout had. However, the only other extant document about such an exchange in the early 1600s is a Dutch record, which is discussed later.

In 1615, John Mason was appointed governor of the colony at Cupids, and in the next two years explored the coast of the Avalon Peninsula from Conception Bay around to Placentia. Mason had intended to visit and trade with the native inhabitants and promised to give his correspondent, Sir John Scot, "a tast of the event."[75] On his travels, Mason collected much information about the Newfoundland coast, but he did not encounter Beothuk.[76] In his *Brief Discourse* on Newfoundland, published in 1620, Mason concluded that there were "but few Saluages in the north, and none in the south parts of the Countrie; by whom the planters as yet neuer suffered damage, against whom (if they should seeke to trouble vs,) a small fortification will serue being but few in number, and those onely Bow men."[77] Mason's opinion that the Beothuk population was relatively small was probably correct, though he erred when he claimed that they all lived in the northern part of the island.

In the annals of Cupids, attempts at barter with Beothuk in Trinity Bay were recorded again in 1619. In that year Thomas Rowley, Willoughby's new agent, wrote that he intended to go to Trinity Bay for the purpose of trading.[78] Sir Percival Willoughby had tirelessly promoted the development of his property at Heart's Content and Rowley was finally ready to build a house there close to Beothuk camps. Once this was accomplished, he intended to "se[e] what good beginning we may have w[i]th them the end of the next fishing [season]." To be equipped for barter, he asked the company to send out two dozen hatchets, leads, looking glasses, beads, and a drum.[79] Judging from the correspondence that has survived, no trade goods were shipped to Newfoundland and Rowley appears not to have accomplished what he had planned. He may have found, like others before him, that providing a livelihood and other obligations took all his time and energy. As it turned out, the fishery alone could not defray the expenditures of the settlement, and other sources of income did not materialize as quickly as had been expected. In time the colony became a steady financial drain on its shareholders and the Newfoundland Company was unable to sustain itself. Although it is mentioned in documents until 1631, the company was floundering for many years and eventually dissolved.[80]

COLONIES FOUNDED BY OTHER ENGLISH PROMOTERS

Shortly after the Newfoundland Company had initiated settlement on the island, the Bristol Society of Merchant Venturers acquired land grants and founded the fishing community of Bristol's Hope in Conception Bay.[81] William Vaughan initiated a settlement in Aquaforte on the Avalon Peninsula in 1617 and land grants were also taken up by Henry Cary, later Viscount Falkland. "South Falkland" included Renews and part of the Placentia Bay coast; "North Falkland" encompassed much of the north shore of Trinity Bay and all, or parts, of Bonavista Bay.[82] In the 1620s, Sir George Calvert, later to become Baron Baltimore, founded a colony directly north of Cary's "South Falkland" and built a stately home in Ferryland.[83] In the 1630s this home and a grant for "Newfoundland" were acquired by David Kirke.[84] All the colonies were located on the Avalon Peninsula, away from the areas inhabited by Beothuk. With the success story of the French in the Gulf of St Lawrence as an example, trade with the natives was often discussed as an opportunity for making easy profits. But in the early stages of settlement, the struggle to make the colonies viable and to procure a daily living seems to have occupied the inhabitants to the exclusion of other ambitions. In any event, neither of the colonies survived long enough to allow the time and energy for contacting the nearby Beothuk. As a result, communication and trade failed to develop.

Only one of the patrons, Lord Falkland, included the native population in his plans. His instructions to settlers show that he was poorly informed. Fearing the loss of men from his colony, Falkland sternly warned his settlers not to live among the natives. Instead, he encouraged them to take some of the native children from their parents and bring them up in the plantation, ensuring that the children were less than five or six years old so that they could more easily be integrated into the English community.[85] Falkland's second scheme was to promote another settlement in "North Falkland" (Random Sound?), with the purpose of excluding the natives from Trinity Bay.[86] He reasoned that if the natives' territory were reduced it would be easier for them to defend themselves against "foreign enemies," leaving one to conjecture who, other than Falkland's settlers, might have constituted such enemies.

A prominent promoter of Newfoundland colonization, Captain Richard Whitbourne, had a more favourable opinion of its native population. Whitbourne had visited Newfoundland on fishing and trading voyages from the 1570s onwards and in 1615 had been commissioned by the vice admiralty to settle disputes among the fishermen. Three years later, he acted as governor of Vaughan's colony in Aquaforte.[87] Whitbourne navigated the coast from the Northern Peninsula and the Gulf of St Lawrence to St George's Bay and from there to Cape Race, Trinity Bay, and Bonavista Bay.[88] Despite his long residence in Newfoundland and his many travels around its coast, Whitbourne met none of its native people. He nevertheless hoped that good relations with them could be achieved. In his *Discourse and Discovery of New-Found-Land*, published in 1620, Whitbourne repeatedly assured the reader that in time trade would be established to the benefit of the English.[89] He described the Indians as "rude" and "sauage" people who neither believed in God nor had any form of government. In their habits, customs and manners, they resembled the Indians of the continent from whence he supposed they came.[90] He considered them ingenious and of subtle disposition and believed that they could be brought to "obedience." While they avoided the part of the country that was settled by the English they might be induced to assist the English in opening up the interior.[91] Although Whitbourne thought the native population was confined to the north of Trinity Bay, the journal and letters of Guy and Crout provide good evidence that the Beothuk lived in Trinity Bay and Placentia Bay. In addition, Beothuk tools and a fireplace have been unearthed in archaeological excavations at Ferryland, on the southeast coast of the Avalon Peninsula – between two strata containing European earthenware – showing that Beothuk had come to this part of the island after Europeans started to fish there.[92] If Whitbourne and Mason's opinion that there were only a few natives in Newfoundland had become known to wider circles in England, it may have discouraged entrepreneurs and traders from coming to the island and thus precluded serious attempts at establishing a fur trade with the Beothuk.

FAILURE TO CONVERT THE BEOTHUK

Although the conversion of the native "savages" had been cited as a compelling reason for the colonization of Newfoundland, neither the merchants who financed settlements nor the British Crown, which sold land grants and levied taxes on Newfoundland fish, made provision for missionizing the native population. Yet instructions to civilize and convert them continued to be issued, and there was constant rhetoric about the work of bringing "the poor infidels ... to the worship of God and their own salvation ... to the everlasting honour to his Majesty."[93] Whitbourne even hinted at the possibility of spreading the "true Christian Faith" to the adjoining regions, including the countries in possession of the king of Spain whose inhabitants were presumably already missionized by Catholic priests.[94] His vision of converting Indians beyond the boundaries of Newfoundland was shared by Eburne and others.[95] The Carmelite priest Simon Stock, for example, who requested permission to accompany Baltimore to Newfoundland, planned to establish a Catholic mission on the Avalon "to thwart the English heretics" and to convert Indians in other parts of North America to the Catholic religion.[96] In the event neither Anglicans nor Catholics were able to realize their plans because funds were not forthcoming and missionaries in this part of the world were scarce. The few clerics who came to Newfoundland either travelled with fishing admirals and stayed only during the summer, or, if they were attached to a settlement, seldom remained for more than a season.[97] While French colonists on the mainland were often accompanied by Roman Catholic missionaries, mainly from the Jesuit and Recollect orders, who came to christen and convert the aboriginal population, the Church of England did not have an equivalent institutional arm. The Society for the Propagation of the Gospel, which was to take on this missionary function, was not founded until nearly a century after colonization had begun. Its first Newfoundland minister, the Reverend John Jackson, arrived in St John's in 1703; he was forced to leave within two years because of financial and other problems. Other ministers followed at intervals, but until the second half of the eighteenth century missionaries seldom stayed for longer periods of time. Financial support pledged by the communities that had requested the services of a minister was often insufficient and working conditions were difficult to endure. The severe climate and travel on foot or in open boats for long distances to visit scattered communities exposed the clergy to much physical hardship. Poor diet caused scurvy and other symptoms of malnutrition and many of the clergy were thus hampered by ill health.[98] Beset with these problems the life of the clergy was often a struggle for survival and under these circumstances ministers were clearly unable to take on the additional task of converting the native people of the country, with whom no means of communication existed.

INTERACTION WITH SEASONAL FISHING CREWS

During the seventeenth century Beothuk and settlers seem to have been able to exploit resources without interfering much with one another. In contrast, fishing crews who came to Newfoundland for the summer season appear to have caused friction, probably because they were more numerous, and because their practice of going ashore in different locations was more intrusive. Whitbourne, for example, estimated in 1620 that in a good year a contingent of more than sixty English ships fished on the northern shore of Trinity Bay.[99] With an average crew size of twenty men, this would have amounted to an English migrant population of up to twelve hundred in the north part of Trinity Bay alone. Projecting a proportional number of fishing crews along the remaining coast, it is clear that the numbers were considerable and that this seasonal influx of Europeans would have disturbed the Beothuk.[100] The number and size of boats and crews increased as the century progressed. According to the Newfoundland census for 1699, 5,120 seasonal fishermen from England made use of 465 stages in different harbours. These figures must be added to those of the permanently settled population in Newfoundland, which amounted to 3,171 English people including women and children.[101] The sheer number of seasonal fishing crews and their greater mobility as compared with permanent settlers would more often have brought seasonal fishermen than year-round residents into contact and conflict with the Beothuk.

Two English sources from the early 1600s describe such conflicts in Trinity Bay. The first incident was reported by Whitbourne (1620), who indicated that the English sailors involved in strife belonged to "Tapson" (probably *Topsham*), a seasonal fishing craft.[102] The sailors, who had been robbed by Indians when their vessel was anchored in the harbour of Heart's Ease on the northwest shore of Trinity Bay, were searching for the culprits when they discovered three Beothuk "tents." They frightened the occupants away by firing their guns and then carried off three canoes, a great store of skins, ochre, food, weapons, and other things, some of which they presented to Whitbourne. Whether these Beothuk were actually the ones who had stolen articles from "Tapson" was not ascertained. It also remains unclear whether the Beothuk who had plundered the vessel actually resided in Trinity Bay or whether they had come from Bonavista Bay, whence Indians were reputed to come at night into Trinity Bay to steal sails, lines, hatchets, hooks, knives, and similar gear.[103]

The second incident of conflict was reported by David Kirke of Ferryland in 1639. According to Kirke, John Guy had agreed with the Beothuk he traded with at Bull Arm in 1612 to meet them again the following summer. Accordingly, the Beothuk had come to the designated trading place. The crew of a passing fishing vessel, who knew nothing about Guy's arrangement, feared that the assembled natives were hostile and "let fly their shott" at them.[104] Immediately upon this attack the Beothuk retired into the woods and "from that day to this" did much "mischief" to the fishermen in Trinity Bay and farther to the north.[105] Their tendency to retaliate when wronged was certainly well known and usually took the form of taking equipment from, rather than attacking, fishermen.[106] Kirke did not specify whether the crew who shot at the Beothuk were seasonal fishermen, but since the few permanent settlers of the area were probably apprised of Guy's intentions, it is likely that they were.

Both accounts suggest that fishing crews were ill disposed towards the native population and retaliated vigorously to avenge theft, occasionally using firearms to ensure that they kept the upper hand. Reciprocal thievery may have been set in motion by the aggressive acts of fishing crews, as claimed by Kirke, or by the Beothuk's habit of taking revenge by pilfering European goods. Initially Beothuk appear to have threatened unwelcome visitors by endangering their equipment, as recorded from the harbour of "Pesmark" where they cut mooring ropes. In response, Europeans may have used violence against Beothuk, who soon learned to flee from their camps when fishermen approached. It is possible that sailors fired their guns in order to retrieve stolen goods or to rob the Beothuk rather than to hurt them, but their threatening behaviour would have engendered distrust and hindered the development of communication and trade. Without regulations governing conduct towards the native population, the Beothuk were subject to a wide range of behaviour, much of it dishonourable. By the end of the seventeenth century the Beothuk had become elusive. Contact with Europeans may not have been entirely severed at this stage, but only a few more misadventures sufficed to destroy the delicate balance of mutual tolerance.

BEOTHUK CONTACT WITH THE DUTCH AND FRENCH

Among the extensive records of Dutch fishing voyages, only two documents mention trade with native people, and only one of these could concern Beothuk. The Dutch who appear to have exchanged goods with them in 1606 were men from *Witte Leeuw*, a heavily armed trading vessel from Amsterdam. The record states that they privateered a Spanish and a Portuguese ship, from which they extorted train oil, cod, and guns after having "traded with the Indians." This occurred in St Mary's Bay in Newfoundland. Presumably, these Indians were Beothuk, perhaps from the band in Trinity Bay that met with John Guy six years later.[107]

In 1637, about thirty years after *Witte Leeuw* had come into Newfoundland waters, the captain of the Dutch vessel *Fortuyn* was taken to court and accused of having tarried eight or nine days on shore at "Terra Nova" in order to barter with native people for personal profit.[108] Since the term "Terra Nova" denoted Newfoundland as well as southern Quebec and Labrador, we have no way of knowing whether the captain of *Fortuyn* had actually traded with Beothuk.

Contacts between the French and Beothuk seem to have been similar to those with the English. Captain Wheeler of HMS *Tiger*, which patrolled the northern district between Fogo Island and Petit Nord, recorded in 1684 that the French were at "utter defiance" with the Indians, who were numerous on that coast.[109] These "Indians" may have been Beothuk or Inuit. Beothuk certainly resorted to Notre Dame Bay but Inuit also came there to trade with Frenchmen. Commander Graydon reported in 1701 that the French kept guard boats in every harbour throughout the fishing season to prevent the Indians of the country and "what nations soe ever" from plundering their boats in the night. He also stated that "great hatred" existed between the "Canada Indians" (taken to be Inuit) and the Newfoundland Indians (Beothuk).[110] Though the French may have sought protection from Inuit attackers whose feud with the French is well documented (see chapter 3), Beothuk may also have done "mischief" on occasion.[111] For example, the "Red Indians" in Hare Bay were said to have been skilled in stealing fishing boats, which they burned to obtain nails. Since it was the French who fished close to Hare Bay, the stolen boats would have been French.[112] As a rule, Beothuk were not known to be aggressive; Indians discovered by a French officer in the southern part of the island in 1694 "were so unprepared for war that a small party of Europeans could chase them away."[113] Assuming that these Indians were Beothuk (since Micmac were usually affiliated with the French and had guns), the description of their fear of guns fits that given in English sources.

Despite the Beothuk's reticence, some French crews tried to communicate with them. According to the testimonial of Thomas Mitchell, who was captured by the French in 1697 and taken to their fishing grounds in Notre Dame Bay, he (or the French) saw several native people on the shore. They tried to speak with them, but the natives, presumably Beothuk, would not come close.[114] Given that Frenchmen had attempted to attract Beothuk in this area, pieces of Normandy pottery and glass beads (similar to those found in French fishing stations at Petit Nord) that were excavated on a Beothuk site in Dildo Run, Notre Dame Bay, would suggest that the French left items of small value on the shore to initiate communication.[115] Although there is no evidence that they succeeded in making contact, two sources claim that relations between Beothuk and the French were better than those between Beothuk and the English.

One source is the journal of Edward Burd, supercargo on the merchant ship *The Christian of Leith.* Burd claimed that the few Indians who resided to the north lived "in greater friendship with the french than with the English, who treated them with great severity," and that the French used the Indians in their attacks on English settlements.[116] Most likely, Burd was talking about two different populations, the Micmac, who had become allies of the French, and the Beothuk in the north, who had been poorly treated by the English. William Taverner, an English settler and trader, commented at about the same time that the Indians (Beothuk in Notre Dame Bay) were affiliated neither with the French nor with the English. During a journey by sea from Cape Bauld to the Avalon Peninsula, he had seen three Indians and more than "50 fierce" (presumably Indian men) on the coast. Taverner believed that these Indians (Beothuk) were "a nation yt is settled by themselves between the English and the French," and that they had no connections with the French.[117]

It is therefore questionable whether Banks, who visited Newfoundland in 1766 and asked local settlers about the Beothuk, was correctly informed when he wrote: "Of the Indians that inhabit the interior parts of Newfoundland, I have as yet been able to learn very little about them ... They are, in general, thought to be very few … but why that should be imagined I cannot tell, as we know nothing at all of the interior parts of the Island, nor ever had the least connection with them, *tho' the French we are told had*"(emphasis added).[118] Since Banks did not elaborate on the nature and extent of relations between French and Beothuk, and since his is the only report that claims actual connections between the two, they are unlikely to have amounted to more than occasional small trade.

CHAPTER THREE

Relations between Beothuk and Their Native Neighbours

In the course of the seventeenth century Beothuk not only had to adjust to inroads on their traditional territory by white fishing crews and colonist/settlers, they also had to contend with hostilities and encroachment by native neighbours. Micmac groups increasingly hunted and trapped on the west and south coast of Newfoundland, Inuit adversaries came across the Strait of Belle Isle to Petit Nord and Notre Dame Bay, and Montagnais hunters began to exploit resources on the Northern Peninsula. English and French records from the early historic period seldom mention relations between ethnic groups. However, some clues can be extrapolated from native oral traditions.

MICMAC HUNTING AND TRAPPING

In the second half of the seventeenth century, Micmac hunting and trapping on the Newfoundland south coast probably in combination with other factors, resulted in open conflict between them and the Beothuk (Fig.3.1).

Micmac oral tradition, as recorded by the anthropologist Frank G. Speck in 1922, contends that Micmac resided in Newfoundland in early, even prehistoric, times. They were known as *Sa'yewe'djki'k*, or "the ancients"; later newcomers joined them.[1] Archaeologically, prehistoric Micmac occupation in Newfoundland has not been ascertained. Surveys and excavations conducted in Placentia and Hermitage bays, Bay D'Espoir, the Burgeo region including Grandy's Brook and White Bear Bay, La Poile Bay, Cape Ray, and on the Port au Port Peninsula have consistently exposed either Maritime Archaic or Recent Indian tools or Palaeo-Eskimo material, but no Micmac remains.[2] Nor are there any reliable European documents of Micmac visits to Newfoundland during the sixteenth century. References to Indians in Newfoundland in the works of Crignon, Thevet, and de Laet merely describe native people in general terms but give no specific features that would clarify their ethnic identity.[3] A Micmac presence in Newfoundland at that early date can only be deduced from Micmac and Beothuk traditions; for the latter we must rely on the Beothuk captive Shanawd-

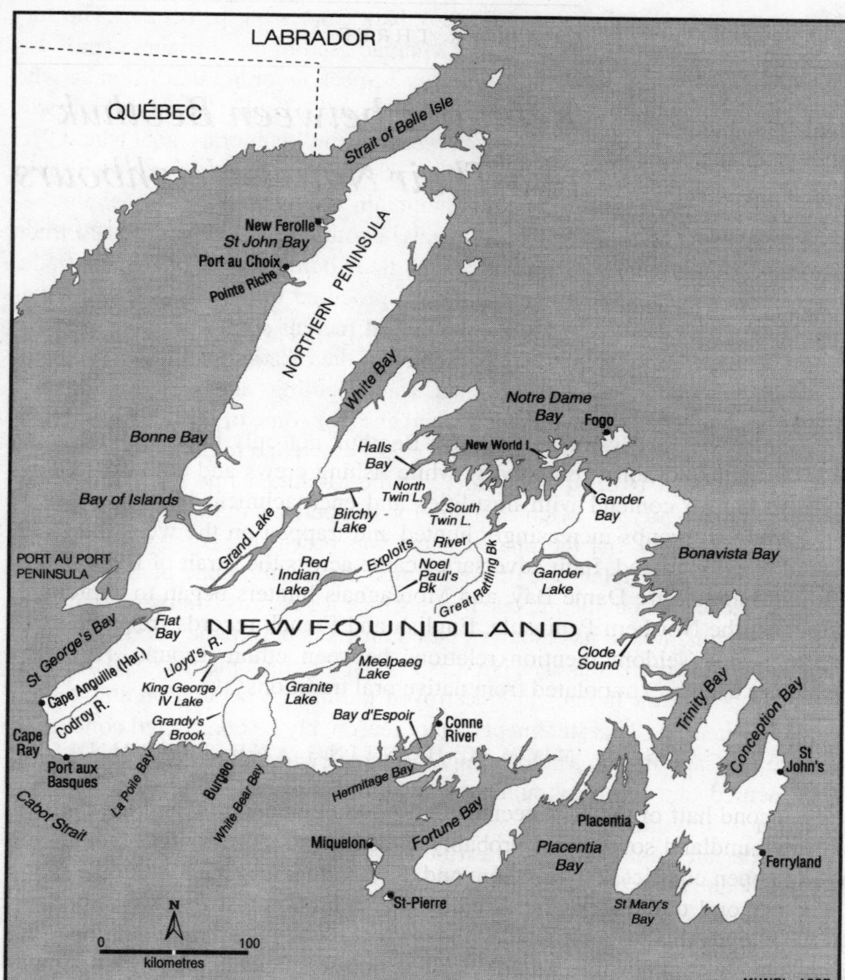

Fig.3.1 Map of Newfoundland showing places to which Micmac resorted during the sixteenth, seventeenth, and eighteenth centuries.

ithit, who told Bishop John Inglis in 1827 that "the Micmacs … have been visitors here [in Newfoundland] for centuries."[4]

Once Micmac had mastered the art of building seagoing bark canoes, they were capable of paddling across the hundred-kilometre-wide Cabot Strait, and travel to Newfoundland would have become a matter of motivation rather than of the ability to do so. Birchbark canoes were built by native people for centuries (if not millennia) before European contact.[5] In the early seventeenth century, Father Biard, Marc Lescarbot, and Nicolas Denys all commented on the

Micmac's skill in building and navigating bark canoes on the ocean.[6] The surveyor J.B. Jukes was told in 1839 that Micmac used to cross in these frail vessels from Cape Breton Island to Cape Ray.[7] Speck recorded that Micmac who formerly travelled this route would stop over at St Paul's Island, which was therefore called by Micmac *Tuywe gan moniguk*, or "temporary goal island."[8]

The earliest documents indicating Micmac visits and resource exploitation in Newfoundland date from the 1600s. Champlain's account of native people (believed to refer to Micmac and Montagnais) coming to Newfoundland to trade with fishing crews in the 1620s indicates their participation in the fur trade, though it does not prove that the furs were procured in Newfoundland.[9] Likewise, Gosnold's report in 1602 of unidentified Indians somewhere off the New England coast who were able to inform him of the location of Placentia cannot be considered evidence that Micmac were hunting and trapping there.[10] Bourque and Whitehead have made a good case for some of these native people being Micmac middlemen/traders who regularly travelled to the island.[11] Father Biard's mention in 1612 of "Presentic" as the Micmac name for "Newfoundland" (it was actually the Micmac name for Placentia) would support the view that their knowledge that the place existed was based on visits rather than on hearsay.[12] Several scholars are of the opinion that, while none of this circumstantial evidence is convincing, taken as a whole it suggests Micmac familiarity with Newfoundland and its resources based on visits before the 1600s.

In the 1650s (approximately), Nicolas Denys, a French pioneer settler, stated that the Cape Breton Indians had destroyed the moose population and "abandoned the island."[13] This statement cannot reasonably be considered conclusive evidence for Cape Breton Micmac migration to Newfoundland, although it cannot be denied that the Newfoundland south coast would have been a logical choice for their winter hunt.

A decade later, John Mathews testified that "Indians" who usually came to "kill beaver and other beasts for ffurs" had been seen in St Mary's Bay in 1662.[14] Subsequent developments make it likely that these Indians were Micmac who traded with the French at their fort in Placentia, built in the early 1660s. The rumour, spread among the English, that this fort was maintained as a defence against the Indians (Micmac) who "come off from the Maine and molest them [the French] in their Beaver trade" was soon recognized as a falsehood.[15] Far from being fearful of Micmac, the French evidently supported Micmac trapping in Newfoundland.[16] This connection enabled Micmac to get a firmer footing on the island and to make territorial advances in the wake of Anglo-French conflicts in the 1690s. As Catholic converts who had in the past been trading partners with the French, the Micmac immediately became their allies and Micmac families soon settled in the neighbourhood of the French fort.[17] Indians – not only Micmac – became an important element in d'Iberville's winter war of 1695–96.[18] During the War of the Spanish Succession (1702-13), Cape Breton Micmac again joined forces with the French in their attacks on the English; better equipped for winter travel than the French, they penetrated through inaccessible countryside and raided English communities in Fortune and to the north.[19] In

1705, twenty-five Micmac families arrived in Placentia with the intention of establishing themselves in Newfoundland with French assistance. The rest of their people were expected in the coming spring.[20] By 1707–08, French commanders recorded that sixty Micmac families had wintered in Fortune Bay while others lived temporarily on St Pierre Island; still others had "destroyed" the caribou and beaver hunt in parts of southern Newfoundland. In the woods these "savages" were free like the wolves and bears.[21] As the war progressed, the French realized that they could not control the Micmac and began to urge their departure; however, there is no evidence that Micmac complied.[22]

Although Beothuk and Micmac would have been aware of each other's presence, it is uncertain whether they had contact at that time. Some Beothuk still resorted to the southern part of the island since they were seen there in 1694.[23] Also, three Beothuk burials, two in Placentia Bay and one close to Burgeo, the latter including iron hatchets, indicate that the Beothuk buried some of their dead off the south coast well after contact.[24] While some scholars have argued in the past that the southern region was vacant and had been taken over by Micmac without the need for prior displacement of Beothuk, opinions on this point have more recently changed.[25] Micmac and Beothuk traditions of friendly relations could be interpreted to mean that at some stage, Micmac exploited this territory with the Beothuk's consent. They could also mean that the Beothuk were not in a position to defend this part of their territory against trespass and withdrew from the area to avoid open conflict with their Micmac neighbours. While both interpretations are speculative, they would account for the historical fact that Beothuk were the first in this region but later lost control of it.

After the Treaty of Utrecht (1713), the French were forced to leave their fort in Placentia; the Micmac, who had resided in Placentia and Fortune bays, also abandoned this part of the coast. William Taverner, who surveyed the population and resources of the Newfoundland south coast, thought that the Micmac no longer came there because the departure of the French had deprived them of their trading partners, who supplied them with provisions and guns they were now forced to obtain in Quebec.[26] If Taverner's survey is to be believed, in 1714–15 Micmac were found only at Cape Ray and at the harbour of Anguille. This part of the country offered an abundance of fur bearers, and near the coast caribou collected together in herds of a thousand head, making the area desirable for wintering over. St George's Bay, a short distance to the north, was wooded and had plenty of caribou but showed no signs of native occupation, although Sr Estienne Mousnier, captain of *Saint-Antonie* from Quebec, said "savages" may previously have come there.[27]

THE BEOTHUK IN MICMAC TRADITION

Our knowledge of relations between Beothuk and Micmac in Newfoundland comes largely from the oral traditions of both people. Micmac traditions were collected in the 1820s by John Peyton, Jr, justice of the peace in the Bay of

Exploits, and by William E. Cormack, founder of the Boeothick Institution. Geologist and surveyor J.B. Jukes, who published Peyton's information in 1842, also questioned Sulleon, a Micmac from the St George's Bay band, in 1839. A fourth source is the informant of anthropologist Frank G. Speck, who had a lifelong interest in northeastern native cultures and published his research on Beothuk and Newfoundland Micmac in 1922. All accounts agree on the main point: that Micmac and Beothuk coexisted peacefully in or near St George's Bay until disagreements turned harmony into enmity and bloodshed. There are, however, variations on this theme, probably due to local differences and to the considerable lapse of time between the actual events and their later retelling for the written record. The change in relations was confirmed by two Beothuk captives and by the daughter of a Beothuk/Micmac couple.

There are essentially three versions of the critical turning point in relations between the two peoples. The first, reported by John Peyton, Jr (as recorded by Jukes), came from an old Micmac who said that hostilities first erupted when a group of Micmac, descending the river near St George's Bay, fell in with a party of Beothuk. In their canoes the Micmac had concealed the heads of two murdered Beothuk for which they wished to collect rewards from the French.[28] The Beothuk, upon discovery of this treachery, invited the Micmac to a feast, seating each Micmac between two Beothuk. At a signal, every Beothuk stabbed his Micmac neighbour.[29] Cormack recorded the same story in 1827 and noted that information about these events could only be gleaned from Micmac tradition.[30] He was later able to question the Beothuk Shanawdithit and found that she concurred with the tradition.[31]

The second version is based on the testimony of Sulleon, as recorded by Jukes. Sulleon gave a confused account of the way the Beothuk slew the Micmac at a feast but said nothing about Micmac possessing Beothuk heads. In addition to the gory banquet, Sulleon related that a group of Roman Catholic Micmac from Nova Scotia, who had settled in the western part of Newfoundland, "were armed with guns and hunted the country, making great havoc amongst the game," and that soon afterward a quarrel between these Micmac and the "Red Indians" arose.[32]

The third version, recorded by Speck, contends that Micmac had camped alongside the Beothuk in St George's Bay in wintertime, when quarrels arose over a Micmac's killing of a black weasel. This act was taken as an omen of misfortune and a violation of a taboo, since the animal had not attained its proper white winter hue. The incident led to the killing of a Beothuk boy, and within a few days "feeling became so intense that a fight ensued in which the Red Indians were beaten and driven out." Because Micmac also cited the destruction of a tabooed animal as the reason for their war against the Iroquois, Speck referred to these traditions as "folktales."[33]

Since as a rule the function of an oral tradition is not to explain the actual cause of an historic event but rather to validate current social relations, these two tales – the first about the taking of Beothuk heads for reward and the

Beothuk's subsequent revenge and the second about the killing of a tabooed animal – should not be taken literally with respect to details.[34] For example, the setting of a feast at which bloody revenge is taken on enemy forces is a common motif in folktales.[35] Regardless of possible causes, hostilities appear to have begun in the area of St George's Bay, presumably between the Beothuk who lived there and the Micmac who came there to hunt. It is historical fact that the Micmac emerged as the victors and henceforth controlled the area, while the Beothuk retreated. Micmac tradition claims that they did not pursue the Beothuk, who nonetheless remained terrified and avoided contact.[36]

MICMAC IN BEOTHUK TRADITION

The Beothuk point of view on their relations with Micmac was transmitted by two Beothuk informants, Tom June and Shanawdithit. June's testimony, given in 1768, was paraphrased by Lieut. John Cartwright, who recorded that there existed between "Canadians" (Micmac) and Beothuk "so mortal an enmity that they never meet but bloody combat ensues."[37] No mention was made of the circumstances in which this enmity arose. Shanawdithit was captured in 1823 and retained in the Peyton household for several years. John Peyton, Jr, who had ample opportunity to talk to her, kept no notes (or if he did, none survive), though he asked Shanawdithit about these matters. When Bishop John Inglis visited the Peytons on Exploits Islands in July 1827, either Shanawdithit or Peyton told him that "originally they [the Beothuk] had intercourse with the Micmacs and they could partially understand each other … the Micmacs who have been visitors here [in Newfoundland] for centuries were formerly on friendly terms but their enmity has been implacable and of the deadliest character for about 150 years, from the following circumstance."[38] In Bishop Inglis's notes this is followed by the statement that the French had offered a reward for every Beothuk, dead or alive, "probably on account of depredations, as they are sad thieves," and by the story of the Micmac's taking of heads and the Beothuk's fierce revenge.

Quoting Peyton as his source, Jukes wrote in 1839 that the "Red Indians" in general and Shanawdithit in particular had a great dread of Micmac, and when two of them came to Peyton's house she went into hiding. Shanawdithit called the Micmac "Shannoc," meaning "bad Indians," or "bad men."[39]

Thomas Peyton, John's son, later recalled that Shanawdithit, while staying in the Peyton household, "exhibited the greatest antipathy to the Micmacs, more especially towards one Noel Boss, whom she so dreaded that whenever he made his appearance, she would run screeching with terror and cling to Mr P. for protection."[40] Shanawdithit called Noel Boss "Mudty Noel" (Bad Noel) and claimed that he once fired at her across the Exploits River as she was stooping down to clean venison. In describing how she was injured in the back and leg, she would act the part, limping away after being shot.[41]

From September 1828 onwards, Shanawdithit spent several months under the tutelage of William Cormack, in St John's.[42] According to his notes (published anonymously by John McGregor), her account of the Beothuk's rupture with the Micmac coincides with Micmac traditions. "About the end of the seventeenth century, they were numerous and powerful as their Mik-mak neighbours, with whom they were at that period in habits of friendly intercourse. A solitary tradition tells us that they had incurred the displeasure of the French fur-traders, whose nation then held sway in those regions. A reward was offered for the scalps, heads, or bodies, of the Boeothics. The Mik-maks, tempted by the premium, slew two Boeothics, and carried off their heads." They were accidentally discovered by some Red Indians "in the prow of the Mik-mak canoe that was about to convey them to the quarters of the French commandant at Marasheen." Here follows the story of the feast at which the Micmac were slain. "The Boeothics retired to the remote districts of the interior. War ensued; and the intercourse of the Mik-maks with Europeans, which taught them the use of firearms, gave them murderous ascendency over the primitive Boeothics, who had no arms but bows, arrows, and wooden spears."[43] Although one might suspect that some of the details were Cormack's, both Micmac and Beothuk traditions describe the events that led to hostilities between them in broadly similar terms.

Santu, daughter of a Beothuk man and his Micmac spouse, told Speck in the early 1900s that "the Micmac … came to Newfoundland a long time ago and for a while, with the white people, fought her people [the Beothuk]."[44]

There has been much argument and speculation about whether Micmac actually scalped Beothuk. According to Micmac tradition, they killed and beheaded Beothuk in order to qualify for rewards from the French, who paid cash for enemy scalps. While there is no unequivocal evidence that the Micmac actually did this, there are ample records both of scalping in Newfoundland and of rewards given by the French. Thus, for example, during the French siege of St John's in the 1690s in which some Micmac were fighting on the side of the French, an English eyewitness described how Indians removed the scalp of the settler William Drew.[45] In the War of the Spanish Succession, the English gave cash rewards for the scalps of "French Indians," while the French paid for scalps both of "English Indians" and the English themselves.[46] As late as 1747–48, a party of forty Micmac from Isle Royale who were wintering in Newfoundland plundered isolated houses, captured twenty-three English, and then held them prisoner. When twelve of the prisoners were transferred to the neighbourhood of Saint John, New Brunswick, they overpowered and killed their Micmac guards and their families. In retaliation, the Micmac put the remaining Newfoundland English to death and claimed rewards for their scalps from the French in Quebec. This incident is probably the one referred to on a "Plan of the Bay of 3 Islands," drawn in 1764, on which the river from Grand Lake to the bottom of White Bay bears the notation "It was this way the Cape Breton Indians used to pass – encouraged by the French – to kill our people employed in the winters seal fishery."[47] While the scalping of Englishmen does not prove that Micmac also scalped Beothuk, the fact that they used the reward system to their advantage by killing and scalping Newfoundland settlers suggests that their own accounts of taking Beothuk heads may not be too far-fetched.

The exact date when fighting between Beothuk and Micmac began is uncertain. Bishop Inglis's suggestion, based on Shanawdithit's account, of 150 years of enmity counting back from the 1820s would mean there had been friction between the two groups since about 1670. However, it is uncertain whether Bishop Inglis fully understood Shanawdithit's manner of reckoning time. According to Peyton, as published by Jukes, the conflict arose about "100 years ago," that is, in the 1720s. Jukes's Micmac source, Sulleon, placed the confrontations in the early 1700s, saying that a body of Micmac came to the western part of Newfoundland "at the beginning of the last [eighteenth] century" and "soon" quarrelled with the Beothuk.[48] In view of subsequent events, Peyton and Jukes's estimates are probably quite close to the actual timing of hostilities in St George's Bay, although relations may have begun to deteriorate much earlier. Jean Alphonse de Saintonge, who accompanied Roberval on his voyage to northeast Canada in 1542–43, recorded as early as 1544 that the native people from "Cape Breton make war against those from Newfoundland when they go fishing and never grant life to anyone whom they capture unless it be an infant or a young girl."[49] Cormack's account places this state of affairs even further in the past. He cites a Micmac informant who told him that "when several tribes [Beothuk and Micmac] were upon an equality in respect of weapons the Red Indians were considered invincible and frequently waged war upon the rest until the latter [Micmac] got fire arms."[50] This tradition implies that the Beothuk, in their dealings with Micmac, were warlike and belligerent, thus contradicting the idea promoted by some writers of fiction and history alike that they were of mild and unaggressive disposition.[51] It also indicates that in the confrontations in which Beothuk were beaten, the Micmac were armed with guns while the Beothuk defended themselves with bows and arrows, a circumstance referred to in Micmac oral traditions recorded by Cormack, Jukes, and Millais.[52] Speck's informants, on the other hand, recounting the same events a century later, had the Micmac conquer the Beothuk without the help of firearms, which, however, they "soon after" obtained.[53]

THE EFFECT OF MICMAC HOSTILITIES ON THE BEOTHUK

According to both Cormack's and Speck's Micmac informants, the Beothuk from St George's Bay, having been beaten by their Micmac foes, retreated into the interior of the country. Since the Beothuk depended on coastal resources, such a retreat would have been temporary because, to survive, they would have had to find a new coastal habitat. It is possible that the defeated Beothuk first moved into the lower reaches of Bonne Bay; this proposal is supported by a record to the effect that Montagnais trappers knew of Beothuk hunters in that area in 1718.[54] The harbour there lacked good anchorage for fishing vessels and may have been avoided by the French and Basques, thus making it attractive for Beothuk.[55] Alternatively, the Beothuk may have taken refuge at the bottom of White Bay, which was not favoured by French fishing crews and was within easy reach of caribou migration routes across Grand and Birchy lakes.[56]

According to Jukes's informant Sulleon, about thirty years after the original fighting Micmac confronted Beothuk in a "battle" at the northern end of Grand Lake and overpowered them. In this encounter every Beothuk man, woman, and child was put to death.[57] The victory brought the entire western region, including Grand and Birchy lakes and the access to White Bay, under Micmac control, a territorial gain that was confirmed by Lieutenant Parker and by other naval officers who patrolled the Newfoundland coast and recorded the presence of Micmac camps at Cape Ray (1715, 1763), Port aux Basques (1726–27), Codroy (1768), Anguille (1715, 1763), St George's Bay (1788, 1789, 1793), Bay of Islands (1770, 1793), Pointe Riche (1767), and Ferolle, St John Bay, and Port au Choix (1767, 1788).[58] In the 1760s and 1770s, the Micmac from these camps appear to have confined their hunting and trapping expeditions to the hinterland of their coastal camps, and to the area around Grand Lake and the bottom of White Bay.[59] In the south, Micmac came to harbours west of Placentia, particularly in the areas of Fortune and Bay D'Espoir (1766) and trapped around many lakes and river systems inland from these locations.[60] Others returned to Cape Breton Island and elsewhere in Nova Scotia because, without permission, Micmac were not allowed to stay in Newfoundland beyond the month of October.[61]

Lieut. John Cartwright, who assessed Beothuk/Micmac relations after his exploration of Beothuk country in 1768 (see chapter 6), remarked, "We know that the Canadians range all of the western coast." The Beothuk Tom June had told him that "the two nations did not see the least sign one of the other during the whole winter," which Cartwright took to mean that fear kept them apart.[62] While his interpretation may be valid, it should also be noted that at the time, the hunting habits of the two populations were different enough to ensure that their paths would rarely have crossed.[63] Some Beothuk bands hunted and trapped during the winter season in the hinterland of Notre Dame and Bonavista bays; other groups intercepted migrating caribou herds on the Exploits River and Red Indian Lake in fall and remained close to the kill sites until the following spring. In contrast, the Micmac focused on trapping furs for trade around lakes and rivers inland from the middle of summer until the beginning of winter. At the end of the trapping season, they assembled at or near the mouths of large rivers on the south and west coasts, where eels could be speared through the ice and caribou could be tracked down in their winter habitat not too far from the coast.[64]

Eventually, however, Micmac began to encroach on Beothuk territory to extend their trapping range. According to Peyton's account of Micmac tradition, they entered Beothuk country from the south via Shannock Brook (Noel Paul's Brook), which led to a fight between the two peoples at the confluence of Shannock Brook and the Exploits River. As before, the Micmac were the victors.[65] Following the Beothuk's repeated defeats in which many of them lost their lives, the Micmac appear to have become the traditional foes of all Beothuk and enmity between the two groups became entrenched.

CONFLICT BETWEEN INUIT AND FISHING CREWS

In the late 1500s, Inuit from Labrador began to frequent the Strait of Belle Isle.[66] Purportedly they were belligerent and hostile towards the fishing crews who were employed in the cod and whale fisheries. Inuit were most extensively involved in conflicts with the French who fished on the northern Newfoundland coast between Cape Norman (north of Pistolet Bay) and Cape St John (Notre Dame Bay), an area known as Petit Nord (Fig. 3.2).[67] As noted in chapter 2, Captain Wheeler of the British Royal Navy, who enquired into the French fishery in 1684, found the French to be "at utter defiance" with the "Indians," who were numerous in the northern part of the island and "never reside their [*sic*] but in summer and have their arms by them." The French constantly kept armed boats along the shore so as to protect themselves "from the canoes of the Indians and what nations soe ever."[68] Evidently more than one ethnic group resorted to this region; they would have been visiting Inuit and resident Beothuk.

Because Inuit aggression against the French has often been attributed to the Beothuk, relevant facts are briefly reviewed here. According to several French accounts from the early 1600s, hostilities originated in the 1580s when Inuit had camped opposite the northern entry to Quirpon and French fishermen from St Malo who wished to trade with them had anchored in the same location. When the night watch of the St Malo crew heard a noise they fired, fearing an attack, and killed the wife of one of the "chiefs." Ever since this event, the natives were said to cross the strait in their sealskin-covered "canoes" to avenge this deed.[69] As a result the French requested armed boats to patrol the coast and protect them in 1609–10.[70] References to patrol boats, which can be found in French and English records until the eighteenth century, often claim that fishing crews needed protection from "hostile Indians," although the evidence clearly shows that the agressors were Inuit.[71]

One of the people who believed that the hostile natives in the north were Beothuk was David Kirke from Ferryland. In a letter to Archbishop Laud dated 1639, Kirke describes a major attack of about eighty (Newfoundland) "Indians" who killed sixteen French fishermen in Les Ouages Harbour (St Julien) whilst the latter were piling up their fish. Clothing themselves in the apparel of the murdered French, the attackers proceeded to Petty Masters (Croque Harbour), where they killed another twenty-one Frenchmen. They were said to have returned home in great triumph, carrying the heads of the slain.[72] The context in

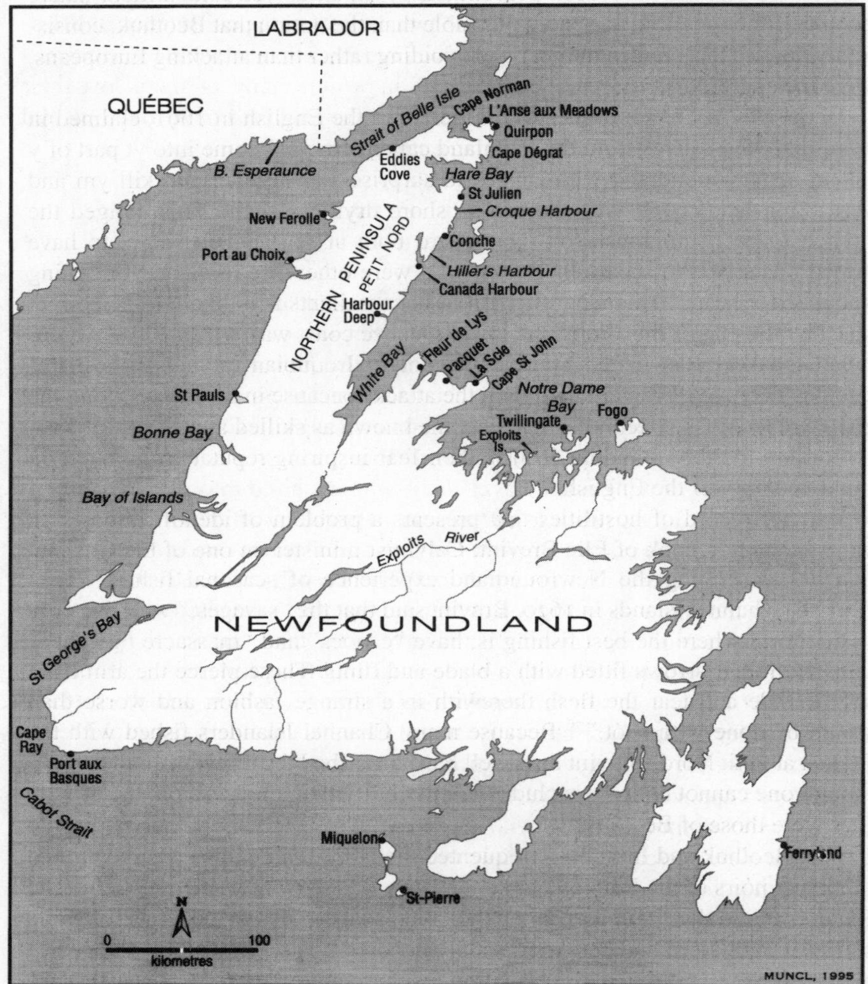

Fig.3.2 Map of Newfoundland showing places to which Inuit and Montagnais resorted from the sixteenth to the mid-eighteenth century.

which Kirke described this incident suggests that the killing had occurred well in the past and may have been the incident that precipitated the St Malo fishermen's request for armed protection.[73] Given that the Beothuk were neither embroiled in a feud with the French nor known to have used European clothing or to have assembled in large numbers (as has been the practice of Inuit), it is considered certain that the assailants were Inuit.[74] However, Inuit were not recorded to have beheaded their victims, and the reputed cutting off of heads as trophies remains a problem. It could have been an embellishment of the story, or the massacre could have been perpetrated by other, as yet unidentified, native people. Either possibility is more plausible than the notion that Beothuk, consistently described as few in number and avoiding rather than attacking Europeans, were the aggressors.

Jacqueauly, a French officer who deserted to the English in 1691, claimed in 1714 that "the natives from the mainland called 'Iroqois' come into yt part of y Island of Newfoundland with canoes to surprise y fishermen and kill ym and very often land & kill ym who are on shore drying y fish." This obliged the French to be continuously on their guard both at sea and on shore, to have armed boats, and to secure their men who were otherwise in danger of "being knockt on y head." This identification of the assailants is unlikely to be correct since by the end of the 1600s, the lower Quebec coast was inhabited by Algonquian speakers and visited by Inuit but not by Iroquoian raiding parties. Iroquoians may have been credited with the attacks because in their wars along the St Lawrence river system they had become known as skilled and cruel warriors. According to Abbé Baudoin (1696), their fear-inspiring reputation lingered on in the memory of the English.[75]

Another record of hostilities that presents a problem of identification is an entry in the notebook of Elie Brevint, Calvinist minister on one of the Channel Islands. Describing the Newfoundland experience of seasonal fishing crews from the Channel Islands in 1620, Brevint said that the "savages," who live only in the north where the best fishing is, have "canoes" and "massacre the Christians with their arrows fitted with a blade and flints. These pierce the arm from side to side and tear the flesh therewith in a strange fashion and worse than would be done with shot."[76] Because many Channel Islanders fished with the French at Petit Nord, Brevint may well have described the effect of Inuit arrows, though one cannot entirely exclude the possibility that, on occasion, the projectiles were those of Beothuk.

That Beothuk and Inuit both frequented the Northern Peninsula is mentioned in the memoirs of the Raudots, father and son, which were written in 1720. The Raudots claim that Inuit as well as the "red savages" destroyed French fishing stages at Petit Nord and cut the ropes of anchored boats, which they stripped of all useful materials.[77] Their explanation for these guerilla activities was that the Inuit needed iron to make arrows, knives, and spears, which they could not procure by other means. Since Inuit are known to have traded with Frenchmen and Basques, this rationale applies more convincingly to the Beothuk, who had come to incorporate iron tools into their technology but had no opportunity of acquiring such items, since they did not trade with Europeans. In contrast, some Inuit traded with Frenchmen and Basques despite the existing discords. In the 1690s, for example, Inuit were trading with Quebec ships for amunition, axes, and the like and in the early 1700s exchanged furs for firearms and other goods with the French in Notre Dame and Basques in Port au Choix.[78] But the quantitiy of furs involved was relatively small until the French negotiated a treaty with the Inuit in 1756, after which trade relations became more significant.[79]

Conflicts between English fishing crews and Inuit were rarely recorded. This changed with the annexation of Labrador by the British Crown in 1763, when Newfoundland governors became responsible for solving the problem of Inuit interference in the Labrador fishery.[80] Having received several reports that English, American, and Newfoundland fishing crews had been "impudent, treacherous and cruel" towards the Inuit and had on many occasions "plundered and killed" them, Hugh Palliser, the incumbent governor, met with a large Inuit assembly in Pitts Harbour in 1765 to make peace.[81] Assisted by the Moravian missionary Jens Haven, who had become familiar with the Inuit language in the course of his work in Greenland, Palliser established trade relations with them.[82] He proclaimed Inuit to be under the protection of the British government and ordered naval officers to supervise all transactions with them and to remain in Quirpon, Croque Harbour, and Château Bay in Labrador until all Inuit had left for their northern settlements.[83] By 1786 British naval officers who patrolled the Strait of Belle Isle no longer mentioned southern visits by Inuit, and although stragglers were encountered, for example in 1798, by the end of the eighteenth century Inuit voyages to the south had become the exception rather than the rule.[84] In the early nineteenth century Inuit seldom travelled south, much to the chagrin of the English, who would have liked to trade with them.[85]

BEOTHUK/INUIT CONFLICT

The earliest direct information about relations between Inuit and Indians in Newfoundland comes from Commander Graydon, who recorded in 1701 that "great hatred" existed between "Newfoundland Indians" (believed to mean Beothuk) and the "Canada Indians" (believed to mean Inuit).[86] It was Graydon who reported the arrival of Inuit umiaks to trade with the French in harbours between Fogo and Croque. This infiltration of Inuit into Notre Dame Bay, a coast and island area extensively exploited by Beothuk, is likely to have resulted in tension or actual fighting.

While no other officer described the ill feelings between the two populations quite as clearly, Lieut. John Cartwright stated in 1768 that the "Esquimaux" formerly "ranged far enough to the southward to have fallen in with Red Indian canoes and … that they then treated all they met as enemies. The Esquimaux in harassing them kept to their own element, the water, where their superior canoes and missile weapons provided for killing whales, made them terrible enemies to encounter."[87] This information could have been given by the Beothuk boy Tom June, captured in 1758, whom Cartwright had consulted with regard to his tribe. Cartwright added that in more recent times, the spread of English settlements in the north kept Inuit from coming far enough south to interact with Beothuk.[88]

Since Graydon's and Cartwright's reports actually address relations between Beothuk and Inuit and describe them in terms of enmity and hatred, it is assumed that their portrayals of the situation were fairly accurate.[89] However, while some Inuit may have met Beothuk with hostile intentions, others may have contacted Beothuk groups in a more peaceful manner. This is alluded to by Charlevoix, who wrote in 1744 that on the Newfoundland coast only "Eskimaux" were to be seen, but that these people had often spoken of "other tribes [inland] with whom they have commercial intercourse."[90] Since the Labrador Inuit were not a single, unified group, their relations with Beothuk may have been similar to those with the French, where a long-lasting animosity among some groups did not prevent others from engaging in barter.[91]

The tradition that Inuit and Beothuk were hostile nevertheless persisted. In 1797, for example, Magistrate John Bland informed Governor Waldegrave that the Beothuk and Inuit were said to have been in "perpetual hostility," though he did not know the basis of their dissension. As far as Bland could tell, a great many years had elapsed since the Inuit had any footing south of Cape Charles, and he thought that the present generation of Newfoundland natives would "scarcely know that there is such a people as the Esquimaux."[92] In this it turned out that Bland was mistaken: the Beothuk captive Shanawdithit, who lived with the Peytons in Exploits Bay in the 1820s, related that her people knew and "despised" the Inuit "for their filthiness"; she did not allude to contacts or conflicts.[93]

Although stories of hostility referred to events that occurred much earlier, ill-informed statements prevailed. In 1810, when Governor Duckworth issued a proclamation to "Micmacs, Esquimaux and other American Indians" requesting that they live in peace with Beothuk, Inuit and Beothuk would no longer have come into contact, since by then Inuit no longer travelled to Notre Dame Bay.[94] An article on the capture and death of the Beothuk woman Demasduit published in the *London Times* in 1820 concluded with the misleading comment: "Whether they [the Beothuk] had fled to some other part of the island or had been exterminated by the Esquimaux, who, to obtain furs with which they are covered are known to invariably murder them at every opportunity, could not be ascertained."[95] Even Lieutenant Buchan, a veteran in Beothuk affairs, committed an error by noting on his 1811 "Sketch of the River Exploits" that "Esquemaux pass from Great Rattling Brook to St Georges Bay"; this river was part of a traditional Micmac route and was not used by Inuit people.[96] As late as 1827, Bishop Inglis, reporting to the Society for the Propagation of the Gospel on his visit to Newfoundland, noted that the "Esquimeaux," like the English, French, Micmac, and "Mountaineers" (Montagnais), "shoot at the Boeothick as they shoot at the Deer."[97] Since Inuit no longer came far enough south to interact with Beothuk, Inglis was obviously misinformed.

BEOTHUK/MONTAGNAIS RELATIONS

English and French accounts from the sixteenth and seventeenth centuries rarely differentiate between native groups but refer to them as "savages," "Indians," "Esquimaux-Indians," or "Esquimaux," regardless of ethnic affiliation.

This undifferentiated usage has resulted in much uncertainty about the identity of the people that were described, as was the case with the Inuit who killed thirty-seven French fishermen at Petit Nord. Another incident of mistaken identity was that of the "Indians" who were employed by the French and Basques in the whale and cod fisheries in the Strait of Belle Isle (on the Labrador side). Captain Whitbourne believed that they were Beothuk who lived on the north and west coast of Newfoundland. Basques had informed him that they were an "ingenious and tractable people ... ready to assist them with great labour and patience in the killing, cutting, and boyling of Whales; and making the Traine-oyle, without expectation of other rewards, than a little bread, or some such small hire."[98] Whitbourne was so impressed with this tale that he planned to go there to trade with them and make "trayne oyle" as did the Basques. In the event, he was unable to follow through with his plan because the owners of the ship with which he intended to travel would not permit him to go there. In retrospect it is clear that he was misinformed and that the Indian helpers in the whale fishery would not have been Beothuk. This assertion is based on a report on the Basque whale fishery in the Strait of Belle Isle, published in 1625 by the Spaniard Lope de Isasti. Isasti, like Whitbourne before him, described the Indians as ingenious and tractable, working with skill and patience for little reward. He said that they were called "montaneses" (people of the mountains), taken to mean Montagnais, or "canaleses" (people of the channel or strait). According to Barkham, the wording of the text clearly shows that the Indian assistants were known by two different names.[99] The "canaleses" could therefore not have been Beothuk, as some scholars have suggested. This makes sense inasmuchas Beothuk in other parts of the island were said to be elusive and unapproachable, and it is unlikely that those who lived on the Northern Peninsula or on the west coast would have freely mingled with, and even worked for, the Basques.

Isasti also mentioned hostile "esquimals," who were reputed to be cannibals. They came to the Strait of Belle Isle to attack the Basques with bows and arrows; fortunately, the friendly Indians (Montagnais) would warn the Basques of impending assaults, implying a prior animosity between the Indians and Inuit.[100]

Since neither Isasti nor Whitbourne ever visited the Strait of Belle Isle but used almost identical phrases to describe the Indians, their information is assumed to have come from the same source, namely, Basque (or French) whalers who had worked there.[101]

A question that Isasti did not address is whether the "montaneses" were in the habit of travelling across to Newfoundland. Considering the relatively short distance involved, some Montagnais may have intermittently exploited resources on the Northern Peninsula or in western Newfoundland.[102] However, there is no evidence that Montagnais parties hunted and trapped in Newfoundland on a regular basis before they became affiliated with the French. This affiliation began around 1702, when Courtmanche received a concession to erect posts for prosecution of the seal and cod fisheries on the north shore of the

Strait of Belle Isle and recruited Montagnais to assist him.[103] To supplement diminishing resources in Labrador, the French encouraged Montagnais to go on trapping expeditions to Newfoundland and fitted them out with supplies.[104] On occasion, French employees were dispatched with the Montagnais trappers, probably to ensure that the pelts were not sold to the English but were brought back to the French trading post in Labrador.[105]

Commander Percy of the Royal Navy, reporting on the French fishery in northern Newfoundland in 1720, recorded the presence of "a sort of French Indians" who, to the detriment of English furriers, take "a considerable quantity of fur in winter and sell them to our [English] trading people."[106] Two years later, "Canada Indians" were said to "have for some years past come thither to catch fur."[107] While the reports do not explain who these Indians were, William Taverner, an English settler and trader who complained about their extensive trapping in Newfoundland, identified them as "Mountaineers." He noted that the French governor in the Gulf of St Lawrence – presumably de Brouague – frequently equipped as many as seventy or eighty Montagnais trappers with boats and other necessities. On their arrival in Newfoundland, usually in the month of September, they dispersed in small parties between Cape Dégrat and St George's Bay, trapped for furs throughout the winter season, and returned to Labrador in the following April "loaded with furs & other skins."[108] Taverner had been credibly informed by several inhabitants of Port aux Basques who had wintered amongst the Montagnais that this had been their practice ever since the Treaty of Utrecht in 1713, when France was forced to surrender all settlements and fortifications in Newfoundland.

That Montagnais hunted and trapped on the Northern Peninsula and on the west coast in the early eighteenth century does not prove that they had communication with Beothuk. Yet there seems to have been some contact since Montagnais trappers appear to have been the only people who were informed about the northern Beothuk's whereabouts and practices. They had told the French intendant Raudot that "red savages" lived in Hare Bay at Petit Nord; they painted themselves red from head to foot, were numerous, used birchbark canoes, and hunted caribou with the aid of pole fences. In one location the informants had found a lake of roughly four kilometres in circumference surrounded by poles, with a single space left for caribou to enter. The animals could thus be killed in the water, which was easier than pursuing them on land. The houses of the "red savages" had oval sleeping hollows, suggesting that occupants "rest with their body almost curled up like dogs when they sleep."[109] Apparently, the informants had not seen Beothuk in this position and only presumed that they slept rolled up, which implies that any encounter they might have had with Beothuk was brief.

"Red savages" also hunted caribou in Belle Bay (Bonne Bay) but would run away as soon as they saw a European.[110] De Brouague, who wished to extend his fur business, nevertheless asked the French who accompanied a Montagnais party on their trapping excursion to attract the "red savages" and, if possible, to trade with them. But when they arrived at Bonne Bay, where they had hoped to meet with Beothuk, the "red savages" had just left.[111] Since the Beothuk were known to flee from Europeans, their hasty retreat at the approach of Montagnais with Frenchmen at their heels would have been a foregone conclusion. One might speculate that the Montagnais would not have been overly anxious to draw Beothuk into trade, since they were potential competitors for furs in the region.

The evidence suggests that by the 1720s, relations between Montagnais and Beothuk were sporadic at best and based on mutual tolerance rather than close ties. The Beothuk would not have been so elusive had the Montagnais been trusted as friends, and the Montagnais would not have tried to meet with the Beothuk had there been a history of warfare. As it was, Beothuk and Montagnais shared what may originally have been traditional Beothuk trapping territory in northern and western Newfoundland, and Montagnais trappers did not take advantage of their guns to evict Beothuk from these regions. Several factors, all of them speculative, could account for the Beothuk's seclusion and avoidance of Montagnais. In the 1720s relations between Beothuk and Micmac, who were affiliated with the French, deteriorated to the point of open aggression and the subsequent defeat of the Beothuk. While there is no evidence that Montagnais were drawn into this conflict, their association with the Micmac and their participation in the French fur trade could have rendered them suspect to the Beothuk. In addition, trade – whether with Europeans or Montagnais middlemen – may have been unacceptable to the Beothuk because it would inevitably have affected their traditional way of life and curtailed their independence. Another inhibiting factor may have been that previous contact with Montagnais had brought smallpox (or other diseases) to the Beothuk. In the seventeenth century, the Labrador Montagnais had been decimated by smallpox and possibly measles, and if the Beothuk had been infected after visits from Montagnais, relations would have suffered.[112]

Despite various deterrents, there is likely to have been communication between the two, possibly for as long as Montagnais came to Newfoundland. Hostilities between Beothuk and Montagnais have never been recorded, and neither the captive Beothuk boy Tom June, questioned by John Cartwright in 1768, nor Shanawdithit, who gave information about her people in the 1820s, alluded to enmity with Labrador Indians.[113]

From the 1740s onwards, when the Montagnais' attachment to the French relaxed and their trapping activities in Newfoundland temporarily ceased, relations undoubtedly became tenuous. Following the Treaty of Paris in 1763, when Labrador came under British jurisdiction, Governor Hugh Palliser recorded that the "Mountaineer" lived west of the Strait of Belle Isle and traded with settlers from Quebec and with New England whalers. The natives who inhabited "without the Strait and to the northward" were Inuit. "Of their [Montagnais] numbers or places of abode very little is known, they come down to the coast in greater or lesser numbers according to the treatment they have met with the preceding year."[114] Palliser described them as harmless but addicted to stealing and drinking to excess and believed that under proper regulation they could be brought into a profitable trade. In 1773, the patrolling officer of the Royal Navy, Lieutenant Roger Curtis, confirmed that the Montagnais in Labrador lived a good way into the country, mainly trapped for furs, and came every year in their birchbark canoes to the southern Labrador coast to trade with Canadian merchants for spirits, firearms, ammunition, and blanketing.[115] Curtis described their way of life in detail but made no mention of Montagnais trapping parties coming to Newfoundland. They were said to be hostile towards Inuit, but there was not the slightest hint that they were in contact with Beothuk.

Montagnais parties resumed excursions to northern Newfoundland in the 1780s, possibly as a result of Governor Palliser's encouragement. They no longer came only for the trapping season but went furring inland in winter and traded on the Newfoundland coast in summer. In the absence of English traders they sold their furs to the French.[116] In the summer of 1785, twenty "Canadian Indians" (presumed to be Montagnais) were recorded at Great and Little Quirpon, and in the following year sixty Montagnais came in canoes from Labrador to Quirpon, Carouge (Cape Rouge Harbour?), Conche, and Pacquet Harbour. They penetrated a great way into the country and caught considerable quantities of fur, which they traded for muskets, powder and shot, traps, boats, sails, and clothes.[117] Two years later twenty-one Montagnais were encountered at Ferolle and Port au Choix.[118] As the French had taken great pains to convert the Montagnais to their own faith, parties travelled from the Newfoundland west coast to St Pierre and Miquelon to be married or to have their children christened by the resident priest.[119] Among the English, the Labrador Montagnais were reputed to be "treacherous drunkards and thieves" who were generally under French influence.[120] The British naval officers who patrolled the Labrador coast seem not to have trusted them and are likely to have scrutinized their habits and affiliations with care. Yet there are no reports that they were in contact with Beothuk.

INFORMATION ON MONTAGNAIS FROM SHANAWDITHIT

It is unfortunate that none of the records of Montagnais hunting and trapping practices in Newfoundland give a clear indication of their relations with Beothuk. Though the apparent absence of strife encourages the conclusion that they did not foster hostile attitudes, it is nevertheless disappointing that there is so little evidence for the widely quoted contention that the two groups were on friendly terms. This contention rests largely on Shanawdithit's remarks to John Peyton, Jr, in the 1820s, which Peyton relayed to Bishop Inglis of Nova Scotia on the occasion of his visit to Exploits Islands in 1827 and, a decade later, to the geologist and surveyor J.B. Jukes. Bishop Inglis noted in his diary: "The traditions of the Boeothick represent their descent from the Labrador Indians but the language of one is wholly unintelligible to the other."[121] Jukes recorded his conversation with Peyton as follows: "They [the Beothuk] were acquainted with another tribe of Indians whom they called Shaunamunc, and with whom they were very friendly. These came from the Labradore, but were not Esquimaux, whom the Red Indians also knew and despised ... The Shaunamuncs were dressed in deer-skins and not seal-skins, but their deer-skins were not reddened ... The Red Indians traded with these Shaunamuncs; receiving stone-hatchets and other implements from them and they mutually visited each other's countries."[122] Jukes was of the opinion that the Shaunamunc would have been the "Mountaineers on the Labrador shore."

Knowing that the information comes from a single source, that is, from Shanawdithit through Peyton, Jr, the two statements can be seen as supplementing each other, referring to Labrador Indians as ancestors of the Beothuk, or as people descended from the same ancestors as the Beothuk, and as the Beothuk's trading partners. Certainly, Shanawdithit's information about trade between Beothuk and what may have been Labrador Montagnais (or their ancestors) suggests amicable interactions. The archaeological record supports this conclusion.[123] Regrettably, there is as yet no other direct evidence that might confirm this relationship or place it within a clearer historical context.

CHAPTER FOUR

Competition for Resources on the Coast

REDISTRIBUTION OF BEOTHUK IN THE EARLY 1700S

During the first half of the eighteenth century the relatively peaceful coexistence between English settlers and Beothuk came to an end. The Avalon Peninsula became more widely settled by English colonists and was to remain a stronghold of the English fishery. In the course of Anglo-French conflicts in the 1690s, French forces and their Indian allies advanced overland from Placentia to Trinity Bay in order to attack English settlements. Since the Beothuk's portage path from Come by Chance to Bull Arm was the most convenient route, the French are likely to have carried their boats across on this path and to have scared the Beothuk away.[1] In subsequent years this part of Trinity Bay increasingly attracted English settlements, which forced the Beothuk to relinquish their camps at Dildo South and in Bull Arm. A census from 1711 states that 250 English residents lived in "Dildo South and adjacent places" where a hundred years earlier John Guy had seen Beothuk mamateeks (mamateek is the Beothuk term for house).[2] Though the Beothuk moved further north, they nevertheless continued to make forays into Trinity Bay until the 1770s, probably by crossing the narrow headlands from neighbouring Bonavista Bay.[3]

Bonavista Bay, with its deeply indented coastline and profusion of islands, afforded a reasonable degree of seclusion and security for the Beothuk and remained part of their territory. In 1720, Commander Percy of the Royal Navy reported that the inhabitants of Bonavista Bay were aware of the presence of native people but had no commerce with them. They were "a Savage people not as yet acquainted with the use of guns; In the summer season they come to the southward, have been seen near Bonavist. In the winter they go farther northward in Canoose made of Birchin Rinds which they sawe together with the sinnews of Bucks and pay the Seams with Turpentine."[4] That Beothuk frequented Bonavista Bay throughout the eighteenth century has been confirmed through archaeological excavations on the best-known site in this bay, known as The Beaches.[5]

The coast and islands in Notre Dame Bay, extending from Ragged Harbour on the Strait Shore to Cape St John on the Baie Verte Peninsula, became the Beothuk's major resort. Here they camped on sequestered beaches in inlets and river mouths and evaded fishermen by slipping out of view among the numerous headlands and islands. Although French as well as English crews fished for cod in the bay throughout the seventeenth century, encounters with Beothuk seem to have been rare.[6]

For the winter season the Beothuk moved away from the coast to hunt and trap. Many of their winter quarters were located on the banks of the Exploits River and Red Indian Lake and on other lakes. Since the French fishing crews went back to France for the winter, there would have been no conflict with them over inland resources; in fact French records rarely mention the Beothuk. However, a great number of English settlers from Fogo, Twillingate, and Bonavista took over French fishing places for the winter to trap fur bearers and catch seal.[7] Many of them also hunted and trapped inland and thus competed with the Beothuk for fur-bearing animals.

On the Northern Peninsula, Montagnais parties began to exploit resources so that the Beothuk could no longer roam freely on this part of the island. However, some Beothuk were said to have hunted caribou in the vicinity of Hare Bay.[8] But in spring and summer they were barred from much of the coast by the presence of French fishing stations and visiting Inuit from Labrador. The entire Newfoundland west coast as well as the inland area around Grand and Birchy Lakes was taken over by the Micmac, who, sometimes alongside the French, also replaced the Beothuk on the south coast and in Placentia Bay.

Of necessity, in the 1700s, the dramatic decrease in areas available to the Beothuk for ensuring subsistence would have led to a redistribution of bands and to a heavier exploitation of animal populations in the reduced territory. To make matters worse, as the century advanced the English encroached more aggressively into the region to harvest salmon and trap fur bearers. While the immediate consequences of this development cannot readily be quantified, it is possible to document the steady growth of the English salmon and fur businesses and, by implication, a progressive exclusion of the Beothuk from what had traditionally been their major sources of food.

THE GROWTH OF THE ENGLISH SALMON FISHERY

The Beothuk's subsistence economy was based on the exploitation of terrestrial as well as marine species, available at different times of the year. In June and July, following the seal- and egg-collecting season, salmon was their major resource. Every year large numbers of salmon enter Newfoundland rivers to spawn. They not only provided immediate subsistence but also, when dried or smoked, constituted an important reserve. Failure to procure a good supply during the annual salmon runs would have been a calamity.[9] In the early days of settlement, when settlers and summer fishing crews caught salmon solely for their own consumption, the Beothuk continued to have access to major salmon rivers in Bonavista and Notre Dame bays and would have been able to obtain sufficient quantities for their subsistence.[10] The situation changed when the English started a commercial salmon fishery that quickly expanded into rivers from which the Beothuk were accustomed to harvest their supplies. Around 1708, George Skeffington of Indian Bay had begun to build houses and stages for processing and curing salmon on several rivers north of Cape Bonavista. To improve the servicing and patrolling of his salmon posts, he had also cleared the land alongside the rivers "near fourty miles [sixty-four kilometres] up the country."[11] By the early 1720s his men caught salmon in Freshwater Bay (Gambo River) at the bottom of Bonavista Bay; at Ragged Harbour River on the Straight Shore; in the Gander River, one of the most productive salmon runs in Newfoundland (later to produce 145,800 kilograms of salmon annually); and in Dog Creek (now Horwoods River).[12] In his petition for rights to the salmon fishery in these rivers, Skeffington expressly stated that they had never been exploited by summer fishing crews; but he did not mention that native people had formerly fished there.[13] William Keen, a Bonavista merchant who joined Skeffington in the business, recorded harvests of seven hundred tierces a season (a tierce being about 162 kilograms), an amount that he hoped would increase in the future.[14] According to Captain Scott, the naval officer who patrolled the northern district in 1718, further fine salmon rivers "capable of employing some hundreds of men in the salmon fishery" were still lying "unimproved."[15]

After 1717, quantities of salmon caught or sold were reported in the answers to questionnaires on the Newfoundland fishery called "Heads of Enquiry," issued by the Board of Trade in England. The answers were submitted annually by the naval commanders of the Newfoundland convoys and, after 1729, by the officers who were appointed governors of Newfoundland for the summer season. The figures for salmon are only approximations since locally consumed or traded fish was not included; in addition, the methods by which information was collected tended to produce figures that were considerably smaller than the actual amounts.[16] They nevertheless show the significant growth of the English salmon fishery and indicate the reduced access to salmon that was imposed on the Beothuk. Between 1717 and 1735, quantities of salmon fished by the English in Newfoundland ranged from 200 to 900 tierces (32,400 to 145,800 kilograms) per year, with an average of about 600 tierces (close to 100,000 kilograms).[17] From 1736 to 1755, annual catches averaged ca. 1,245 tierces (201,690 kilograms); from 1756 to 1784, ca. 1,760 tierces (285,120 kilograms); and from 1785 to 1800, ca. 3,400 tierces, which amounted to 550,800 kilograms of salmon. Although these figures comprise salmon catches from rivers all around Newfoundland, the majority of salmon runs, and the most productive ones, were those in Notre Dame Bay, particularly in the Gander, Exploits, and Indian Arm rivers.[18]

In the early years of the salmon fishery, the salmon catchers constructed weirs that hindered the fish from proceeding upriver to spawn. As the salmon found their paths to the spawning grounds blocked, they would congregate below the weirs, where the men could dip them out or catch them in seines.[19] At a later stage, weirs, or "rack works," were supplemented with gill and stake nets, particularly in river estuaries and in the tidal areas near the river mouths, where weir construction was impractical.[20] With the expansion of the fishery, competition among the English became fierce. Salmon was often caught by a succession of traps and nets, and salmon catchers would sometimes set nets in such a way that they prevented salmon from entering already existing works.[21] An example is given in chapter 7 in which the servants of the owner of a salmon station were punished for placing nets directly in front of the nets of a competitor.

THE BEOTHUK'S EXCLUSION FROM SALMON RIVERS

In the early 1700s, Beothuk who camped on The Beaches and elsewhere in Bonavista Bay may have caught their salmon in Freshwater Bay, while those from Boyd's Cove and other places in eastern Notre Dame Bay would have relied on salmon from nearby Dog Creek and Gander Bay. When Skeffington's posts barred them from these rivers they responded by breaking down weirs and by killing some of Skeffington's men, though the records do not disclose at which of the salmon posts this destruction occurred.[22] It was the first time in documented history that the Beothuk had resorted to violence. Skeffington informed the patrolling officer that the salmon fishery had been: "obstructed by the Islander Indians, killing some of his men, breaking down his dams, taking away some of his Nets and robbing him of his provisions and other necessaries. This happened to him last summer and several times before but [he] has not met with any obstruction from them this year."[23]

Skeffington's use of the term "Islander Indians" is another first in the records, since this designation clearly identifies the Indians as Beothuk. Prior to this date, native people of different ethnic origin were often referred to as "savages" or "Indians," and these unspecified terms can cause confusion with respect to their identification. While Skeffington made it clear that the culprits were Beothuk, it was another few decades before government officials, and settlers in general, consistently differentiated between Beothuk and other native people in Newfoundland.

According to a communication by William Keen to the Board of Trade in 1720, Skeffington had planned to go back to the salmon posts with thirty to forty men; presumably these men were armed.[24] This large force may have temporarily frightened the Beothuk away, though they had not yet accepted the loss of the salmon rivers to the English. In 1724 Skeffington again complained of being disturbed in the salmon fishery "very much by the Indians who come once or twice a year to gather oker and this last time killed him a man." Though the killing was perpetrated by Beothuk who had come to collect ochre, the conflict clearly centred on access to salmon. Skeffington also intimated to the patrolling officer that if the government would allow him two boats with six men each he would undertake to keep "the country always clear of the Indians," presumably having in mind the country around his salmon posts.[25] There is no evidence that Skeffington's request was considered, nor do the records mention whether he attempted to avenge the death of his men. Given that he thought the Beothuk should be driven from the country, it is quite possible that he or his men took the law into their own hands to punish and scare them, for he did not report further conflicts.[26] Edward Burd, supercargo on the merchant ship *The Christian of Leith*, wrote in his 1726 journal: "The Indians are now pretty much worn out, only there are still some towards the northward living wild in little huts in the woods, they live upon the wild fowl that they kill, upon some fish that they catch when they go out in their canoes, which are made of the rinds of trees … the English … treat them with great severety."[27] Three years later Skeffington's salmon fishery changed hands; new salmon posts were erected in rivers in western Notre Dame Bay, particularly the Exploits River, which became widely known for its productive salmon runs.[28] This swift extension of the salmon fishery into most parts of Notre Dame Bay severely reduced the Beothuk's chances of catching enough salmon to meet their needs. Rather than stepping up their aggression they seem to have retreated; patrolling officers reported in the early 1730s that Beothuk were seldom to be seen in Notre Dame Bay.[29]

From the 1730s onwards, the English began to establish fishing and salmon stations in every sizeable bay and inlet in greater Notre Dame Bay. According to John Cartwright, the Beothuk, whom he tried unsuccessfully to contact in 1768, "used formerly to kill considerable quantities of salmon in the rivers and small streams; but the English have now only left them in possession of Charles's and another brook."[30]

Within a year or so, a salmon station with a crew of three men was also operating at Charles Brook. This was the first year the salmon catchers had tried this brook, which "had hitherto been constantly occupied by Indians to whom it answers very well; that soon after they came here, several large canoes full of indians came into the mouth of the brook, but immediately retired again; and that they still remained hid in the neighbouring woods, but had not yet done them any mischief; they however, added that the natives often made their appearance on the opposite side, and used threatening tones and gestures."[31]

Being prevented from taking salmon at one of the two remaining good salmon rivers would have been a severe blow to the Beothuk, since the more productive of the thirty-three principal salmon and trout streams in Notre Dame Bay (listed by a fishery warden in 1885) were already occupied by the English.[32] A few streams, such as Jumper's Brook, Burnt Bay Brook, Little Rattling Brook, Brown's Arm Brook, Badger Bay Brook, and the Terra Nova River in Bonavista Bay may still have been available; at least, there are no records that licences for salmon posts were sought for these rivers. But the absence of records does not prove that settlers did not go there to catch trout and salmon.[33] The Beothuk may also have been able to exploit streams that the English had temporarily vacated, as was the case in 1786 at Northwest and Southwest brooks in Green Bay.[34] However, the overall quantities they were able to obtain are likely to have been pitifully small in comparison with the amounts they had formerly caught.

During the 1760s the English salmon fishery became fiercely competitive. The method of catching salmon by a succession of traps and nets led to violence and unfair practices. To counteract this development Governor Byron made it unlawful to "obstruct or hinder others from spreading or hauling their nets, whether by cutting down trees into the River, by directing them into other people's nets, by shooting their nets within or upon the nets of another, and running boats willfully upon the nets of other."[35] These measures did not prevent the pirating of salmon or of nets, nor did they prevent the depletion of the breeding stock. As a result, a new set of rules issued in 1775 prohibited the placing of weirs and nets in a manner that would entirely obstruct the passage of salmon upriver.[36] Yet throughout the greater part of the season salmon rivers were often completely barred with nets, which led to a steady reduction of salmon. During the period from 1800 to 1829, salmon catches dropped to an average of 2,695 tierces (465,590 kilograms) per annum from a previous average of 3,400 tierces (550,800 kilograms) and continued to decline.[37]

In 1786, the English set salmon nets on the Exploits River for forty-four kilometres "up the country." Catching devices in other rivers were placed for an average of twenty-two kilometres from the river mouths upriver, so that the salmon catchers occupied and controlled substantial portions of these rivers.[38] The Beothuk protested against this intrusion into their country by taking away gear or occasionally killing a man. Capt. George Christopher Pulling, who enquired into relations between the settlers and Beothuk in 1792, was told that during the previous few months alone, the Beothuk had taken several salmon nets from Harry Miller on the Exploits River, thirty pounds sterling worth of nets from Richard Richmond, and more nets from Mr Clark of Fogo. At Twillingate a Beothuk party had stolen four salmon nets, twelve pounds of seine twine, a frying pan, and other trifles. Joseph Hornet from Indian Arm complained that if he did not keep watch every night while his nets were set, the Beothuk would steal some of them every year.[39]

Pulling also heard that Beothuk had killed a young man on his way to take salmon out of a pond at Ragged Harbour in 1780. The man who had accompanied him was nearly killed but managed to fetch his gun and wound one of the attackers.[40] Salmon catcher Thomas Rowsell was ambushed, killed, and beheaded by Beothuk while he was dipping salmon from his weir at South West Brook in New Bay. His body was found pierced with arrows and stripped of clothing. It was said by some that Thomas Rowsell, as well as his brother

George who fished in Halls Bay, had previously been friendly with the Beothuk, "comparatively speaking," though their master, Matthew Ward, was known to be a notorious enemy of the native people.[41] However, J.P. Howley later recorded that Thomas Rowsell was reputed to be a great Indian killer who "never ... spared one of the natives."[42] Rowsell's friends avenged his death by ambushing a party of Beothuk in two canoes at Moore's Cove, near Shoal Tickle, and discharging their buckshot at them. "It was never known how many were killed as the canoes drifted away."[43]

While the majority of the salmon catchers were indifferent or actually hostile towards the Beothuk, some were kindly disposed. Tradition has it that Thomas Rowsell's brother George never molested the Beothuk. Salmon catcher Genge occasionally put out a salmon for the Beothuk at Indian Arm, and John Quinn, who lived at this post in 1816, was on equally friendly terms with them.[44] The Beothuk seem to have trusted only a few individuals and continued taking gear whenever the opportunity arose. This tactic was not conducive to improving their access to salmon; instead, it caused further deterioration of relations with the English.

SEA TRAVEL TO BIRD COLONIES BECOMES HAZARDOUS

Less dramatic, but nevertheless contributing to the Beothuk's difficulties in supplying themselves with food, was their loss of access to seabirds and their eggs. In early summer, seabirds such as gannet, murre, puffin, and razorbill that breed in large coastal colonies made a significant addition to their diet; according to Henry Crout (1613), the Beothuk would drive "penn gwynnes" from the shore into their boats on an island north of Dildo South in Trinity Bay.[45] In 1768 John Cartwright wrote: "During the egg season they [the Beothuk] are supposed to feed luxuriously; and by no means to want after the young have taken to wing; for in archery they have an unerring hand that amply supplies their wants."[46] The Beothuk preserved egg yolks in powder form, or as sun-dried cakes, or made a kind of sausage by stuffing eggs together with other ingredients into seal guts.[47] They were said to return to their inland habitations in the fall "laden with Birds [and] Eggs," presumably preserved in the ways described.[48] Among the numerous bird-nesting places, the most prolific breeding colonies that Beothuk regularly visited were those of the great auk on Funk Island. George Cartwright recorded in his diary: "It is a singular, almost incredible fact that these people [the Beothuk] should visit Funk Island ... The Indians repair thither once or twice every year, and return with their canoes laden with birds' eggs; for the number of sea-fowl which resort to this island to breed are far beyond credibility."[49]

Already in the sixteenth century, explorers and other travellers visited the bird colonies on Funk Island to provision themselves *en route*.[50] The tradition was continued by Newfoundland fishermen and settlers, who were well aware of this excellent source of meat and eggs. Fowling as a pastime was widely pursued, and the prodigious number of seabirds on Funk Island made this colony a favoured birding place.[51] In 1770 George Cartwright observed that "the bird islands are so continuously robbed [by the settlers] that the poor Indians must now find it much more difficult than before to produce provisions for the summer and this difficulty will annually become greater."[52]

Cartwright's words were prophetic. The Beothuk were increasingly prevented from obtaining their accustomed quantities of birds and eggs. When travelling to the bird colonies in their canoes, they were persecuted by armed bird catchers. In July 1792, for example, McDonald and four other men from Tilton Harbour on Fogo Island fired moleshot directly at two Beothuk canoes that were heading to Funk Island. They supposed they had wounded some of the Beothuk, who paddled off to the Gannet Rocks about one kilometre north of Funk Island, where they collected what birds and eggs they could find.[53] Since birchbark canoes are easily damaged by gunshot, sea travel became extremely unsafe. To avoid being shot, and probably also to take advantage of calm seas, Beothuk often canoed to sea in "the thickest Fog," a feat the settlers greatly admired but that would have been hazardous for the Beothuk.[54]

The problem for the Beothuk of gaining access to seabirds was confounded by the rapid decline of the bird population. English bird catchers who went to Funk Island not only collected birds and eggs for food but killed large quantities of the flightless great auk for their feathers. They constructed stone corrals or compounds into which they drove the birds for killing, scalding, and plucking and used the birds' carcasses, which had a thick layer of fat, as fuel.[55] Laws prohibiting this practice were eventually issued, but enforcement came too late to prevent extinction of the great auk. By about 1800 the species no longer existed in Newfoundland.[56]

CHAPTER FIVE

Hostilities over Hunting and Trapping

From fall to spring terrestrial mammals were the Beothuk's main food resource. For those bands that intercepted the large migrating caribou herds that passed across the Exploits River and Red Indian Lake and who wintered there, preserved caribou meat constituted the bulk of their winter diet. Small fur bearers, seal, migratory and overwintering birds, and lake fish would have supplemented caribou.[1] Beothuk bands that remained, during the winter season, closer to the coast where caribou passed in smaller numbers relied to a greater extent on seal, bear, beaver, and other small mammals.[2] While Newfoundland's resources were plentiful, the sizes of animal populations and of specific herds fluctuated, and migratory patterns were liable to change. Formerly, the Beothuk would have been able to adjust their hunting patterns to changes in the distribution of their prey. Once the English and other native groups hunted and trapped in Newfoundland, it would have been difficult for the Beothuk to offset cyclical reductions of animal populations or changes in their migrations. In addition to decreased territory, their diminished flexibility would have interfered with the Beothuk's subsistence economies, although such interference cannot readily be documented or quantified. Nevertheless, information on the development of the English fur business in Newfoundland, citing the quantities of furs sold, can show how the Beothuk were progressively excluded from one of their major resources.

THE ENGLISH FUR BUSINESS

Once fishermen began to live permanently on the island, hunting and trapping became an essential part of their economy. In 1612–13, John Guy, governor of the colony at Cupids, sent a hogshead of sample pelts to England; letters from the colony mention the consumption of caribou and bear meat, the trapping of muskrat, fox, otter, and marten, and the colonists' desire to learn from experts how best to take beaver and other fur bearers.[3] Prior to the 1670s, documentation on hunting is scanty, but one may assume that most settlers availed themselves of terrestrial mammals (as well as seal) since the fishing and hunting seasons complemented each other. Moreover, hunting and trapping not only provided them with meat but the profits from fur sales could have offset occasional poor catches of fish.

In 1681, Captain Story of *HMS Antelope* recorded that settlers from Bonavista Bay went "furring mid September and take no provisions with them but bread and salt, finding beaver, otter and seals enough to feed on. They carry guns and kill also a great deal of venison, which they salt down for the winter. They return about 1st of May."[4] Other reports stress that the meat procured by hunting was the settlers' chief form of subsistence, while the profits from furs were not on the whole a major factor. In the latter part of the 1600s the English largely hunted inland from Trinity and Bonavista bays. The French Abbé Baudoin, who took part in d'Iberville's winter war against the English in 1696–97, claimed that more than two hundred English trappers spent all winter in the woods and penetrated into the deepest part of the forests up "to the gates of Placentia." They were excellent hunters and trackers who took beaver as well as caribou and bear and knew the island perfectly by land, even the part that was dominated by the French.[5] The French, Baudoin concluded, were afraid of the woods; they mostly hunted in the south and inland from Placentia and only occasionally sought fur close to their fishing grounds north of Cape Freels. Since the French did not winter over at their northern fishing stations in Notre Dame and White bays and on the Northern Peninsula, some of the English went trapping in White Bay and others "caught good furs at Petit Nord."[6]

Starting in 1677, the "Heads of Enquiry" on the Newfoundland fishery routinely included the question whether trade was carried on in furs. Answers to the enquiries sent by the naval commanders of the Newfoundland convoys and, after 1729, the officers who were appointed governor for the summer season stated quantities and sometimes types of furs that had been procured (as a rule, seal takes were not included under furs). They also contained information on the areas where inhabitants trapped and whether they had traded for fur with Indians (see Table 5.1).[7] The reports rarely differentiate between various ethnic groups and do not mention that the Beothuk were elusive nontraders.[8] It is assumed that the trading Indians would generally have been Micmac, Montagnais, and possibly also Inuit, whose trade relations with the French are well documented.[9]

In the seventeenth century no conflicts between Beothuk and English hunters were recorded, though the latter clearly entered Beothuk territory. Presumably, the limited catches of the English, mostly destined for personal consumption, made no appreciable inroads on the animal population, and English hunting practices may not have interfered significantly with those of the Beothuk.

In the 1720s trapping by the English became an established business. Its considerable growth is reflected in the figures recorded in the annual reports of the

Newfoundland fishery under "pound sterling worth of furs sold." These figures cannot easily be translated into numbers of animals or species trapped since they would have been influenced by varying quantities of pelts, fluctuating prices, and variation in the records (often, not all districts were accounted for).

For the period from 1722 to 1754, the figures for annual sales of furs range between £220 and £976 sterling with an average of £615 (see Table 5.1). The amounts recorded for 1725 and 1726 are exceptional: in 1725, £4,592 worth of furs were sold (£2,650 in Trinity alone) and £1,900 worth in 1726. Certainly these catches were inordinately large, and it is possible that seal pelts were included in the figures. The large harvests may also have been due to a sudden increase in the number of trappers, referred to as furriers in the Newfoundland records. Commander Bowler, in his report for 1726 and again for 1727, states that several persons who had come out to work in the fishery in Conception, Trinity, and Bonavista bays had stayed behind in winter to "employ themselves with furring." This resource, so he thought, had hitherto only been exploited by a few of the permanent inhabitants.[10]

BEOTHUK AND FURRIERS CLASH

The annual records do not bear out Bowler's claim that the settlers had generally neglected furs, but the sharp rise in amounts sold in 1725 and 1726 may indeed have come about when men from the summer fishery joined the local furriers. The hunting and trapping methods of this larger contingent of men, or their exploitation of areas farther inland, led to altercations with Beothuk. In 1729 Commander Beauclerk reported to the authorities that "by their constant cruel usage to the Indians wherever they meet them all traffic with them is entirely cut off."[11] Beauclerk did not cite details and it is uncertain whether he referred to conflicts that had arisen over hunting and trapping; but his wording implies repeated aggressive behaviour by settlers or furriers over an extended period.

Writing in 1732, Captain Falkingham stated, "I cant learn that the furriers have any commerce with the Indians but that several of the Indians had been formerly distroyed by the furriers and since several Englishmen have been distroyed by the Indians."[12] These killings of Beothuk, the first that were officially recorded, indicate a turning point in relations due to significant interference with Beothuk hunting and trapping. While it is not proven that the Beothuk were mistreated and killed by fishermen/furriers who worked only temporarily in Newfoundland, it is reasonable to speculate that transients would have been less concerned about the long-term effects of poor relations with the native population than would the permanent settlers, who became saddled with the resulting problems.

The Beothuk may have responded for a time by avoiding encounters with the English, because in the following decades they were rarely mentioned in the records. In 1732, an officer of *HMS Drake* wrote: "I can give you no account of the Indians that inhabit this island for they are now very seldom seen hereabouts."[13] Three years later Captain Lee reported: "Some people here tell stories of Indians [who] have been seen some years ago, I am certain they have no traffic now nor did I see one person in Newfoundland [who] had ever seen an Indian."[14] It appears that this temporary disappearance of the Beothuk eliminated them not only from the patrolling officers', hence the governors', reports but also from the minds of the authorities who were responsible for their welfare.

INTERMITTENT SMALL TRADE WITH BEOTHUK

Beothuk only occasionally exchanged furs for European goods. This was usually by the "dumb (or silent) barter" method in which articles were laid out in the absence of the trading partner. As noted in chapter 2, Beothuk probably bartered with a Dutch trader in St Mary's Bay in 1606 and are known to have traded with the colonists John Guy and Henry Crout in Trinity Bay in 1612 and 1613. However, both Guy and Crout implied that the Beothuk offered only a few pelts that were hardly worth the effort of coming to Trinity Bay. In the late 1800s, residents of Harbour Grace claimed in conversation with J.P. Howley that "in the early days of settlement" (presumably in the 1600s), Beothuk had camped on the beach at Carbonear in Conception Bay and exchanged furs for iron tools.[15] It is likely that here, too, only a few furs changed hands. A more profitable trade with settlers developed in the vicinity of Bonavista Harbour, whose inhabitants told George Cartwright in the 1760s that a satisfactory barter had formerly been carried on in their neighbourhood: "They [the settlers] used to lay a variety of goods at a certain place to which the Indians resorted, who took what they were in want of, and left furs in return. One day a villain hid himself near the deposit, and shot the woman dead, as she furnished herself with what pleased her best."[16] Since that time, so Cartwright was assured, the Beothuk had ceased trading and had become hostile towards settlers.[17] It is impossible to pinpoint the date of this unhappy event; it may have occurred twenty or thirty years before Cartwright heard about it. Because these occasional exchanges of goods seem to have been the only form of communication that existed between Beothuk and English, the termination of barter in Bonavista Bay, limited as it may have been, put an end to friendly relations altogether.

Trade for furs has sometimes been inferred from the presence of European goods in excavated Beothuk sites and in burials. But the types of goods that are recorded – fragments of pottery, glass, and clay pipes, pieces of iron and other metals, spoons, broken kettles and iron pots, bits of cloth and cord, nails, knives or blades, hatchets, axes and chisels – could all have come from deserted fishing stations and need not have been received in exchange for furs. Glass (or trade) beads, however, are unlikely to have been obtained in this manner. Beads have been unearthed in Beothuk sites at South Exploits, Badger Brook, Red Indian

Falls (where about a thousand beads were found), and Boyd's Cove (which yielded close to seven hundred blue-and-white trade or seed beads). They were also found in a burial at Devil's Cove in Green Bay and possibly in another on Rencontre Island near Burgeo.[18] By themselves trade beads do not conclusively prove trade; in fact, there is evidence that beads were left by the English to signal their desire for trade and friendly contacts. For example, a document in the governor's correspondence file dated 8 June 1808 lists ten dozen glass-bead necklaces that were to be left for Beothuk in an attempt to open amicable relations.[19] Beads were also among the presents that Captain Buchan took on his excursions to Red Indian Lake in 1811 and in 1820.[20]

At the Boyd's Cove site, thought to have been occupied by Beothuk between 1650 and 1730, beads were excavated together with sherds of Normandy stoneware of the type that was traded by the French with Montagnais in northern Newfoundland and Labrador.[21] According to Thomas Mitchell (reporting in 1697), the French had been anxious to communicate and trade with Beothuk in Notre Dame Bay; so it is conceivable that the Beothuk from Boyd's Cove obtained both the beads and the stoneware from French crews who fished in this area.[22]

FACTORS THAT PREVENTED A REGULAR FUR TRADE

Why the Beothuk never engaged in an organized fur trade is undoubtedly a complex question. The conditions that led to such a trade with other northeastern native groups – plentiful animal resources, people skilled at catching them, and Europeans interested in trade relations – were also present in Newfoundland. If European acts such as the occupation of traditional Beothuk campsites and the exploitation of resources without the Beothuk's consent, or the capture and killing of members of their tribe, or the intrusion of the fishery on their summer habitat are quoted as causes of Beothuk unwillingness to communicate, one need only remember the circumstances that other native groups on the Atlantic Seaboard had to contend with. They not only experienced similar disturbances to their way of life and resources but were also often forced to tolerate fortified trading posts and extensive land claims by the English, who wanted to farm. Despite these negative aspects of colonization, many of the mainland tribes succumbed to the offer of trading for European goods. As the Beothuk experience with Europeans is unlikely to have been materially different from that of other native groups, their persistent refusal to cooperate was presumably due to different factors.

Pastore has argued that the Beothuk's ability to procure iron objects from seasonally vacated fishing premises diminished their need for trade and that the Beothuk therefore showed little interest in bartering. This caused early English settlers to do their own trapping, an unusual phenomenon that would have helped to prevent the development of a regular trade with the Beothuk.[23]

Already in the 1550s they were reputed to be people with whom one could not "deal." Crout was unable to communicate with the Beothuk whom he saw near Hopeall in 1613, while the French who attempted to contact Beothuk in Notre Dame Bay in 1697 received no response to their signals.[24] Moreover, when exchanges were actually made the Beothuk offered very few furs, thereby failing to stimulate the interest of potential traders: it was the Beothuk's unwillingness to engage in worthwhile barter that kept traders away. As a consequence, Newfoundland settlers, who might otherwise have developed a lucrative trade with them, set about acquiring the skills of trapping and preparing skins themselves and then sold them through local merchants. Thus, the development of a fur business by English trappers was the result of the Indians' failure to trade, and not the cause.

Factors other than the economic might have played a role. For example, following hostile encounters and captures in the early days of fishing, the Beothuk may have become wary and reticent because, unlike Inuit, they dispersed during the summer into small groups that were relatively defenceless. Under these circumstances, they may have chosen to avoid encounters altogether rather than expose themselves to the risk of being mistreated. In any case, as Pastore has pointed out, the Beothuk's need to trade was reduced because they were able to supply their immediate wants by scavenging seasonally vacated fishing premises, or by confiscating traps set in the woods or nets placed into rivers.[25]

It is also likely that their strong adherence to traditional values and behaviour, combined with an early rejection of Europeans and their culture, was salient to the Beothuk's failure to engage in trade. In this they differed from other northeastern groups, who came to emulate certain European customs. The Beothuk continued with many of their traditional practices, such as the extensive use of red ochre as body paint and the use of bows, arrows, and spears in favour of guns, long after other tribes on the Atlantic Seaboard had abandoned them. Although they were quick to appreciate the useful qualities of European metal tools, kettles, canvas, rope, and other materials, they incorporated these materials into their technology and did not, to any great extent, replace their own methods. For example, they changed the shape of iron axes to fit their requirements in a cutting tool; they set iron blades into curved handles to turn them into crooked knives and used nets to make ropes and sails to cover mamateeks (houses).[26]

Another possibility, though an entirely speculative one, is that the Beothuk realized the threat to their culture inherent in a trade with Europeans. With good reason, they may have feared that animal stocks would become depleted and that the way resources were traditionally exploited and shared would undergo unwanted changes. Adaptation to trade with Europeans could also have disturbed traditional family and group patterns, interfered with food gathering, and rendered the Beothuk vulnerable to European influence and pressures.

An interesting observation was made by Samuel Hearne, a Hudson's Bay Company trader who was working among the northern Chipewayans in the

1760s. These people, like the Beothuk, captured caribou with the aid of fences and pounds. Hearne remarked that this relatively easy method of procuring the necessities of life did away with any incentive to procure surplus pelts for trade. In Hearne's opinion, hunting unneeded furs brought the natives no real benefit because it interfered with their traditional method of moving along with the caribou and exposed those who deviated from this proven custom to the risk of famine. Only the more industrious among the Chipewayans obtained furs for trade, "but gain nothing from this additional trouble, since the real wants of these people are few and easily supplied with the help of few tools. In fact those who endeavour to possess more are always the most unhappy and may only be slaves and carriers to the rest, while those whom they [Hudson's Bay traders] call indolent and mean spirited, live generally in a state of plenty and consequently must be the most happy and independent also."[27]

THE GROWTH OF THE ENGLISH FUR BUSINESS

In the second half of the eighteenth century the fur business was in the hands of permanent settlers. Most families in Trinity and Notre Dame bays had at least one member who worked a trapline. According to a report from 1773, of the sixty-one men engaged in trapping, twenty-three came from Trinity Bay, two from Bonavista, thirty-four from Fogo and Twillingate (which explains why conflicts repeatedly involved men from Fogo), and two from White Bay.[28] Some men traded on their own account, while others worked for merchants who supplied them with provisions.[29] The value of furs sold by the English between 1755 and 1800 ranged from £388 to £3,890 sterling with an average of about £1,486 per annum. Furs kept for personal use were not included in these figures. Sealskins were usually, but not always, listed separately, which is the cause of certain discrepancies in the records (see Table 5.1).

A rough estimate of catches in Newfoundland in the year 1763 based on quantities of furs obtained and on prices paid to residents of Croque Harbour has been computed as follows: the figures were prorated from Croque, assuming a total of £1,500 sterling for all of Newfoundland. In 1763 the English would have procured approximately 3,415 pelts: 265 fox, 335 otter, 480 marten, 1,500 beaver, and 835 "catt" (ermine?).[30] If the quantities caught by French, Micmac, and Montagnais trappers taken together amounted to two-thirds of those brought home by the English, their share would have been 2,300 odd pelts. Accordingly, the number of fur bearers killed in 1763 in Newfoundland would have amounted to roughly 5,700. In comparison with the average annual harvest of furs in Newfoundland today (4,862 fur bearers, considering only the species listed above), the number projected for 1763, excluding those taken by the Beothuk, is seventeen percent higher than that recorded for the 1970s and 1980s. While we do not know the size of the animal populations as a whole and therefore cannot calculate the percentages that were trapped in 1763, the estimated number of pelts procured by English furriers nevertheless gives some idea of the heavy exploitation of fur bearers in the late 1700s. Competition from the English would therefore have been a significant threat to the Beothuk since it reduced their chances of trapping these same animals. Bands that lived furthest from a major caribou migration route and relied heavily on the meat of bear, beaver, and other terrestrial mammals for their winter diet were probably the most severely affected.[31]

George Cartwright observed in the 1770s: "I fear that the [Beothuk] race will be totally extinct in a few years, for the fishing trade is continually increasing … the bird islands are … continually robbed … our furriers are considerably increased in number, and much improved in skill, and venture further into the country than formerly, by which the breed of beavers is greatly diminished."[32] Cartwright's contention that the furriers continued to venture farther into (Beothuk) country and that the beaver population had notably declined confirms what other reports and the official figures of furs traded by the English indirectly suggest. His conclusion – that under these circumstances the Beothuk would become extinct – has unfortunately also proven correct. Specific evidence of trappers intruding into what would have been the Beothuk's domain comes from officers of the Royal Navy and local informants. Lieut. John Cartwright wrote in 1768 that John Cousens, owner of a salmon station on the Exploits River, usually went trapping in fall. On one occasion, when he had planned to kill beaver on Middleton and Mary Anne lakes, he found on his arrival that Beothuk had already set up camp there and he was forced to retreat.[33] On his map Cartwright also marked "tilt pond" on the upper run of Great Rattling Brook, a name that indicates that a furrier's tilt was located there.[34] In 1778 the furrier Thomas Dicks carved his initials into a tree at Indian Pond.[35] Capt. William Parker's chart of Newfoundland, drawn up in 1770, bears the notation "this lake [Gander] is laid down by the account of the furriers," who were evidently familiar with the country thereabouts.[36] Captain G.C. Pulling was told in 1792 that Richard Richmond, Nicholas Eaton, and Jason Lilly trapped on Great Rattling Brook, where their tilts were built about sixteen kilometres apart, the last one sixty-four kilometres up the brook; William Cull trapped for furs on Northern and Peters brooks to the north-west of Peters Arm.[37] During the early 1800s William Elliot trapped at Gander Bay Pond and netted thirty dozen martens in addition to beaver and otter, and a furrier in Pacquet Harbour caught a hundred beaver, as well as foxes, cats, bears, and other fur bearers.[38]

Faced with extensive encroachment by the English, the Beothuk responded by confiscating traps and frightening furriers. Richard Richmond was dismayed one morning to discover fresh footprints left by Beothuk around his tilt at Rattling Brook. The Beothuk had not only reconnoitred but had also taken his traps so that he was forced to pack up and leave. William Cull, on seeing their tracks a short distance from his tilt on Northern or Peter's Brook, felt the hair on his head "stand on end" for he had nothing but his hatchet to defend himself should a Beothuk suddenly attack him.[39] He rushed back to his tilt to fetch his gun, loaded it with drop shot, put on his snow shoes ("Indian rackets"), and set off in pursuit of the Beothuk. After two days he gave up the chase, collected his traps from the trapline to prevent their being stolen, destroyed those he could not carry away, and returned home.

Both Richmond and Cull lived alone in their tilts during the trapping season, as was the custom among furriers, so the Beothuk could have killed either of them if they had so chosen. It is therefore remarkable that throughout the latter part of the eighteenth century, when hostilities had intensified to the highest pitch, not one furrier was attacked on his trapline or killed in his tilt. In fact, the furriers who had suffered nothing worse than the loss of traps seem not to have considered that they were at the mercy of the Beothuk while trapping in Beothuk country and could easily have been shot. Instead of appreciating the Beothuk's restraint, many were indignant about their losses, and some of them set out to raid Beothuk winter camps to take revenge. In the course of these raids they not only stole furs – on one raid furriers carried away a hundred caribou skins – and destroyed the Beothuk's possessions but also injured and probably killed some to them.[40]

Disturbance of Caribou Migration Routes

Whether the hunting of caribou by English furriers caused disturbances among the herds and thereby adversely affected the Beothuk's caribou drive is not known. The English do not seem to have killed caribou for their furs; the official records rarely list caribou skins among the furs that were sold. Perhaps these skins were not readily marketable. However, settlers traditionally hunted caribou for meat, which they salted down for winter consumption. With the expansion of the settler population the English may have stepped up the caribou hunt to meet growing demands, which could well have interfered with the Beothuk's hunting pattern.[41] In the fall, when large herds migrating from the Northern Peninsula crossed the Exploits River and Red Indian Lake, the Beothuk intercepted them at lake and river crossings by means of extensive fenceworks and pounds (for a fuller account see chapter 20). They packaged, froze, and stored the meat in special-purpose structures for consumption during the winter months. Since the Beothuk congregated in large groups for the caribou drive, furriers are unlikely to have interfered with the drive directly. But it is possible that their hunting practices and use of guns had an impact on the migration patterns of the herds. While the Cartwrights in 1768 recorded about fifteen kilometres of Beothuk fenceworks on the Exploits River below Badger, Lieutenant Buchan in 1811 and Cormack in 1827 saw fences only on the upper course of the river and at Red Indian Lake, whence they continued in a northerly direction for about forty-nine kilometres.[42] This shift further inland may indicate that by the early 1800s, the caribou herds had diverted from their former migration routes and were crossing the Exploits River closer to Red Indian Lake, which would have forced the Beothuk to build new fences. We have no direct evidence whether these changes led to smaller catches; what we do know is that the remnant of the Beothuk group experienced starvation.

THE EFFECT OF ENGLISH SEALING ON THE BEOTHUK

Contemporary reports and faunal remains from archaeological sites show that seal played a major role in the Beothuk's seasonal cycle of exploitation. Fresh seal meat and oil supplemented their food intake during early winter after the migrating caribou herds had passed and were a major resource in spring, before bird eggs and salmon could be taken. Several seal species were available in Newfoundland waters, including harp, harbour, grey, ringed, bearded, and hooded seals. Of these, the harp seal was and still is the most numerous. Harp-seal herds, amounting to several hundred thousand animals, migrate southward along the Newfoundland coast in late December and return northward in February and March to whelp on the advancing ice pack. In late December and early January, when seals passed the headlands and offshore islands, the Beothuk would have hunted them from their canoes. Their sealing harpoon, whose detachable head was tied to a thong, was designed for harpooning a seal in the water (or through the ice) and retrieving the animal with the aid of the thong. The strongly hogged sheer (upturned sides) of their canoes prevented the shipping of water when heeling to take a heavy object such as a seal aboard. In late February and March, the Beothuk could have hunted seal on land-fast ice, or on the ice floes that came close to shore.

As with other renewable resources in Newfoundland, the English were quick to make use of seal. Already in 1579 Whitbourne went seal hunting in Trinity Bay, and official reports from the 1680s and 1690s mention that the residents of Newfoundland "in the wintertime … hunt for deer [caribou], beaver, otter, bear, martin, fox and seals on whose flesh they feed for the greatest part of that season."[43] The English also produced seal oil, which was eminently saleable and soon became the basis of a profitable business; in 1720, £2,000 sterling worth was exported to England. Beginning in the early 1700s, answers to the Heads of Enquiry on the Newfoundland fishery routinely include data on seal oil and sealskins. Catches of seal, predominantly but not exclusively harp seal, fluctuated but grew steadily larger as more fishermen were employed in the industry.[44] On the northeast coast there were major processing centres at Trinity, Bonavista, Greenspond, and Fogo.[45] The English usually caught seal in open water. They set nets in harbours or in narrow passages between headlands and islands during the seals' southward migration at the end of December; in some places nets were also set between April and June.[46] From the 1780s onwards, sealers began to hunt harp seal from open boats, but catches did not improve much until decked schooners started to travel to the whelping patches on the ice fields.[47] From an average of about 31,000 seals caught annually between 1786 and 1792, the number of pelts brought back by schooners went up in 1819 to 218,000 and in 1823 to 687,000, the largest catch ever recorded.[48]

Considering the large size of harp-seal herds and the relatively small number taken by the English in the eighteenth century, there should have been no shortage of this species for Beothuk consumption. However, while the animals may have been plentiful, Beothuk seal-hunting parties may have found it difficult to gain access to those headlands and islands where harp-seal herds passed on their migration. Not only might the English have set their nets in the most promising places but their communities were often built at the entrance to a bay or close to a headland, which prevented the Beothuk from going there. A few less-bountiful sealing beaches may have been available so that the Beothuk could harvest a minimum of animals. Strife between Beothuk and English sealers has not been recorded.

A high percentage of the seal bones found in Beothuk middens at The Beaches in Bonavista Bay and at Boyd's Cove in Notre Dame Bay have been identified as harbour seal, showing that the Beothuk hunted this nonmigratory species as well.[49] From spring to fall, harbour seals stay close to land where they whelp; they favour inlets and estuaries and sometimes work their way up river; they do not move offshore until the inlets freeze over.[50] Today the once-sizeable harbour-seal population in Newfoundland is insignificant.[51] The large proportion of harbour-seal bones in Beothuk middens could be due to the location of the sites close to inlets and estuaries where the seals would have been available. The Beaches site, for example, is adjacent to a long shingle bar, a perfect place for harbour seals to haul out and whelp. It has been occupied by Maritime Archaic Indians and Palaeo-Eskimos as well as Recent Indians and historic Beothuk, suggesting that it was an excellent place for pursuing a subsistence livelihood. The fact that harp seals were hunted from exposed headlands or islands and presumably processed at the kill site could explain why so few harp-seal bones found their way into the middens of camps in the inner reaches of bays. But hunting harp seal in the open sea with harpoons (the Beothuk did not have large nets) was hazardous, and the Beothuk may traditionally have favoured harbour over harp seals, since this species could be killed on shore. When Beothuk found themselves excluded from beaches close to harp-seal migration routes, they may well have attempted to rely more heavily on the harbour seal. However, harbour seals, which were also pursued by the English, are vulnerable to overexploitation. During the whelping season they assemble in relatively small groups of perhaps a few hundred (rather than tens of thousands), and an increased harvest could have caused a depletion of this seal population and a notable reduction in yet another resource.

Table 5.1
Quantities of Furs Sold by the English, 1677–1827

Year	*Value of Furs in £*	*Reference**	*Remarks*
1677	500	CO 1/41,145a	
1681	500	CO 1/47,52	beaver, otter, seal, caribou
1691	2, 000	CO 1/68,259	beaver, otter, fox, cat, seal
1692		Ibid., 266, 293	small quantities, little furs
1698		CO 195/2,II: 306	small gain f. fur, catch fowl
1699		Ibid., 373	small value; deer, bear, beaver
1700		CO 195/2,428	little furs; for food: deer, bear, beaver
1701		CO 195/3,5, 13	deer, beaver, otter, seal
1702		CSPC 1702,1154	little furs
1705		CO 194/3,93	good furs
1706		CO 195/4,310	trade nearly ruined by French
1707		CSPC 1706–08,1211	small quantities
1708		CSPC 1708–09,223	sell to New Engld.traders
1710		CO 194/4,554	beaver, otter, fox, marten
1711		CO 194/5,22	little profit; deer, otter, beaver, marten, fox, seal
1712		Ibid., 56	few beaver & other
1714		Ibid., 103	trade with Micmac
1715		CO 194/6,28, 44	beaver & other furs
1716		CSPC 1716–17,70	furs
1717	3,000	Ibid.	no trade with Indians
1718	3,000	CSPC 1717–18,751	beaver, otter, fox, seal
1719	40	CO 194/6,312	per person
1720	2,000	CO 194/7,7	
		CSPC 1720–21,260	considerable quant. by French Indians
1722	780	CSPC 1722–23,330–7	beaver, fox, marten – no trade with Island's Indians
		CO 194/7,153	Canad. Ind. trade w. English
1723	780	Ibid., 205	Bonavista & northward
1724	790	Ibid., 240–2	Bonavista & northward
1725	4,592	CO 194/8,14	Trinity Bay alone £2,650
		CO 194/7,269	French operate in Fortune and Bay d'Espoir

* All records from the Colonial Office and the Calendar of State Papers, Colonial, America, and West Indies, that are cited here have been consulted in the Public Record Office, Kew, UK.

Table 5.1 *(Cont'd)*
Quantities of Furs Sold by the English, 1677–1827

Year	*Value of Furs in £*	*Reference**	*Remarks*
1726	1,900	Burd Journal PANL MG 231	beaver, fox, otter & other
1727	890	CSPC 1726–27,1743	prob. more; no trade w. Indians
1729	500	CSPC 1728–29,940	less than £500; trade lost due to cruel use of Indians
1730	925	CO 194/9,59–60	
1731	582	Ibid., 112–13	
1732	391	Ibid., 211	no trade w. Indians; Indians
		CO 194/24,118	were killed & so were furriers
1733	182	CSPC 1733,347	Trinity Bay & north; no traffic with the Indians
1734	400	CSPC 1734–35,362	furs and venison; no traffic with the Indians
		CO 194/9,177	Cape Bret. Ind. at Cape Ray, create fear f. settlers and furriers
1735	485	CSPC 1735–36,119	no Indians seen
1736		Ibid., 324	French traffic with Indians
1738	712	CO 194/24,142	no traffic with Indians
1739	895	Ibid., 150, 169	no traffic with Indians
1740	690	Ibid., 169, 195	no traffic with Indians
1741	880	Ibid., 252	no traffic with Indians
1742	739	Ibid.; PC 5/9,76	no traffic with Indians
1743	550	CO 194/24,285, 292	no traffic with Indians
1745	270	CO 194/12,32	no traffic with natives
1746	312	Ibid., 45	no traffic with Indians
1748	326	CO 194/25,20	no traffic with Indians
1749	220	Ibid., 49	no traffic with Indians
1750	920	Ibid., 90	no traffic with Indians
1751	675	Ibid., 106	no traffic with Indians
1752	874	CO 194/13,47	no traffic with Indians
1753	976	Ibid., 113	no traffic with Indians
1754	406	Ibid., 151	no traffic with Indians
1755	1,000	Ibid., 196	no traffic with Indians
1757	3,890	Ibid., 238	no traffic with Indians
1758	1,090	CO 194/14,7–8	no traffic with Indians
1759	3,380	Ibid., 40	no traffic with Indians

Table 5.1 *(Cont'd)*
Quantities of Furs Sold by the English, 1677–1827

Year	Value of Furs in £	Reference*	Remarks
1760	2,075	CO 194/15,2	Placentia alone £1,200, no traffic with Indians
1762	388	Ibid., 65	
1763	1,800	Graves Papers, NAC, microf. A-133	
1764	2,760	CO 194/21,24	
1765	980	Ibid.	addit. £1,000 truck w. Indians
1766	1,728	CO 194/16,317	
1767	2,041	CO 194/18,13–14	
1768	1,593	Ibid., 40–1	
1769	1,077	CO 194/28,121	trade w. Indians, £50 Codroy & Bay of Islds.
1770	1,028	CO 194/30,7	
1771	1,109	Ibid., 84	
1772	900	CO 194/21,24	£136 truck w. Indians
		CO 194/30,175	French in the north complain about Eskimos
1773	1,359	CO 194/31,92	no truck with Indians
1774	827	CO 194/32,54	£30 truck with Indians
1776	1,135	CO 194/33,38a	
1778	641	CO 194/34,54	no truck with Indians
1779	2,432	Ibid., 89	furs and seal
1782	752	CO 194/35,152	no trade with Indians
1784	540	CO 194/21,24	no trade with Indians
1785	1,640	CO 194/36,57	£25 truck Cape St John to Quirpon, £200 Placentia
1786	2,575	Ibid., 253	good furring from Cape St John to Quirpon
		CO 194/21,23–4	£225 truck with Indians, French i. Quirpon fur & seal
1787	1,093	Ibid., 24	
1788	1,901	Ibid.	
1789	1,040	Ibid.	
1790	1,334	Ibid.	
1791	2,405	Ibid.	£100 truck
1792	2,280	CO 194/23,494	£50 truck
1793	1,086	Ibid.	
1794	1,860	WO 1/15,295	

Table 5.1 *(Cont'd)*
Quantities of Furs Sold by the English, 1677–1827

Year	*Value of Furs in £*	*Reference**	*Remarks*
1795	977	co 194/39,3	Greenspd., Fogo, Trepassy
1797	935	co 194/40,5	£100 truck w. Indians in Hermitage Bay
1798	45	co 194/42,242	
1800	580	Pole Papers, PANL, MG 205	many areas not reported
1801	580	Ibid.	prob. same as 1800, trade with Micmac
1803	1,070	co 194/44,114	£450 truck w. Indians at Harbour Breton & Gt. Jervis
1804	1,475	co 194/45,19	no truck with Indians
1805	830	Ibid., 201	Fogo & Expl.; no truck w. Indians
1806	510	co 194/46,78	Fogo not recorded
1807	3,685	co 194/47,54	£3, 000 Burin; Fogo not recorded
1808	1,240	co 194/48,7	no truck with Indians
1809		co 194/49,14	quantities uncertain, no truck with Indians
1810	5,362	Ibid., 49	hides £1,180, beaver £1,291, seal skins 118,050
1811	140	co 194/51,37	Fogo not recorded; no trade with Indians
1812	571	co 194/54,38	mostly Fortune Bay; £120 truck in Fortune
1813	585	co 194/55,29	£331 truck most. Fortune Bay
1814	1,932	Ibid., 103	£350 truck
1816	2,390	co 194/59,27	£300 truck
1817	1,500	co 194/61,22	£500 truck
1818	1,120	Ibid., 158	£200 truck
1819	840	co 194/62,150	£410 truck with Indians
1820	950	co 194/64,23	£400 truck with Indians
1821	900	Ibid., 143	£400 Hrb. Breton
1822	1,290	co 194/65,121	£500 truck with Indians;
		Howley 1915,59	on the westcoast £1,300
1823	1,120	co 194/66,172	£300 truck with Indians
1826	912	co 194/72,390	£59 truck w. Indians near Hrb. Breton
1827	1,609	co 194/74,355	

CHAPTER SIX

Lieut. John Cartwright Explores Beothuk Country

PREPARATION AND EXPLORATION

The first governor to act upon his concern for the welfare of the native people in Newfoundland and Labrador was Hugh Palliser (1764–68).[1] Labrador had come under English government with the Treaty of Paris in 1763, and resolving interference in the fishery due to conflicts with Inuit had become the responsibility of the Newfoundland governor. After meeting with Inuit at Pitts Harbour in 1765 (see chapter 3), Palliser had ordered fishing crews on the Labrador coast to treat the native people with civility and fairness.[2] In 1768, after numerous accounts of cruel and inhumane treatment of the native population in Newfoundland had come to his attention, Palliser commissioned Lieut. John Cartwright to lead an expedition into the interior of the country to make contact with them. John Cartwright's brother George, later to become an entrepreneur and owner of seal and salmon stations in Labrador, apparently had conceived the idea of a mission into Indian country and had convinced Palliser to implement his plan.[3] Governor Palliser instructed John Cartwright to gather detailed information about the Beothuk so that in time, friendly relations could be effected and the Beothuk could be rendered "useful subjects to his Majesty."[4] Perhaps to justify the expense of the expedition, Palliser also directed him to explore the unknown interior of the island and examine the practicability of travelling across the island from Notre Dame Bay to the south coast. John Cartwright was at the time first lieutenant of *HMS Guernsey* and surrogate judge for Trinity and Conception bays. Having become genuinely concerned about the native population he was an excellent choice for the task.[5] In July 1768, he sailed to the Bay of Exploits in a shallop of *HMS Liverpool*, accompanied by ten seamen, Rev. Neville Stow, chaplain of *HMS Guernsey*, and his brother George.[6] By the end of August preparations for the expedition had been completed. Cartwright hired John Cousens, a local planter and furrier, as a guide and Cousens's establishment at "Indian Point" (now Gills Point) served the party as a meeting place before and after the expedition.[7] He also consulted with "Cousens's Indian," the

Beothuk captive (Tom) June, who told him about a Beothuk settlement by a large lake.[8] June, captured as a child in 1758, had been reared in Fogo and was said to have made frequent trips back to the heart of the country to meet with his parents. June would have been a perfect guide and one wonders whether Cartwright had tried to recruit him and whether June (or his employer, John Cousens) had declined.

On 24 August the men rowed up the Exploits River as far as "Start Rattle" (upriver from Jumpers Brook) where they left their boats in the woods. The following morning the party divided into two groups in order to search both river banks simultaneously. John Cartwright and John Cousens headed one group, George Cartwright and Rev. Neville Stow the other. Every man carried his own provisions consisting of fourteen pounds of bread and seven of meat, to be augmented by hunting along the way. They were equipped with fowling pieces, hatchets, and other implements; the most trustworthy among them had heavy rifles, and the others carried pistols only for defence. Trekking upriver they soon discovered many "wigwams" most of which appeared to have been erected the previous winter. They also came upon extensive fenceworks built for the interception of migrating caribou herds. Cartwright was greatly impressed with the magnificence of the "great falls" (Bishop Falls) and the romantic appearance of the scenery. At "Sewel Point," east of Bishop Falls, many remnants of split roots led him to conjecture that the Beothuk must stop at this place to repair their canoes *en route* to their summer habitat on the coast. The party spent the night in one of the "wigwams" and pushed on early the next morning, searching for beaver as they went. Dwellings and caribou fences continued on either side of the river but the habitations were deserted, leading Cartwright to conclude that the Beothuk had gone for the summer to the coast. At Little Red Indian Pond, a change in the forest vegetation from young birch and poplar to established fir, pine, and larch indicated that about seventy years previously a fire had consumed all the woods on both sides of the river from the entrance of the bay up to that point.[9] The Exploits River had such a reputation for harbouring Beothuk that it had never before been traced so far, except by two furriers the previous winter who, seeing at that place a canoe half built and other signs of native habitation, retired with all speed.

At the end of four days' travel many of the men had worn out their shoes and, as game was scarce, their provisions were reduced to a minimum. When persistent rain made progress difficult, several of the men, including George Cartwright, returned to the shallop. Farther upriver three more men fell behind. In a final effort to reach the lake where an Indian winter settlement was said to be located, the remaining party, five of the original fourteen, pressed on until rain and the setting sun forced them to prepare for the night. While the men erected a shelter, John Cartwright struck out on his own and discovered a large lake, which he called "Lieutenant's Lake" (Red Indian Lake) presumably after his own rank. On the following morning the men walked along the shore as far as a cove on the northeast arm of the lake (the area of Mary March Provincial Park) which Cartwright called "June's Cove". In a clearing a few hundred metres from the shore were signs of a large Beothuk settlement, which was in an advanced stage of decay and almost hidden among young wood and high weeds. Cartwright later wrote that it answered "the description of such a place given by the Indian boy June where he said his father dwelt. By his account it was the residence also of great part of their tribe … From the circumstances of its large extent; being well filled with habitations … I should be induced to think that it might have been a settlement for all seasons; the studded houses making it sufficiently warm in winter, without the shelter of the woods."[10]

On their way from June's Cove back to the Exploits River the party passed a Beothuk camp that had been occupied the previous winter. It was situated on the lakeshore between Mary March's Brook, at the northeastern end of the lake, and Indian Point, and consisted of three conical houses and one square house.[11] Archaeological evidence and maps drawn by Capt. David Buchan in 1811 and 1820 and by Shanawdithit in 1828 indicate that the Beothuk changed the location of their winter settlement back and forth from the northeastern arm of Red Indian Lake (Cartwright's "June's Cove," later the location of Nonosabasut's mamateek and burial hut) to the shore between Millertown ("Sabbath Point") and Indian Point (Cartwright's "Takamahaka Point," called "Lookout Point" by Buchan).[12] On 31 August, before retracing their steps along the Exploits River, the party ascended "Mount Janus" (Halfway Mountain) to get a view of the country. They then trekked back as fast as their tattered footwear and the rainy weather would allow and reached the shallop five days later.

Cartwright was greatly disappointed that he had not made contact with the Beothuk, whom he had expected to meet at one or another of their campsites. Quite clearly Cartwright and those whose advice he may have sought had not been aware of the Beothuk's seasonal movements. During the month of August they would still have been on the coast, although it is possible that an avant-garde had already returned inland but gone into hiding when they saw a party of armed men advancing upriver.

John Cartwright reported on his expedition in a letter to Governor Palliser, dated 19 September 1768, to which he attached an unfinished map entitled "A Sketch of the River Exploits the East End of Lieutenant's Lake and Parts adiacent in Newfoundland, taken on the spot by Lieutenant John Cartwright of His Majesty's Ship Guernsey 1768." This sketch map shows the course, tributaries, and mouth of the Exploits River, Great Rattling Brook, the northeast end of "Lieutenant's Lake" (Red Indian Lake), and all of "Eyers's Lake" (Gander Lake).[13] Cartwright had charted the Exploits River as he went, and Cousens, who had travelled on these waterways during his frequent trapping excursions, had provided information on the network of tributaries.[14]

In February 1769, John Cartwright wrote a more extensive report, "Remarks on the situation of the Red Indians, natives of Newfoundland; with some account of their manner of living; together with such descriptions as are necessary to the explanation of the Sketch of the country they inhabit: taken on the spot in the year 1768."[15] This account is not present in the records of the Colonial Office and may not have been submitted officially at the time. It was published in 1826 by Cartwright's niece, F.D. Cartwright, in *The Life and Correspondence of Major Cartwright*. In the 1850s, F.D. Cartwright sent John Cartwright's original manuscript to Bishop Feild in St John's, where it is now in the collection of the Provincial Reference and Resource Library.[16] Presumably, Cartwright communicated the contents of the report to Governor Palliser, who may have discussed it with the secretary of state for the Colonies, the earl of Hillsborough, in England. At least, as of 1769, instructions for Newfoundland governors required them to publish and disperse a proclamation ordering the inhabitants to treat native people fairly or face punishment if they failed to comply.[17] This method of providing protection for the native population was first implemented by Palliser in Labrador, and it is assumed that it was introduced to Newfoundland on Palliser's recommendation, since Palliser himself did not return to Newfoundland after 1768.[18]

Four years later, in 1773, John Cartwright, who by then was no longer stationed in Newfoundland, submitted to the earl of Dartmouth, then secretary of state for the Colonies, a copy of his report of the exploration and an extract of his 1768 letter to Governor Palliser.[19] He attached three maps. The first is of the island of Newfoundland with the rivers and lakes already mentioned but with Lieutenant's, or Red Indian, Lake erroneously amalgamated with "Lake Micmac," or Grand Lake (Fig. 6.1).[20] The second map outlines the previously uncharted coast between New Bay Head and Cape John (now Cape St John) in Notre Dame Bay.[21] Cartwright's efforts at mapping seems to have set a precedent in that instructions to Newfoundland governors from this time forth repeatedly included requests for soundings and maps of the harbours, bays, and uncharted coastlines in northeast Newfoundland.[22] Cartwright's third map is a new sketch of the Exploits River entitled "A Sketch of the River Exploits and the East End of Lieutenant's Lake in Newfoundland," on which Beothuk dwellings and caribou fences are marked by identifying symbols (Fig. 6.2). In a note on this map, Cartwright described the river bed and discussed the possibility of taking a whaleboat up the river into "Lieutenant's Lake" to continue explorations, saying that the several rapids and the great falls would present impediments.[23]

INFORMATION ON THE BEOTHUK

Although John Cartwright did not meet any Beothuk, his report and maps are among the few documents that include first-hand information on their settlements and distribution and rank high on the list of reliable documents. They also represent the first personal account of Newfoundland's aboriginal inhabitants since the colonists John Guy and Henry Crout described their meetings with Beothuk in 1612–13. Cartwright's account includes population estimates and observations on the Beothuk's way of life, means of subsistence, relations

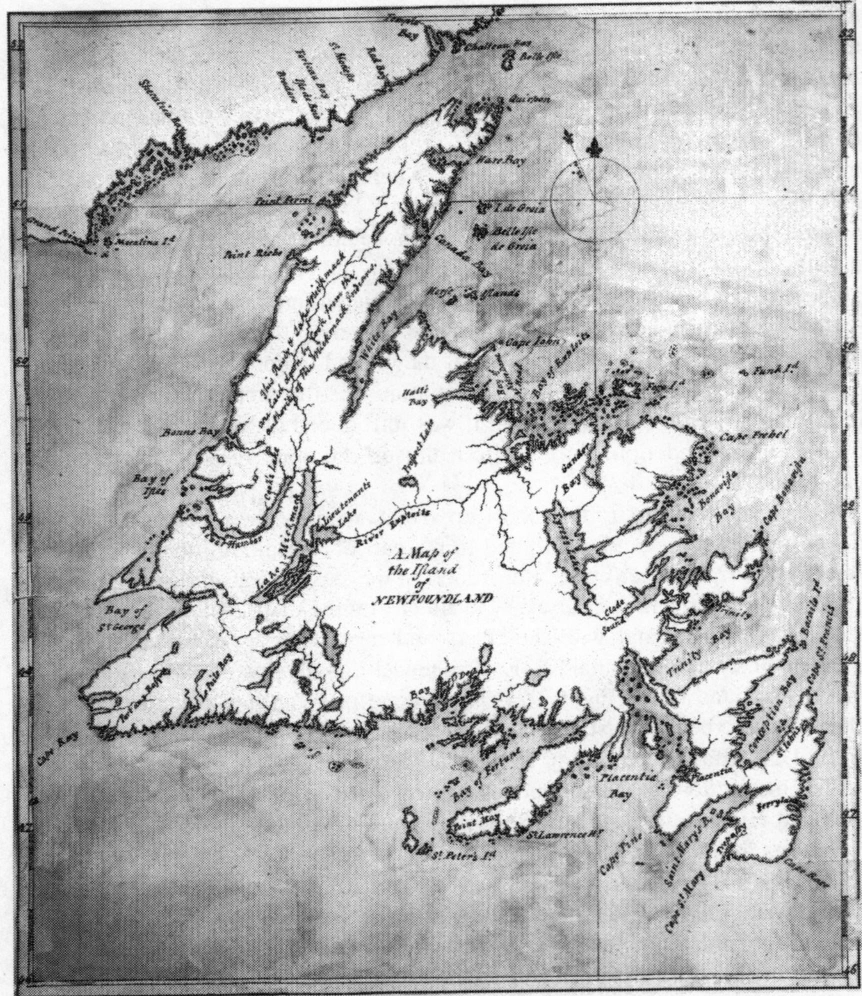

Fig.6.1 "A Map of the Island of Newfoundland," by Lieut. John Cartwright, submitted in 1773. (National Archives of Canada, NMC 14033)

with other native groups, and interactions with English settlers.[24] It also gives descriptions of Beothuk caribou fences and traps, different types of Beothuk dwellings, canoes, bows, and arrows, and their methods of preserving food (discussed at length in Part Two).[25]

If Cartwright had previously believed that Beothuk could be met in the interior of the country in August, he came to realize in the course of his journey that they moved with the seasons. During the summer they lived in small groups on the coast where they took quantities of salmon and hunted game and birds on is-

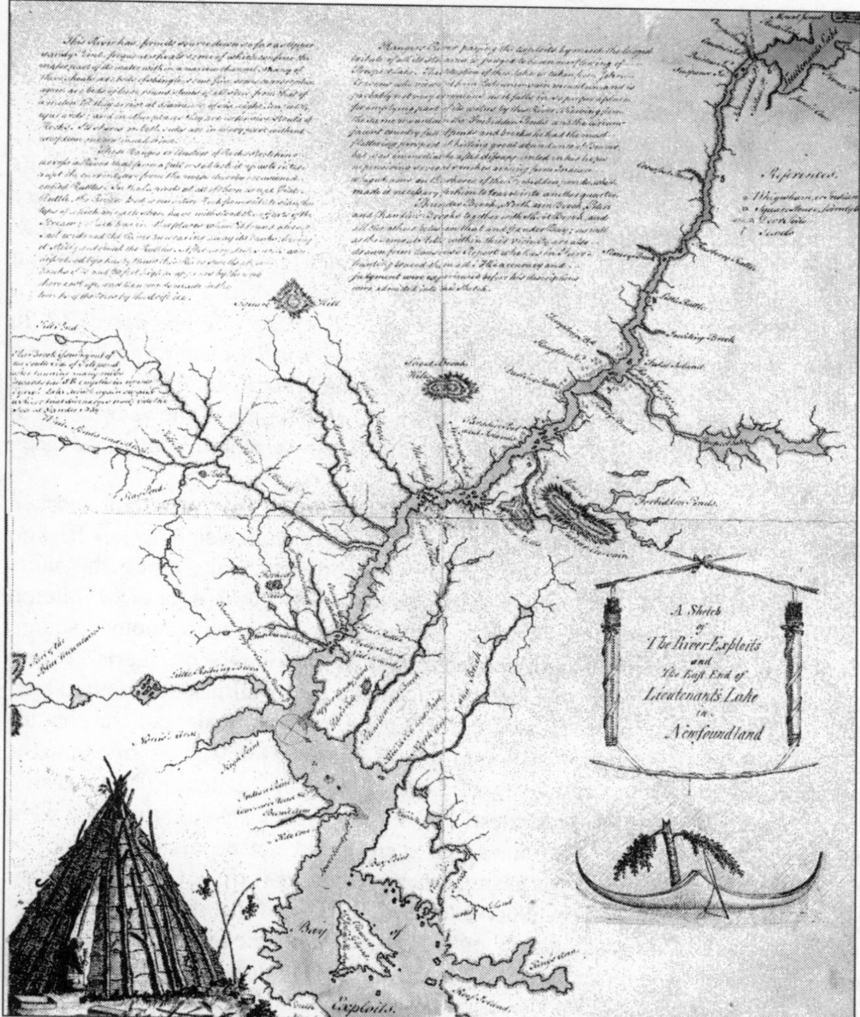

Fig.6.2 "A Sketch of the River Exploits and the East End of Lieutenant's Lake in Newfoundland," by Lieut. John Cartwright, submitted in 1773. (National Archives of Canada, NMC 27)

lands in Notre Dame Bay. Many of these islands abounded with sea-fowl, ptarmigan, hare and other game, and a great number of seals. Larger islands had caribou, foxes, bear, and otters.[26] By 1768 Beothuk came to the coast between Cape St John and Cape Freels, a smaller area than they had covered in the past when they were considerably more numerous.[27] During the winter the Beothuk assembled in a central location "deep in the recesses of the woods," where they hunted for their subsistence.[28] Cartwright presumed that the dwellings on the

Exploits River constituted their principal settlement, which they occupied for the duration of the fall hunting season and the subsequent winter months.[29] Caribou herds, crossing this river in the course of their migration in late fall, provided a reliable food supply, as evidenced by the abundance of horns and bones that lay scattered about the wigwams. In Cartwright's opinion, about one-half to two-thirds of the Beothuk tribe assembled for the caribou drive on the Exploits River, the remainder residing in more remote places around Middleton, Mary Anne, and Gander lakes. With no major caribou routes close by, these areas could support only smaller groups during the winter season, and precariously at that. However, where beaver were plentiful the Beothuk could well have subsisted "without any great dependence on the deer-chase [caribou-drive]."[30] In spring, when the caribou returned north, they did not travel in large herds, so that the Beothuk were not able to procure as much venison as they did in the fall. Even if they had been fortunate in the hunt, at this time of the year the meat was poor and difficult to preserve, and the Beothuk would soon have been forced to come to the seashore.[31]

On the map of the Exploits River submitted in 1773, Cartwright marked thirty-four conical habitations on the south side of the river between Bishop Falls and Red Indian Lake, fifty-two on its northern banks along the same stretch of the river as well as one square house, eight in the area of Middleton and Mary Anne lakes, three on Red Indian Lake along with another square house, and two or more near the river mouth in the vicinity of Charles Brook (see Table 15.1).[32] The sketch map only accounts for dwellings in a limited area but can nevertheless serve as a basis for a population estimate and for conclusions about the size and distribution of inland camps, if allowances are made for additional winter camps elsewhere. On questioning the settlers in Notre Dame Bay about the number of Beothuk still alive, Cartwright was told that they were so seldom encountered in summer that there could not be more than two or three hundred of them left. But infrequency of sightings struck Cartwright as an unconvincing basis for a population estimate. He argued that the Beothuk's way of life and lack of firearms made them silent and inconspicuous inhabitants who did not carelessly expose themselves to sight and whose movements on the coast could be well hidden in the many bays, inlets, and islands between the two capes. Having himself seen as many as ninety-one mamateeks on the Exploits River and at Red Indian Lake, Cartwright postulated a population between three and five hundred. However, he admitted that several of the dwellings had not been used for some time; because the disused houses had been left standing it was difficult to make an accurate calculation.[33]

Based on Cartwright's map and report, a conservative estimate of the Beothuk population in 1768 would be close to 350.[34]

Cartwright also recorded the location and extent of Beothuk caribou fences.[35] On the southern bank of the Exploits River fences were positioned between Great Rattling Brook and Stony Brook, and from Middle Brook well beyond Pamahac Brook. On the northern bank, fences were erected east of Bishop

Falls, east of Badger Brook and west of Badger, all of them parallel to the river. Fences on the northern river bank had wing-type extensions that directed migrating caribou herds to specific river crossings or into compounds or traps.[36] At "Sewel Point" (east of Bishop Falls), where the lack of trees had prevented Beothuk from building solid tree fences, they had placed "sewels," poles to which birchbark flaps were attached. Taken together, the fenceworks measured a total of about thirty kilometres, fifteen kilometres on either side of the river.

Beothuk/Settler Relations

In his report Cartwright stated that the English who had taken possession of the country had made no effort to accommodate the aboriginal inhabitants. Amicable relations once existed, but it was not the conduct of Beothuk that had caused established social bonds to be broken. In Cartwright's opinion any hostility by the "Red Indians" was "founded, on their part upon a just, and, to any uncivilized people, a noble resentment of wrongs. On the part of the English fishers, it [was] an inhumanity which sinks them far below the level of savages. The wantonness of their cruelties towards the poor wretches, has frequently been almost incredible."[37]

There seems to have been no shortage of violence and murder by English fishermen. Cartwright recounted a grisly story of the killing of a pregnant woman, whose hands were displayed to him as a trophy.[38] A second incident, related by him in order to strengthen the case against the fishermen, concerns the wounding or killing of a defenceless woman and the robbing of her child.[39] He thought the Beothuk, who moved about in small groups and had no guns, were particularly vulnerable to harassment during the summer season. "So inconsiderable are they in point of numbers, and subject to such an extreme dread of fire-arms, that they are ever on the defensive. Besides, the necessity of their separating into single families and small parties in order to obtain that subsistence which no one place would furnish to numerous bodies, renders them in general an easy conquest to a single boat's crew."[40] Although no codfisher operated in the island area where the Beothuk foraged for food, it was often visited by salmon fishers, shipbuilders, sawyers, woodsmen, furriers, and hunters who moved from island to island in quest of game.[41] In addition to being persecuted the Beothuk were increasingly denied access to traditional food supplies such as salmon, seabirds, eggs, and fur bearers. This consistent erosion of their resource base was depriving them of their livelihood and under these conditions they would not be able to survive. Cartwright's brother George shared his concern.[42]

Although John Cartwright's detailed report and maps, which illuminate many aspects of Beothuk culture and distribution, are much valued today, at the time his warnings and accusations had little impact on the attitude of the English towards the native population. His account appears to have caused Palliser to report the persecutions to authorities in England, but the proclamations with threats of punishment that were subsequently issued neither prevented further offences nor assured Beothuk access to adequate means of subsistence. Indeed, having failed in his mission to establish good relations, Cartwright had achieved little of immediate benefit to them. Had he succeeded in initiating communication, Beothuk history might have taken a different turn, considering that in 1768 their tribe was still a viable group.

A BEOTHUK CAPTIVE

Governor Palliser not only sent Cartwright on a peace mission to the Exploits River but also planned to contact Beothuk through a captive. Anyone who brought a Beothuk to Palliser would be given a cash reward. This plan had unfortunate consequences and probably caused considerable damage to already-precarious relations since it encouraged a group of furriers to kill a Beothuk woman in 1768 and carry away her little boy. When this child, who was about four years old, was presented to Governor Palliser, he could neither give information about his tribe nor provide words of his language.[43] To Cartwright's dismay, one of "the very villains" who had taken part in the capture came to him "to ask a gratuity for the share he had borne in the transaction." The child was given the name John August "and was the following winter exposed as a curiosity to the rabble at Pool for two pence apiece."[44]

It is quite possible that the task of settling the matter with the child's captors fell to Cartwright, since he was surrogate for the northern district. According to the log of *HMS Guernsey*, the shallop was again sent north two days after Cartwright's return from his expedition, presumably with Cartwright aboard since his report on his trek up the Exploits River was written in Twillingate.[45] The records do not indicate whether the promised reward for a captured Beothuk was paid. All we know is that John August was later employed in the fishery in Catalina and then in Trinity where he died in 1788, aged twenty.[46]

A PROCLAMATION IS ISSUED

Hugh Palliser, whose term as governor ended at the close of the fishing season in 1768, was succeeded by John Byron, appointed from 1769 to 1772. The instructions for Byron, indeed for all governors from 1769 onwards, included the order to issue a proclamation for the protection of the Beothuk.[47] The text for this proclamation reads as follows:

> Whereas it has been represented to the King, that the subjects residing in the said Island of Newfoundland, instead of cultivating such a friendly intercourse with the savages inhabiting that island as might be for their mutual benefit and advantage, do treat the said savages with the greatest inhumanity, and frequently destroy them without the least provocation or remorse. In order, therefore, to put a stop to such inhuman barbarity, and that the perpetrators of such atrocious crimes may be brought to due punishment, it is His Majesty's royal will and pleasure, that I do express his abhorrence of such inhuman barbarity, and I do strictly enjoin and require all His Majesty's subjects to live in amity and

brotherly kindness with the native savages of the said island of Newfoundland. I do also require and command all officers and magistrates to use their utmost diligence to discover and apprehend all persons who may be guilty of murdering any of the said native Indians, in order that such offenders may be sent over to England, to be tried for such capital crimes as by the statute of 10 and 11 William III for encouraging the trade to Newfoundland is directed.[48]

While the proclamation left no doubt that the authorities condemned the persecutions and killings of Beothuk and made them a punishable offence, it did not have the intended effect. Two factors that contributed to its ineffectiveness were the Beothuk's practice of taking revenge by stealing gear, which greatly incensed the settlers, and the latter's reluctance to inform on each other when an atrocity was committed. Being prejudiced against and in fear of the Beothuk, settlers would not have wanted to see one of their neighbours hanged for wounding or killing an Indian. Also, according to the proclamation, offenders who had murdered Beothuk were to be tried by an English court, and witnesses could be sent to England to give evidence. They were given no allowance for their travel, and their absence from the fishery for several months was liable to cause their ruin or that of their families.[49] With the implementation of the Commission of Oyer and Terminer in 1750, capital crimes connected with the fishery could be tried in Newfoundland, yet the proclamations indicated that trials for the murder of Beothuk were to remain an exception to this rule. The clause was finally eliminated in 1789.[50]

The British authorities seem to have been impervious to Cartwright's accusations and did nothing to prosecute offenders. Instead, their interest centred on developing a profitable fur trade with Beothuk, possibly by selling rum to them. Instructions to governors, starting with John Byron in 1769, therefore directed them to use their "best endeavours to conciliate their [the Beothuk's] affections and to induce them to trade with our subjects reporting to us by one of our principal Secretaries of State the best account you can obtain of the number of the said Indians, the places they frequent, the nature and extent of the commerce that is or may be carried on with them and how the same may in your opinion be further extended and improved."[51] Perhaps in response to this new directive, Governor Byron adopted the plan of his predecessor and sent John Cartwright to Notre Dame Bay in July of 1769 to make a second attempt at contacting Beothuk.[52] Cartwright was unsure where to find them and eventually searched near Triton Island. But he not only found it difficult to navigate this intricate coast, which had not yet been charted, but also next to impossible to come close to Beothuk, who habitually posted themselves where they had a commanding view of all means of access and retreated rapidly when strangers approached.[53] Although fishermen sometimes accidentally encountered Beothuk not far from the place where Cartwright had moored his vessel, he himself only once caught sight of a Beothuk canoe, when scanning the sea through his telescope from a hill on Sunday Cove Island. Cartwright's men immediately gave chase with two boats but lost sight of the canoe when it disappeared around a point of land; they nevertheless searched along the coast until dark. On resuming their quest the next morning, the men found a deserted mamateek in a narrow pass within a few yards of where they had looked the night before; the embers of the fire were still glowing.[54] Cartwright concluded that "every days' experience only served to confirm the writer more and more in his opinion that the plan he acted upon was practicable and when it should be regularly pursued, and after the most advantageous manner, that it's ending successfully was very little to be doubted."[55]

A year later in the fall of 1770, John Cartwright returned to Triton Island, presumably to continue his mission. However, his plans came to naught when he was shipwrecked. In a letter filed with the Admiralty Records, Governor Byron reported that Cartwright, whom he had sent to the north in the shallop of *HMS Antelope* "on the business of surrogating," was "castaway upon Troy towne Islands [Triton Island]" but that all his people and most materials were saved.[56] Since this area was not one in which surrogate courts were held but was rather the very place where Cartwright had seen a Beothuk canoe the previous year, it would appear that Governor Byron did not wish to report Cartwright's futile attempts to contact Beothuk and covered himself by claiming that he was shipwrecked while on surrogate duty.

Another opportunity to interact with Beothuk presented itself earlier that year in July. This time it was John Cartwright's brother George who came close to meeting a small Beothuk group. On his way to Labrador he had stopped at Fogo to have his vessel refitted and went looking for Beothuk to pass time. With the aid of his telescope he discerned a few of them on a small island east of Coal All Island, in the vicinity of Comfort Cove. There were six people, two canoes, and two mamateeks, each with a fire in it. George immediately made plans to return at night to take the Beothuk by surprise. As he had a forceful personality he could well have succeeded in communicating with these Beothuk, but whether it could have led to an amicable interchange is a moot point. Neither his English captain nor the Irish cooper who accompanied him were willing to risk their lives on an expedition that threatened danger but offered no prospect of profit, so the nightly raid was never made.[57]

John Cartwright's expedition into Beothuk country and his subsequent searches in Notre Dame Bay held some promise. It was a tragic turn of fate that he failed to contact any Beothuk; for he was well equipped to further harmonious relations with them if the Beothuk had still been willing to make peace. Cartwright was genuinely concerned about the native population, fully supported by the incumbent governors, and acutely aware of the delicate nature of his mission. It is just possible that an encounter with one of the Cartwrights could have tipped the scale towards improved relations. Circumstances were never again as favourable as they had been in 1768 and 1769, and later attempts to conciliate the Beothuk had no real probability of success. As we know from Shanawdithit's revelations, the Beothuk eventually became opposed to any form of interaction and taught their children to foster hate and revenge against the English.[58]

CHAPTER SEVEN

Intensified Conflict between Beothuk and Settlers

In the first two to three decades of the eighteenth century, the Beothuk faced increased competition from the English for access to salmon and fur-bearing animals. This resulted in hostile acts on both sides and in killings of Beothuk and of English salmon catchers and furriers. Following these clashes the Beothuk retreated for a time from areas that were frequented by the English. However, in the early 1760s they again made their presence forcefully known by taking or destroying fishing gear and equipment and sometimes by wounding or killing settlers. The latter, becoming more resentful, retaliated by shooting at Beothuk on sight, raiding camps, and pursuing them as they travelled by canoe. Since no communication between settlers and Beothuk existed, let alone any mechanism for settling disputes, hostilities intensified.

The first three sections of this chapter summarize reports and traditions about hostile as well as friendly encounters between Beothuk and English. They are followed by discussions of circumstances that contributed to the persistence and growth of animosities.

RECORDS OF HOSTILE ACTS BY BEOTHUK

Not long after furriers killed the occupants of a wigwam and captured the Beothuk child June in 1758 (an incident discussed in chapter 9), a group of Beothuk attacked shipmaster Scott and his fishing crew in the Bay of Exploits in the early 1760s (Fig. 7.1). Scott's party had built a fortified residence in the mouth of the bay. When a large number of Beothuk appeared, Scott went among them unarmed "with every sign of amity … and mixed with them … An old man, in pretended friendship, put his arms around his neck; at the same instant another stabbed Scott in the back. The war-whoop resounded, a shower of arrows fell upon the English which killed the other shipmaster and four of his companions. The rest of the party hastened to their vessels and returned to St John's, carrying one of those who had been killed with the arrows sticking in his body."[1]

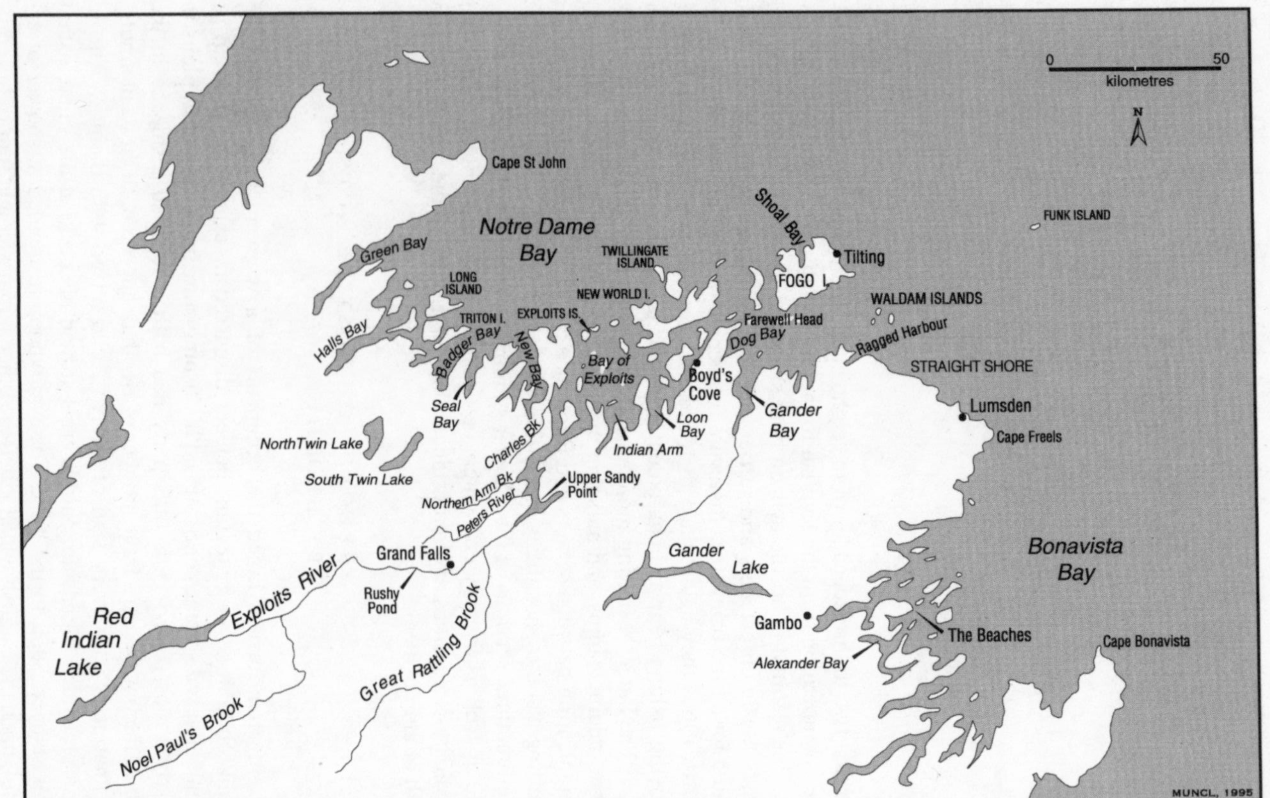

Fig.7.1 Map of northeastern Newfoundland showing places to which Beothuk resorted in the late eighteenth and early nineteenth centuries.

An attempt by five Englishmen to settle in Halls Bay also ended in tragedy. According to Thomas Peyton, who heard the story from Henry Rowsell of Halls Bay, "they were all killed by the Indians. A crew went up from Twillingate shortly afterwards, and found the bodies of those unfortunates, with their heads cut off and stuck on poles."[2]

When Banks visited Newfoundland in 1766, he was told that the English lived in constant warfare with the native population and vice versa. He was given the scalp of a local fisherman, who had been killed by Beothuk while swimming to his ship. A year later his companions had found the scalp with the whole face attached, which they immediately recognized as that of Sam Frye.[3]

In answer to George Cartwright's enquiries about the Beothuk in the 1760s, most of the settlers' complaints focused on the Beothuk's practice of taking their equipment – many settlers had lost sails, fleets of nets, hatchets, kettles, and tools. Similar complaints were voiced in 1792 when Capt. G.C. Pulling questioned settlers and fishermen in the districts of Bonavista and Notre Dame Bay about their relations with the Beothuk. Presumably in retaliation for wrongs suffered at the hands of settlers, fishing crews, and furriers, the Beothuk routinely purloined fishing gear and traps, which outraged the English who did not perceive these thefts as acts of revenge. The Beothuk had taken salmon nets and other articles from several fishermen, robbed residents at Tilting Harbour on Fogo Island of sails and lines, and wounded and killed some of their cows.[4] During the summer of 1792 Harry Miller had lost traps and nets valued at thirty pounds sterling.[5] It should be added here that while Pulling's report does not make much of the taking of traps, many archaeological sites, particularly on the Exploits River, have yielded a profusion of pieces of iron and Beothuk-made tools, some of which were derived from traps.[6]

Sometimes Englishmen were attacked with bow and arrows when at work. As described in chapter 4, a young man was killed while dipping salmon at a pond close to Ragged Harbour in 1780, and salmon catcher Thomas Rowsell was shot in 1789 in New Bay. On other occasions death was avoided; for example, in 1783, when a man named McDonald went duck hunting with a boy in Gander Bay, the boy was nearly killed by a Beothuk who emerged from the woods with a knife in his hand. McDonald rescued the boy by pointing his gun, but it was a close call. The Beothuk ran off with all speed; had McDonald's gun not been out of order he would have been shot.[7] In the following year at about the same place, MacDonald met the same Beothuk, who passed by "at an easy pace" and did not appear to be afraid; neither side offered any injury.

An incident remembered in the northern district for many decades was the Beothuk's ambush of nine men who had gone to fetch rock ballast at Shoal Bay, south of Fogo Harbour. The Beothuk had positioned a decoy pigeon in the entrance of the bay to test whether the settlers had brought their guns. When none of them took aim, the Beothuk correctly assumed that they were unarmed. As their punt approached the shore, Beothuk shot at the occupants with arrows; five men were wounded, three quite seriously. By the time a large party came back to take revenge, the Beothuk had made their escape.[8] Two of Matthew Ward's men were involved in another hostile encounter in the spring of 1792. On rounding a point of land they suddenly came face to face with five Beothuk who shot arrows at them and forced them to retreat. According to the informant, a confrontation in which the English fled had not happened in Notre Dame Bay for several years.[9]

TRADITIONS RECORDED BY J.P. HOWLEY

In his book *The Beothucks or Red Indians*, published in 1915, J.P. Howley relates many traditions about Beothuk that he collected in the late 1800s from residents of the northern bays. Most informants had heard these stories from old people in their community, when they themselves were young. Howley could not vouch for their correctness but believed that most of them contained some "element of truth."[10] A careful scrutiny of the material suggests that several traditions resemble accounts by Pulling and the Cartwright brothers, in a transformed or embellished form; others have not been recorded before, and still others may have been rendered unrecognizable in the process of telling and retelling.

One example of a tradition that is evidently based on a real event but that became embellished over the years is that of the near capture of a settler woman. It was related by Inspector Grimes of the Newfoundland Constabulary who had grown up in Notre Dame Bay and had heard the story when he was young. According to this tale, Beothuk came to Herring Neck on New World Island at a time when only two women, a mother and daughter named Stuckly, were at home. They raided the house and started to carry the daughter away. The mother, coming to the rescue, gave one of the Beothuk a stunning blow with a clothes pole, so that he dropped his burden and ran off. The story was later clarified by one of Mrs Stuckly's descendants, who said that a Beothuk had come close to the house but had neither raided it nor carried away one of the women, nor even come into striking distance, but rather had been chased away by the dogs. The incident had occurred on the south side of Twillingate Island, where the Stucklys lived before they moved to Herring Neck.[11]

On another occasion, Beothuk concealed themselves under the fishing stages in the harbour of Herring Neck. When the fisherfolk retired to their houses, the Indians cut up the sails of a fishing boat and all the fishermen's lines, besides doing other mischief. Though they were detected they made their escape.[12]

Inspector Grimes also related to Howley that a man named Cooper was killed by Beothuk in Notre Dame Bay in the late 1700s.[13] Cooper's brother, in England at the time of the killing, came back to avenge his death. On meeting several canoes in New Bay he riddled them with shot and ball; a number of Beothuk were killed or drowned and not one of the canoes was said to have reached land.

A story that appears to have undergone substantial transformation was told by Mr Wiltshear of Bonavista. A fisherman from the neighbourhood of Cat Harbour (now Lumsden) had his new suit of sails stolen by Beothuk. Searching for the thieves he saw them on a distant hill, shaking their "cossacks" (long, loose coats or gowns) at him in defiance; the garments were made out of the boat's sails and were daubed with red ochre. The fisherman raised a party of twenty-five men who trekked overland to a place where they knew of a Beothuk encampment. On arrival the party found twelve deserted dwellings. Two of the men had been dispatched in a skiff to take the rest of the party home but had been seen by Beothuk, who had given alarm. The Beothuk who had kept a watch had placed a goose as a decoy on the water and, when the skiff drew close, shot at the two men; no injuries were recorded.[14]

Several aspects of this story seem implausible. There are no other reported cases of Beothuk using sails to make clothing; sails were usually taken to cover mamateeks and were occasionally hoisted on canoes. Nor was there much time between the theft and the fisherman's sighting of the defiant Beothuk for sails to be converted into garments, and it seems nearly impossible that the fisherman could tell from a distance that the garments the Beothuk wore had been made from *his* sails. Altogether, the goose decoy, the shooting of the men in the skiff, and the twelve deserted wigwams fit poorly together with the rest of the story, and one cannot help wondering whether this tale was an amalgamation of several separate stories.

J.P. Howley heard a number of stories from Thomas Peyton, son of John Peyton, Jr, who knew several of the old furriers in the employ of his father. Thomas Peyton had never heard of an English settlement being attacked by Beothuk, nor of any white person being carried off, nor of Beothuk scalping anybody.[15] However, old John Boles had told him that on one occasion, while rowing to his salmon nets in Halls Bay, he saw a Beothuk on a cliff raising his bow. Knowing how accurately the Beothuk aimed, Boles held a boat's thwart over his head and the arrow embedded itself in the board. Catching up his flintlock gun, the old man continued, "I peppered his cossack for him."[16] When he was a boy, Thomas Peyton heard that an English youngster had been killed when going ashore for water on the south side of Twillingate Harbour, near Hart's Cove. Peyton also recalled a tradition about two boys who were shot by Beothuk when they went ashore to wash their clothes in Kiar's Pond.[17] A crew sent to search for them found the bodies and saw a party of Beothuk making off. Inspector Grimes had heard of the same incident, though in his version the Beothuk had carried away the boys' heads.[18] Another of Peyton's recollections concerned a boy from New Bay named Rowsell, who was in the habit of going alone into the country to look after his father's traps. One day he did not return, and it was believed that he had either been killed or carried off by Beothuk.[19]

Despite intermittent acts of violence Beothuk did not take every available opportunity to harm the English. George Cartwright had heard many stories of Beothuk having spared the lives of "our people, when they might very easily have put them to death." In one case a fishermen in the Bay of Exploits was about to land in order to look at a trap, when he was surprised by the voice of a Beothuk who was standing on the shore with an arrow in his bow ready to shoot. He motioned with his hand for the fisherman to leave and the fisherman immediately rowed away as fast as he could. He later said he regretted not having had his gun with him as he would have shot the Beothuk "dead upon the spot."[20] Harry Miller told Captain Pulling in 1792 that a few years earlier, when he was standing near his house looking over the water, a group of Beothuk arrived in four canoes and stopped opposite to him. Miller was alone at home at the time and was convinced that the Beothuk knew this. He called out "halloo" to them; they stayed a few minutes and then paddled on at a leisurely pace.[21] An old Micmac once said to Howley, "Red Injun not bad man, if he mind to he could kill every fisherman without letting himself be seen at all."[22]

HOSTILE ACTS BY THE ENGLISH

It is evident that the English never doubted their right to settle in Newfoundland and to exploit the resources without considering the rights and needs of the aboriginal population, whose presence was considered a nuisance at best. The settlers were therefore indignant about the Beothuk's thefts of gear and their habit of cutting loose fishing boats – sometimes directly out of the harbour. Fishermen and furriers vented their anger and frustration by pursuing Beothuk and shooting at them.[23] Feelings sometimes ran high and there were people who thought that it was no crime to kill an Indian.[24]

One of the principal settlers, Harry Miller, reasoned with Pulling: "Why if we were not to shoot at 'em others wou'd & can you blame us now Capn P-g when they steal our nets, Traps, & evry thing they can lay hold of. – Now wou'd not You kill any man that you found robbing Your house or vessel."[25] Isakiah Guy, William Cull, Richard Richmond, and a furrier with the name of Creazy were equally ready to shoot and, in Pulling's words, "think it right & doing themselves Justice to Retaliate."[26]

One of the most brutal recorded murders was perpetrated by a fisherman named Wells in the summer of 1779. On seeing a canoe in a cove near Cape St John, Wells fired directly at its occupants, three or four of whom fell. After landing, some of the Beothuk ran into the woods, but those who had been wounded hid behind cliffs. Wells searched them out, shot them again, and then took their canoe and its contents.[27] An equally gruesome story was told of John Moore from Trinity, who once came across a Beothuk woman and her two children. When she pleaded for mercy by exposing her breasts, Moore or his companion "shot her Dead." One of her two children died while being carried to the boat; the other escaped into the woods.[28]

Thomas Taylor, Richard Richmond, and William Hooper, servants of Harry Miller, attacked a Beothuk family at their camp at Charles Brook Pond, in 1791. The men allowed two women to get away but shot a man, wounded a boy, and captured a girl, known as Oubee.[29] Before arriving at the camp they had become enraged on seeing an empty punt close by, imagining that its owner had been murdered. In fact, Beothuk from Charles Brook Pond had travelled to Cape Farewell where they had been chased ashore by two fishermen, Hicks and Verge, who took their canoe. The Beothuk were thereby forced to walk over a hundred kilometres through the woods to Indian Arm, where they took Mr Lester's punt with three salmon nets in it in order to get back to Charles Brook.[30]

On another occasion, when passing Indian Cove, Thomas Taylor, William Cull, and four other men saw Beothuk wigwams covered with sails. They changed their course to land, but by the time they reached shore the Beothuk had stripped the wigwams and fled into the woods. The settlers carried away two canoes, a salmon net, and everything they considered worthwhile. A party of Beothuk in a canoe, on coming into the cove and seeing them, quickly paddled out of sight.[31] R. Gilham, who crossed the paths of Beothuk in 1788, saw several of them run into the woods and took the canoe that they had left in the land-wash.[32] In the same year, on the Strait Shore, Thomas Peckford and his companions came upon a dozen Beothuk who managed to escape into the forest; Peckford added: "We cou'd not get within shot ... Tis hard to kill 'em without Balls I assure Ye Sir ... for they open their cossacks & throw 'em quite lose round 'em when small shot won't kill 'em thro' it."[33]

According to a tale collected by Howley, a youngster who worked for fisherman Facey from Loon Bay was wounded in the throat by Beothuk while skirting along the coast in his boat.[34] On the boy's return, Facey said, "I'll settle that" and set out to find the culprits. When he came across a wigwam in which two Beothuk were asleep, he called out to them and then fired. Facey later stated that he only gave them a fright but did not kill them.

Among Howley's informants, one of the more suspect is Jabez Tilley of Old Perlican, Trinity Bay. Tilley passed on his collection of tales in the last years of the nineteenth century, more than a hundred years after the alleged events, and Howley found all but two of them "altogether too revolting" to be included in his book. The first, said to have happened in 1775, concerned some Beothuk who had come into Trinity Bay at night to steal sails and other gear. Tilley's informant, a Mrs Warren, and others were up all night splitting fish in a stage close by but were unaware of the robbery. The next day a search party found wigwams near Lower Lance Cove and attacked the Beothuk while they slept. Seven were killed, the rest escaped. One of the Beothuk men was 2.13 metres (seven feet) tall. The fishermen loaded their boats with the stolen articles and everything else they could carry away. There were other lurid details.[35]

The second tale is less easy to believe, for reasons that will be given. Tilley stated that "on one occasion 400 Indians were surprised and driven out on a point of land near Hant's Harbour, known as Bloody Point, and all were destroyed."[36] Considering that Beothuk bands in general and the band in Trinity Bay in particular are estimated to have had between thirty and fifty members, the numbers involved are suspiciously large. Furthermore, these relatively small bands were widely distributed in different bays; larger Beothuk settlements have only been recorded from the Exploits River area close to major caribou routes. Finally, since the best estimate of the size of the entire Beothuk tribe in 1768 is five hundred or less, four hundred Beothuk could not have assembled on a headland in Trinity Bay and been killed. Extensive research for more precise information about the incident has yielded no confirming record, and the only hard fact we have is that Howley was told this "current tradition" in the 1880s (or later) by a resident from Old Perlican. Most likely, the original story, in the course of retelling, was embellished with regard to numbers and brutalities and could even have been "transferred" to Hant's Harbour from a different location. Another place whose name has been attributed by a writer to the brutal murder of Indians is Bloody Bay, an inlet in Bonavista Bay in the lower reaches of Alexander Bay (today this inlet is known as Northwest, Southwest, and Middle Arm).[37] Yet there is no record of any sort that might confirm this claim. Reverend Mr Wilson wrote in 1866 that the location had a history of frequent, hostile encounters between fishermen and Beothuk. "When fishermen would be looking for bait, or getting wood from the shore, they would be assailed by a shower of arrows, and be obliged either to defend themselves with their fire arms, or escape in their boats."[38] Two recent histories of Glovertown (in the district of Alexander Bay) also claim that Englishmen, rather than Beothuk, were killed there. According to Harold Stroud, people in the area believe that the name Bloody Bay is based on the late-eighteenth-century killing by Beothuk of a family of Kearleys, or Carleys.[39] Watson Lane was told that Bloody Bay may have received its name on account of the murder of eleven fishermen by Beothuk; a twelfth man who hid under his overturned boat survived. This is said to have occurred at Curly's Cove, a small cove on the north side of Bloody Bay.[40] These stories suggest that the names Bloody Bay and Bloody Point have spawned a number of conflicting traditions, all concerning bloody encounters; yet there is no actual proof that any of these tales – including that related to Howley in the 1880s – were based on facts.

As regards Indian killers, here too exaggeration and boasting may have created a distorted picture of the actual events. Reminiscent of one of Tilley's tales, Inspector Grimes had heard that Richmond, a noted "Indian killer," said he once saw a dead Beothuk 2.13 metres, or seven feet, tall. Though he would not admit to it, it was commonly believed that he and another man had seen the Beothuk on the shore preparing to send off an arrow and had shot him.[41] Another man reputed to have killed Beothuk, Pollard, had openly made a virtue of his achievements, and a furrier from Twillingate Great Island with the name of Rogers "boasted that he had shot at different periods above sixty" Beothuk.[42] One Noel Boss even claimed to have killed ninety-nine Beothuk and wished to add one more so as to round it off at one hundred.[43] No one can now test the truth of these statements. However, the theme of a person having killed a large number of enemies or wishing to kill more to achieve a personal quota is one that recurs in folktales in many places.[44] It is unlikely that single persons killed large numbers of Beothuk because the Beothuk were not that numerous, particularly in the early 1800s. Perhaps the killers initially indulged in (untruthful) boasting after which the numbers were amplified in the retelling.

Raids on Beothuk Winter Settlements

While the Beothuk were frequently pursued or shot at in chance encounters, Captain Pulling recorded that on two occasions settlers trekked inland during the winter with the specific purpose of raiding Beothuk settlements. In February of 1790 Harry Miller, who owned salmon stations on the Exploits River, sent eight men on such a raid. He claimed that he wanted them to retrieve traps and nets that the Beothuk had stolen during the preceding summer.[45] It should be noted that the Beothuk usually took the metal from traps to fashion tools of their own design and cut up nets for making rope, so that there would have been little left to retrieve. Most likely, the party intended to steal furs from the Beothuk and take bloody revenge; the account of William Richmond certainly suggests that revenge was uppermost in the raiders' minds.

Armed and provisioned, the men set out "fully resolved to kill everyone we saw both *Big & small* to be revenged on them for killing Thomas Rowsell the summer before & stealing from us as they do."[46] After more than four days of travel at the rate of twenty miles a day, they discovered three canoes and four wigwams in a small cove.[47] When the Beothuk recognized the armed furriers they picked up their children and some possessions and fled into the woods; Richard Richmond, who was one of the party, counted up to thirty before losing track. The men pursued the fleeing Beothuk with their dogs and captured two women, one with an infant. After a hearty meal of venison, they packed up as many caribou skins and other things as they could drag away, spent the night in the camp, and, before leaving the next morning, set fire to three of the four wigwams. They also burned all three canoes in revenge for the Beothuk's burning of one of their punts the previous summer.[48] Everything that would have been useful to the Beothuk as well as the stolen articles they had found in the wigwams – a tea kettle, an iron pot, and a trap – they threw into the river; the Beothuk's provisions were left intact. Some of the traps had been worked into spears and arrows, while the salmon nets had been taken to pieces and plaited into rope. The men had intended to bring the women away with them but later decided against it because they could have been held responsible for their support. Captain Pulling questioned seven of the eight men who had been on the trip; they all claimed that no shot had been fired because their conscience had not allowed them to do what they had intended.[49]

An embellished version of this account to which other stories had been attached was recorded in 1816 by the Methodist preacher Busby, in a letter to the Wesleyan Missionary Committee in London.[50] A tradition related by Inspector

Grimes to Howley may concern the same story.[51] In both these versions shots were fired and Beothuk, including a heroic chief, were killed.

Pulling also recorded a raid staged nine years earlier in 1781 by John Peyton, Sr, his partner Harry Miller, and their headman Thomas Taylor. Pulling had already heard about this expedition before speaking to either of the participants, who, when questioned, were very cautious in their replies. Thomas Taylor related that the three men had been walking up the Exploits River for three days when they spotted a group of Beothuk gathered in the land-wash where they had spread caribou skins.[52] The men "thought *best to Fire*" and then pursued the fleeing Beothuk. They caught a young girl and probably also an older woman and others who were wounded. After packing up the skins as fast as they could, they returned home without doing any damage.[53] A lame story in Pulling's opinion because Mr Pittman, a man of veracity, had previously told him that Peyton had bragged about his "glorious expedition" when he came to Trinity shortly after the event. According to Peyton's account, as retold by Mr Pittman, the raiding party had

> discharged all their pieces at the Wigwams when they who were within ran out screaming some were wounded & all of course terrified … In one wigwam was a man which they had so crippled as not to be able to stand who had one of Peytons [traps] in his hand the Bed of which he had been working into arrows on a rock. On their entrance the wounded Indian sitting on his breach fought with the remainder of y/e Trap some little time but soon being conquer'd P-n wrested the Trap from him & *beat his brains out* with it. After acting in this cruel manner and pilfering all they could drag away they march'd home again.[54]

While Mr Pittman could not remember Peyton's story verbatim, that his informant had beaten out a man's brains had made so deep an impression on him that he would never forget it. He was also sure Peyton had said that some of the Beothuk had been killed. Richard Richmond told Pulling, "There must have been great slaughter, for … Peyton had Thirty Six Pistol Balls in his Gun."[55]

George Cartwright recorded in 1783–84 that two years previously, three men, one of whom he knew (presumably John Peyton, Sr), went up the Exploits River in quest of Beothuk to plunder and murder. It is likely that this was the same raid later recorded by Pulling. According to Cartwright's account, the men found a number of Beothuk houses at the mouth of the "great lake from whence the river issues … about seventy miles higher up than boats can go" (presumably Red Indian Lake), inhabited by "about sixty souls."[56] On perceiving the armed men, the Beothuk ran for their lives but made poor headway in the deep snow. The men immediately fired on them and wounded and killed "by their own confession" nearly all. Those who escaped into the woods were half clothed or naked; none of them had implements to procure either food or fuel. The three men proceeded to load three sledges with the things they considered to be most valuable from the Beothuk houses and then returned home. Cartwright added that they probably burned down the wigwams, so that any remaining Beothuk would have perished. In 1793, when called as a witness during the Parliamentary Enquiries into the State of the Trade to Newfoundland, Cartwright claimed that there had been over a hundred inhabitants and that the burning of the wigwams was a fact.[57]

Other tales of raids that circulated among northern settlers contain similar motifs and it is impossible to discern whether they were independent incidents or embellished versions of the same story.[58]

In the context of the story of the Peyton raid, George Cartwright said he believed from the conversations he had with fishermen in northern Newfoundland that there were "very few who would not have done the same thing."[59] It is difficult, however, to see how this condemning statement could be true. Many of the fishermen may have retaliated for loss of gear in some form, but there is no evidence that more than a few of them behaved in as brutal a manner as Peyton, Sr, and his companions. Pulling reported that not everyone was hostile towards the Beothuk, and that "every man who I have convers'd with on the subject of Civilizing those harass'd mortals joins me in [the] opinion of the probability as well as utility of the undertaking."[60]

A close look at the records reveals that the list of men who persecuted and killed Beothuk is quite short, and some of the names recur with disturbing frequency. There were others who suffered theft and attack by Beothuk without seeking revenge – John Quinton and Thomas Haysom, for example, who had been among those who were attacked in Shoal Bay, or Mr Clark's planter and the fisherman Hornet, both of whom had lost gear through Beothuk thievery.[61] In fact, to their credit, most of the settlers and fishermen in the northern bays appear to have behaved in a reasonable manner. They may have turned a blind eye to persecutions that they could not prevent but would not themselves have gone out of their way to harass or kill Beothuk. "God forbid all northern Furriers & Salmon catchers shou'd be alike," as Pulling said when commenting on W. Elliot's story that "he did not meddle with anything belonging to them."[62] Elliot, while duck hunting, had found a Beothuk camp from which the occupants had fled on hearing his shots, leaving behind roasted birds, caribou skins, and other articles. He thought that they would come back, as he had previously known them to do when he had "routed" them in a similar way.

Tradition has it that Thomas Rowsell's brother George never molested Beothuk and that they in turn did him no injury, except to help themselves occasionally to a salmon from his weir. They would even meet him face to face and call him by name, "so bold were they with him."[63] Hollet, a salmon catcher who lived on one of the northern brooks, had frequently met with Beothuk and related that they "once play'd him a trick by taking away his Boat while he was absent from it & carrying over the other side the river & when He came to the place where he had left it they stood laughing & making Fun of the old man on the other side & He was obliged to walk some distance e're He cou'd cross the river but when he came to his Boat he found it had not receiv'd the smallest Injury."[64]

J.P. Howley was told that old man Genge, who lived alone at Indian Arm, used to put out a salmon or other food for the Beothuk. He frequently saw Beothuk but he never interfered with them and in turn, they did him no harm. They sometimes came to his salmon dam and dexterously speared a fish while he was present at the other side of the river; they would also pick the seaweed out of his nets as they were hung up to dry.[65] According to Thomas Peyton's notes, John Quinn, who carried on the salmon fishery at Indian Arm after 1816, was also reputed to have been friendly with the Beothuk, who oftentimes speared a salmon on his rackwork. They never attempted to injure Quinn, but "occasionally he would miss a piece of rope or some small article which he supposed they had taken."[66]

Factors behind English Animosity

In order to come to terms with the disturbing fact that some of the English persistently persecuted and injured Beothuk, it may be useful to identify factors that could have contributed to their behaviour. With the exception of Harry Miller and John Peyton, Sr, who owned fishing establishments in the Exploits region and employed men on their stations for the purpose of catching salmon and, in winter, for trapping, the majority of those who came into conflict with the Beothuk were employees, or boatkeepers who worked in the fishery during the summer and trapped in winter. Being part of what Governor Milbanke described as the "lower order," they were not only poorly off but also dependent on employers and merchants who sometimes "ruled as despots."[67] While the influential and wealthy found ways to avoid justice, servants were often convicted for small crimes.[68] At times, they were even used as "whipping boys."[69] In 1725, for example, Watts and Clarkes were ordered by their employer, Jos. Randell, to set salmon nets directly in front of nets already set by Skeffington and others, to prevent them from catching salmon. When Skeffington complained, the servants were taken to a surrogate court and sentenced to five to ten "lashes with a catt of Nine Tails on the bare back." Surrogate courts were usually headed by ships' commanders who routinely enforced discipline among seamen with the lash.[70] In the following year three more of Randell's men were punished for the same offence, while Randell, who had ordered them to act as they had, went unscathed.[71]

In addition to what seems to have been a biased system of justice, punishments for offences were often extremely severe, particularly with respect to property transgressions. This way of exacting justice in the late 1700s had been imported to Newfoundland from Britain; the stocks, flogging, imprisonment, and deportation were common sentences.[72] Furthermore, the death sentence was given for what would today be considered minor offences. Thus James

Reily, who had stolen some items of clothing and surgical instruments, was sentenced to death under British law, but since this was his first offence, mercy was shown and he was merely taken to the public whipping post where the letter T was branded on his hand with a red-hot iron.[73] The death sentence for Matthew Dempsey, convicted of picking a lock and removing a pawnbroker's duplicates, was reduced to deportation to Newfoundland, while William Gibbeons, who had attempted to break into a house, was flogged and deported to Newfoundland for want of bail.[74] In a Newfoundland surrogate court in 1784–85, a man named Clark was sentenced to death for stealing some goods from a shipwreck; it took a petition to the governor by the prosecutor and by the French captain whose ship had been robbed to have Clark pardoned.[75]

Because punishment for theft was severe, one may ask whether persons who lived under the threat of these laws were likely to stand idly by when Beothuk stole equipment or destroyed boats of considerable value. In addition, boatkeepers and planters who made a scarce living could not be expected to react with equanimity to thefts that interfered with their fishing and trapping and caused them real hardship. While one can argue that the Beothuk had a just cause, neither the settlers and fishing crews nor the authorities in England and the governors who represented them in Newfoundland would have doubted the right of the English to settle and fish in Newfoundland. In fact, British colonial policies promoted the appropriation of native lands without assuming any responsibility for the safety and well-being of the rightful owners. Intermittently these policies had been supported by the Church, which argued that by virtue of being non-Christians the native population was inferior; some proponents of the Catholic church had even claimed that by being heathen, native people had forfeited their rights.[76]

Given these circumstances and opinions, a sympathetic understanding of the Beothuk's situation would have been rather remarkable among Newfoundland servants and boatkeepers, who, as Governor Waldegrave saw it, did all the work and took all the risks, while others reaped the profits.[77]

For much of the eighteenth century the northern district, an outpost with its share of ruffians, was removed from the arm of law and justice. As William Keen wrote in 1728: "For want of an authorised person to administer justice we [in Bonavista] are exposed in the winter season to insults of ill minded men who, knowing they cannot be punished in Newfoundland commit many outrages, robberies and murders. There is no officer of justice here."[78]

While Bonavista eventually acquired a magistrate, his presence was no guarantee of order. In 1759, residents of St John's complained that after the troops had left, robberies were committed "every day, magistrates insulted in execution of their duties and a chief justice was murdered."[79] In the absence of a system of justice that would effectively curb disorderly conduct, even a few lawless and rowdy men could do much mischief. Chief Justice Reeves later wrote of the area of the northern bays that it was "a lawless part of the Island where there are no Magistrates resident within many miles, nor any Control from the short visit of a Man-of-War during a few days in the Summer; so that people do as they like, and there is hardly any time of Account for their actions."[80]

One factor that made the situation more complex was that two of the "Indian killers," John Peyton, Sr, and Harry Miller, were respected members of the community who employed men in the salmon and fur business.[81] Instead of setting a good example and using their influence to discourage violence by their servants, they promoted the persecution of Beothuk and personally took part in at least one destructive raid.[82] In 1797 Magistrate John Bland of Bonavista stated in his letter to Governor Waldegrave that Peyton, Sr, in the course of his residence in the Bay of Exploits, "has rendered himself infamous for his persecution of the Indians. The stories told of this man would shock humanity to relate, and for the sake of humanity, it is to be wished are not true."[83]

FAILURE TO CONTROL PERSISTING PERSECUTION

Essentially five groups of people or agencies could be held responsible for allowing fishermen and furriers to persecute Beothuk unchecked: the principal inhabitants in the northern district who, by virtue of their position, were respected and had some authority in the community; owners of business establishments who heard about the ill treatment of Beothuk on their visits; representatives of the judicial system, such as magistrates and patrolling officers, who were usually informed of transgressions; the Newfoundland governors to whom they reported; and Colonial Office officials, who were ultimately responsible for the native population in British colonies.

In order to bring about better relations with the Beothuk, the principal inhabitants of the area not only needed insight into the problems of both sides but also had to be motivated to resolve them. While a number of them may have sympathized with the Beothuk's plight and wished for better relations, believing themselves to be powerless they refused to become involved, though by being silent, they acquiesced in the deeds of those whose violence they may well have abhorred.

As far as the merchants who visited the northern district were concerned, George Cartwright claimed during the 1793 Parliamentary Enquiries into the State of the Newfoundland Trade that he could not recollect an instance at which the merchants had used "their influence and endeavours to prevent" the harassment of Beothuk. In Cartwright's opinion these persons did "not trouble their heads about the matter, for fear it should affect their own interests."[84] Certainly, there is no record that any members of mercantile families used their influence to promote a more humane attitude towards the Beothuk or to curb persistent persecution. Mr Jeffrey, a Newfoundland merchant who was called as witness during the enquiries, had "heard of many instances of very inhuman treatment of … [the Beothuk] in the North part of the island" and thought the matter required investigation.[85] However, at the time he had neither reported this state of affairs to the authorities nor asked that they conduct such an investigation.

Since there were no magistrates in the immediate neighbourhood of areas frequented by Beothuk, that is, between Cape Freels and Cape St John, bringing offenders to justice was difficult because magistrates in other districts were too far away to exert authority.[86] Moreover, while persecutions of Beothuk were widely talked about, they were not witnessed by independent observers who could have given evidence against the culprits in court. Beothuk who had suffered injuries could not be called as witnesses, and the men who were present when crimes were committed were either implicated or unwilling to see their friends hanged or imprisoned for the sake of Beothuk, whom they did not know and for whom they had little regard. One may speculate, though, that had similar numbers of Englishmen been murdered in the northern outposts, means would have been found to stop the killings and prosecute the killers.

In contrast to the inhabitants of the northern communities and visiting traders and merchants, who may have feared that meddling would interfere with their business, the naval officers who patrolled the Newfoundland coast had no such interests to protect. It was their duty to collect information on the fisheries and settlements in all major harbours and to communicate this information to the governor, who summarized their reports for the Colonial Office in Britain. But with the exception of a report from 1732 that states that there had been clashes between furriers and Beothuk, governors' submissions to the Colonial Office rarely mention the native population beyond the standard phrase "No traffic with the Indians."[87] As conflicts between settlers and Beothuk were common knowledge, naval officers may not have transmitted what they had heard to the governor, perhaps because they perceived a need to report that everything was under control in their district.

The first record in years in which a naval officer addressed the problem of poor relations with Beothuk at length is that of Capt. R.C. Reynolds. In his 1786 report to Governor Elliot concerning the fishery in Twillingate, Fogo, Bay of Exploits, and Bonavista, he stated that:

> the Native Indians never come near those settlements but with hostile, savage, intentions. They generally roam about in small Parties and conceal themselves at the back of the Mountains till they see a favourable opportunity for their purpose – then descend (always by night) upon our settlements and carry off everything they find that's portable, leaving marks of waste and devastation behind them.
>
> When they are in the neighbourhood it is dangerous for our people to be stranding those savages lying in wait behind the Bushes shoot their arrows at them which often prove fatal.
>
> Our planters say no kindness can induce, no treatment prevail on them to have the smallest intercourse or traffic with us. But this implacable disposition proceeds perhaps from a remembrance of former wrongs.[88]

Though Reynolds stressed danger from Beothuk as the main problem and claimed that the planters had been rebuffed when showing kindness towards them, he gave no examples of such kindness. He also failed to relate any of the "former wrongs," the most prominent one, still fresh in the mind of the people, being the bloody raid on an Indian camp staged by Miller and Peyton only five years earlier.

Officer Reynolds's interpretation of the inhabitants' complaints was obviously one sided. Able seaman G.C. Pulling (aged nineteen), from *HMS Thisbe* gave a different account. The information he was able to collect during *Thisbe's* five-week sojourn in Trinity Bay in the fall of 1785 caused him concern about the Beothuk's survival. Wishing to bring their precarious situation to the attention of authorities in England, Pulling submitted a statement that began: "To correct the flagrant cruelties which I am well assured have been for many years past exercised on the native Indians of Newfoundland (commonly known by the name of Red Indians) I beg leave to submit the following ideas to His Majestys Government."[89]

This document, which is discussed at length in the next chapter, suggests that the problem was as much the persecution of Beothuk as the danger they posed to fishermen. It also proves that information of this type was readily available to an interested person. Pulling's statement, which he sent privately to an undisclosed recipient, is supported by a report filed in 1787 by the commander of *HMS Mulin*, Edward Parkenham, who wrote that the trade for furs "might be rendered much more advantageous – as well as the intents of humanity advanced – if their [the settler's] improper and often cruel treatment of the Native Indians did not exclude all intercourse with them."[90]

Some information about persecutions obviously reached governors who may have been reluctant to admit that Beothuk were being abused within their jurisdiction. For example, Governor Richard Edwards's statement in 1779 that there had "not been any Indians seen upon the Island for several years" clearly contradicts the evidence since by then conflict with Beothuk had greatly accelerated.[91] There also seems to have been a streak of prejudice at work against Beothuk, which led to a blind eye being turned on the situation. Few governors made an effort to comply with Colonial Office instructions to obtain information on the size and location of Beothuk settlements and to investigate ways of improving trade with them. Nor did they enforce orders "to use their utmost Diligence to discover and apprehend all persons who may be guilty of murdering … Native Indians."[92] For example, when Irish hunters captured the Beothuk boy known as June and killed his mother and another child, the incumbent governor neither reported the murder nor laid charges.[93]

Since the governors' main goal was supporting the fishery and maintaining order, one can see how inertia, lack of information, and an inability to visualize solutions could have led to an unwillingness to admit the existence of reprehensible behaviour towards the Beothuk population and to initiate appropriate changes, which is not to say that such inertia should be excused.

The secretaries of state for the Colonies and other officials in positions of responsibility clearly did not live up to their mandate, let alone to their moral obligation as representatives of a Christian monarch. Their main concern appears to have been the growth of the fisheries, which brought revenue, and presumably the security of their own position, which made it inadvisable to support unpopular measures. Distant as they were from the troubled area, it was easy to ignore requests for measures, such as a peace mission or the creation of a reserve, that would have ensured greater security for the native population as well as access to important food resources.

People at all levels of authority showed a complete disregard for the humanity of the Beothuk and failed to take any responsibility for them. Among the settlers, fear, ignorance, and unrestrained emotion overrode their sense of decency and moral obligations. Merchants were too self-serving to care about the aboriginal population, magistrates, naval officers, and governors turned a blind eye so as not to become involved in unpopular measures, and officials in Britain ignored their responsibility for the sake of personal and public gain.

WHY THE BEOTHUK CONTINUED TO TAKE AND DAMAGE EQUIPMENT

It may be useful to ask what advantages accrued to the Beothuk by acquiring European goods, and whether they outweighed the damages they sustained as a consequence – assuming that they were aware that their thievery triggered retaliation.

Pilfering goods and equipment from Europeans, a widespread habit among native people, was frequently commented upon by early explorers. Jacques Cartier, for example, specifically noted that the natives on the Atlantic coast of North America were skilful thieves.[94] The Beothuk were no exception. Unwilling to expose themselves to contact or trade, they soon found that they could obtain European materials not otherwise available to them by stealth. Fishermen repeatedly complained about Beothuk pilfering in the 1620s; over time, rather than abating, this annoying habit increased.[95] As a rule, the Beothuk appear to have stolen and destroyed property indiscriminately since they could rarely track down individuals who had wronged them, and presumably also because all Europeans shared the blame of usurping their land and resources. Sir David Kirke, who settled in Ferryland in 1638, thought that the stealing was the Beothuk's way of taking revenge for the injustices they suffered.[96] Certainly, the unmindful behaviour of Europeans, their capture of members of the tribe, and their interference with the Beothuk's subsistence activities may well have been the major cause of the thefts.

Other contemporary writers, such as the Raudots and George Cartwright, rationalized stealing as the Beothuk's only means of obtaining goods they needed.[97] The Beothuk occasionally had the option to trade, but the barter arrangements in Trinity Bay (as described by Kirke) and in Bonavista, where a woman had been shot, had shown that the English could not be trusted and exchanges rarely occurred. While the Beothuk had been capable of subsisting by their traditional methods before European goods ever came their way, the reduction of their territory would have called for more efficient hunting and trapping techniques, and European tools such as iron axes for fence building may have become essential. The Beothuk clearly coveted metal tools, fishing nets, sails, and twine, which suggests that the rationale proposed by the Raudots and Cartwright has validity.

An argument that is sometimes made, namely, that among Beothuk property was largely considered a community asset and that taking tools from Europeans may not have been considered theft, cannot be substantiated. We know nothing about the Beothuk's traditions in this regard and it is unlikely that they failed to recognize the nature and consequences of their "borrowing." Having been exposed to the practices of Europeans for several centuries, the Beothuk are bound to have realized that their thievery was strongly resented and that they were taking risks. It would appear that they continued with their practice in defiance of the English because it provided an outlet for their mounting anger and frustration over continued injustices. Indeed, Shanawdithit later disclosed that from infancy her people were taught to take revenge for the innumerable wrongs that were inflicted on the tribe by the whites.[98]

The persistent stealing and destruction may have had additional functions. Le Jeune, a Jesuit missionary with the Huron, said that "to steal and not to be discovered was considered to be a sign of superior intelligence to them. Utility is not always the sole object of their thefts."[99] On several occasions the Beothuk expropriated or destroyed gear without material benefit to themselves, for example, cutting loose fishing boats from their moorings and allowing them to drift to rocky shores.[100] Well planned and cunningly executed, such feats would have provided an opportunity for showing bravery and would have boosted the morale of an otherwise disheartened people. They may also have strengthened the unity of the group, brought prestige, and been recorded in legends and songs, thus playing a significant role in their cultural survival. The most notorious incident of this type was the cutting adrift of Peyton's vessel in 1818 while it was loaded with salmon and ready to sail for St John's. Shanawdithit, who had taken part in this venture, later described the Beothuk's excitement on the occasion. "Stealing man's boat" was among the many topics of songs that she listed; perhaps this song celebrated the stealing of the boat belonging to Peyton.[101] Yet the Beothuk paid dearly for this adventure. When the Peytons pursued them to their winter camp at Red Indian Lake to retrieve stolen goods, Demasduit was captured and their leader Nonosabasut and his brother were killed.

CHAPTER EIGHT

Plans to Conciliate the Beothuk

It became increasingly evident that proclamations ordering Newfoundland residents to live in peace with the Beothuk and requesting magistrates to bring wrongdoers to justice were ineffective. If persecutions were to be halted, other methods had to be found. In the 1780s and 1790s, four men submitted proposals to authorities in Britain promoting new measures to provide protection for the Beothuk and to improve relations. These men were George Cartwright, merchant and owner of fishing and sealing stations in Labrador; George Christopher Pulling, officer in the Royal Navy; Chief Justice John Reeves, law advisor to the Board of Trade, and William Waldegrave, governor from 1797 to 1799.

GEORGE CARTWRIGHT'S PLAN FOR AN INDIAN RESERVE

George Cartwright, whose sealing and fishing stations stretched between Cape Charles and Hamilton Inlet on the Labrador coast, had been successful in contacting and befriending the Inuit who resorted to that area. Buoyed by his success, Cartwright turned his attention to the Newfoundland Beothuk. Since accompanying his brother John on the exploration of Beothuk country up the Exploits River in 1768, he had been interested in these Indians. In 1784, he submitted a proposal to the Colonial Office entitled "The Case of the Wild or Red Indians of Newfoundland."[1] The "Red Indians," he stated, were by then confined to the country between Cape Freels and Cape St John and their number had been reduced through murder and famine. Since they had been dispossessed of salmon brooks and denied access to bird islands, they were "put to the greatest difficulties to procure a scanty subsistence, and can do that only at the hazard of their lives; which our people not only never spare when they chance to meet with them, but even often go in quest of them on purpose to murder and rob them. If some effectual measures be not taken to prevent it, that unhappy race of mortals will soon be extirpated."[2]

Cartwright recounted details of Peyton and Miller's raid of a Beothuk winter camp in 1781 and of the murder of a pregnant woman on another occasion, which he had heard from men who had been involved in the atrocities.[3] In Cartwright's opinion it was only natural that the Beothuk were taking revenge by stealing tools, or by killing. Every summer they lurked about fishing harbours and had become so desperate that they had shown much bravado and daring in their exploits. The people who committed offences were planters and servants who lived in areas frequented by Beothuk, or who were employed in the cod fishery there. The merchants who could have intervened were not willing to do so as it would put them to expense and trouble. Some believed that "the Indians ought either to be extirpated, or caught and made slaves … to work at the fisheries."[4] Since the proclamations were treated with contempt, more effective measures to curb the persecutions were required and it was "high time for Government to interfere, and either make friends of, or extirpate them. Let Justice and humanity determine." He also believed that the Beothuk would not survive unless they received protection and were given a territory in which they could hunt and fish without competition and molestation from the English.

Cartwright proposed that the coast between Gander Bay Point (Dog Bay Point?) and Cape St John be declared a royal district. Between mid-August and the first of November all persons would be permitted to enter this area for the purpose of cutting hay, collecting wood, felling timber, or gathering berries; for the remainder of the year only His Majesty's vessels should be allowed to go there. To enforce the observance of this plan the district should be patrolled by a schooner shallop of about thirty tons with two six-oar boats, two swivel guns, eighteen stands of arms, a master, two mates, a carpenter's mate, and fourteen seamen. The vessel should also carry an assortment of hardware, beads, woollens, nets, and other articles as presents for the Beothuk. Once a reconciliation had been effected, the quantity of gifts should gradually be diminished "in proportion as traffic might be supposed sufficiently to supply the wants of the Indians."

Responsibility for making contact with Beothuk and enforcing the various rules was to be in the hands of a superintendent of Indian Affairs who would have full jurisdiction within the royal district. Cartwright believed that an attempt at contacting Beothuk could be dangerous and would require knowledge of their character, customs, and manners. It would also take time and patience. Since he had accumulated some of this knowledge and had been successful among the hostile Eskimos in Labrador, Cartwright was confident that he could achieve conciliation and offered himself as a suitable candidate for the position of superintendent, for which he expected a most moderate payment.[5] He had already talked about his plan to some of the merchants whose fisheries were adjacent to the proposed district, and who would consequently be most affected by the intended exclusion, but they "saw so little inconvenience therefrom, and were so sensible of the justice and humanity of the scheme, that they much approved of it." Considering that some merchants were reputedly in favour of extirpating the Beothuk, they might not have approved wholeheartedly of these ideas. In the event, Cartwright's plan was not adopted, presumably because it involved considerable expense. Moreover, neither the Newfoundland governors nor the Colonial Secretary in England would have been inclined to limit the English fishery in the northern bays; nor would they have favoured a scheme that prevented settlers from trapping, thereby affecting their ability to procure a living during the winter season.

A PROPOSAL BY GEORGE CHRISTOPHER PULLING RN

In the autumn of 1785, *HMS Thisbe*, with able seaman Pulling on board, visited Newfoundland on her way from Halifax to England.[6] It will be recalled that during a five-week sojourn in Trinity Harbour, Pulling heard about the conflicts between northern settlers and Beothuk, who, armed only with bows and arrows, were no match for the gun-bearing settlers. To bring their precarious situation to the attention of authorities in Britain, Pulling submitted a proposal to "His Majesty's Government" expressing his conviction that it would be feasible to gain the confidence of the Beothuk and to establish a trade that would benefit the merchants as well as the salmon catchers and furriers.[7] The latter had already promised their assistance, provided that past incidents could be "buried in oblivion." Pulling offered to head a mission into Beothuk country and suggested that he be made surrogate for the northern district so that he could be vested with the necessary authority. It would be best to employ a vessel of about two hundred tonnes with accommodation for about thirty men, including officers and marines. The vessel was to go out early in the spring and to be stationed in the Bay of Exploits, which was considered a convenient location from which to operate.

Pulling's proposal may have been inspired by the plan submitted by George Cartwright as it incorporates some of Cartwright's ideas. Since Cartwright had done business with Messrs Lester and Stone in Trinity Harbour in the summer of 1785 and had stayed at Stone's house, he may well have discussed his ideas with these men, which they could have passed on to Pulling when he came to Trinity in the fall of that year. From a practical point of view Pulling's proposal was more feasible than Cartwright's as it avoided a ban on fishing and trapping by the English in part of Notre Dame Bay. Bestowing on the leader of such a mission the authority of a surrogate also dispensed with the need to create the position of superintendent. In addition, Pulling had already kindled good will among northern settlers and enlisted the support of salmon catchers and furriers who were implicated in previous conflicts. However, there would be expenses.

Pulling does not seem to have received a reply at the time, but on 5 March 1792, by then commissioned as a lieutenant in the Royal Navy, he was granted "leave of absence" on half pay to accept the position of captain on the merchant ship *Trinity* in Newfoundland.[8] This temporary change of service would have allowed him to collect information unofficially in Newfoundland's northern district about relations between inhabitants and Beothuk.[9] Whether he had a commission from the Admiralty or initiated this investigation with their agreement cannot be said. Chief Justice John Reeves, who came to Newfoundland at the same time, might have had a hand in this arrangement since Pulling subsequently reported to Chief Justice Reeves, providing him with evidence about relations with the Beothuk in the Parliamentary Enquiry into the State of Trade to Newfoundland held in 1793.[10]

Pulling began his enquiry with a boat master in Lester's employ; he then questioned owners of fishing stations, planters, furriers, and salmon catchers who lived or worked in areas that were frequented by Beothuk.[11] By the end of the summer he had accumulated many eyewitness and second-hand accounts of encounters with Beothuk from inhabitants of Trinity Bay, Greenspond, Fogo Island, and the Exploits River. Pulling prepared a preliminary report, entitled "Facts relating to the Native Indians of Newfoundland, collected from the Salmon Catchers and Furriers, who reside near those parts frequented by the Indians," in which he scrupulously recorded the dates and locations of the incidents he described and the names of the people who had been involved in them.[12] He also identified all informants and often narrated the events in their own words. This method of recording, as much as its contents, renders the report indisputably authentic and provides solid evidence of persisting hostilities between settlers and Beothuk.[13]

On his return journey to England, Pulling compiled a final report titled "A few facts by G.C. Pulling respecting the native Indians of the Isle of newfoundland, anno Domini 1792."[14] It contains the testimonies from the preliminary report to which further accounts of conflicts were added, along with observations on the Beothuk's way of life and customs and on the wide spectrum of attitudes expressed by settlers. While some of the residents felt anger or even hatred towards the Beothuk, others were sympathetic or kindly disposed and believed in the "possibility and utility of civilising" them.[15]

Since the success of a peace mission to the Beothuk would have depended in part on Pulling's ability to communicate with them, he made use of the opportunity to meet the Beothuk girl Oubee and to gather information from her on her language. This girl had been captured in 1791 at a camp near Charles Brook and was now living in Mr Stone's household in Trinity. Pulling obtained from her 111 Beothuk words or phrases and attached this wordlist, which is the earliest recorded Beothuk vocabulary, to his report.[16] It bears the caption "The following words of their language are all I can yet procure"; the first entry reads "Ou=bee ... The name of y/e Indian Girl who lives w/th Mr Stone."[17] A copy of this vocabulary found its way to the Reverend Mr Clinch, Anglican minister in Trinity, who sent it to Governor Pole in 1800.[18] Until recently it was believed that the wordlist was compiled by Clinch and copied by Pulling. The evidence, however, suggests the reverse.[19]

In a letter to Chief Justice Reeves, who had asked Pulling for his ideas on how to initiate communication with Beothuk, Pulling reiterated his plan for sending a naval vessel to the Exploits bay or river and offered his services as commander.[20] He added that one hundred pounds sterling's worth of apparel, trinkets, beads, and so forth should be brought and left in wigwams or disposed of in some other manner to convince Beothuk of the good intentions of the English. Pulling emphasized that the salmon catchers and furriers of those parts would have to be assured that "no notice will be taken of any cruelties that they may already have been guilty of But that every step will be taken to bring to Justice all those who shall in future wilfully Injure or Molest them [the Beothuk]."[21]

At the end of the fishing season of 1792 Pulling left Newfoundland for England via Naples. In March 1793, on the last leg of the *Trinity's* homeward journey, the ship was captured by the French. Pulling was brought to Marseilles and detained there until late fall. There is circumstantial evidence that Pulling sent his final report either directly to the committee appointed to hold a parliamentary enquiry or to its chairman, Sir Charles Jenkinson, Baron Hawkesbury (later to become first earl of Liverpool). Chief Justice Reeves may have received only the earlier and shorter version. His testimony at the enquiry was, however, based on the information gathered by Pulling.[22] Reeves stated that violence against Beothuk was continuing unabated and he promoted Pulling's idea of sending a sloop to the northern district for their protection. Yet neither Pulling's report nor the peace mission, as proposed by Pulling and recommended by Reeves, are mentioned in the official records of the Enquiries, and it is doubtful whether they were even discussed.[23] Though Pulling's investigations had proven that the conflicts between settlers and Beothuk had reached a level that threatened the Beothuk's survival, administrators and politicians were apparently unwilling to take costly and possibly unpopular measures to rescue the Beothuk from extinction but readily embraced Pulling's suggestion that former cruelties towards them by fishermen and furriers of the area should be "buried in oblivion."

In his letter to Reeves from Marseilles in which Pulling reported the capture of his ship, he added that "I shall think little of the loss I've met with if no other Person is sent out on the business I have so much at heart [the mission to the Beothuk]."[24] Immediately after his return from France, in early November 1793, he approached the secretary of the Admiralty in London and offered to find suitable men for a winter expedition if the Admiralty intended to employ him for that purpose.[25] To his probable disappointment, his plan of a peace mission was rejected and Pulling was sent to the West Indies, which effectively prevented his further involvement on behalf of the Beothuk.

CHIEF JUSTICE JOHN REEVES'S ENDEAVOUR

John Reeves, law adviser to the Board of Trade, was sent to Newfoundland in 1791 to preside over the newly created Court of Civil Jurisdiction and, a year later, over the Supreme Court of Judicature that superceded it. The historian

Prowse described Reeves as an admirable official, industrious, painstaking, firm, and resolutely impartial.[26] During his term of office Reeves took a special interest in the situation of the native people, who were, as he argued, "the King's subjects."[27] He may well have played a role in Pulling's change of service to allow him to investigate relations between settlers and Beothuk. After Reeves returned to England in December 1792, he presented a report on the judicial system in Newfoundland to Henry Dundas, secretary of state for Colonial Affairs, to which he attached a statement about the "Wild Indians."[28] According to Richard Routh, Collector of Customs, Reeves's report did him great honour. In the twelve years of his service as collector, Routh had regularly been informed that Beothuk were "shot at by the Furriers and Inhabitants with the same want of feeling that a deer or a bird would be killed," and he may have been relieved that the persecutions were finally brought to the attention of higher levels of government. Routh himself seems never to have reported them.[29]

As mentioned before, Reeves specifically broached the subject of the deplorable state of the Beothuk in the Parliamentary Enquiries and pointed out that they were

> more peculiarly our own people than any other of the Savage Tribes; they and everything belonging to them is in our Power; they can be benefitted by none others; they can be injured by none others; in this Situation they are entitled to the Protection of the King's Government, and to the benefit of good neighbourhood from His Subjects; but they enjoy neither. They are deprived of the free use of the Shores and the Rivers, which deprivation should entitle them to some compensation from us; but they receive none; instead of being traded with, they are plundered, instead of being taught, they are pursued with Outrage and with Murder.[30]

Reeves described these outrages in vivid terms, contending that the English themselves had received little benefit from government in the past and had therefore "paid off upon the Indians what was meted out to them."[31] Referring to Pulling's investigations, Reeves observed that persons who had been involved in the outrages were prepared "to make themselves useful in commencing any new system of treatment and conduct," provided "they were relieved from the danger of enquiry into what has passed," a request he considered to be a clear admission of their guilt. In accordance with Pulling's plan, Reeves proposed that the Beothuk should be protected from violence by executing the present laws against offenders, though he conceded that in this distant part of the island the fear of law provided little security and was therefore not sufficient as a deterrent.

In Reeves's opinion attempts to gain Beothuk confidence were not hazardous, given that a similar effort in Labrador, where the native people were said to be more intractable, had already been successful.[32] Either the Moravians, who were experienced in working with the native people in Labrador, should be encouraged to send a missionary to the Beothuk in Newfoundland, or local furriers should be employed under the direction of someone with a talent for such enterprise.[33] In either case, any such party should be provided with a small force to support its members. If one of the sloops of war on the Newfoundland station were to "winter in the Bay of Exploits or Gander Bay for protecting such a project in the season, this would be as much force as would be needed." Reeves argued that it was the duty of the English to grant Beothuk the rights of religion and civil society, principles that might have appealed to the commission where pleas for humanity had not. He also believed that it would be to the advantage of the English to establish an unrestricted trade. However, despite Reeves's authoritative arguments and the ample documentation behind them, the commission did not advocate changes in policy with regard to Newfoundland's native population.

Aware of the commission's reluctance to take remedial action, Reeves continued to promote ideas for creating better conditions for the Beothuk with the authorities in Britain. He urged the former chief justice of Newfoundland, D'Ewes Coke, to use his influence with Lord Castlereagh (then secretary of state for the War and Colonial departments) to convince him that the deteriorating situation of the native people in Newfoundland required attention, arguing that the Beothuk "are as much British Subjects as people born in the Strand [in London]."[34] In 1807, Reeves also assisted in providing a painting that depicted Englishmen and Beothuk trading, which, together with presents, was to be left at one of the Beothuk's usual resorts.

GOVERNOR WALDEGRAVE'S ATTEMPTS AT IMPROVING RELATIONS WITH BEOTHUK

As noted earlier, Vice Admiral William Waldegrave, governor of Newfoundland from 1797 to 1799, was the first governor in years to take an active interest in the fate of the Beothuk. As others had before him, Waldegrave issued a proclamation directing all persons to refrain from persecuting the native population, whereupon John Bland, magistrate at Bonavista, informed him that proclamations had thus far proven to be ineffective.[35] Bland's letter resulted in a lively correspondence with the governor. Some of the northern hunters, he wrote, "regard an Indian as fair game: & destroy him with no more remorse than they shoot a Deer."[36] He believed that eradication of the Beothuk's animosity would take time and entail expenditures that the government alone could afford. Government intervention was also required to effect changes in attitudes and behaviour among the English settlers. The first step would be to obtain possession of Beothuk; "kind treatment, trifling presents and a friendly dismission" would then open the way to further communication.[37] Soldiers from the garrison in St John's should be employed to lessen expenses, perhaps accompanied by a few Eskimos to communicate with them. Guides should be chosen from among the furriers and winter residents who were well acquainted with the interior parts of the country. These men should be paid liberally and furnished with a "covering for the body to resist the force of an arrow," to minimize the need for firearms. Bland thought it would be best to trace the Beothuk to their winter quarters inland rather than intercept them in summer on their way to the islands. The plan was to be executed with prudence and discernment, its purpose – to show a sincere offer of peace – perpetually borne in mind. Bland also suggested that John Peyton, Sr, whose bloody raids he condemned, be expelled from the Bay of Exploits and that the fishing rights to this region be granted to someone better disposed.

According to Bland several persons had objected to a conciliatory scheme, claiming that the Beothuk would always be hostile towards Europeans either because they were malignant by nature or because a deep sense of injury would cause them to reject any peaceful overture. In contrast, Bland considered the Beothuk capable of gratitude for kindness and thought the experiment worth a trial. With remarkable insight and compassion he argued:

> It ought to be remembered that the Savages have a right to this Island, and every invasion of a natural right, is the violation of a principle of Justice. They have been progressively driven from South to North, and their removal has been produced by a slow and silent operation, it has nevertheless had all the effect of violent compulsion. In proportion as their means of procuring subsistence became narrowed, their population must necessarily have decreased, and before the lapse of another Century, the English nation, like the Spanish, may have affixed to its Character the indelible reproach of having extirpated a whole race of People.[38]

Waldegrave thought Bland's plan was sound but held out no hope that it would be found expedient by the authorities in Britain, who might look upon it as "bordering on Quixotism."[39] If Waldegrave had been hesitant to approach the Colonial Secretary in these matters, a communication from the Reverend George Charles Jenner, minister in Harbour Grace, may have convinced him that it was his duty to act immediately.[40] Jenner, while working as a medical practitioner in Trinity Bay, had become acquainted with Capt. G.C. Pulling and had received from him a copy of his preliminary report on settler/Beothuk relations. Precipitated by Waldegrave's proclamation, Jenner sent this report to Waldegrave and assured him that all information had been authenticated.[41] In response, Waldegrave wrote to the Duke of Portland, secretary of state for the Colonies, to request a change in policy with regard to the Beothuk so as to save "the sad remains of this unhappy persecuted race of People" from destruction.[42] He enclosed his proclamation, his correspondence with Bland, and Pulling's report, which had not previously been in the public domain, and asked for further instructions, which he promised to execute with zeal and punctuality; but he received no answer.

In February 1798, Waldegrave followed up his campaign of providing evidence that the Beothuk were persecuted by forwarding a copy of Capt. Ambrose

Crofton's investigations.[43] Crofton had been told that the Beothuk made the Bay of Exploits their headquarters during the winter and in summer resorted to the area between Cape St John and Cape Freels as well as to Fogo and Funk Island, where they collected birds and eggs or plundered the inhabitants: "A constant warfare has always been kept up between them and the fishermen. The depredations committed by the latter has [*sic*] been hitherto kept secret, and its a misfortune that no person of respectability is resident during the winter months near to the Bay of Exploits."[44] Mr Chaytor, the magistrate at Fogo and agent for Mr Lester of Poole, resided there only for a few months in the summer and was too preoccupied with his business to attend to the functions of a magistrate.[45] In Crofton's opinion the situation of the Beothuk was becoming intolerable, and steps would have to be taken to avoid further deterioration. Since the Beothuk were unacquainted with the use of firearms and quit their wigwams upon the report of a musket, they were relatively defenceless.

"From motives of economy," Croften proposed to combine measures for the protection of the Beothuk with a survey of the coast, which was dangerous to approach. A small vessel should be sent to the Bay of Exploits and while part of the crew conducted the survey, others could attempt to communicate with the Beothuk. He advised leaving the vessel or part of her crew in an appropriate location for the winter so as not to jeopardize all the "good that might have been produced during the summer." If this plan could not be adopted, Crofton thought that people from the island of Fogo might be willing to seek out the Beothuk. Respectable merchants from Poole such as Messrs Lester, Slade, and Handcock could also be asked to lend support.[46]

Governor Waldegrave continued to press for new approaches to secure the Beothuk's protection and requested permission to employ a vessel for that purpose. He also considered it "advisable to appropriate a certain part of the coast and a proportion of the interior of the Island for the exclusive use of the … Indians." Infractions should be severely punished.[47] Waldegrave cautiously added that, in forming the limits of the boundaries, great care should be taken "not to injure the present establish'd Fisheries or Commerce of the British Inhabitants." Receiving no reply, he curtly requested that his submissions – including the reports from Pulling and Crofton, as well as Reeves's evidence given before the Lord's Committee in 1793 – be laid before the duke of Portland, in whose humanitarian leanings he seems to have placed much faith.[48] But he received neither new instructions nor permission to proceed with the proposed plan because the secretary of state did not consider it appropriate to attend to this matter while Britain was engaged in war.[49] In the fall of 1799, Waldegrave left Newfoundland for good with no immediate prospect of "something [being done] for the Indians."[50]

CHAPTER NINE

The Capture of Beothuk to Make Peace

Ever since the English established permanent settlements in Newfoundland, the settlers had attempted to meet native Indians to trade with them. They believed the best way of making contact would be to visit their camps and make reciprocal exchanges of people. Later the capture of Beothuk was favoured. Even after relations had become precarious, the idea of taking one of the Beothuk by force, showing kindness, and then releasing him or her with presents dominated plans to conciliate the Beothuk. Throughout the records the theme of "capturing Indians" persists until the Beothuk had disappeared from the island.

This chapter discusses various ideas and schemes for making contact with Beothuk or procuring captives to use as messengers of good will and describes the fate of Beothuk people who fell into the hands of the English. Records and traditions about white people who were said to have lived among Beothuk are also reviewed.

SEEKING FRIENDLY RELATIONS THROUGH EXCHANGES

In the early 1600s the council for the Newfoundland Company believed that friendly relations and cooperation with the native people could be achieved by having some of them live with the English. The first governor of the colony in Cupids, John Guy, was therefore advised that it would be of benefit "if you can vppon ackquaintance made with them and with there good lickinge consent send over one or to of experience in these Countrys to be kept vntill wee could Learne ther language or ther oures for there further discoverie of Countrie wee wish you herin to Followe ou[r] advise and otherwise not to meddle with them."[1] It is noteworthy that the council considered it worthwhile to send Beothuk to England so that they could teach their language to some of the English and vice versa. That the Beothuk's consent for such a scheme was required was clearly understood.

In a letter to Sir Percival Willoughby written in 1613, Henry Crout, one of the colonists in Cupids, said that he hoped in "continuance of tyme we shall procure some of them [Beothuk] and leaving some of vs in place as the french do at Canada." Crout obviously agreed with the council's suggestion and indicated that the colonists were not afraid of interacting with the native population.[2] The French had exchanged people on numerous occasions; for example, in 1541 Cartier had left two French boys in exchange for a native girl entrusted to him five years earlier, and de Monts and Champlain had exchanged young men with tribes they met.[3] Crout assured Willoughby that he knew "wher is one [white person] to be procured w[hi]ch can speake ther langguad very well w[hi]ch hath bin five years a mongst them."[4] He evidently considered that this person would be a suitable go-between who could assist in making appropriate arrangements. Crout was certainly aware of the need to approach the Beothuk carefully. He also wished to discourage the taking of captives, which several men in the colony were keen to do, since in his estimation it would jeopardize future relations to the detriment of the company. He warned that "if the [Beothuk] should be touched or taken parforce ther wilbe never no hoop of any good to be done by them for the are bentt to revenge."[5] As it turned out, nothing came of the proposed exchange. The Beothuk avoided contact and the small English population in Newfoundland was too preoccupied with making a living to become involved in an exchange program of uncertain benefit.

THE CAPTURE OF BEOTHUK

A century later, conflict over access to salmon runs and fur bearers led to clashes and to the deaths of both Beothuk and Englishmen. As a result, the Beothuk became increasingly elusive and it was now quite difficult to catch even a glimpse of them, let alone to make contact. The plan of having Englishmen living with the Beothuk and vice versa was entirely forgotten and probably was no longer feasible. But the Board of Trade in Britain continued to promote the idea of cultivating good relations with the native population so as to profit from trade in furs, and William Taverner, a planter and trader, asked the Board to employ him to capture Beothuk and "bring that whole Nation to head with us which would be of great advantage to us."[6] On a journey from Cape Bauld to the Avalon Peninsula in 1729, Taverner had seen about fifty "fierce" (interpreted to mean fierce Beothuk men) and therefore knew where to find them. It is nevertheless difficult to visualize how he hoped to accomplish what he promised, considering that open hostilities between Beothuk and English had quite recently taken place. Taverner could hardly have expected to obtain the consent of Beothuk to accompany him to St John's. Capturing some by force would have required substantial support and could easily have caused bloodshed and violence: hardly a promising incentive for profitable trade. As it was, the board seems not to have been interested, so Taverner's ability to procure Beothuk was not put to the test.

Within the following two decades, relations between settlers and Beothuk deteriorated further. Neither the inhabitants in the northern district nor the Newfoundland governors made any efforts to improve understanding or to promote peace; when Beothuk people were taken captive, no one showed an interest in using the opportunity to make contact with their people.

The first Beothuk to fall into the hands of settlers was a nine-year-old boy (or girl). In 1758, Irish hunters from Fogo had opened fire on finding a Beothuk mamateek, killing a woman and a child. They had brought away with them the only survivor, "a nine year old girl."[7] When Governor Edwards heard about the incident, he sent orders, apparently disobeyed, that the captive should be brought to St John's.[8] There was no search for the hunters until justices of the peace from the area complained about the situation; the culprits were not apprehended.[9] In January 1759 Edwards mentioned the capture of the Indian girl, whom he had "brought Home" (to England), in a letter about supplies in the forts of St John's but made no reference to the murder. This letter would not have come to the attention of the Board of Trade or the Privy Council, which might have followed up on the killings.[10] Although Edwards's note suggests that he personally brought the captive to England, the child probably travelled on one of the English fishing vessels in Edwards's convoy, perhaps on the ship owned by the person who later raised the child; Edwards probably never met the child himself and therefore remained ignorant of its gender. Ten years later, in 1768, John Cartwright recorded that he had talked to a Beothuk captive whom he referred to as "the boy June" and "Cousens' Indian."[11] Presumably June was at that time employed by John Cousens. Nothing has been recorded about June's capture and it is likely that he was the child, believed by Governor Edwards to have been a girl, that had been abducted by the Irish hunters. Edwards may have been misled about the captive's gender because June, the month in which he was taken, is a name generally given to girls. If two Beothuk had been captured, first a girl and then the boy June, the fate of the girl after she had been taken to England as well as the circumstances of the capture of June remain shrouded in mystery.

In 1768 June told Cartwright of a Beothuk settlement on the northeastern arm of Red Indian Lake (across from today's Millertown), where he said his father dwelt. Cartwright later found this settlement and marked it on his map as "June's Cove."[12] Other informants also stated that June was a boy, that he returned to Newfoundland after a visit to England, and that he was raised and employed in the fishery in Fogo. He reputedly became "uncommonly expert in all branches of the Newfoundland business."[13] June was said to have made frequent visits to his parents in "the heart of the country" and to have induced his master to spend a day with his parents and siblings, who pitched their tent nearby at Gambo and dwelt therein during the whole of one winter.[14] Local tradition has it that June lost his life "sometime before 1788" when he upset his skiff while entering the dangerous gut into Fogo Harbour.[15]

When Sir Hugh Palliser became governor in 1764, June was working in the fishery in Fogo. Although Palliser was greatly interested in the Beothuk, there is no record that he attempted to obtain information from June about possible means of contacting his people. Neither did he send June back to the Beothuk with tokens of peace nor use him in any other way to initiate friendly relations with his tribe. Instead, Palliser offered a reward for "a live Indian" that led, in August 1768, to the capture of a second boy, known as John August, or August.[16] As described earlier, furriers had come across this boy and his mother, killed the mother on the spot, and carried the boy away, said to have been about four years old at the time, too young to give any useful information,[17] August was taken to England the following winter and "displayed as a curiosity to the rabble at Pool for two pence apiece."[18] He was later brought back to Newfoundland where he was reared in an outport community and subsequently employed in the fishery. In 1785 August worked for Mr Child in Catalina, Trinity Bay, and shortly after for Mr Thomas Street in Trinity.[19] August died in October 1788, aged twenty-four, and was buried in the Trinity churchyard. The entry in the church register reads: "October 29th 1788. Interred John August (a Native Indian of this Island) a Servt. of Jeffrey & Street."[20] Those who knew August well said that he frequently expressed his wish to meet the murderer of his mother so that he might avenge her death.[21] Magistrate William Sweetland later claimed that for many years, August spent two or three weeks each year away from the settlement; it was thought that he visited his family in the interior during these times, "though he did not commit his secret to any one."[22]

Just as Governor Palliser had missed the chance of questioning June, George Cartwright appears not to have taken the opportunity to contact August. We know that he visited Catalina and Trinity in 1785 and knew of August; he recorded in his diary that Mr Child had only two people working for him, "one of whom is the Red Indian who was caught about seventeen years ago."[23] Strangely enough, Cartwright did not obtain August's opinion on how a conciliation could be achieved; nor did he advocate August's return to his people as an intermediary.

The third Beothuk captive, taken in July 1791, was the girl Oubee. A group of fishermen searching for Beothuk who were believed to have stolen salmon nets and traps came to a small Beothuk camp by a pond, close to Charles Brook.[24] When they approached the mamateek, two women emerged whom they allowed to flee, but they shot and killed a man and wounded a child. They took Oubee, who was later described as "a child" (presumably less than ten years old), "as a fair prize" and claimed that she "did not seem averse to accompany them."[25] When the circumstances of her capture came to the attention of John Bland, magistrate for Bonavista, he reported the incident to Governor Milbanke. However, no charges were laid and the offenders were not punished.[26]

Oubee was taken into the family of Mr Thomas Stone in Trinity, where Captain Pulling contacted her in 1792 and collected from her a vocabulary; as already noted, this was the first time that Beothuk words were recorded. Oubee accompanied the Stone family to England for the winter of 1792–93 and again in December 1793, when the Stones quit Newfoundland and moved permanently to England. She died there in or before 1795.[27]

Not one of the captives who became associated with the English and learned to communicate in their language was sent back to their own people to promote peace. No attempts were made to obtain from them information about their culture, nor were they consulted on how to approach their people. It is a regrettable fact that these unique opportunities to improve relations with Beothuk were allowed to pass unheeded. As John Bland later stated: "The language, religion and customs of the different nations of the world have ever been objects of research with the enlightened of all countries but [with respect to the Beothuk in Newfoundland] no person … has hitherto felt his curiosity exited on such a subject … I cannot help holding an opinion that we know almost as little of the Newfoundland Indian as we do of the inhabitant of the interior of Africa."[28]

Beothuk were also taken in raids some of which I have already described, such as John Peyton, Sr's raid with two other men on a Beothuk winter camp in 1781, when they found a frightened young girl in one of the mamateeks. Having been assured that she would not be harmed, the girl was said to have remained with them "very contented." Some evidence suggests that an older woman and possibly others who had been wounded had also remained in the camp.[29] Although there would have been no difficulty in taking the girl away with them, the men decided against it because they feared that, as she grew up, she might have children who would become the responsibility of her captors.[30]

During another raid, undertaken in 1790, a young, good-looking woman with an infant and an older female were taken. The men had intended to bring them back to their fishing community but changed their minds since they too were concerned about the possible expense. According to eyewitnesses, the women had soon become "pretty reconciled" and "seemed desirous" of going back with the men.[31] Captain Pulling interpreted this willingness as proof that at least the "young people" among the Beothuk were not averse to interaction.[32] Considering Shanawdithit's disclosure that all Beothuk who had been in contact with whites would be sacrificed to the *munes* of the victims slain by whites, the desire of the Beothuk women to accompany their captors may have been motivated by fear of punishment rather than by good will towards the English.[33]

Thus, between 1758 and 1791 at least seven Beothuk were captured: five children and two women. With the possible but unlikely exception of the raid in 1790, one or more Beothuk had been killed in the process of obtaining these captives. Of the five children, three were carried off and taken in by families in fishing villages; an infant and a young girl as well as two (or more) adults taken in raids were allowed to remain in their camp because their captors wished to avoid any responsibility for their support or for that of their offspring.

CAPTIVES AS CONCILIATORS

By the early 1800s, the efforts of Chief Justice Reeves and others to bring about changes in the attitude towards native people began to bear fruit inasmuch as the ill treatment of Beothuk was becoming public knowledge. This general awareness generated pressure on Newfoundland governors to show their concern and to attempt to reverse the trend. We have seen, however, that the governor's well-intentioned efforts were singularly unsuccessful. The degree of hostility that existed was clearly underestimated; hence notions of how to approach the problem were naive. The governors and their advisors believed that the taking of captives was the key to conciliation and seem to have expected that an opportunity to view the material goods of the English was sufficient to convince captives that it would be beneficial for their tribe to cooperate. Obtaining captives was therefore considered to be of paramount importance even though the use of force to achieve this goal was more likely to entrench hostility than to reduce it. Creative ideas about effecting a peaceful coexistence through the mediation of captives were also lacking. It was generally believed that once they had been treated kindly and sent back to their people with presents, the problem of hostile relations would be resolved.[34] It is noteworthy that the natives, who were viewed as "uncivilized" and "untutoured savages," were expected to learn the English language and accept the English way of life as desirable, while the English saw no need to familiarize themselves with the language and customs of the natives. The experience of missionaries and others, however, indicates that native people were unequal to the burden imposed on them unless their exposure was fairly long.[35] Lieut. Roger Curtis, for example, who had visited Inuit in Labrador, was convinced that carrying native individuals to England was of little consequence since they "acquired no useful knowledge." He therefore advocated that if peaceful relations were sought, it would be more appropriate to have a capable English volunteer live among the native people.[36]

James Hutton, a Moravian missionary who had witnessed the fate of Labrador Inuit after they had been in England, wrote in 1773 that all attempts at impressing natives with the material achievements of the English were utterly misguided.[37] Mikak, the Inuk woman who had been taken so much notice of in England, had not told her people about the power of the English and the splendour of their civilization, presumably because she feared that her tales would not be believed. She had therefore failed to convince other Inuit of English superiority, though inculcating the necessary awe had been a major objective of her journey. The English had also rudely "stared and gaped" at the "savage Apparition" in a manner that was "offensive to modesty and Humanity," so that

Mikak had been unable to form a respectful idea of the British nation. On her return to Labrador, the valuable presents she had received had aroused envy and ill will among her people and created distinctions hitherto unknown. Hutton felt that contact with English civilization had made Mikak more wretched and less content; it "spoiled [the Inuit] for that State of Life to which God has called Them."[38]

Particularly objectionable was the risk of contracting European diseases. Infectious diseases not only threatened the life of captives but, when carried back to their native communities, endangered the rest of their people. The five Inuit who were taken by George Cartwright to England in 1773 were a prime example; all five contracted smallpox and only one woman, Caubvick, survived. After she was brought back to Labrador, the disease spread to her kin.[39]

An added problem was that Beothuk who had been held by the English and later returned to their people would likely be punished. The Beothuk religious principle whereby those who had been in contact with whites were sacrificed has already been mentioned. Shanawdithit expressed on several occasions that she feared she might be put to death for having lived with the English, and Demasduit's wish to remain with her captors if only she could have her child with her is likely to have been based on similar fears.[40] Beothuk were also taught that any person who made peace with the whites would not be admitted to the "happy island" after death, nor would their graves be furnished with the items they required for the long journey there.[41] If these threats were as genuine as Shanawdithit claimed, captives would have had good reason to fear the consequences of their English sojourn on their return, and they would hardly have wished to testify to the kindness and good intentions of English people since any such testimony would have added to their guilt.

Despite the serious drawbacks outlined above, governors persistently promoted the idea that captives were the most promising means of improving settler/Beothuk relations. Governor Charles Morice Pole (1800–02), who was "anxious both as a public and private man" to improve relations with the Beothuk, sent Lieutenant Le Breton to the northern district to obtain "possession of two or three Indians." Le Breton returned with stolen bows, arrows, and other Beothuk implements but no captives.[42] In a correspondence between the governor and John Bland, justice of the peace for Bonavista, the latter proposed to station a select military party in the neighbourhood of the Exploits River. Rowsell, one of the permanent residents in the area who had offered to conduct such a party to a Beothuk settlement, was confident that by these means several Beothuk could be taken captive.[43] However, in his communication with the secretary of state for the Colonies, Governor Pole refrained from suggesting a military expedition; he may have considered Bland's scheme too elaborate and costly to be accepted. Instead, he recommended that a reward be offered to any resident who captured two or three Beothuk, a measure for which he received approval.[44]

In the following year Captain Edgell, commander of *HMS Pluto*, reported to Pole that relations between settlers and Beothuk had deteriorated badly, allegedly in the wake of brutal murders of Beothuk.[45] Edgell believed that Beothuk came to Twillingate and adjacent islands at night to plunder in retaliation for raids on their winter camps in which the settlers had taken furs and perhaps also the lives of their kin. Even though the Beothuk were "very shy and in great dread of fire arms," they never missed an opportunity to kill an inhabitant. In response to his enquiry how Beothuk could be captured, he was told that when they were leaving the Bay of Exploits, Gander Bay, or the islands they visited, such as Twillingate and Fogo, one would have to watch their movements, either in spring as they quitted the interior of the country, or at the latter end of September as they returned to their winter settlement. It had been the settlers' experience that "on approaching their wigwams, the Men instantly fly to the woods, but the women and children remain apparently without fear." It should therefore not be difficult to secure a woman or a child.[46] Since Governor Pole's appointment was not renewed, he was unable to act upon these recommendations, and attempts at taking Beothuk were temporarily suspended because Pole's successor, Governor James Gambier, was strongly opposed to the forcible removal of Beothuk from their people. Instead, he advocated a permanent establishment of the type already proposed by Cartwright, Pulling, and Waldegrave. It was to consist of "a discreet Officer with fifteen or twenty men furnished with arms and provisions to enable them to pass the winter in the vicinity of the habitations of the Indians where, by making them presents of such articles of small value as are most useful to them, an amicable and conciliatory disposition may be manifested to them which may gain their confidence and encourage them to form a friendly intercourse with the officer and his party to whom they should make known their grievances and ill treatment they receive from the Furriers."[47] While it is doubtful whether a group of armed soldiers could have instilled confidence in the Beothuk, the effectiveness of the plan was never tested. The Right Honourable Lord Hobart, secretary of state for the Colonies, was not willing to allocate a vessel or the money for presents and additional crew and the plan was shelved.

WILLIAM CULL CAPTURES A BEOTHUK WOMAN

In September 1803, during the second year of Governor Gambier's term, a young Beothuk woman was seized as she was paddling her canoe to collect birds' eggs from an islet in Gander Bay. Her captor, William Cull of Fogo, conveyed the woman to St John's and received fifty pounds sterling for his expenses and loss of time.[48] The exact circumstances of the capture are not recorded but it seems unlikely that she was wrested from a group of seventeen Beothuk as was claimed twenty years later by James Dobie, surgeon of *HMS Egeria*.[49] The name of this Beothuk woman has not been recorded but there are several descriptions of her. The Reverend Mr Anspach wrote that she had black eyes, skin of a "copper colour," and hair much like that of a European and would not suffer her bundle of fur clothes to be taken away.[50] She showed a "passionate fondness for children" and an interest in the music played by a band; but she could not be prevailed upon to dance. Gold ornaments and feathers greatly attracted her, and in the shops, where she was allowed to take what struck her fancy, she preferred brightly coloured things.

Vice Admiral Erasmus Gower, who came to Newfoundland after the woman had been sent back to her people, summarized what he had been told about her:

> To judge of the disposition and manners of her tribe from … this woman … we should be inclined to think favourably of them. I understand she was gentle, inoffensive, and generally cheerful. She appeared to be very succeptive of the kinder affections, and was particularly fond of young children. When taken she was wrapped in a single garment of Seal Skins, curiously sewed together, which was made to cover her from head to foot. This, as well as her body, was smeared with a composition of grease and red earth or oker.[51]

During the woman's stay in St John's, Governor Gambier introduced her into a large assembly and she was greatly astonished and pleased at the sight of the company: "The principal merchants and ladies of St John's vied with each other in cultivating her good graces … presents poured in upon her from all quarters and she seemed to be tolerably contented with her situation."[52] Having thus favourably impressed the captive, a scheme of communicating with the Beothuk tribe with her assistance could have been devised. However, Gambier had no idea of how to use this unexpected opportunity effectively. With a surprising lack of insight he and his advisors appear to have believed that the captive's exposure to the English way of life and a few presents, accompanied by assurances of good intentions in a language she could not understand, would induce confidence in her and convince her tribe to overcome their animosity. After the Beothuk woman had "received every indulgence and gratification that could be afforded her," she was supplied with a variety of articles and William Cull was asked to bring her to the spot where she had been taken. He was allowed fifteen pounds sterling for fishing lines, saws, nails, shoes, kettles, blankets, hatchets, knives, and other items that he was to offer to the Beothuk in exchange for furs or as presents. Cull was also authorized to take into custody and send to St John's any person who could be proven to have ill treated Beothuk.[53] These measures, "together with the account the woman on her return will give of the kind treatment she has received will, it is probable produce a further intercourse, which if followed up by proper measures would, it is to be hoped, tend to the civilizing and improving the condition of those miserable creatures."[54]

No attempts were made to obtain information about the whereabouts and size of the Beothuk group or about their complaints; nor was the captive consulted as to what would be a suitable way of improving relations with settlers. It seems not to have entered Gambier's mind that this woman's knowledge could be invaluable to the English with regard to establishing contact with her people. By placing the burden of initiating contact and trade with the Beothuk onto the shoulders of a single northern settler who had neither the funds, the time, nor the inclination to pursue such a dangerous and elusive goal, Governor Gambier sidestepped his responsibility to do all in his power to improve conditions for the Beothuk.

Bringing the captive back to a Beothuk settlement turned out to be more troublesome than anticipated. Cull was unable to find men who would accompany him into Beothuk territory in winter and he had little choice but to take the woman into his home. During her extended residence with his family, Cull and his wife (or one of his son's) learned enough of the Beothuk language to let her know that it was their wish to be on friendly terms with her people.[55]

In 1804, when Vice Admiral Erasmus Gower succeeded Gambier as governor of Newfoundland, the Beothuk woman was still residing with Cull. It now fell to Gower to order the justice of peace at Fogo, Andrew Pearce, to select four reliable men to accompany Cull and the captive on her way up the Exploits River. Although Gower would have been aware that many previous attempts to befriend the Beothuk had failed, he gave no clear directions and, promising further awards, left it to Cull and his men to "open an amicable trafic with the Indians, which by means of the woman seems highly probable."[56] Thus Governor Gower, like Gambier before him, failed to "use his best endeavours to cultivate the Indian's affections," as the instructions he had received directed him to do.[57] He seems to have hoped that the northern settlers would befriend the Beothuk of their own volition, even though he had been told that Beothuk were often shot "without remorse." Not until August 1804 did Cull and his companions convey the woman up the river "as far as we possibly could," but they did not dare to approach a Beothuk camp. When the party checked out the spot ten days later and found that the woman had gone, Cull assumed that "the rest of the Indians had carried her off in the country." Cull subsequently wrote to the governor's secretary that he would not wish to have anything more to do with the Beothuk: "The people do not hold with civilizing the Indians, as they think they will kill more than they did before."[58] Capt. Edward Chappell later claimed that Cull killed the woman for the sake of her presents, a charge Cull vehemently denied. He even asked Cormack how to sue Chappell for libel, although he admitted at the same time that he had shot more Beothuk with his long "Fogo" duck gun than he could remember.[59] Sometime later Governor Gower was informed that the former captive had "visited some of our settlements alone, and it is anxiously hoped that she will bring some of her friends with her and that our people may have good sense and humanity enough to avail themselves of so favorable an opportunity of establishing an amicable intercourse with them."[60] One may wonder why the woman came back alone. Could she have been rejected by her people because she had lived for so many months among the English? Or perhaps she never tried to join them because she was afraid of punishment. Cormack believed that she "never gained her tribe."[61]

LURING THE BEOTHUK WITH A PAINTING

Vice Admiral John Holloway, governor of Newfoundland from 1807 to 1809, launched a creative campaign to bring about peace between settlers and Beothuk, though unfortunately neither of his schemes was successful. Determined to put an end to persecutions, he threatened in a proclamation that all persons who harmed the Beothuk would be punished "to the utmost rigor of the law," just as if the offence had been committed against himself. When some fishermen were reported to have stolen a Beothuk canoe, Holloway ordered the offenders to be brought to St John's where they were "dealt with according to law," though no other mischief had occurred.[62] It was the first time that fishermen had been apprehended for robbing the Beothuk. If it was the incident later recalled by Mr Wiltshear, the court dismissed the case after the culprits had spent ten days in prison.[63]

Holloway offered a reward of fifty pounds sterling and reimbursement of expenses "to such a person who shall be able to induce or persuade any of the males of the Tribe of Native Indians to attend them to the Town of St John's."[64] It is difficult to understand how this well-meaning governor could have been so poorly informed as to believe that Beothuk could be contacted at will and induced to board the ships of their English foes.

Holloway also planned to send a mission to the Beothuk with presents, but the idea was not approved by the Privy Council.[65] Undaunted, Holloway subsequently promoted the idea of leaving pictures in places usually resorted to by Beothuk, together with small quantities of trade goods. The pictures were to represent "Indians and Europeans in a Group, each in the usual Dress of their Country, the Indians bringing Furs, etc. to traffic with the Europeans, who should be offering Blankets, Hatchets, etc. in exchange."[66] While it was naive to think the Beothuk could be lured into trade and trust through a picture and presents, at least communication was finally being sought by means that deliberately avoided the risk of confrontation. Chief Justice John Reeves believed that the plan "promised immediate and complete success." He used his influence to gain support for it among officials in Britain and personally commissioned a painting by Miss Cuoran for Holloway to take to Newfoundland (Plate 9.1).[67] Once the Privy Council for Trade had approved of the scheme and allocated one hundred pounds sterling for presents, Lieutenant J.W. Sprott, commander of *HMS Herring*, was sent to the Bay of Exploits to deposit the painting and gifts in a suitable place.[68] If the Beothuk did not approach him, he was to leave so that they could help themselves to the articles he had left, and he was to replenish the supply intermittently from his stock of ten dozen glass-bead necklaces, eighteen tin pots, sixty blankets, sixty yards of coating, thirty-six hatchets, shirts, pottery, and nails. If Sprott could entice Beothuk onto his schooner, he was to reward them with presents and bring them back to shore. If they paid a second visit he was to persuade two of them at most to come away with him, but under no circumstances was he to use force. The northern settlers were to be informed of the nature of his mission and told that those found offending against the Beothuk would be prosecuted. Holloway even threatened to transport culprits to St Domingo and dispossess their families.[69]

By the end of the summer no Beothuk had approached Lieutenant Sprott; nor had any of the gifts been taken, and Holloway reported that his attempts at opening an exchange had so far failed.[70] In reply, the secretary of the Privy Council, William Fawkener, said mockingly that the united efforts of "our friend Reeves and Miss Cuoran [the painter] could not tame and catch a single Indian," demonstrating that he neither understood the difficulties of making contact nor cared much about it. Lord Redesdale was more sympathetic but, in consideration of the long-term persecutions of the Beothuk, had no hopes for success from a second expedition.[71] Holloway nevertheless wanted to give the scheme another chance and, in the following spring, ordered Lieutenant Sprott to sail from England directly to the Bay of Exploits.[72] Once more, the Beothuk kept away and Holloway had to admit defeat.[73]

INSTRUCTIONS TO CONVERT BEOTHUK

In the same year (1809) the Wesleyan Missionary Committee in Britain instructed their minister in Trinity, John Remmington, to go northward to spread the gospel to the native population in Newfoundland.[74] This policy of including the Beothuk in their plans was unique among religious groups in Newfoundland and deserves credit. However, considering the circumstances, Remmington could not have succeeded even if he had tried. He would not have had the means to procure the necessary equipment or pay guides, and he could not have counted on the help of volunteers because the people in this region did not want to have anything to do with the Beothuk.[75] He probably soon realized the impracticability and hopelessness of such an undertaking and wrote to the committee that he had attended to the request and gone to Bonavista but had been unable to find Indians there.[76] In a subsequent letter Remmington alluded to the fatigue, pain, and great peril of journeying through the island wilderness, but whether this was in reference to a fruitless search for native people further afield cannot be ascertained.[77] A year later (1810), the Methodist ministers William Ellis and Samuel McDowell from Carbonear reported to the committee that it was not in their power to do anything about the natives who lived far to the north. In their opinion the most promising scheme would be to fit out a naval vessel that "should lie in wait on the sea coast to meet with them [Beothuk]," a plan that had already been promoted by several Newfoundland governors and that was to be revived in the years to come.[78]

RECORDS OF WHITE PEOPLE CAPTURED BY BEOTHUK

Not all records and stories of capture describe the taking of Beothuk. There are also some fairly well documented cases and several traditions of white persons having lived with the Indians. The earliest is the person (presumably a man) mentioned by Henry Crout in 1613 who was said to have stayed with the Beothuk for five years. Since Crout knew where to find him, it is assumed that this man had voluntarily joined and later left the Beothuk and had not been held captive.[79]

There were also traditions circulating among the fisherfolk in the late 1800s of white people who were captured by or associated with Beothuk. One of these traditions, recorded by J.P. Howley, claims that a man was forcibly carried off while he was cutting timber in Exploits Bay. The Beothuk had aroused his curiosity by throwing snowballs into the saw pit and seized him when he climbed up to investigate. A year later, so the story goes, this man fled towards a passing settler's boat while Beothuk discharged arrows in his direction. A woman with an infant entreated him to return, but seeing that her pleas were to no avail, she drew a knife from her belt and cut the infant into two parts, throwing one after the fleeing man. John Peyton, Jr's son Thomas, who lived in the Bay of Exploits in the early 1800s, said to Howley that he had never heard this story and did not believe it.[80]

Another abduction is related in the epic "The Last of the Aborigines, A Poem founded on Facts," by George Webber. Webber was told by northern planters that a three-or four-year-old English boy had been taken by Beothuk. Sometime later an Indian man approached the home of the bereaved parents, who killed him. Webber assumed that the Indian had intended to bring the parents to their child. No other source confirms the events described in the poem.[81]

In the late 1960s, when Charlie Furey from Harbour Main was ninety-one years old, he related the following story to Dr Cyril Byrne of St Mary's University. Around 1729–30, William Moores, one of the first settlers in Harbour Main, Conception Bay, was on friendly terms with the chief of a group of Indians from that area. He became enamoured of the chief's wife (or daughter) and married her after killing the chief.[82] The tradition does not specify whether Moores lived thereafter with the Indians or remained in his community. It is doubtful whether this story is based on fact since it has not surfaced in other collections of folk tales from the area.

The question whether white women were captured by the Beothuk cannot be answered with any degree of certainty. There are two versions of a colourful but unconvincing story in which Beothuk carried off three women. These were recorded by J.P. Howley and the historiographer H.F. Shortis. Howley was told that, in the early days of settlement, men from Carbonear pursued a Beothuk canoe in Trinity Bay; all the occupants escaped except for the chief's daughter, who was sick. They abducted the girl and she remained with the settlers until her people recaptured her in a raid when the fishermen were absent. The Beothuk raiders also took three English women in retaliation. In the following spring, the women returned unscathed and dressed entirely in "deer skins." They gave a favourable account of the treatment they received and described the Beothuk as civilized rather than savage people. In Shortis's version, the women came back the following day "safe and sound" but not in fur robes.[83] If there is any basis to this tale, Shortis's version is the more plausible.

In 1811, Lieut. David Buchan saw a European-looking woman at a Beothuk winter camp at Red Indian Lake (his excursion is discussed in the next chapter); he recorded the situation as follows:

> Conceive my astonishment at beholding a female bearing all the appearance of an European, with light sandy hair, and features strongly similar to the French, apparently about 22 years of age, with an infant which she carried in her cossak, her demeanour differing materially from the others … Instead of that sudden change from surprise and dismay to acts of familiarity [displayed by the other occupants of the camp], she never uttered a word, nor did she recover from the terror our sudden and unexpected visit had thrown them into.[84]

As Buchan's detailed report of his meeting with Beothuk is considered to be completely authentic, it is highly probable that the woman he saw was indeed of European origin. However, when Cormack asked Shanawdithit about her in 1828, she did not admit to knowing anything about this woman. Perhaps Shanawdithit really had no idea where the European-looking woman had come from, unless she concealed what she knew for fear that it would reflect unfavourably on the Beothuk.[85]

Since we have no record of a woman missing from one of the English communities, the female in the Beothuk camp could have been the survivor of a shipwreck. According to Santu Toney, daughter of a Beothuk man and his Micmac spouse, shipwreck victims were sometimes taken into a Beothuk group; Santu believed that her grandmother on her father's side was a white woman who had been rescued from a wreck.[86] Santu was born around 1837. Theoretically, her grandmother could have been the white woman described by Buchan and her father the infant this woman had carried.[87]

If the European-looking woman did not come from a shipwreck, she could have been the issue of a union between a Beothuk and a white person; the possibility that a man or woman who was temporarily held captive, or who had voluntarily joined the Beothuk, could have produced a child cannot be excluded. Or it may be that a Beothuk woman was coerced into sexual relations. In 1792,

G.C. Pulling recorded a "hear say story of two Indian women having been sometime in Company with the Rowsells at Halls-bay this summer [1791]."[88] The story was later refuted by Mr Moses Chaytor, Lester's agent, who claimed that it was "entirely without foundation as he [George Rowsell] has not seen an Indian this summer." While the wording suggests that the Rowsells may not have associated with Beothuk women in the summer of 1791, they or others may have done so previously. It is also possible that Beothuk women were sexually coerced during raids on their camps. Records about raids indicate that men were systematically killed while women were sometimes spared, which may on occasion have led to sexual relations, although there is no evidence to prove it.[89] Talking about the raid in February 1790, Richard Richmond said to Pulling that the young woman they captured was very modest. "When Thos Taylor took her child to look at it & put his hand upon her knee when she supposing He meant to take greater libertys push'd back his hand & seem'd much displeas'd."[90] The woman captured by Cull in 1803 was said to have become outraged if any man approached her.[91] One scholar has compared the events in Newfoundland with the situation in New Zealand, where white sealers raided native villages in order to carry off the woman. But the comparison is not valid.[92]

When the book was already in print I found the translation of a journal by Jean Conan, a Breton sailor, in which he wrote about being shipwrecked in 1787. After the shipwreck Conan and three others ran into a group of eighteen Indians (believed to have been Beothuk) at Shoe Cove and stayed in their camp for several days. Fearful that the Indians would kill and eat them, the sailors were instead fed and Conan reports that he was seduced by a young girl who cried when a French boat arrived to rescue the men (Bakker and Drapeau 1994).

CHAPTER TEN

Lieutenant Buchan's Efforts to Make Contact

THE DISTRIBUTION OF BEOTHUK IN THE EARLY 1800S

With the extension of English settlements into greater Notre Dame Bay, the Beothuk became increasingly confined both geographically and in terms of the time they would spend in areas resorted to by the English. During the summer months, the Beothuk travelled in their canoes along the coast and among the islands between Cape St John and Cape Freels.[1] Under cover of night, they made forays into the fishing harbours to obtain tools and equipment.[2] They routinely visited Fogo and Twillingate islands to catch seals and to procure other means of subsistence, and it is recorded that in 1809, they shot Michael Turpin at Sandy Cove/Fogo and another English youngster on the south side of Twillingate Harbour.[3] From Fogo and the Straight Shore, where they were said to have maintained a camp with twelve mamateeks near Cat Harbour (now Lumsden), they crossed over to the Wadhams and Funk Island off the east coast for seabirds and eggs.[4] But as long as the settlers remained in their winter houses on the mainland shore (as opposed to their summer homes on the larger islands), the Beothuk would not venture to the bird rocks for fear of being discovered and shot. This considerably shortened the bird and egg-collecting season.[5]

As access to coastal resources diminished, the Beothuk remained inland for longer periods of time. In 1792 Lieutenant Pulling had been told that they came down the Exploits River at the end of May; by 1801 the Beothuk were said to come out to the islands in June and July.[6] This change in the timing of their summer dispersal would have led to a more interior-oriented subsistence economy, and to new strategies for securing food in spring. Most likely, small parties were dispatched to hunt seal, take smelt and inshore groundfish, and collect clams and mussels before the main body of the bands moved to the coast. Furthermore, salmon catching, which would formerly have been a community affair, may have been assigned to specific groups. Lieutenant Buchan, who in

1810 asked settlers about the number, way of life, and habits of the Beothuk, concluded that the majority remained all year on the ponds and rivers inland, and that only a small division came to the coast.[7] Tell-tale signs of former Beothuk camps abound on the banks of the Exploits River; between Grand Falls and Red Indian Lake alone about ninety housepits have been identified on twenty-two sites.[8] However, analysis of faunal remains from Beothuk inland and coastal camps does not support Buchan's contention.[9]

Although the Exploits River and Red Indian Lake were generally considered to be the heartland of Beothuk territory, some Beothuk resorted to the Gander Lake region and to lakes inland from New Bay and Badger Bay. In the 1820s, when Beothuk no longer used the Exploits River as a route to the coast, the area around South Twin Lake became a major refuge.[10] Some Beothuk may also have survived on the Northern Peninsula in the vicinity of Hare Bay.[11]

PREPARATIONS FOR A MISSION TO THE BEOTHUK

In the fall of 1809, Governor Holloway engaged William Cull and six other furriers to travel up the Exploits River in winter "in quest of the [inland] residence of the native Indians."[12] Holloway seems to have hoped that the party would attempt to meet with Beothuk, but in the event the men were not willing to risk a hostile confrontation and turned back once they were within striking distance of Beothuk habitations. Cull's narrative of the expedition, as recorded by the governor's secretary in July 1810, contains the following information: On 10 January 1810, William Cull, accompanied by John Cull, Joseph Mew, John Waddy, William Waddy, Thomas Lewis, James Foster, and two Micmac guides, set out on their journey. Travelling upriver, they passed deserted Beothuk houses and caribou fences and examined one of the two storehouses they saw on their way. It was filled with the meat and skins of about a hundred caribou and quantities of other pelts. Cull also found lids of tea kettles that had been given to the woman he had previously captured and returned. He took three beaver and nine marten skins and left in exchange one pair of swanskin trousers, one pair of yarn stockings, bits of printed cotton, needles, pins, thread, and twine. Shortly afterwards, the party saw two Beothuk on their way to the storehouses who, on discovering the furriers, disappeared from sight. The men conjectured that the Beothuk's settlement could not be far and decided to turn back.[13] Cull later told Captain Buchan that they had also "fallen in with a wigwam sufficiently large to contain from 50 to 60 persons [and had seen] several indications displayed by the Natives of bartering and tokens of peace as leaving things in exchange and Bows without strings."[14] Cull's claim that barter was occasionally effected was later confirmed by "Old Tom," who lived on one of the numerous islands in the Bay of Exploits. This old man recalled that when he was a boy (1800–10, approximately), he had seen half a dozen Beothuk trading with his father at the mouth of the Exploits River.[15]

Sir John Thomas Duckworth, who succeeded Governor Holloway in 1810, was well aware of the unresolved problems concerning the native population. He published two proclamations, the first addressed to the "Micmac Indians, Esquimaux and other American tribes frequenting the Island of Newfoundland," the second to the Newfoundlanders, asking them "to live in kindness" with their native neighbours. He also offered a reward of one hundred pounds sterling to any person who could establish friendly relations with them.[16] In a letter to the earl of Liverpool, Duckworth admitted that he was not authorized to propose a reward but justified his offer on the grounds that the object was of such importance and the difficulties of finding Beothuk so great that a substantial reward was required to tempt settlers into giving it a try.[17]

Impressed with the "popular and affectionate manner" of Duckworth's proclamation, the Reverend Edmund Violet, Methodist minister in St John's, approached the governor to express his conviction that it was the obligation of the civilized world to help those who were, by the providence of God, less fortunate. He conjectured that if he or his kind "were … placed precisely in the condition in which they are fixed, it would be … divine charity to save us from it."[18] In the ensuing correspondence, Violet suggested a mission into Beothuk country to make initial contacts.[19] A party comprising eight or ten seamen and someone familiar with the area should be headed by an intelligent, enterprising, and persevering individual of intrepid spirit and humane motives. To entice the Beothuk, useful articles should be left in places they frequented and replenished intermittently.[20] If Beothuk were taken, they should receive presents and be allowed to go; they should also be given to understand that others would be treated with the same kindness. An expedition of this nature would have to be repeated for several years and would entail considerable expense, which only government could afford. But the benefits would be honour to the country, a peaceful coexistence with the Beothuk, possibly a profitable trade, and valuable information on the resources of the interior.

BUCHAN'S EXPEDITIONS

Governor Duckworth, a man of "great discernment" who has been credited with daring and skill as a naval officer, approved of Violet's plan and decided to send an expedition up the Exploits River.[21] Records of a request by Duckworth for permission have not been found. Either the documents are lost or, more likely, Duckworth proceeded without obtaining official sanction.[22] As a celebrated officer, he may have had influence with the Admiralty and may not have felt intimidated by the possibility of disapproval.[23]

Duckworth appointed Lieut. David Buchan, commander of HMS *Adonis*, as the officer in charge because he considered him to be a "man of no ordinary turn of mind, of considerable fortitude and perseverance," and knowledgeable about winter travel in the interior.[24] Duckworth instructed Buchan to sail to Notre Dame Bay, obtain further information on the Beothuk there, and hire two guides to follow Cull's route. Buchan was to use his own judgement with regard to provisions, arms, articles for the Beothuk, and the number of men he should take.[25] Duckworth also left it to Buchan to conduct the expedition as he saw fit and was willing to rely wholly upon his diligence to take advantage of whatever circumstances might occur. Nonetheless, he cautioned Buchan not to allow guns to be fired in the neighbourhood of the Beothuk and to consider the health of his men above all.[26] After his return from the expedition in the spring of 1811, Buchan was to collect information on the fishery in several Newfoundland and Labrador harbours. But should he have entered into any agreement with the native people to come down to his ship in the summer, he was to attend to this first and foremost and disregard all other parts of the order. Giving priority to contacting the Beothuk may not have been in line with government policy and probably for this reason Duckworth labelled his order "most secret."[27]

After all preparations for the expedition had been completed, Lieutenant Buchan proceeded to the Bay of Exploits and anchored HMS *Adonis* at Peters Arm. He selected twenty-three men and a boy from the crew of *Adonis* to accompany him and hired William Cull, Mathew Hughster, and Thomas Taylor as guides. The party was armed with seven muskets, three fowling pieces, six pistols, and six cutlasses. Provisions, consisting mainly of bread, sugar, cocoa, pork, salt fish, spirits, rice, and tea, were packed along with other equipment and some presents for the Beothuk on twelve sledges. The entire baggage, including the sledges, weighed 1,629 kilograms.[28]

On Sunday, 13 January 1811, at 7:00 A.M., the men set out with great hopes for the success of the venture. They travelled up the Exploits River for eleven days, covering on average about twelve kilometres per day. At night they camped in quickly prepared shelters, leaving caskets of food in three of them for the return journey. The men had to contend with biting winds, drifting snow, sleet, and rain. At night, it was sometimes too cold to sleep. Progress was difficult. The sledges had to be pulled over ice ridges or conducted up steep banks while the baggage was carried separately; paths had to be cut, broken sledges repaired, and the baggage repacked when sledges became unfit for further use. Fatigue and sometimes swollen and inflamed legs added to the men's discomfort.

When they came to the upper part of the river, the men found old wigwams and a storehouse, as well as caribou fences on either bank. On the eleventh day (23 January), the open river prevented them from taking their sledges any further. Buchan continued with half the party, taking supplies for four days; the other men stayed behind. The advance party soon noted tracks made by Beothuk. On turning a point, they came to a large lake, now frozen; on it were two bodies in motion that could have been "men or quadrupeds." The party took shelter in the woods and prepared for the night, which proved to be excessively cold. At 4:00 A.M. the following morning, fortified by a dram of rum, they set out again in utmost silence, passing quantities of carcasses and quarters of frozen venison on the way. At length they crossed the lake and soon saw six canoes and three wigwams. Buchan wrote: "The bank was now ascended with great alacrity and silence, being formed into three Divisions, the Wigwams were at once secured, on calling to them within, and receiving no answer, the skins which covered the entrance being removed, we beheld a group of men, women and children lying in the utmost consternation; they were some minutes without motion or utterance."[29] This nonhostile meeting between Beothuk and Englishmen represents a highpoint in the history of attempts at communication with the native people. But before the English were able to take advantage of their unique opportunity, Buchan committed the tragic error of misinterpreting the Beothuk's feigned ease towards their unwelcome guests as a signal of genuine confidence and trust:

> My first object was now to *remove their fears which was soon accomplished* by our shaking hands, and showing every friendly disposition, the women embraced me for my attentions to their children; from alarm they became curious and examined our dress with great attention and surprise, they kindled a fire and presented us with Venison steaks … everything promised the utmost cordiality; knives, handkerchiefs and other little articles were given to them, and they offered us skins, I had to regret their language not being known and the presents at a distance of at least twelve miles, occasioned me much embarrassment.[30]

After three and a half hours of friendly interchanges with – in Buchan's opinion – every appearance of the greatest amity, Buchan conveyed his wish to go back to the place where he had left his baggage and then return; four of the Beothuk indicated that they would accompany him. Corporal James Butler and Private Thomas Bouthland asked to be left behind to repair their snowshoes, others were equally anxious to stay. Buchan complied with the first request to show the Beothuk his confidence in them, which they noted with satisfaction.[31]

Accompanied by the four Beothuk, Buchan and his men retraced their steps. Two of the Beothuk, one a "chief," soon turned back, directing the others to continue.[32] When the party had almost reached the base camp, the third Beothuk ran away, while the fourth remained and was pleased to see the presents. Although the meeting at the Beothuk's winter camp had gone well, Buchan was uneasy about the flight of the three Beothuk, fearing that they might misrepresent his intentions.

On the following day, only eight men stayed behind; the remaining nineteen set out for the Beothuk settlement. On reaching it they found the wigwams deserted and left in disarray, though there were no signs of violence. The Beothuk man who had stayed with Buchan seemed perplexed. Buchan was now anxious for the safety of his two men. He indicated by signs that the Beothuk was free to go but that Buchan wished for the others to return and asked him to tell his people not to hurt his two marines. The Beothuk smiled meaningfully and pointed to the west side of the pond but would not leave. He put one of the wigwams in order and showed Buchan a staff that belonged to their chief. Buchan's party settled down for the night, leaving half of the men on watch at all times.

On 26 January, fourteen days after they had left the schooner, the men rose early, distributed blankets, shirts, and tin pots in each of the three wigwams, and attached some articles to the chief's staff before they left. The plan was to return in two days' time. The Beothuk accompanied them, running ahead, but suddenly halted and then took off at speed. Buchan soon discovered the reason for his departure: the bodies of his two marines were lying on the ice, pierced by arrows; their heads had been cut off and carried away and there was no trace of their garments.[33] The men were greatly affected, but sorrow soon gave way to a desire for revenge. Buchan, assuming that they were being watched, became alarmed for the safety of the eight men who had remained with the sledges and therefore decided to return forthwith. Marching downriver, they saw tracks in the snow and conjectured that Beothuk might be waiting in the forest to attack them. However, the tracks were those of two marines who had come up to view the lake; all was well at the camp. Buchan resolved to return to the schooner because the Beothuk most likely expected revenge rather than kindness and therefore constituted a serious hazard for his party. Moreover, the rapid thaw would soon make their retreat on the river impracticable. The ice was already separating from the banks so that the sledges could no longer pass. Buchan made his men fill their knapsacks with provisions before they set off. Without sledges and eager to leave this inhospitable part of the country behind, the men covered between twenty-nine and fifty-one kilometres per day, though many of them were severely fatigued. Within four days, at noon on 30 January, they arrived at *HMS Adonis*.

Although Buchan would have been well informed about the continued harassment of Beothuk and was anxious to succeed in making peace, he had obviously underestimated the Beothuk's hostile attitude, hardened over centuries of persecution. Instead of treating the Indians as equals and respecting their position, he seems to have associated their "primitive" way of life with primitive reasoning and believed therefore that friendly gestures and a few presents could assuage their mistrust. While Buchan thought that he had inspired trust in the Beothuk, it was the Beothuk who had inspired trust in him, which brought about the tragic conclusion of his expedition.

Buchan's disappointment and regret over the outcome of the expedition gradually gave way to new hopes and a determination to make a second attempt. He ordered sledges and casks to be made, and once the men had recovered from their previous exertions, another expedition set out. On 5 March 1811, Buchan left the schooner with a party of twenty-nine men equipped with provisions for twenty-two days. He made sure that every man was provided with proper clothing and spares. As the recent thaws had levelled the ice, travelling conditions proved favourable until heavy snowfalls and low temperatures forced them to remain in camp for three days. On the ninth day they arrived at a storehouse by the river, which the Beothuk had visited since Buchan's party had passed it on their previous journey. They had removed the prime venison, dug up the ground, and perforated the skin cover of the store with many arrows. Buchan concluded that the Beothuk had come downriver in their canoes and had shot arrows at the store in case Buchan's party was concealed there. Seeing that they had acted so warily and were evidently prepared to resist, Buchan abandoned any further pursuit. The party left red shirts in the storehouse in exchange for some venison and turned back. Travel was hampered by snow, hail, and sleet and it took them five and a half days to reach the schooner.[34]

SHANAWDITHIT'S VERSION OF THE EVENTS

Seventeen years later, the captive Shanawdithit related what she recalled of Buchan's expedition to W.E. Cormack, Magistrate Sweetland, and John Peyton, Jr (as recorded by Bishop John Inglis).[35] She told Cormack in 1828 that at the time of Buchan's visit, her tribe had been much reduced but still enjoyed their favourite hunting grounds around and adjacent to Red Indian Lake and the Exploits River. In the winter of 1810–11, they camped in three groups on different parts of the lake; the principal camp, located at its eastern end, consisted of three mamateeks inhabited by forty-two people. Of these, one mamateek was Shanawdithit's father's and she was in it at the time. A smaller encampment of two mamateeks occupied by thirteen people lay ten to thirteen kilometres to the west; a third camp of two mamateeks and seventeen people was situated near the lake's western end. Buchan came to the principal encampment and took all the Beothuk prisoner. After several hours of cautious mimed civilities, which included an agreement to exchange two hostages, Buchan departed to fetch a supply of presents that he had left downriver. Soon after he had gone, the Beothuk became fearful that he would return with a larger force to carry them off to the coast. Their suspicions grew when one of the Beothuk who had travelled with Buchan came back. They resolved to break camp and join the rest of the tribe. To ensure concealment they first killed the two marines. Shanawdithit told Magistrate Sweetland that the hostages had been treated with kindness until then. It was the chief (who had deserted Buchan's party on the first day) who proposed to put the hostages to death immediately. The others opposed it strenuously but were eventually persuaded. Four Beothuk took the marines out on the lake and shot them down with arrows from behind. Shanawdithit said to Peyton, Jr, that some of the Beothuk wanted to kill the marines right from the beginning because they were fearful, though others violently objected, "but upon one of the Marines refusing to give up his Jacket to some who wished to take it away, he and his companion were immediately pierced with arrows." Shanawdithit's mother severed the heads from the bodies. In haste the Beothuk packed up their belongings and crossed the lake, carrying the heads of the two marines with them. One of the heads, stuck on a pole, was left at the north side of the lake. They travelled along the lakeshore to the nearest encampment and told the people there what had happened. The next morning all Beothuk joined in the westward retreat. On the second day, they were joined by the Beothuk man who had stayed with Buchan until he discovered the slain marines; this man was Shanawdithit's uncle. They all crossed the lake and sent a messenger to the third camp, whose members joined them as well. To avoid discovery, the entire tribe retired to an unfrequented part of the forest some distance from the shore, carrying with them their winter stock of provisions. They built six mamateeks and danced and sang for two hours around the head of the marine, which they had brought with them and stuck on a pole. They remained in this camp for the rest of the winter. With the arrival of spring, a small group went back to the principal camp to fetch a supply of venison. Afterwards the tribe became "scattered and continued dispersed in bands frequenting the more remote and sequestered parts of the northern interior."[36]

Shanawdithit made two sketches of the events (Plates 10.1 and 10.2, lower part). Sketch 1 shows the upper part of the Exploits River and the northeastern end of Red Indian Lake on which she marked the place where Buchan had left his baggage, his track to the Beothuk's principal camp, the three mamateeks, Buchan's return to his previous camp, the killing of the marines, the route of the fleeing Beothuk, the location of their two smaller camps, and that of their final refuge. A circle around a head on a pole marked A and another marked B show the two places where the Beothuk celebrated the killing of the marines; a note indicates that they danced and sang at point A after their arrival at their new winter camp and at point B on their return in the spring.[37] Sketch 2 (lower part) deliniates part of the lakeshore and Buchan's party returning to his camp accompanied by four Indians.

Shanawdithit's story and sketches largely coincide with Buchan's narrative and confirm his conclusion that the murder of the marines was not the result of poor conduct by the victims but was committed after the Beothuk who fled from his party had returned.

Buchan's Concluding Remarks and Map of the Country

Buchan's diary of the expedition as well as his "Concluding Remarks" contain considerable information on the Beothuk's appearance, clothing, use of ochre as body paint, cooking habits and methods of preserving caribou meat, household vessels, canoes, arrows with iron points, metal axes, snowshoes, summer and

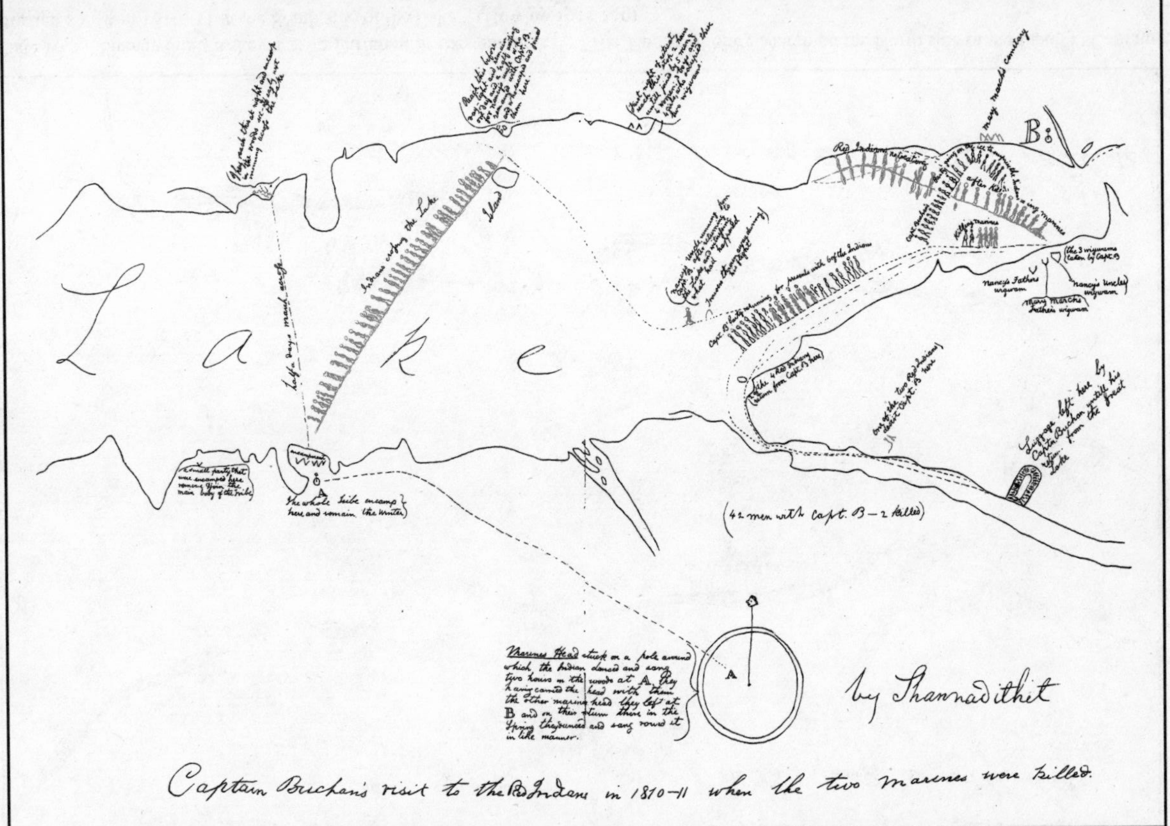

Plate 10.1 Shanawdithit's sketch 1: "Captain Buchan's visit to the Red Indians in 1810–11, when the two Marines were killed." (Howley 1915,238)

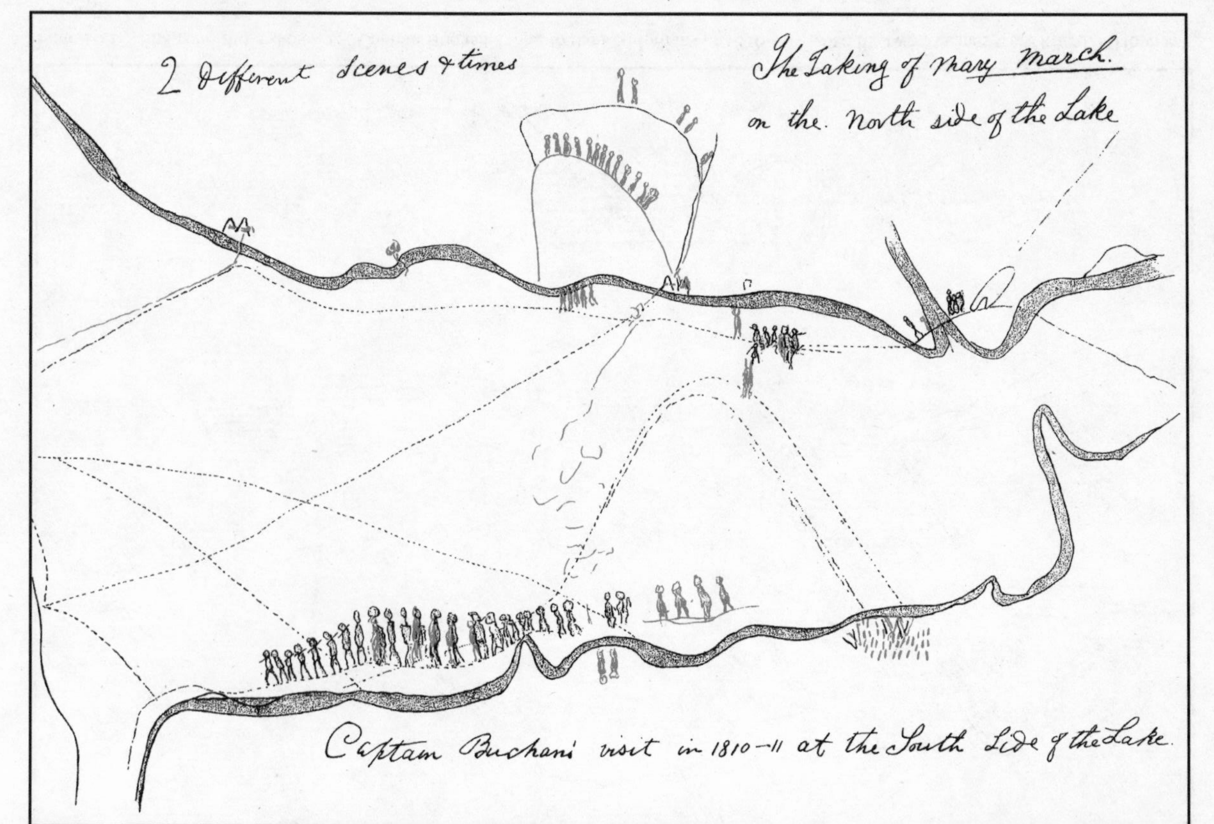

Plate 10.2 Shanawdithit's sketch 2: "2 Different Scenes and times"; "The Taking of Mary March on the North side of the Lake"; "Captain Buchan's visit in 1810–11 at the South side of the Lake." (Howley 1915,240)

winter mamateeks, and storehouses; this information will be discussed in Part Two in the appropriate chapters.

Buchan also submitted a map of the course of the Exploits River and the northeastern end of Red Indian Lake (Fig. 10.1).[38] It indicates the location of his party's overnight camps on the river on both journeys, a dock and path, four Beothuk storehouses, three mamateeks at the principal settlement, and another one across the northeastern arm of the lake (marked "old"), roughly in the spot where Nonosabasut's burial hut was later found.[39] Buchan also noted an Indian path from the Bay of Exploits to New Bay (see Table 15.1).

Buchan believed that the Beothuk lived in independent companies but had one principal chief.[40] He also thought that their subsistence adaptation had undergone vital changes since they formerly may have lived mostly on fish and sea fowl, lacking proper weapons to kill caribou. Their spears were made from iron, which formerly would not have been available.[41] In the process of settling the coast, the English had forced the Beothuk to retreat inland. Buchan argued that many of them no longer came down to the sea for the summer, though elsewhere he stated that "from necessity, all come to the sea coast in summer"; their canoes had been seen in various places between Cape St John and Cape Freels.[42] Those who remained inland lived next to ponds and rivers to procure food for the winter. During the winter season the Indians removed to well-built, larger houses of the type Buchan had seen at Red Indian Lake. In his estimation, the enormous quantities of caribou meat and neatly dressed furs he had seen in that camp exceeded by far the amount that the occupants would have needed for their own use. He conjectured that those Beothuk who came to the coast to collect sea foods, iron articles, and whatever else might be of use to them exchanged these items for venison and skins with the Beothuk who had stayed behind.

Lieutenant Buchan estimated that there were about thirty-five adults in the principal camp, two-thirds of them women, and at least thirty children, most of whom were not older than six years: "Never were finer infants seen." However, he later told William Carson that none of the people in the camp could have been older than fifty, and those who came close to it "were in a state of decrepitude."[43] Elsewhere in his report, Buchan put the number of people in this camp at seventy-five but believed it absurd to suppose that the whole tribe resided in that camp alone. He was convinced that their total number was considerable.[44] In the late 1820s Buchan told Dr Carson that in his opinion, the tribe did not exceed 150 members; yet in his testimony in 1836 before the Select Committee enquiring into the situation of Aborigines in British Settlements, he claimed that, at the time of his expedition, there could not have been fewer than four hundred Beothuk in existence.[45] When Governor Duckworth gave an account of Buchan's expedition to the earl of Liverpool in the fall of 1811, he claimed that Buchan had found convincing proof that the numbers of Beothuk had been greatly underestimated and that the tribe amounted to at least three thousand persons.[46] This figure is certainly incorrect, but Buchan's

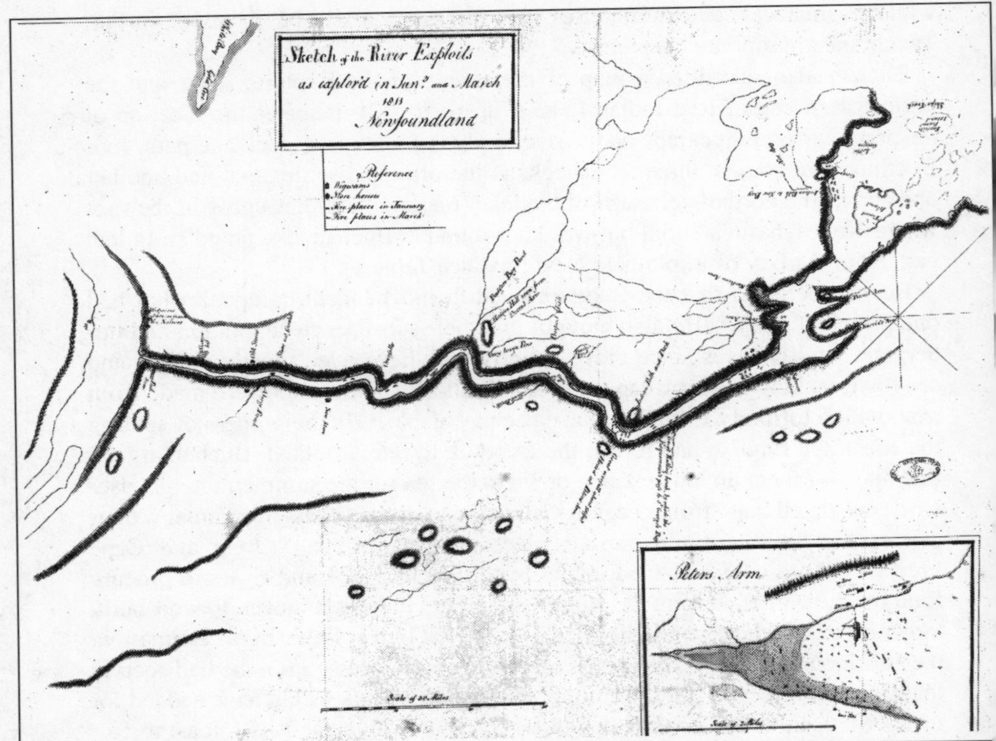

Fig.10.1 "Sketch of the River Exploits as explor'd in Jan.y and March 1811 Newfoundland," by Lieut. David Buchan. (Public Record Office, London, MPG 589, CO 194/50)

estimate of four hundred individuals is equally spurious. Shanawdithit accounted for each person in the three camps, listing their gender and age, and arrived at the figure seventy-two for the entire tribe (she did not include possible survivors on the Northern Peninsula). This discrepancy in numbers between Shanawdithit's information and the reports by Buchan led the surveyor general Noad to believe that she deliberately concealed the true size of her tribe.[47] However, subsequent events indicate that Buchan's figures, rather than Shanawdithit's, were erroneous.

In his report of the expedition to Governor Duckworth, Buchan had great praise for the perseverance and almost unexampled good conduct of his people in every instance, in the face of so many obstacles.[48] Had it not been for the disastrous fate of the two marines, he would have considered his journey fortunate beyond all expectations, considering that it was the first time communication with the Indians had been achieved. Buchan then requested permission to follow up on his attempts by searching for them in summer when they were travelling among the islands between the Wadhams and Cape St John. In Buchan's opinion, the aim of bringing "the natives into civil society" was one of national importance and, if successful, "would wipe away a certain degree of stigma brought on us by the former barbarity of our countrymen."[49]

Without further explanation, Lieutenant Buchan now favoured the capture of Beothuk as the most promising means of bringing about communication.[50] At the Parliamentary Enquiry in 1836, he actually declared that Governor Duckworth's instructions not to use any coercive measures had prevented him from taking some of the Beothuk down to the ship – a step that he would have preferred. He would have treated the Beothuk well and then released them over a period of several years.[51]

Governor Duckworth fully supported Buchan's endeavours and approved of his conduct and the decisions he had made in the course of the expedition. He readily agreed to the proposal to go again in quest of Beothuk in the following summer. He also reported on Buchan's expedition to the earl of Liverpool, and this report was subsequently submitted to the prince regent.[52]

BUCHAN'S SUBSEQUENT SEARCHES

In the spring of 1811 Buchan's departure for the northern district was much delayed, and by the time *HMS Adonis* arrived at Fogo to take up the search for Beothuk, the summer was well advanced.[53] The first two boats were not dispatched until 6 August 1811; a third one left Fogo on 2 September for Ragged Harbour on the Straight Shore, where Beothuk had recently been seen. As Buchan had not yet recovered from the extreme hardships he endured during the winter expedition, he was unable to travel on the small boats himself and put his officers in charge.[54] All three crews returned without having seen any Indians. Buchan then sailed to the Bay of Exploits, where he sent a search party upriver as far as the Nut Islands. The men found several campsites with the remains of seal, birds, and eggs, and a place where the Beothuk had built and repaired canoes; at one point they were in such close pursuit that the footprints of the Beothuk were still to be seen on a sandy beach. Evidently, that summer, the Beothuk had not come down the Exploits River but had travelled by way of ponds and small rivers from the northeastern end of Red Indian Lake to the Badger Bay ponds and New Bay, conveying their canoes on well-cut portage paths. From Badger Bay they had passed across to the Triton Islands; from New Bay they had portaged across a neck of land and entered the Bay of Exploits at Winter Tickle. A large, grassy space marked by sleeping hollows showed that Beothuk had been there in significant numbers. From this point they usually travelled eastward as far as Cape Freels and westward among the Triton Islands as far as Cape St John.[55]

Buchan, still optimistic and anxious to succeed, believed that if he could start the search early in the season he would surely meet Beothuk in the eastern part of Notre Dame Bay. He therefore requested permission to remain on the Newfoundland station for the winter of 1811–12 so as to go northward in early spring.[56] Duckworth was in favour of Buchan's scheme but gave strict orders not to risk the lives of his people or his own.[57]

According to plan, *Adonis* remained in St John's harbour for the winter and Buchan made preparations for another search. Since his crew was not large enough to man the three additional boats he had fitted, he asked Duckworth for ten supernumeraries and a petty officer.[58] Perhaps to justify the expense, Duckworth asked the Admiralty for permission to have Lieutenant Buchan survey the coast between Cape Bonavista and Cape St John, but his request was refused. This did not stop Duckworth from allocating to Buchan the additional crew he had requested.[59]

By May 1812, Buchan had four boats in readiness for the search, each provided with four weeks' worth of provisions. But unfavourable ice conditions delayed their departure. Even at the end of June it was difficult for *Adonis* to proceed beyond Fogo.[60] Buchan therefore sent three small boats out to take post at any one of about fourteen places between Cape Freels and Exploits Bay such as Dog Bay, Farewell Islands, Great and Little Beaver coves, Dildo Tickle, Indian Arm, Burnt Bay, and the Comfort Islands. He was, however, uncertain whether the seamen would be equal to the task since they were not accustomed to lie in wait in the woods, which were now swarming with mosquitoes.[61] In mid-July, he sailed *Adonis* to New Bay and then entered Badger Bay through Laole Tickle, a place known to be popular with the Beothuk. He deposited provisions at Ward's Island, where the fisherman Wells had a homestead, and dispatched two fast rowing boats to reconnoitre Badger and Seal bays.[62] Buchan took the third boat to New Bay and then to Halls Bay, rowing thirty to forty-eight kilometres a day. While he did not find anything of interest, the crew in Badger Bay had come across the remains of roasted venison beside a fireplace whose embers were still glowing. On his way to Exploits Bay Buchan received orders to sail to Twillingate, where news of the war with America awaited him. He promptly recalled all boats.[63] Master W. Thomson reported that, due to the lateness of the season, the settlers had remained longer than usual in their winter houses and the Beothuk had therefore stayed amongst the islands, unwilling to travel to the bird rocks until the English had moved out to their summer homes.[64] As a result they had lost the egg season. The Beothuk would not move about again until the young birds were fit for taking, approximately between mid-August and September. At that time the Indians could be expected in substantial numbers around Badger Bay, Seal Bay, and the Tritons.

Buchan, who must have been wondering whether his goal was attainable, asked Duckworth for permission to employ six boats until October, which would "next to a certainty" allow them to obtain captives. He now knew more about the Beothuk's habits and the paths they took to the coast since they had given up travelling down the lower Exploits River.[65] While waiting for a reply he sent one boat to the neighbourhood of the Triton Islands but had to recall it ten days later when ordered to return to St John's. The crew reported fireplaces and a new wigwam but had been unable to catch up with its occupants.[66]

Buchan's unrivalled perseverance, matched by Governor Duckworth's continued encouragement and support, had promised eventual success. However, the commencement of war defeated all further plans. As the main objective of the naval force was the defence of the island and its fishery, no vessel could be spared to search for Beothuk.

MEETINGS WITH BEOTHUK REMAIN UNATTAINABLE

In 1813, Vice Admiral Sir Richard Keats replaced Duckworth as governor of Newfoundland. Keats soon recognized that new approaches were needed if communication with the Beothuk was to be achieved. The hundred pounds sterling offered to anyone who established an exchange with them on a firm and settled footing had not been claimed. Keats presumed that the Beothuk keenly remembered the ill treatment they had experienced and for this reason declined all contacts, "unallured by the temptation of traffic and strong liquors."[67] In Keats's opinion, occasional communication would be of no permanent advantage either to the Beothuk or the English. The most effective way of securing their confidence would be to establish a post in Beothuk country, display kindness, and engage in an equitable exchange for several successive seasons. Before Keats received a reply to his proposal, Vice Admiral Francis Pickmore had taken over as governor. Although W.E. Cormack later claimed that Governor Keats sent Lieutenant Buchan in *HMS Pike* to the Exploits River to initiate trade, there are no records of any such expedition.[68] However much Buchan may have wished to continue with his mission, other tasks took priority. In the summer of 1815, he was assigned to take back St Pierre and Miquelon for the British Crown. The following winter, when Buchan was left in charge of the colony while the incumbent governor returned to England, unprecedented hardship and economic disaster struck Newfoundland. Buchan's compassionate and courageous management of famine, fire, and unrest received the highest praise.[69] In 1816, after he had been promoted to commander, Buchan's return to Newfoundland on *HMS Pike* was delayed until September. According to the captain's log, he immediately set off for Twillingate Harbour and sailed from there through Beothuk island territory as far as Cape St John.[70] But the limited time at his disposal and the lateness of the season precluded the dispatch of search parties.[71] As the economic conditions in Newfoundland remained bleak for another year, further action on behalf of the Beothuk was not taken.

Relaxed vigilance over the activities of the northern settlers seems to have resulted in renewed violence. According to Shanawdithit's sketch 5, "accompanied with 2 others old Mr Peyton killed woman at A 14c 15 years ago on the Exploits River" (Plate 10.3). The sketch suggests that the men disturbed the occupants of a winter mamateek, possibly in the vicinity of Rushy Pond, and that

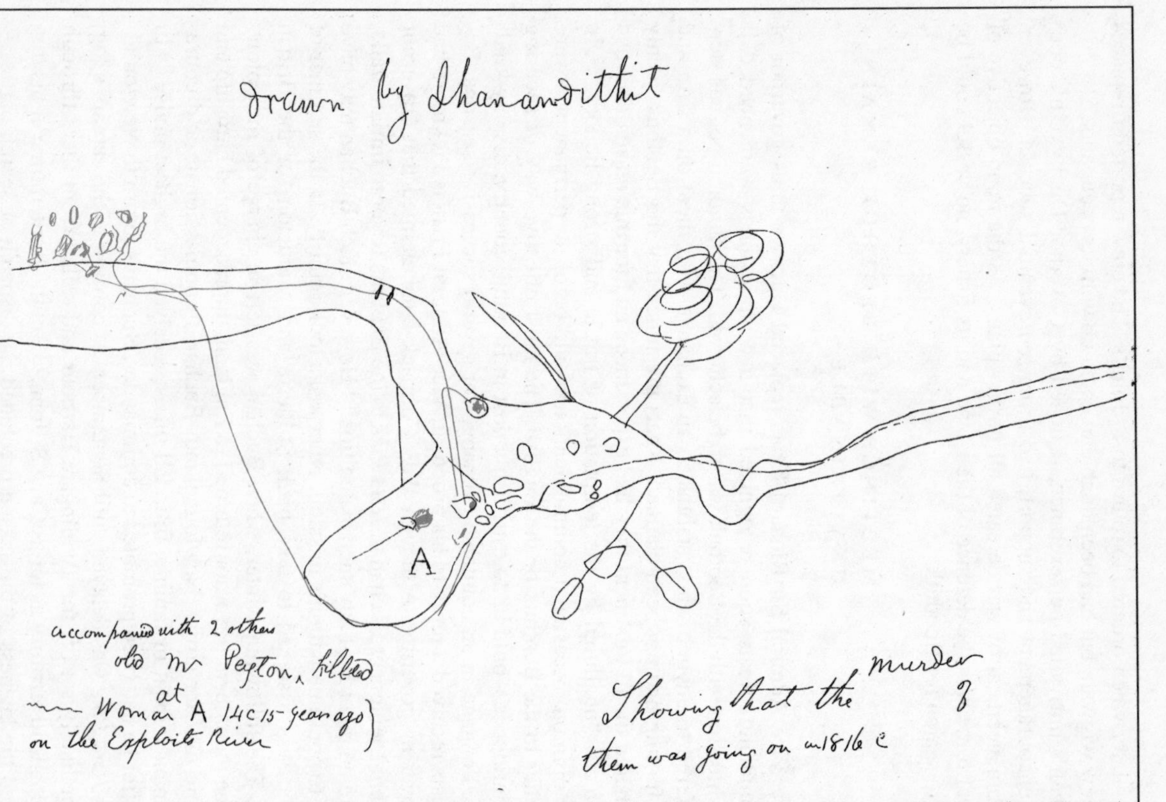

Plate 10.3 Shanawdithit's sketch 5: "accompanied with others old Mr Peyton killed Woman at A 14 C 15 years ago on the Exploits River. Showing that the murder of them was going on in 1816c." (Howley 1915,245)

about ten to twelve Beothuk escaped and reassembled at a distance on the river bank. One woman was intercepted by Peyton and struck down. On another occasion, in 1817, a man named Rogers from Twillingate Great Island and three others discovered nine Beothuk asleep on a small island far up the bay (presumably Notre Dame Bay). They rowed up quietly and shot all of them. Mr Slade, who was told about this murder by Rogers, visited the spot and found there a pile of bleached human bones.[72] In the summer of 1818, Shanawdithit's "brother, mother, sister and a young child were shot ... when attempting to reach an island, in a canoe, to collect the eggs of wild fowl."[73]

The Beothuk in turn continued to thieve. John Gale, who had a fishing station at the bottom of White Bay, contended that in April 1817, "Red Indians" had taken property from his winter house to the amount of fifty pounds sterling.[74] As Peyton, Jr, was later to say, they had never attempted any personal injury towards him and his family but considered whatever came their way "fair game for plunder."[75] In 1823 James Dobie, surgeon on *HMS Egeria*, was told that Beothuk stole salmon nets and boat tackle and would even set fire to old houses in order to obtain ironwork for arrows.[76]

CHAPTER ELEVEN

Micmac and Montagnais versus Beothuk: The Final Phase

MICMAC ENCROACHMENT INTO BEOTHUK TERRITORY

During the nineteenth century, Micmac continued to make steady inroads into Beothuk territory. They had settlements on the island, they interacted with the expanding European population, and, in contrast to the Beothuk, they had guns. By the early 1800s many Micmac families lived permanently in Newfoundland. St George's Bay had become the seat of their largest and most thriving community, with a fluctuating population of between sixty and 150 individuals (Fig. 3.1).[1] The settlement was said to have been sanctioned by the English in the 1780s, when a Micmac elder or chief was given a tract of land in this bay in payment for his services during the English/American war.[2] The second largest Micmac settlement was located on the south coast in Bay D'Espoir. The two communities were connected by an overland route, which was also used for travelling to the centre of the island.[3] In addition, Micmac hunting and trapping parties came seasonally to Newfoundland from Cape Breton Island and Nova Scotia. In 1810 as many as two to three hundred Micmac were gathered in Bay D'Espoir.[4] The periodic influx of trappers was one of several factors that led to the Micmac's steady advance inland into areas that had formerly been exploited by Beothuk – eastward from St George's Bay and northward from Bay D'Espoir and other points along the south coast.

As Newfoundland governors began to adopt a more protective attitude towards the Beothuk, the role of Micmac and their interaction with Beothuk was more closely scrutinized by the naval officers who patrolled the coast. Already in 1798, Capt. Ambrose Crofton reported that Micmac, who had guns, "may prove an implacable enemy" to the native Indians. Three years later Capt. H.F. Edgell said Beothuk were persecuted by settlers and "hunted by the Micmacks" from St George's Bay. He concluded that it would not be surprising if the number of native (Beothuk) people decreased dramatically.[5] In 1808, Governor Holloway stated that the Micmac who visited Newfoundland from Cape

Breton or Nova Scotia were at "Enmity with this unfortunate Race of Native Indians," and that the Beothuk remained hidden in the interior "from Dread of the Micmacs."[6] In response to these unfavourable accounts, Sir Thomas Duckworth and subsequent governors issued proclamations ordering Micmac to live in peace with the native Indians.[7] Captain William Parker, after making enquiries about the general conduct of the Cape Breton Micmac, reported in 1810 that they were at open war with the natives in Newfoundland and killed them whenever they could.[8] Even the then Captain Buchan, who was well versed in matters concerning the Beothuk, later attributed their rapid decline and extinction to persecutions by Micmac as well as by English.[9]

It was not long before Micmac regularly came to White Bay – in 1812 fifty Micmac wintered there – and then moved inland. The fisherman Gill, who fished in White Bay, reckoned that they were going to cross into Halls Bay, which was still part of the Beothuk's resource base. He considered the Micmac to be "a scourge to the Natives on whom they breath[e] eternal enmity."[10] In 1815, Governor Keats expressed apprehension about the Micmac's increasing incursions into Beothuk territory and believed that "the arrival of these [Micmac] newcomers will prove fatal to the native Indians of the Island."[11] John Peyton, Jr, also accused the Micmac of harassing Beothuk, though it is possible that he did this to divert attention from accusations that members of his own family had murdered Beothuk.[12] Capt. Hercules Robinson, who patrolled the Newfoundland coast in 1820, reported to Governor Hamilton that the Micmac waged a "war of extermination" against the Newfoundland natives.[13] Robinson's claim may have been exaggerated, but there is good evidence that at least some Micmac were hostile towards the Beothuk and made no attempt to disguise their feelings: they told the surgeon of *HMS Egeria*, James Dobie, that they would shoot Beothuk like dogs. Dobie was led to believe that the Micmac had always considered it a duty to murder Red Indians and that only the influence of their priests could stop the persecutions.[14]

In combination, these reports suggest that the Micmac who lived in Newfoundland as well as those who came to the island to hunt and trap were generally hostile towards the Beothuk. While it is difficult to gauge how accurate the assessments were, the Micmac's increasing incursion into Beothuk country, even allowing for bias, was bound to precipitate conflict and fuel the Beothuk's hostile feelings.

By 1822, according to William Epps Cormack, there were some 150 Micmac living in Newfoundland, many of whom had been born there. On the west coast they had settled at St George's Harbour, Flat Bay, Codroy River, Bonne Bay, and Bay of Islands; on the south coast, at White Bear Bay; and in Bay D'Espoir, close to Weasel Island. Small groups had crossed the island and had established themselves at Clode Sound in Bonavista Bay and in Gander Bay, which had until recently been strongholds of the Beothuk.[15] In 1822, a man presumed to have been Micmac made his way to Moreton's Harbour, New World Island, where he excited much curiosity among the residents, many of whom had never seen an Indian.[16] Four years later, a Micmac arrived at Fogo Island to ask the resident minister, Rev. John Chapman, for a Bible and a spelling book. He was the first Micmac that Chapman had seen on the island.[17] The Micmac paid deference to a number of individuals in St George's Bay but considered Cape Breton, where their chiefs resided, to be their headquarters. Cape Breton was also the location of their burial ground.[18]

In the 1820s, Micmac still considered a great portion of the interior to be Red Indian territory, possessed and hunted exclusively by Beothuk. The southern border ran about fifteen to twenty-five kilometres to the north of the Micmac camp on King George IV Lake, where the Micmac routinely began and ended their travels to and from the west coast by canoe.[19] When Cormack walked across Newfoundland in 1822, he was escorted by a Micmac guide, Joseph Sylvester, who took him for the last part of their journey along this well-established route that ran through several lakes, including Meelpaeg and Granite lakes.[20] Even though they acknowledged the Beothuk's claim to the central part of the island, many of the northern lakes, and the Exploits River, Micmac were quite familiar with those areas and frequently trespassed upon them. In the winter of 1810–11, for example, Buchan's party saw two Micmac canoes at the confluence of the Exploits River and Rattling Brook, though the Micmac usually camped at Wigwam Brook at the mouth of the Exploits River to hunt and trap in that region.[21] Similarly, it was a Micmac who advised Cormack of a large Beothuk camp on South Twin Lake (Cormack investigated the camp in 1827), which had become a refuge for the Beothuk now that they were increasingly disturbed on the Exploits River and at Red Indian Lake. Two of the Micmac Cormack had spoken to had several times "fallen in with the Red Indians, and on one occasion had obtained possession of their camp."[22] Another Micmac hunter had once come across a lone Beothuk mamateek on Hodges Hill (north of the Exploits River) in which all the furnishings were intact, though the occupants had disappeared.[23] Micmac frequently travelled up the Exploits River and complained about Beothuk stealing their axes whenever they encamped in "Red Indian country."[24] A Micmac informant who was questioned about the "Red Indians" by Capt. Edward Chappell in 1817 said, "Killee all men [Micmac] dat dem see,"[25] implying lasting antagonism.

According to Cormack, the Micmac practice of plundering Beothuk for their furs was common knowledge, and they studiously concealed the nature and object of their trips into Beothuk country from the English. He also believed that Micmac jealously guarded their monopoly on the fur trade and deliberately kindled a fear of firearms in the Beothuk.[26] Micmac were evidently able to infiltrate virtually all Beothuk territory and in encounters usually had the upper hand. In the end, the Beothuk had no safe place to stay.

Micmac/Beothuk encounters were not always overtly hostile. In 1824 a meeting took place on the Exploits River about half way between the coast and Red

Indian Lake. Micmac exchanged friendly gestures across the river with a party of Beothuk; Shanawdithit was a member of that party.[27] On another occasion, a group of Micmac frightened the occupants of three Beothuk canoes on the Exploits River with a gun shot; the Beothuk fled but one of their canoes, with two small children in it, drifted to the Micmac side of the river. The Micmac informant, Mathy Mitchel, claimed that the children disembarked and ran away.[28] Another Micmac informant recalled that his grandparents once saw a Beothuk couple on the Exploits River; they fled and left their small child in their canoe. The Micmac were said to have left food with the child.[29] It is possible that incidents of this kind tempted Micmac to take a Beothuk child away.

RECORDS OF KIDNAPPING AND INTERMARRIAGE

Several Micmac traditions describe either the kidnapping of Beothuk or their marriage into a Micmac group, or both. According to one story, three Micmac hunters gave chase to Beothuk and overtook a young woman when the strap on her snowshoe broke. She was taken back to the Micmac camp, and although she initially resisted all attempts to befriend her, she later married her captor.[30] In another case, two women were captured by Micmac but were soon returned because the Micmac were fearful of an evil spell.[31] Beothuk boys or men were also absorbed into the Micmac tribe. The Beothuk Gabriel is said to have come from the interior to the Micmac settlement in the Codroy Valley; nothing further is known about the events that led him to join the Micmac; but he later married a Micmac woman.[32] Another case of a Beothuk-Micmac couple is that of the parents of Santu Toney. Santu's father was a Red Indian who, as a baby, when among his own people, had been stained red. He was "taken" by Micmac as a young boy, reared by them, and converted to Christianity. He married a Micmac woman and their daughter Santu was born around 1837. After her mother died, Santu and her father moved to Nova Scotia around 1846. Since he had been alive at least into the late 1840s, he could qualify as the last surviving Beothuk. Santu stated that her parents were not the only Beothuk-Micmac couple in the Micmac group; some of the descendants of these couples may still have been scattered here and there. However, Santu did not cite specific examples.[33] The Micmac John Paul, when questioned by Speck around 1915, considered it quite possible that some Micmac had married Beothuk survivors, a fact that had been kept secret due to "fear of retaliation or at least molestation at the hands of the English, since such a stir had been raised over them [Beothuk]."[34] As recently as 1958 the Micmac Charlie Brake of South Branch, Codroy River, who was born around 1890, claimed that his grandmother had been a Beothuk.[35] According to a publication by the Conne River Indian Band Council, "there are several people in Conne River today who believe that they may have Beothic blood in their family lines through intermarriages that occurred three generations ago."[36] In two of the three cases recorded by Silas

Rand and Frank Speck in which a Beothuk had joined a Micmac group, the Beothuk had not done so voluntarily.

In contrast, the Micmac and Montagnais associated quite freely with each other. Towards the end of the eighteenth century, Montagnais hunters from the Lower Quebec Coast who trapped for furs in Newfoundland became closely linked with Micmac groups by taking spouses from among Newfoundland Micmac.[37] Speck recorded that "from early colonial times … intermarriages between them [Montagnais] and the Micmac were so common that more than half of the older Indians in Newfoundland today [ca. 1915] have Montagnais among their grandparents."[38] In the process of integration, Montagnais may have come to identify with Micmac interests and to have adopted the Micmac's uncompromising attitude towards Beothuk. For example, James John, a Montagnais, and his Micmac wife, who hosted Cormack on his trek across the interior of the island in 1822, were unwilling to divulge information about the Beothuk. All John would say was that the country about ten kilometres to the north was considered to belong to the Beothuk, who during fall and winter lived at "the Great Lake of the Red Indians" (Red Indian Lake). Yet at that time, hardly any of the Beothuk were still alive.[39]

In 1828, when Cormack sent John Louis, John Stevens, and Peter John (two Abenaki and one Montagnais) to the Exploits River to look for Beothuk survivors, he seems to have sensed in them an undercurrent of fear, or a reluctance to approach the Beothuk peacefully. Cormack therefore instructed the men to "avoid coming into contact with the Red Indians under any circumstances however favourable they may appear to be."[40] He probably took this precaution because he did not have confidence in the men's ability to approach Beothuk with sufficient restraint or to conduct a meeting in a pacific manner.

BEOTHUK RESPONSE TO MICMAC ENCROACHMENT

Few accounts touch on the Beothuk's response to the Micmac's continued encroachment on their territory. There are few records of retaliation, which suggests that the Beothuk rarely resorted to violence. However, John Peyton, Jr, considered the Beothuk to be a "fierce and savage race" when compared, presumably, with Micmac and Montagnais, who, in his opinion, were "partly civilized."[41] Shanawdithit revealed to Cormack that "from infancy all her nation were taught to cherish animosity and revenge against all other people; that this was enforced by narrating, during the winter evenings, the innumerable wrongs inflicted on the Boeothics by the white men and by the Mik-maks; … and that if the Boeothics made peace and talked with … the Micmacks, who … belonged to the bad spirit, that they would not, after they died, go to the happy island."[42] She also said that any member of the Beothuk group who had come in contact with Micmac would be sacrificed to the spirits of the victims of Micmac aggression.[43] Although Shanawdithit communicated to Bishop Inglis (probably through John Peyton, Jr) that the enmity of the Micmac had been "implacable and of the deadliest character," her disclosure to Cormack suggests that, on the other side, the Beothuk never forgot the defeat and losses they suffered at the hands of Micmac. By instilling unabated thirst for revenge in every member of the tribe, and by threatening punishment for peaceful interaction, Beothuk fanned the flames of animosity.

Since the Micmac were armed with guns, the Beothuk may not seriously have contested their superiority in confrontations. Yet a desperate sense of outrage could have incited them to revenge whenever possible. Noel Mathews, one of Howley's Micmac canoe men, told Howley that a Micmac hunter was said to have been murdered at Red Indian Lake when he approached a Beothuk mamateek. His wife, who had remained hidden from view, later found her husband's headless body in the deserted camp.[44] In a different version of this story, the wife made her way to St George's Bay to tell her people that her husband had failed to return. A group of Micmac thereupon set out and, finding their dead companion in a mamateek, pursued the Beothuk to wreak vengeance upon them.[45]

According to Micmac lore, recorded by Chappell and Speck, the Micmac's fear of Beothuk never completely disappeared. This is echoed by Cormack, who searched for the remains of the Beothuk tribe in 1827 and stated that the Red Indians had been the terror of other natives in Newfoundland and were "even feared yet."[46] When Cormack put up camp with his three Indian guides on the foundation of a Beothuk mamateek at Red Indian Lake, two of the guides were obviously uneasy; Cormack wrote: "None of the Indians of the other tribes had ever encamped near this lake fearlessly." After the Beothuk had disappeared from the island, a Micmac told Howley, "Red Injun not bad man"; he may not have been the only Micmac to feel this way.[47] Micmac attitudes towards Beothuk were evidently ambivalent, ranging from traditionally fostered fear, anger, and contempt to an inclination towards personal benevolence or even respect.

MICMAC VIEWS ON THE DEMISE OF THE BEOTHUK

Opinions among Micmac on the demise of the Beothuk vary considerably and have changed over time. In the 1830s some Micmac believed that starvation brought about their untimely end. Others thought Beothuk survivors had remained in the interior or moved to Labrador.[48] In the early 1900s, Micmac questioned by Speck would say that the Beothuk had been doomed by an unconquerable fear of their fellow man, Micmac as well as European.[49] This view implies that the demise of the Beothuk was the result of their own timidity and therefore beyond anybody's control. Along the same line, the spokespeople of the present-day Conne River Band Micmac have stated that the Micmac's presence in Newfoundland did not have a detrimental effect on the Beothuk.[50]

CHAPTER TWELVE

The Captive Demasduit

The story of Demasduit, or Mary March as she was known to the English, is one of the best-authenticated of the recorded histories of Beothuk captives. Parts of the story, notably her capture, were described by several people whose accounts have survived to this day. Needless to say, there are discrepancies among the different accounts due to the relative astuteness of the observers and their memory for detail, the time lapse between actual events and their narration, and the tendency of some informants to play down or actually suppress unfavourable aspects of the story.

Demasduit had a captivating personality and charmed people who met her, particularly among the citizens of St John's. As a result, many changed their views on the Beothuk and became motivated to promote a peaceful settlement with the remnant of her tribe. Her death from a consumptive illness before she could be returned to her people and mediate peace put a tragic end to what had looked to be a promising scheme.

In the following account, Demasduit's story is told as far as possible in the words of people who participated in the events. Critically important is the account from the Beothuk woman Shanawdithit, who was captured later and related the story of Demasduit from the point of view of the Beothuk.

BEOTHUK TRANSGRESSIONS PRECIPITATE A CONFRONTATION

The background to the capture of Demasduit was shaped by an increase in Beothuk thieving and resulting clashes with English settlers. The central figure on the English side was John Peyton, Jr, son of the notorious antagonist of Beothuk, John Peyton, Sr. Peyton, Jr, ran a busy salmon fishery and fur trade in the Bay of Exploits and Exploits River region. He reported to Governor Hamilton in 1819 that the Beothuk had, over the last few years, continually pilfered his tools and equipment and, on occasion, cut the mooring ropes of his boats.[1] He gave many details. In 1814 Beothuk had gone into the tilt of John Morris, one of his furriers, and carried away or destroyed provisions, equipment, and all of the furs. They had also taken seven traps set in beaver lodges, a loss amounting to about fifteen pounds sterling. Two months later, a new set of salmon nets was cut from its moorings, and traces of red ochre on the buoys indicated to Peyton that they had been taken by Beothuk. In 1816, Beothuk had carried away the sails and tackle from one of Peyton's fishing boats in the harbour of Exploits Burnt Island and had cut the boat adrift; that same night they had also cut the ropes of a boat belonging to George Luff in the same harbour. In October 1817, Beothuk had stolen fourteen of Peyton's best marten traps and had shot an arrow through the roof of the cat-house. Over the years, they had also pilfered knives, axes, traps, hooks, lines, rope, canvas, and other useful articles from Peyton's stations, most of them of little value but a nuisance to replace. Peyton had not retaliated. But in September 1818, the Beothuk had become so emboldened as to commit a major theft that Peyton was not willing to ignore.[2] On the night of 18 September, between midnight and half past one, Beothuk cut adrift a boat from his wharf at Lower Sandy Point in the Bay of Exploits.[3] It had been loaded for market and Peyton was merely awaiting daylight and the turn of the tide before setting off. The cargo consisted primarily of salmon and furs, but stowed in the boat's cuddy were clothes, bedding, and several articles of value, including two silver watches, guns, pistols, ammunition, and cooking utensils. Knowing that Beothuk were in the neighbourhood, Peyton had kept a strict watch until midnight, after which he and the crew had gone to lie down. But Peyton had become restless and visited the wharf again only to find the boat missing. Since it was a very dark night, he was forced to wait until early morning before he could set out on a search. At length he "found the boat hauled up in a small creek at the mouth of Charles' Brook away down on the other side of the bay. She was completely rifled, everything of a portable nature, including the cordage and sails being carried off [though the cargo was not damaged]. The guns alone, battered and broken and otherwise rendered perfectly useless, were found in the bed of the brook not far away."[4]

Shanawdithit, who had been one of the raiding party, later told Peyton that for several days they had watched all his movements from a tall birch tree on a ridge behind his house known as Canoe Hill. When Peyton last inspected the wharf before he retired, the Beothuk were already hidden in their canoe beneath it, but they kept so perfectly motionless that he did not notice their presence.[5]

John Peyton, Jr, went to St John's to bring the matter before Governor Hamilton and to request permission to try to regain his property. He also expressed his wish to open friendly communication and to let the Beothuk know that he was prepared to barter with them.[6] Peyton later specifically referred to his "most anxious desire" to take Beothuk prisoner and to Governor Hamilton's encouragement to "capture one of the Indians alive."[7] In the 1820s, W.E. Cormack claimed that Hamilton had offered a reward of one hundred pounds sterling to any person who could bring a "Red Indian" to St John's.[8] However, there is no record of such an offer. The last public proclamation to mention a reward was the one made by Governor Richard Keats some five years earlier: "If any person shall succeed in establishing on a firm and settled footing an intercourse [with the Beothuk] so much to be desired, he shall receive One hundred pounds as a reward for his meritorious services. But if any of His Majesty's subjects … shall exercise any cruelty, or be guilty of any ill treatment towards this inoffensive people, they may expect to be punished with the utmost rigour of the Law."[9] Keats's offer may have been renewed verbally when Peyton visited Governor Hamilton. Hamilton's correspondence certainly suggests that he was interested in procuring a captive, although he nowhere specifically mentions that he had given John Peyton encouragement to do so. One cannot help concluding that either this encouragement or the offer for a cash reward may have enticed Peyton to concentrate on the capture, rather than on establishing friendly relations.[10]

THE TAKING OF DEMASDUIT

On 1 March 1819, John Peyton, Jr, left his house at Sandy Point accompanied by his father and eight furriers. He told his men that the objective of the excursion was to take some Beothuk prisoner and, through them, try and make friends with the rest. He ordered them not to start any hostilities unless they received orders directly from him.[11] Trekking upriver, the party passed old mamateeks, fireplaces that had recently been used, and storehouses. In one of them they found five of Peyton's marten traps and the jib of his boat. In order to travel with greater speed, the Peytons and their men left most of their provisions in one of the storehouses. They then took a route that diverged from the Exploits River and led them directly to the northeast arm of Red Indian Lake. It took them five days to get there.

The events that followed were later reported by John Peyton, Jr, in a letter to Governor Hamilton written immediately after the event, and by Governor Hamilton in his official report to Earl Bathurst. They were also recorded in the late 1800s by J.P. Howley, who had heard the story first from John Peyton, Jr, and then from John Day, one of Peyton's men. "E.S." (presumed to have been a member of the mercantile Slade family), who accompanied the Peytons to Red Indian Lake, published his version of what happened on that fateful expedition in an English newspaper in 1829. Shanawdithit told of the Peytons' arrival at their camp in conversation with W.E. Cormack in 1828.

In his letter to Governor Hamilton, John Peyton, Jr, reported that, on coming to the lake, he saw several Beothuk running away when he showed himself openly. By divesting himself of his snowshoes, jacket, and gun, he caught up with a woman and held her. Seven or eight Beothuk were in sight and two advanced towards his party after the woman had called out to them. One had a hatchet hidden under his cassock but was disarmed by Peyton's men. This Beothuk first took hold of Peyton, Jr, who shook him off. He then tried to wrest a gun from several of Peyton's men and from Peyton's father. After a struggle in which the Beothuk grasped Peyton, Sr, by the throat, Peyton, Sr, and two of the furriers shot him. The other Beothuk fled.[12]

In his official report to Earl Bathurst, Governor Hamilton stated that when Peyton met a party of Beothuk, they all ran away with the exception of a woman who exchanged friendly gestures with him and his men; "the other Indians did not possess the same peaceful sentiments." They approached in increasing numbers, laid hands on some of Peyton's men, and in the ensuing struggle, when Peyton, Sr's life was in imminent danger, one of the Beothuk fell to a musket ball. The other Beothuk then dispersed and the party returned home, accompanied by the woman.[13]

Many years later, when John Peyton, Jr, told the story to Howley, he said that the woman he pursued stopped and made supplications for mercy by exposing her breasts. Peyton tried to drag her back, but some of the Beothuk who had fled turned around and approached him. A powerful-looking man furiously brandished a bright new axe and would have killed him "had not [my] men just then arrived on the scene and prevented it. The Indians then moved off." Taking the woman along, the party went into one of the wigwams where they found many pilfered articles. Peyton thought that the three wigwams altogether housed no more than fourteen or fifteen Beothuk.[14] In this account, Peyton did not mention the killing.

John Day, one of Peyton's men, recalled that Demasduit, who was ill and weak at the time, carried her baby in her arms until her husband took it from her when he saw that she could not keep up. He then handed the child to another man so that he could rescue his wife, whose hands had been tied by her captors with a handkerchief. When the Beothuk man was prevented from freeing her, he struck down two of Peyton's men and then grasped John Peyton, Sr, by the collar. Old Peyton called out for help, asking, "Are you going to stand by and let the Indian kill me?" Whereupon one man shot the Beothuk, another stabbed him in the back with a bayonet, and others struck him with the butts of their muskets. The Beothuk was a powerful man and Day believed that in hand-to-hand combat he would have been a match for all of them. When he lay dead on the ice, they measured him; he was well over six feet (1.83 metres) in height.[15]

By far the most detailed account was given by "E.S." in an article in the *Liverpool Mercury* published in 1829, ten years after the event.[16] According to the author, each man who took part in the expedition was equipped with a musket, bayonet, and hatchet. Every servant had a pistol, and he and Mr … (E.S. consistently omitted Peyton's name) had a second pistol, a dagger, and a double-barrelled gun instead of a musket. Provisions, blankets, and other necessaries were carried on a light sled, dragged in turn by one of four dogs. Mr …'s objective was to open friendly communication with the Beothuk and he exhorted his men not to use undue violence. If the Beothuk continued to avoid him he planned to take one or two of them captive. On approaching the lake, some men incautiously fired at a passing caribou and within minutes the lake was covered with Beothuk. Men, women, and children rushed from three wigwams; the last to emerge were three men, a woman, and a child. When the woman fell behind, Mr … divested himself of his bag, gun, and hatchet and overtook her. She fell on her knees and begged for mercy by exposing her breasts. Of several Beothuk in sight, three laid down their bows and came closer. One, the captive's husband, advanced with a branch of spruce and made a long oration, his gestures becoming animated and his eyes "shooting fire." He then shook hands with many of the party and attempted to take back his wife. Finding himself opposed, he brandished an axe but was disarmed. Mr … intimated that the woman must go with him but that the Beothuk man might come also; they would both regain their liberty the next day. When he led the captive towards one of the wigwams, her husband became furious and strove to drag her away. One of the furriers stabbed him in the back with a bayonet. The Beothuk knocked him down and did the same to others who tried to hold him. When he brandished his dagger, Mr … fired his pistol and the Beothuk fell. Blood flowed from his mouth and nose, his eyes flashed fire, and he uttered a yell that made the woods echo. The men covered the body of the slain man with boughs and went to one of the wigwams. It was not until the captive was obliged to leave the remains of her husband that she gave way to grief and vented her sorrow in heartbreaking lamentations. Mr … fired several shots over the heads of the nearby Beothuk, who fled. There were at least several hundred of them.

After the party had retired for the night into one of the wigwams, both Mr … and E.S. bitterly reproached the man who had first stabbed the Beothuk. While he had acted violently, there had been no need for such a brutal response. The Beothuk had only done what every man ought to do, "to come to rescue his wife from the hands of the captors and nobly lost his life in his attempt to save her." The captive was tied securely and the party decided to take her back so that she could be used as an intermediary in the hope of developing friendly relations.[17]

Shanawdithit, who was later asked about the capture of Demasduit, told Cormack that in 1819 her tribe was reduced to thirty-one members. They were occupying three winter mamateeks on the north side of Red Indian Lake when a party of nine armed Englishmen came up from the coast to carry some of them away.[18] On seeing a small group of Beothuk, the English gave chase and overtook and seized Demasduit. Her husband, chief Nonosabasut, went amongst the armed men to convince them that he wanted the woman back. His brother approached also. A parley and altercation took place as the white men insisted on taking Demasduit, while her husband strove to rescue her. He was shot on the spot and his brother, who then tried to run off, was shot as well. According to Shanawdithit, Demasduit and Nonosabasut were married five years after Lieutenant Buchan's visit (1811) and "the general breaking up," and her only child was born four years later (Cormack questioned these figures since the timing could not be correct). The infant died two days after Demasduit had been abducted.[19]

Shanawdithit graphically illustrated the events in sketch 2 (Plate 10.2, upper part), on which she drew three mamateeks on the north side of Red Indian

Lake approximately opposite the camp that Buchan had found in 1811.[20] Red figures and semicircular lines represent Beothuk and the routes they took when they fled. A red figure close to the white men and another prone on the ice probably depict Nonosabasut, first haranguing the intruders and then lying dead. Demasduit is represented by the red figure in the midst of six black (pencilled) figures.

After the unfortunate confrontation, which took place on 5 March 1819, John Peyton, Jr, and his party stayed overnight in one of the wigwams, keeping watch at all times.[21] When the men were asleep, Demasduit tried to escape. She placed her outer robe on the snow and noiselessly crawled along, dragging the robe behind either to deaden the sound or to obliterate her tracks. She had gone a considerable distance before her absence was noticed, but she was soon recaptured. She made no further attempt to escape and from then on kept close to Peyton, Jr.[22] When Demasduit understood she was to accompany the party, she placed herself in the sled that was drawn by dogs and directed the men by signs to cover her and to lace her moccasins.[23] Rev. John Leigh later told Captain Robinson that "by her helplessness, by the attention she appeared habitually, to expect at the hands of others, and by her unacquaintance with any laborious employment, she indicated either a superiority of station, or that she was accustomed to a treatment of female savages very different from that of all other tribes."[24]

In his report to Governor Hamilton, Peyton expressed his regret at the death of the Beothuk but explained that if they had been able to "intimidate or persuade him [Nonosabasut] to leave us ... we should have been most happy to have spared using violence." However, if Peyton's main objective had been to gain the confidence of the Beothuk and make friends, he would have released Demasduit to show his good intentions. His failure to do this despite Nonosabasut's growing anger and frustration indicates that he was more concerned with procuring a captive than with effecting a peaceful meeting, and in his report he deliberately glossed over the cause of Nonosabasut's aggressive behaviour. Under the circumstances, Nonosabasut could not have been expected to retreat peacefully. Indeed, had Peyton let go of the captive as requested, more amicable relations might very well have begun.

Peyton assured the governor that his objective was still to establish good relations with the Beothuk so as to protect his property and to rescue them from the misery and persecution to which they were exposed.[25] He offered to return the captive to her people and at the same time open up communication with them. Peyton reckoned that such an undertaking would cost about four hundred pounds sterling and asked Governor Hamilton to finance his expedition. But the governor refused. Instead, he brought the death of Nonosabasut before the grand jury, which concluded that Peyton's party had not intended to gain possession of a Beothuk by violence and bloodshed. The jury decreed that "the deceased came to his death in consequence of an attack upon the party in search of them, and his subsequent obstinacy in not desisting when repeatedly menaced by some of the party for that purpose, and the peculiar situation of the searching party and their men was such as to warrant their acting on the defensive."[26] As there was no evidence to corroborate Peyton's story, the jury recommended that four of the party should be brought before the court at the end of the fishing season so as to establish the innocence of the Peytons and their men more completely. Accordingly, in June 1819, Governor Hamilton ordered Captain Glascock to stop on his way to Notre Dame Bay in Twillingate and call before him, in conjunction with Magistrate John Leigh, the persons who were engaged in the expedition to take down their testimony. If any of them seemed culpable, Glascock was to bring them to St John's to be tried in the Supreme Court.[27] Governor Hamilton later wrote to Earl Bathurst that the grand jury had investigated the case in detail and concluded that the party were "fully justified under all the circumstances in acting as they did."[28]

In the 1850s, Surveyor General Joseph Noad examined the records of Nonosabasut's death and the court's conclusion and expressed his opinion in a lecture as follows:

> It may not be forgotten that the Indian was surprised in the "heart of his own country" … invaded by armed men of the same race with those who had inflicted on his tribe irreparable injuries – his wife was seized by them – his attempts to release her, which ought to have been respected, were violently resisted … he continues, with a courage and devotion to her which merited a far different fate, singly his conflict with ten armed men – he is shot, and his death is coldly ascribed to his "obstinacy." Had the Indian … without feeling or emotion witnessed the separation of the mother from her infant child, then indeed little sympathy would have been felt for him – and yet it is precisely because he did show that he possessed feelings common to us all … that he was shot.[29]

The Role of Rev. John Leigh in the Capture

The Reverend John Leigh, appointed by the Society for the Propagation of the Gospel to minister to the communities of Twillingate and Fogo Island, arrived in Newfoundland in the fall of 1816. He had come from England on *HMS Pike*, commanded by Capt. David Buchan, who may have kindled his interest in Newfoundland's native population.[30] In his first letter to the missionary society, Leigh reported that the natives were harassed and even murdered by settlers. That two natives of the tribe who had many years before worked for their livelihood in the fishery proved that they could be civilized. They had frequently visited their kin but never brought any of them back. Leigh's idea was to capture two boys of about twelve to eighteen years old and, after two or three years, allow them to go back to their friends; "they no doubt would return and would in all probability bring others with them." Leigh would have tried the experiment immediately had he been able to afford it, because he was anxious to do all in his power "to raise these our fellow creatures from a state of darkness and wildness."[31]

Though Leigh was not in a position to put his plan into practice, he knew of two "respectable persons" who had offered to "take ten or twelve of them in the summer, by mild means, at the rate of £100 [sterling] per head or £150 for half that number." Leigh had so far been unable to communicate this offer to the governor but would do so after the governor's return from Britain. Most likely, the people who had offered to capture Beothuk for a fee were the John Peytons, father and son. Leigh may have presented this idea to Governor Hamilton and thus predisposed him to permit the Peytons to set off on their fateful excursion in 1819. After the event, Leigh informed the society of Peyton's meeting with Beothuk at Red Indian Lake, his capture of a Beothuk woman, and the necessity, in this encounter, "of shooting one Gallant but unfortunate poor creature who came to her rescue," this creature being her husband. He recommended that more of the tribe be taken and that the woman be used as an interpreter.[32] The society was dismayed by Leigh's report and expressed "disapprobation of their missionary's taking part in any measure for the civilisation and conversion of the Natives which are either violent or fraudulent in themselves or may be attended with fraud or violence in their execution."[33] Although the society assumed that Leigh abhorred violence in any cause and that his share in the proceedings was due to his zeal in the cause of civilization, he seemed to have paid too little attention to the nature of the means employed. Having been involved in a scheme that led to the death of a man, he must be considered a party to proceedings that the society could not sanction. Indeed, the measures being considered for catching more Beothuk could well result in further deaths.[34]

Distressed over this censure, Leigh defended himself by ignoring the events that led to Nonosabasut's death and claiming that he had merely tried to prevent the governor from sending the captive to England. He thought that by conducting her safely back to her people with presents, her tribe could be convinced that there was no intent to injure them, and he had great hopes that friendly relations could be achieved with her help. Upon Leigh's protesting his innocence, the society investigated no further. However, since he had advocated the capture of Beothuk despite the absence of safety precautions to avoid violence, he could be considered partially responsible for Nonosabasut's death and that of his brother. His trust in the use of "mild means" by the Peytons, one of whom was reputed to be an "Indian killer," had been as misplaced as his opinion that the Beothuk's desire to avenge the murder of their leader would evaporate once the captive was brought back to them with presents. Leigh had clearly been naive to expect the Beothuk to react any differently from the friends of Thomas Rowsell and Cooper, who were said to have "waged a war of extermination" in revenge for the killings of the two men.[35] Unfortunately, Leigh was not the only person to misjudge the Beothuk's outrage.[36] Governor Hamilton and others appear to have shared his unrealistic assessment of the situation, believing that centuries of injustice and killings could be assuaged with a few baubles.

DEMASDUIT

Once the Peytons had safely conveyed Demasduit from Red Indian Lake to the coast, they placed her under the care of the Reverend John Leigh in Twillingate. The women who took care of her washed the ochre from her person and clothed her in English garb.[37] Demasduit was named Mary March after the month in which she had been captured.[38] For some time she was ill at ease in Leigh's household and twice during the night attempted to escape to the woods. Thereafter she was carefully watched and a few weeks later seems to have been tolerably reconciled to her situation, enjoying "the comforts of civilization, particularly the clothes."[39] Her own clothes, made of caribou skins tastefully trimmed with marten, she would neither put on nor part from.[40] Rev. John Leigh (as recorded by Robinson) described her as being

> tall and rather stout, having small and delicate limbs, particularly her arms. Her hands and feet were very small and beautifully formed and of these she was very proud, her complexion a light copper colour, became nearly as fair as an European's after a course of washing and absence from smoke, her hair was black, which she delighted to comb and oil, her eyes larger and more intelligent than those of an Esquimaux, her teeth small, white and regular, her cheek bones rather high, but her countenance had a mild and pleasing expression.[41]

As Demasduit spent many weeks in his household, Leigh came to know her fairly well and later recalled some of her character traits, abilities, and behaviour to Capt. Hercules Robinson, who recorded much of Leigh's account. Demasduit ate sparingly and disliked spirits but was fond of sleep. She was playful and endowed with an astute "perception of anything ridiculous" (an unmarried man seemed an object of great ridicule to her), and her general "knowledge of character showed much archness and sagacity." She had a remarkable innate sense of delicacy and propriety and a power of mimicry that quickly enabled her to speak the language she heard. Before she could express herself, she described people she could not name, such as a shoemaker, tailor, blacksmith, and a man who wore glasses, "with a most happy minuteness of imitation." Leigh also found that Demasduit could be quite obstinate. She was glad to be of help but only if she were not asked to assist. Once Demasduit understood English reasonably well, Leigh compiled a Beothuk vocabulary of about 180 words, which he sent to the Society for the Propagation of the Gospel.[42]

Demasduit rarely spoke freely about her people but told Leigh once that they lived in separate mamateeks, her own housing sixteen. She routinely divided trinkets that were given to her into sixteen shares and once secreted some blue cloth in her room, which she converted into sixteen pairs of moccasins. Robinson recorded that she had two children (he probably erred here; Shanawdithit later said she had only one), which was "the tie that held her to her wigwam." Although she had adjusted to life in Leigh's household, she seemed to "drag a lengthened chain," and "all her hopes and acts appeared to have a reference to her return."[43] Leigh drew a crew and a female figure representing Demasduit in a boat that was going upriver; when he portrayed the people stopping at a wigwam and then returning, Demasduit cried "No, no." Leigh then altered the sketch by leaving the woman behind at the wigwam, whereupon Demasduit responded joyfully, "Yes, yes good for Mary."

In spring, after the breakup of the ice, Leigh took Demasduit to St John's, where she remained for a short time.[44] Governor Hamilton, in his official report, described her as a woman of about twenty-three years, "of a gentle and interesting disposition and acquiring and retaining without much difficulty any words which she was taught."[45] Many years later, Mr Curtis, who had seen Demasduit in Twillingate, said she was of medium height and slender and "for an Indian very good looking."[46]

While in St John's, Lady Hamilton, the first governor's wife to reside in Newfoundland, painted a watercolour portrait of Demasduit in miniature. She portrayed her as an attractive, sensitive young woman with black eyes and short cropped black hair, clad in a skin robe that was trimmed with fur. The portrait was said to be a striking likeness and is the only fully authenticated picture of a Beothuk (Plate 12.1).[47] The original, now in the National Archives in Ottawa, was later copied by several artists.[48]

The Methodist clergyman John Lewis, who had several interviews with Demasduit in St John's, described her as having a pleasing countenance and a complexion that was not much darker than that of English women employed out of doors. She was of medium size, with a good figure and delicate hands. Her manner was mild and she had a cheerful disposition.[49] When Demasduit was taken to the Methodist chapel (as well as to the Anglican church), her demeanour was appropriate to the occasion, but she seemed indifferent to the singing and preaching. Lewis, who was unable to determine whether she "had any idea of a Deity," may have considered the concept of a Divine Being necessary for the successful instruction of Demasduit and her people in the Christian faith.[50] His wish to test her perception suggests that he had not ruled out the possibility of so instructing the Beothuk. However, he realized that the circumstances of her capture had prejudiced attempts at making peace with the tribe and thought it would have been better if a man had been caught, rather than a women whose husband lost his life in her defence. This fact could invoke "jealousy" among her people, he said, perhaps meaning that they might suspect her to have been violated while with the English.[51]

As a woman, Demasduit may have been a less-convincing intermediary with her own people; among the English in St John's, her female gentleness appears to have been of advantage. With her modesty and intelligence, she won the hearts of many citizens who had the opportunity to meet her. Wherever she went she was treated with great consideration and loaded down with presents.[52] It was generally hoped that once this friendly captive returned to her kin, she would describe to her people what she had seen and how kindly she had been

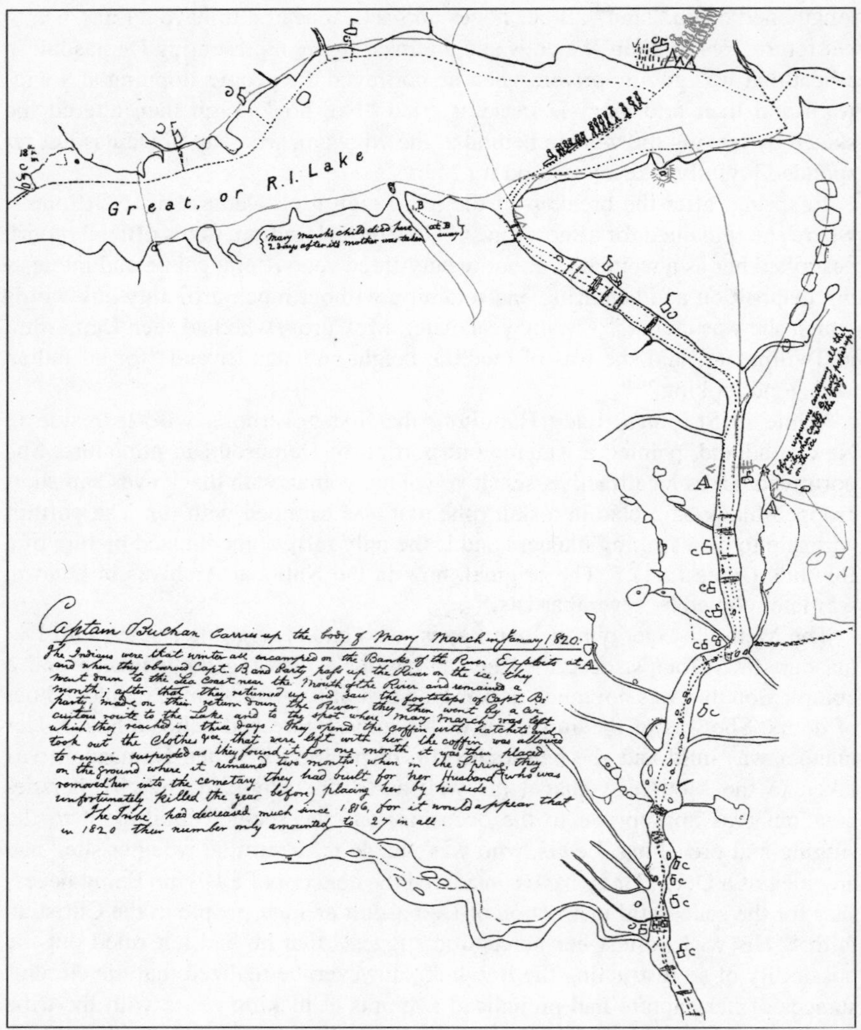

Plate 12.2 Shanawdithit's sketch 3: "Captain Buchan carries up the body of Mary March in January 1820." (Howley 1915,241)

treated. Indeed, her account was expected to convince her tribe that the whites honestly wished for good relations. In retrospect, it is difficult to understand how the citizens could have believed that friendliness towards a single captive could have turned the Beothuk's anger and hostility into an attitude of trust and friendship. Not only had the Beothuk suffered too long to dismiss past injuries lightly but Demasduit's testimony of the kind intentions of the English may not have had much credibility among her kin, since, according to Shanawdithit, her association with the English was a punishable offence.[53] It was presumably for this reason that Demasduit said on several occasions she would remain with the English if only she could retrieve her infant child.[54]

Plans to Use Demasduit as Mediator

It was elsewhere observed that many citizens of St John's were so greatly impressed by Demasduit's gentleness and tact that they revised their attitude about the ill-reputed "Red Indians." In an article in the *Mercantile Journal*, an anonymous author made the following statement:

> In consequence of ... habitual persecution and cruelty, which every well informed person in this Island knows are not exaggerated in the relation, we could not but believe that the Red Indians were the most ferocious and intractable of the savage tribe – impelled by no moves but those of hunger and hostility. And it is with no less of astonishment than pleasure, that we find, in the young woman which has been brought amongst us, a gentle being, sensibly alive to every mild impression and delicate propriety of her sex. Indeed her appearance and manners are so different from any thing which we could be led to anticipate, that many persons were induced to believe the whole story to be an imposture, and that the woman was in reality one of the friendly tribes of Indians, who had volunteered a visit to St Johns [sic].[55]

In a bid to enlist general support, the author reflected on the "horrible" fact that Demasduit's people, who presumably resembled her, were still exposed to "wonton cruelty" and argued that by virtue of priority the Beothuk had a better title to the island than the English. Although others had made statements of this kind – for example John Cartwright (1768) and Chief Justice Reeves (1793) – never before had such a frank admission been made public. Exhorting the British Government to "restore these injured people to confidence, security and the enjoyment of their full rights," the article appealed to the public to take a decided part in this affair, which its author regarded as one of "national importance."

A follow-up article, published on 3 June, informed the public of a meeting of the principal inhabitants of the town, who had unanimously agreed to make every effort to communicate with the Beothuk, using Demasduit as mediator.[56] A subscription of £120 sterling was collected and a committee of six men elected: Attorney General James Simms, Dr William Carson, Rev. John Leigh, Mr Thomas H. Brooking, and Mr William Haynes, with Chief Justice Forbes in the chair.[57] The committee proposed to dispatch an expedition in the coming winter. Under the leadership of competent citizens, thirty men who were accustomed to travel in the interior were to deliver the captive, together with presents, to the Beothuk winter camp at Red Indian Lake and induce two or three of the "chiefs" to accompany them to Twillingate. Should the Beothuk show hostility, the men were to remain in the neighbourhood and woo them with daily acts of kindness. The expedition was to go ahead if attempts by naval officers to return the captive during the summer were unsuccessful, and if government did not intend to repeat such attempts in winter.[58] Since Demasduit was to play a major role as mediator, she was to be cared for in Twillingate by Mrs Cockburn or Mr Burge, who would start teaching her English.

The citizens' determination to become involved in the planning and execution of appropriate measures towards Beothuk instead of leaving the matter to government was an important new development. Chief Justice Forbes submitted the proposal to Governor Hamilton, who agreed to send the captive back to Twillingate but was determined to retain his authority over any attempts at befriending the Beothuk. Hamilton immediately directed Captain Glascock, commander of *HMS Sir Francis Drake*, to bring Demasduit to any one of the native settlements on the coast and to use the opportunity to contact the Beothuk.[59] He was to consult with the Reverend Mr Leigh and John Peyton, Jr, on how best to achieve these goals. Presents for the Beothuk were subsequently delivered to *HMS Drake*, among them thirty double blankets, two dozen red shirts and other items of clothing, twenty-four knives, four hundred sewing needles, seventy-two sail needles, hatchets, files, saws, axes, nails, fish hooks, twine, fourteen pounds of soap, tin kettles, dishes and pans, as well as some butter, cheese, tea, and sugar, and twenty-four small looking-glasses and strings of beads.[60]

On his way north, when passing the harbour of Twillingate, Glascock fired two guns as a signal for Leigh to deliver Demasduit to *HMS Drake*.[61] When she arrived on board, Glascock found her in a delicate state of health. Demasduit was suffering from consumption, a disease she had contracted either while she was still living among her own people or during her stay with the English. In the ensuing weeks her illness, probably aggravated by emotional stress and exposure in small open boats, repeatedly prevented her from accompanying search parties.[62]

Captain Glascock moored his ship in Fortune Harbour, on the headland between the Bay of Exploits and New Bay, and proceeded with the cutter and gig to New Bay. He was accompanied by John Peyton, Jr, who had offered his assistance. They found no fresh portage paths signifying the Beothuk's arrival at the coast, and Glascock presumed that they were still encamped inland. He therefore took the cutter up the Exploits River as far as the lower waterfall (Bishop's Falls) and entered the woods to look for signs of Beothuk habitations. Here too, however, were no recently occupied wigwams, which led Glascock to conclude that, fearful of the English, the Beothuk no longer lived on the lower Exploits River. Reconnoitres at Indian Arm and Badger Bay were equally unrewarding. Glascock then took Demasduit to Seal Bay, where they caught a glimpse of a Beothuk canoe before it disappeared around a point. Demasduit "exhibited an apathetic indifference" to the sight of the Beothuk and was unwilling to follow them into the woods. She did not wish to join her tribe unless she was brought either to the group from which she had originally been taken or else to one of the large settlements.[63]

On 30 June, Master Trivick from *HMS Drake* signalled a canoe sighted in Badger Bay, but the Beothuk fled. Knowing that he would not be able to track them down once they had gained the shore, Trivick had a musket fired to throw them into confusion. The Beothuk nevertheless escaped. After landing, Trivick discovered several wigwams and placed presents in them; when he returned two days later, the Beothuk had carried the presents away together with their gear.[64] Thomas Peyton later wrote that his father, John Peyton, Jr, believed they could have caught up with the Beothuk had not the officer in charge stopped the men from rowing to get the arms chest out. John Peyton was vexed to think "of a boat's crew commanded by a British officer, not being able to do this without weapons."[65]

After Glascock's return from Seal Bay, he attempted to contact Beothuk on the neck of land between the Bay of Exploits and the southern arm of New Bay. Two parties advanced at the same time, one from each bay, and met halfway. But the camp there had long been deserted. The Beothuk were avoiding this favoured spot as they were avoiding the lower Exploits River. On a final search in Badger and Seal bays, Demasduit showed Glascock a hidden path that led to recently inhabited mamateeks, but she adamantly refused to be left there.

Having failed in his mission and exhausted his men, Glascock decided to give up the search. He delivered Demasduit to Twillingate and then sailed to St John's.[66] In his report to Governor Hamilton, Glascock stated that between 18 June and 14 July, the gig and cutter of *HMS Drake* had kept continual night guard and had rowed for upwards of 150 kilometres along the coast. The crew and officers had shown much zeal and fortitude, even though they had greatly suffered from exposure and from the "tormenting tortures of every description of insects," which had deprived them of sleep at night. Mr Peyton, Jr's exertions had been "unexampled."[67]

CAPTAIN BUCHAN'S FINAL ATTEMPT TO MEET BEOTHUK

As Glascock had failed to deliver Demasduit to her people, Governor Hamilton assigned the task to Capt. David Buchan, now commander of *HMS Grasshopper* and just returned from an exploratory expedition into the arctic seas.[68] Buchan's concern for the Beothuk and his previous experience in following their trails made him an excellent choice, and he would have had the confidence of Governor Hamilton as well as the Citizens' Committee. After consulting with Rev. John Leigh and investigating local circumstances, Buchan suggested another winter expedition and Governor Hamilton agreed. Hamilton authorized Buchan to supplement his crew with hired men and to purchase whatever supplies he considered desirable. He also had delivered to his ship a large selection of presents for the Beothuk consisting of twine, knives, pots and kettles, needles, looking-glasses, and strings of beads.[69] The planning and execution of the enterprise was left to Buchan's ingenuity and discretion.[70]

On 25 September, Captain Buchan sailed *HMS Grasshopper* to the Bay of Exploits and moored the ship at Peter's Arm.[71] At the end of November, John Peyton collected Demasduit from Twillingate and delivered her aboard.[72] Demasduit's health had declined markedly since Buchan had last seen her in August.[73] He immediately provided her with warm clothing and appointed a woman to look after her. But it soon became apparent that, even if the ship's surgeon could keep her alive through the winter, she was in no state to travel on foot inland.[74] Buchan therefore decided to go without her and attempt to bring some of her people back to Peter's Arm. Demasduit would not hear of it, arguing that he would not be able to find the Beothuk; she also said, "Gun no good." Going over a map of Buchan's previous route, Demasduit delighted in speaking of the mamateeks and made Buchan understand that she wanted only to collect her child, with whom she would then return. She remained cheerful, but her deteriorating health caused Buchan serious concern. Then, on 8 January, at 2:00 P.M, Demasduit suddenly died. Dr Carson later stated that she had succumbed to consumption.[75] Her gentle manner and patience under suffering had endeared her to those around her, and her death caused much sorrow. Her last wish had been to see John Peyton, Jr, and she is said to have "ceased to respire with his name upon her lips."[76] Demasduit had always seemed much satisfied when he was near and had looked up to him as her protector.[77]

Without instructions for this turn of events and unable to return to St John's because of ice, Buchan decided to convey Demasduit's remains to the place of her former residence and pursue the original plan of attempting to make contact with Beothuk. Forty-nine men, including Officer C.C. Waller, two midshipmen, a boatswain, John Peyton, Jr, and a few of Peyton's men, were fitted out with equipment and food for forty days. An additional ten men and an officer were to accompany the party for the first forty kilometres of their route to help pull the sledges on this most difficult part of the journey.[78] According to the captain's log of *HMS Grasshopper*, the ship's surgeon found all but one of the men fit for the expedition. The provisions consisted of 665 kilograms of bread (presumably hard tack), 1,227 kilograms of beef and pork, 305 kilograms of flour, along with cocoa, sugar, tea, and about 170 litres of rum.[79] The food and drink as well as the presents for the Beothuk were packed on twelve sledges and catamarans.[80] The party was equipped with snowshoes made by John Peyton and moccasins manufactured by the ship's crew, perhaps from the 120 sealskins that had been delivered to the ship earlier.[81] They brought nineteen muskets, twenty pistols, appropriate ammunition, and twelve pole-axes.[82]

Due to the unusual mildness of the winter, travel conditions on the Exploits River were poor and Buchan waited until 21 January before setting out. Even so, the obstacles encountered by the party were nearly insurmountable. The ice was exceedingly treacherous and often broke, on one occasion tumbling several men, including Buchan, into the water. The roughness of the ice surface jolted the sledges apart and only four out of the original twelve remained operable. By

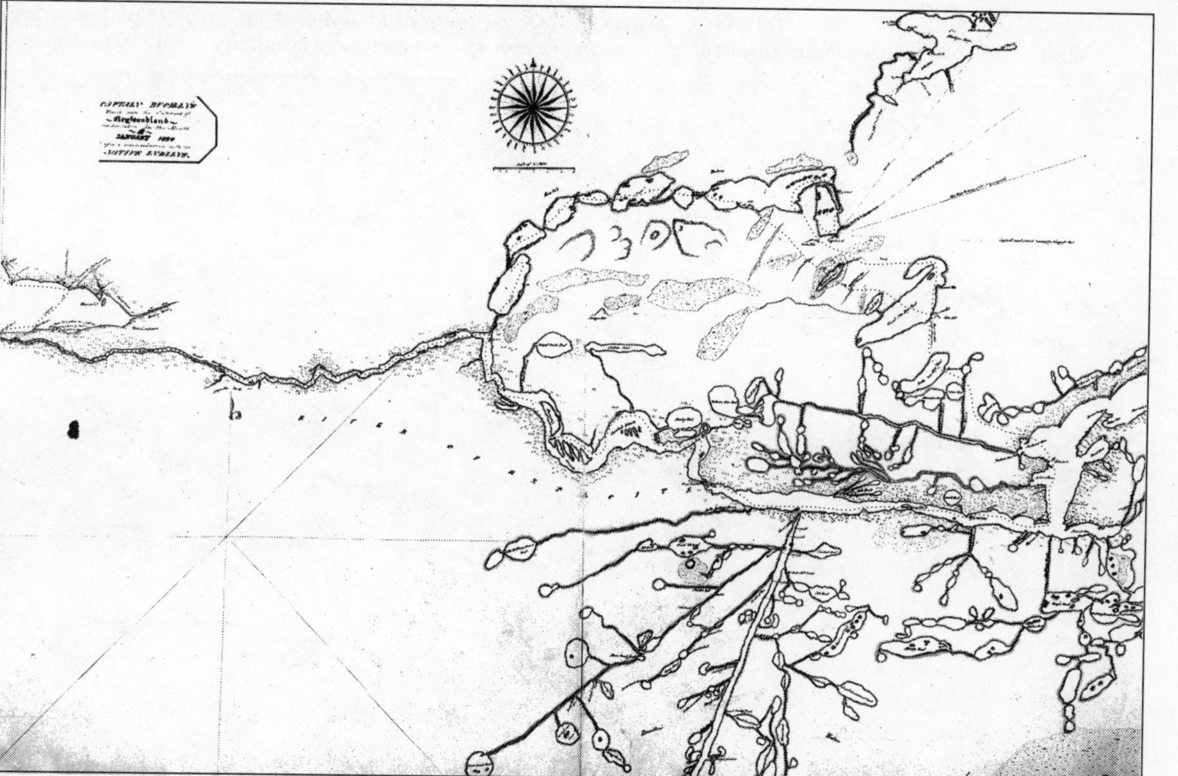

Fig.12.1 "Captain Buchan's Track into the Interior of Newfoundland in the month of January 1820, to open a communication with the Native Indians," part 1. The broken line shows Buchan's track. The track to New Bay is not marked. (By permission of the British Library, Add. 57703 f.1 Mss.51222)

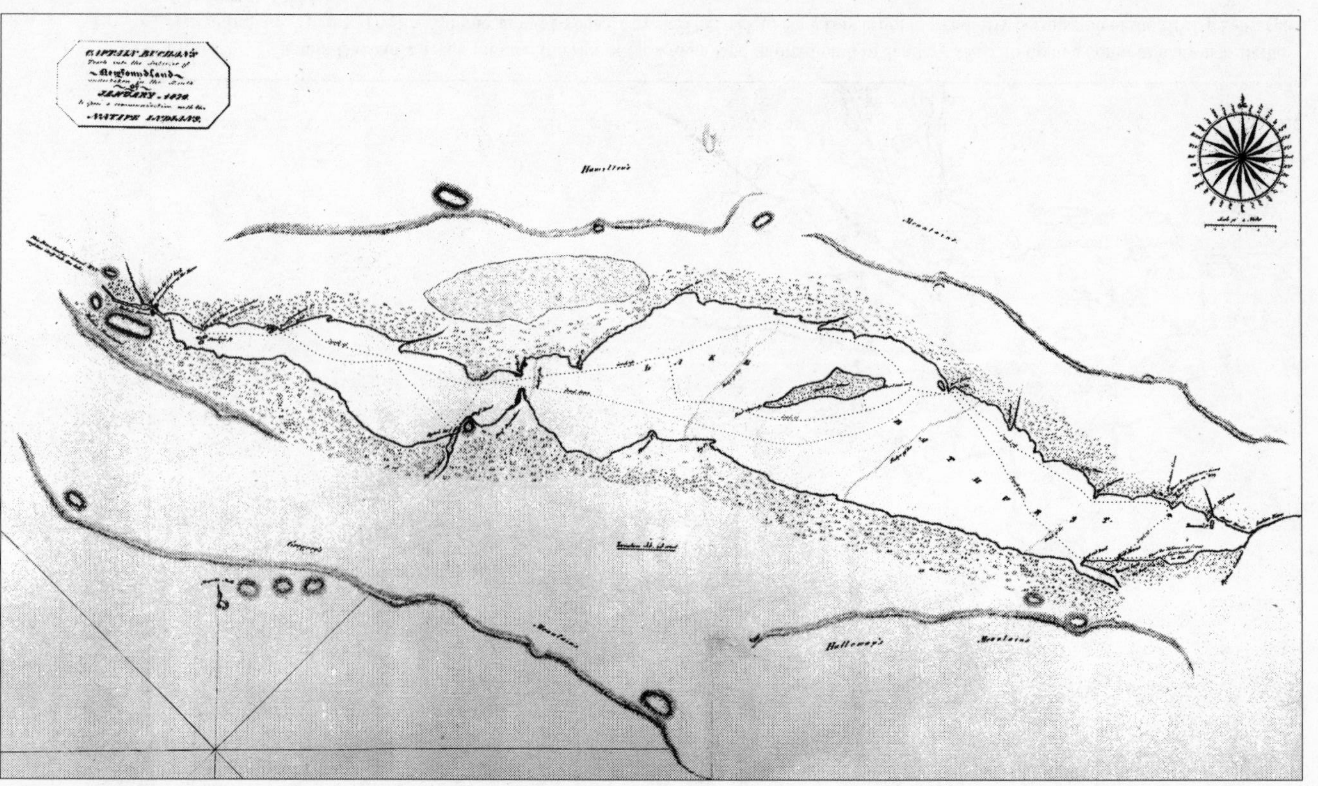

Fig. 12.2 "Captain Buchan's Track into the Interior of Newfoundland in the month of January 1820, to open a communication with the Native Indians," part 2. The broken line shows Buchan's track. (By permission of the British Library, Add. 57703 f.2 Mss.51222)

the time they got half-way upriver, fourteen of the men, suffering from frost burns, were no longer fit to continue and had to be sent back.[83]

The party found no recent signs of Beothuk until they reached a second "overfall," presumably a sequence of rapids, known as Red Indian Falls about nineteen kilometres west of Badger. Shanawdithit's sketch 3 (Plate 12.2) depicting these events suggests that the Beothuk were camped at a small lake off the Exploits River (probably Little Red Indian Pond).[84] It was probably in this area that Peyton's snowshoe struck against a freshly frozen caribou liver. Supposing that Beothuk could not be far, he offered to make a search with a few of his men. However, Buchan would not consent to dividing the party.[85] A short distance upriver, where Buchan had seen a small storehouse in 1811, a very large one had been erected in its place. It was uncovered and many skins and portions of caribou meat were concealed in the snow. There was a raft drawn up on the bank, and sledge marks showed the direction in which the Beothuk had travelled. The disorderly state of some nearby wigwams, which had apparently been occupied in the early part of the winter, suggested that they had been left in haste. After depositing all but the most necessary food and equipment at the storehouse, Buchan's party continued their journey and on 11 February reached the former residence of Demasduit on the northwest side of Red Indian Lake. The frames of two wigwams were still standing, while a third had been turned into a burial hut of curious construction, in which the body of what was presumed to have been Demasduit's husband Nonosabasut had been placed, together with "all his worldly treasure." Demasduit's coffin, which had been conveyed so laboriously to the site, was unpacked. "It was neatly made and handsomely covered with red cloth ornamented with copper trimmings and breastplate. The corpse, which was carefully secured and decorated with the many trinkets that had been presented to her, was in a most perfect state, and so little was the change in the features that imagination would fancy life not yet extinct."[86] Captain Buchan had a tent to which a Union Jack had been attached pitched close to the wigwams and the coffin suspended in it. Demasduit's coat and presents, including two wooden dolls that she had particularly treasured, as well as the sledge for the coffin, were also deposited in the tent.[87]

Although the chances of meeting with Beothuk were slim, Buchan continued his search along the northwest shore of the lake. On 14 February, having covered a distance of about seventy kilometres, the majority of the men were given a rest, while a small party under Peyton's direction investigated the lake's southeast extremity up to the confluence of Lloyd's River. In several places Peyton found abandoned wigwams; faint tracks of snowshoes and moccasins indicated that the occupants had moved further east. As provisions had became scarce and several of the men were unwell, Buchan had little choice but to turn back. On his way he left presents here and there, including iron spears and arrowheads that had been made by the ship's armourer. To attract attention he suspended red flags with the presents.[88] Once Buchan had reached the last cache of stores on the Exploits River, he sent fourteen men on the shortest possible route to the sloop. He himself, together with John Peyton, Jr, and the remaining twenty men, explored the chain of lakes connecting the Exploits River with Badger Bay. They passed old wigwams and saw several cut trees and the tracks of snowshoes and sledges, but none were very recent. On 26 February, Buchan dispatched the remainder of the party to the sloop with the exception of John Peyton, Jr, and two other men, with whom he explored the country inland from New Bay. Three days later they arrived at *HMS Grasshopper*, having been absent for forty days.[89]

Buchan did not admit defeat. With indefatigable optimism, he immediately prepared four small boats to continue the search once the ice had moved. On 19 March he sent Officer Waller and John Peyton, Jr, with thirteen men and provisions for two weeks to explore the lakes inland from Badger Bay. Buchan himself was not well enough to accompany them. The men soon discovered a portage path used by Beothuk to travel from the interior to the Badger Bay coast, but no Beothuk.[90] Shortly after they had left, William Cull informed Buchan that he had recently seen smoke rising from what he believed to be a Beothuk camp near Hodges Hill, close to the junction of Badger Brook and the Exploits River. "Loath to leave any thing undone that might lead to an intercourse with the natives," Buchan immediately dispatched Midshipman Barnard, with Cull, Cull's two sons, and three other men, to investigate. They returned ten days later with nothing to report.

As great quantities of ice were still blocking the entrance to the bays between the Exploits River and Cape St John, Buchan was unable to send his men out in boats and decided to return to St John's to await further orders from the governor. In commemoration of his excursion, the largest island in Red Indian Lake and a community close to the lake were later named Buchan Island and Buchans. The Blue Mountain Tolt, south-west of Gander Lake, was renamed Mount Peyton.[91]

In his report to Governor Hamilton, Buchan noted that he had omitted nothing within his power to attain the desired object of his mission, notwithstanding the "infinite labour and difficulties" that attended his journey. He praised John Peyton, Jr's unremitting zeal and attention and that of his officers, concluding: "It is impossible for me to hold out success when so much depends on fortuitous circumstances but I will venture to say that it is my opinion that there would be a great probability of it by following up the operations without intermission until the last of August."[92]

Buchan also submitted two maps entitled "Captain Buchan's Track into the Interior of Newfoundland undertaken in the month of January 1820 to open a communication with the Native Indians" (Figs. 12.1, 12.2).[93] One shows the Exploits River and Great Rattling Brook and their tributaries, along with the chain of lakes connecting the former with Badger Bay; the second outlines Red Indian Lake (called Lake Bathurst by Buchan) and the surrounding country. According to the geologist J.B. Jukes, these maps were drawn up by one of Buchan's officers with the assistance of John Peyton, Jr. On the first map, seven

Beothuk wigwams are marked on the banks of the Exploits River and six on other rivers and ponds. The map of Red Indian Lake shows six Beothuk wigwams and a burial site on the lakeshore, and an apparatus for drying skins set next to a wigwam close to the junction of Lloyd's River.

Of some importance are the fifteen tilts shown on these maps occupied by English furriers during the trapping season. One tilt is drawn next to the Beothuk's cemetery (where Nonosabasut was interred) on the northwest shore of Red Indian Lake, and three others on the lakeshore farther south. Ten tilts dot the shores of lakes connecting the Exploits River with Badger Bay and New Bay, and another is noted at the mouth of Great Rattling Brook. In addition, the names of six ponds and brooks south of the Exploits River, such as Tilt Pond, suggest that tilts had been built there. While contemporary documents seldom refer to the furriers' intrusion into Beothuk hunting territory, Buchan's maps are indisputable evidence of their encroachment. By the 1820s, the English had infiltrated the Beothuk's last resort.

Shanawdithit's Story

Eight years after Buchan had deposited Demasduit's remains at Red Indian Lake, Shanawdithit described the events on sketch 3 (Plate 12.2). It shows the course of the Exploits River, with its falls and rapids, and the shore of Red Indian Lake; Buchan's party as it crossed the lake; the suspended coffin and the sled he left behind; his route to and from the lake; and the party's overnight camps. The many minute details Shanawdithit recalled indicate that the Beothuk had followed Captain Buchan and examined his campsites *en route*. Her sketch also gives the different positions of Beothuk camps. Three mamateeks drawn at the exit of the Exploits River from Red Indian Lake probably represent abandoned habitations. To the southwest, where Victoria River flows into the lake, a small red dot and the letter B bear the notation: "Here Mary March's child died two days after its mother's abduction." Red lines show the route by which the Beothuk travelled back and forth. The sketch marks two letters "A," one on the right bank of the Exploits River (looking downstream) next to one mamateek, and another one on the left bank close to three mamateeks, with the note: "Three wigwams containing all the tribe when Capt. Buchan and party passed up on the ice with the body."

The lengthy inscription, written by William E. Cormack for whom Shanawdithit made the sketch, reads:

Captain Buchan carries up the body of Mary March in January 1820. The indians were that winter all encamped on the banks of the River Exploits at A. and when they observed Capt. B. and party pass up the River on the ice, they went down to the Sea coast near the mouth of the River and remained a month; after that they returned up and saw the footsteps of Capt. B.'s party made on their return down the River; they then went by a circuitous route to the Lake, and to the spot where Mary March was left which they reached in three days: They opened the coffin with hatchets and took out the clothes etc. that were left with her the coffin was allowed to remain suspended as they found it for one month; it was then placed on the ground where it remained for two months, when in the Spring they removed her into the cemetery they had built for her husband (who was unfortunately killed the year before) placing her by his side.

The Tribe had decreased much since 1816, for it would appear that in 1820 their number only amounted to 27 in all.

THE SEARCH FOR BEOTHUK IS SUSPENDED

Having made considerable efforts to contact the Beothuk, all of which had failed, Governor Hamilton did not consider it advisable to attempt anything further during the current season.[94] A year later, the governor was still unable to report to Earl Bathurst any progress with regard to the Beothuk, but he sent him a Beothuk canoe whose construction he considered to be a curiosity.[95] This canoe may have been the one that Mr Wiltshear and other fishermen from Green Bay had presented to Governor Holloway in 1807.[96]

Judging from the reports and letters in the Colonial Records in England and from the Governor's Correspondence in Newfoundland, it seems that after Buchan's futile expeditions in the winter and spring of 1820, Newfoundland governors ceased to sponsor attempts at finding Beothuk. However, the expeditions and Demasduit's sojourn in St John's appear to have changed public opinion about the Beothuk's character and intentions. For example, Captain Hall, commander of *HMS Carnation*, who had served two seasons on the Newfoundland station, recorded in 1820 that "the red Indians who [*sic*] we have always understood to be mischievous, savage and watching to attack the white inhabitants, are quite the reverse … they are the most miserable creatures imaginable, wild as foxes & timid & cowardly as hares. Very few now remain."[97] Hall also thought that it was the Beothuk's timidity, rather than their vengefulness, that accounted for the repeated failure to approach them.

The positive impression Demasduit had made on people in St John's seems to have stirred their keen and lasting interest in the native population. The Citizen's Committee was apparently disbanded after Demasduit had died, but the emerging spirit of responsibility – and the willingness to act – remained. Indeed, it is quite possible that the committee's ideas inspired William E. Cormack and influenced his decision to search for remnants of the Beothuk tribe in the interior of the country in 1822 and again in 1827.[98]

CHAPTER THIRTEEN

1822–27: The Boeothick Institution

WILLIAM E. CORMACK SEARCHES FOR BEOTHUK

In 1822, three years after Demasduit had visited St John's, William E. Cormack, an entrepreneur with scientific interest and a philantrophic bent, decided to explore the unknown interior of Newfoundland and search for the remnants of the elusive Beothuk. Born a Newfoundlander in 1795 or 1796, Cormack had grown up in Scotland and studied natural sciences at the universities of Glasgow and Edinburgh.[1] In the winter of 1821–22, he returned to Newfoundland to take over family business interests; within months of his arrival he conceived the plan of walking across the island, with a friend and a native guide. To train himself and test his equipment, he departed in July 1822 with Joseph Sylvester, a Micmac, on a trial excursion to Placentia, and from there to Trinity and Conception bays.[2] When affronted by a settler on the journey, Sylvester promptly rolled up his bundle and threatened to quit the expedition; Cormack had to work hard to persuade him to stay.[3]

The trial walk convinced Cormack that the expedition should not be attempted until the beginning of fall, when food – animals, birds, and berries – was at its most plentiful and available. Accordingly, at the end of August, he and Sylvester went by boat via Bonaventure to Random Bar, at the western end of Random Sound in Trinity Bay, whence they intended to walk across the island to St George's Bay. The inhabitants of Bonaventure considered the venture foolhardy: the men would surely fall prey to wolves, if they were not attacked by "Red Indians."[4] Cormack's friend, Charles Fox Bennett, who later became prime minister of Newfoundland, was to be the third member of the party but at the last moment was unable to go.[5] Cormack later claimed that Governor Hamilton opposed the undertaking and had prevented Bennett from taking part in the expedition.[6]

At sunrise on 5 September, the two travellers set off from Random Bar on their arduous trek due west across country.[7] They were equipped with a hatchet, tin kettles, three blankets, a telescope, two compasses, a fishing rod and tackle, various other articles, and about fifteen kilograms of provisions. They also carried a double-barrelled fowling piece each, pistols, and between them about two kilograms of gunpowder and ten kilograms of bullet and shot.[8]

Those who knew Cormack described him as a tall, wiry individual, physically able to endure high levels of hardship and toil. His temperament, reputedly lively and sympathetic, would sustain him under the most trying of circumstances.[9] Throughout the trek, Cormack made copious notes on the geological formations and character of the land and identified the flora and fauna of each region. The journey was difficult. The heavy loads, oppressive heat, and myriad bloodthirsty insects made progress slow. Sylvester evidently felt at home in the country and slept soundly while Cormack lay awake, beset by apprehensions and thoughts "of no ordinary kind."[10]

On 10 September, after enjoying magnificent views of the coast and country, they entered what Cormack termed "the interior." By this time their provisions were nearly exhausted and they were forced to live on what they could shoot – geese and ducks, beaver, and an occasional caribou. They also caught trout and picked berries. Though they frequently saw wolf tracks, the animals fled at their approach. On passing a distinctive mountain that formed a landmark, Cormack named it Mount Sylvester after his guide. By 10 October, they were in what Cormack believed to be the central part of the island, where the Beothuk were thought to live, but they found no traces. Both men began to feel the effects of their unceasing exertion, and Sylvester had to be encouraged to continue with promises of additional rewards and appeals to his honour.[11] At Meelpaeg Lake they rested at the camp of the Montagnais James John and his Micmac wife. John drew maps of the country on sheets of birchbark, which have been preserved in the Newfoundland Museum, and told the travellers that the "Red Indian's" country lay about ten to eleven kilometres to the north. He added that at this time of the year, the Indians would be at the Great Lake (Red Indian Lake), farther north still.[12] Cormack and Sylvester continued westward, but winter weather made walking even more tedious and the nights became very cold. Snowstorms added to their difficulties and the two men were often unable to find dry ground to sleep on or enough wood to keep a fire going. Though they frequently shot a caribou, thousands of which were passing on their eastward migration, the food they had was no longer adequate to support their fatigued bodies, and Cormack realized that his strength was failing. Sylvester obstinately insisted on going further south than Cormack had planned, and Cormack suspected that his guide was deliberately avoiding Beothuk country. However, Cormack did not dare to separate from him. On 29 October, the travellers met a Micmac family at a lake that Cormack named "Wilson's Lake." Gabriel, their host, confirmed that the country of the "Red Indians" was sixteen to twenty-four kilometres to the north and that the Beothuk would now be at the Great Lake.[13] He agreed to accompany the two men to the coast, and two days later they set up camp on George IV Lake, said to be the southernmost lake frequented by Beothuk.[14]

On 2 November, the three men reached St George's Harbour. Sylvester, "who had with painful constancy" accompanied Cormack across the island, joined his countrymen to spend the winter; Gabriel returned to his family, and Cormack who was extremely fatigued, rested in the home of Mr Philip Messervey, the principal inhabitant of the community.[15] He then set out on foot and by boat to Fortune Bay, some two hundred miles to the east, where he caught a vessel bound for Britain. Cormack submitted a lengthy report to Lord Bathurst; he also drew a map of the interior of the country with his route marked due west from Random Sound. He had crossed the island too far to the south to pass through Beothuk country (Fig. 13.1).

Although Cormack's energies and possibly his finances were exhausted, he did not abandon his plan to meet Beothuk. However, several years were to pass before he would make another attempt.

THE KILLING OF TWO BEOTHUK

Within weeks of Cormack's failure to find Beothuk, two English furriers from Twillingate, James Carey and Stephen Adams, killed a Beothuk man and woman in Badger Bay. They concealed their deed for three months but confessed after three Beothuk women, Shanawdithit and her mother and sister, were captured. It was later established that the murdered Beothuk were Shanawdithit's paternal uncle and his daughter.[16]

Carey was brought before the Supreme Court, where he testified that on 23 January, while he was out on the shore of Badger Bay, he saw two persons in the distance.[17] He fired a gun to test whether they were friends or Beothuk – the latter usually fled at the report of a gun – but the two seemed unafraid. When Carey realized that they were Beothuk, he ran into his house to fetch his partner Adams. The furriers motioned to the Beothuk to keep back but they continued to advance, holding large knives in a menacing manner; at a distance of about five metres, Carey and Adams fired their guns and both Beothuk fell. Later account of the event states that the man was shot first while the woman calmly awaited her death; in yet another version, the woman was said to have been accidentally shot, in consequence of which her companion attacked the furriers.[18]

After John Broom, chief magistrate for St John's, had made his deposition, Magistrate John Peyton, Jr, was called as a witness. Peyton testified that Carey and Adams were justifiably afraid of Beothuk, who were generally well armed and had killed five men in the last twenty years.[19] The men he employed were constantly obliged to look out for their security; indeed, one of his men had been shot at by Beothuk and another one wounded. Carey had always expressed his wish to make peace with the Beothuk and had been a volunteer with Capt. David Buchan in 1819–20.[20] Captain Buchan and Rev. John Leigh, also witnesses for the defence, confirmed Peyton's statements and pointed out that the Beothuk were dangerous and appeared to have been armed with deadly

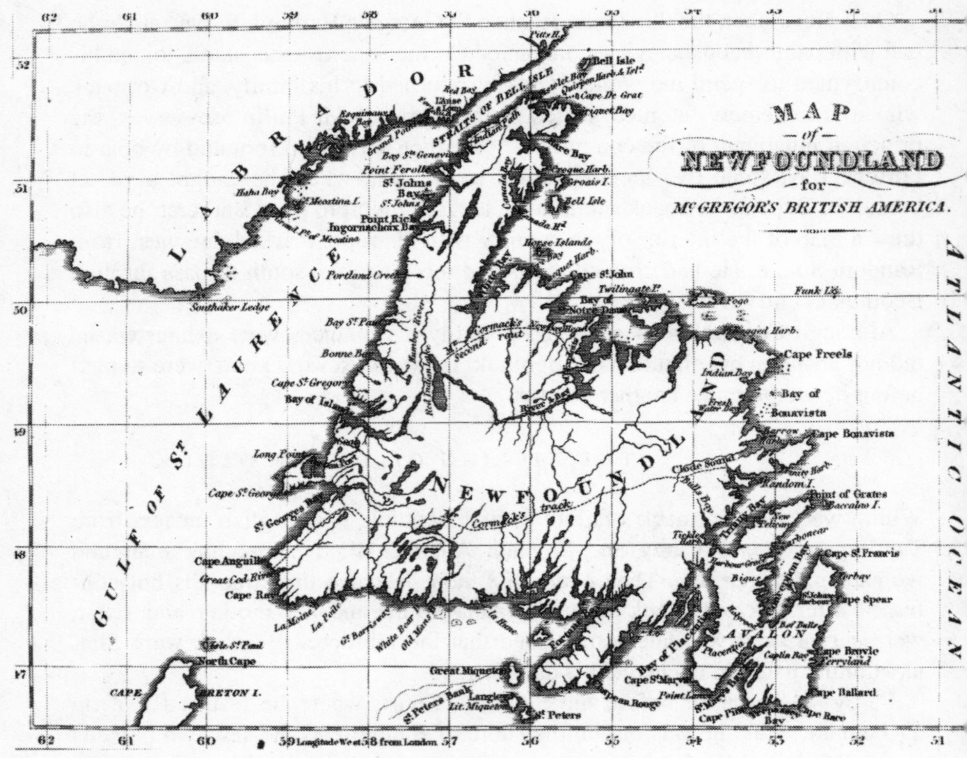

Fig.13.1 W.E. Cormack's routes across Newfoundland in 1822 and 1827. (McGregor 1832,1:141)

weapons.[21] Leigh had seen one Englishman wounded with nine arrows and believed that in the last twenty-five years eight settlers had been killed by Beothuk and three severely wounded, while only three Beothuk had been killed by settlers. He suggested that Carey had acted in self-defence.[22] Supreme Court records state that Chief Justice R.A. Tucker, in his charge to the jury, observed that "the question for their consideration was whether in their opinion the situation of the prisoner was such that it became *necessary* to his own safety for him to act as he did. If it was, the homicide was excusable. But that at all events the Jury were bound to believe that the prisoner fired at the Indians under the influence of fear and that undoubtedly the same indulgence which the law extends to the passion of *Rape* is at least due to the passion of fear which is in its nature a less criminal one than that of Rape" (emphasis in the original).[23] The jury was to determine whether the prisoner had acted in self-defence or was guilty of manslaughter – the circumstances of the crime ruled out "murder." After a few minutes of deliberation, the jury returned a verdict of "not guilty."[24]

In retrospect, it seems reasonable to say that Carey is unlikely to have stated the facts accurately. There are records indicating that he boasted about the killings, which would have been an unconvincing response to a frightening case of self-defence.[25] Most difficult to explain is why the two Beothuk, a man and a woman, would have advanced on armed whites, brandishing knives. This would surely have been a suicidal act. There is no record that the judge asked to see the alleged knives or that an alternative reason for the Beothuk's approach was suggested. It is at least as likely that the Beothuk were starving (a fact later confirmed by Shanawdithit) and came for help. Howley pointed out that the Beothuk man – Shanawdithit's uncle – was the same man who accompanied Captain Buchan in the 1811 episode described in chapter 10; he may have judged from his experience with Buchan that some of the English were friendly, and he may therefore have hoped for assistance from these two men.[26] In any event, it seems clear from the way the trial was conducted that no one, least of all the judge, was trying particularly hard to obtain a verdict of "guilty." Public opinion at the time appears to have been in favour of the culprits, although a few years later, residents claimed that justice was generally meted out in favour of the Beothuk. In the 1880s, for example, Thomas Peyton was of the opinion that in a trial that took place around 1810, the fishermen accused of having killed the occupants of a canoe would have been hanged had not John Peyton, Jr, and others vouched for their innocence.[27]

THE CAPTURE OF SHANAWDITHIT, HER MOTHER, AND HER SISTER

In April, about three months after they had killed the Beothuk man and his daughter, Carey and Adams captured three Beothuk women. Noting their tracks in the snow, the two men, joined by William Cull and others, had decided to search. About ten kilometres from Carey's house, the party found an old Beothuk woman sheltering in a wigwam; they took her to Cull's house for the night.[28] They had also seen a man leaving the wigwam but were later unable to find any trace of him.[29] When the furriers brought the old woman to John Peyton, Jr, Peyton told them to take her back to Cull's house and to look for other Beothuk. Two weeks later they found in another wigwam two young women who agreed to go with them once they understood that they already had the older woman. The men then brought all three women to John Peyton, Jr, at Exploits Island.

Shanawdithit's story of the circumstances concurs. Starving, she had gone with her mother and sister (and apparently others) to the coast at Badger Bay to search for mussels (see sketch 4, Fig. 14.1).[30] When the furriers accidentally met them, the women had allowed themselves to be taken. It was Shanawdithit's father who had slipped away just before the furriers took her mother from the mamateek. While crossing a creek he had broken through the ice and drowned. One or two others escaped to the interior.[31] On another occasion, Shanawdithit said that her father and another person died early in 1823 and that the three women went to Badger Bay in consequence of his death.[32]

There is another version that connects the two other women to Shanawdithit's lover (discussed in the next chapter), who died in or after 1818: "She and her lover's two sisters were left helpless and destitute of food during one of the most severe winters remembered. All the inland waters and the bays were frozen up; the snow lay several feet deep on the ground. Impelled by hunger, they ventured to the coast, and were, as has been stated, captured. The other women died soon after."[33] But the claim that the two other women were her lover's sisters has not been substantiated; presumably, when Cormack took down this information, he misunderstood what Shanawdithit was trying to convey.

Peyton, Jr, took the three women to St John's, intending to place them under the charge of Governor Hamilton. They arrived there on 18 June 1823. Since Hamilton had not yet returned from England, Peyton informed Capt. David Buchan, who was acting on the governor's behalf, that one of the women was "far gone in a consumption" and required medical aid; the health of the other two had been precarious ever since they had come to stay with him.[34] Buchan instructed the high sheriff, John Bland, to look after the women's needs and asked Mr Watt, surgeon of *HMS Grasshopper*, to attend to their health.

Two Methodist ministers, the Reverends Mr Wilson and Mr Ellis, visited the three women. They were housed in the courthouse in a comfortable room with beds but preferred to sleep on their "deer skins" in a corner.[35] In his diary entry for 23 June 1823, Wilson described the old woman, who seemed to him to be in good health, as "morose, [having] the look and action of a savage. She would sit all day on the floor with a deer-skin shawl on, and looked with dread or hatred upon every one that entered the court-house."[36] In a letter to the Methodist Missionary Society, he withheld these impressions and claimed that he "could see nothing savage or barbarous either in the women's manners or in their countenance. The old woman appeared to have passed through much trouble."[37] Captain Buchan estimated that she was about forty-three years old, though she bore "all the marks of premature old age."[38] One of the daughters, about twenty-four years old, was ill with an "affection of the lungs" that Buchan believed would soon cause her death. The doctor recommended that she be bled and demonstrated the procedure on another person, but when he brought the lancet close to the girl's arm, both she and her companions became so furious that he had to abandon the idea.[39]

The youngest of the three, Shanawdithit, was thought to be about twenty, perhaps twenty-three. Buchan described her as being "of a very lively disposition and quick apprehension."[40] When first taken she was covered with red ochre and grease, which the women who took care of her had quite a job washing off.[41] In the Reverend Mr Wilson's opinion she was in good health: "Her complexion was swarthy, not unlike the Micmacs; her features were handsome; she was a tall fine figure and stood nearly six feet high, and such a beautiful set of teeth, I do not know that I ever saw in a human head. She was bland, affable and affectionate."[42] Shanawdithit reacted with curiosity and amusement to the tick of Wilson's watch and grimaced into a looking-glass, but a black pencil and a piece of paper put her into raptures; she drew the shape of a deer perfectly, in one flourish, starting at the tip of the tail. When Wilson left, he shook hands with the three women.[43]

The main purpose of Wilson's visit seems to have been to assess whether the Beothuk could be converted to Christianity. Though he did not describe how he came to this opinion, he concluded that "they have minds capable of ... receiving instruction, and could an intercourse once be opened with this degraded part of our species, and the Gospel be sent amongst them, no doubt but amongst them as well as amongst long neglected and despised Hottentots, many would soon be brought to worship the God that made the world, and to seek salvation through that saviour, who has bought them [by] his blood."[44] That his view was ethnocentric and judgmental would not have occurred to Wilson, in his missionizing zeal.

A day later, Wilson saw the three women in the street. They were dressed in English clothes, but "over their dresses they all had on their, to them, indispensable deer-skin shawls." Shanawdithit, who had torn off the front of her bonnet, had decorated her forehead and arms with tinsel and coloured paper. Having been allowed to choose presents, the women had taken a few trinkets but had largely selected pots, kettles, hatchets, hammers, nails, and other articles of ironmongery. The sick woman, who was hardly able to walk, was determined to have her share of these treasures, a spectacle Wilson found painful to watch. Mr Wheeler, who was later questioned by J.P. Howley, remembered how people everywhere, especially the young ones, stopped to look at the women. When children crowded around them, Shanawdithit pretended to catch some of them, which caused them to scatter in all directions. Shanawdithit reacted with "unbridled laughter," as if their fear pleased her; she was not the least abashed by anything.[45]

Captain Buchan, anxious to return the women to their people without delay, asked John Peyton, Jr – who had offered to bring them to a spot from which they could conveniently rejoin their tribe – to take them back to the Exploits River.[46] The various accounts of subsequent events are all more or less in agreement with each other. According to John Peyton, Jr, he delivered the women to Charles' Brook and gave them a small boat. They appeared perfectly happy to be left there and Shanawdithit indicated that she would look for others of her tribe and bring them back with her.[47] When the women ran out of food, they walked along the bank of the river to the nearest English station, whence they were brought to John Peyton, Jr, on Exploits Island. Peyton had a tilt built for them on the shore of the bay near his own dwelling and supplied them with food. The mother frequently gave the sick girl (called Easter Eve by the settlers) a vapour bath, but her illness grew worse and she soon died.[48] The mother herself died sometime later of consumption.[49] Her name was Doodebewshet, but she was locally known as Betty Decker. She once said that it was she who had severed the heads of the two marines Buchan had left behind as hostages at Red Indian Lake in 1811. Some settlers called her Old Smut because, judging from her countenance, they believed her to be capable of any cruelty and to have been the instigator of every wicked act perpetrated by the Beothuk.[50] After Doodebewshet's death, John Peyton, Jr, took Shanawdithit into his household.[51]

Thomas Peyton, his son, recalled many years later that the elder daughter had died at Charles' Brook. Shanawdithit and her mother had paddled to Lower Sandy Point and told the men at the salmon station that the girl had gone "winum, asleep, dead," whereupon the men had gone to bury the body. The mother died a few days later at Sandy Point. Shanawdithit sewed her body into a blanket before it was buried, after which she was brought to Exploits Island to John Peyton, Jr's house.[52] According to Cormack, as recorded by Howley, the mother and one daughter died within a few days of each other shortly after they had arrived, in their wanderings along the riverbanks, at an English fishing station.[53]

Mr Curtis told Howley some sixty years after the event that, when the women were first taken, Cull brought them for shelter and food to his house, not to his own. Poor weather detained the party for a week at Curtis's house. At that time Mr Curtis was in John Peyton, Jr's employ and lived at "Indian Point." The women could use no salt, very little pork, no sweetening, no butter: in fact they ate very little of anything.[54] According to Curtis, his employer later took the women to St John's on the new schooner *Anne*, which Curtis had just built. After they had been brought back to Exploits Island, they lived "in a hut outside our door" until Peyton gave them their liberty and furnished them with a small flat boat for the summer.[55] The women paddled down Exploits Bay and landed on the western shore of Point of Bay, where the mother died. The daughters wrapped her body in birchbark and buried her. They then went to Lower Sandy Point where the cooper Pike lived. The elder sister died there a week later. Nance (Shanawdithit) paddled in the small boat "back to us" at Exploits Island.[56]

Since these details were related long after the events, it is not surprising that there are discrepancies in the different accounts. However, all versions agree that Shanawdithit was the only survivor and was taken into the household of John Peyton, Jr.

In a letter to the *Evening Telegram*, Amy L. Peyton, author of *River Lords, Father and Son* (the story of the two John Peytons), commented that in the summer of 1823 the younger Peyton, then thirty years old, along with his youthful bride Eleanor, aged seventeen, had accepted Shanawdithit into their household "when no one else would bother."[57] This statement has a ring of truth. There is no indication that anybody other than John Peyton showed an interest in Shanawdithit at that time. After the capture of Demasduit in 1819, Peyton had delivered her to the Church of England minister in Twillingate, John Leigh, who had presumably offered to look after her. But in 1823, Leigh no longer lived in Twillingate and Peyton could not reasonably have asked Leigh's successor, Rev. John Chapman, or any other resident in the area to accept the responsibility of housing the Beothuk captive. Peyton seems not to have approached Governor Hamilton about Shanawdithit's future, perhaps because his relations with the governor had been strained since the death of Nonosabasut and the subsequent trial. Governor Hamilton was evidently quite content to leave Shanawdithit in obscurity, an attitude that Cormack later decried.[58]

However, Peyton's decision to keep Shanawdithit in his home may not have been entirely altruistic. Shanawdithit proved to be an intelligent and capable helper in the Peyton household. She is unlikely to have been a financial burden, since she worked for her keep and would not have received much of a wage. At any rate, in October 1823 Peyton charged the government fifty-one pounds, fifteen shillings, and four pence for board and lodging for "Nancy" from 1 August to 16 October (and for other expenses connected with the three Beothuk women), which he duly received.[59] Peyton may also have felt that he owed a debt to the Beothuk – or he may have wished to prevent Shanawdithit from disclosing his father's murder of a Beothuk woman in 1814–15 (see Shanawdithit's sketch 5, Plate 10.3). Whatever the reasons that kept her with the Peytons, Shanawdithit seemed to be as happy in their household as could have been expected, and the warmth of a family, with children who loved her, perhaps eased her adjustment to life among the English.

John Peyton, Jr, later said that while Shanawdithit lived with them, she "acted as a kind of servant" but did "pretty much as she liked."[60] Mr Curtis confirmed the informal nature of her position and said that she took on the functions of a servant of her own volition. Mr Gill, whose mother had been employed by the Peytons when Shanawdithit lived there, recollected that Shanawdithit was very pert at times and openly defied Mrs Peyton when she was cross with the servants. Shanawdithit would laugh in her face and say, "Well done Misses, I like to hear you jaw, that right", or, "What de matter now Missa Peyton, what you grumble bout."[61]

In the 1880s, the few people who could remember Shanawdithit or had heard about her told Howley that she was tall and had a good figure, though she was inclined to be stout; her hair was jet black; she looked rather like a Micmac, as she was about the same colour and broad featured.[62] Shanawdithit was usually called Nance, or Nancy April, from the month in which she was taken. She was described as a very industrious and intelligent person who performed the usual household work with satisfaction; making the fires, preparing tea, sweeping and scrubbing the floors, washing clothes, cooking and sewing.[63] She was also very gentle and loved children.[64] Her co-workers were impressed by her ability to draw or copy anything and to bite patterns into folded birchbark filaments, creating designs of leaves, flowers, or animals. They also remembered her skill at carving elaborate combs out of caribou horn.[65] Towards men, Shanawdithit was very modest; when someone attempted an unwanted familiarity, she repulsed him so rudely that he would never again approach her.[66] She was said to have indicated that "her tribe was very strict about the moral law and visited severe penalties on any one who transgressed. Burning alive at the stake being the fate of the adulterer, which was witnessed by the whole tribe who danced in a circle around the victim."[67] On one occasion, Shanawdithit showed the greatest partiality to a fisherman who had a bright red beard and hair; she even sat on his knee, much to the confusion of the shy man.[68] Occasionally Shanawdithit fell into a "melancholy mood" and went off into the woods for several days, saying that she was going to talk to her mother and sister, or that "all gone widdun [asleep] Nance go widdun too, no more come Nance, run away." Usually she came back singing and laughing, or talking aloud to herself, claiming that she was speaking to her mother and sister: "Yes they here, me see them and talk to them."[69] Though the young woman was not easily abashed, she was fearful of Micmac. One of them, "Mudty Noel" ("bad Noel Boss"), had once shot at her from across the river when she was washing venison and had wounded her severely in the back and legs. As described earlier, she would act the part, when telling this story, by limping away after being shot at. When Noel Boss, or even his dog, made his appearance, she would run screeching with terror and cling to John Peyton, Jr, for protection. It should be noted here that Shanawdithit had also been shot in her hand and leg by "the English."[70]

Much of what Mr Curtis and Mr Gill recounted was confirmed by Mrs Jure, who had worked for the Peyton family while Shanawdithit was a member of the household.[71] Mrs Jure recalled that Shanawdithit had cherished some fine clothes given her by Captain Buchan; Buchan had brought her a pair of silk stockings and shoes in which she took great pride. Both Mrs Jure and Mr Gill claimed that Shanawdithit was a married woman and had left one or two children behind, but the assertion that Shanawdithit had a family cannot be substantiated.[72] Though Shanawdithit later told Cormack that she had had a "lover" who froze to death when he fell asleep from exhaustion, she did not mention having children of her own, nor did she list children among the occupants of her father's mamateek on Badger Brook, where she lived before her capture.[73]

In 1825, two years after Shanawdithit had joined the Peyton household, Chief Justice R.A. Tucker, who had presided over Carey's trial, informed Governor Cochrane's secretary that a Beothuk woman who might be the only survivor of her tribe was residing with Mr Peyton. Tucker gave a brief account of her capture and of the decline of the tribe, concluding that "whatever curiosity may be felt regarding it [this race] can be gratified by her alone."[74] Cochrane was evidently not interested; a note scribbled on the back of Tucker's letter reads: "Write a letter … that if he could obtain any more definite details it might be worthwhile to send them here but that his present communication was necessarily too vague."[75] Chief Justice Tucker made no further attempt to stimulate Governor Cochrane's interest.

In June 1827, Bishop John Inglis of Nova Scotia came to Newfoundland to visit Anglican communities in St John's and in out-harbours along the coast. He travelled on *HMS Orestes*, stationed in Halifax, under the command of Capt. W.H. Jones.[76] While in St John's Bishop Inglis met William E. Cormack, who talked to him about his search for the aboriginal inhabitants of the island in 1822. Inglis was moved by the story of the Beothuk, who had resisted contact with the English for so long, and he put a journey into Beothuk country on his itinerary for his "personal gratification." In subsequent correspondence with Cormack, he proposed to place any surviving Beothuk under protection near their best hunting grounds and to give them some clothing, food, fishing gear, and arms and ammunition to "enable them to live."[77] After visits to Greenspond, Fogo, and other places, *Orestes* moored at Exploits Island to call on John Peyton, Jr, who later accompanied them on their trip up the Exploits River.[78] Inglis admired the beauty of the river, whose banks were lined with fine stands of trees interspersed with natural meadows. Several places bore traces of Beothuk, who had lived there until four or five years ago; these sites offered a commanding view both up and down the river and were well chosen for securing seals, caribou, salmon, and wild fowl. On their return trip, Peyton showed Inglis the wharf at Sandy Point from which Beothuk had stolen his boat.

Bishop Inglis also met Shanawdithit, who was said to be the last of her race. He kept a diary of his conversations with her and with John Peyton, who told him much of what he had heard from her; a copy of this diary is preserved in the National Archives of Canada. Inglis sent an abbreviated version to the Society for the Propagation of the Gospel, where part of it can still be found in the archives.[79]

Inglis described Shanawdithit as a rather graceful woman, about twenty-three years old, with a mild and pleasing countenance, and a fine disposition. She was fond of Peyton's three young children, who would "leave their mother to go to her."[80] Inglis thought that she looked remarkably well in the clothes given her by Captain Jones. Although he did not explain the purpose of this gift, the captain's log book shows that *HMS Orestes* had moored at Exploits Island the previous year. Since Jones later gave a Beothuk birchbark canoe model, labelled "Made by Shanawdithit," to the Royal Naval College, it is inferred that he had asked Shanawdithit to make the model for him and brought her clothes in return for the favour.[81]

John Peyton told Inglis that the Beothuk believed themselves to be descended from Labrador Indians, that they buried implements with the dead, used incantations, and feared a powerful monster from the sea. Inglis concluded that "of their religion there seems to be little trace."[82] He also recorded several details about the Beothuk's encounter with Buchan's party in 1811, the circumstances in which Shanawdithit and her mother and sister were taken in 1823, and of their enmity with the Micmac.[83]

At church, Shanawdithit's "deportment was serious and becoming." She knelt when others were kneeling, she perfectly understood that the community was engaged in a religious service, and she seemed struck by their solemnity. Inglis regretted that she had not received sufficient instruction to be baptized and confirmed. As Mr Curtis put it, "Peyton's religion was very unobtrusive and he never had prayer in common in his house in which Nance might have joined." Curtis also never saw anything in Shanawdithit's conduct to indicate a belief in God.[84] Inglis realized that taking Shanawdithit for instruction to Halifax was out of the question; should any more of her people be discovered, it was important that she be in Newfoundland. He therefore obtained John Peyton, Jr's promise to instruct her so that she would be ready for confirmation, should Inglis meet her again.[85] It appears that Rev. John Chapman of Twillingate had already attempted to teach Shanawdithit some rudiments of Christian belief. In a letter to the Society for the Propagation of the Gospel written in 1826, he said: "The female I mentioned last autumn is greatly improved in her manners since that time; though the state of her mind does nothing in favour of the scheme of innate ideas: for as to any knowledge or notion of a Supreme Being her mind appears to be almost totally destitute, *even now* though she is by no means of a dull apprehension, but quite the reverse." (emphasis in original).[86] Shanawdithit was presumably unwilling to accept the religious beliefs of her captors. Considering the dramatic events in her life, such as her capture and subsequent subjection to English habits, standards, values, and language, it is surprising that she adjusted as well as she did; one might conclude that her traditional beliefs, which allowed her to communicate with her mother and sister, had encouraged and sustained her during this difficult time and that she was determined to hold on to them.

It is most unfortunate that so little information about Shanawdithit was recorded during her five-year stay with the Peytons, and that no one preserved what she had transmitted to John Peyton, Jr, and his family. According to Amy Peyton, John Peyton "was a learned person for the times, very concise and thorough, with an obsession to jot down every detail." Yet he appears to have written nothing about Shanawdithit or anything she told him, unless such writings were subsequently lost.[87]

THE FOUNDING OF THE BOEOTHICK INSTITUTION

In the summer of 1827, if not earlier, W.E. Cormack decided to make a second attempt at finding remnants of the Beothuk tribe. He toyed with the idea of fitting out a party, to include four native guides and seven hired men, that would be large enough to carry extensive equipment and surround a Beothuk camp.[88] Cormack hoped that government would provide five or six of the men and thought to solicit a letter from Earl Bathurst to Governor Cochrane to promote his undertaking.[89] In the event, he seems to have abandoned this plan, becoming convinced that the governor was interested neither in the Beothuk nor in the extensive but hitherto unused resources of the interior.[90] Since Cormack could not shoulder the expense of a large party (his business faltered within a year), he settled on a plan to take just three native guides. He was convinced that his success in completing his previous walk was in part due to the smallness of his party. Many people together could not have sustained themselves and the chances of casualties occurring would have multiplied. In addition, he judged that the toil and deprivations had been such that "hired men or followers of any class, would not have endured them."[91] Bishop Inglis suggested that Cormack take John Peyton and Shanawdithit along. Peyton was not available, though he hinted that he might accompany Cormack in the following winter (1828–29).[92] Shanawdithit did not go with the party either, possibly because it was impractical, or more likely because she refused. Cormack later said that she "constantly persisted in refusing to accompany any of the expeditions in search of the Boeothics."[93]

It was planned to begin the expedition at the end of September and Cormack made arrangements for John Louis (or Lewis), an intelligent and able Abenaki, to join him at John Peyton's at Exploits.[94] John Louis was quite familiar with Beothuk country; in 1822 he had actually seen a Beothuk party at Red Indian Lake.[95] Cormack gratefully accepted Judge A.W. Des Barres's timely offer to travel with him at the beginning of September to Twillingate, where Des Barres, a senior assistant judge of the Supreme Court and judge of the Northern Circuit Court, was to open the northern circuit.[96] In the course of the trip Des Barres proposed to Cormack that he form a "Boeothick Institution" whose objective would be to open communication with the Beothuk, enlist public support, and raise funds; other benefits such as knowledge about the resources of the country would also accrue.[97] Cormack readily agreed to the proposal. On 2 October 1827, a meeting of interested persons was held at the Twillingate courthouse, with Des Barres in the chair, to found an institution of the kind proposed.[98] Cormack, the founder, outlined the primary objectives thus: "to open a communication with and promoting the civilisation of the Red Indians, and of procuring, if possible, an authentic history of that unhappy race of people, in order that their language, customs and pursuits, might be contrasted with those of other Indians and nations."[99] He anticipated that in the course of the institution's researches, much information about the unknown interior would also be obtained. Cormack continued his address with a brief history of the Beothuk, proposing that their hostile encounters with, and defeat by, Micmac had caused a notable decline in the once numerous and powerful tribe. Moreover:

> European weapons have been directed against them, from every quarter, and in latter times too often at the open breasts and unstrung bows of the unoffending Boeothucks. Sometimes these unsullied people of the chase have been destroyed wantonly, because they have been thought more fleet and more evasive than men ought to be; at other times,

at the sight of them, the terror of the ignorant European has goaded him on to murder the innocent. Civilization might weep. Incessant and ruthless persecution, continued through so many generations, has given these sylvan people an utter distrust and abhorrence at the very signs of civilization.[100]

Cormack announced his intent to make an excursion into Beothuk country to try and "force a friendly interview with some of them before they were entirely annihilated." He believed that it would take many such interviews over a period of several years to reconcile the Beothuk to the approaches of the English. Several people in Newfoundland and in England had already offered their support.

All those present voted for the formation of the Boeothick Institution, which was to be supported by voluntary subscriptions and donations. All officers agreed to do their duties gratuitously.[101] Bishop John Inglis was voted patron, Judge Des Barres vice patron and Cormack president and treasurer.[102] Cormack later mentioned that, for reasons he did not disclose (probably of a political nature), neither the governor nor the chief justice could be named patron or vice patron of the institution.[103] It was reckoned that £250 sterling would be required annually to support its activities.[104]

At the meeting it was unanimously resolved that John Peyton, Jr, should be given thanks for the valuable information he had provided and that Shanawdithit should be "placed under the paternal care of the institution; the expense of her support and education to be provided out of the general funds." John Peyton was not present at the meeting and he later voiced his objection when Shanawdithit was removed from his home.

In keeping with the resolution to publish the proceedings of the Boeothick Institution in the newspapers, a statement was sent to the *Royal Gazette*, which had shown the greatest interest in the institution. Copies were sent to Dr Barrow and to Sir Charles Hamilton and notices went to newspapers in Britain.[105]. Cormack told John Peyton, Jr, about the formation of the institution and Peyton's election as resident agent and corresponding member.[106]

On the day the Boeothick Institution was founded, the grand jury of the Twillingate circuit court stated that steps should be taken to protect the "Red Indians" and prevent a recurrence of the crime and murder that had hitherto been exercised against them.[107]

An institution for the benefit of the aboriginal population was not a new concept. The Citizen's Committee, formed when Demasduit came to St John's, had been intended to serve similar purposes, including the promotion of a more honest appraisal of the Beothuk's situation. Following the lead of an anonymous author who had appealed to the citizen's conscience and feelings in 1819, Patrick Morris, in his 1827 pamphlet "Remarks on the State of the Society, Religion and Morals" in Newfoundland, stated: "The unoffending native Indians were hunted down like wild beasts and had to take refuge in their woods and wilds; where they wisely preferred their own barbarism to the exterminating civilisation that was offered them by their Christian visitors."[108]

CORMACK AND THE BOEOTHICK INSTITUTION CONDUCT SEARCHES

After the formation of the Boeothick Institution Cormack went to Gander Bay to engage James John, an elderly Montagnais, and Morris Lewis, an adventurous young Micmac from Newfoundland, to accompany him and John Louis on his second expedition. He would have liked to take Joseph Sylvester along but was unable to find him.[109] At the end of October, Cormack stayed for a few days with the Peytons on Exploits Island. In planning his route, he had evidently relied on John Peyton, Jr's knowledge of the Beothuk's whereabouts. According to a note he wanted to "Ascertain from Paton [*sic*] and others every point on the course where the Indians have been seen at."[110] However, his host was absent at this time, although he had seen to it that a boat and crew were placed at Cormack's disposal; he may also have sent Cormack information about a suitable route earlier by mail.[111]

Departure was delayed until the end of October, when poor weather conditions prevented the party's sailing directly to Halls Bay as intended. Instead, they entered the country at the mouth of the Exploits River on 31 October 1827 and from there took a northwesterly route to the area inland from New Bay, Badger Bay, and Seal Bay.[112] Their equipment was probably similar to what Cormack had taken on his previous trip and found eminently suitable. This time he reduced the quantity of provisions, expecting that they would subsist largely on caribou and beaver, which they planned to shoot on the way.[113] Cormack also took a Beothuk vocabulary of two to three hundred words; this was probably the Demasduit vocabulary collected by Rev. John Leigh, who had given a copy of it to John Peyton, Jr.[114] Bishop Inglis recorded that the party was equipped with "shields to protect them from arrows" as well as various hieroglyphics and emblems of peace, though Cormack, in his report on the expedition, did not mention such items.[115] After four days of travel, they found a Beothuk settlement at the east end of "Badger Bay Great Lake" (South Twin Lake; see Table 15.1).[116] It was located at the start of a route along a chain of lakes that connected Badger Bay with the Exploits River about thirty miles from its mouth. Another path, going eastward, led to the lakes near New Bay. The settlement consisted of the remains of eight or ten winter mamateeks, each large enough for up to eighteen or twenty people, and each with a small square or oblong storage pit next to it. There were also vestiges of summer mamateeks, a vapour bath, and a canoe rest. Cormack inferred that the Beothuk who had been there had two canoes. Among the articles strewn about on the ground were a fairly new two-and-a-half-metre ochred spearshaft, parts of old canoes, and fragments of skin clothes. Cormack's party moved on to Halls Bay and then to the highlands south of White Bay. By then it was mid-November, the country was covered with snow, and the ponds were frozen. Caribou were migrating from the mountains to the low mossy barrens farther south, and Cormack assumed that the Beothuk would be stationed at caribou routes to provision themselves for winter. For two days the men looked in vain from hilltops for tell-tale smoke from Beothuk camps. They then pressed on to Red Indian Lake, hoping to find Beothuk there. After ten days of strenuous travel they had their first glimpse of the majestic lake, but no canoe disrupted its placid surface; the Beothuk seemed to have deserted it.[117] Cormack's party spent a few days surveying remains of various kinds on the east end of the lake. In several places they saw small clusters of winter and summer mamateeks; they also found a storehouse in ruins, and not far off a building for drying and smoking venison in perfect condition. The wreck of a little-used birchbark canoe about 6.71 metres (twenty-two feet) long had been thrown up among the bushes; Cormack surmised that its occupants might have drowned. It became evident that the Beothuk, who had once been the terror of Europeans and of native people alike, might no longer exist. One night, when they camped on the foundation of an old Beothuk mamateek, two of Cormack's guides became very uneasy, "as if they thought themselves to be usurpers of Red Indian territory."[118]

Searching on the northwestern side of the lake opposite the Exploits River, the party came across Beothuk caribou fences leading to the water. They also discovered a Beothuk cemetery (see List 1A); a burial hut housed the remains of adults and children wrapped in caribou skins, and a pine coffin "containing a skeleton neatly shrouded in muslin." This perplexed them until one of the party realized these were the remains of Demasduit. The remains of a man next to her were assumed to be those of her husband Nonosabasut. Of the variety of articles that had been deposited with the dead, Cormack took away a skilfully made birchbark-canoe replica, the pelisse (dress) of the "chief's infant daughter," two human figurines, a wooden replica of a bird, birchbark dishes and cups, iron pyrites, and the skulls of Nonosabasut and Demasduit. He later donated most of these items to Professor Jameson for the collection of the university museum in Edinburgh.[119] An article attributed to Cormack's friend John McGregor claimed that the male skull "bore the marks of several wounds, one of which had cleaved the lower jaw; it however reconnected in healing; another wound was evidently caused by a shot."[120]

Cormack now pinned his hopes on finding Beothuk on the banks of the Exploits River. While gliding downstream on a succession of rafts, the party passed Beothuk caribou fences from the lake downward on both banks for about forty-nine kilometres. The fences had openings here and there where the animals could approach the river and swim across; the Beothuk used to hide at these openings and shoot at passing animals. But now the fences were decayed. Cormack supposed that "not many years ago there must have been hundreds of Indians to have kept up these fences and pounds. As their numbers were lessened so was their ability to keep them up for the purposes intended; and now the deer pass the whole line unmolested."[121] The party landed at various spots but found no traces of Beothuk that were as recent as those seen at South Twin Lake. The few Beothuk who had survived seemed to have taken refuge in some sequestered spot, probably in the northern part of the island. On 29 November, the party reached the mouth of the Exploits River again after thirty days of strenuous travel, having made a circuit of over three hundred kilometres through Beothuk territory.[122] Cormack called on the Peytons at Sandy Point where they had moved for the winter. He presented such "a gaunt, haggard and worn out appearance from the excessive toil and privation he had undergone" that John Peyton, Jr, failed to recognize him at first.[123] On his return trip to St John's Cormack stayed for a few days with Rev. John Chapman and his wife (Cormack's sister) in Twillingate.[124] In 1829, he published a full report of his expedition through his mentor, Professor Jameson, in the *Edinburgh New Philosophical Journal*.[125] The map showing Cormack's route as printed in McGregor's *British America* (1832) is reproduced in Fig. 13.1. Bonnycastle's map from 1842 marks Cormack's 1827 trek as well as the "former summer residence of Red Indians" inland from Halls Bay and the Bay of Exploits, and "Red Indian hunting grounds and hunting fences" north of the Exploits River (Fig. 13.2).[126]

On 12 January 1828, the members of the Boeothick Institution were summoned for a meeting in St John's, at which W.E. Cormack reported on his recent expedition.[127] He presented the institution with "several ingenious articles, the manufacture of the Boeothicks," that he had brought back and with a Beothuk vocabulary of two to three hundred words – presumably another copy of Demasduit's wordlist. In accordance with the objectives of the institution, Cormack had also collected minerals and gathered information "on the natural condition and production" of Newfoundland's interior. Since he had not been able to contact any Beothuk, Cormack suggested that they employ John Louis, John Stevens, and Peter John (Abenaki and Montagnais) to search through Beothuk country for any remnants of the tribe.[128] The plan was accepted. Having undertaken to lay the proceedings of the institution before the secretary of state for the Colonies (Earl Bathurst), Cormack sailed for Britain two days later.[129]

In February, at a subsequent meeting in the courthouse in St John's, the conditions of employment for the three men, as outlined by Cormack, were adopted: In addition to the sum granted for their services, the men were to be paid a gratuity of one hundred dollars if they discovered the whereabouts of the Beothuk.[130] John Louis, designated chief of the party, was to start the expedition on or before March 10 from Fortune Bay. The men were to proceed to White Bear Bay to consult with the Micmac; from there they would travel overland to St George's Bay, search the country around Grand Lake and to the west of Red Indian Lake, then on to White Bay, whence they would return to the Exploits River and confer with John Peyton for further instructions. The projected route covered more than eight hundred kilometres as the crow flies, not including John Louis's initial trek from St John's to Clode Sound to inform the two other members of the party. It took the men four months to complete the journey.

In the event that they discovered a Beothuk camp, the men were told to exercise great caution and "avoid coming in contact with the Red Indians under any

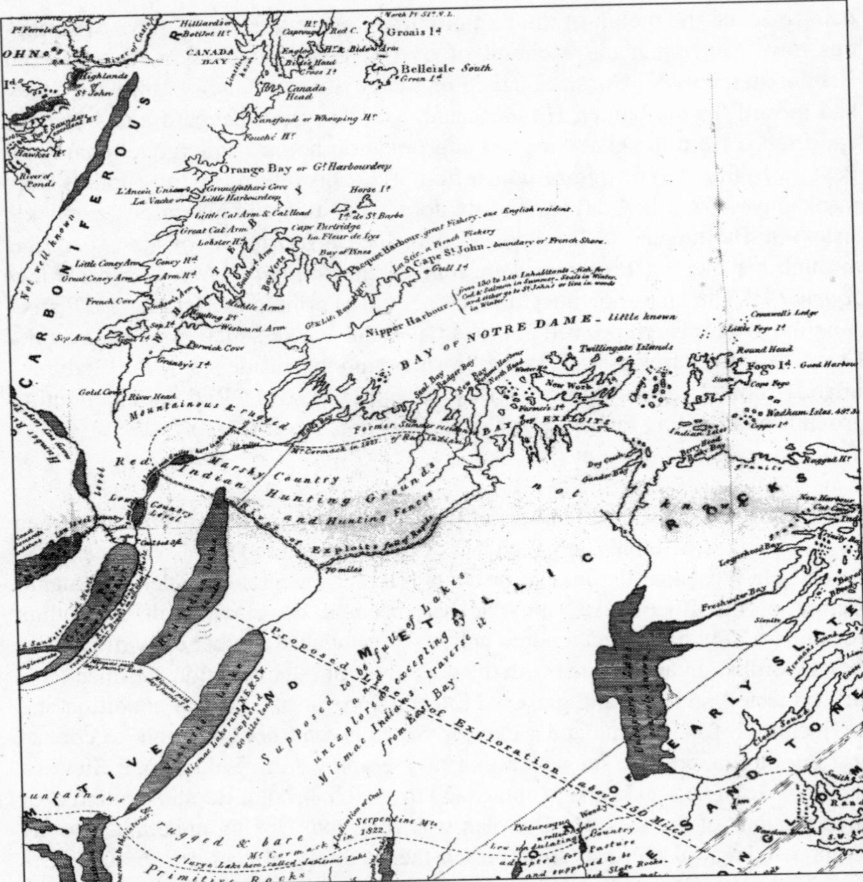

Fig.13.2 Cormack's route in 1827 and "Former Summer residence of Red Indians; Red Indian Hunting Grounds and Hunting Fences." (Bonnycastle 1842,1:Fig.5)

circumstances however favourable they may appear to be." John Louis was to ascertain as correctly as possible the numbers of Beothuk now in existence and the country they occupied and was then to return to St John's so that "another expedition upon a more matured plan and other measures ... may be adopted by the Institution."[131]

The three men were "almost confident" of finding Beothuk; yet their search proved unsuccessful.[132] They had first gone to Bay D'Espoir to collect relevant information from Micmac and from there had followed the prescribed route via Grand Lake to Red Indian Lake. They had then built a canoe and spent a week examining the lake's creeks and coves for recent traces of Beothuk. Finding none, they had paddled down the Exploits River to Mr Peyton's establishment where they had procured passage to St John's, arriving in town on 20 June 1828.[133]

Four days later, at a meeting of the subscribers to the Boeothick Institution at Perkin's Hotel in St John's, Cormack, who had since returned from Britain, announced that the men had failed to find recent signs of Beothuk. As they had not explored the vicinity of White Bay, he suggested that they be employed once more and accompanied by a white settler (in the event, no settler was engaged for the job). The gratuity for the men was raised to $150. Since this part of the coast was largely fished by the French, Cormack thought it would be prudent to send a letter to the French commandant informing him of the purpose of the search party and asking for his assistance.[134] To defray the costs of this new expedition, he also requested further contributions.[135]

John Louis was instructed to proceed with his party on board the schooner *Eclipse* to Croque Harbour, where he was to deliver Cormack's letter to the French commandant. He was to follow the commandant's instructions or, if no information about the Beothuk was forthcoming, to search north and west of Croque Harbour, then traverse the country on an inland route in a southerly direction, and subsequently search around White Bay. From there they were to travel to the house of Mr Peyton at Exploits Island. They were to examine carefully all lakes and rivers *en route*, leaving no part of the country unsearched. John Louis was to make a plan of the areas they had investigated so that Mr Peyton would be able to give the institution his opinion and observations thereon.[136]

The three men set off once more, but again returned without having found any recent signs of Beothuk, though old marks abounded everywhere from White Bay to Notre Dame Bay. The French authorities had not been able to give them any useful information but had been exceedingly helpful in providing men, boats, ammunition, and provisions.[137]

At a meeting of the Boeothick Institution in October, the members were acquainted with the result of the latest expedition, which tended to confirm their fears that the Beothuk, if not totally extinct, were in the process of dying out. If a remnant still existed, it was thought to be so small and to occupy such a limited space that it had been passed by unnoticed.[138] In a letter to John Peyton, Cormack expressed his profound discouragement that the three men had not been able to give him unequivocal testimony as to whether the Beothuk were or were not extinct. Cormack believed some of them might have hidden out on the Baie Verte Peninsula or at a lake inland from Badger Bay.[139] Rumour had it that traces of Beothuk had been seen close to Nipper's Harbour in Green Bay.[140] But the institution was unwilling to employ the men again as they had twice returned without completing the prescribed route. John Louis and John Stevens, aware of public dissatisfaction with their performance, had volunteered to go without pay to Green Bay to put the matter at rest. According to one source, they went to "the Exploits" with a Mr Knight but found that the rumour of Beothuk in Green Bay was unfounded.[141]

Capt. David Buchan later stated that there was hardly a part of the coast of Newfoundland that he had not visited between 1826 and 1829 (at times) in company with Sir Thomas Cochrane.[142] On one occasion they had seen old traces of Beothuk up the Bay of Exploits but nothing that would indicate recent occupation. From the evidence of this trip they had concluded that the Beothuk no longer existed.

Having been confident that the Beothuk could be contacted and saved from extinction, and having spent considerable energy and resources trying to prove this point, Cormack was deeply disappointed to find that his efforts had been in vain. However, as Bishop Inglis and John Stark were to say, he had reason to feel some satisfaction in having done his utmost in the general cause of humanity.[143]

CHAPTER FOURTEEN

Shanawdithit

A PROTÉGÉ OF THE BOEOTHICK INSTITUTION

It was mentioned in the last chapter that the Boeothick Institution, at its founding meeting, had resolved to place Shanawdithit under its care.[1] This resolution, later renewed, was not acted upon until the three native scouts returned from their second unsuccessful search for any remaining Beothuk. It now became evident that Shanawdithit might be the sole survivor. Since she alone could provide the institution with information on the tribe's language and customs, her transfer to St John's became of imminent concern.[2] Although Captain Buchan later claimed that she was transferred to St John's by order of government, the responsibility for bringing her away from the Peytons on Exploits Island rests with the Boeothick Institution, particularly its president, W.E. Cormack.[3] In a letter defending the transfer, Cormack confirmed that John Peyton, Jr's consent had not been sought and that he had not been present when it was first proposed, but: "Besides what took place here last winter on the subject, when you [John Peyton, Jr] were here in summer there was a good deal said about bringing her round to instruct her, and it was intended to mention it to you as a proposition, but it was delayed day after day until you had gone."[4] In September 1828, John Stark and Andrew Pearce sailed to Exploits Island in Pearce's yacht in order to take Shanawdithit to Twillingate and send her from there to St John's. When they arrived, John Peyton was not at home, and although Mrs Peyton was quite willing to let Shanawdithit go, she would not give permission. Presumably, Stark and Pearce convinced her that it was for the good of all concerned to have Shanawdithit transferred and that her husband would not wish to have it otherwise, since three days later Mrs Peyton sent Shanawdithit to Twillingate, where the Reverend John and Mrs Chapman looked after her with great kindness until her passage to St John's was arranged.[5]

Shanawdithit arrived in St John's on 20 September 1828.[6] John Stark urged Cormack in a letter to have her vaccinated immediately by Dr Carson: "Pray let nothing prevent this."[7] He further suggested that she be given new clothes and that a close watch be kept over her by placing her under the care of a moral, steady woman. Stark thought "*no one* should be allowed to see her" without special permission, presumably to spare her the embarrassment of being visited by the merely curious.[8] Attorney General Charles Simms, who had taken a great interest in the Beothuk, could probably advise what else should be done for Shanawdithit's comfort and well-being.[9]

John Peyton, Jr, strongly objected to Shanawdithit's removal from his home in his absence. He immediately asked T.H. Brooking, a member of Governor Cochrane's council and formerly a member of the Citizen's Committee founded to bring Demasduit back to her people, whether "the Judge" (Des Barres?) had directed her transfer, or whether Governor Cochrane had anything to do with it. Brooking assured Peyton that she had been brought to St John's solely under the direction of the Boeothick Institution, and that nothing could be done with respect to any claim Peyton might wish to make against those who removed his charge until he came to St John's.[10] Cormack later wrote: "Most fortunately with the assistance of two gentlemen similarly interested in the subject as myself I obtained the guardianship of the last survivor"; "she belongs to those who are most kindly to her, and now that she is among us here let us forget the past."[11] John Peyton, Jr, never laid charges, but he was annoyed that his authority over what he considered to be "his charge" had been ignored, particularly since he had been an active supporter of the Boeothick Institution.

John Peyton may have grown fond of Shanawdithit; she also had been an industrious and intelligent helper in the Peyton household and the Peyton children had come to love her.[12] However, the Peytons, preoccupied with their business and their growing family, had made little effort to teach Shanawdithit the language skills that would have helped her to gain confidence and interact with others more effectively. Cormack recorded that "on her arrival in St John's she spoke so little English that those only who were accustomed to her gibberish, could understand her."[13] Although Peyton had asked Shanawdithit many questions about her tribe's history and culture and had shown himself to visitors, who recorded their conversations with him, to be knowledgeable in this regard, he seems not to have collected information in a systematic fashion. Neither, apparently, did he record what she told him nor preserve Shanawdithit's drawings.

In contrast, Cormack clearly recognized that Shanawdithit's store of information was invaluable. The focus of his association with her was to teach her English and thereby acquire knowledge about her people. Without Cormack's foresight and determination to salvage what Shanawdithit was able to communicate, a large portion of what we know today about the Beothuk would have been lost. Cormack seems to have expected John Peyton, Jr, to share his views when he wrote to him:

I am certain you would have coincided in opinion with us, in thinking it highly proper, as well as incumbent on the people of Newfoundland, to have her instructed, and I know

> that you would have given every facility in your power, to promote this object, by sending her round now. Your being absent when she came away from the place, was quite an accidental thing, and under the circumstances, you must consider that everything was done for the best, and with the best intentions ... Much is due to you and Mrs Peyton for taking care of this woman as long as you have done.[14]

As for Shanawdithit, no one knows how she felt about the upheaval of a transfer to St John's.

While many government officials and other citizens were willing to do their share, Governor Cochrane withheld his approval from the Boeothick Institution and was not prepared to take any responsibility for Shanawdithit. Cormack became critical of Cochrane's and other governors' attitudes, stating: "It is a melancholy reflection that our Local Government has been such as that under it the extirpation of a whole Tribe of primitive fellow creatures has taken place."[15] He also accused the government in Newfoundland of lacking "moral will" and acting like the strong man who kills the weak instead of measuring his strength against an equal.[16] In his address at the founding of the Boeothick Institution, Cormack asserted that "the British have trespassed in this country and have become a blight and a scourge to a portion of the human race; under their power a defenceless and once independent proud tribe of men have been nearly extirpated from the face of the earth, scarcely causing an enquiry how or why."[17] Blame also lay with the authorities in England. In the 1820s, for example, Earl Bathurst freely admitted that "there was reason to believe that our people had frequently put them [the Red Indians] to death without sufficient provocation, and in some instances I am ashamed to say, they were shot at in mere sport. There was no wonder that they flew from all our approaches."[18] Yet neither the earl nor other officials in the Colonial Office had taken any initiative to stop the atrocities.

SHANAWDITHIT IN ST JOHN'S

Once Shanawdithit had settled in Cormack's house, she was instructed in the English language and soon acquired the skills that allowed her to express herself with reasonable confidence. Cormack supplied her with paper and pencils of various colours and found that she had a talent for drawing. Soon she was able to communicate in broken English, helped by her illustrations.[19] Only a portion of the information Shanawdithit gave to Cormack has been preserved; Cormack never published any of his notes, nor did he complete his history of the Beothuk, of which roughly twenty handwritten pages survive. He appears to have left some of his manuscript material with John McGregor, with whom he stayed after leaving Newfoundland in January 1829. McGregor published the material anonymously in 1836. Other notes have found their way back to Newfoundland, probably through the efforts of the Honourable Joseph Noad, Surveyor General. J.P. Howley, who later had access to this portion of Cormack's papers, included all information that directly concerned the Beothuk in his classic work *The Beothucks or Red Indians*. Other notes expressing Cormack's ideas and attitudes that have not previously been printed are cited in this chapter.

Cormack recorded only a few observations about Shanawdithit. He remarked on her lively disposition and strong sense of gratitude, and on her great affection for her parents and friends.[20] A more extensive description of Shanawdithit is included in the 1836 article attributed to John McGregor:

> Her name in her own language was pronounced Shaa-naan-dithit. She was the last of the Boeothics. Her person, in height above the middle stature, possessed classical regularity of form. Her face bore striking similarity to that of Napoleon, and the olive cast of her complexion added to the resemblance. Her hair was jet black; her finely pencilled brows – her long, darting lashes – her dark, vigilant, and piercing eyes, were all remarkably striking and beautiful. Her teeth were white, even, and perfectly sound. Her hands and feet, small and well formed. She never laughed. Her smile was an exertion to do so, not a feeling[21] …
>
> Her manners were easy and graceful – her temper generally calm; but on occasions, when some of the servants treated her, as she thought, with disrespect, her fierce Indian spirit kindled – the savage eye darted fire and vengeance; and the uniform kindness of Mr Cormack alone would subdue the tempest which raged in the bosom of Shaa-naan-dithit.[22]

Dr William Carson, who cared for Shanawdithit throughout her lengthy illness, characterized her as "a tall, strong, well formed female, about 28 years of age, of amicable disposition tractable, high spirited and proud. She felt most keenly the slightest degradation. My acquaintance with her and the still more interesting female Mary March gave me a high opinion of the disposition and abilities of the Red Indians."[23] Carson also thought that Shanawdithit was "majestic, mild and tractable, but characteristically proud and cautious."[24]

At the time of Shanawdithit's transfer to St John's, Cormack advocated that a likeness of her be made.[25] Whether this was actually done cannot be confirmed unequivocally, though there is circumstantial evidence that at least one of two miniature paintings of a Beothuk woman by the artist William Gosse may portray Shanawdithit (frontspiece and plate 14.1).[26] Gosse came to Newfoundland from England in 1822 to join his uncle's firm, Gosse & Ledgard, in Carbonear and from the 1830s to 1845 worked as a professional artist in St John's.[27] It is possible that he saw Shanawdithit during her residence in St John's in 1828–29; he may even have been asked to sketch her. Considering the great interest in Shanawdithit and the extensive efforts that were made to preserve as much information about the Beothuk as possible, it would be surprising if no one had taken steps to have her portrait painted. In his *Newfoundland in 1842*, Sir Richard Bonnycastle concluded his summary of Shanawdithit's story by saying that he had seen a miniature of her "which without being handsome, shews a pleasing countenance, not unlike in expression to those of the Canadian Tribes round with prominent cheek bones, somewhat sunken eyes, and small nose."[28]

It is evident from a comparison of Lady Hamilton's miniature of Demasduit with Gosse's two watercolours that Gosse had used the Hamilton painting as a template for his two portraits – the clothing and hairstyle are alike, as is the angle of portrayal.[29] The inscription on the back of portrait no. 1 reads: "A female Red Indian of Nfld. 'Mary March,' that was captured in the Month of March 1819. – Painted by W. Gosse at St Johns Nfld. July '41. Fm an original by Lady Hamilton, May 1821 [should be 1819]." The inscription on the back of Plate 14.1 reads: "A female Red Indian named Mary March, painted by W. Gosse, July 1841, from an original by Lady Hamilton, May 1821 [1819]." Though the settings of all three miniatures are alike, Lady Hamilton portrayed Demasduit as a sensitive young woman with a mild and pleasing expression and a spark of liveliness, while the Beothuk woman in Gosse's watercolours is more stolid and slightly older, with broader facial features, her mouth is firmly closed. The penetrating and reproachful look of the woman on the frontispiece is striking; she seems to have internalized the tragedy of her tribe, to be the captive who "never laughed".[30] The Beothuk woman portrayed in Plate 14.1 has fairly bland features and differs from that on the frontispiece. The obvious changes to the facial features in comparison with Lady Hamilton's Mary March show that Gosse did not simply reproduce this miniature, even though the inscriptions on his portraits claim that they were copied from that picture.[31] Since Bonnycastle had seen a portrait of Shanawdithit in or before 1842, the date "July 1841" given for both Gosse miniatures would fit the time frame.

In 1856, the Society for the Propagation of the Gospel in London published what is obviously a reproduction of Gosse's portrait (Plate 14.1) in the *Mission Field*, engraved by W. Dickes (Plate 14.2).[32] It was labelled "Shanawdithit" and accompanied by the text: "Our frontispiece is the portrait of a woman who is believed to have been the last survivor of the Boeothicks, the aboriginal people of Newfoundland."[33] The same issue of the *Mission Field* contains Bishop Inglis's record of his 1827 visit to Exploits Island and his conversation with Shanawdithit.[34] One may speculate whether William Gosse, who returned to England in 1845, provided the Society with the miniature shown in Plate 14.1 and indicated to the publishers of the *Mission Field* that it portrayed Shanawdithit.

SHANAWDITHIT'S STORY OF HER PEOPLE

Topics that were of particular interest to Cormack were the Beothuk's encounters with Englishmen and the decline of the tribe. In response to his questions, Shanawdithit related details of encounters she had witnessed and gave a complete census of the Beothuk population from the time of Captain Buchan's visit to their principal settlement on the northeastern shore of Red Indian Lake in the winter of 1810–11, to the spring of 1823.[35] At that time of Buchan's visit,

Plate 14.1 Miniature portrait no.2 of "A female Red Indian named Mary March painted by W. Gosse, July 1841, from an original by Lady Hamilton" which may portray Shanawdithit. (Collection of the Newfoundland Museum)

(sketch 1, Plate 10.1) the principal camp consisted of three mamateeks. One housed fifteen – four men, five women, three children, and three other children; the second housed twelve – four men, two women, three girls, and three children; the third, with three men, three women, two single women, five children, and two other children, housed a further fifteen, for a total of forty-two. A second camp on the north shore of Red Indian Lake (not seen by Buchan) had two mamateeks, housing thirteen people: three women, four men, and six children. A third camp at the southwestern shore of the lake (also not seen by Buchan) had two mamateeks, one with two men, four women, and three children, the other with three men, three women (one pregnant), and two children, seventeen people altogether. The total population of the three camps was seventy-two.

Plate 14.2 Portrait of "Shanawdithit" in *The Mission Field*, 1856. (By permission of the United Society for the Propagation of the Gospel, London)

The occupants from all three Beothuk camps later came together and wintered over in a sequestered spot at the southeastern end of Red Indian Lake.[36] In the following one or two years, twenty-two members of the tribe died in the Exploits River region, at Red Indian Lake, and in Green Bay, so that "in the second winter afterwards" (probably meaning the winter of 1812–13) only fifty people were left. More died of want and hardship, particularly inland, in subsequent years and some were shot by the English. Then, in 1818, the year before Nonosabasut was killed, Shanawdithit's "brother, mother, sister, and a young child, were shot … when attempting to reach an island, in a canoe, to collect the eggs of wild fowl. Her father, who had been a chief and a swift hunter, died some moons after; and her lover, at a time when they were perishing for want of food, followed a deer for some days over the country, which was covered with snow, and lying down to rest, he fell asleep and was frozen to death."[37] This disturbing story is contained in the 1836 article published anonymously by McGregor. The author of the article interjects here that Shaa-naan-dithit (his unique way of spelling her name) would at that time have been little more than sixteen years of age. As she was said to have been about twenty when she was taken in 1823, she might have been sixteen at the time. Shanawdithit's statement that she was taken by furriers five years later together with her "mother" and her sister while her "father" escaped but drowned could indicate that she may have been adopted into another family after her biological mother and father had died.[38]

According to the notes taken by Cormack, the whole tribe numbered only thirty-one individuals in 1819. They all camped together in three mamateeks on the northwestern shore of Red Indian Lake where Peyton's party found them. One housed thirteen persons (including three married couples), the second housed twelve persons (including three married couples), and the third housed six persons (including one married couple). With the capture of Demasduit and the deaths of Nonosabasut, his brother, and Demasduit's child, the tribe was reduced to twenty-seven people (Shanawdithit's sketch 2, upper half, Plate 10.2, and sketch 3, Plate 12.1).[39]

Shanawdithit's information appears specifically to have concerned the band(s) that wintered on the Exploits River or at Red Indian Lake and resorted to the coast in Notre Dame Bay. There is some evidence that another Beothuk group lived on the Northern Peninsula. Reports by Montagnais hunters, recorded in 1720, mention a Beothuk camp in the vicinity of Hare Bay, and as late as 1800, a hunter from Griguet claimed to have come across a Beothuk family about twenty-four kilometres inland from the coast.[40] Shanawdithit either did not know about this group or was uncertain whether these northern people were still alive; it is also possible that she deliberately omitted any mention of them.

In the winter of 1819–20 Shanawdithit's people (Cormack refers to them as "the whole tribe") camped at "Badger Bay Waters" (the chain of lakes between the Exploits River and Badger Bay.) No deaths occurred during that winter. In the following summer the group split into two parties; one group went to Red Indian Lake; the remaining six men, five women, four boys, and two girls moved to the banks of the Exploits River.[41] In 1822–23, at the onset of winter, the tribe – still numbering twenty-seven persons – camped in four mamateeks at a lake between the Exploits River and Badger Bay (Shanawdithit's sketch 4, Fig. 14.1).[42] Shanawdithit's father's mamateek housed five people: her father, mother, sister, herself, and another person.[43] Shanawdithit's paternal uncle's mamateek housed seven people: her uncle and his daughter and five other persons. All five subsequently died.[44] The third mamateek housed nine people, one of whom subsequently died.[45] The fourth housed six people, two of whom subsequently died.[46]

By April 1823, according to Shanawdithit's sketch 4, the group had moved further down the lake, marked A on the sketch, where they camped in three mamateeks. By that time eight of the twenty-seven people had died.[47] The annotation on the sketch lists the nineteen survivors of the camp at point A as follows: "5 men, 4 women, 1 lad, 2 children = 12." They are identified as Shanawdithit's uncle, his daughter, Shanawdithit's brother and his two children (a girl and a boy), Demasduit's mother and sister (the uncle "was married to one

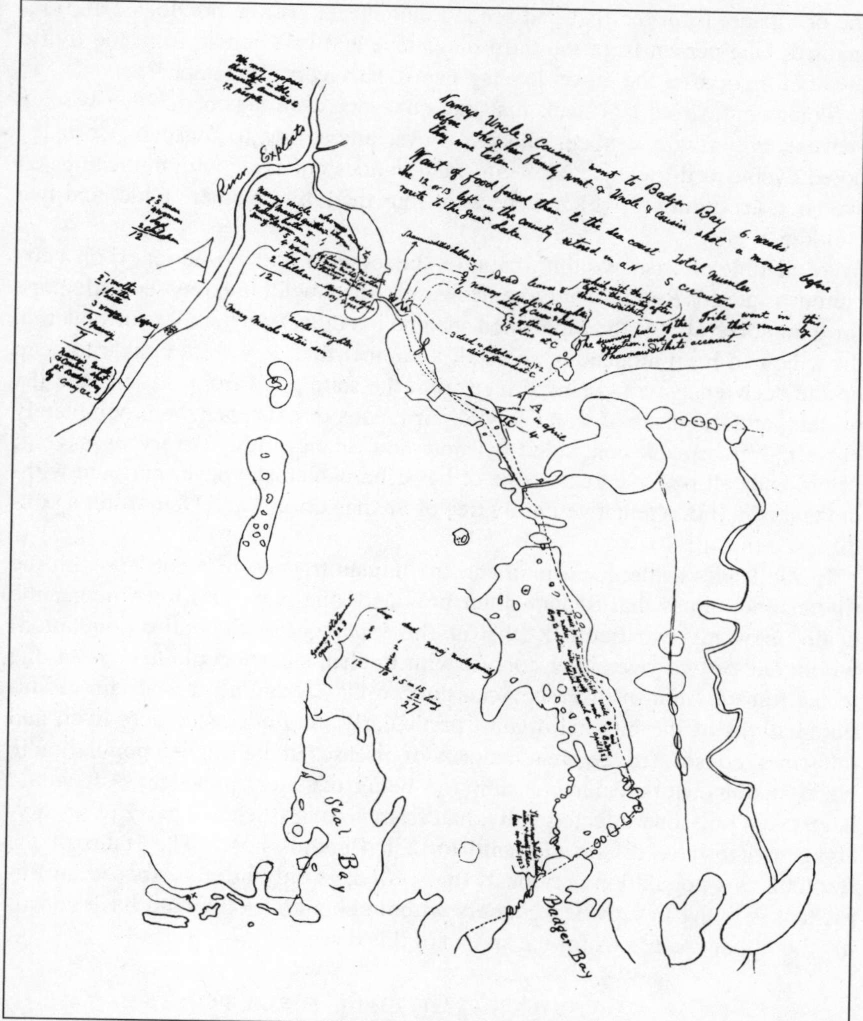

Fig.14.1 Shanawdithit's sketch 4: Beothuk camps on lakes inland from Badger Bay and on the Exploits River, in the winter of 1822–23. (Howley 1915,243)

of them"), Demasduit's sister's son, two of her brothers, one of whom was called Longnon, and Longnon's wife and son. In addition: "1 mother, 1 father, 1 sister, 3 women [whose relationship to the group is not revealed], 1 Nancy = 7."

After the move Shanawdithit's father and another person from his mamateek died, whereupon she and her mother and sister went to the coast in search of mussels; a month earlier, her uncle and his daughter were shot.[48] Thus, none of the occupants from the first and second mamateeks (of the previous camp) remained. One person from the third mamateek and two people from the fourth died before or after the move, leaving twelve survivors altogether.[49]

Shanawdithit told Cormack that the survivors were six men, three women (wives), two single women, and two boys, amounting to thirteen (Cormack noted twelve or thirteen).[50] This information does not agree with the listings on sketch 4, according to which there were four men, five women, a lad, and two children.[51]

At the time of Shanawdithit's capture, the remnant of the tribe set off on a circuitous route for Red Indian Lake. However, Shanawdithit expressed little hope for their survival: "At the time when she and the other two females surrendered, the tribe had been reduced to so small a number that they were unable to keep up the deer-fences; and being driven from the shore, and from the fish and the oysters, and the nests of water-fowl, their means of existence were completely cut off."[52] Cormack concluded his notes on Shanawdithit's story by saying: "Here ends all positive knowledge of her tribe, which she never narrated without tears."[53] (For a tentative family tree of Shanawdithit's and Demasduit's families, see Fig. 14.6.)

If one leaves aside, for a moment, the human tragedy that unfolds with the figures and names that Shanawdithit provided, one may question whether the death of twenty-two Beothuk (that is, thirty percent of the entire population) within one or two years after contact with Buchan's party could have been due to the transmission of disease. According to Dr Carson, acute and chronic inflammations of the internal organs, particularly the lungs, stomach, liver, and intestines, constituted the great majority of diseases in the English population in Newfoundland, tubercular consumption being the most prevalent.[54] It would have taken only one infected individual from among Buchan's party of twenty-eight men to have dispersed bacilli to their Beothuk hosts. The status of the Beothuk as a population previously unexposed, or only briefly exposed, to Europeans – living in crowded quarters without enough food would have constituted optimal conditions for the spread of this disease.

SHANAWDITHIT'S SKETCHES

As mentioned earlier, Cormack kept Shanawdithit supplied with paper and pencils, and she often communicated with him by means of drawings or sketches to which Cormack added explanatory notes. Ten of these sketches are now in the collection of the Newfoundland Museum. Since the originals are faded, J.P. Howley published the hand-drawn copies that are reprinted in this book (with the exception of sketch 6, which is a photograph of the original);[55] added here are two further sketches, one of which has not been published previously.

Sketches 1 to 5, referred to in previous chapters, illustrate encounters between Beothuk and Englishmen. Sketch 1 shows Captain Buchan's visit to the Red Indians in winter 1810–11 when the two marines were killed (Plate 10.1).

The House in St. John's in which Shawnawdithit lived
(Roopes) drawn by herself.

Fig.14.2a Shanawdithit's sketch 10: "The House in St John's in which Shawnawdithit lived (Roopes) drawn by herself." (Howley 1915,249)

Sketch 2 represents two different scenes and times, the taking of Mary March on the north side of Red Indian Lake and Captain Buchan's visit in 1810–11 at the south side of the lake (Plate 10.2; the original has 1815–16, which is crossed out and replaced with 1810–11). In sketch 3, Captain Buchan carries up the body of Mary March in January 1820 (Plate 12.2). Sketch 4, untitled, shows Beothuk camps on lakes inland from Badger Bay and on the Exploits River in the winter of 1822–23 (Fig. 14.1). Sketch 5 illustrates old Mr Peyton's killing of a woman on the Exploits River in 1814–15 (Plate 10.3).

Sketches 6 to 9 mostly represent artifacts that are discussed in Part Two of this book under the appropriate headings (see Figs. 19.1, 20.2, 22.3, 24.1). Two notes on the back of sketch 8 are unexplained. One note that was crossed out reads: "summer dress of woman, summer dress of man, boy, girls." Had Cormack asked Shanawdithit to describe these garments, or draw them, or, maybe to make one as later referred to in a letter?[56] And then, on the back of the same sketch the sentence "Nancy is a bad girl." What would have made Cormack write down this phrase – had Shanawdithit been stubborn or capricious? We will never know.

In combination, these sketches tell us a great deal about historic events as seen through the eyes of Shanawdithit and about some aspects of Beothuk culture. In contrast, sketches 10, 11, and 12 give us glimpses of her experience as a

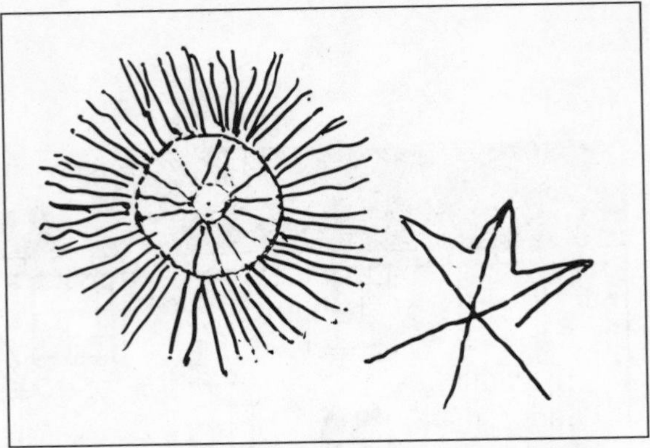

Fig. 14.2b Two small figures on the back of Shanawdithit's sketch 10. (Collection of the Newfoundland Museum)

captive among the English. There is sketch 10: "The House in St John's in which Shawnawdithit lived (Roopes) drawn by herself" (Fig. 14.2a). This appears to have been a house owned by Mr Roopes, perhaps rented by Cormack, with whom she was said to have stayed. The small house drawn underneath may be Cormack's rendition of it, which would indicate that Shanawdithit drew the front and back views of the house next to each other, making it appear twice its size with two chimneys rather than one. On the back of this sketch are two small geometrical figures whose significance is not known (Fig. 14.2b). The two drawings that were not published by Howley are sketches 11 and 12. Sketch 11, untitled, shows the profile of a person (Fig. 14.3). This drawing is filed in the Colonial Office records in the Public Record Office, Kew, UK. It was enclosed in a letter from Capt. David Buchan to R.W. Horton, 24 November 1824.[57] Buchan actually sent "two specimens, the production of the Native Indian Female, that was brought to me at St Johns, in June 1823, and who still continues under the care of Mr Peyton."[58] The second drawing is missing. The profile could be Captain Buchan's mother; Mr Gill told Howley that Buchan once showed Shanawdithit a portrait of his mother "which she copied very accurately."[59] Upton suggested that it was a portrait of Buchan; Fardy thought that it was a self portrait.[60] Sketch 12, also untitled, shows the interior of a room (Fig. 14.4). On the upper margin of the drawing, which is twenty by sixteen centimetres, is the note "In philosophical Journal Apl. 1829," and on the lower margin "1827," both in Cormack's hand. Though the artist is not named, it is assumed that the drawing was made by Shanawdithit.[61]

Stray notes by Cormack, as published by Howley, would indicate that Shanawdithit produced several other drawings that have been lost: "Men singing to Ash-wa-meet, with Eagles feathers and deers ears in cap. Eagle Gob-id-in. Woodpecker Shee-buint. Lump fish Ae-she-meet. Little bird Ob-seet. Black Bird-Woodch. Blunt-nosed fish Mo-co-thut. Profiles of man and woman."[62]

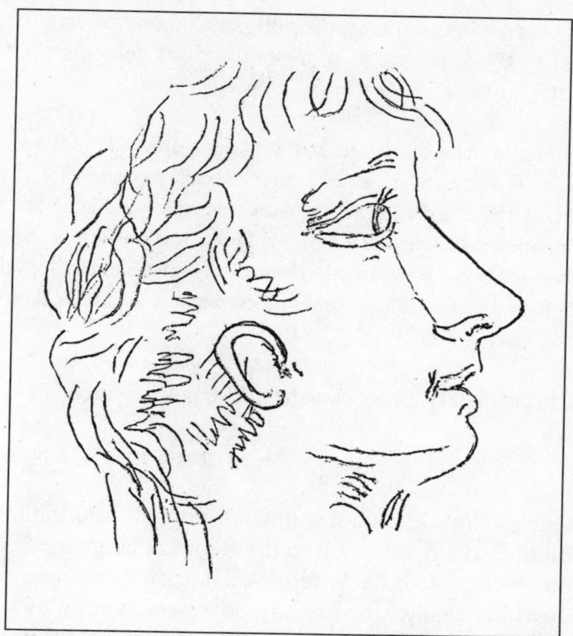

Fig.14.3 Shanawdithit's sketch 11: Profile of a person. (Public Record Office, London, CO 194/68 f.250)

Fig.14.4 Sketch 12: Interior of a room, presumed to have been drawn by Shanawdithit. (By permission of David Howley, St John's)

According to the article published anonymously in 1836, Shanawdithit, when asked by Cormack to represent various subjects relative to the customs of her tribe, always

> preferred the red crayons and with them drew the profiles of various persons of her nation. That they were resemblances seems probable; for if taken from her, and if afterwards requested to draw the same persons, the likenesses exactly resembled those she previously sketched. That of her father was uniformly the same – the features, particularly the nose, were strictly Roman. She also sketched groups, exhibiting the Boeothics in their camps, villages, and in their canoes; also rude sketches of their mode of hunting and snaring deer.[63]

Unfortunately, these sketches have not survived.[64]

INFORMATION ON BEOTHUK CULTURE

One of Cormack's notes reads: "Note all Red Indian words," apparently a reminder to pay attention to the Beothuk language.[65] Several circumstances indicate that Cormack followed up on his intention. As mentioned in the previous chapter, he already possessed a copy of the Demasduit wordlist, to which he added words elicited from Shanawdithit. On 10 January 1829, Cormack sent a Beothuk vocabulary "gathered from a female of that tribe at present residing in my house here" to the Natural History Society in Montreal, after being elected a member.[66] In the 1880s, the linguist Latham uncovered among his papers a copy of the wordlist that Cormack had taken with him to Britain and that had come to Latham in a roundabout way.[67] It concludes with Beothuk terms for "don't be afraid," "not hurt you," and "we come to be friends," which were presumably intended for use in a hoped-for encounter.[68] About 120 terms in this vocabulary are new or diverge notably from those in wordlists obtained from Oubee and Demasduit in 1792 and 1819, bringing the number of known Beothuk terms to 325, along with twenty-one numerals and the names of months. They represent only a rudimentary portion of the Beothuk language as they include few verb forms and lack grammatical and structural information, so that the proposed affiliation of Beothuk with the Algonquian phylum cannot be asserted beyond all doubt.

Shanawdithit also made a full "dress" of her people, which Cormack may have taken to Britain together with the other Beothuk artifacts he had collected.[69] Most of these artifacts, but not the "dress," are now in the National Museums of Scotland, Edinburgh. A painted leather coat, believed to have come from Shanawdithit, that was donated by descendants of the Simms family to the Newfoundland Museum in 1965 would not be of Beothuk origin; experts in the field consider it to be a typical Naskapi man's coat.[70]

Other topics on which Cormack intended to gather information, listed on scraps of paper, were Beothuk traditions about their origin, "great men of character" among their tribe, their mode of counting, how they recorded events, how large the tribe had been in the past, whether they had any exterior form of worship, their government, and what Shanawdithit's people said or thought "of all other men for all were to be enemies to them."[71] To some of these questions we have no answers.[72] But Shanawdithit responded at length to the last query and her story explains why attempts of the whites at making peace were doomed to fail. She revealed that

> from infancy all her nation were taught to cherish animosity and revenge against all other people; that this was enforced by narrating, during the winter evenings, the innumerable wrongs inflicted on the Boeothics by the white men and by the Mik-maks; that a tradition of old times told that the first white men that came over the great lake were from the good spirit, and that those who came next were sent by the bad spirit; and that if the Boeothics made peace and talked with the white men which belonged to the bad spirit, or with the Mic-maks, who also belonged to the bad spirit, that they would not, after they died, go to the happy island, nor hunt, nor fish, nor feast in the country of the good spirit, which was far away, where the sun went down behind the mountains.[73]

Moreover, "it was an invariable religious principle laid down by her people to sacrifice to the *munes* of the victims slain by the whites and Mik-maks any Boeothic who had been in contact with them."[74] This information affords a rare insight into the mechanism of social control that Beothuk elders used to implant aversion to making peace with their enemies. Presumably the threat of death prevented Beothuk from entering into any communication with the English or with the Micmac. It may in part explain why they avoided naval parties as well as Cormack and his native emissaries, and why they disbelieved Captain Buchan's assurances of his good intentions. It would also explain why Shanawdithit had consistently refused to accompany any of the expeditions in search of the remnant of her tribe.

Another paragraph in the article of 1836 informs us that Shanawdithit's "father and her lover and her mother were with the good spirit, and that she would go there too; but that she would not go back to the Red Indian Lake, because she would be killed there, and not be buried with the things she should want for her journey."[75] These disclosures throw a chilling light on the fears that would have weighed heavily on Shanawdithit's mind while among the English. The threat of becoming a sacrifice to the *munes* if a captive was to return to his or her people could explain why Demasduit wanted to retrieve her child but remain with the English. It may also be the reason why the unnamed Beothuk woman who was captured by William Cull in 1803 and taken back by him into the woods to join her tribe returned to the English settlement alone (discussed in chapter 9).

CORMACK'S VIEW OF THE BEOTHUK

In the course of his association with Shanawdithit, Cormack came to believe that the Beothuk were a heroic and self-reliant people, nobler than and superior to any other North American tribe.[76] He also thought that they represented man at a time more remote than any history; their clothing, armour, and present circumstances were probably "similar to what such might have been previous to the discovery of America by Europeans." Indeed, in Cormack's opinion, the Beothuk were a group of people "unknowing and unknown to civilisation … [who] provided information on the development of man from primitive to civilised." At a time when Cormack still hoped that the Beothuk might be conciliated and subsequently recover he wrote: "It would be extremely interesting … to observe their transition from the primitive savage to the first state of civilisation; to observe their mind illuminated at once; the primitive feelings, sentiments, and language at such a period of intellect would be valuable acquisition to know."[77] While Cormack had shown much compassion for the intolerable situation and suffering of the Beothuk, he nevertheless seems to have viewed them as an interesting phenomenon rather than as humans with capabilities very much like his own.

With regard to Shanawdithit and other possible survivors among her people, Cormack wanted

> to continue to hold out the reward for their discovery and friendship of the Red Indians, and to protect and instruct Shanawdithit, the only surviving Boothic [*sic*], and to learn from her all we can that relates to her tribe … The withering survivor of this extirpated tribe who is now amongst us deserves our peculiar care and sympathy. This woman we fear can no longer be viewed as likely to be instrumental in bringing about a reconciliation between her relations and the whites. It is now too late to tell her tribe that they ought not to have been destroyed like wild beasts. She must merely be considered as a prime specimen of a child of nature, deserving the attention and regard of man in his polished state on that account, and entitled to his protection and support, owing to the peculiar circumstances in which he has been the means of placing her. To secure her against being a second time sent into obscurity, depending on the bounty of a few private individuals for her existence, and from which she has been lately dragged. I intend, when in England this winter to introduce her to the notice of some Institutions who can appreciate such a primitive individual for the knowledge to be acquired of human character, moral and physique by studying her.[78]

In the end, however, Cormack's desire to protect the Beothuk and rescue them from extinction went unfulfilled. Nor did he take Shanawdithit to England to be studied by scientists. Shanawdithit's health was rapidly deteriorating, and the Beothuk tribe was "expiring because [they were] unable to resist the destroying inroads of the whites. They have never surrendered to their power, nor solicited their alliance or protection, because they have been taught to expect nothing but death and fatality at their hands."[79] Admitting defeat Cormack noted, "We have exerted ourselves and we can do no more."[80]

SHANAWDITHIT'S DEATH

In early November 1828, after Shanawdithit had stayed for about six weeks in Cormack's house, she may have been transferred to the home of Attorney General Charles Simms, "one of the warmest advocates here for humanity towards her people." This suggestion is based on a letter from Cormack to John Peyton, Jr, dated 28 October 1828, in which Cormack said that Shanawdithit "leaves me next week to live with Mr Simms, the Attorney General, who has undertaken to superintend her instruction."[81] He sent a similar message to Bishop Inglis. Since Cormack was a bachelor, it may have been considered inappropriate to have Shanawdithit stay with him for any length of time; there may also have been financial considerations. Family traditions, related to me by Regina O'Keefe, a descendant of Dr Charles Renouf, support the idea that she was transferred in November 1828.[82]

Other evidence indicates that this transfer did not take place. In his letter to the Natural History Society in Montreal dated 10 January 1829, Cormack mentioned that Shanawdithit was, at that time, residing in his house. John McGregor, who hosted Cormack after he moved to Britain at the end of January 1829, made a similar statement. Shanawdithit's residence with Cormack until his departure in January 1829 is also mentioned in her obituary, published in the *Public Ledger*, St John's, in which the writer states that she had been offered "an asylum ... in the house of James Simms, Esq. ... since the departure of Mr Cormack from this island."[83] Thus, the intended transfer may have been delayed until Cormack left Newfoundland. The discrepancies in the records show how even a simple fact, such as Shanawdithit's domicile between November 1828 and the end of January 1829, can be obsured in contradictions.

When Shanawdithit, her mother, and sister gave themselves up to furriers, all three women were said to have been in a precarious state of health. As described earlier, two of them died within a few weeks from "pulmonary consumption."[84] It is almost certain that Shanawdithit suffered from the same disease when she was taken, but her health deteriorated less rapidly than that of her mother and sister. Though her co-worker in the Peyton household, Mrs Jure, did not mention health problems, she did say that Shanawdithit sometimes became sulky or "too lazy to do anything," which could have been due to emotional stress or to physical weakness.

After Shanawdithit arrived in St John's she was probably vaccinated by Dr Carson, as so urgently requested by John Stark, and Dr Carson is likely to have examined her for any signs of ill health at the same time, though we have no record of it. A paragraph in the 1836 article referring to Shanawdithit's ordeal prior to her capture states: "Impelled by hunger, [she and two other women] ventured to the coast, and were, as has been stated, captured. The other

Fig.14.5a Braid of Shanawdithit's hair. (By permission of Regina O'Keefe, Manuels)

women died soon after. She, although her youth adapted her more readily to a new mode of living, was never after in good health; and, as she grew up, her predisposition to consumption – a disease common, it appears, to her tribe – was apparently sapping her vitals."[85] Elsewhere the author writes that Shanawdithit "from the first exhibited a predisposition to pulmonary disease: yet her appetite was sharp and she ate more food than most European women."[86] Cormack, when referring to her health, said, "Shanawdithit lived nearly nine months under the protection of the Institution, during a considerable portion of which time she was unwell."[87]

As Cormack realized that his days in Newfoundland were numbered, he asked Bishop Inglis to keep an eye on Shanawdithit to prevent her from "sinking into abject dependance … on the mercy of the Local Government." Inglis promised to enquire for her and to contribute to her welfare.[88] In January 1829, Cormack became insolvent, and he left Newfoundland at the end of the month.[89] If Shanawdithit had not earlier been transferred to the home of Attorney General Charles Simms, she would have joined his household at this time, presumably appreciating the company of a large household; before she came to St John's to stay with Cormack, her one question had been whether he had any family.[90]

According to Surveyor General Noad's lecture (1852) Shanawdithit had presented Cormack with a braid of her hair and two stones, "a rounded piece of granite and a piece of quartz."[91] When Cormack left for Britain the stones and

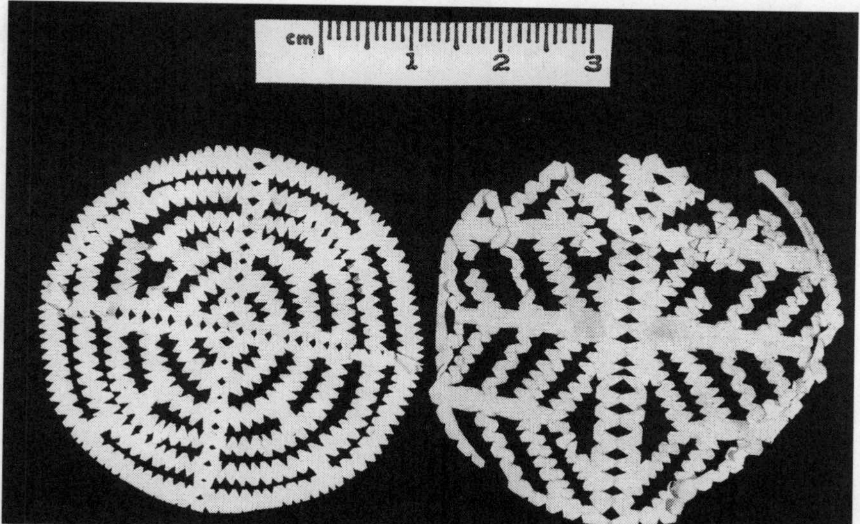

Fig.14.5b Paper cuttings (watch glasses) made by Shanawdithit. (By permission of Regina O'Keefe, Manuels)

the hair were placed in the Museum of the Mechanic's Institution; they are now lost. In 1876 T.G.B. Lloyd noted that he too owned a lock of Shanawdithit's hair, and another braid and two delicate paper cuttings (watch glasses) have been handed down in the Renouf family (Figs. 14.5a and 14.5b). They are now in the possession of Regina O'Keefe.[92]

For many months it was hoped that careful attention to Shanawdithit's needs under Dr Carson's able supervision would bring about an improvement in her health. However, after a lengthy struggle her disease worsened, and her strength rapidly declined. Eventually it was considered necessary to send her to the hospital, where she died on 6 June 1829 of the same consumptive disease that had killed all four women who had fallen into the hands of the English since 1819.[93] An obituary published in the *Public Ledger* closed with this statement: "With Shananditḣit has probably expired nearly the last of the native Indians of the island; indeed, it is considered doubtful by some whether any of them now survive. It is certainly a matter of regret, that those individuals who have interested themselves most to support the cause of science and humanity, by the civilisation of these Indians, should have their labours and hopes so unfortunately and suddenly terminated."[94]

W.E. Cormack's obituary for the *London Times*, published 14 September 1829, was largely a requiem on the disappearance of the Beothuk tribe.

This interesting female lived six years a captive amongst the English, and when taken notice of latterly exhibited extraordinary strong natural talents. She was niece to Mary

Plate 14.3 Monument on the south side of St John's Harbour in memory of Shanawdithit's grave.

March's husband, a chief of the tribe, who was accidentally killed in 1819 at the Red Indian Lake in the interior while endeavouring to rescue his wife from the party of English who took her, the view being to open a friendly intercourse with the tribe.

This tribe, the Aborigines of Newfoundland, presents an anomaly in the history of man. Excepting a few families of them, soon after the discovery of America, they never held intercourse with the Europeans, by whom they have ever since been surrounded, nor with the other tribes of Indians, since the introduction of fire arms amongst them …

There has been a primitive nation, once claiming rank as a portion of the human race, who have lived, flourished, and become extinct in their own orbit. They have been dislodged, and disappeared from the earth in their native independence in 1829, in as primitive a condition as they were before the discovery of the New World, and that too on the nearest point of America to England, in one of our oldest and most important Colonies.[95]

Dr Carson performed a post-mortem examination on Shanawdithit and found that her skull exhibited certain peculiarities.[96] He presented the skull to the Royal College of Physicians in London for further study.[97] In 1938 it was transferred to the Royal College of Surgeons and was subsequently destroyed by a bomb during World War II.[98]

Shanawdithit was buried in the old graveyard on the south side of St John's harbour, as recorded in the Church of England Cathedral Parish Register of St John's: "1829. Buried, June 8th. Nancy Shanawdithe[?] aet. [age] 23, South Side (very probably the last of the aborigines), F. Carrington, Rector."[99] In 1903 the old South Side graveyard was dismantled to make room for the railway, and today a plain stone cairn with a plaque reminds us of Shanawdithit's grave (Plate 14.3).[100] The text reads: "This monument marks the site of the Parish Church of St Mary The Virgin during the period 1859–1963. Fishermen and sailors from many ports found a spiritual haven within its hallowed walls. Near this spot is the burying Place of Nancy Shanawdithit, very probably the last of the Beothics who died on June 6th 1829." Cormack said she was in her twenty-ninth year.[101]

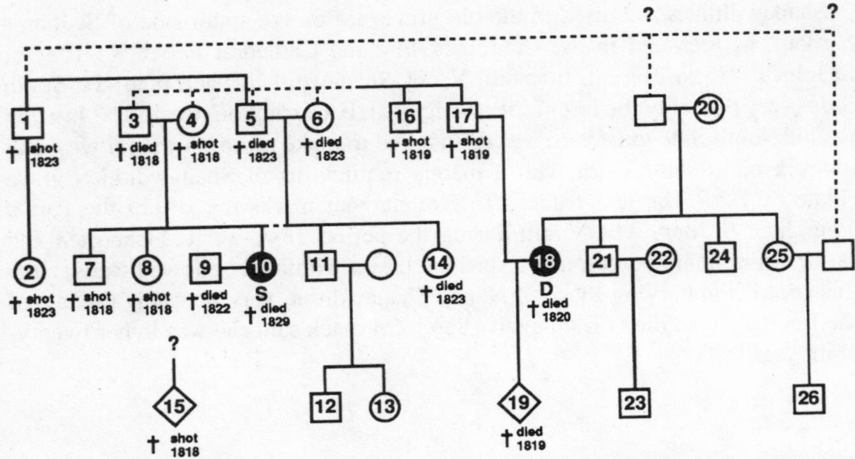

Fig.14.6 Tentative family tree for Shanawdithit **(S)** and Demasduit **(D)** and key. The family tree as presented here is probably not correct in all details because the available information is inconsistent and incomplete. It is nevertheless included to give a general idea of the identity of Beothuk survivors in 1823.

Problem areas are as follows:

a) Shanawdithit's biological father and mother died in 1818 and she was subsequently adopted (?) by another couple, presumably related to one of her biological parents. Her brother and sister, who were shot in 1818 (together with her mother), are assumed to have been siblings; the sister who was captured together with Shanawdithit and brother Longnon may have been offspring of her adoptive parents.

b) Shanawdithit was niece to Nonosabasut. We have no clue whether he was a maternal or paternal uncle and whether he was related to Shanwdidthit through her biological or her adoptive(?) parents. For this reason, the connecting line between each set of Shanawdithit's parents and Nonosabasut and his brother is a broken one.

c) Shanawdithit's paternal uncle was a brother of her adoptive father. He was married to one of the four women listed on sketch 4 under location A: Demasduit's mother, Demasduit's sister, Longnon's wife, and the uncle's daughter. This note is interpreted to mean that he was married to either of the two former.

1 Shanawdithit's (adoptive?) paternal uncle (brother of no.5) was shot at Badger Bay in the spring of 1823. He was married either to Demasduit's mother (no.20), or to Demasduit's sister (no.25). See note c) above.[1]
2 Shanawdithit's (adoptive?) cousin (daughter of no.1) was shot at Badger Bay in the spring of 1823.[2]
3 Shanawdithit's father died in 1818.[3]
4 Shanawdithit's mother was shot on the way to an island in 1818.[4]
5 Shanawdithit's (adoptive?) father died or drowned when escaping the captors of Doodebewshet in 1823.[5]
6 Shanawdithit's (adoptive?) mother, Doodebewshet, captured in April 1823, died of consumption in 1823.[6]
7 Shanawdithit's brother was shot on the way to an island in 1818.[7]
8 Shanawdithit's sister was shot on the way to an island in 1818.[8]
9 Shanawdithit's lover froze to death in the winter of 1822- 23(?).[9]
10 **Shanawdithit**, born approx. 1800–03, was captured in Badger Bay in the spring of 1823 and died of consumption on 6 June 1829.[10]

11 Shanawdithit's (adoptive?) brother was alive in 1823.[11]
12 Shanawdithit's (adoptive?) brother's son was alive in 1823.[12]
13 Shanawdithit's (adoptive?) brother's daughter was alive in 1823.[13]
14 Shanawdithit's (adoptive?) sister was captured with Shanawdithit in Badger Bay in the spring of 1823; she died of consumption in 1823.[14]
15 Child (possibly related to Shanawdithit's family) was shot on the way to an island in 1818.[15]
16 Nonosabasut's brother was shot at the taking of Demasduit on Red Indian Lake in March 1819.[16]
17 Nonosabasut, a Beothuk chief, husband of Demasduit, was Shanawdithit's uncle; he was shot at the taking of Demasduit on Red Indian Lake in March 1819.[17]
18 **Demasduit**, born approx. 1796–97, was married to Nonosabasut [in 1815?] and had a child in 1819; she was captured on Red Indian Lake in March 1819 and died of consumption onboard *HMS Grasshopper* on 8 January 1820.[18]
19 Infant child of Demasduit and Nonosabasut died two days after Demasduit's capture in March 1819.[19]
20 Demasduit's mother, possibly married to Shanawdithit's (adoptive) paternal uncle (no.1), was alive in 1823.[20]
21 Demasduit's brother Longnon was alive in 1823.[21]
22 Longnon's wife was alive in 1823.[22]
23 Longnon's son was alive in 1823.[23]
24 Demasduit's brother was alive in 1823.[24]
25 Demasduit's sister, possibly married to Shanawdithit's (adoptive?) paternal uncle (no.1), was alive in 1823.[25]
26 Demasduit's sister's son was alive in 1823.[26]

Computer design by Brian Payton, St John's

1 Shanawdithit's sketch 4; Cormack Papers 20/84 (in Howley 1915,224).
2 Shanawdithit's sketch 4; Cormack Papers 20/84 (in Howley 1915,224).
3 "Sketches of savage life," 1836,323.
4 Ibid.
5 Shanawdithit's sketch 4; Cormack Papers 20/84 (in Howley 1915,224, 229); Bishop Inglis, Diary, 2 July 1827, NAC, microfilm 713.
6 Shanawdithit's sketch 4; Cormack Papers 20/84 (in Howley 1915,224); Howley 1915,180; Dr W.Carson, MD, Answers to questions by the Royal College of Physicians of Great Britain, 1830, Governor Cochrane to Viscount Goderich, 7 February 1831, PRO, CO 194/81, f.59a.
7 "Sketches of savage life," 1836,323.
8 Ibid.
9 Ibid.
10 Buchan to Governor Hamilton, 28 June 1823, PRO, CO 194/66, f.66 (in Howley 1915,172); "Sketches of savage life," 1836,323; Wilson to the Methodist Missionary Society, 12 August 1823, MMS: LR, North America, Newfoundland 1823/24, Box 4, file 4f, no.14. Shanawdithit's sketch 4; Cormack Papers 20/84 (in Howley 1915,224); *Public Ledger*, St John's, 12 June 1829, cited in *Conception Bay Mercury*, 19 June 1829,3 (in Howley 1915,231); Carson, 1830, Cochrane to Goderich, 1831, PRO, CO 194/81, f.59a.
11 Shanawdithit's sketch 4.
12 Ibid.
13 Ibid.
14 Ibid.; Cormack Papers 20/84 (in Howley 1915,224); Howley 1915,180, 181; Carson, 1830, Cochrane to Goderich, 1831, PRO, CO 194/81, f.59a.
15 "Sketches of savage life," 1836,323.
16 Cormack Papers 20/84 (in Howley 1915,228).
17 "Sketches of savage life," 1836,323; Cormack's obituary of Shanawdithit, *The London Times*, 14 September 1829, cited in Howley 1915,231; Cormack Papers 20/84 (in Howley 1915,228).
18 Governor Hamilton to Earl Bathurst, 27 September 1819, PRO, CO 194/62, f.61–64 (in Howley 1915,119–20); Robinson 1834,217; Cormack Papers 20/84 (in Howley 1915,227–8); Shanawdithit's sketch 2, upper part; Buchan's report of his second expedition to Governor Hamilton, 10 March 1820, PRO, CO 194/63, f.64–77 (in Howley 1915,121); Carson, 1830, Cochrane to Goderich, 1831, PRO, CO 194/81, f.59a.
19 Shanawdithit's sketch 3; Cormack Papers 20/84 (in Howley 1915,228).
20 Shanawdithit's sketch 4.
21 Ibid.
22 Ibid.
23 Ibid.
24 Ibid.
25 Ibid.
26 Ibid.

CHAPTER FIFTEEN

Epilogue

With the death of Shanawdithit in June 1829, many people believed that the Beothuk were now extinct, but no one knew this for certain. In the 1830s, Governor Henry Prescott (1834–40), after careful investigation and enquiry, officially adopted the opinion that all Beothuk had died.[1] However, since there were, according to Shanawdithit's own testimony, some twelve or thirteen Beothuk survivors from her band at the time of her capture in 1823, it is likely that some of them were still alive after Shanawdithit had died, a notion that is supported in records and folklore memories of sightings and encounters with Beothuk after 1829.

SIGHTINGS IN NEWFOUNDLAND AND LABRADOR

Around 1827, a Beothuk was seen fishing in a river in the interior and four years later, a woman and a man or boy were observed crossing a lake.[2] Frank G. Speck was told in the early 1900s that "many years ago" hunters had seen a canoe with Beothuk on Grand Lake.[3] In September 1834, the *Conception Bay Mercury* and the Carbonear *Star* reported that a party of ten or twelve Beothuk had shot arrows at grasscutters at Western Arm, about twenty-five kilometres from Fogo. The grasscutters retreated and reached their boat without injury. When they returned to the place well armed, they were unable to find their assailants.[4] In 1841, Micmac in the interior had seen "two strange Indians armed with bows and arrows, whom they had no doubt belonged to the Red Men"; on being discovered, these men fled with great rapidity.[5] The Micmac who reported the incident were prepared to swear an affidavit attesting to the truth of their statement. However, in 1845, when Micmac allegations that Red Indians had been seen around Grand Lake came to the notice of Governor John Harvey, Harvey sent the commander of *HMS Hyacinth* to investigate the matter. The commander subsequently reported that local trappers who were familiar with the area had never found any traces of Beothuk; they believed the allegations had been a ruse to keep English trappers away.[6] In 1886, enquiring about Beothuk in Halls and Exploits Bay, J.P. Howley was told that, several years after Shanawdithit's death, Beothuk were killed in White Bay.[7] As late as the 1960s, Charlie Furey from Harbour Main told Cyril Byrne that he had heard that Beothuk had lived in the watershed area of Bay St George in the 1840s and 1850s and were said to have intermarried with the whites.[8]

Other informants claimed that Beothuk had been seen on the Northern Peninsula. A settler from Griguet, south of Quirpon, told George Webber that, around 1800, he had unexpectedly met a Beothuk family about twenty-four kilometres from the coast.[9] John Stevens, who had been employed by Cormack to search for Beothuk in 1828, later told Mr Peyton that signs of the Red Indians had been observed near Quirpon around 1838.[10] In the 1960s, George Decker, who assisted the Ingstads in their discovery of the Norse site at L'Anse aux Meadows, said that in his great-grandfather's day (presumably in the 1820s and later), Beothuk were living near L'Anse aux Meadows, and that this area had been "their last refuge."[11]

There were also rumours and tales that Beothuk had crossed the Strait of Belle Isle and lived in Labrador, sometimes causing problems. Although it is possible that there is a grain of truth in these tales of sightings and strange Indians, they cannot be considered reliable sources. In the early 1850s, Micmac told Surveyor General Joseph Noad that the whole tribe had crossed over to Labrador some twenty-five years before (ca. 1827).[12] Lieut. Col. Richard H. Bonnycastle recorded that in the summer of 1831, people who were employed in the Labrador salmon fishery were frightened by the sudden appearance of a fierce-looking group of natives in the Bay of Seven Islands; these strangers were totally different from the "warlike Mountaineer" of the interior. Seeing three ships of war riding in the bay – carrying the visiting governor general and his entourage, including Bonnycastle – the strangers became alarmed and disappeared as suddenly as they had come. Bonnycastle assumed that these mysterious natives had been Beothuk.[13] In the fall of 1873, the geologist T.G.B. Lloyd was informed by inhabitants of Battle Harbour, Labrador, that about half a century earlier a tribe of Red Indians had been living near this community, opposite Belle Isle. They were said to have been a source of trouble to the fishermen and, on one occasion, to have killed two white children and stuck their heads on poles.[14] In the late 1800s, Mr Watts from Carbonear learned from a "reliable source" that hunters near Forteau, Labrador, had come upon a camp of natives who fled as soon as the hunters showed themselves, leaving their equipment behind.[15] The hunters believed these natives to have been Beothuk. Other men from Carbonear who used to fish in the Strait of Belle Isle had heard from Naskapi in Labrador of a strange race of big men who were seen on several occasions.[16]

Surveyor J.B. Jukes, who collected information about the Beothuk in 1838–40, came to believe that remnants of the tribe had integrated into Montagnais bands in Labrador.[17] But the idea has not been corroborated. While Frank G.

Speck found that Penobscot, Maliseet, and Micmac from the western end of the St Lawrence had incorporated knowledge of the Beothuk into their oral traditions, he was unable to obtain any equivalent information from the Montagnais; Speck concluded that the Beothuk had little or no impact on them.[18] He later recorded possible evidence for a link between Beothuk and the St Augustin Montagnais band on the Lower North Shore that must, however, be regarded as tenuous.[19]

When Speck asked Santu, the descendant of a Beothuk/Micmac union, about the possible fate of Beothuk survivors, she claimed that relations between Beothuk and Inuit as well as Labrador Indians had been friendly, and that some Beothuk were said to have joined "them" (Inuit or Innu?). She recalled that a paternal uncle or great-uncle (a Beothuk?) once returned from Greenland, where he had intermarried with Inuit.[20] Since Santu was suffering from increasing senility, her recollections of friendly relations with Inuit may have pertained to Micmac rather than Beothuk; for example, Nancy Jeddore's Micmac father, born in 1777, spent many years among Inuit.[21]

The scattered information concerning the whereabouts of Beothuk survivors, though largely unauthenticated, nevertheless suggests that some of them continued to exist out of sight of the English. One may speculate that the families from the Exploits River band who, in 1823, left the camp at Crooked Lake in the direction of Red Indian Lake may have remained secluded at Newfoundland's interior lakes for some years.[22] Survivors from a group near L'Anse aux Meadows on the Northern Peninsula, if such a group existed, may eventually have crossed over to Labrador. Whether these survivors remained independent or amalgamated with Montagnais/Naskapi (or Inuit) cannot be said.

NEWFOUNDLANDERS AND BRITONS BEGIN TO ACKNOWLEDGE RESPONSIBILITY

From the time of John Guy and Henry Crout onwards, there were people among settlers and, later, naval officers, St John's citizens, and visitors to the island who empathized with Newfoundland's native population. As conflicts and violence increased, some of these people spoke out against the deteriorating situation, for example Lieut. John Cartwright in 1768 and his brother George in 1784, Lieut. G.C. Pulling in 1792, and Magistrate John Bland in the 1790s. It has been seen that several Newfoundland governors tried to improve the conditions of the Beothuk. Finally, citizens' groups such as the Citizens Committee and the Boeothick Institution were formed to take positive steps towards making peace with them. None of them were successful.

After Shanawdithit's death, which was believed to mark the demise of the tribe, many people belatedly realized that the Beothuk had become extinct through neglect and open hostility in which the English had played an ignominious role. An article published in the St John's *Royal Gazette* in September

1832 argued that the Beothuk had been dispossessed of their land and resources unlawfully and without regard to their rights or their ability to survive.[23] In the author's view, the fate of the Beothuk was a distressing and perplexing page in Newfoundland's history and the circumstances of their demise "revolting to our humanity [and] repulsive from the dishonour which countrymen of our own who profess to civilization and Christian truth" have brought upon their compatriots. In addition to dispossessing the Beothuk of their land, the Beothuk's neighbours, settlers and other native peoples alike, "all acted in a spirit of lawless spoliation" and hunted the Beothuk like wild beasts, often just because they had stolen nets or iron tools or taken revenge for wrongs they had suffered. With eloquence and conviction, the author developed the argument that, under the circumstances, the Beothuk had a right to steal and should not be judged by "our domestic morality," since they were clearly "in a belligerent state" with the usurpers of their land, although war had not been openly proclaimed. If the Beothuk had taken revenge for ill treatment, it should be remembered that in the morality of a native person, "revenge is good, unconditionally"; it is a sacred duty to avenge an injury, and doing so is sanctioned through ancestral practice. In the case of the Beothuk, reciprocal outrage and injustice came to form the links of an unbroken chain, and "through a space of nearly three centuries, the hand of these poor Boeothics has been against every man, and every man's hand against him."[24]

The fact that such penetrating and insightful thoughts about native rights and ethics, coupled with a strong condemnation of the behaviour of the English towards the Beothuk, were published in St John's within three years of Shanawdithit's death shows that people in Newfoundland had become more self-critical and were beginning to question the circumstances under which the Beothuk had perished.

Britain's attempt at reappraisal and self-reproach took the form of the 1836 parliamentary inquiry referred to earlier into the impact of British settlement on the native populations of Africa, Australia, and the Americas. Of the North American colonies, Newfoundland was the first to be investigated. Capt. David Buchan, called as witness, testified to the persecutions of Beothuk by settlers and to the failure of most Newfoundland governors, as well as authorities in Britain, to intervene.[25] He confirmed that the effect of the "visitation of civilised and christian men" in Newfoundland had been the destruction of its native population. With regard to contacting the Beothuk, Buchan reported on his belated and unsuccessful attempts at making peace with them and concluded that "there appears to have been always a fatality in every thing that was undertaken."

The report that was subsequently issued by the Select Committee notes that the native population in Newfoundland had once been numerous and resorted to every part of the coast until the arrival of the English:

> We occupied the stations where they used to hunt and fish thus reducing them to want, while we took no trouble to indemnify them so that doubtless many of them perished by

famine; we also treated them with hostility and cruelty and many were slain by our own people as well as by the Micmac Indians who were allowed to harass them.

Under our treatment they continued rapidly to diminish … In the colony of Newfoundland it may therefore be stated that we have exterminated the natives.[26]

The proceedings, however, served only as a painful reminder of the neglect and ill will that had influenced most decisions concerning the Beothuk; by 1836 there was nothing to be done.

While British officials laid the matter aside, responsibility for the disappearance of the Beothuk has come to rest heavily on the shoulders of Newfoundlanders. Initial reassessment of their past role in the demise of the tribe has led to a continuing search for facts, reappraisal of events, and feelings of guilt and remorse among an increasing segment of the population. These feelings have yet to be resolved.

Table 15.1
Beothuk Sites or Encounters Recorded in Documents

The location of recorded campsites and places of encounter are listed by area chronologically so as to facilitate an overview of regional distribution in time.

Recorded sites that have been excavated are included in Table 16.1. In some cases it has not been possible to correlate the recorded sites with excavated ones, particularly those on the Exploits River and at Red Indian Lake; hence there may be an occasional overlap.

Date	*Location*	*Type of Site or Encount.*	*Informant/Reference*
AREA I: SOUTHCOAST INCLUDING PLACENTIA BAY			
1594	"Pesmarck," (Presque?)	Indians cut mooring ropes of boats	Crew of "Grace" (Quinn 1979,4:64)
1612	passage hrb. (come by chance)	wigwams, fishg. gear	guy and crout (cell 1982,72, 84)
AREA 2: CONCEPTION AND TRINITY BAY			
1612	savage hrb. (dildo south) path to dildo pond	wigwams, artifacts	guy and crout (ibid., 70, 83)
1612	Dildo Pond and Isld.	3 wigwams, 1 square house, manned canoe	Guy and Crout (Ibid.)
1612	Stock Cove	9 wigwams	Guy (Ibid. 72)
1612	Truce Sound (Sunnyside?)	8–9 wigwams, canoe, 8 men in 2 canoes	Guy and Crout (Ibid., 72, 84)
1613	Small (Hopeall?) Isld.	1 wigwam	Crout (MMss. Mix 1/24)
1620	nr. Heart's Ease	3 wigwams, 3 canoes, provisions	Whitbourne (Cell 1982:193)
1775	Lower Lance Cove	campsite	J.Tilley (Howley 1915:269)
AREA 4: NOTRE DAME BAY EAST, STRAIGHT SHORE, ATLANTIC ISLDS.			
1770	Isld. nr. Solid Isld. Dildo Run	2 wigwams, 2 canoes	G.Cartwright 1792,1:17 (in Howley 1915:46, 47)
1770	Small Isld. east of Coal All	1 wigwam	Ibid., 4 (in Howley 1915,49)
1787	Shoal Bay, Fogo Isld.	a group of Beothuk	Pulling (Marshall 1989:121)
1792	Ragged Hrb. coast	4 manned canoes	Pulling (Ibid., 122)
1792	Ragged Hrb. Pond	1 wigwam	Pulling (Ibid.)
1792	Wadham Islds.	2 canoes	Pulling (Ibid., 120)
1792	Gannet Rocks	2 canoes	Pulling (Ibid.)
1766	Funk Isld.	canoes	Banks (Lysaght 1971,133)
1770		dto.	G.Cartwright 1792,1:10 (in Howley 1915,56)
1792		dto.	Pulling (Marshall 1989, 120–1, 128)
1817?	Cat Harbour (North Lumsden)	12 wigwams	Wiltshear (Tocque 1846, 285 in Howley 1915,276)

Table 15.1 *(cont'd)*
Beothuk Sites or Encounters Recorded in Documents

Date	Location	Type of Site or Encount.	Informant/Reference
AREA 5: BAY OF EXPLOITS			
1792	Indian Cove,	3 wigwams, (previously there were 7 or 8)	Pulling (Marshall 1989,128)
1768	Charles Brook	2+ wigwams	J.Cartwright's map (Fig.6.2)
1791	Charles Brook Pond	1 wigwam	Pulling (Marshall 1989,128)
1819	same location	old wigwams	Glascock (in Howley 1915,115)
AREA 6: EXPLOITS RIVER			
1768	Betw. Grt. Rattl. Brook & Stony Brook, SE bank	caribou fences	J.Cartwright's map (Fig.6.2)
1768	Betw. Bishop Falls & Grand Falls, NW bank	3 clusters of 2 wigwams, 3 single wigwams, 1 camp with 3 wigwams	Ibid.
1768	Same stretch of river, SE bank	2 clusters of 2 wigwams, 3 single wigwams	Ibid.
1768	At Grand Falls NW bank	3 clusters of 2 wigwams, caribou fences, sewels, gaze, path, drying rack, raft	Ibid., J. Cartwright's report (in Howley 1915, 42–3)
1811	East of Grand Falls, NW bank	2 wigwams	Buchan's report, 1811 (in Howley 1915,73)
1811	At Grand Falls, NW bank	path	Ibid.
1768	Betw. Grand Falls & Badger Brook, NW bank	2 single wigwams, 5 clusters of 2 wigwams, 3 clusters of 3 wigwams, 1 camp with 4 wigwams, caribou fences	J.Cartwright's map (Fig.6.2)
1768	Same stretch of river, SE bank	4 single wigwams, 4 clusters of 2 wigwams, 1 camp with 3 wigwams, 1 camp with 4 wigwams	Ibid.
1768	At Badger Br. both river banks	extensive caribou fences upriver and downriver	Ibid.
1814/15	Rushy Pond	1 mamateek (?)	Shanawd. sketch 5, (Plate 10.3)
1811	Rushy Pond Marsh, NW bank	caribou fences and sewels	Buchan's report, 1811 (in Howley 1915,74)
1871	Opp. Quesawetquek Brook (Joe Brook?), NW bank	wigwam pits	Howley Papers, CNS Archive, Box 4, file 280
1781	3 days travel up the Exploits River, ca. 60 miles from Sandy Point	several wigwams	Pulling (Marshall 1989,135)

Table 15.1 *(cont'd)*
Beothuk Sites or Encounters Recorded in Documents

Date	*Location*	*Type of Site or Encount.*	*Informant/Reference*
1820	Badger Brook	2 wigwams	Buchan's map, 1820 (Fig.12.1)
1811	Isld. 3 km upriver fr. Badger Brook, NW bank	old wigwam, caribou fence across the isld. and several km upriver on either bank	Buchan's report, 1811 (in Howley 1915,75)
1811	Upriver fr. rapids (Red Indian Falls) NW & SE banks	several km of caribou fences	Ibid.
1811	3 km upriver fr. rapids (Red Ind. Falls), SE bank	1 storehouse carcasses left nearby	Buchan's report, 1811 (in Howley 1915, 75, 82)
1820	same area	1 lg. storehouse several wigwams, 2 rafts	Buchan's report, 1820 (in Howley 1915, 123–4)
1811	Isld. ca. 6 km upriver fr. above	1 storehouse	Buchan's report, 1811 (in Howley 1915, 75)
1811	ca. 3 km further upriver on projecting rock	pile of caribou horns, frame of wigwam	Buchan's report, 1811 (in Howley 1915, 75, 82)
1809	same place	storehouses	Seen by W.Cull, Buchan's report, 1811 (in Howley 1915,75)
1768	betw. Badger Brook & Noel Paul's Br., NW bank	2 camps with 2 wigwams 1 single wigwam 1 square house	J.Cartwright's map (Fig.6.2) J.Cartwright's report (in Howley 1915,42)
1768	same area, SE bank	4 single wigwams 1 cluster of 3 wigwams	J.Cartwright's map (Fig.6.2)
1820	same area	2 clusters of 2 wigwams 1 cluster of 3 wigwams	Buchan's map, 1820 (Fig.12.1)
1820	Lake NW of Expl. River (Little Red Indian Pond?)	3 mamateeks	Shanawd. sketch 3 (Plate.12.2; Howley 1915, 242)
1820	same area, SE bank	1mamateek	Ibid.
1790	ca. 80–100 miles fr. mouth of Expl. River (approx. Noel Paul's Br.)	4 wigwams, canoes	Pulling (Marshall 1989,124)
1768	upriver from Noel Paul's Brook, NW bank	3 single wigwams	J.Cartwright's map (Fig.6.2)
1768	same stretch of river, SE bank	1 wigwam	Ibid.
1820	close to Red Indian Lake NW bank	1 wigwam	Buchan's map, 1820 (Fig.12.1)
1820	same area	3 mamateeks	Shanawd. sketch 3 (Plate 12.2)

Table 15.1 *(cont'd)*
Beothuk Sites or Encounters Recorded in Documents

Date	*Location*	*Type of Site or Encount.*	*Informant/Reference*
AREA 7: RED INDIAN LAKE AND OTHER LAKES			
Red Indian Lake			
1768	Betw. Expl. River & Millertown	1 single wigwam, 1 square house 1 cluster of 2 wigwams	J.Cartwright's map (Fig.6.2)
1811	same area	3 mamateeks	Shanawd. sketches 1, 2 (Plates 10.1, 10.2)
1820	same area	3 wigwams	Buchan's map, 1820 (Fig.12.2)
1827	same area	clusters of summer & winter wigwams in ruins, 1 smoking house, 1 small store (log) house, 1 wreck of a canoe	Cormack 1829,322
1876	same area	series of wigwam pits the largest 33' (10m) diameter	Lloyd 1876a,223
1811	a distance SW of Mary March Brook	4 mamateeks, cemetery, marine's head on pole	Shanawd. sketch 1 (Plate 10.1)
1811	same area	1 old wigwam	Buchan's map, 1811 (Fig.10.1)
1820	same area	2 wigwams, cemetery (1 tilt)	Buchan's map, 1820 (Fig.12.2) Buchan's report, 1820 (in Howley 1915,124)
1827	same area	cemetery, caribou fences leading to the lakeshore	Cormack 1829,323–5
1876	5 km to the the north fr. above	remains of 55 km of caribou fences across a marsh on the SE side of Grand Lake, some repaired and used by Micmac	Lloyd 1876a,224
1820	SW of cemetery	3 wigwams	Buchan's map, 1820 (Fig.12.2)
1820	SW end of Red Ind. L.	1 wigwam, 1 drying rack	Ibid.
1880s	Lloyd's River nr. Red Indian Lake outlet	2 caribou traps & fences, a look-out	Howley's map (Fig.20.3)
1811	SE shore of Red Indian Lake, prob. Bluff Head	5 mamateeks, marine's head on pole	Shanawd. sketch 1 (Plate 10.1)
1811	SW of the above	1 wigwam	Ibid.
1876	Junction of Victoria River	3 wigwam pits	Lloyd 1876a,223
1819	Same area "B"	where Mary March's Child died	Shanawd. sketch 3 (Plate 12.2)

Table 15.1 *(cont'd)*
Beothuk Sites or Encounters Recorded in Documents

Date	*Location*	*Type of Site or Encount.*	*Informant/Reference*
Other Lakes			
1768	Middleton Lake and Mary Anne Lake	2 clusters of 2 wigwams 1 camp of 3 wigwams 1 single wigwam	J.Cartwright's map (Fig.6.2)
1822–23	Betw. Joe's & Paul's Lake	3 mamateeks	Shanawd. sketch 4 (Fig.14.1)
1823	Crooked Lake, NW shore	3 mamateeks	Ibid.
1823	Betw. Crooked & South Twin Lakes	portage path	Ibid.
1820	Rocky Pond (?)	1 temp. wigwam and tree with tuft & red/white circles	Buchan's report, 1820 (in Howley 1915,125)
1820	On Brook issueing fr. NE end of South Twin Lake	2 wigwams	Buchan's map, 1820 (Fig.12.1) Buchan's report, 1820 (in Howley 1915,125)
1827	South Twin Lake	8–10 winter mamateeks, summer mamateeks, canoe rest, portage paths to Badger Bay and to lakes inland from New Bay	Cormack 1829,322
1803	Gander Lake	Beothuk sighted in canoe	Governor Gambier (in Howley 1915,63)
AREA 8: NOTRE DAME BAY WEST, INCL. NEW, SEAL, BADGER, HALLS AND GREEN BAY			
1769	prob. Woodford Cove, Halls Bay	1 wigwam	J.Cartwright's map (NAC. NMC 14032)
1876	Indian Brook betw. Grand Lake & Halls Bay	a few wigwam pits	Lloyd 1876a,224
1820	Badger Bay	Beothuk in canoe	Captain Trivik (in Howley 1915,126)
1820	Wild Bight, Badger Bay	1 wigwam, Indian path	Buchan's map, 1820 (Fig.12.1)
AREA 9: THE NORTHERN PENINSULA AND THE WEST COAST			
1800	Griguet, 24 km inland	a Beothuk family of four	Webber 1978,98, fn. 5
1720	Hare Bay	a camp and caribou fence around a lake	Morandière 1962,1:22
1718	Bonne Bay	a camp	Ibid.
1594	St George's Bay	a camp of about 40 to 50 Indians	Quinn 1979,4:64, doc. 560

Appendix One

Letter from Henry Crout to Sir Percival Willoughby, August [1613], MMss. Mix 1/24, Willoughby Papers, Middleton Manuscripts, Nottingham University, Nottingham, UK. Published by permission of the Honourable Michael Willoughby and the Department of Manuscripts, University of Nottingham. The transcript was provided by Gillian T. Cell, College of William and Mary, Williamsburg, Virginia, US. Letters underlined indicate expansions of contractions in the original; letters or words in square brackets are supplied after careful measurement of space, where the document is damaged.

August [1613]. Henry Crout to Sir Percival Willoughby. In Cupers Coue the of August/

Right

Worshippfull yt may please you to vnderstand: that yours the 15th & 12th of may I haue Received By Iohn combers// who by great chaunce we did meett comynge Forth of Trynitie bay comying into the old perllican in a shipp of London // otherwise I do not knowe howe he would haue gotten vnto cupers cove untill the end of the Fishinge viage / / we wear agayne at the very bottome of trynitie bay with our shallopp being 5 of us // only to see wher thos wear still inhabittinge in the freshe watter lake which we did see the last year // but before we wentt vnto that lake we went into another sound: wher hattn did Imagine the last wintter of the Irone stone // but comyng ther ashoore vnto the place and taking the vew of it he sayeth yt is none // but sayeth by any man Iugmentt that doe see it would think it to be verie Irone stone // at bellill the lik is no man but would thinke yt wear meattell // his skill I do not knowe // some triall he hath taken with him iith Iuly we departed this sound and wentt towards solvage bay // in the morninge we passing by a litle plessante Ila[nd] at the rissinge of the sune we first espyed a canno ha[uled] vpon the rocks: and presently we had espied a solvage th[er] which made vs to put ashoore at the Iland: cominge as[hoore] we perceaved the solvages wear newly gone from th[er] house into the wouds For we found the stonnes to be w[arm] in the mydest of ther house which they had made ther Fier vpon // our men wear verie Importunate to haue stay[ed] 2 or 3 dayes and to watch the woods: only For to haue ta[ken] them // wherat I would not giue my Consent and besids th[ey] would haue taken away ther canno/ which I would not suffe[r] neither which made our men to storue much at it: in the end w[e] wentt into the house which was covered with some skynnes and they lay one with Fine long green grasse for ther pillow at ther heades and some vnder them // but by all Imagination th[ey] could not be but a man his wyffe and child: and may ape[ar] by showes and other things which we brought with vs // so having Fully parvsed ther house and sondry reste meatte vp[on] ther wooden speets // we lefte in ther house both beskitt a[nd] cheese one Lynnen Cape and one napkinge: and so d[eparted] without medling with any thing: from thence departing went v[nto] the bottom of mountt eagell bay: but thos which we did see th[er] last winter wear gone all abroad acoastinge all the s[ummer] for eeges and birds agaynst the wyntter which in one Il[and] to the northwardes they may fill bottes with penn gwynes [dri]ving them into ther boottes from the shoore for they are not able [to fly] thos egges and birds they dry for ther wintter

[fo. 1v] [And the] next da[ye we] r[eto]rned [agayne] from mountt eagell baye and in the morninge cam vnto the Iland wher we found the solvages house the daie before but at our retorne they and ther canno and provition wear gone except some 2 speets of ther rost meatt they had lefte behind them // which I do Thinke they lefte for vs so from thence Rowinge homwards we wear not scarse one leage they made vs a signe from the mayne with a Fier for to come vnto them which presently we retorned thinkinge to haue spoken with them: but again[st] our comyng vnto the place they had hanged out such small store of skines as they had vpon poolles one a beache as it wear in a markett place // we made all the maynes we could with a fladg of truce and signes to come and speeke but they wear fearfull being so fewe we see them runing to and froe in the woods but would not come neer vs // so seeing the would not thes few skynnes as the had we troucked & left vpon every poole in steed of eche skynne knyves aquavitie lynnen and other thinges which we esteeme twice to the valew of them only to giue them Content at the first // I do insure you in very shorte tyme the wilbe brought to be verie famyller as the are with the frenchmen in canada which do company dayly togeather and troucke for very Rich skynnes which the solvages do trad from one hand to another amongst them selves and bring to the french which I do presume to do the lik with thos people in a shorte time but if the should be touched or taken parforce ther wilbe never no hoop of any good to be done by them // for the are bentt to revenge if the be any way wronged // the maye hear after do vs mishcheefe or ells the will do it vnto some fishermen // I do writt this because I do leave some in this place which haue a intentt to take some of them parforce which I haue told them allredy my openyon which if the do I will insure you it may be a great lost in tyme vnto the Company // I knowe wher is one to be procured which can speake ther langguad very well which hath bin five years a mongst them // and in continuance of tyme we shall procure some of them and leaving some of vs in place // as the french do at canada as at my retorne I shall informe your worship of all bussines more at large // I ame very sorowe that Iohn combers and my selfe can by no maynes find out any Aryes or hawkes this year which we have laide hard waite in all places wher the haue bin accoustomed to breed heartofore but no news of any this year: we do Imagine it is the long and cold spring this year hath bin the accation of it blowing so cold against the hie cleaves // for we haue made search thorowe out // and no fisher man allso haue not had the sight of any all this year [fo.2] me thinks the com[pany ma]keth [too few fishing] viages which if it were well cons[idered] and g[ood advice] taken they might fr[ay] much of the charge towardes the [colony] vntill such time as the land and ground be mannvred: they [haue] heartofore sent fishermen which haue had no great eperience [*sic*] which to my knowledge hath bin a great lost vnto the companye // but thos that have fished this year I hope will make the company Reasonable proffitt yet good courses beinge taking ther might be greatter good done // For corne I do insure you if it wear sowen in tyme yt would prove exceeding good: but that we sowd The last wintter cometh Forth too late and wilbe scarcly Ripe tyme inought so well yeared and cearned as possible any Corne maybe this is at Instant the best tyme for putting of it into the ground // wherty it maybe vp Free before the Cold weather do take it for in the wintter the snowe do[th] kept it warme and doth norishe it // all kind of yearbes & Routtes ells doth prove exceeding well // I haue sent by this shipp vnto master Slany a barrell of maker[ell] in pykell which I haue intreated him to deliver you the one hal[f] allso I haue sent you in this shipp a littell barrel of Sammon and some makerell to fill it up which is marke in this marke P.W. in the one of the headеs: which I will writt master nvnne for the receapt of it dowtting that your worshipful is in the Country: I hope to bring some few herring and some lobbstars by the way of bristowe with me [I hope] at our Comyng at bristow we shall receive some letter or o[rder] Ther From you // because we haue noe accquantance [ther] and for my owne part I can not showe my selffe before an[y man] for wantt of apparrell // For I do insure you hear is n[oe] provition not for me nor any others scarse at all // hear will remayne some 30 in all this wintter bartell Hatton & Rossell cometh with me master thomas and Iohn Combers // I hope we shalbe in england or London so soone as this shipp hopping in god we shalbe Redy within this 6 days so I end with my dailye prayers vnto the allmightie for your prousperous success in all your acctions and affaires

Your worships to comand // Henry Croutt

Endorsed: To the right worshippfull Sir Percivall Willughby Knight these be delivered In London at Carlille house in Lambeth marsche

[Also on the back in Francis Willoughby's hand:] From H. Croute in newfoundland 6

APPENDIX TWO

Biographies of Major Informants

To acquaint the reader with the background of the most prominent seventeenth-, eighteenth-, and nineteenth-century informants, their biographies are given here. Added is the biography of J.P. Howley, author of *The Beothuck or Red Indians*, who collected much of the material that has been used in this work.

BUCHAN, DAVID

David Buchan was born in Scotland in 1780. At the age of ten he was signed on in the Royal Navy as cabin boy; a year later he was employed on an East Indian trader. In 1796 Buchan returned to the Royal Navy as able seaman and quickly advanced through the ranks. He served as master on *HMS Nettby*, which was instrumental in sinking and capturing several French ships in the English-French war. Buchan married Marie Ayde in 1802 or 1803 and the couple had three children. Their daughter, Sophie Maria, was baptized in Newfoundland in 1813.[1] In 1806 Buchan was commissioned lieutenant and from 1808 onwards intermittently served on the Newfoundland station. One of his first assignments was to survey Newfoundland's south coast. In the summer of 1815 he was given the task of retaking St Pierre and Miquelon for the British Crown; a year later he was promoted commander. In the winters of 1815–16 and 1816–17, in a series of fires in which most of St John's was destroyed, Buchan, in the absence of the governor, averted starvation and distress among the residents through his prudent actions. In 1818, as commander of *HMS Dorothea*, he was placed in charge of an arctic expedition with orders to find a northern passage to the Pacific Ocean. After six months of perilous travel through ice, the party had to return.

Buchan first encountered Beothuk in the winter of 1810–11 when he headed a naval peace mission into Beothuk country. He discovered the Beothuk's major camp at Red Indian Lake and exchanged civilities and presents with its occupants. But once he had left, the Beothuk killed the two marines Buchan had left behind as hostages and fled. Encouraged by Governor John Thomas Duckworth, Buchan searched for Beothuk in the following two summers on the coast of Notre Dame Bay. However, the Beothuk evaded him. In 1819 he was called upon to return the Beothuk captive Demasduit to her people. Unexpectedly the Indian woman died onboard his ship, whereupon Buchan conveyed her coffined remains to the Beothuk camp at Red Indian Lake. He then tried in vain to find Beothuk inland from Badger and New Bay. When Shanawdithit and her mother and sister were brought to St John's in 1823, it was Buchan who saw to it that their needs were met and that they would be returned to their people without delay.

In 1820, acting as surrogate judge, Buchan, together with the Rev. John Leigh, sentenced two fishermen to be whipped. This sentence outraged the community and the accused took him to court. Buchan was acquitted but the incident led to increased pressure for judicial reforms. Buchan was promoted captain in the Royal Navy in 1823 but was later that fall taken off the active list. He was appointed high sheriff for Newfoundland in 1825. In 1835 Buchan resigned from this position and subsequently may have been employed by the East India Company; he is last heard of on one of its ships, *Upton Castle*, in 1838.

To commemorate Buchan's efforts and his meeting with the Beothuk, two communities, a lake and a brook at or close to Red Indian Lake, and two islands, one on Red Indian Lake and one in Dildo Run, were named after him.[2]

CARTWRIGHT, GEORGE

George Cartwright was the second son of William Cartwright, a landholder in Nottinghamshire, England, and his wife Anne. Born in 1739, he was educated at Newark and later at Randall's Academy in Heath, UK. At the age of fifteen or sixteen, he entered the Royal Military Academy at Woolwich and, after a military career abroad, returned to England in 1760 with the rank of captain.[3] Cartwright made his first voyage to Newfoundland in 1766, accompanying his brother John, a lieutenant in the Royal Navy, on a cruise around the northern Newfoundland coast. On his second trip to Newfoundland in 1768, he took part in an expedition into Beothuk country that was headed by his brother John.[4] Two years later George Cartwright started a new career in Labrador, where he operated several fishing and sealing stations between Cape Charles and Hamilton Inlet. During his time in Labrador Cartwright took a great interest in the native populations, befriended Inuit of the area, and in 1772 brought five Inuit to England. They contracted smallpox and only one woman, Caubvick, survived. In 1784 Cartwright submitted a lengthy report to authorities in England on the precarious situation of the Beothuk in Newfoundland and suggested ways of putting an end to their persecution. He also asked for an appointment as "superintendent of Indian Affairs" so as to implement his plan.[5] His proposal was not accepted.

In 1786 Cartwright's ventures in Labrador failed and he returned to England. In 1792 he published the journal of his daily activities in Labrador, his observations on the flora, fauna, and meteorology of the country, and his encounters with native people.[6] Cartwright continued to be interested in Labrador affairs and jotted down ideas and practical suggestions for setting up and running a fishing station in a manuscript entitled "Additions to the Labrador Companion."[7] In 1793, Cartwright was asked to give evidence about the persecution of the Beothuk before a committee of the House of Commons.[8]

In the early 1800s Cartwright was appointed barrack master at Nottingham, where he became known as "Old Labrador." He died in 1819, aged eighty. A settlement at the entrance to Sandwich Bay and two islands off the Labrador coast bear his name.[9] A memorial in the entrance of Sandwich Bay commemorates the contributions to the province by George Cartwright and by his brother John.[10]

CARTWRIGHT, JOHN

John Cartwright, third son of William and Anne Cartwright, was born in 1740 at Marnham, Nottinghamshire. He, too, attended school at Newark and was afterwards sent to Heath Academy. John has been described as a remarkably gentle person but full of courage and energy. In 1758 he entered the Royal Navy and in 1759, serving under Lord Howe on *HMS Magnamine*, took part in several engagements with ships of the French fleet. He was commissioned lieutenant in 1762 and a year later was given command of a naval ship.[11] In 1766, by then first lieutenant on *HMS Guernsey*, Cartwright was appointed surrogate (judge) on the Newfoundland station (Trinity and Conception Bay) and later deputy commissary to the Vice Admiralty Court.[12] During his service in Newfoundland, he was sent by Governor Hugh Palliser with a naval party to explore the interior of the country and to establish friendly relations with the Beothuk. In August 1768 the party advanced along the Exploits River to Red Indian Lake, where they saw many Beothuk habitations and fenceworks but failed to meet Beothuk. Cartwright submitted a lengthy report and four maps with much valuable information on Beothuk distribution and culture.[13] In the following two years he tried to contact Beothuk on the coast but had to discontinue his search when he was shipwrecked.[14] He returned to England in 1770.

John Cartwright took an interest in many subjects but increasingly focused on political issues. In 1774 he published a pamphlet on American independence in which he sympathized with the cause of the colonists and thus felt obliged to turn down an offer by Lord Howe to serve in his fleet in the war against the Americans. This decision effectively terminated his naval career.

In 1775 Cartwright was appointed major of the Nottingham Militia; he was discharged sixteen years later. In 1780 he married Anne Catherine Dashwood. As the couple had no children, they adopted their niece Francis Dorothy, who later published Cartwright's writings in *The Life of Major Cartwright* (1826). After the death of his father, John Cartwright ran the Marnham estate but later moved to London. He was the author of some eighty publications, among them *Radical Reform of Parliament* in which he favoured universal suffrage, *Declaration of Rights*, and *The State of the Nation*, which earned him the name of "Father of Reform." He also helped to found societies for the abolition of the slave trade, the liberty of the press, and parliamentary reform. In 1819 he was fined for attempting to spread contempt of government.

Although John Cartwright was generally held in high esteem, he was unsuccessful in his bids for a seat in Parliament. He nevertheless continued with his political activities and was said to have been one of the most generous-minded public men of his time. John Cartwright died on 23 September 1824; in Britain, a monument in his honour was erected at Burton Crescent, London, which was later renamed Cartwright Gardens.[15]

CORMACK, WILLIAM EPP(E)S

William Epps Cormack was born in May 1795 (or 1796) in St John's, the son of a Scottish merchant and the daughter of William Epp(e)s, a St John's merchant.[16] The family moved to Scotland around 1805 where William went to school and later studied natural sciences at the universities of Glasgow and Edinburgh. Professor Robert Jameson, founder of the Edinburgh Museum and editor of the *Edinburgh Philosophical Journal*, became his mentor. In 1818 Cormack settled a group of Scottish immigrants in Prince Edward Island and later became justice of the peace in Charlottetown. In 1821 or 1822 he moved to St John's, Newfoundland, to take over family business interests in the shipping trade. Within a few months of his arrival, he decided to explore the island on foot and establish contact with the elusive Beothuk. After a trial walk across the Avalon Peninsula, Cormack and his Micmac guide, Joseph Sylvester, set out in early September on their arduous journey from Random Sound, Trinity Bay, to St George's Bay. They arrived on the west coast two months later. Cormack met no Beothuk but his account of the botany, geology, and mineralogy of Newfoundland's interior remains a classic.[17] Cormack sent specimens of Newfoundland minerals to Doctor Jameson in Edinburgh and was later to add Beothuk artifacts to Jameson's collection. In later travels he sent plants or seeds to the Linnean Society in London, to Kew Gardens, and to the Scottish Highland Society. Over the years, Cormack also corresponded with Sir William Hooker, Professor Faraday, Doctors Ure and Hodgkin, and the historian John McGregor, a close friend.

In early October 1827, Cormack founded the Boeothick Institution with the purpose of promoting the civilizing of the Beothuk and of procuring authentic information about this people.[18] In a second attempt to make contact, Cormack and three Indian companions found many traces and a cemetery, but the Beothuk remained elusive. He had Shanawdithit, the last known Beothuk, transferred to St John's and elicited from her much information on Beothuk history and culture.[19] In 1829 Cormack was elected a member of the Natural History Society in Montreal and in 1833 was awarded a medal for the best essay on the fishery in North America.[20] At the end of January 1829 he returned to Britain when his Newfoundland business failed. Seven years later he removed to Australia where difficulties with government agencies forced him on to New Zealand. He exported spars to London for the Admiralty, ran a watchmaker's business in Auckland, and was appointed justice of the peace.[21] Frustrated by government policies affecting his landholdings, he returned to England in 1847. Following the discovery of gold in California, Cormack immigrated to San Francisco in 1853 and later moved on to New Westminster, British Columbia, where he engaged in local politics, advocating law reform, representative government, and equality for the Indians. In 1864 he accepted the position of superintendent of Indian Affairs for the district of New Westminster. Cormack died on 29 April 1868 and was buried in the small cemetery of Holy Trinity Church on the Indian reserve in New Westminster.[22]

In Newfoundland a community, a mountain, and a lake commemorate Cormack's contribution to the province.[23] A memorial erected on the road to Random Island celebrates his daring trek across the country in 1822.

CROUT(E), HENRY

In February 1612 Henry Crout purchased a half share in the Newfoundland Company, founded for the purpose of settlement in Newfoundland. In the same year, he joined the first English colony in Cupids, Conception Bay, where he represented Sir Percival Willoughby's interests and acted as guardian to his son, Thomas Willoughby. Crout attempted without success to cross the peninsula dividing Conception and Trinity bays so as to reach the place where Willoughby's lot was located. In the fall of 1612, he accompanied the governor of the colony, John Guy, on an expedition to Trinity Bay; on this journey they met Beothuk and shared a meal with them. In a series of letters to Willoughby, Crout recorded activities and events in the colony and many details of the journey to Trinity Bay that validate and extend Guy's report. He also kept the colony's official journal. In 1613, Crout returned to Trinity Bay with a small crew and traded with Beothuk; he left for England later that year but was back in Newfoundland in 1616. Willoughby, who became dissatisfied with Crout's management of his affairs, dismissed him a year later.[24]

GUY, JOHN

John Guy, presumed to have been born in Britain, was prominent in the civic and commercial life of Bristol. He was elected to the Common Council in 1603, was a member of the Bristol Society of Merchant Venturers, and became one of the principal subscribers to the North Virginia Company. Guy first visited Newfoundland in 1608 and wrote a tract advocating the settlement of the island.[25] In 1610 the London and Bristol Company appointed him as governor of their colony on the Avalon Peninsula. Guy arrived that year in Newfoundland with thirty-nine colonists and established a settlement in Cuper's Cove, now called Cupids. He returned to England in late summer 1611 and came back to Newfoundland with more colonists in early 1612. In October/November of that year he explored Trinity Bay and made contact with the Beothuk in Bull Arm. His journal contains a lengthy description of this meeting, the earliest detailed record on the Beothuk's appearance and their material culture. In April 1613 Guy suddenly left for England. He may have come back to Newfoundland for a few months in 1614. But as his relations with the company became strained, he probably left the island for good in that year. John Guy served as mayor of Bristol in 1618 and represented Bristol in the House of Commons where he supported the Newfoundland planters. Before his death in Bristol in 1629, Guy received a lot in Newfoundland which he called Seaforest. He bequeathed this lot to his sons.[26] A plaque in the community of Cupids commemorates Guy's attempts at colonization.

HOWLEY, JAMES PATRICK

Born in 1847 in St John's, Newfoundland, James P. Howley was one of four sons of Richard Howley and Elisabeth née Burke. He was educated at St Bonaventure's College, St John's. In 1868 he became assistant to Alexander Murray qv. FGS on the Geological and Topographical Survey of Newfoundland. Upon Murray's death in 1887, Howley was put in charge of the Survey Office and later became director of the Geological Survey.

Inspired by Alexander Murray's conviction of the importance of a museum, Howley collected innumerable exhibits and devoted much time to identifying acquisitions. He later became curator of the Geological Museum and built it into a respected institution.

Howley was a prolific writer. Among his best-known publications are the *Geological Map of Newfoundland* and the monograph *Record of the Geological Survey*; his *Geography of Newfoundland* became the standard textbook on the subject in schools. In recognition of his contribution to science and history, he was made fellow of the Royal Geological Society in 1882 and was subsequently honoured by several other scientific and cultural institutes and associations.

During his early years in the field, Howley developed a great interest in the by then extinct Beothuk. He questioned local inhabitants, particularly in the Notre Dame Bay area, befriended the Peyton family in Twillingate, and took every opportunity to add Beothuk artifacts to the museum collection. Howley also accumulated a large number of documents relating to the Beothuk, which he published in his 1915 classic *The Beothucks or Red Indians*. James P. Howley died in St John's in January 1918.[27] A community, a lake, and a mountain in western Newfoundland were named in his honour.[28]

PEYTON, JOHN SR

John Peyton, Sr, was born at Wimbourne in southwest England in 1747 or 1749.[29] He came first to Labrador in 1770 to work for George Cartwright, whom he accompanied on an exploratory trip to the Bay of Exploits in search of Beothuk. After serving two summers with Cartwright, he settled in Fogo to carry on a cod fishery. About 1775 he moved to the Exploits River and, in partnership with Harry Miller, ran salmon-fishing stations there for the next twenty-five years.[30] During the salmon season he lived at Upper Sandy Point (now Peterview); for the winter he usually returned to England. In 1788 John Peyton, Sr, married Anne Galton who remained in Wimbourne. The couple had two children, John, Jr, and Susan. After Miller's death in 1800 Peyton, Sr, bought his shares and thereby gained full rights to the salmon-fishing properties on the Exploits River. Peyton, Sr, was a shrewd business man and is said to have claimed the fishery of the whole Bay of Exploits; if anyone set a net he would have one set immediately in front of it.[31] In 1812 he brought his son, John Peyton, Jr, to Newfoundland to help in the business, which John, Jr, eventually took over.

Peyton, Sr, had the reputation of being a brutal "Indian killer." In 1781 he participated in an excursion to hunt down Beothuk in retaliation for thefts. In 1814 or 1815, he chanced on a Beothuk camp on the Exploits River and killed one of the occupants. He also took part in the expedition to Red Indian Lake in 1819 in which Demasduit was captured and her husband Nonosabasut and his brother were killed.

In 1823 Peyton, Sr, made a last trip to England to visit his wife. He died in 1829 and was buried on Exploits Island.

PEYTON, JOHN JR

John Peyton, Jr, was born in 1793 in Wimbourne and attended school at nearby Christchurch. He afterwards worked at the Navy Pay Office in London.[32] In 1812 Peyton, Jr, came to Newfoundland and worked one season as a "youngster" (an unmarried apprentice). Stationed at Upper Sandy Point, he patrolled the river to protect the Peyton river claim; during the hunting season he trapped for furs. John Peyton, Jr, later joined his father's business and started to export salt cod from a station on Exploits Island. He spent the salmon season (spring and early summer) at Upper Sandy Point, resided during mid-summer and fall on Exploits Island, and returned to Upper Sandy Point for the winter. In 1815–16 Peyton, Jr, took over his father's business and extended it by starting a shipyard on Exploits Islands and later a second one at Indian Point in the Exploits River estuary. Two years later, in 1818, he was appointed justice of the peace for the northern district.

John Peyton, Jr, was more benevolent towards the Beothuk than his father and did not retaliate when he suspected that the Indians had taken some of his tools. However, after Beothuk had cut loose one of his boats he sought permission from Governor Hamilton to retrieve his property and, if possible, to capture a Beothuk. In March 1819 the John Peytons, father and son, and a party of furriers tracked down a group of Beothuk at Red Indian Lake and captured Demasduit. Her husband, chief Nonosabasut, who attacked Peyton, Sr, was killed, and so was his brother. The grand jury declared that the Peytons had acted in self-defence.[33] Peyton, Jr, subsequently assisted in attempts to return Demasduit to her people and, after she had died, accompanied Captain Buchan to Red Indian Lake, where they left her remains.

In February 1823, John Peyton, Jr, married the seventeen-year-old Eleanor Elizabeth Mahaney from Carbonear. A few months later, the Beothuk Shanawdithit was taken by trappers with her mother and sister and brought to the Peytons on Exploits Island. After the mother and sister had died, Shanawdithit remained in the Peyton household, where she assisted with household duties for five years.

John Peyton, Jr, was well acquainted with Cormack and provided him with information about the Beothuk. He also became resident agent of the Boeothick Institution, founded by Cormack in October 1827. He strongly objected, however, when, in his absence, Shanawdithit was transferred to St John's under the auspices of the institution.

John Peyton, Jr, and his wife had four sons and four daughters. The oldest son, who went to school at Christchurch, was lost at sea on his return from England. The family moved to Twillingate in 1836 and Peyton was appointed stipendiary magistrate; he kept this position into his eighty-seventh year. He died in 1879 and was buried beside his father on Exploits Island. A mountain, a brook, several lakes, and a point of land in Bay D'Espoir were named after the Peytons.[34]

PULLING, GEORGE CHRISTOPHER

George Christopher Pulling was born in 1766, the third son of George Pulling, a landholder in Hampshire, England, and his wife Mary Anne née Joliffe. He joined the Royal Navy as able seaman at the age of twelve. In 1786, after a visit to Trinity Bay while serving on *HMS Thisbe*, Pulling submitted a proposal to authorities in England on how to stop cruelty towards the Beothuk. Five years later, by then a lieutenant, Pulling was granted leave of absence on half pay to make a proper investigation of relations between settlers and the Beothuk in the northern district. On his homeward journey, during the winter of 1792–93, Pulling was taken prisoner by the French, which prevented him from giving evidence before the Parliamentary Enquiry into the State of Trade to Newfoundland in March-June 1793. Pulling prepared a lengthy report, which he probably sent, together with a Beothuk vocabulary, to the chairman of the enquiry, the first earl of Liverpool. Pulling advocated sending a peace mission to the Beothuk under his command, but the idea was not approved. Instead, he was sent to serve in the West Indies. After a successful attack on a Spanish convoy, Pulling was promoted post captain in 1802. He married Elizabeth Moser of Kendal in 1803; the couple had five sons. In 1807 Pulling became captain of the land-based *Sea Fencibles* at Bristol. He died in 1819 at the age of fifty-three.[35]

TONEY, SANTU

Santu was born at Indian Point, Red Indian Lake, around 1837. She claimed that her father, named "Kop," was one of the last surviving Beothuk. When Kop was young, he had been taken by the Newfoundland Micmac, reared by them, and converted to Christianity. His wife, Santu's mother, was a Micmac from the Newfoundland band. She died when Santu was quite young. At the age of about ten Santu and her father moved to Nova Scotia, where she grew up. She married a Mohawk and the couple spent time in New Brunswick and Nova Scotia and then roamed throughout the Great Lakes area and the northeastern states and eastern Canada. When her husband died, Santu returned to Nova Scotia and married Toney, a Micmac chief. They lived near Yarmouth. The couple had four or five children. Santu later separated from her husband and, with her youngest son, drifted about the New England states, earning a living through basket making, bead working, and fortune telling. Her son, Joe Toney, still lived with her when the anthropologist Frank Speck first met her. After her husband's death Santu returned to Yarmouth. She died in 1919.

Speck met Santu in 1910 in Gloucester, Massachusetts, and interviewed her on several occasions. Santu was able to recall interesting information about her father's people, the Beothuk, and a Beothuk song. She also told Speck of the tradition that her father's mother had been a shipwrecked (apparently white) woman who was rescued by the Beothuk and had remained with them. However, interviews with Santu were difficult because she was unable to concentrate on anything for very long and her memory was sometimes hazy. Speck thought that she did not always differentiate between Beothuk customs and those of the Micmac/Montagnais, among whom she had lived. He made great efforts to authenticate Santu's claim that she was descended from a Beothuk man and was satisfied with the evidence he was able to collect.[36]

WHITBOURNE, RICHARD

Sir Richard Whitbourne, originally from Exmouth in Devonshire, England, made his first voyage to Newfoundland in 1579. He continued to make trips to the island and witnessed Sir Humphry Gilbert's arrival in Newfoundland in 1583. Whitbourne commanded his own ship and three others in engagements with the Spanish Armada in 1588 and was recommended for his part in the action by Lord Howard. His ships were engaged in fishing in Newfoundland and in trade in the Mediterranean. In 1615 he was commissioned by the High Court of Admiralty to hold vice-admiralty courts in Newfoundland. In 1618 he became the first governor of Sir William Vaughan's Newfoundland colony on the Avalon Peninsula. Whitbourne travelled extensively around Newfoundland's coast from the Northern Peninsula and the Gulf of St Lawrence to St George's Bay, and from there to Cape Race, Trinity Bay, and Bonavista Bay. He advised Lord Falkland on the founding and management of his colony in the southern part of the Avalon Peninsula between 1622 and 1626 and was knighted by Falkland in 1625. Whitbourne later served as lieutenant on *Bonavista*; details of his further career are not known.[37] In 1622 he published *Discourse and discovery of New-found-land*, followed two years later by *A discourse containing a loving invitation ... to all Adventurers ... for the advancement of his Majesties most hopeful Plantation in the New-found-land.* In these publications Whitbourne provided much information on the geography, climate, and resources of the island. He gave practical advice on settlement and the fishery and voiced his opinion about the Beothuk, whom he considered to be harmless and few in number. A community on the Avalon Peninsula was named after him.[38]

PART TWO

Ethnography

Introduction

The ethnography presented in this volume is a review of Beothuk cultural traits and practices. The source material used for this study are Beothuk artifacts, accounts, drawings, and wordlists obtained from Beothuk captives, archaeological data, unpublished and published contemporary reports and maps, and other documents; all are referenced in the notes. In order to extend the known data I have undertaken an intensive and systematic search for new documentation. The new material was analyzed and integrated with known sources, and all data were collated under specific subject headings. The available information is discussed in twelve chapters, each focusing on a particular theme. Taken together, these chapters provide a complete, up-to-date assessment of what is known about Beothuk culture. Numerous illustrations of Beothuk artifacts, campsites, and burial places are included here, as are Shanawdithit's drawings, which are a unique source of information.

Despite the addition of new material to the known sources, the information at our disposal is nevertheless limited. Not only is there a paucity of documentation but cultural aspects are often recorded in a fragmented manner, or out of context. Comparisons with practices among other native groups have helped to contextualize and validate pieces of information or to deduce the significance of Beothuk practices that could otherwise not be understood. As a rule, these comparisons are not intended to infer a diffusion of cultural traits or deduce possible affiliations, although resemblances between Beothuk artifacts and those of other tribes that have hitherto not been noted are pointed out.

Our knowledge base is not only restricted, it also lacks balance. As with the historical data presented in Part One, much of the available information was recorded by Englishmen rather than obtained from Beothuk themselves, so that the Beothuk voice is nearly absent from the record. Beothuk material culture is also more extensively documented than less-tangible traditions. For example, several contemporary documents give details of house and canoe construction while information on band organization, alliances, marriage patterns, and Beothuk cosmology is lacking. Discussion of these topics relies heavily on deductions from artifacts and archaeological reports aided by comparisons with practices of other native groups; other topics have been omitted for want of reliable data.

It should also be noted that most records of aspects of Beothuk culture date from the second half of the eighteenth century onward and almost exclusively describe Beothuk practices and artifacts that have been observed among bands that staged caribou drives in the watershed of the Exploits River and subsequently wintered close to slaughtering sites inland. The Beothuk captives who provided additional information were members of these bands. Cultural traditions from bands that remained relatively close to the coast throughout the year have rarely been documented. While the caribou hunters on the Exploits River may have become the dominant group, their culture traits do not necessarily represent those of the entire Beothuk tribe.

Assuming that Beothuk culture, like that of other populations, was a dynamic entity subject to continuous change, an attempt has been made to trace the development of cultural adaptations over time. Though extensive shifts in the Beothuk's geographical distribution, accompanied by a dramatic population decline, are bound to have led to cultural adjustments, for the most part, such adjustments cannot be traced from the fragmentary information that has survived and pertains largely to prevailing circumstances in the last few decades of the Beothuk's existence. It was also not possible to establish with any degree of certainty whether traits characterizing this late period represent traditions of long standing or originated after contact, or whether and how they might have changed. An exception are modifications in Beothuk technology. As European metal goods became available, the Beothuk used this new material in the manufacture of projectiles; iron axes enabled them to apply new methods in fence and house construction. Other traits, such as the use of red ochre and the placement of grave goods (also recorded in the prehistoric Maritime Archaic Indians in the Atlantic Provinces), appear to be based on ancient traditions that may have remained relatively intact among the Beothuk.

Many documents that contain information on Beothuk cultural traits were written in a specific historic context that is only briefly referred to in Part Two. For details, the reader is advised to consult the relevant chapters in Part One. For easy reference, major events in Beothuk/English relations and those with other native groups are listed in the chronology that follows.

CHRONOLOGY OF MAJOR EVENTS

1497 Discovery of Newfoundland by John Cabot.

1560s-1700s Conflict between Beothuk and Inuit.

1594 The crew of the English fishing vessel *Grace* discovers a Beothuk camp at St George's Bay and later experiences hostile acts from Beothuk at Presque, Placentia Bay.

1612 John Guy and a party of colonists explore Trinity Bay and meet Beothuk with whom they feast and trade.

1613–14 The crew of a fishing vessel are said to have shot at Beothuk in Trinity Bay.

1694 Beothuk refuse contact with French fishing crews.

1719 Salmon posts are erected by Skeffington and others in Freshwater Bay, Gander Bay, and Dog Creek; Beothuk protest by killing some of the salmon catchers; this is the first record of Englishmen being killed by Beothuk.

1720s Confrontations between Beothuk and Micmac take place in St George's Bay; the Beothuk are defeated.

1729–31 English furriers kill Beothuk and Beothuk retaliate by killing furriers.

1730s Barter between Beothuk and settlers in Bonavista Bay terminates after a Beothuk woman is shot while selecting a trade item.

1750s Renewed confrontations between Beothuk and Micmac occur at Grand Lake; Beothuk are defeated again and lose access to Newfoundland's west and south coasts.

1758 The Beothuk boy June is captured by furriers and his mother and a child are killed.

1760 Shipmaster Scott attempts to build a station in the Bay of Exploits; in an encounter with Beothuk, Scott and five of his men are killed.

1760s Captain Hall is killed by Beothuk when he tries to settle in Halls Bay.

1768 Governor Hugh Palliser sends Lieut. John Cartwright to explore the Exploits River and to contact the Beothuk; Cartwright, who did not meet Beothuk, submits a detailed report about the Beothuk's way of life and two maps of the river on which he marked Beothuk habitations; he also reports that Beothuk are persecuted by fishermen and settlers.

1768 Furriers capture the Beothuk boy August and kill his mother.

1781 John Peyton, Sr, his partner Miller, and their headman raid a Beothuk winter camp on the Exploits River; many Beothuk are wounded or killed.

1784 George Cartwright submits a proposal to the Colonial Office suggesting that a reserve be set aside for the Beothuk; his proposal is not accepted.

1790 Eight English furriers raid a Beothuk winter camp on the Exploits River and wound occupants; they burn three of four houses and carry away caribou skins.

1791 Fishermen capture the Beothuk girl Oubee; a Beothuk man and child are killed in the encounter.

1792 Capt. G.C. Pulling questions northern fishermen and furriers about relations with the Beothuk. He submits a lengthy report and a Beothuk wordlist collected from Oubee; his report shows that Beothuk are consistently persecuted. He suggests remedial action and states that many residents are in favour of his plan; Chief Justice Reeves supports his proposal.

1797–1806 Governors William Waldegrave, Charles Morris Pole, and James Gambier submit proposals to authorities in Britain to improve relations with Beothuk. The plans call for sending a peace mission, capturing Beothuk to be used as mediators, and setting aside a Beothuk reserve. None of the proposals are approved.

1803 A Beothuk woman is captured by William Cull and returned to the Exploits River the following year.

1807–09 Governor John Holloway sends one of his officers with trade goods and a painting of trading Englishmen and Beothuk into Beothuk country; he is unable to contact Beothuk.

1811 Governor Thomas Duckworth sends Lieut. David Buchan on a peace mission into Beothuk country. Buchan, with twenty-three marines and three furriers as guides, treks up the Exploits River in midwinter and finds the Beothuk's principal settlement at Red Indian Lake. He believes he has convinced the Beothuk of his friendly intentions and leaves two hostages; during his absence the Beothuk kill the marines and flee.

1814–15 John Peyton, Sr, kills a Beothuk woman on the Exploits River, near Rushy Pond.

1818 Settlers and fishermen kill Shanawdithit's brother, mother, sister, and a young child on their way to an island where they intended to collect bird eggs; Shanawdithit's father, a swift hunter, dies a few months later.

1819 In March of this year, the John Peytons, father and son, with eight of their men capture Demasduit (Mary March) at Red Indian Lake; her husband, Nonosabasut, and his brother are killed in the encounter. The Peytons claim to have acted in self-defence. Rev. John Leigh collects a Beothuk vocabulary from Demasduit.

1820 On 8 January 1820 Demasduit succumbs to pulmonary tuberculosis. Captain Buchan brings her coffined body to the Beothuk camp at Red Indian Lake.

1822 William E. Cormack, an explorer and entrepreneur, and the Micmac Joseph Sylvester walk across Newfoundland from Trinity Bay to St George's Bay in search of Beothuk; they fail to meet any.

1823 Two furriers kill a Beothuk man and his daughter; taken to court they are declared to be "not guilty."

1823 Shanawdithit, her mother, and sister, ill and starving, give themselves up to furriers; the mother and sister die within a few weeks. Shanawdithit is taken into the household of John Peyton, Jr, on Exploits Islands.

1827 In October William E. Cormack founds the Boeothick Institution whose aim it is to open communication with the Beothuk and promote their civilization.

1827 In November, Cormack and three native guides search Beothuk territory for the remnants of the tribe; the party finds only abandoned camps and a cemetery.

1828 The Boeothick Institution sends two Abenaki and one Montagnais to search for Beothuk inland from St George's Bay, around Red Indian Lake, on the Exploits River, on the Northern Peninsula south of Crocque Harbour, in White Bay, and on the coast of Notre Dame Bay; the men are unsuccessful in finding survivors, though they come across many signs of Beothuk habitation.

1828 In September Shanawdithit is transferred to St John's under the auspices of the Boeothick Institution. William E. Cormack questions her extensively about the history and culture of her people.

1829 On 6 June Shanawdithit dies of pulmonary tuberculosis. Though some of her people would still have been alive, either in the interior of Newfoundland or in Labrador, the Beothuk tribe as a cultural entity has become extinct.

CHAPTER SIXTEEN

Position of Beothuk in Newfoundland Prehistory

MARITIME ARCHAIC INDIANS

The earliest inhabitants of Newfoundland were Maritime Archaic Indians, who lived for several millennia on the southern Labrador coast until some of them crossed the Strait of Belle Isle to Newfoundland around 5000 BP (BP stands for Before Present, reckoned from AD 1950; see Fig. 16.1).[1] Maritime Archaic Indian sites have been found around the entire Newfoundland coastline. Best known are the cemeteries at Port au Choix and on Twillingate Island (the Back Harbour site) and a campsite at The Beaches in Bonavista Bay. Maritime Archaic Indian remains have also been recovered inland at Red Indian Lake and on the Exploits River. The location of their coastal sites and the presence of slate lances (or bayonets) suggest that these Indians pursued sea mammals such as porpoise, small whale, perhaps even walrus; toggling and barbed harpoons indicate seal hunting, and fish spearpoints and plummets (small ovate stone weights) imply the spearing and netting of fish. Barbed points may have been used as bird darts. In fall and winter, the Indians would have hunted terrestrial mammals, either from inland camps or by going on short-term hunting expeditions. Among the chipped stone tools produced by Maritime Archaic Indians are knives, projectile points, bifaces (chipped or flaked stone tools modified on both faces), thumbnail scrapers, and large prismatic blades (long, narrow, parallel-sided flakes), the latter (otherwise associated with Palaeo-Eskimo cultures) unique to Bonavista Bay. Most conspicuous are their large stone axes, adzes (edged tools hafted at right angle to the handle), and gouges (with a curved bit), which suggest wood working, and their long, ground and polished slate spears and bayonets, not used by other natives in Newfoundland. Only in the cemetery at Port au Choix have bone and antler tools been preserved; the graves also contained bone pendants, red ochre, a whale effigy in stone, and other objects that may have had a magical purpose. A series of carbon dates from Maritime Archaic Indian sites suggests that they lived in Newfoundland until about 3000 BP (1050 BC).[2] They are believed either to have left the island, to have become

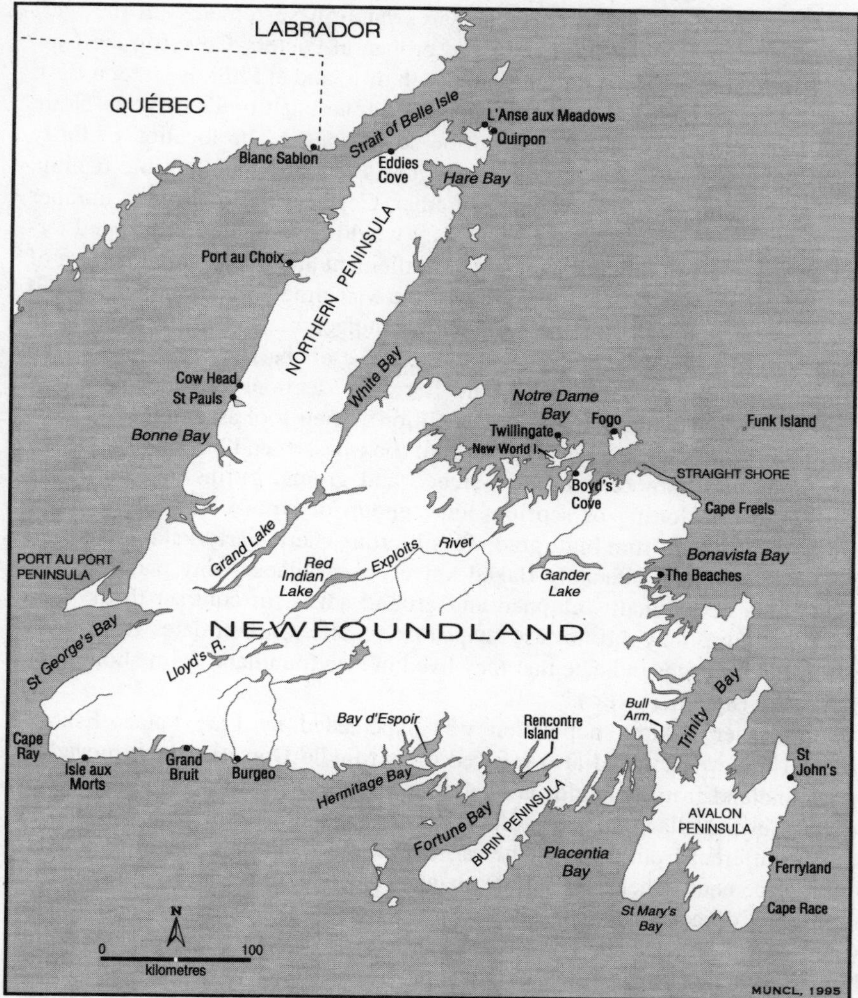

Fig.16.1 Map of Newfoundland showing the location of prehistoric Indian and Eskimo archaeological sites.

extinct, or to have become "archaeologically invisible" before the arrival of Early Palaeo-Eskimo groups from Labrador.[3]

EARLY AND LATE PALAEO-ESKIMO

In Newfoundland, the Early Palaeo-Eskimo people, who belonged to the Groswater phase of the Palaeo-Eskimo tradition because their tool types are identical to those found in Groswater Bay, Labrador, camped on sheltered beaches as well as on headlands.[4] For example, Groswater-phase remains on the west coast have been excavated at Cow Head proper, at Factory Cove (on the Cow Head Peninsula), at Broom Point to the north of it, and at Phillips Garden East, close to Port au Choix; other sites have been found at Boyd's Cove in Notre Dame Bay, and at Isle aux Morts on the south coast.[5] The location of Early Palaeo-Eskimo camps close to the sea suggests sea-mammal hunting, fishing, and bird catching during spring and summer. Considering the limited number of animal species that were available, they would have hunted or trapped terrestrial mammals in fall and winter. The settlement and exploitation pattern of these early Eskimos differed from that of the Maritime Archaic Indians as did their cultural traditions, methods of tool manufacture, and artifact types. In contrast to Maritime Archaic Indian tools, those of the Early Palaeo-Eskimo are small and finely flaked with thin, flat cross sections (another name for Palaeo-Eskimo is Arctic Small Tool Tradition). Their tool assemblage is identified by the presence of high side-notched (box-based) end blades (used as arrow points and harpoon blades), notched and ground burins and burin-like tools (used for slotting or scoring bone, antler, or wood), and circular side blades, all chipped from high-grade fossiliferous chert. Early Palaeo-Eskimos also made scrapers, bifacially flaked knives, microblades (tiny parallel-sided flakes) and, occasionally, chipped and ground adzes. In contrast to the later Eskimo culture, they did not use soapstone vessels. Carbon dates from Early Palaeo-Eskimo sites indicate that they lived in Newfoundland from about 2800 to 2100 BP (850 to 150 BC).[6]

This earlier Eskimo population was superceded by Late Palaeo-Eskimo groups (in Newfoundland also referred to as Middle Dorset), which moved to Newfoundland from Labrador around 2000 BP (50 BC) and occupied much of coastal Newfoundland.[7] Their artifact types and manufacturing techniques were notably different from those of the earlier Eskimo tradition, indicating population replacement rather than culture change. The new migrants would not have been direct descendants of the Early Palaeo-Eskimo population, although they would have been related. The subsistence strategy of the Late Palaeo-Eskimo differed from that of the earlier Eskimo tradition inasmuch as they placed greater emphasis on the exploitation of outer coastal resources, though regional adaptations varied. On the northeast coast, campsites of the Late Palaeo-Eskimo tradition are located in proximity to harp-seal migration routes, and on the south coast and in Trinity Bay, close to beaches where harbour seals routinely came ashore.[8] There is evidence that some Late Palaeo-Eskimo also hunted caribou on the Exploits River.[9] Among their larger campsites were those at Port au Choix on the west coast, at the Pittman Site in White Bay, at Cape Ray on the southwest coast, and at Stock Cove in Bull Arm, Trinity Bay.[10] The Late Palaeo-Eskimos dwelled in semisubterranean houses. Their tool assemblage is identified by tip-fluted triangular end blades (used on harpoons) and tabular burin-like tools fashioned from locally available cherts and nephrite, in addition to large numbers of microblades, ground slate tools, and angular vessels, amulets, and other objects made from soapstone.[11] They also produced intricate bone and ivory carvings, many representing animal forms. Carvings found in Newfoundland – as opposed to Labrador – are often stylized. The majority of carbon dates associated with Late Palaeo-Eskimo sites fall between 1700 and 1400 BP (AD 250 and 550), indicating that during this period the tradition was at its peak. After 1400 BP the population appears to have declined. The most recent carbon date from a small site in Placentia Bay is close to 1000 BP (AD 950).[12]

THULE ESKIMO

A third Eskimo culture, the prehistoric Thule Eskimo, advanced in the fourteenth century from the arctic regions into northern Labrador; by the mid-sixteenth century their descendants, the Inuit of the historic period, had spread down the Labrador coast as far as Hamilton Inlet.[13] Skilled in sea-mammal hunting, they exploited migrating Greenland whales and harp seals as well as resident populations of ringed seals and walrus. In the second half of the sixteenth century, Inuit groups made forays into the Strait of Belle Isle and were said to have come in conflict with Beothuk.[14]

RECENT INDIANS

Around 2000 BP (50 BC), when Late Palaeo-Eskimo immigrants were taking possession of many coastal areas in Newfoundland, a second Indian population appears in the archaeological record of the island. According to archaeological convention, these later Indians are referred to as Recent Indians so as to distinguish them from the preceding Maritime Archaic Indians and from the "historic" Beothuk, who lived in Newfoundland during the period for which we have historic records, beginning with the discovery of the island by Europeans around AD 1500.[15]

Notable differences in tools from different Recent Indian sites have led archaeologists to divide the Recent Indians into three distinct groups. They are named after their type sites (the site where a specific type of material was first found): "Cow Head complex," "Beaches complex," and "Little Passage complex" (the term complex refers to the distinctive tools and other remains of a particular population).[16] Tools from the Cow Head complex, originally found at Cow Head on the west coast of Newfoundland, have also been excavated at Port au Choix, L'Anse aux Meadows, Cape Freels, and on several smaller sites on the northeast and southwest coast.[17] Based on artifact typology and four carbon dates ranging from about 1950 to 1150 BP (AD 1 to AD 800), the Cow Head population represents the earliest of the Recent Indian groups. Their subsistence adaptation has not yet been defined though the location of camps close to the sea suggests that they made use of a variety of marine resources, probably supplemented by some hunting inland. Cow Head Indian tools include fairly crude expanding broad-stemmed projectile points, lanceolate, ovate, and bipointed bifaces and side scrapers.[18] These tools differ substantially from those of the Maritime Archaic Indians but not enough to preclude the possibility of a cultural relationship between them.

Plate 16.1 The Beaches, a multicomponent site in Bonavista Bay, where Maritime Archaic Indian, Palaeo-Eskimo, Beaches, Little Passage Indian, and Beothuk tools have been excavated.

Since there is no evidence of an Indian population in Newfoundland for the thousand-year period between the most recent traces of the Maritime Archaic Indians and the earliest remains of the Cow Head (Recent Indian) people, the connection between the two populations remains an unresolved question. A few of the Cow Head tools, among them corner-notched projectile points, have been seen as a possible stylistic link with the succeeding Beaches complex.

First identified at The Beaches site in Bonavista Bay (Plate 16.1), remains from the Beaches population have largely been excavated in Bonavista and Notre Dame bays, though some sites have also been found at Port au Choix and on the south coast.[19] Their lithic assemblage is characterized by medium-sized side- and corner-notched projectile points, triangular bifaces, and thumbnail scrapers, made from locally quarried cherts (Plate 16.2). The Beaches complex lasted from about 1150 to 750 or 850 PB (AD 800 to AD 1100 or 1200).[20] Geographically and chronologically, the Beaches complex appears to have been relatively limited. Several archaeological sites with Beaches material also contained Little Passage tools. Site stratification and artifact typology indicate that Beaches-type tools predate those of the Little Passage complex and that they are closely related.[21]

Before the trail from the Beaches to the Little Passage complex is pursued further, it should be mentioned that Beaches tools, particularly the diagnostic projectile points, are typologically close to those of the contemporaneous Recent Indians in Labrador the Point Revenge complex (named after the type site in Hamilton Inlet).[22] This complex covers the period from about 950 to 300 BP (AD 1000 to 1650).[23] Point Revenge sites have been found on the Labrador coast between Saglek Bay and the Quebec Lower North Shore. The campsites of both the

Plate 16.2 Prehistoric native stone quarry in Bloody Bay, Bonavista Bay. (By permission of Ned Pratt, St John's)

Point Revenge and Beaches Indians were located in inner coastal regions, which would indicate that both peoples had a similar subsistence economy. Also, some Beaches projectiles were made from Ramah chert, a raw material that was quarried in northern Labrador and used predominantly by Point Revenge Indians.[24] As more evidence of this nature accumulates, the likelihood that the Beaches and Point Revenge complexes are related is gaining acceptance.[25] Their geographic distribution and persistence in Labrador into the historic period make the Point Revenge Indians the most likely progenitor of the Labrador Montagnais/Naskapi.[26] If a relationship between Labrador Point Revenge Indians and Newfoundland Beaches (and the subsequent Little Passage) Indians can be substantiated, then the historic Beothuk and Montagnais/Naskapi would be related, perhaps through a common ancestor. A relationship is implied in Beothuk tradition, which claims their descent from "Labrador Indians."[27]

LITTLE PASSAGE INDIANS

Little Passage remains from the third group of Recent Indians in Newfoundland, were first identified at the L'Anse à Flamme site, in a narrow passage leading from Hermitage Bay to Bay d'Espoir. In contrast to the limited distribution of Beaches remains, evidence of Little Passage occupation has been found in all major bays of Newfoundland: near Eddies Cove, at Port au Choix, St Pauls, and on the Port au Port Peninsula on the west coast, in the Burgeo area, in Hermitage Bay, and in Placentia Bay on the south coast, in Trinity and Bonavista bays to the east, and in Notre Dame Bay to the north-east. Material from the Little Passage complex has also been excavated at sites along the Exploits River and at Red Indian Lake (see Table 16.1). Camp distribution taken in conjunction with the tool assemblage of these Indians points to their exploitation of a large variety of marine foods during spring, summer, and early fall, and to their hunting of caribou, beaver, and other fur bearers from inland camps, often situated in the vicinity of the coast. Some of the Little Passage Indians seem to have modified this seasonal pattern and moved further inland along the Exploits River and up to Red Indian Lake, presumably to intercept migrating caribou herds that cross these waterways in fall. Tool types associated with the Little Passage people are triangular bifaces, thumbnail scrapers, side- and corner-notched projectile points (smaller than the Beaches points,) tiny corner-notched or expanding-stemmed projectiles, ovate bifaces, linear flakes, and flake points (Plate 16.3). The typology of Little Passage tools as they developed from Beaches tools would place the beginning of this complex between 850 and 750 BP (AD 1100 to 1200).[28] With the beginning of a written history of Newfoundland and its aboriginal people around 450 BP (AD 1500), the Little Passage Indians are referred to as (historic) Beothuk. They were the same population, but for convenience of classification, the prehistoric phase of these Indians has been designated by archaeologists as Little Passage, and the historic phase as Beothuk.

Since all prehistoric native peoples in Newfoundland were hunters and fishers, and since major resources tend to occur in specific locations, many excavated sites were found to have been occupied by several Indian and Eskimo populations. One of the largest of these multicomponent sites is the one at Cape Freels on the northeastern extremity of the Bonavista Peninsula, close to the migration route of harp-seal herds. Remains of Maritime Archaic Indians, Palaeo-Eskimo, Cow Head, Beaches, and Little Passage Indians on the long, sandy beaches of this cape show that groups from these populations have intermittently camped there.[29] Other large, multicomponent sites are those at Brighton Tickle Island in western Notre Dame Bay (Plate 16.4.) and at The Beaches, a narrow neck of land in the recesses of Bonavista Bay, which was probably frequented by harbour seal (Plate 16.1).[30] A stone quarry at Bloody Bay, in close proximity to the Beaches site, was used by Maritime Archaic and Recent Indian populations (Plate 16.2). In some areas the remains from different populations were found in distinct layers, suggesting that centuries passed before the sites were used again. In others, tools from different peoples were found in close association, or actually mixed. Either little soil had accumulated in the interim period, or user populations of such sites followed each other in short succession. One may speculate whether Indian and Eskimo groups living contemporaneously in Newfoundland between 2000 and 1000 BP (50 BC to AD 950) would have competed for coveted resource centres. If relationships in prehistoric times

Plate 16.3 Little Passage Indian tools from Inspector Island. Top row: projectile points; 2d row: two scrapers, two microblades; 3d row: bifaces (knife blades). (Provided by Ralph Pastore, St John's)

can be deduced from what has been recorded in the early historic period, the two groups would have grudgingly tolerated and avoided each other at best and may sometimes have resorted to fighting. But despite their avoidance, Indians and Eskimos were well aware of each other's technology and are thought to have adopted tools from one another. Toggling harpoons, for example, whose heads detach and turn whilst in the wound, were employed by Maritime Archaic Indians long before the Palaeo-Eskimos were using them.[31] In turn, the Early Palaeo-Eskimos might have been the first to bring into northern Labrador the bows and arrows that were subsequently adopted by Maritime Archaic Indians, though the evidence for this transfer is, as yet, tenuous.[32]

THE NORSE

The Norse, who came from Greenland to L'Anse aux Meadows on the Northern Peninsula around 950 BP (AD 1000), do not appear to have influenced aboriginal technology. According to the Graenlendinga and Eirik's sagas, they ex-

Plate 16.4 Brighton Tickle Island, a multicomponent site, where Maritime Archaic Indian, Palaeo-Eskimo, and Little Passage Indian tools have been found. (Provided by Gerry Penney, St John's)

changed milk and cloth with native people in Vinland (which may have been L'Anse aux Meadows) but refused to trade arms.[33] Resulting hostilities caused the Norse to leave. One or more parties returned to the Vinland settlement for short visits, but the Norse eventually refrained from attempts at colonizing on this side of the Atlantic.[34] The "scraelings" (the Norse term for native people) of Norse sagas could have been Newfoundland or Labrador Indians or Late Palaeo-Eskimos.[35] The sagas mention the use of skin boats and war slings, suggesting an Eskimo population, but it is possible that they incorporate what fourteenth-century Norse knew about Greenland Eskimos since the sagas were not written down until the Norse had come into contact with Eskimos – called scraelings – in Greenland. Excavations in the area of L'Anse aux Meadows have exposed Maritime Archaic and Cow Head Indian artifacts, as well as Late Palaeo-Eskimo remains. Given the chronology of native occupation in Newfoundland, the Indians belonging to the Cow Head complex are likeliest to be the native people who defeated the Norse.[36] Norse visits may have lived on in the Indians' oral tradition but do not seem to have made a lasting impact on their culture; there is no indication that they adopted Norse methods of extracting bog iron to fashion iron tools or other Norse techniques.[37]

THE BEOTHUK

A close association between the tools used by the prehistoric Little Passage Indians in Newfoundland and those of the historic Beothuk has been observed on several sites, most clearly at Boyd's Cove in Notre Dame Bay (Plate 16.5).[38] This association is believed to represent the prehistoric/historic contact component of the Beothuk, and to indicate a direct cultural as well as genetic line of descent. Thus, the Beothuk are believed to have developed their culture *in situ* in Newfoundland and not to have been new migrants. Beothuk occupied the same campsites at which their Little Passage ancestors had lived, and their settlements on the coast suggest marine orientation with a limited back-up system for hunting terrestrial animals, as proposed for their prehistoric ancestors. Whether the extensive interception of migrating caribou herds along the Exploits River and at Red Indian Lake that resulted in the more interior-oriented subsistence economy of some Beothuk bands was a prehistoric phenomenon or developed in the historic period has not been established. The lithics used by Beothuk are largely identical to those of the Little Passage Indians, although over time they changed in size and shape. The projectile points became steadily smaller and their surface was less retouched; that is, the tools were less often sharpened through pressure flaking along the edges. These modifications, already noted in prehistoric Little Passage specimens, persisted into the eighteenth century. Hafting notches were made broader and shallower and in time were shifted from the corners to the base, so that the more recent points are stemmed rather than corner notched.[39] With the introduction of iron, the Beothuk produced stone tools more sparingly and by the mid-eighteenth century had largely replaced them with tools manufactured from iron implements.

Plate 16.5 The Boyd's Cove site, located on a level terrace, here seen across Indian Brook, where Beaches, Little Passage, and Beothuk Indian artifacts have been excavated. (Provided by Ralph Pastore, St John's)

Table 16.1
Prehistoric and Historic Archaeological Sites with Cow Head, Beaches, Little Passage Indian, and/or Beothuk Remains

All prehistoric sites listed in this table contain "Recent Indian" remains; if they have been identified as originating with either the Cow Head, Beaches, or Little Passage complex, this is indicated under the heading "Affiliation." Historic Beothuk sites are listed as "Beothuk." The heading "Site Name" is self-explanatory.

All sites and burials are listed by area so as to facilitate an overview of regional distribution. If a Borden number was allocated it is stated; in the case of general sites it is listed under "Borden No." in the case of burials it is listed with the location.

All burials, listed separately, are taken to be (historic) Beothuk, which is indicated by the heading. The date marks the year in which a burial was found. Many burials have been discovered by local residents or visitors whose names are listed under the heading "Informant." Most of these burials are not recorded in detail.

All entries in the table are referenced for easy access to the original records.

Area 1: South Coast, Including Placentia Bay

Site Name	*Borden No.*	*Affiliation*	*Reference*
Melbourne (Sot's Hole, Burgeo)	CjBj-1	Litt. Pass.	Penney 1984a,64
Upper Burgeo Cornelius Isld.	CjBj-7	Litt. Pass.	Penney 1984a,62
Boat Hole Brook	CkBm-1	Beaches Litt. Pass. Beothuk	Penney 1989a,13
Couteau Cove-2	CkBm-2	Beaches Litt. Pass.	Penney 1989a,13
L'Anse à Flamme Hermitage Bay	CjAx-1	Litt. Pass.	Penney 1984a,19
Furby's Cove-2 Hermitage Bay	CjAx-4	Litt. Pass.	Penney 1984a,64
Isle Galet Bay d'Espoir	CkAx-1	Litt. Pass.	Penney 1984a,166
Gt.Brule Marasheen Isld. Pl.B.	CjAm-1	Beothuk	Linnamae 1971,11
Tack's Beach King's Isld.Pl.B.	CjAn-1	Litt. Pass.	Linnamae 1971,13
West of Burgeo and Islands	CjBk-1-4 CjBj-10, 11	Rec. Ind. Rec. Ind.	Ken Reynolds pers. com. 1996

Beothuk Burials

Site Name	*Date*	*Informant*	*Reference*
Rencontre Isld. Lower		Smith McKay	Dawson 1860,468
Burgeo Group CjBj-2	1847	Blackmore	Patterson 1892,157 Howley 1915,334
Hangman's Isld. Placentia Bay	1880s	Warren/Dahl	Howley 1915,292–3
Indian Hole Tilt Isld.Pl.B.	1880s	Warren/Dahl	Howley 1915,293–4

Table 16.1 *(cont'd)*
Prehistoric and Historic Archaeological Sites with Cow Head, Beaches, Little Passage Indian, and/or Beothuk Remains

Area 2: Avalon Peninsula, Conception Bay, Trinity Bay

Site Name	*Borden No.*	*Affiliation*	*Reference*
Ferryland	CgAf-2	Litt. Pass. (pre-1621)	Tuck 1989b,301
Stock Cove	CkAl-3	Beaches Little Pass. 17th cent. Beothuk	Robbins 1982,199
(same location		9 houses	Guy in 1612 [Cell 1982,72])
Thornlea Collier Bay	CjAk-2	Rec. Ind.	Rutherford and Gilbert 1992,18
Frenchman's Isld.	ClAl-1	Litt. Pass. Beothuk	Evans 1982,215
Samson's Head Cove Gt. Mosquito Cove	CkAl-4	Beaches (Litt.Pass.?)	Thomson 1989,16
Russel Pt Dildo Pond	CiAj-1	Litt. Pass. Beothuk	Gilbert and Reynolds 1989,6–7

Area 3: Bonavista Bay

Site Name	*Borden No.*	*Affiliation*	*Reference*
Sailors Site	DeAj-1	Beaches	Carignan 1977,216–17, 272–3
The Beaches, Alexander B.	DeAk-1	Cow Head Beaches Litt. Pass. Beothuk	Devereux 1965b, 1969; Carignan 1975a, 200–1, 214–15, 1977,264–7; Tuck 1992; MacLean 1990b, 1991, 1993
Fox Bar	DeAk-3	Beaches Litt. Pass.	Carignan 1977,216, 272–3
Shambler's Cove opp. Greenspond Isld.	DgAj-1	Beaches Litt. Pass.	Tuck 1983,31, 43
Chandler Reach	DdAj-2	Rec. Ind.	Tuck 1980,24
Cary Cove	DeAl-3	Rec. Ind.	Carignan 1975b,38
Sailor's Isld.	DeAk-6	Rec. Ind.	Tuck 1980,56
Long Islds.	DdAj-2	Rec. Ind.	Tuck 1980,56
Bloody Bay Cove-1	DeAl-1	Beaches	Carignan 1975a,220-1; 1977,215–16, 268–71
Cape Freels 1	DhAi-1	Beaches Litt. Pass.	Carignan 1977,234-5; MacLean 1990a,10
Cape Freels 2	DhAi-2	Beaches Litt. Pass.	Carignan 1977,236–43
Cape Cove 2	DhAi-6	Beaches	Austin 1984,119–21
Cape Cove 3	DhAi-7	Cow Head Beaches Litt. Pass.	Austin 1984,119–21

Table 16.1 *(cont'd)*
Prehistoric and Historic Archaeological Sites with Cow Head, Beaches, Little Passage Indian, and/or Beothuk Remains

Beothuk Burial

Site Name	*Date*	*Informant*	*Reference*
Fox Bar DeAk-2			Carignan 197_, 1973

Area 4: Notre Dame Bay East, Straight Shore, Atlantic Islds.

Site Name	*Borden No.*	*Affiliation*	*Reference*
Inspector Isld.	DiAq-1	Beaches Litt. Pass. Beothuk	Pastore 1983, 1989b
Boyd's Cove	DiAp-3	Beaches Litt. Pass. Beothuk	Pastore 1983, 1986a
Indian Lookout Isld., near Fogo	DjAn-2	Beothuk	MacLeod 1966

Beothuk Burials

Site Name	*Date*	*Informant*	*Reference*
Straight Shore, opp. Indian Islds.	1834	Dr Winter	Lloyd 1876a,227; Howley 1915,334
nr. Musgrave Hrb., ocean beach	1948	Jos. Mouland	Anna Sawicki pers. com.
Phillips Isld. nr. Fogo DjAn-1	1940s	R. Hoddinott	MacLeod 1966,App.II
Seal Cove, Fogo	1887	Thomas Farrell	"Disc. of Red Ind. Remains," 1887
Spirit Cove, New World Isld. DiAr-3	1936–37	Lloyd Watkins	Marshall 1973, 1974b

Area 5: Bay of Exploits

Site Name	*Borden No.*	*Affiliation*	*Reference*
Southwest Hrb. Upper Black Isld.	DiAs-2	Beothuk?	Devereux 1969:4
Birchy Isld.		Beothuk	Devereux 1965b
(Birchy Isld. Sandy Point		1 wigwam pit	Thom. Peyton in Howley 1915,284)
Winter Tickle		Beothuk	Jenness 1934,30, Old Syst.Cat. NF. VIII A No.170–72

Beothuk Burials

Site Name	*Date*	*Informant*	*Reference*
Comfort Isld. DiAr-1 (cemetery)	1888	George Hodder	Howley 1915,332; MacLean 1990a,10
Musslebed Isld.	1974	K. Manuels	Marshall 1974b

Table 16.1 *(cont'd)*
Prehistoric and Historic Archaeological Sites with Cow Head, Beaches, Little Passage Indian, and/or Beothuk Remains

Yellow Fox Isld.	1886	J.P.Howley	Howley 1915,291
Swan Isld.-2 DiAs-9 (cemetery)	1886	J.P.Howley	Howley 1915,289 MacLeod 1966, App.III
Swan Isld.-1 DiAs-1	1970s	Don Locke	MacLean 1990a,11
Long Isld. Bay of Exploits	1927	D.Jenness	Jenness 1929,36
High Greco Isld. DiAt-3	1925–30	J.Haynes	Devereux 1965b

Area 6: Exploits River

Site Name	*Borden No.*	*Affiliation*	*Reference*
Rattling Brook (Bay of Expl.I)	DgAt-l	Litt. Pass.	MacLean 1990a,10
Rushy Pond-1	DfAw-10	Rec. Ind.	Schwarz 1992b,29
Wigwam Brook (North Angle)	DfAw-1	Beothuk	LeBlanc 1973; Locke 1974,14, 19–25; MacLean 1990a,6; Thomson 1982,28, 30–1
Beaver Isld.	DfAw-2	Beothuk	MacLean 1990a,6
(same location	1811		Buchan's report, 1811, Howley 1915,83)
Boom Isld.	DfAw-3	Litt. Pass. Beothuk	MacLean 1990a,7
Aspen Isld.1	DfAw-4	Beothuk	Locke 1974,8, 15; MacLean 1990a,7; Thomson 1982,34
Aspen Isld.2	DfAw-5	Beothuk	MacLean 1990a,7; Thomson 1982,32
Aspen Isld.3	DfAw-6	Beothuk	MacLean 1990a,7; Thomson 1982,34
South Exploits site	DfAw-7	Beaches Beothuk	Locke 1974,15, 19–26; MacLean 1990a,7; Thomson 1982,34
Four Mile Rapids	DfAv-1	Beothuk	MacLean 1990a,6
Pope's Pt, Badger	DfBa-1	Beothuk	Devereux 1964; 1965a; 1970; Locke 1974,34; MacLean 1990a,8
Two Mile Isld. 1 (Cartwright Fatal Isld.)	DfBa-2	Beothuk	Locke 1974,20, 24–6; MacLean 1990a,8; Thomson 1982,26
Two Mile Isld. 2 (Cartwright Fatal Isld.)	DfBa-3	Beothuk	MacLean 1990a: 8; Thomson 1982,26
Two Mile Isld. 3	DfBa-4	Beothuk	MacLean 1990a,8
Slaughter Isld.1	DfBa-5	Beothuk	MacLean 1990a,8; Thomson 1982,26, 29
Little Red Ind. Brook-1	DfBa-6	Beothuk	Howley n.d.,1888; Locke 1974,3, 21; MacLean 1990a,8

Table 16.1 *(cont'd)*
Prehistoric and Historic Archaeological Sites with Cow Head, Beaches, Little Passage Indian, and/or Beothuk Remains

Small Point site	DfBa-8	Rec. Ind. Beothuk	Schwarz 1992b,31
Red Ind. Falls 1	DfBb-3	Beothuk	Locke l974,9, 21, 28; MacLean 1990a,9; Thomson 1982,19–20
Red Ind. Falls 2	DfBb-4	Beothuk	Locke 1974,9; MacLean 1990a,9; Thomson 1982,20–1
Red Ind. Falls 3	DfBb-2	Beothuk	Locke 1974,9, 20, 22, 31; MacLean 1990a,9
Red Ind. Falls 4	DfBb-6	Beothuk	Locke 1974,9, 21; MacLean 1990a,9; Thomson 1982,22
Red Ind. Falls 5	DfBb-1	Beothuk	Locke 1974,9; MacLean 1990a,9; Thomson 1982,23
Red Ind. Falls 6	DfBb-5	Beothuk(?)	Thomson 1982,25
Noel Paul's Br.1	DeBb-1	Beothuk	Locke 1974,28; MacLean 1990a,4; Thomson 1982,13–15
Noel Paul's Br.2	DeBb-2	Beothuk	Thomson 1982,16
Noel Paul's Br.4 (Noel Paul's Brook South)	DeBb-4	Beothuk	MacLean 1990a,4
Little Brook site	DeBb-5	Beothuk	MacLean 1990a,4
Noel Paul's Br.5 (No Name Site)	DeBc-1	Beothuk	MacLean 1990a,4 Thomson 1982,18

Area 7: Red Indian Lake and Other Lakes

Site Name	*Borden No.*	*Affiliation*	*Reference*
Indian Point	DeBd-1	Litt. Pass Beothuk	Locke 1974, Site I: 24–6, 28, 32–5, 40; MacLean 1990a,5; Devereux 1970; Sproull Thoms. 1982,174
(same location		3 mamateeks	Shanawd. sketch 3, 1820)
(same location		21 wigwam pits	Lloyd 1876a,223)
(same location		7+ wigwam pits & lookout tree	Speck 1922,22)
Red Ind. Lake	DeBd-2	Beothuk	Locke 1974, Site II: 27, 28, 32; Site III: 21, 31; MacLean 1990a,5
Red Ind. Lake North	DeBd-4	Beothuk	MacLean 1990a,5
June's Cove 1 NW end of lake	DeBd-3	Beothuk	MacLean 1990a,5
(Red Indian Lake, NW end of lake)		Beothuk abandoned settlement for all seasons, sev. studded houses	Cartwright's report, 1768, Howley 1915,43)
Deer Lake Beach site	DhBi-6	Beaches	Reader 1994,17–31

Table 16.1 *(cont'd)*
Prehistoric and Historic Archaeological Sites with Cow Head, Beaches, Little Passage Indian, and/or Beothuk Remains

West Pond, Halls Bay	DiBb-1	Rec. Ind.	Penney 1988,21, 42
King George IV Lake 1	DbBl-1	Rec. Ind.	Penney 1987b,4
Marshland's site Gambo Pond	DeAn-1	Beaches Litt. Pass.	Schwarz 1992a,37
Burnt Cabin site Gambo Pond	DdAo-8	Litt. Pass.	Schwarz 1992a,43
Triton Br.1 Gambo Pond	DdAp-2	Beaches Litt. Pass.	Schwarz 1992a,47

Beothuk Cemetery

Site Name	*Date*	*Informant*	*Reference*
Red Indian Lake northwest shore Nonosab. burial hut	1827	W.E. Cormack	Cormack 1829,323–4

Area 8: Notre Dame Bay West, Incl. New, Seal, Badger, Halls and Green Bays

Site Name	*Borden No.*	*Affiliation*	*Reference*
Badger Bay V, Little Cove Hrb.	DiAv-6	Rec. Ind. tent rings	Penney 1988,31
Badger Bay III Gull Isld.	DiAw-8	Rec. Ind.	Penney 1988,32
Oil Isld.	DiAw-15	Litt. Pass.	Schwarz 1984,18
Brighton Isld. Tickle, Triton Isld.	DjAv-4	Litt. Pass.	Penney 1988,18; MacLean 1990a,11
Robert's Cove, Triton Isld.	DjAv-5	Rec. Ind.	Penney 1988,19
Paddock's Cove, Long Island	DjAw-10	Rec. Ind.	Penney 1988,34
Sunday Cove Isld.		Litt. Pass.	Owen Bryant 1906, Harvd. Univ. Peabody Museum Arch. File 06-30
Eaton's Point, Halls Bay	DiBa-1	Rec. Ind. (Beothuk?)	Locke pers. com.; Penney 1988,42

Beothuk Burials

Site Name	*Date*	*Informant*	*Reference*
Charles Arm DiAt-2	1960s	W.Parmiter	Devereux 1966
Robert's Arm (Devil's Cove) DjAw-16	1960s	Anthony & Burton	Garth Taylor 1964; Rowsell (Canada 1972)
Big Isld. Burial I DjAw-17	1886	Tilley & Coffin	Howley 1915,332; Patterson 1892,156
Big Isld. Burial II DjAw-18			Howley 1915, 332; Patterson 1892,156
Triton Isld.	1875		Jenness 1934,26, 37; Old Syst. Cat. NF.VIIIA No.90–4

Table 16.1 *(cont'd)*
Prehistoric and Historic Archaeological Sites with Cow Head, Beaches, Little Passage Indian, and/ or Beothuk Remains

The Launch I Long Island DiAv-2	1912	Winsor & Budgell	Marshall 1974b
North China Head Long Isld. DjAw-1	1941	Ryan & Rowsell	Ryan 1948,41; Devereux 1966; Marshall 1974b; 1978
Long Island Green Bay	(pre-1927)		Jenness 1929; Old Syst. Cat. NF.VIIIA No.95–124
Pigeon Isld. nr.Long Isld.	(pre-1927)		Ibid., No.169
Area 9: Northern Peninsula, Strait of Belle Isle, Newfoundland West Coast			
Site Name	*Borden No.*	*Affiliation*	*Reference*
L'Anse aux Mead. Norse site	EjAb-1	Cow Head Beaches	Ingstad 1985,1: Fig.8 J.A.Tuck pers. com., Loring 1992,454
nr. Eddies Cove	EiBb-1	Litt. Pass.	Geologist Dan Bragg, 1991, pers. com.
Spence site Port au Choix	EeBi-36	Cow Head Beaches Litt. Pass.	Renouf 1992; 1993
Cow Head	DlBk-1	Cow Head	Tuck 1978c
St Pauls Bay-1	DlBk-5	Litt. Pass.	Penney 1989b,12
St Pauls Bay-2	DlBk-6	Rec. Ind.	Penney 1989b,12
Port au Port	DdBq-1	Litt. Pass.	Simpson 1984,128–9
Codroy Valley	ClBu-2	Litt. Pass.	Penney 1994,16
Blanc Sablon	EiBg-1B	Litt. Pass.	Pintal 1989,43
Beothuk Burial			
Site Name	*Date*	*Informant*	*Reference*
Indian Cliff, betw. Bradore & Blanc Sablon, Labrador	1888	Edward Jones	Wintemberg 1928, 1936,25

CHAPTER SEVENTEEN

Distribution and Size of the Beothuk Population

INTRODUCTION

Though the Beothuk were the only residents of Newfoundland at the time of discovery, we are not certain of their geographical distribution. The key questions discussed in this chapter are which areas of Newfoundland were occupied by Beothuk aboriginally, and how their distribution was affected by the increasing immigration of Europeans. Related to the foregoing are questions about the size of the Beothuk population and the rate at which it declined over 330 years.

To determine the original state of the Beothuk population historic documents as well as archaeological records have been consulted; both types of data have drawbacks. Sixteenth-century accounts that mention native people are rare, and, to repeat a point made earlier, if they refer to "natives" they often fail to specify whether these people were resident or visitors, and where the meetings or sightings took place. This dearth of information hampers attempts to map Beothuk occupation in the 1500s and makes it difficult to estimate the size of the tribe. The database has therefore been extended by drawing on reports from the seventeenth and, occasionally, early eighteenth centuries that indicate consistent Beothuk habitation in certain areas. Information from archaeological records is also limited since relatively few Beothuk sites have been found, and fewer still can be dated from around the time of contact in the early 1500s. To provide a broader information base, campsites inhabited by the forebears of the Beothuk, the prehistoric Little Passage Indians, have been included in this review.

Taken together, the historic and archaeological data give a fairly convincing picture of the dispersion of the Beothuk over most of Newfoundland in or before AD 1500, and of their gradual exclusion from some inland and coastal areas in the course of the seventeenth, eighteenth, and early nineteenth centuries.

GEOGRAPHICAL DISTRIBUTION

Beothuk presence in Newfoundland is discussed in nine sections, eight of which cover major bays or stretches of coast, while the ninth covers the region around the watershed of the Exploits River, Red Indian Lake, and other inland lakes.

Area 1: South Coast including Placentia Bay. There is considerable archaeological and historical evidence that the Newfoundland south coast was intermittently occupied by Little Passage Indians and that their descendants, the Beothuk, continued to come to this coast until the end of the seventeenth century. Prehistoric Little Passage campsites have been found in Hermitage Bay, Bay d'Espoir, and in the area around Burgeo. Remains of Beothuk occupation have been excavated from sites at Couteau Bay, carbon dated ca. AD 1500, and at Lower Burgeo, dated ca. AD 1600. Two Beothuk graves have been recorded from Placentia Bay and one from Rencontre Island in the Lower Burgeo group; this last burial contained iron tools acquired from Europeans.[1]

Among the earliest documents that mention Newfoundland's native population is Crignon's account of a voyage by the brothers Jean and Raoul Parmentier in 1529 (see chapter 1). According to this account, the coast between Cape Race and Cape Breton was well populated by "cruel and austere people" with whom it was impossible to trade or to converse.[2] It was about six decades later in 1594, when Placentia Bay had become a busy fishing centre, that native people who were presumed to have been Beothuk cut the mooring ropes of boats from the English fishing vessel *Grace* in the harbour of Pesmark, probably present-day Presque, on the Burin Peninsula. Whether these Beothuk lived there permanently or had come there only to hunt or fish cannot be ascertained. John Guy, governor of the English settlement at Cupids, mentioned in his 1612 diary that the Beothuk from Trinity were in the habit of going to Placentia Bay to catch salmon in the Come By Chance River.[3] Another record states that the crew from a Dutch vessel traded with Indians in St Mary's Bay in 1606.[4]

A later reference to the presence of Beothuk on the south coast can be found in a 1694 report by a French officer from the fort in Placentia, who encountered a group of native people, believed to have been Beothuk, in the "southern part of the island."[5] While Beothuk may have continued to come to some areas on this coast, the records suggest that from the early eighteenth century onwards they no longer exploited resources on a regular basis in southern Newfoundland.

Area 2: Avalon Peninsula, Conception Bay, and Trinity Bay. In the 1980s and 1990s stone tools and flakes believed to be of Beothuk origin were unearthed at Ferryland, on the Avalon Peninsula. They were found above a layer of fishbones and Devonshire pottery, which suggests that Beothuk paid visits there in the late sixteenth or early seventeenth century, probably during the absence of the English.[6] Captain Whitbourne was therefore wrong in his belief that the "savages" had never come south of Trinity Bay.[7] However, the sparse evidence for native activities on the Atlantic coast of the Avalon Peninsula would indicate that such visits were rare events.

Prehistoric Little Passage remains have not, as yet, been discovered in Conception Bay, which was one of the first places to be colonized by the English. One would nevertheless assume that the Beothuk were familiar with the resources of the bay and may have exploited them since prehistoric times. For example, the *English Pilot* recorded in 1689 that Indians came to Ochre Pit Cove in Conception Bay to obtain ochre (probably an iron oxide since there is no ochre deposit).[8] Also, according to nineteenth-century lore, "in the early days" Indians, presumably Beothuk, had camped on the beach of present-day Carbonear and had traded furs with the English in exchange for iron goods.[9] By the 1700s, Beothuk seem to have grown reluctant to enter the bay as much of the coast was fished by transient crews or taken up by permanent settlements.

In Trinity Bay, specifically at Dildo Pond, Stock Cove, and on nearby Frenchman's Island, in Bull Arm, Little Passage tools and Beothuk remains were excavated by archaeologists in the 1980s and 1990s.[10] Beothuk habitations at Dildo Pond were described by John Guy as early as 1612 (Plate 2.1). Together with a party of colonists he had seen Beothuk dwellings at this lake and subsequently met Beothuk in Bull Arm.[11] Guy had also noted Beothuk camps at four other places, namely, at the harbour of Dildo South, Stock Cove, in the area of Sunnyside, and in Placentia Bay close to the Come By Chance River. Other accounts from the same period mention Beothuk camps on a small island, on the shore east of Hopeall, and in the vicinity of Heart's Ease.[12] The Beothuk were probably frightened away from this part of Trinity Bay by French and mainland Indian forces who carried their boats overland from Placentia to Trinity Bay in the 1696–97 campaign against the English. By the early 1700s, the Beothuk had been largely displaced by English settlers but still made forays into Trinity Bay until the 1770s.[13]

Area 3: Bonavista Bay. As noted in chapter 16, the large shingle bar in Alexander Bay/Bonavista Bay known as The Beaches has yielded ample archaeological evidence of occupation by Maritime Archaic Indians, Palaeo-Eskimos, Beaches and Little Passage Indians, as well as historic Beothuk (Plate 16.1).[14] A multiple Beothuk grave has been found one to two kilometres away at Fox Bar (Plate 25.3).[15] The Beaches site would have been favoured by native groups not only because it was conveniently located for hunting seal and other marine life but also because it was close to a much-frequented source of rhyolite tuff, a type of stone used for the manufacture of tools (Plate 16.2).[16] Little Passage remains have also been recorded at a number of other beaches and islands along the heavily indented coast of Bonavista Bay and inland from the bay at Gambo Pond (see Table 16.1).[17]

A large number of stone tools from ancient and recent Indian populations, including Beaches and Little Passage Indians, have also been excavated on the long, sandy beach at Cape Freels on the northern headland of Bonavista Bay.[18] This extensive native site is situated in close proximity to the migration route of harp seal. Although no Beothuk housepits or hearths have been found (signs of occupation were probably destroyed by shifting sands and repeated floods), it is thought likely that Beothuk would also have come to this beach.

Among contemporary accounts of Beothuk in Bonavista Bay is an eyewitness report from 1536 describing how English travellers sighted Beothuk in a canoe and pursued them; at the end of the chase, all they found was an abandoned camp.[19] A century later, fishermen were said to have been hesitant to enter Bonavista Bay on account of the Indians there.[20] Commander Percy of the British Royal Navy reported in 1720 that in the summer season, inhabitants had seen them near Bonavista.[21] As more English settled in this bay, Beothuk lost access to resources in some areas, though they continued to make use of The Beaches and possibly other locations in Bonavista Bay until the end of the eighteenth century.[22] After 1800 Beothuk no longer visited the bay, probably due to a severe population decline, which forced them to reduce their range, and to the threat of harassment by resident fishermen.

Area 4: Notre Dame Bay East, Straight Shore, Atlantic Islands. Considered under this heading are the coast between Cape Freels and Comfort Cove, including the Straight Shore, and the offshore islands including Fogo, Twillingate, New World Island, the Wadhams, and Funk Island.

Archaeological evidence of Beothuk residence comes largely from two excavated campsites, one at Boyd's Cove on the main shore (Plate 16.5), and one on neighbouring Inspector Island. Carbon dates from shell and charcoal samples from Boyd's Cove, supported by artifactual evidence, suggest that this site was occasionally occupied by prehistoric Indians and used intensively by Beothuk from about AD 1650 to 1730.[23] Within a maze of islands and shoal waters, Boyd's Cove would have been a safe place to approach by canoe but dangerous for European boats. The Beothuk appear to have abandoned this campsite when the English established a salmon station in Dog Bay, to the east of Boyd's Cove. Seven Beothuk burial places, which contain European material among the grave goods, are further evidence of a Beothuk presence in the area. They were found on Fogo Island, on an islet near Fogo (Plate 25.6), on New World Island (Plate 25.2), on the Straight Shore, and on islands in Comfort Cove.[24]

Beothuk are also known to have travelled to Funk Island, the Wadhams, and other small islands in the North Atlantic where they collected canoeloads of seabirds and their eggs, particularly from a colony of the now-extinct great auk.[25] Their voyages were not recorded before 1766, but it is reasonable to assume that the Beothuk made these trips long before Europeans had become aware of it.[26] By 1812 Beothuk were still going to the bird islands, though they did not venture from their camps in the Bay of Exploits until the settlers had moved from their winter houses in this area to Fogo and other places for the summer.[27] Visits by Beothuk to Fogo and Twillingate islands, which continued into the early nineteenth century, occasionally resulted in conflict. Beothuk persisted in taking equipment and ambushing and wounding or killing Englishmen, and islanders are said to have shot and killed Beothuk.[28] Beothuk also came to the Straight Shore, north of Cape Freels, where their camps were seen at Ragged Harbour Pond in 1780, at Ragged Harbour in 1792, and at Cat Harbour (now North Lumsden) after 1817.[29] In 1803 a Beothuk woman was seized in her canoe on her way to an islet in Gander Bay.[30]

Area 5–7: Bay of Exploits, Exploits River and Red Indian Lake. Stone tools of the Little Passage type found on several sites at Red Indian Lake and on the Exploits River indicate prehistoric inland hunting.[31] The main attraction was the caribou herds that passed through this region on their seasonal migration. Some Beothuk bands continued with the inland hunting pattern of their prehistoric forebears, as shown by a large semisubterranean dwelling at the Indian Point site that was associated with a carbon sample dated ca. AD 1595.[32] Beothuk graves on islands in the Bay of Exploits support the conclusion that Beothuk resided in this region (Plate 25.4).[33]

A profusion of campsites on the Exploits River that date from the late eighteenth and early nineteenth centuries confirm what is known from many contemporary accounts, that the Beothuk favoured this river and its watershed until the early 1800s.[34] In the second half of the eighteenth century the term "Beothuk country" was synonymous with the area around the Exploits River and Red Indian Lake, at that time considered to be the heartland of Beothuk occupation. It was here, in 1768, that Capt. John Cartwright mapped eighty-seven Beothuk mamateeks (the Beothuk term for house) and about thirty kilometres of caribou fences along the river banks.[35] During the following three decades, English furriers repeatedly penetrated into the watershed area of the Exploits River, occasionally trekking upriver to attack Beothuk winter camps.[36] Between 1811 and 1827 Captain Buchan and W.E. Cormack encountered Beothuk dwellings, storehouses, and caribou fences on the Exploits River and at Red Indian Lake and a cemetery on the lake's northern shore.[37] Logging operations, changing river beds, and a dam that considerably raised the water level of Red Indian Lake in the early 1900s have disturbed and obliterated many sites and thus rendered much of the archaeological record inaccessible.

Area 8: Notre Dame Bay West. The bays and large islands in the western part of Notre Dame Bay attracted prehistoric Little Passage Indians as well as their descendants, the Beothuk. Surveys of this part of the bay have disclosed a considerable number of native sites; however, they have not yet been excavated and occupation dates are not available.[38] Additional proof of a Beothuk presence in this area comes from eight Beothuk graves found on Long Island (Plate 25.5), Triton Island, and Big Island, and at Robert's Arm, some containing European materials among the grave goods.[39]

Accounts from western Notre Dame Bay portray a long and turbulent history of conflict between Beothuk and English settlers. A Captain Hall, the first person to attempt settlement in Halls Bay, is said to have been killed by the Beothuk. After moving into the area in 1772, members of the Rowsell family frequently pursued the Beothuk and, in turn, were robbed and ambushed by them.[40] Eruptions of violence were also recorded at New Bay, where both English and Beothuk were killed.[41] A camp on South Twin Lake (recorded in 1827) was one of the last large winter camps that the Beothuk maintained. It was connected by portage paths to Badger and New bays. It is a measure of the importance of these bays and islands to the Beothuk that they remained their main resource base during spring and summer until 1823.[42]

Area 9: Northern Peninsula, Strait of Belle Isle, West Coast. Recent Indian/Beaches-type tools have been unearthed at the Viking site at L'Anse aux Meadows on the northernmost tip of the Northern Peninsula. Carbon dates associated with these tools suggest that Indians occupied the site before and after the Vikings lived there.[43] Little Passage tools have also been found in a small cove near Eddies Cove, north of Pointe Riche, and Little Passage- and Beaches-type tools on the Spence site at Port au Choix.[44]

The importance of the Northern Peninsula as a convenient point of departure or landing for native people travelling to and from Labrador is evidenced by English sixteenth- and seventeenth-century maps that identify a route from Labrador across the Strait of Belle Isle as "Indian Passage"; its end point in Newfoundland may have been "Savage Cove."[45] In addition to its strategic position for travel, this northerly coast offered easy access to seals and whales in the Strait of Belle Isle, and it is possible that the "Newfoundland savages" who, according to Whitbourne, lived "in the North and West part of the Country" (in 1579) were Beothuk.[46] To date, however, no Beothuk remains have been found near the straits.

Beothuk houses and caribou fences were seen in Hare Bay around 1719.[47] The native people there were said not to have traded with Europeans and to have obtained nails and other metal items by burning fishing boats. In the early 1800s, a hunter from Griguet claimed that he and his companion met a Beothuk family about fifteen miles inland from the coast.[48] If this information can be trusted, it implies that some Beothuk continued to live in the far north of the island, even though the French had an extensive fishery there and Montagnais came across from Labrador for the hunting season. In the 1830s, when it was generally believed that the Beothuk no longer existed in Newfoundland, rumours circulated that a few survivors had left the island for Labrador via the Northern Peninsula.[49]

On Newfoundland's west coast (south of the Northern Peninsula), Little Passage Indian remains have been found at St Pauls and at the Port au Port site on the eastern shore of the Port au Port Peninsula.[50] This last site was ideally situated for catching migrating harp seal and may have been a seasonal hunting camp; the Indians' main settlement was probably located at the mouth of St George's River, where in 1594 the crew of the English vessel *Grace* from Bristol "found the houses of the savages made of firre trees."[51] Most likely Beothuk groups continued to live there for another century; Micmac tradition claims that their own settlement in St George's Bay – probably dating to the early 1700s – was preceded by Beothuk occupation.[52] Native people described as "red savages" were also said to have hunted in the vicinity of Bonne Bay around 1718.[53] However, Beothuk occupation of this sequestered bay and of St George's Bay has not been ascertained archaeologically. A history of confrontation with Micmac indicates that the Beothuk lost access to this part of the island in the early part of the eighteenth century.

The evidence leaves no doubt that Beothuk and their prehistoric forebears, the Little Passage Indians, had at one time or another exploited resources in every major bay of the island and had hunted inland from these bays, particularly in the watershed area of the Exploits River. Eighteenth- and nineteenth-century accounts give a fairly convincing picture of the Beothuk's wide distribution and subsequent exclusion from many parts of their traditional land and coast. Already by the end of the seventeenth century the Beothuk had been pressured away from the south coast, from Placentia, St Mary's, and Conception bays. A few decades later, the Beothuk from Trinity Bay had been replaced by English settlers. They continued to visit a few areas in Bonavista Bay and to have access, no longer exclusive, to the coast and islands of Notre Dame Bay. Although Beothuk made trips to the bird islands in eastern Notre Dame Bay into the early 1800s, it was the large islands and the hinterland of western Notre Dame Bay that became their last refuge. Some Beothuk may have lived on the Northern Peninsula and survivors may have gone from there across to Labrador. On the west coast, areas such as St George's Bay and Bonne Bay were taken over by Micmac between about 1720 and 1740. These territorial changes severely diminished the Beothuk's resource base, which became too small and did not include sufficient access to major species to support their population.

APPROXIMATE SIZE OF THE BEOTHUK POPULATION

Determining the size of the Beothuk population at the time of contact has largely been a matter of educated guesswork; accurate data for band sizes, or the size of the Beothuk population as a whole, are lacking. The extent of specific camps can be deduced with reasonable accuracy from archaeological investigations and historic accounts, but these records are not suitable for an estimate of the entire Beothuk population. Although resources in every major region were exploited either prehistorically or after contact with Europeans, bands may have rotated from one bay to another, or they may have lived in one bay but also exploited the resources of a neighbouring one, as did the Beothuk from Trinity Bay who went to Placentia Bay to catch salmon. If this kind of exploitation scheme was generally practised, the entire Beothuk population might have been considerably smaller than has often been assumed.

Estimates of Band Size

To gain an idea of the size of Beothuk groups that occupied a specific area, approximate figures have been deduced from descriptions of Beothuk camps in St George's and in Trinity bays. In 1594 the crew of the English fishing vessel *Grace* saw native houses in St George's Bay. They estimated the size of the group at forty to fifty based on footprints the occupants had left when they fled, and presumably also on the number and size of their houses.[54] This estimate fits well with figures for group sizes extracted from later documentation.

In 1612, John Guy reported several campsites in Trinity Bay: "some houses" at Dildo South, nine houses at Stock Cove, eight to nine houses at the head of Bull Arm, four houses at Dildo Pond, and "some houses" close to a salmon river (probably Come By Chance) in Placentia Bay.[55] In the following year a shelter just large enough for three occupants was seen on a small island off the south shore of Trinity Bay, and Beothuk were seen on the nearby shore.[56] Camps were also set up close to the breeding colonies of birds – one camp was recorded in the vicinity of Heart's Ease in 1622.

It is postulated that in 1612, the camp at Dildo South was the base camp of the Beothuk in Trinity Bay, and that they moved for short periods to Bull Arm and to Stock Cove; in the salmon season they would have gone to the Come By Chance River in Placentia Bay. In late fall the group transferred to a hunting camp or camps at Dildo Pond and possibly elsewhere and remained there for the winter. In accordance with this subsistence pattern, calculation of the size of a band is based on the eight to nine mamateeks in the base camp, of which one or perhaps even two may no longer have been in use, since it was the Beothuk's habit to leave old or unoccupied mamateeks standing.[57]

The houses recorded by Guy on the coast, being summer habitations, may have been large enough for five to six individuals (three to eight people per house have been recorded for coastal summer mamateeks).[58] Assuming that seven to eight houses, each occupied by five to six people, accommodated the entire band, it would have numbered between thirty-five and fifty-five individuals.

Only one archaeologically excavated site at Boyd's Cove has prompted an estimate of group size. Boyd's Cove is believed to have been a base camp with a network of temporary exploitation camps as has also been suggested for Dildo South in Trinity Bay.[59] Judging by the number and successive use of the mamateeks and by the faunal remains, Pastore suggests that between thirty and forty-nine people may have lived there at any one time.[60]

Contemporary Estimates of the Size of the Beothuk Population

John Mason, governor of the English colony in Cupids in 1616–17, and Richard Whitbourne, governor at Aquaforte in 1618, who had both travelled extensively around the Newfoundland coast, were of the opinion that the native Indians were "few in numbers."[61] In the 1760s, settlers in Notre Dame Bay claimed that only two to three hundred Beothuk were still alive. Lieut. John Cartwright, after he investigated Beothuk country in 1768, concluded that the native population was "inconsiderable ... in point of numbers" and estimated the size of the tribe at between three and five hundred individuals.[62] On his map of the Exploits River Cartwright marked eighty-seven houses on the banks of the river. Because many of these had not been used during the previous hunting season, he was not able to make "an accurate calculation of the inhabitants."[63] He believed, however, that during the hunting season up to two-thirds of the Beothuk lived close to the Exploits River, while the remainder of the tribe had their winter camps in more remote places such as Gander, Middleton, and Mary-Anne lakes.

Cartwright's 1768 estimate of a maximum population of five hundred seems not to have been challenged. Banks was told in 1766 that the Indian population amounted to "less than 500," while G.C. Pulling, who had questioned many local residents on this topic, suggested in 1792 that there were five to six hundred Beothuk. The figure of six hundred was mentioned in an 1801 report by W. Sherrett, the commanding officer of the Newfoundland Forces.[64]

Governors Holloway (1807) and Duckworth (1810) and Chief Justice Reeves (1808) supposed that not more than five to six hundred Beothuk were still alive, while Governor Keats (1815) believed that only "a few hundred" of them were left.[65] Lieut. David Buchan observed in 1811 that the Beothuk camp at Red Indian Lake housed between sixty-five and seventy-five Beothuk, but he noted that this would not have been the entire tribe. In the late 1820s he suggested a figure of 150 individuals. Some sixteen years later in 1836, Buchan told the Select Committee on Aborigenes that the tribe would have amounted to four or five hundred people in 1811.[66]

The one estimate that is considerably at odds with the others is that of Governor Duckworth. In his official report of Buchan's 1811 expedition he wrote: "We had greatly underestimated the numbers of the Indians ... they cannot amount in the whole to less than three thousand persons."[67] This figure is so different from Buchan's that it is assumed to result from a misunderstanding.

As described in chapter 14, the captive Shanawdithit later claimed that the camp Buchan visited in 1811 housed only forty-two people, and that the entire tribe amounted to no more than seventy-two.[68] She not only provided these figures but specified the gender of the people in each house in both the main camp as well as the two smaller camps on the northern and southwestern shores of the lake.

In 1819, when the John Peytons, father and son, captured Demasduit (Mary March) at the Beothuk's principal camp on Red Indian Lake, John Peyton, Jr, thought that the three mamateeks did not house more than fourteen or fifteen individuals altogether.[69] In contrast, E.S., an agent from one of the mercantile firms in Fogo who accompanied the party, claimed that the Indians who had fled from the camp amounted to several hundred men, women, and children. In 1829, this same agent expressed the opinion that Shanawdithit could not have been the last of the tribe "by many hundreds."[70] Rev. John Leigh, in whose house Demasduit stayed in March 1819, thought the Beothuk tribe at that time numbered about three hundred.[71]

Shanawdithit's detailed descriptions and drawings, which she made for William E. Cormack in 1828, indicate that by 1819 the Beothuk tribe had been reduced to thirty-one people and was dwindling. In the spring of 1823 only nineteen Beothuk remained. Shanawdithit referred to this group as "her uncle's family." (see Fig. 14.6). By the time Shanawdithit was captured, no more than twelve (or thirteen) Beothuk were still alive in the interior.[72]

The discrepancy between her numbers and the figures quoted by the English – with the exception of Peyton, Jr – are certainly substantial. Surveyor General Noad reviewed whatever was known about the Beothuk in the 1850s and concluded that Shanawdithit would have purposely concealed the true size of her tribe.[73] Yet subsequent developments would support her figures rather than the official ones, since few Beothuk were seen after 1823.

Retrospective Estimates of the Size of the Beothuk Population

Twentieth-century estimates of the size of the Beothuk population at contact range from five hundred to fifty thousand. The first figure was suggested by the anthropologist James Mooney, who accumulated a large body of population data for Indian tribes north of Mexico. His figures, based on contemporary estimates from the 1600s and early 1700s, were posthumously published by Swanton in 1928. They are still widely quoted. For the Beothuk population Mooney adopted a figure of five hundred, presumably based on Cartwright's 1768 estimate since none of the earlier documents are helpful with respect to population size.[74] One needs to remember, however, that by this time the Beothuk were almost certainly undergoing a population decline.

Based on John Cartwright's map and report, I estimate the Beothuk population in 1768 at close to 350 individuals. This estimate is based on the assumption that of the eighty-six conical dwellings Cartwright marked on his map of the Exploits River, only half, that is, forty-three mamateeks (plus a square house), had been inhabited during the previous hunting season (the other houses are likely to have been abandoned some time earlier). With five people in each conical mamateek plus fifteen in the square house, the population along the river banks would have amounted to 230 individuals. In Cartwright's opinion, this group constituted about one-half to two-thirds of the entire tribe, the remainder occupying more remote areas. Considering other evidence about Beothuk presence and group size, it is suggested that the families who wintered on the Exploits River in 1768 represented two-thirds of the Beothuk population; accordingly, the size of the total population would have been around 345.[75]

The anthropologist Diamond Jenness suggested that at the time of first contact with Europeans, the Beothuk population would have amounted to five hundred, a figure he probably took from Mooney's work.[76]

The anthropologist A.L. Kroeber, in his publication on "Cultural and Natural Areas of Native North America" (1939), also put the Beothuk population at five hundred.[77] The aim of Kroeber's work was to study the relationship between ecological factors and cultural phenomena. After calculating the population density of each tribe – based on population estimates from archival records and size of territory – he grouped the tribes by "natural area" according to similar environmental factors. Kroeber was able to demonstrate that similar environmental conditions were associated with similar population densities.

In Kroeber's scheme, the Beothuk were placed in the category of "Eastern Subarctic" hunters and gatherers, together with Montagnais/Naskapi, Têtes de Boule (Attikamek), and Cree (excepting Plains Cree). His average population-density figure for the whole of the eastern Subarctic was 1.11 (individuals) per one hundred square kilometres. This figure has subsequently been used by other researchers to calculate a probable Beothuk population size. It should be remembered, however, that Kroeber had included an assumed Beothuk population figure of five hundred in his calculation, and that the purpose of his research was not to establish the size of populations but to compare population densities. For the Beothuk Kroeber had tabulated a population density of 0.40 (individuals) per one hundred square kilometres, for the subarea inhabited by Montagnais/Naskapi and Tête de Boule a population density of 0.44 (individuals) per one hundred square kilometres, and for the area inhabited by Cree a density of 1.43 (individuals) per one hundred square kilometres.[78]

If one were to draw on Kroeber's calculations for an estimate of the Beothuk population size, one would have to exclude the figure for the Beothuk and use only the population density of other northeastern groups. Dividing the 112,300 square kilometres of the Newfoundland landmass into 1,123 units of one hundred square kilometres each, one could multiply this number of units by 0.44 (as given for Montagnais/Naskapi and Tête de Boule), or by 1.43 (as given for Cree), or by 1.1 (calculated for these three groups together).[79] The resulting figures for the Beothuk population would be 494 people based on Montagnais/Naskapi plus Tête de Boule population density figures, 1,605 people based on the population density figure of the Cree, and 1,235 people taking the figures for the three groups together.

Kroeber also looked at population density per length of tidal shoreline and concluded that there is a measurable relationship between access to marine resources and population density. In a very rough way, the population density for one hundred square kilometres of land use equalled that for one mile of tidal shoreline.[80] However, because Kroeber included in his calculation the entire Newfoundland shoreline of 3,050 miles (4,900 kilometres) in combination with the population estimate of five hundred Beothuk, the population density worked out to be 0.16 (persons) per mile of shoreline. When Kroeber included this low density in his calculation for the "Northern Area" (not identical with the area of "Eastern Subarctic"), it evidently skewed his calculation, which came to 0.40 (persons) per mile of shoreline (or a total of two thousand persons distributed over a shoreline of 5,550 kilometres).[81]

Anthropologist Fred Eggan, who reviewed Mooney's figures for population sizes at contact, suggested a land-support capacity of just over one person per one hundred square kilometres for the northern interior Subarctic.[82] Presumably this capacity figure was based on Kroeber's work. A calculation of the Beothuk population size based on Eggan's figure suggests just over 1,123 people at the time of contact.

For his estimate of the precontact Beothuk population, the historian L.F.S. Upton utilized a combination of Eggan's and Kroeber's studies on population densities in the northeastern Subarctic. Upton arrived at a population figure of 1,123 based on Eggan, and at 3,050 based on Kroeber's shoreline figure. He then averaged the two and suggested a population of about 2,000.[83]

Leo F. English, a Newfoundland writer, believed that the Beothuk numbered 15,000 to 20,000 people at contact, while Keith Winter, in his popularized account *Shanaditti*, estimated 50,000; neither provide a rationale for their figures.[84]

Archaeologists in Newfoundland suggest that the Beothuk population at contact might have been five hundred (Tuck) or less than one thousand (Pastore).[85]

It should be clear from this discussion that any attempt at estimating the size of the Beothuk population is fraught with uncertainty. Methodologies such as those used by Kroeber and others demonstrate that population estimates are often based on too much supposition and too little hard fact. No estimates based on general environmental conditions could completely simulate those of the Beothuk, who used inland and coastal resources on a seasonal basis. The estimates also ignore the likelihood that there was no maximum exploitation and that at any one time only portions of Newfoundland were inhabited by Beothuk people. However, it is true that comparisons with other regions serve as a guideline as to plausible upper limits for population size.

In sum, then, information from two reports (1594, 1612) and from the excavated Beothuk site at Boyd's Cove suggests that Beothuk bands would have numbered about thirty to fifty-five people. Estimates for the size of the entire Beothuk population at the time of contact vary. Early historic records emphasize the smallness of the native population in Newfoundland; contemporary estimates, recorded from the 1760s onwards, range from two hundred to six hundred; the figure of five hundred, as suggested by Cartwright in 1768, was generally accepted. The Beothuk captive Shanawdithit said that by 1811 the tribe had decreased to seventy-two people and, at the time of her capture in April 1823, had dwindled to twelve or thirteen. With her death in 1829, the Beothuk tribe is considered to have become extinct. Retrospective population estimates of the Beothuk at contact, based on land-support capacities and on the attendant population densities of other subarctic hunters, fishers, and gatherers, range from about five hundred to 1,600. Newfoundland archaeologists suggest an original population of between five hundred and one thousand.

CHAPTER EIGHTEEN

Aspects of Social Organization

Historic accounts of Beothuk contain little direct information about social organization, although some general features can be extrapolated from Beothuk culture traits coupled with information on the social organization of other northeastern Algonquian tribes. Most of the details that are known were not collected until the mid-1700s. By that time significant changes had occurred in the size and distribution of the Beothuk population, which in turn would have affected other areas of their culture. Information from the eighteenth and nineteenth centuries would therefore largely reflect social organization as it had developed through the impact of European and other native groups.

Because our database is scanty, only five aspects of social organization are examined in this chapter: l) tribal structure and cooperation among bands; 2) ceremonies and celebrations; 3) band leadership; 4) differences in social status; 5) the presence of shamans.

TRIBAL STRUCTURE AND COOPERATION AMONG BANDS

The ethnohistorian A.W. Trelease has postulated that among Algonquians the smaller village community or band was the important social and political unit, while the tribal unit was largely linguistic and cultural. A significant feature of the social organization among Algonquians was their preference for living in independent bands that constituted, beyond the family, the primary functional unit of society.[1] These bands are likely to have been of the type usually found among hunting and fishing people, defined by the anthropologist Rogers as units of two or more hunting groups that habitually gathered together in one season and continued with a relatively stable membership for a greater length of time.[2] The geographic separation of these bands would have fostered self-sufficiency and caused each group to conduct its daily affairs independently. Cooperation among bands, while common in times of emergency, was not generally practised.

The size of Beothuk bands in the seventeenth and early eighteenth centuries is estimated to have ranged between thirty and fifty-five.[3] In the 1760s the Beothuk who assembled for the fall hunting season by the Exploits River, believed to have numbered over two hundred individuals, would have belonged to several bands.[4] In the early 1800s, as described earlier, the principal Beothuk winter settlement at Red Indian Lake, visited by Capt. David Buchan in 1811, consisted of three large dwellings occupied by forty-two Beothuk. Two smaller settlements elsewhere on the shore of the lake with two dwellings each housed thirteen and seventeen Beothuk respectively.[5] Since by that time the Beothuk tribe had decreased significantly, it is possible that these three camps constituted the remnants of three different bands and their numbers do not necessarily indicate original band size.

The discussion of cooperation between bands is limited to the questions whether Beothuk bands cooperated in subsistence activities and lent material assistance to each other in conflicts with outsiders, and whether their reluctance to trade with Europeans and to acquire firearms would have been based on consent among all bands.

One conspicuous feature in Beothuk/European relations is the absence of attacks by Beothuk on encroaching fishermen and settlers. One may argue that, at least in the sixteenth and early seventeenth centuries, the small size of Beothuk bands and their dispersal throughout the island would have made it difficult to assemble sufficient force to tackle Europeans who were armed with guns. However, these factors do not seem to have determined the Beothuk's reluctance to resort to organized resistance, because even at a time when their territory had decreased and united action against encroachment and hostilities by settlers would have been more feasible, it did not occur. There is also no evidence that the Beothuk band in St George's Bay, which came into conflict with Micmac in the early 1700s and was largely eradicated, was supported in these confrontations by other bands. While the available documentation does not allow for conclusions about Beothuk policies on organized resistance, the absence of records to this effect suggests that material assistance between bands may not have extended to defence.

With regard to cooperation in subsistence activities, Cartwright's map suggests that, by the 1760s, several bands participated in the annual caribou drive on the Exploits River. He proposed that "the small parties into which they [Beothuk] were divided for ranging the islands [in summer]" met inland in "a common center compos[ing] one extensive and numerous society."[6] His map of the Exploits River indicates that the eighty-seven mamateeks were widely distributed over a seventy-kilometre stretch of this waterway.[7] Thirty-four conical mamateeks are marked on the southeastern bank of the river between Bishop's Falls and Red Indian Lake, and fifty-two conical and one square mamateek on the northwestern bank. Of these, eighteen mamateeks stood by themselves; in nineteen locations two dwellings were built next to each other, in six locations clusters of three mamateeks were noted, and in three locations clusters of four.

Some of the clusters are likely to have formed one large camp, particularly those that were situated at the opening in caribou fences, each maintaining and patrolling a specific part of the fenceworks.

In the early 1800s, when the survival of the tribe was increasingly threatened, families cooperated. One incident that caused them to unite was Captain Buchan's appearance at their principal settlement at Red Indian Lake in 1811. As recounted in Part One, Buchan had spent several hours trying to convince the Beothuk of his friendship, but they did not trust his intentions and killed the two marines he had left behind when he went back to his previous camp to fetch presents. They then fled to a secluded location where they were joined by the occupants of two other camps.[8] In the winter of 1819 all thirty-one survivors of the tribe joined again at the northeastern arm of Red Indian Lake, presumably to increase their chances of providing sufficient food and greater security. In the winter of 1822–23 the remnant of the tribe, by now reduced to twenty-seven, camped in one location, presumably to meet the challenge to their survival together.

In contrast to other North American tribes, the Beothuk never became involved in the fur trade. Only a few Beothuk individuals exchanged goods with white settlers in "silent barter" (in the absence of the trade partner) on a small scale; at no time were significant quantities of furs traded. This abstinence from trade may have been based on resentment and animosity towards the whites – certainly violent encounters with Europeans affected relations from the early contact period on, and few trade opportunities arose as a result. Possibly the prediction that trade relations could lead to depletion of resources or to dependency on European goods contributed to the Beothuk's reluctance to embark on regular exchanges of furs, and most likely there were other reasons.[9] However, since Beothuk bands throughout Newfoundland acted in like manner, their general avoidance of trade could reflect agreement on this issue.

The Beothuk's rejection of European guns may have been based on a similar understanding among bands; we know of no deviation from this position throughout the more than three centuries of existence alongside Europeans, though the Beothuk routinely acquired other European hardware. When guns did come into their possession, they did not seem to value them. In 1818 for example, when they took Peyton's vessel in Exploits Bay, the Beothuk destroyed two guns and a pistol, breaking and sinking the firearms together with the ammunition.[10]

CEREMONIES AND CELEBRATIONS

Perhaps the most significant Beothuk tradition was their annual ochring ceremony, which appears to have been unique among seaboard Algonquians, at least during the late historic period. According to the informant Santu, daughter of a Beothuk/Micmac couple, all members of the tribe received a new application of red ochre on the face and body once a year.[11] This coating was a mark of tribal identity. Infants born during the previous year were given their first coating as a sign of their initiation into the tribe. The paint was meant to last for a year but under certain conditions it could be renewed in the intervening months. To be told to remove the paint prior to the next ochring ceremony was considered a form of punishment. When a husband or wife died, the surviving spouse would wash with heated water decocted with the shavings of dogwood.[12]

Santu claimed to have been told by her father that the ochring ceremony was celebrated every spring. In the early 1800s (when the Beothuk were confined to the upper Exploits River and its watershed) it was held at Red Indian Lake. The event was said to have been accompanied by dancing, feasting, and games and to have lasted for about ten days, during which the community enjoyed, to use Santu's phrase, "a big time." A notation in the *English Pilot* (1689) records Beothuk visiting a cove south of Bay de Verde, Conception Bay, in order to procure ochre and apply it to themselves.[13]

The coating of canoes and, perhaps, other material objects with ochre may also have been attended by a special ceremony. A possible ochring site was recorded by Cormack in 1827, at an abandoned Beothuk camp on Badger Bay Great Lake (South Twin Lake), which he believed to be a "favourite place of settlement."[14] Cormack had noted daubs of fresh red ochre on a canoe storage rack and believed that a canoe had recently been ochred there. At the Indian Point site Helen Devereux found two parallel, irregular patches of red ochre the length of a canoe that may have originated from the daubing of ochre on such a craft.[15]

Another ceremony involving the community was that of dancing in a circle around an object of special interest, as depicted in Shanawdithit's sketch of celebrations after the killing and decapitating of Buchan's two marines (Plate 10.1). One head had been "stuck on a post around which the Indians sang and danced two hours"; the other head had been stored in a different location where a similar ceremony was held some months later.[16] Appropriate songs on these occasions may have been those entitled "Whiteman's Head" and "Whiteman's Jacket," the latter perhaps relating to the blue jackets of Buchan's marines. According to Shanawdithit's account, "upon one of the two marines refusing to give up his jacket to some who wished to take it away he and his companion were immediately pierced with arrows."[17] The Beothuk practice of impaling the heads of Englishmen on poles is recorded repeatedly in contemporary accounts.[18]

On other occasions the community joined for the recitation of historic events or for songs and games. Shanawdithit revealed to Cormack that from infancy all members of the tribe were taught to foster animosity and feelings of revenge against all people around them. This was reinforced by "narrating, during the winter evenings, the innumerable wrongs inflicted on the Boeothics by the white men and by the Mik-maks."[19] Such recitations were probably done by an authorized person when a band was assembled in winter.[20]

Songs not only accompanied ceremonies and feasts. According to Shanawdithit they also told of special events; sometimes the occupants of two or three mamateeks sang together.[21] Topics recorded by Cormack include other Indians, dead men, white men's houses, white men's guns and stages, white men's dishes, beads, buttons, nets, hatchets, shirts, Indian bows and arrows, canoes, and boat stealing. This last topic may have alluded to the Beothuk's stratagem of cutting fishermen's boats from their moorings.[22] Singing songs about natural phenomena, animals, and other resources in order to pass on knowledge about nature and to express respect and appreciation for their environment would have revived and verified communal traditions and memories. Drums or other musical instruments that accompanied the singing and dancing of other native tribes have never been mentioned in connection with Beothuk.[23]

Myths explaining the creation of the universe, and different natural phenomena would also have been retold, as was the practice among other native peoples.[24] Unfortunately, none of them have been recorded fully. Shanawdithit only remarked in passing "that 'the Voice' told them that they [Beothuk] sprang from an arrow or came in the ground."[25]

BAND LEADERSHIP

In general, hunter-fisher-gatherer band societies were egalitarian. A limited form of leadership was provided by an older, experienced male who was respected for qualities such as wisdom and charity. Elman R. Service describes this leadership role as "charismatic," or one of "informal influence." While there is no detailed information on Beothuk leadership, it is reasonable to assume that Beothuk bands were headed by individuals whose qualities and roles were similar to those described for other hunter-fisher-gatherer band societies.[26] Influence may have been informal and a leader would only have kept his status as long as performance warranted. Privileges may have concerned status symbols rather than extensive authority or exemption from certain tasks.[27] Accounts by casual European observers indicate that Beothuk chiefs differed from the rest of the group in their attire and bearing. (Although these leaders are referred to in documents as "chiefs," in anthropological parlance the term tends to be associated with a more formal power position. Though we are not certain about the extent of the authority of Beothuk leaders, I use the term here for want of another.)

The man identified by John Guy in 1612 as the chief of the Beothuk band he encountered in Trinity Bay was the only one to wear mittens and footwear. The last to join the assembled group, he behaved in a "civil" manner and carried an "oare" in his hand.[28] Perhaps this oar was a staff of office. Guy said that he "seemed to have some command over the reste," suggesting that he not only stood out on account of his outfit, civility, and manner of approach but also by the way the other Beothuk conducted themselves around him.[29]

The presence of a chief was also mentioned in nineteenth-century descriptions of Beothuk who wintered in encampments on the Exploits River and at Red Indian Lake. As detailed in the chapter on hunting techniques, these

Beothuk intercepted migrating caribou herds every fall and for this purpose built fences up to sixty kilometres long. Not only did the maintenance of the fences require considerable organization but the timing of the caribou drive and the positioning of participants had to be orchestrated if the hunt were to be successful. Presumably, this task would have been allocated to a chief or leader with the authority and skills to manage the preparations and the drive itself. Hunting activities by Beothuk who wintered closer to the coast may have required leadership of a different type, more suited to smaller groups.

When the survival of the tribe was at stake in the early 1800s, leaders could have assumed greater authority than was the norm. However, accounts of Beothuk chiefs indicate that their general role was to influence rather than command their people. In the 1860s or 1870s Inspector Grimes, a native of Notre Dame Bay and member of the Newfoundland Constabulary, related a story that he had heard in his youth concerning an encounter on the Exploits River in the late 1700s between a large body of "Red Indians" and a party of furriers. The encounter ended in a "pitched battle" during which a huge and powerful man, who appeared to be a Beothuk chief, had tried to induce his party to rush towards the furriers and overwhelm them.[30] When the men refused to comply he ran forward alone and was killed, whereupon the others fled. The furriers said that, had the Indians followed, they could easily have overpowered the furriers before they had time to reload their guns.[31]

Capt. David Buchan, who trekked up the Exploits River to the Beothuk's winter settlement at Red Indian Lake, believed that they lived in "independent companies" but had one principal chief. Buchan met this chief, who has gone down in history as the man responsible for the killing of his two marines at that settlement. He wore a conspicuous high cap, owned an ochre-covered "mythological emblem," and generally indicated by his behaviour that he was the man in charge. When he returned, having left Buchan's party, "he called his brethren together, and proposed to put the marines to death immediately, but this the others would not consent to do, and opposed it for a long time most strenuously, nevertheless, the chief eventually gained his point by having persuaded them of the necessity of doing so."[32]

Although it has been claimed that the chief must have been of a "sanguinary temperament," this is hardly a fair statement. He had apparently done what he believed to be best for his people, and while he had hotly argued the case for killing the marines, the deed was not done until his council consented (for a full account of the story, see chapter 10).

The last known Beothuk chief, Nonosabasut, was described as a powerfully build man of great physical strength. His caribou-skin coat was lined with beaver and other furs and he had a bushy beard, an uncommon feature among Beothuk.[33] When the Peytons and half a dozen furriers caught up with his group at Red Indian Lake and captured his wife Demasduit in 1819, he laid down his bow, approached the party with a branch of a fir tree, and delivered a long oration. He then shook hands with many of the English and strove to take back his wife. Prevented from doing so, he tried to force her release but was shot and stabbed to death in the ensuing struggle.[34] Shanawdithit recounted that he was the most powerful chief and hunter of the tribe. Her father, a swift hunter, had also been a chief.[35]

DIFFERENCES IN SOCIAL STATUS

Nonosabasut was laid to rest by his people in a burial hut built on the foundation of his mamateek at their camp on the northeastern arm of Red Indian Lake. This tomb was extremely elaborate relative to the commonest mode of interment wherein the body was wrapped in birchbark, placed on the ground, and then covered with a heap of stones.[36] A large variety of articles (described in greater detail in the chapter on mortuary practices) were deposited with Nonosabasut in the hut. Demasduit's remains were later placed by his side after Captain Buchan had returned them in a coffin to the camp upon her death in 1820. The remains of their child, who had died shortly after Demasduit's capture, and those of other children were interred in the same burial hut. The care taken in the disposal of Nonosabasut and his family and the numerous gifts deposited with them indicate special status.[37]

There is also evidence that the mamateek of a Beothuk chief was larger than those of the rest of the group and set apart from them. Shanawdithit's sketch of the Beothuk settlement at Red Indian Lake (Plate 10.1) depicts the mamateek of her uncle (presumed to have been the chief at that time) as larger than the other dwellings and different in shape.[38] Buchan said in 1811 that two wigwams stood close together and a third one about ninety metres away. When the anthropologist Frank G. Speck investigated a Beothuk campsite at Red Indian Lake in the early 1900s, he counted seven round pits and one large, rectangular one. His Micmac guide claimed that the rectangular one had been the foundation of the dwelling of a Red Indian "chief." Differences in the size of dwellings were also observed by archaeologists at two Beothuk campsites on the Exploits River that had several small housepits and one larger one.[39]

It is evident from what we know of Demasduit that women, too, could hold special status among the Beothuk. Demasduit may have held such status as the wife of a chief. Her privileges included a place in the elaborate burial hut and may also have extended to aspects of daily life. For example, after her capture by the English, Demasduit placed herself in the sleigh and directed the men by signs to cover her over. She also held her legs out to have her moccasins laced.[40] She was said to have habitually expected attention from others and to have been "unacquainted with any laborious employment." To her captors her behaviour indicated "a superiority of station."[41] However, as Barbara Neis has pointed out, Demasduit's refusal to lace her boots or do housework may have been her way of protesting her capture.[42]

Shanawdithit, who was captured four years later, was also said to have expected small attentions as her right.[43] Yet she was a diligent, adept worker and cook. During the years she lived with the Peytons, she performed the usual household chores such as washing and scrubbing to their satisfaction. But while the two women differed in their willingness to work, both were said to have resented anything approaching rough, harsh, or unseemly conduct on the part of men.[44] Several Beothuk women, when caught by Englishmen, were said to have appealed to their pursuers' sympathy by laying bare their breasts and thus disclosing their sex.[45] This may have been done to indicate to the English that they were not armed, or because women were sometimes spared.

Among the Beothuk as among most North American Indian tribes, a man had only one wife; at least, Shanawdithit consistently referred to couples when speaking of married persons.[46] The Reverend Mr Leigh and W.E. Cormack questioned Demasduit and Shanawdithit respectively on this point. Leigh later told Captain Robinson that "polygamy does not appear to have been practised."[47] Cormack, in his notes of interviews with Shanawdithit, confirmed this.[48]

Marriages were celebrated by way of "a prolonged feast which rarely terminated before the end of twenty-four hours."[49] Mr Gill, whose mother had been a servant with Shanawdithit in John Peyton, Jr's household, said the Beothuk were "very strict about moral law" with respect to marriage. They inflicted severe penalties on anyone who transgressed, "burning alive at the stake being the fate of the adulterer, which was witnessed by the whole tribe who danced in a circle around the victim."[50] Whether this alleged punishment was actually practised or had become exaggerated over time in the story's retelling cannot be ascertained.

PRESENCE OF SHAMANS

Shamans have been described as the "interface" between the people and the powers that embodied the environment on which native people depended. Some shamans were capable of achieving powerful visions or making alliances with other animate beings and soliciting their assistance. Their task was to keep relationships with these powers harmonious so as to ensure success in hunting and other activities. Shamans also had the knowledge to conduct appropriate rituals and ceremonies, including sacrificial offerings, and they were called upon to perform curing ritual for the sick.

It is suggested that healers and specially empowered individuals would also have been present in Beothuk bands, although the evidence is largely circumstantial. Tusks found together with a cache of bone carvings in a cave burial on Long Island/Green Bay and in a grave in the Bay of Exploits may have served a shaman as "sucking tubes" for removing invasions from the body of an afflicted person.[51] We also know that Shanawdithit's mother, Doodebewshet, possessed knowledge of herbal remedies as well as of the workings of special powers.[52] When one of her daughters became seriously ill she threw herbs into a fire, whose smoke the girl was to inhale while she herself uttered "incantations" described by one informant as "horrid shrieks."[53] It may be recalled that she was also the person who decapitated Captain Buchan's two marines.[54] Although Shanawdithit did not say what position her mother held within the tribe, the fact that she secured the heads for subsequent ritual may indicate special status.

Other circumstantial evidence for the presence of shamans includes a necklace of carved bone pieces with an animal tooth in the centre, and a "medicine bag." Both items were found in Beothuk burial places, the first at Robert's Arm and the second at Comfort Cove.[55] Necklaces of a similar kind were among the paraphernalia of northwestern Athapaskan shamans and were said to represent animal spirit helpers.[56] This interpretation may also fit the Beothuk carvings. The Beothuk "medicine bag" contained a number of carved bone charms, "strings of wampum," a brilliant piece of iron pyrite, and several bird skulls.[57] All objects suggest a belief in protection and, by interpolation, the presence of a shaman, who would have mediated the ceremonies that surrounded the acquisition or employment of such objects. Medicine bags, or shamans' bags, were widely used by shamans of other tribes. LeClercq obtained from a Micmac shaman what he called a "juggler's bag," which held "miniature artifacts as well as representations of animals and children, a wooden bird and dew claws," believed to have special powers.[58] In Micmac folklore a Micmac hunter stole from a Beothuk man a leather bag that contained "little bones of animals, deer, moose, fox, wild-cat, every animal that goes in the woods." Because the objects were potentially magical, his companion warned the thief about their possible ill effects.[59]

CHAPTER NINETEEN

Food Consumption and Subsistence Economies

FOOD CONSUMPTION

As hunters, gatherers, and fishers, the Beothuk exploited terrestrial fauna, marine resources, birds, and bird's eggs, as well as edible plant foods. Their most important resources, caribou, seal, and salmon, were migratory species. In response to these animals' habits and habitats, the Beothuk moved in an annual cycle from inland locations to the coast and vice versa. Information on the types of food they consumed and the subsistence economies they had developed to provide nourishment throughout the seasons comes largely from contemporary reports, from accounts by Shanawdithit, and from the faunal remains found by archaeologists on Beothuk sites.[1]

Historic Accounts of Beothuk Subsistence

Before 1700, accounts by explorers, captains of fishing vessels, and settlers invariably describe food collection on the coast during the summer season. Cabot claimed that the native people in Newfoundland ate fish, especially salmon, more than anything else but also consumed fowl and fruits.[2] Crignon said in 1529 that they hunted seal and porpoise and caught seabirds on offshore islands. He claimed that the Beothuk did not fish for Atlantic cod, the mainstay of the European fishery, which feed in deep water, often around the headlands of bays.[3] Instead, they largely fished in the inner reaches of bays, probably using spears or small nets rather than deep-water fishing gear. This would explain why they rarely interfered with the European cod fishery. In 1536 Hoare wrote that the natives roasted bear meat, while Alphonse de Saintonge (1542–43) and Mallart (1545–47) reported that they fished and gathered fruits.[4] The chronicler Thevet, writing around 1557, showed the Newfoundland Beothuk catching porpoise, polar bear, salmon, and dogfish, and collecting lobster, mussels, and oysters. He also claimed that they drank rendered seal oil.[5] Another account, written in the fishing season of 1594, refers to native people roasting caribou meat and plucking cormorants.[6]

At the end of the fishing season, the Beothuk were thought to retire from the coastal regions with their catch of seal, porpoise, and seabirds to "warmer countries but we know not where."[7] This observation of Crignon's (1529) may refer to the Beothuk's move away from the coast for the winter. André Thevet (1557) simply talked about the Indians who "lived inland" and gathered fruit but did not practise agriculture.[8]

John Guy and Henry Crout, from the English settlement at Cupids, found fresh beaver meat and the lower limbs of recently killed caribou in a small Beothuk lakeside camp in Trinity Bay. In an encounter the Beothuk presented the colonists with a white wolfskin and offered beaver, fox, marten, and a birdskin for trade.[9] Captain Whitbourne said in 1622 that their store of skins included caribou, beaver, bear, seal, and otter. He also described how the Beothuk cooked quantities of birds, some the size of ducks, and that they stored hard-boiled egg yolks in containers.[10] It was widely known that the Beothuk stocked up on seabirds and eggs; on one island to the north, so it was said, they drove "penn gwynes" into their boats from the shore.[11] This may have been Funk Island, about sixty kilometres north-east of Bonavista Bay, where great auk nested in large colonies.[12] During the egg season the Beothuk were said to feed luxuriously. According to John Cartwright, the multitude of islands where they hunted abounded with sea fowl, hare, and other game. He also said that they took ptarmigan, which were easy to catch in cold weather, and thought that in winter these birds may have been a "kind of domestic poultry to the Indians."[13]

Of the fourteen species of land mammals that are native to Newfoundland, caribou, found throughout the island, were one of the Beothuk's major sources of meat. Their method of trapping these ungulates in pounds was first mentioned in 1720 when Montagnais hunters reported such an enclosure near Hare Bay on the Northern Peninsula.[14] In 1768 John and George Cartwright described caribou fences and traps along the banks of the Exploits River, and in 1811 Captain Buchan noted "incredible" amounts of caribou meat at the Beothuk's winter settlement at Red Indian Lake.[15]

In early summer the Beothuk depended upon salmon. According to John Cartwright, they "used formerly to kill considerable quantities of salmon in the rivers and small streams, but the English have now only left them in possession of Charles's and another brook."[16] When the English placed a salmon post at the mouth of Charles Brook itself, the Beothuk relinquished the river with great reluctance as it left them with only one "petty rivulet" for catching this anadromous fish.[17]

Two records mention that the Beothuk ate roots and, if pressed for food, consumed the inner bark of spruce trees.[18] They drank water, soup, broth, and seal oil.[19] When John Guy offered them beer they hardly touched it but showed a liking for "aquavitae" (presumably brandy or a similar spirit).[20] This is the only recorded incident of the Beothuk consuming alcohol. Demasduit, who lived for close to a year among the English (in 1819) disliked wine as well as spirits.[21]

Preserved and stored reserves of food supplemented the Beothuk's daily catches. Records give frozen caribou meat, dried or smoked meat (generally known as pemmican), rendered caribou fat, seal oil, seal fat on skin, seal stomachs filled with intestines, dried lobster tails, dried fish, sausages made from a variety of ingredients, dried or smoked salmon, and dried and powdered eggs (Fig. 19.1).[22]

Occasionally the Beothuk received food from Europeans as offerings or in exchange for furs. Thus, Guy gave them bread, butter, raisins, and biscuits; Crout placed biscuits and cheese in one of their mamateeks.[23] Settlers who raided a Beothuk camp on the Exploits River in 1781 shared their bread with two captured women, one of whom ate "very hearty."[24] But European-type food neither became part of the Beothuk's regular diet nor affected their subsistence patterns.

Information on Food Sources Inferred from Faunal Remains

A limited amount of information on Beothuk food consumption can be gleaned from faunal remains at excavated sites. Unfortunately, only a few campsites have yielded faunal material that was sufficiently intact for species identification.

Of the 181 calcined bones from the L'Anse à Flamme site in Hermitage Bay only thirty-five could be identified. Twenty-eight came from seal, two from beaver, one from caribou, one from dolphin or porpoise, and three from unidentified birds.[25]

Ninety percent of the mammal-bone residue on The Beaches site in northwestern Bonavista Bay was harbour seal with some harp seal. The remaining bone material was identified as caribou, black bear, and polar bear. Excavated middens contained bones from Canada geese, ducks, cormorants, and quantities of clam shells and univalves.[26]

On the sandy beaches of Cape Freels, which have frequently been washed over by the sea, faunal remains consisted exclusively of shell middens, though the main attraction of this beach would have been its proximity to the migration route of harp seal.[27]

The most extensive faunal analysis comes from the archaeological site at Boyd's Cove on the eastern shore of Notre Dame Bay, which was formerly inhabited by prehistoric Little Passage Indians as well as by Beothuk. In the course of one excavation season alone, 2,900 bones and teeth and twelve kilograms of shell were recovered from the site.[28] Analysis of this material indicates that Beothuk caught smelt, sculpin, goosefish, sea raven, and winter flounder (minimum number of individuals [MNI=10) as well as clams and univalves (MNI=45). Mammal bones included black bear (MNI=1) and polar bear (MNI=3), caribou (MNI=6), beaver (MNI=3), otter and marten (MNI=8), and different species of seal, particularly harbour and bearded seal (MNI=10).[29] The

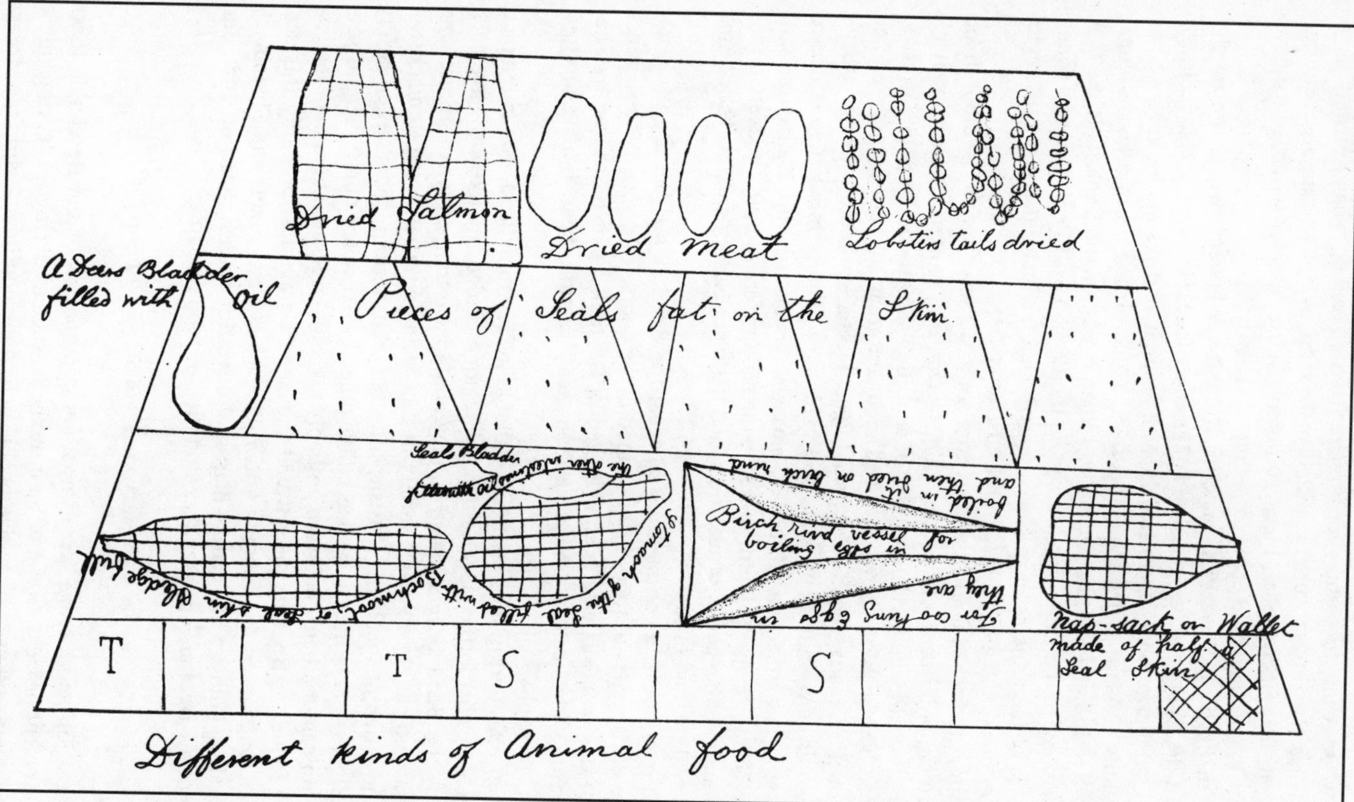

Fig.19.1 Shanawdithit's sketch 7: "Different kinds of Animal food." (Howley 1915,246)

single white-whale tooth may have come from a beached whale, or may have been traded. Bird bones were identified as the remains of Canada goose, cormorant, loon, sandpiper, jaeger, black guillemot, murre, greater scoup, old squaw, eider duck, gull, and bald eagle (together, MNI=20).[30]

The majority of the faunal material from the Wigwam Brook site on the banks of the Exploits River consisted of caribou bone. However, it also included a small number of bones from seal, beaver, arctic hare, fox, and loon, as well as clam shells.[31] Clam and scallop shells have also turned up in archaeological sites at Red Indian Falls and Little Red Indian Brook on the Exploits River.[32] A bone sample from a Little Passage site on the Port au Port Peninsula was found to consist of the remains of beaver and caribou, a few marten, some bald eagle, goose or duck, and a small bird of the auk family.[33]

To sum up, archaeological and written sources show that the Beothuk lived off caribou, polar bear, black bear, wolf, beaver, fox, marten, otter, arctic hare, porpoise, whale, and various species of seal such as harbour, harp, and bearded varieties. The seabirds they consumed included great auk, cormorant, sea and eider duck, Canada goose, loon, sandpiper, jaeger, guillemot, murre, greater scoup, oldsquaw, gull, ptarmigan, and bald eagle. The Beothuk also collected birds' eggs and made use of lobster, mussels, oysters, scallop, clams, and univalves. They caught salmon, smelt, winter flounder, sculpin, goosefish, sea raven, and dogfish and ate fruit, roots, and the inner bark of spruce. They drank water, seal oil, and broth.

This may not be a complete list of what the Beothuk ate, but it gives a fair picture of the types of food they obtained in the course of a year. A subsistence base of this nature is also acknowledged in Beothuk songs passed on by Shanawdithit, which centre around caribou, seal, salmon, bear, birds and eggs, fishes, and shells.[34]

When considering the resources available in Newfoundland, one is tempted to add to this list further species that, while not recorded, are likely to have been used by the Beothuk. For example, they could have trapped lynx, ermine, and muskrat and caught a greater variety of fish including trout, capelin, mackerel, eel, and different species of flatfish; collected crab, shrimp, and a larger variety of molluscs, and berries as well as edible plants. Also, at least until the mid-seventeenth century, harp seal were probably taken in larger numbers than the few bones found on Beothuk sites would indicate. It was most probably this seal species that caused the Beothuk to build camps at Cape Freels and Shambler's Cove, since both are adjacent to harp-seal migration routes. (See Fig. 19.2, diagram of the Beothuk's seasonal exploitation of food resources.)

Preservation and Storage of Food

Preservation and storage were important components of the Beothuk's food-procurement process. Some of their methods, such as drying (or jerking) meat, were known and used by native people across the continent, while the storage of meat packages in storehouses appears to have been unique to the Beothuk. One process involved the cutting of the meat into strips that were dried or smoked in a "smoking or drying house."[35] A structure of this type, drawn by Shanawdithit (sketch 6, Fig. 22.3), shows lattice-work shelves and open studded walls, the latter presumably designed to allow the air to circulate freely. Dried (or smoked) meat not only kept unspoiled for a long period of time but was easy to carry and could be eaten without further preparation. According to John Guy, who tasted meat "dryed in the smoake, or wind," it "savoured very well."[36] Both George Cartwright in the 1790s and William E. Cormack in the 1820s recorded that the Beothuk preserved caribou and seal meat by drying it.[37]

Other methods of preserving meat were less labour intensive and depended upon cold or freezing weather. These methods allowed the Beothuk to process the immense quantities of meat obtained from their caribou drive, during which several hundred animals could be killed relatively quickly. Caribou can weigh three hundred kilograms and upwards so a single animal yields a large quantity of meat and fat. Venison with a high percentage of fat was divested of bone and stowed in large chunks in boxes made of birch or spruce bark, each box containing about seventy-five to a hundred kilograms. Tongues and hearts were placed in the middle of the package. Captain Buchan estimated that the boxes were 0.9 by 0.9 by 0.4 of a metre, while containers seen by another eyewitness were cubes of about 1.2 to 1.5 metres. Lean venison was left in quarters and stored in bulk, sometimes with the skin left on the flesh.[38] Once frost set in, the meat froze and remained unspoiled for the winter. As Cartwright succinctly remarked, "so long as the frost holds there is no want of salt," referring to the settlers' method of salting their meat to preserve it.[39] Large packages and quarters were deposited in storehouses (see Shanawdithit's sketch 8, Fig. 20.2). Packages were also kept inside winter mamateeks or in pits lined with birchbark either next to dwellings or at some convenient place in the forest.[40] Caribou leg bones, ready for extracting the marrow, were suspended on poles inside or outside mamateeks; at the Red Indian Lake settlement Buchan counted about three hundred bones.[41]

The Beothuk rendered caribou fat into clear grease and stored it in birchbark containers. Seal blubber was heated to produce oil, which was kept in caribou or seal bladders or in seal stomachs.[42] In her drawing entitled "Different kinds of Animal food," Shanawdithit sketched caribou and seal bladders "filled with oil" and "seal fat left on the skin," which appears to have been stored in this manner (Fig. 19.1). Other food items on her drawing were dried salmon, dried meat, and dried lobster tails. Before they were placed into the storehouse they may have been exposed to drying breezes on small racks. Cartwright described such a rack as "a slight frame made of sticks pricked into the ground and crossed with others ... which gave it the appearance of a machine for drying salmon upon."[43] Small structures of this type on Shanawdithit's sketch 6 (Fig. 22.3) probably represent such racks.

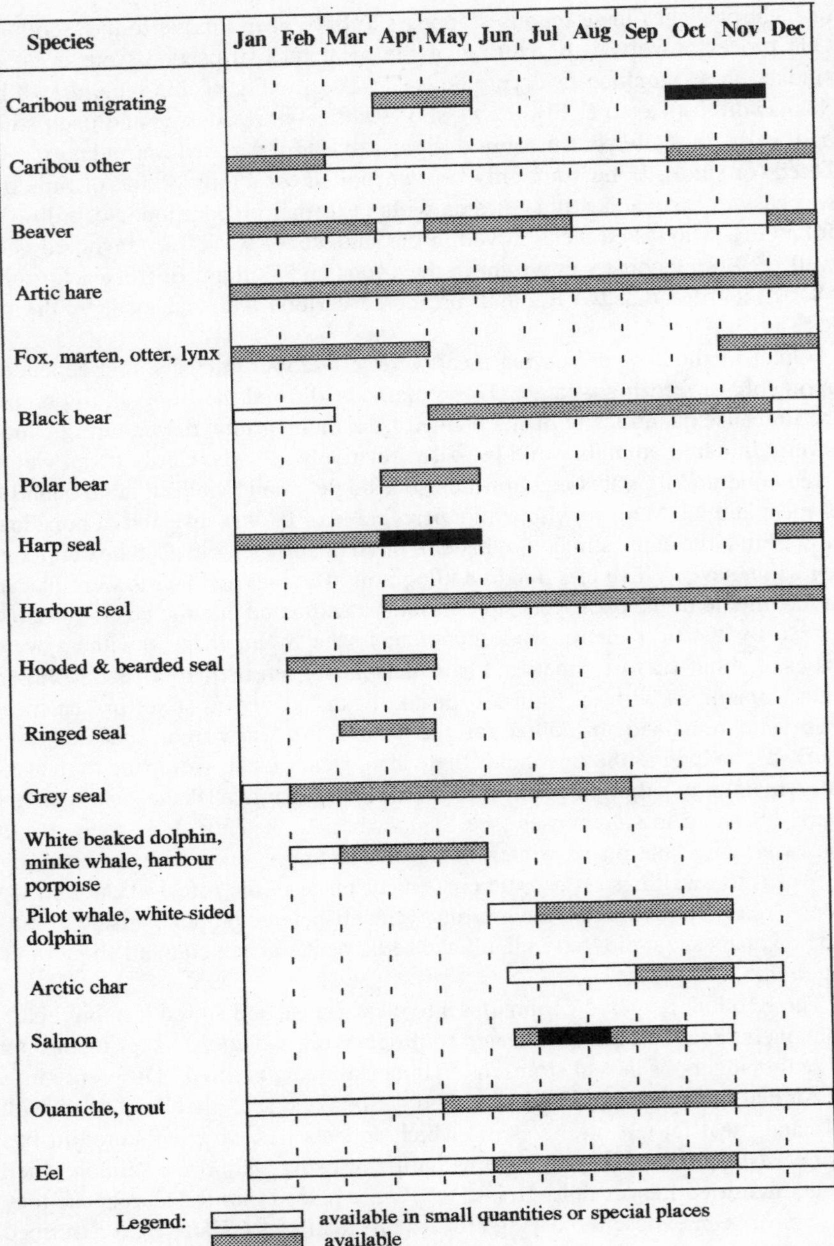

Fig.19.2 Diagram of the Beothuk's seasonal exploitation of food resources. (Provided by Brian Payton, St John's)

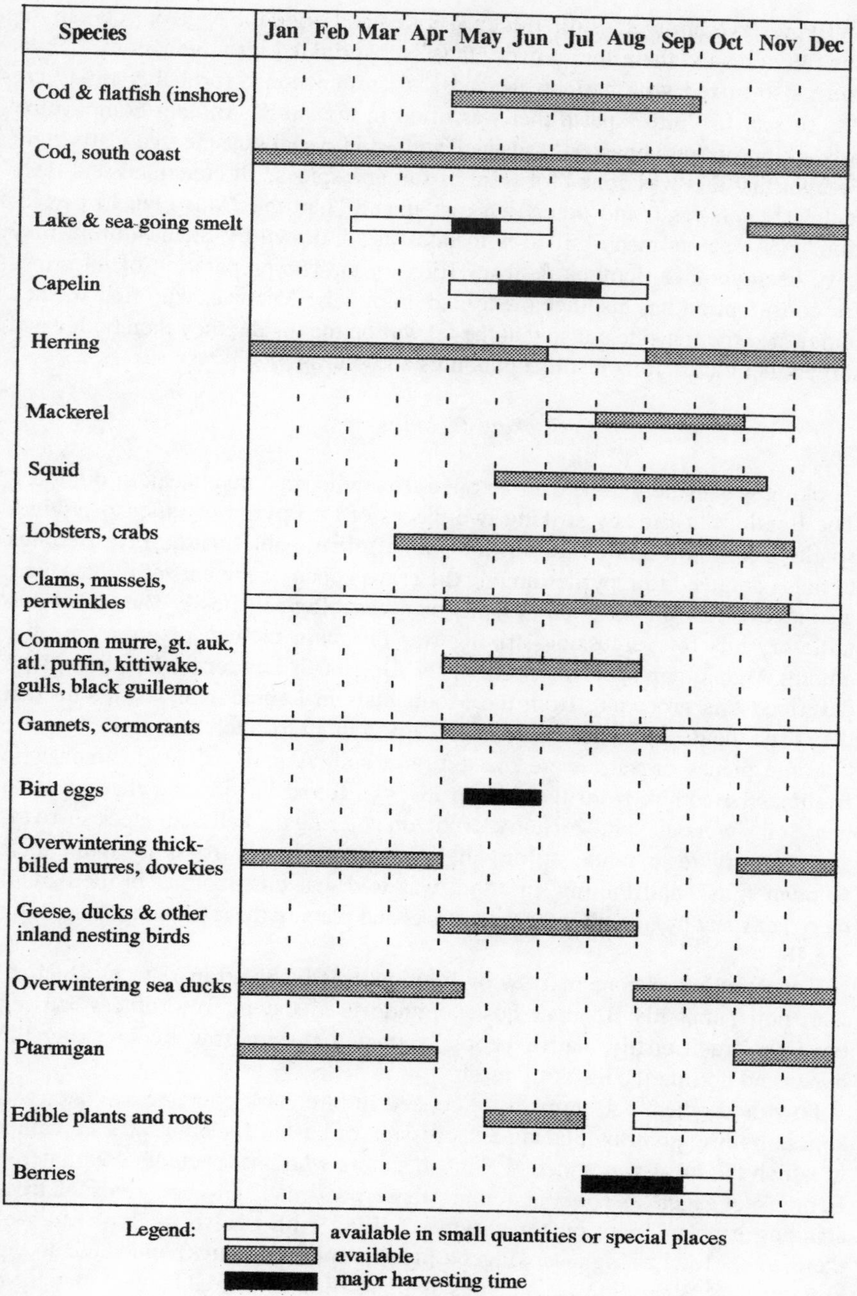

Species	Jan	Feb	Mar	Apr	May	Jun	Jul	Aug	Sep	Oct	Nov	Dec
Cod & flatfish (inshore)												
Cod, south coast												
Lake & sea-going smelt												
Capelin												
Herring												
Mackerel												
Squid												
Lobsters, crabs												
Clams, mussels, periwinkles												
Common murre, gt. auk, atl. puffin, kittiwake, gulls, black guillemot												
Gannets, cormorants												
Bird eggs												
Overwintering thick-billed murres, dovekies												
Geese, ducks & other inland nesting birds												
Overwintering sea ducks												
Ptarmigan												
Edible plants and roots												
Berries												

Legend:
available in small quantities or special places
available
major harvesting time

To preserve birds' eggs the Beothuk boiled and dried the eggs or yolks in the sun, and crushed them into powder that they sprinkled into their broth.[44] Eggs were also mixed with caribou fat and seal "cruncheons" (probably finely cut bits of seal fat) into a paste that was dried in the sun.[45] Another composition was a kind of "pudding" or "sausage" stuffed into seal gut; George Cartwright thought that this was done "for want of salt and spices." It contained seal flesh and fat, liver, eggs, and other rich matter and "had the *Haut gout* to perfection."[46] A seal stomach "filled with intestines," drawn by Shanawdithit, may have been another Beothuk delicacy (Fig. 19.1). The preparation of intestines for consumption has also been recorded among the Micmac, who first washed and turned them inside out so that the fat was on the inside; they then boiled and turned them into "rolls just like puddings and sausages."[47]

Cooking Techniques

Cooking was usually done over an open fire, either in a mamateek or outdoors. The Beothuk lit fires by striking two pieces of iron pyrite together to produce sparks that would ignite bird down or other inflammable matter. Five Beothuk burials contained iron pyrites among the grave goods; fragments of pyrites were also recovered from several housepits on archaeological sites.[48] The use of metallic crystals for percussion striking was the main method of producing fire among Algonquian speakers north of the Gulf of St Lawrence. Le Jeune, who described this procedure from the Montagnais in Labrador in 1634, said that they used the down-covered skin of an eagle's thigh to catch the sparks.[49]

Large pieces of meat were roasted on a spit. A party of Englishmen who frightened Beothuk from their camp in 1536 found "a fire and the side of a beare on a wooden spit."[50] Henry Crout, on entering a small mamateek in 1613, saw "sondry reste matte up[on] their wooden speets" (roast meat on their wooden spits), and Pulling, in 1792, was told that the Beothuk broiled small pieces of meat by impaling them on sticks and placing these around the cooking fire.[51]

Consumption of bone marrow by Beothuk was recorded in 1811 by Buchan, who noted that his Beothuk hostage/guide used the marrow of caribou leg bones.[52] Traditionally, native people extracted the marrow by breaking the bones and boiling the resulting mash.[53]

Fowl and other food items were cooked in birchbark containers. Water was kept at boiling point by placing a succession of heated rocks into the container to which the meat was added.[54] English sailors who unexpectedly encountered Beothuk engaged in cooking found "three pots made of such rinds of trees standing each of them on three stones boiling with twelve fowls in each of them, every fowl as big as a widgeon [a species of wild duck] and some so big as a duck."[55] When European kettles and pots became available, they may have replaced bark containers for boiling and heating liquids. As early as 1612 Guy found a brightly polished copper kettle in a mamateek at Dildo Pond and a small copper kettle at the Beothuk fishing camp in Placentia Bay. These household vessels may have been traded.[56] In the second half of the eighteenth century, when relations between Beothuk and English had become hostile and trade had been suspended, the Beothuk were said to have taken kettles along with other gear from fishing premises.[57] In the 1800s, if not earlier, they used European metal pots for all or most of their cooking. At least, the bark dishes that Buchan saw in Beothuk mamateeks at Red Indian Lake were not "applied to any purpose of cookery." Instead, the Beothuk appear to have cooked their food in iron broilers, two of which they had conveyed out of Buchan's sight.[58]

While meat generally seems to have been roasted on spits and sticks and fowl and other food items boiled in birchbark or, later, in iron pots, other cooking methods may also have been employed. Santu, for example, claimed that "flesh to be eaten was thrown on the fire and only partly roasted. Her father, she remembers, would eat little or no vegetal food nor bread. His diet consisted mostly of halfroasted meat."[59]

SUBSISTENCE ECONOMIES

In order to make good use of Newfoundland's resources, the Beothuk evolved specific exploitation patterns that corresponded with the habits of the most productive migratory animal species on the island, namely, caribou, seal, and salmon. In accordance with the seasonal migrations and habitats of these species, the Beothuk wintered inland, then moved in spring to the coast to catch seal and, later, salmon. Although these staples constituted the bulk of their diet, the Beothuk supplemented them with other resources throughout the year.

Regional differences in the availability of migratory species would have determined the focus of the subsistence economy of each Beothuk band or group. For example, harp seal were plentiful along the northeastern coast and around the Port au Port Peninsula and would have played a greater role in the food intake of Beothuk who exploited these regions than among the bands that lived in Trinity Bay, where harp seal are scarce. Similarly, Beothuk who camped close to highly productive salmon rivers in Notre Dame Bay would have relied far more on salmon as a major source of food than bands on Newfoundland's west coast, which boasts few large salmon rivers.

Details of Beothuk subsistence economies have not been described in contemporary documents. However, by considering the location and size of Beothuk campsites one can deduce the animal species they relied upon. Settlement patterns can also give clues to the nature of band coalition and dispersal in the seasonal process of providing food, the degree to which particular species were caught, whether camps were established close to the most productive food resources, or whether a more central position was preferred from which a variety of species could be monitored and secured. Significant aspects of the Beothuk's subsistence can also be deduced from the types of tools that have been found on archaeological sites. In combination, these different avenues of enquiry provide sufficient data from which to reconstruct Beothuk subsistence economies with some degree of certainty. The graph in Fig. 19.2 summarizes the Beothuk's seasonal exploitation of major food resources throughout the annual cycle.

A Subsistence Economy Based on a Generalized Marine and Interior Adaptation

To reconstruct the Beothuk's aboriginal mode of subsistence, settlement and exploitation patterns of their prehistoric forebears, the Little Passage Indians, are examined because considerably more Little Passage than early historic Beothuk campsites are known. This information can provide a baseline, assuming that the Beothuk way of life, at least for a century or so after European immigration, was similar to that of their prehistoric ancestors.

Of about thirty known Little Passage sites, approximately eighty percent are situated on the coast and twenty percent inland.[60] Assuming that the distribution of these camps is representative of the Little Passage settlement pattern (taking into account that very little archaeological-survey work has been done in the interior), the preponderance of coastal sites suggests that their subsistence economy was oriented towards coastal exploitation. Following a study of the size, location, and composition of lithic tools from eighteen Little Passage sites, seventeen on the coast and one in the interior, Fred A. Schwarz proposed that the activities of a given group or band centred around a coastal basecamp.[61] By his criteria a basecamp was typically located at the bottom of a bay in a relatively sheltered spot, close to a river system that offered quick access to and from the interior. It was fairly large, that is, it yielded a sizeable collection of lithic tools among which most artifact classes were represented.[62] Such a basecamp was a relatively permanent settlement where a group or band intermittently assembled, and where meat and skins were processed and tools manufactured.

Connected with a basecamp, in the Schwarz model, were two types of satellite camps: central exploitation camps, which were situated in sheltered locations on the coast or inland and were central to a variety of resources; and temporary exploitation camps, which were of a more transient nature, being set up on headlands, or on islands, or inland.[63] Characteristic of the subsistence economy associated with this network of camps was a considerable diversification in the use of marine foods and a moderate backup system for hunting terrestrial animals. Schwarz described this pattern as a "generalised marine and interior adaptation."[64] According to this model, the Indians caught several species of seal, whale, porpoise, salmon and other fish, seafood, and birds on the coast between March or April and November; in late fall and winter they left their basecamps to hunt bear, beaver, caribou, and other terrestrial animals inland from smaller camps.[65] Most social functions such as feasts and ceremonies were probably held in the coastal basecamps, between spring and fall. Examples of basecamps supported by peripheral exploitation camps, cited by

Schwarz, were the archaeological sites at Boyd's Cove (Plate 16.4), The Beaches (Plate 16.1), and L'Anse à Flamme.[66] Other networks of base and exploitation camps have been proposed for Hermitage Bay, Burgeo, and St George's Bay, where so far only signs of former exploitation camps rather than of basecamps have been located.[67]

Significantly, none of the designated or proposed prehistoric coastal basecamps are situated in proximity to present-day caribou migration routes with the possible exception of Boyd's Cove, which is relatively close to those on the Exploits River. Little Passage hunters from basecamps on the Avalon Peninsula and at St George's and Bonavista bays would have pursued caribou immediately inland from their basecamps, since these areas support smaller herds that do not travel long distances.[68] Caribou on the Avalon Peninsula remain within the confines of the peninsula and do not migrate across the narrow neck of land near Bull Arm, as has often been assumed.[69] As these herds move about in small companies during the winter season, the elaborate hunting techniques used by the Beothuk on the Exploits River would not have been appropriate. Instead, caribou would have been secured by less-productive methods that could be employed throughout the winter, such as small enclosures, snares, or tracking animals on foot. With smaller takes of caribou other species were relied upon, such as bear and larger numbers of smaller fur bearers, evident at Boyd's Cove, or by beaver, as observed at Trinity Bay. As Cartwright was later to say: "Where beaver abound a proportional number of Indians may very well subsist without any great dependence on the deer [caribou] chase."[70]

Historic Beothuk Model of Adaptation

Schwarz's model of a system of coastal basecamps supported by exploitation camps also fits the settlement pattern of some historic Beothuk. It can be illustrated by using descriptions of camps in Trinity Bay in 1612, 1613, and 1622, and by a 1594 record of a Beothuk camp at St George's Bay.[71]

Sites in Trinity Bay. On their exploration of Trinity Bay in 1612, John Guy and his party discovered a Beothuk camp at the bottom of Dildo Arm. Located in a sheltered position, it was central to a variety of marine resources and gave easy access to inland hunting. At that time it was probably the basecamp of the Beothuk who lived in Trinity Bay. At the end of October the occupants had already moved to their inland camp(s) at nearby Dildo Pond, where Guy found signs of successful beaver and caribou hunting, suggesting that both species played a role in the Beothuk's fall subsistence (Plate 2.1).[72] As Henry Crout later recorded, small herds of caribou roamed the Avalon Peninsula, and the many ponds had a "great store of beavers" that the Beothuk hunted, particularly during the winter months. In the summer of 1613, when Crout returned to the camp at Dildo Arm, it was deserted because the Beothuk had gone birding and egg collecting on islands, so he presumed.[73]

Guy's party also noted a camp at the bottom of Bull Arm (now the community of Sunnyside), which had the characteristics of a central exploitation camp. The Beothuk could have gone from there to catch seal at Stock Cove, said to be visited by them "at their coasting" and to Placentia Bay to catch salmon.[74] A path cut from Bull Arm through the woods to Beothuk houses at the mouth of Come By Chance River suggests visits during the annual salmon run; the Beothuk may also have exploited Placentia Bay's large harbour-seal population.[75]

A camp in the vicinity of "Heart's Ease" (recorded by Whitbourne in 1622), which contained a variety of skins, birds, and dried egg yolks, may have been another exploitation camp. It was conveniently situated for hunting seal and for birding and egg collecting.[76] At the time sailors discovered this camp, the Beothuk were in the process of cooking large quantities of food, as if for a feast; some of them were wearing an unusual headdress, presumably signifying a special occasion.[77] Camps recorded on an island near Hopeall and on the adjacent coast appear to have been small and of a more temporary nature.[78]

Sites in St George's Bay. During the fishing season of 1594, sailors found a native camp in the lower reaches of St George's Bay. Its occupants, estimated at forty to fifty people, had fled, leaving behind plucked and dressed cormorants and caribou meat in the process of being roasted on spits.[79] St George's Bay was an ideal place for a basecamp since it offered fresh water, a good landing beach, and access to a wide variety of marine and terrestrial species. Harp seals pass the nearby Port au Port Peninsula on their migrations and, at least today, grey and harbour seals visit. In the 1500s there may also have been walrus. The coast between St George's and Rose Blanche is also famous for whale becoming trapped in the ice that is driven to shore.[80] In the early 1700s, the region was known for its thousand-head caribou herd, an abundance of fur bearers, and the presence of eels on the shore throughout the winter season (Anguille being named after this species).[81] Nearby outcrops of chert at the Port au Port Peninsula that were quarried for tool manufacture were an additional attraction, as was a deposit of ochre north of the Barasway River.[82] A Little Passage Indian site on the Port au Port Peninsula, probably used as a temporary camp for hunting seal, demonstrates the importance of the peninsula as a hunting post that the Beothuk, like their prehistoric forebears, probably used.

A Second Subsistence Economy Model with a Focus on Caribou Exploitation

Several Beothuk bands followed a different subsistence pattern, which entailed assembling and wintering on the banks of the Exploits River or at Red Indian Lake. Details of this system of food procurement were not known until 1768, when John and George Cartwright explored the Exploits River.[83] It revolved around the interception of caribou herds on their seasonal migration in fall and again in spring, followed by a period of food gathering on the coast from late spring to early fall. These ungulates migrate in late October or early November from their summer grazing grounds to more favourable habitats for winter forage, where they usually disperse into smaller groups. When the snowcover melts and ice on lakes and rivers begins to break up, usually around March or April, the animals return to their summer range.[84]

Prior to the construction of the railway line and the Trans-Canada Highway, caribou herds from the Northern Peninsula migrated every fall to southern Newfoundland; their route led across Sandy and Birchy lakes, the Exploits River, and the northern end of Red Indian Lake. It was a renouned caribou migration and represented the largest concentration of animals in Newfoundland. Taking advantage of these seasonal migrations, the Beothuk constructed extensive fenceworks and enclosures to intercept the herds at lake or river crossings.[85] During migration, herds consistently follow their lead animal and can be driven into traps or towards narrow openings in fenceworks and taken in large numbers with relative ease.

In 1768, as noted earlier, John Cartwright recorded about thirty kilometres of fencing, fifteen kilometres on either bank of the Exploits River, often with leads into the forest with wing-type extensions. The conical mamateeks and square houses he mapped on the river banks and at Red Indian Lake showed that the caribou hunters wintered in the vicinity of the slaughtering sites.[86] Capt. David Buchan described Beothuk camps and fences in 1811 and 1820, and W.E. Cormack in 1827.[87] The location of many of the houses has since been confirmed by archaeological surveys and excavations.[88]

As noted in the preceding section, the Beothuk caribou hunters developed methods of preserving large quantities of surplus meat for the winter by drying or packaging it in bark sheets and then freezing and storing it in substantial storehouses.[89] This practice was not observed among Beothuk in other regions; nor was it known among Micmac who concentrated on small-game hunting in fall and, according to European observers, did not practice extensive food storage.[90] Montagnais/Naskapi who intercepted large herds, as did the Beothuk, stored the meat in dried form and are not known to have kept frozen meat in storehouses.

According to eyewitness accounts from 1792, at a time when English fishermen dominated the coastal waters, the Beothuk moved inland for the caribou drive at the end of September.[91] This timing would have allowed about a month for repair of houses, fences, and enclosures (traps) before the herds appeared. Their inland winter settlements served as activity and social centres where feasts were celebrated, such as the one occasioned by the beheading of the two marines in 1811, and (at least in the early 19th century) the annual ceremony of applying a new coat of red ochre to every person. An early-nineteenth-century cemetery across from the Indian Point campsite suggests burial rituals.[92]

During their sojourn in the interior the Beothuk lived on the meat procured through the caribou drive – Captain Buchan thought that the amounts of venison the Beothuk had packed up were "incredible." They would also have hunted smaller fur bearers and migratory birds such as ducks and geese. Trout and landlocked salmon, fished through the ice, as well as overwintering game birds and plant foods probably supplemented their diet.[93] To catch harp seal, hunters would have had to travel to the northeastern coast where the seals pass in December and January on their way south, and again in late February and March when they migrate northwards and whelp on ice floes.

In contrast to the *en masse* movements of caribou herds in fall, the return migration of the animals in March or April, though along the same routes, was usually a more individualistic adventure and would not have warranted a massive caribou drive. Also, at this time of the year the meat of the caribou is of poor quality and not suited for the methods of preservation used in late fall.

In the 1790s, the Beothuk were said to have left their inland settlements between the first and twentieth of May, paddling down the Exploits River in their canoes, two, three, or sometimes four of them together.[94] Once on the coast, they hunted seabirds and collected birds' eggs and in June and July assembled at river mouths to catch Atlantic salmon. Harbour seal could be hunted during the open-water season in inlets, estuaries, and the lower parts of rivers including the Exploits. The Beothuk also caught the occasional whale (or dolphin), which, according to Shanawdithit, "afforded them more abundant luxury than anything else."[95] For the summer months, bands appear to have dispersed in smaller units. John Cartwright recorded in 1768 that they divided into small parties "for ranging the islands."[96] Beothuk groups sighted in Notre Dame Bay in the second half of the eighteenth century numbered only a few individuals; coastal camps contained no more than one or two mamateeks.[97]

The evidence suggests that Beothuk bands with a "generalised marine and interior adaptation" intermittently assembled at a coastal base camp between spring and fall, March to November approximately. They would have celebrated most of their communal ceremonies and feasts in these basecamps. In winter, when coastal resources were scarce and the weather harsh, they dispersed in smaller groups inland to hunt terrestrial mammals.

The Beothuk whose subsistence pattern focused on the caribou drive had their basecamps inland, near caribou routes, where they lived from early fall to late spring, roughly September to May. They staged their main festivities and ceremonies at these inland camps during the winter. The bird-egg season and salmon run brought them back to the coast, where they dispersed in small groups for the remainder of the summer to hunt and collect seafood on the shore and on islands.[98]

Thus, as a generalization, two different subsistence patterns are proposed. The existence of two distinct economies within one ethnic group was not unique to the Beothuk but has also been recorded for the East Main Cree. Cree bands referred to as "Coasters" predominantly (but not exclusively) exploited resources on the coast, while those who considered themselves "Inlanders" largely hunted big game. In the 1800s the Labrador Naskapi also developed a specialized caribou economy.[99]

Neither the beginning of the caribou adaptation, nor the circumstances of its inception can be established with any degree of certainty. Three prehistoric sites with Little Passage-type tools on the Exploits River and a large earth lodge at Red Indian Lake, carbon dated around 355 +/- 100 BP (AD 1595), suggest hunting trips and occasional wintering farther inland in or before the sixteenth century.[100] Following encroachments of whites on the coast, Beothuk groups may have come to place greater emphasis on the exploitation of migrating caribou herds. In Newfoundland the technology of building enclosures (also used by Montagnais/Naskapi in Labrador and by tribes to the west of them across the Canadian Shield) was first recorded on the Northern Peninsula in 1720; the construction of massive fences of the type described by the Cartwrights may not have been attempted until metal tools were available.

It is proposed that some Beothuk bands developed methods for staging caribou drives and preserving surplus meat in storehouses at a time when other bands still maintained a "generalised marine and interior adaptation" centred on coastal basecamps. According to the faunal analyst who examined remains from the Boyd's Cove site, occupied between ca. 1650 and 1730, the variety of food species represented in the sample revealed a picture of people who were "at ease in their environment."[101] Less than three decades later the main camp of the caribou hunters (Tom June's people) was located at June's Cove on Red Indian Lake (ca. 120 kilometres from the sea coast) where their ancestors are believed to have wintered 150 years earlier. A Beothuk settlement in this location and the extensive fenceworks and more than eighty mamateeks on the Exploits River in the 1760s indicate that this group was flourishing in the mid-1700s.[102] In times of caribou scarcity, they may have shifted their winter camps to locations that offered easy access to the interior as well as to the coast, a move that would have allowed them to procure a greater variety of food species.[103]

During the second half of the eighteenth century, the ranks of caribou hunters may have been swelled by Beothuk from coastal basecamps who were pressured away from their traditional range, but it is considered unlikely that the inception and development of a caribou economy for winter subsistence came about when disillusioned Beothuk sought refuge inland.[104]

By the early nineteenth century the majority of Beothuk had moved to the watershed area of the Exploits River; hunting operations had been shifted upriver closer to Red Indian Lake and fences had been extended to at least twice the lengths recorded in 1768.[105] Though these measures may have temporarily assured an adequate take of caribou for the winter months, decreased access to beaver and other fur bearers, harp and/or harbour seal, salmon and other coastal resources during spring and summer severely reduced the Beothuk's subsistence base. Starvation combined with disease, disruption of group composition, and probably other negative factors greatly diminished their numbers and decreased their ability to make optimal use of the resources left to them. As Shanawdithit later said, they were unable to keep up the caribou fences, and, "being driven from the shores and from the fish and the oysters, and the nests of water-fowl, their means of existence were completely cut off."[106]

CHAPTER TWENTY

Tools and Utensils, Hunting and Fishing Techniques

TOOLS

The Beothuk hunting, fishing, and gathering way of life involved cyclic moves from inland camps to the coast and vice versa. Mobility was paramount and precluded an accumulation of material possessions outside of a restricted range of implements that could easily be carried. These circumstances prevailed among many native groups with the result that native people were often highly versatile in the use of the few tools they possessed. In 1771, Samuel Hearne, an English trader from Prince of Wales Fort in Hudson Bay, observed Chipewayans building a canoe and noted that "all the tools used by an Indian in building his canoe … consist of a hatchet, a knife, a file and an awl; in the use of which they are so dexterous, that every thing they make is executed with a neatness not to be excelled by the most expert mechanic, assisted with every tool he could wish."[1] This versatility and adroitness was no doubt also characteristic of Beothuk craftspeople.

Stone, Bone, and Iron Tools

Originally the Beothuk made their tools from raw materials found in the surrounding environment. Chopping and cutting tools and projectile points were chipped from fine-grained local chert and rhyolite. A major quarry containing thousands of rhyolite shards was discovered in 1990, in Bloody Bay/Bonavista Bay (Plate 16.2). Smaller quarry sites have been recorded from the north coast of New World Island, and from East and West Bay on the Port au Port Peninsula.[2] These materials possess the structural elasticity required to avoid frequent cracks or breakage and they fracture concoidally. Bifacial chipping is clearly seen in the Beothuk's lithic artifacts. As a rule, bifaces (relatively flat tools worked on either face and usually sharpened along either of the outer edges) and knives were hafted to handles. They were used for chopping, cutting, splitting, chiselling, and carving wood, bark, roots, meat, and skins. Stone scrapers, also produced by the chipping method, were employed to clean remnants of flesh from skins, remove pith, and scrape bark, wood, gum, and other materials; grinding stones were used on raw materials, including charcoal and ochre. Tools typical of the Little Passage and early historic Beothuk assemblages are triangular bifaces, thumbnail scrapers (often made of random flakes), corner-notched and side-notched projectile points, and tiny, carefully flaked corner-notched or expanding-stemmed projectiles in which the central hafting part expands downward into a "stem" (Plate 16.3).[3] Other stone tool types from excavated sites, such as grinding stones, ovate bifaces, linear flakes, and flake points, were used by many native groups and do not necessarily identify origin from Little Passage or Beothuk people.

Only a few bone artifacts have survived due to the highly acidic nature of Newfoundland's soil, which rapidly decomposes biostructural material. For example, the Beothuk had bone awls for piercing skins, bark, or other soft materials and probably made beamers from longbones to remove fur from skins.[4] They would also have used bone or antler tools for pressure flaking stone tools.

A blunt bone needle found in a Beothuk grave may have been used to make or repair nets or receptacles (Plate 20.1c), and a bone netting tool of unique design could have been used in the manufacture of snowshoes (Plate 20.1b).[5]

A barbed bone point, perhaps from a fish spear, was collected by Jenness on Triton Island/Green Bay.[6] Bone was traditionally used for harpoon heads, which were surmounted by a stone or, later, by an iron point (Plates 20.1a, 20.2).

Following European contact, the Beothuk acquired iron objects and tools, which expanded their technology and replaced traditional materials and methods of production. In 1612 John Guy left a hatchet, a knife, scissors, and needles with Beothuk in Trinity Bay in exchange for furs. He also noted that they already possessed a European fish-splitting knife, a fishing reel, fish hooks, fishing line, and lead.[7] Some of these objects may have been traded with passing fishing crews, others may have been purloined. In the 1600s Beothuk were said to have come at night to Trinity Bay to obtain hatchets, hooks, and knives from fishing premises. Those Beothuk who lived on the Northern Peninsula were accused of taking fishing boats in order to procure nails.[8]

By the mid-eighteenth century the Beothuk fashioned many of their artifacts from iron. Arrowheads and hatchets depicted on John Cartwright's map of the Exploits River clearly show that they were made of this material (Figs. 6.2, 20.1).[9] The Beothuk evidently knew how to reshape iron by heating it and beating it out on a stone.[10] Anvil stones were not only observed by settlers who entered Beothuk dwellings but have since been found in excavations of Beothuk mamateek pits.[11] When J.P. Howley, author of *The Beothucks or Red Indians*, enquired with settlers in Notre Dame Bay about the Beothuk in the 1880s, the fisherman Wells was "positive they knew how to heat and forge iron, he says they would keep it several days in the fire to render it soft. They used an old axe, set into a junk of wood, with the sharp edge turned up, upon which they would

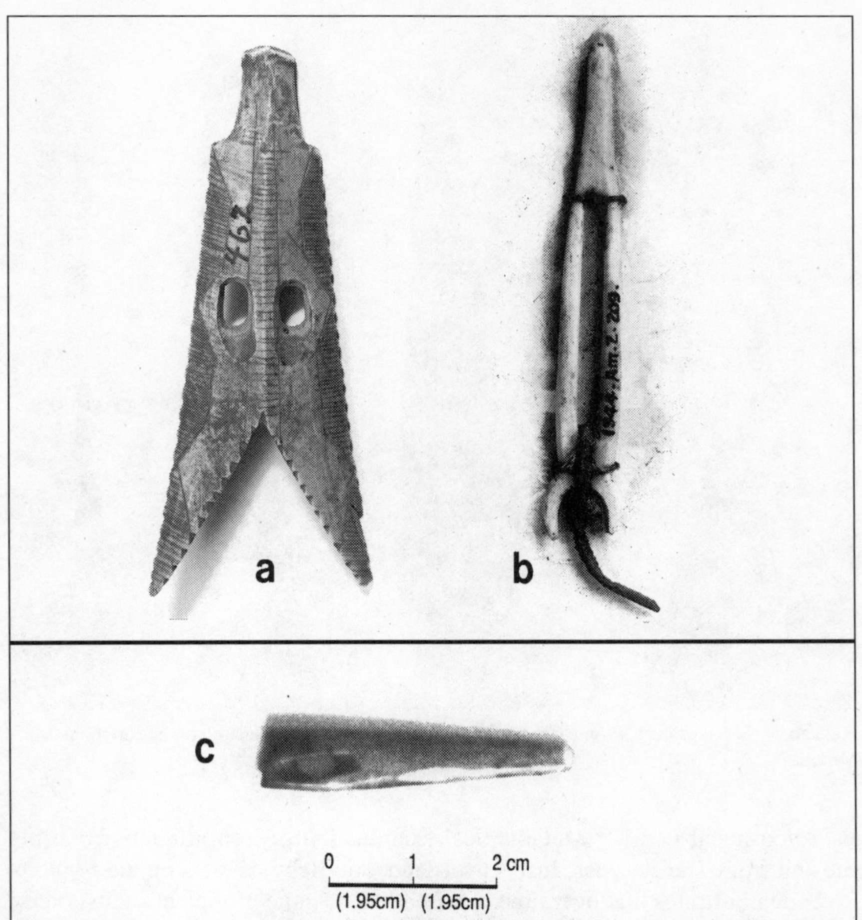

Plate 20.1a Harpoon head without blade, incised with pattern and rubbed with ochre. (By permission of the Ethnographic Museum of the University of Oslo, Norway; photograph Ann Christine Eek, neg.EM 462)

20.1b Netting needle. (By permission of the British Museum, London neg.mm 028323)

20.1c Bone needle from burial at Musgrave Harbour. (Provided by Anna Sawicki, Charlottetown)

work the iron back and forth, till it assumed the requisite shape and then grind it down sharp on a stone."[12] By this method the Beothuk modified axeheads into smaller, more rounded implements, after cutting away the flaring corners or "wings"; in one instance they had flattened a small axe at one end and given it a pick-like shape at the other.[13]

Many iron projectile points, scrapers, fish spears, awls, and other objects found on excavated sites had been made from parts of traps, nails, or other pieces of metal (Plate 20.2). The Beothuk site at Boyd's Cove alone has yielded

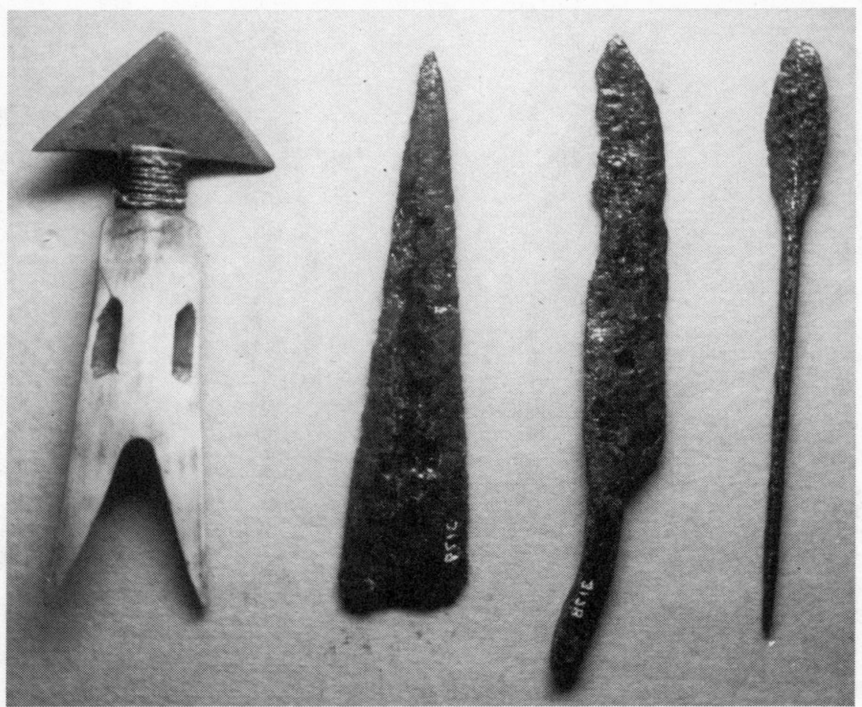

Plate 20.2 Metal projectiles and harpoon head with metal blade. (Collection of the Newfoundland Museum)

ca. 1,700 metal items.[14] Metallurgical examination of iron artifacts from this site and from The Beaches, Inspector Island, and Beothuk sites on the Exploits River demonstrates that over time, the Beothuk became proficient ironworkers; the workmanship of some of the projectile points produced in the latter half of the eighteenth and early nineteenth centuries is clearly superior to that of earlier pieces.[15]

Although the Beothuk appear to have made iron tools at least from the 1700s onwards, stone hatchets were nevertheless still present in the early 1800s. A member of the English party that discovered a Beothuk settlement at Red Indian Lake in 1819 recorded that the "sides of the tenement were covered with arms," among them "axes of iron and stone hatchets."[16] If the observer was correct, then stone implements had not, even at that late date, been completely eradicated from the Beothuk's tool assemblage.

Bows, Arrows, and Quivers

Beothuk bows were about 1.5 to 1.7 metres long and were made either of maple, mountain ash, spruce, pine, or a hard and tough type of fir, locally known as

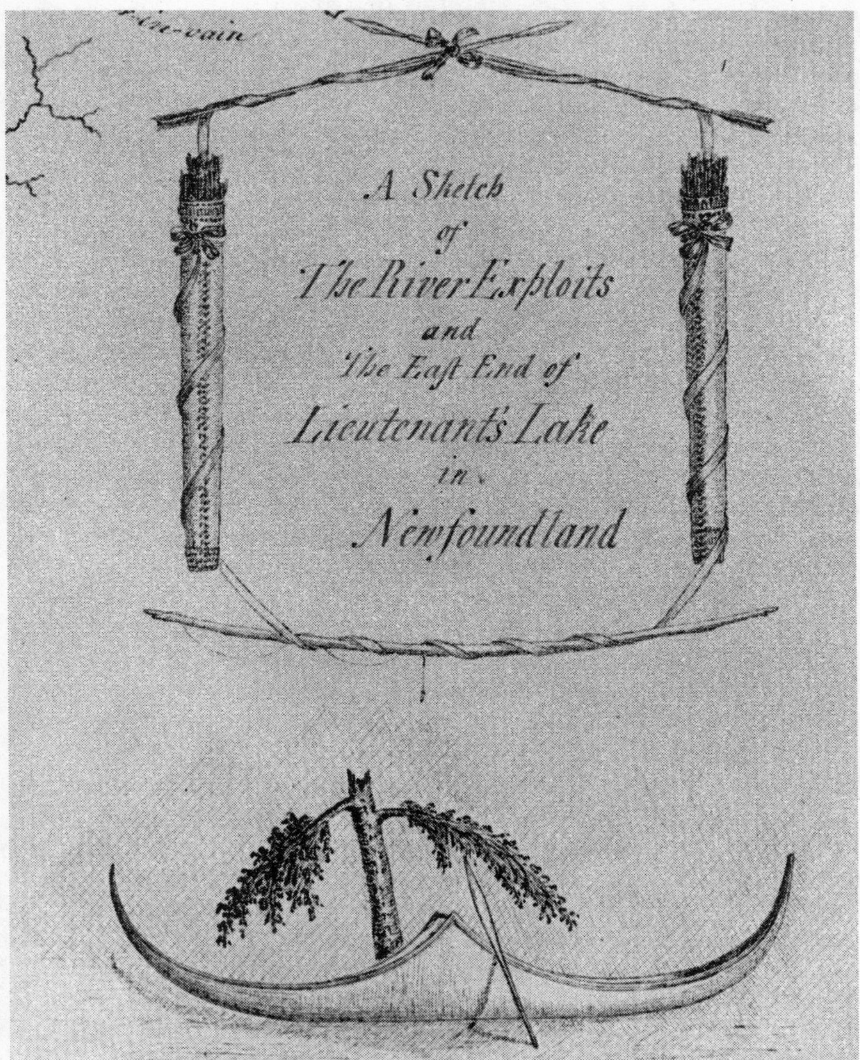

Fig.20.1 Bow, arrows, quivers, and canoe with paddle from John Cartwright's "Sketch of the River Exploits and the East End of Lieutenant's Lake in Newfoundland," 1773. (National Archives of Canada, NMC 27)

"boxy fir," which was seasoned over a fire.[17] Cartwright, who had seen and sketched a bow, arrows, and quiver (Fig. 20.1), described the bow as follows:

The sticks are not selected with any great nicety, some of them being knotty, and of very rude appearance; but under this simple rustic guise they carry very great perfection; and

> to those who examine them with due attention admirable skill is shown in their construction. Except in the grasp the inside of them is cut flat, but so obliquely and with so much art, that the string will vibrate in a direction coinciding exactly with the thicker edge of the bow. This seems to be essential to the true delivery of the arrow, but is a principle that appears not to be generally understood among archers.[18]

Fisherman Wells from Notre Dame Bay said the central part of the bow (presumably the area where it was held) was thick but flattened towards either end, "where the spring chiefly lay." He had also noted "a strip of skin fastened along the outer, or flat side of the bow. The hand grasping the bow passed inside this strip with the arrow placed between the fingers to guide it … [a Beothuk] could arrange five or six arrows at a time between his fingers and shoot them off, one after the other, with great rapidity and unerring aim."[19] The bow was strung with plaited (or twisted?) deerskin. Wells considered it to be a powerful weapon and he and other fishermen said that the Beothuk were extremely skilled in their use.[20] Captain Buchan, who may have seen Beothuk using their bows, explained that to raise the bow a man had to free his right shoulder from his garment and kneel down on his right knee. Holding the bow in his left hand, he would keep it in a perpendicular position so that its lower end was supported against his left foot.[21]

Arrows were made of well-seasoned pine and fletched with two strips of feathers. They were about ninety centimetres long, slender, light, and perfectly straight.[22] In 1529 Crignon claimed that the Newfoundland natives fitted their arrows with stone and "fish bone" points; but the latter type has not been found in archaeological excavations.[23] Cormack confirmed the use of bone for projectile points, although to date only a single bone arrowhead has been unearthed on a Beothuk campsite.[24] In 1768 when John Cartwright described Beothuk arrows, stone and bone projectiles had largely, or perhaps even entirely, been replaced by two-edged iron lances about fifteen centimetres long. George Cartwright said the head is a barbed lance, "made out of an old nail, let into the cleft at the top of the shaft."[25] Projectiles in the Newfoundland Museum collection are between ten and fifteen centimetres long, two-edged, and of lanceolate or triangular form with a tanged (pencil-shaped) end; most of them were reworked from square nails or spikes.[26] According to Captains Pulling and Buchan, the metal projectiles were proportioned to the shaft in such a way that, when missing their target and falling into the water, the arrows would float and could be picked up and reused.[27] For hunting smaller birds, the Beothuk employed blunt arrows whose leading end consisted of a knob of wood.[28]

Hunters carried their arrows in birchbark quivers, depicted by Cartwright as cylindrical tubes, open at one end, with a vertical seam running the length of the container. The edges close to the rim and to the bottom appear to have been decorated with fancy stitching (Fig. 20.1).[29] The Beothuk stored arrows in their houses in cases holding upwards of a hundred. On one occasion, settlers found a store of about five hundred arrows in a mamateek.[30]

Spears and Harpoons

According to Cormack, Beothuk spears – called *amina* – were their chief weapon for killing caribou and other animals. They were "pointed with bone or iron whenever the latter material could be obtained." Spearpoints were also mentioned in G.C. Pulling's 1792 report.[31] Shanawdithit depicted a spear as a ca. three-metre-long wooden shaft tipped with a relatively slender, nearly triangular, iron point (Fig. 20.2).[32] The point was probably hafted by inserting its tang (pencil-shaped hafting end) into a hole in the end of the shaft, a method used by Montagnais. On spearpoints in the collection of the Newfoundland Museum, the haft tends to be considerably longer than the sharpened end. For example, on one slender forty-centimetre-long specimen, the point is about one-sixth of the total length, the remainder being the tang.[33] In 1501 Côrte Real described wooden spears whose "end was burnt in the fire which when they [the natives] throw them, make wounds as if pointed with fine steel."[34]

The Beothuk harpoon, called *a-a-duth* or "Spear for Killing Seals", was illustrated by Shanawdithit as a shaft, approximately 3.7 metres long, surmounted by a detachable head (Fig. 20.2). This head consisted of a bone socket with two spurs into which a triangular iron blade (formerly stone point) was set.[35] T.G.B. Lloyd sketched a harpoon head with a relatively large socket with line holes positioned parallel to each other (probably carved through the thickness of the bone), visible on a specimen collected by the naturalist Peter Stuwitz around 1840 (Plate 20.1a).[36] An iron blade is surmounted on one of several harpoon bone sockets in the Newfoundland Museum. The stem of the blade is inserted in a notch in the neck of the biconvex 10.7-centimetre-long bone socket. Bored obliquely into one face are two parallel line holes that meet at an obtuse angle approximately midway through the thickness of the bone. A single circular hole bored through from the opposite face meets the former two holes. The toggling line, consisting of a considerable length of thong, would have been attached through these holes and then passed down through a notch near the butt end of the shaft.[37] Since there was no foreshaft, the distal end of the wooden shaft would have been tapered to fit into the narrow socket hole. During the hunt, the harpoon head was lodged in the body of the seal with the aid of the shaft, which was then withdrawn; because of the position at which the line was attached, a tug on the line caused the harpoon head to turn sideways. As a result of this toggling action, the harpoon head became firmly embedded in the animal, thus preventing its escape. Once the seal was exhausted it was hauled in. Beothuk may also have used self-pointed bone harpoon heads, with two tandem line holes that were based on a similar design.[38] At least, two specimens of this type in the Canadian Museum of Civilization (Jenness collection) are claimed to be of Beothuk origin.

Clubs, Crooked Knives, and Perforating Tools

The record of Sebastian Cabot's exploration from 1508–09 mentions clubs made of wood. That the Beothuk used clubs was confirmed in 1819 by an eye-

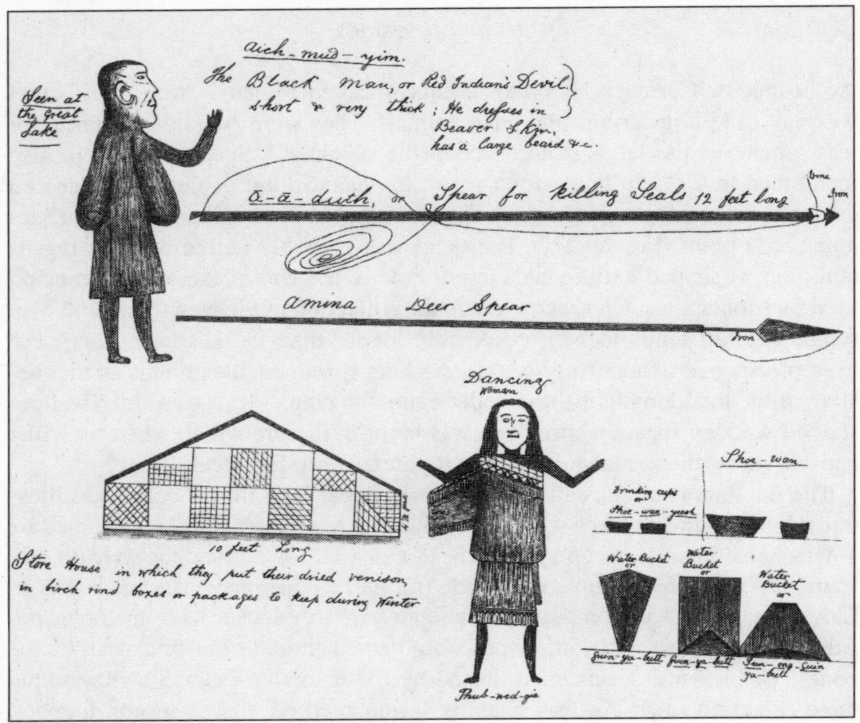

Fig.20.2 Shanawdithit's sketch 8: Black man or Red Indian's devil, sealing harpoon, spear, a dancer, storehouse for dried venison, drinking cups, and water buckets. (Howley 1915,248)

witness, who described clubs among the weapons and tools he saw hung up on the walls of a Beothuk mamateek.[39]

Many North American Indians used crooked knives, a multipurpose tool particularly suitable for whittling wood. Prehistorically, crooked knives were made from a beaver incisor that was modified into a hafted blade with a cutting, scraping, chiselling, or piercing edge.[40] While a fully intact Beothuk knife of this type has not been found, a beaver incisor from one Beothuk site shows clear signs of having been turned into a gouging implement.[41] The metal blade of a knife with traces of red ochre on it that was found in a Beothuk burial site on Big Island, Pilley's Tickle, is curved upwards at the end like that of a crooked knife.[42] Its crudely fashioned wooden handle is not identical to the traditional crooked knives of the Micmac or Montagnais, but it may represent an attempt to make such an implement out of a European knife.

To perforate bone artifacts such as harpoon heads or bone pendants, the Beothuk used the technique of biconical gouging. This involves exerting pressure and scooping with a pointed tool on the two opposing surfaces of the item to be perforated. Modified beaver incisors, silicious stone splinters, and, in historic times, nails and pieces of broken glass may have been employed for this task.

The bow drill was reputedly unknown to the Beothuk as it was to their Micmac and Montagnais neighbours. While the latter groups became familiar with the drill in the late historic period, the Beothuk appear not to have used it.[43]

Perishable Tools

Undoubtedly many Beothuk implements or working aids were made from perishable raw materials such as wood, bark, sticks, roots, shell, and soil and would have constituted a considerable portion of their material-culture kit. For example, Adney, who spent many years observing, practising, and recording Indian canoe-building techniques, mentions the use of broken pieces of shell for cutting, splitting, and scraping; wooden mauls that had been hardened by scorching in fire; bark containers; pieces of dry bark with a bevelled edge; sharpened or pointed sticks; bark spoons; strips of bark; bark torches; stepped or notched sticks; wooden stakes and posts; split-root thongs; clay for girdling trees; and sand or soil accumulations to make up a "building bed" on which to construct a canoe.[44]

Other activities would have called for a similar array of temporary tools. Many of these implements, as the list of canoe-building aids indicates, were surprisingly simple but highly functional. Due to their simplicity and perishable nature, such items, with the exception of birchbark containers, were not recorded by contemporary observers; nor have they been noted in archaeological excavations of Beothuk sites.

UTENSILS

Most household utensils were manufactured from bark, wood, and skin. Wooden roasting sticks have already been mentioned; a wooden spoon (presumably made by Beothuk) was seen in a camp in St George's Bay in 1594.[45] A roughly circular wooden bowl with a flat bottom was collected from a Beothuk mamateek at Red Indian Lake in 1819. This bowl, which is now in the Newfoundland Museum, measures about twenty-five centimetres across and is carved from a single piece of hardwood with two projections, like handles, at the rim (Plate 20.3).[46]

Containers for carrying implements, food, or other items could have been manufactured from a variety of materials. Shanawdithit drew one that was described by Cormack as a "knapsack or wallet" made of half a sealskin, (Fig. 19.1). Receptacles were also made from split roots or other plant matter. An open-mesh bag found in a Beothuk burial site entirely encased a package of food that had first been wrapped in birchbark.[47]

Bark Containers

The majority of Beothuk vessels for cooking and storage, at least until the 1700s, appear to have been made from the bark of birch, fir, and spruce. As early as

Plate 20.3 Wooden bowl taken from Beothuk mamateek at Red Indian Lake, in 1819. (Collection of the Newfoundland Museum)

1594 the crew of the British fishing ship *Grace* found "a dish made of the ryne of a tree sewed together with the sinews of the Deere [caribou], wherin was oil of the Deere."[48] John Guy saw "small coffins [boxes] made of the barke of trees," and Captain Whitbourne said in 1622 that the Indians "used to sew the barkes of spruce and fir trees, round and deep in proportion like a brass kettle, to boil their meat in."[49] Sailors had seen Beothuk cooking in bark pots and described them as "sewn and fashioned like leather buckets that are used for quenching of fire."[50] They also noted bark storage pots for hard-boiled egg yolks.

In his 1773 sketch of a Beothuk camp Cartwright depicted three flat-bottomed boxes – two rectangular and one round – possibly made of bark (Fig. 6.2). Captain Pulling was told by settlers in 1792 that the Beothuk's cooking pots, dishes, and other utensils were made of the bark of birch and fir. Captain Buchan confirmed this, though he thought the cooking was probably done in iron pots that had been obtained from the whites through trade or otherwise.[51]

Shanawdithit's drawing of a series of dishes (sketch 8, Fig. 20.2), to which Cormack added explanatory notes, gives more specific information about the different shapes of bark containers. *Shoe-wan* were low-walled, relatively wide vessels. One type is nearly rectangular in side profile (this may have been a folded dish), the other type is probably oval since in profile both ends flare out. *Shoe-wan-yeesh* (diminutive of *shoe-wan*) were drinking cups of similar proportions but smaller. More substantial containers, presumably the sort mentioned in seventeenth-century documents, were called *quin-ya-butt* and *sun-*

ong-quin-ya-butt, translated by Cormack as "water buckets." They came in three different shapes: one *quin-ya-butt* was narrow at the bottom, becoming wider towards the top, with a rim that was highest where the vertical side seams terminated; another *quin-ya-butt* had a wide bottom, vertical walls, and a horizontal rim. The *sun-ong-guin-ya-butt* had a wider bottom still, and its walls slanted inward to form a relatively narrow horizontal opening at the top. Since no large bark bucket has been preserved, and since Shanawdithit drew the dishes two-dimensionally in profile, it is not clear whether they were cylindrical, square, or rectangular. None of the dishes was drawn with a lid. On sketch 7 Shanawdithit also illustrated a "birch rind vessel for boiling eggs in," but it is difficult to visualize the shape of this dish three-dimensionally (Fig. 19.1).

The Construction of Bark Dishes

The twenty-one Beothuk bark containers that have survived in museum collections come exclusively from burials. They are all made of birchbark, which seems to have been favoured for smaller containers or perhaps for burials. All are painted with a mixture of ochre and grease. Most of these dishes appear to be miniatures of the types of dishes the Beothuk used in everyday life. The sixteen specimens in the Newfoundland Museum are up to fifteen centimetres long, up to ten centimetres high and less than nine centimetres wide.[52] Some are quite flimsily made (Plate 20.4).

Dishes that were removed from Nonosabasut's burial hut at Red Indian Lake, manufactured from thicker bark sheets, were larger, fully finished, and decorated (Plates 20.5a and b, 20.6, 20.7a and b).[53] The stitching on all the dishes was done with fine strands of sinew, spruce roots, or vegetable fibre in a simple in-and-out stitch. On several of the dishes the rim and seam edges are overcast either with a whip stitch or a criss-cross stitch, or reinforced along the rim with pieces of wood.[54]

The simplest style of bark dish, illustrated in Plate 20.5a, was folded from a rectangular piece of bark. The size of this type of dish could vary, but the proportions were usually the same since they were derived by dividing the width and length of a rectangular bark piece into three equal portions.[55] As a rule, the folds were only sewn together along the upper rim of the dish and were not otherwise secured. The upper edge could be pinked. On one of the Beothuk dishes in the Newfoundland Museum the fold was reinforced with a piece of wood inside the rim (Plate 20.4).

More elaborate bark containers were made from a sheet of bark that had been cut into a specific pattern or template that ensured the desired form, provided the piece was folded and sewn together in the correct manner. The seams were stitched and sometimes the rim was reinforced. The template for an oval dish (Plate 20.5b) had a long and narrow rectangular centre from which two winged shapes for the body flared out on either side. The midsection of the centre con-

Plate 20.4 Four bark dishes from the burial of a child on Big Island, Pilley's Tickle. (Collection of the Newfoundland Museum)

stituted the rectangular bottom of the dish. The ends of the midsection, when folded upward, covered the two seams on either of the flared ends inside (clearly visible on Plate 20.4).[56]

The tall cylindrical container shown in Plate 20.4 required a fairly long, rectangular template with small triangular cut-outs and square flaps halfway. The mid-section constitutes the bottom of the container and the two ends, folded upwards, form the body of the cup. Sewn together, this dish has two vertical seams opposite one another, which are protected at their inside base by the square flaps, once bent upwards. This container appears to be a miniature of one of the water buckets, *quin-ya-butt*.

The largest and most interesting of the birchbark vessels comes from Nonosabasut's burial hut and is now in the collection of the Ethnographic Department of the British Museum (Plate 20.6). It is marked "Red Indian Meat Dish for Deer's flesh found … in 1827 by W.E.C." The initials stand for William E. Cormack.[57] The dish is 47 centimetres long, 18 centimetres wide, and 8.5 centimetres high. Essentially two pieces of bark were used in its production. The

Plate 20.5a Folded birchbark dish collected in 1827 by W.E. Cormack from Nonosabasut's burial hut. (Copyright The Trustees of the National Museums of Scotland, 1996, UC 307, neg.10243)
Plate 20.5b Oval birchbark dish, edge reinforced with wooden splint, collected in 1827 by W.E. Cormack from Nonosabasut's burial hut. (Copyright The Trustees of the National Museums of Scotland, 1996, UC 306, neg.10242)

template proper was, in principle, like that of the tall cup but much wider. It was folded in the same manner so that the dish has a seam on each of the two sides. Two small square flaps were folded up from the base to cover the lower part of the inside seams.[58] A second strip of bark, pieced together, runs as a horizontal

Plate 20.6 Birchbark meat dish collected in 1827 by W.E. Cormack from Nonosabasut's burial hut. (By permission of the British Museum, London, neg.cc6975)

band around the outer rim and extends the height of the dish by about 4 centimetres. Its rim is reinforced outside with thin strips of wood that have been wrapped with spruce root before being sewn on. All cut edges of the dish are pinked and all seams are sewn with spruce root. The container is decorated with chevron designs around the upper rim and along the side seams, stitched with spruce root in the manner of porcupine quillwork; porcupine is not native to Newfoundland, so the Beothuk used spruce root instead of quills. Around the container, spaced at intervals below the inner lip, are two-thong fringes (probably the remains of loops).[59] A smaller vessel of the same type, taken from the same burial hut, is in the collection of the Royal Scottish Museum, Edinburgh (Plate 20.7a). It is worth noting that the narrow elongated shape of the dishes, the use of a rim piece with a zig-zag pattern, and the loops for a carrying cord are not found on bark dishes made by any of the other seaboard Algonquians.[60]

Another bark container, also from Nonosabasut's burial hut, is about the size of a large mug (Plate 20.7b). It is made of heavy bark and is nearly square at the bottom but somewhat cylindrical at the top. All cut edges are pinked. Mug-shaped containers of this type have not been recorded among Micmac or Montagnais/Naskapi vessels, but one was collected from Athapaskans in 1970.[61]

The shapes of the two Beothuk water buckets, *guin-ya-butt*, also differ from those manufactured by the Beothuk's Montagnais and Micmac neighbours, while for other Beothuk bark dishes close local parallels can be found. For instance, the folded as well as the small oval containers (Plates 20.4, 20.5a, 20.5b) are similar to Montagnais types and the appearance and construction of the Beothuk water bucket, *sun-ong-guin-ya-butt*, is reminiscent of Montagnais food

Plate 20.7a Birchbark dish collected in 1827 by W.E. Cormack from Nonosabasut's burial hut. (Copyright The Trustees of the National Museums of Scotland, 1996, UC 305, neg.10241)
Plate 20.7b Mug-shaped birchbark container from Nonosabasut's burial hut. (By permission of the British Museum, London, neg.CC6976)

containers and the *rogan* that the Northern Saulteaux used for storing dried meat.[62] However, the Beothuk did not incise patterns into the surface of the bark, as was the custom among other northeastern tribes.

Bitten Patterns

Beothuk produced ornamental figures by biting impressions into folded sections of thin filaments of birchbark, a custom that prevailed throughout the birchbark area that was inhabited by the hunting tribes of northeastern America.[63] Mrs Jure, a servant in the Peyton household, later recalled how Shanawdithit took a piece of (inner) birchbark, folded it up, and then bit with her teeth "a variety of figures of animals or other designs" that became apparent when the bark was unfolded. The fisherman Gill had heard that Shanawdithit produced designs representing leaves and flowers in this manner.[64] During her stay in St John's Shanawdithit also made delicate paper cuttings, locally called "watch glasses" (Fig. 14.5b).

According to Speck, talented Montagnais could produce bitten impressions of hunters with snowshoes, paddles, canoes, and tents, as well as groups of foliage, shrubs, and trees.[65] He regarded these bitten patterns as experimental and source-stages in the process of developing decorations for birchbark dishes, which the Montagnais embellished with cut-out patterns.[66] Among the Beothuk, this mode of bark decoration is not recorded, and the art form of bitten patterns may have represented a purely artistic impulse and technique or been pursued in preparation for decorating other materials. For example, in the 1790s the Beothuk were said to have drawn the shapes of men, women, fish, and other fanciful scrawls on skins; also, the Micmac John Paul told Frank G. Speck in the early 1900s that Beothuk coats were often embellished with painting.[67]

Carved Combs

Seven combs in the Newfoundland Museum collection are tangible evidence of Beothuk skill in carving bone and antler (Plate 20.8).[68] These combs are from 2.75 to 7.5 centimetres long, from 3 to 4.75 centimetres wide, and about 0.25 centimetres thick; their six to fifteen teeth are between 1.5 and 3 centimetres long. One comb has a fine ladder design on both faces and two are perforated for suspension. Though the combs vary in size and shape, a certain uniformity in their appearance indicates a stylistic tradition.

That combs were in daily use was reported by Richard Richmond in 1791. Having invaded a Beothuk camp and taken a young woman captive, Richmond observed that she "comb'd her Childs hair & her own & rub'd seals fat over it." When his companion Thomas Taylor admired the comb, she gave it to him. Taylor later handed it to Captain Pulling when he told him about the incident.[69]

The carving of combs appears to have been a skill that was practised by a number of individuals, including Shanawdithit. Describing Shanawdithit's apti-

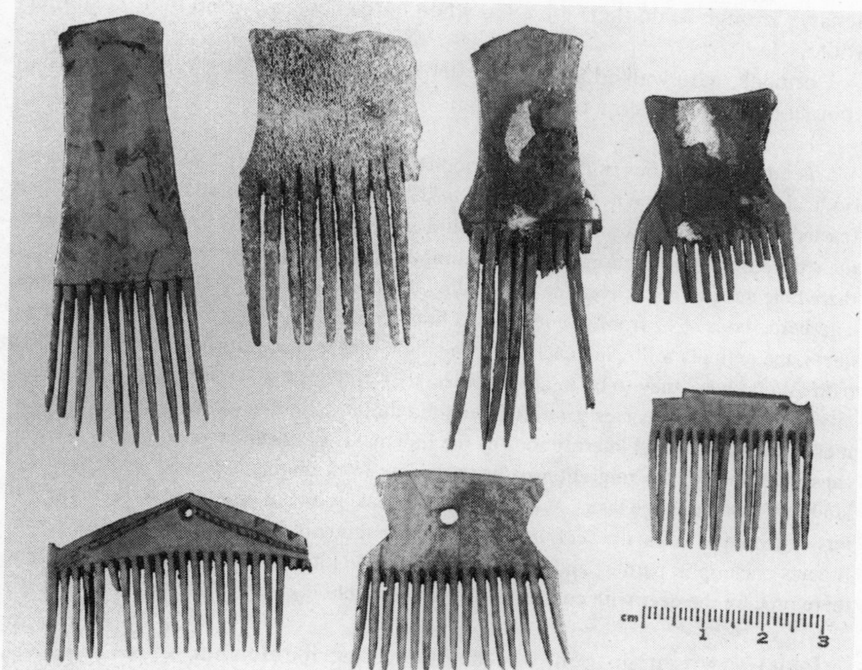

Plate 20.8 Combs carved from bone and antler. (Collection of the Newfoundland Museum)

tude as a carver, her fellow servant Mrs Jure said: "She was very ingenious at carving and could make combs out of deer's [caribou] horn and carve them beautifully." Mr Gill remembered his mother saying that Shanawdithit "made very neat combs out of deers horns and carved them all over elaborately," implying that these combs were decorated.[70]

HUNTING TECHNIQUES

Hunting Caribou

The Beothuk's most effective method of hunting caribou was to obstruct their migration routes with fences or traps, often along rivers or at lake crossings. During their fall migration, the herds stubbornly follow the leading animals; so by funnelling these leaders into fenced-in areas or towards specific river crossings, large numbers of caribou could be trapped. In the 1760s, the migration route of major caribou herds led from the Northern Peninsula across Sandy and Birchy lakes, the Exploits River, and the northern end of Red Indian Lake.[71] The caribou's route varied since obstacles and disturbances could cause the animals to change their paths.[72] Accordingly, fenceworks were extensive enough to do their job even when herds deviated from their customary route.

Cormack, who walked across the island in 1822, gave a vivid account of caribou herds in the process of migration:

We met many thousands of the deer [caribou], all hastening to the eastward, on their periodical migration … When the first frosts, as now in October, nip vegetation, the deer [caribou] immediately turn towards the south and east, and the first fall of snow quickens their pace in these directions … In travelling herd follow herd in rapid succession over the whole surface of the country, all bending their course the same way in parallel lines. The herds consist of from twenty to two hundred each, connected by stragglers or piquets, the animals following each other in single files, a few yards or feet apart, as their paths show; were they to be in close bodies, they could not graze freely … They generally follow the same routes year after year, but these sometimes vary, owing to irregularities in the seasons and interruptions by the Indians … Lakes and mountains intervening, cause the lines of the migration paths to deviate from the parallel; and at the necks of land that separate large lakes, at the extremity of lakes, and at the straits and running waters which unite lakes, the deer unavoidably concentrate in travelling. At those passes the Indians encamp in parties, and stay for considerable intervals of time, because they can there procure the deer with comparatively little trouble.[73]

John Cartwright, in 1768, was the first to describe Beothuk fences and traps, or "pounds" as he called them, which he had seen on the Exploits River in places most amenable for interception.[74] Where there were plenty of trees, the Beothuk had felled them without chopping the trunks completely asunder, taking care that every freshly cut tree would fall on the previous one, thus forming a fence parallel with the river. The weak parts of the fences were filled with branches, limbs, or tops of other trees, or were occasionally secured by large stakes and bindings. These fences were raised to a height of between two to three metres (six, eight, or ten feet) as the place required and were too high to be forced or jumped by the largest animals. They were most effective on steep river banks, where the animals could not get a proper footing when facing the fence. Where tree growth was inadequate for fencing, the Beothuk substituted "sewels" to deter the caribou from leaving the chosen route. Sewels consisted of slender two-metre-long sticks stuck into the ground at an angle, up to ten metres apart. Suspended from their upper ends were narrow strips of birchbark tied together in the form of wings or tassels. Hanging clear of their support, these tassels would move with every breath of wind, emitting sounds when the strips struck against each other. The movement and noise would frighten the caribou and keep them from passing between the sewels. John Cartwright illustrated such sewels on his sketches of a Beothuk mamateek (Figs. 6.2, 23.3).

On the southern banks, fences usually ran parallel to the Exploits River. On the northern banks and at Red Indian Lake, they often had leads extending far into the forest to funnel the animals in a southeasterly direction towards narrow exits by the water. At certain stations along the shore the Beothuk built small crescent-shaped breastworks, or stands, half the height of a man from which they could shoot their arrows at passing caribou. Some of these stands (called "gazes" by the settlers) were raised behind the fence, others were constructed in large spreading trees.[75] John Cartwright marked the fences but not the leads on a map of the Exploits River (Fig. 6.2).

George Cartwright described a caribou pound (or trap) that led to a Beothuk dwelling by the side of the Exploits River. It consisted of two high, strong fences, erected parallel to each other, that formed a narrow lane of some length. From the farther end of each fence extended two very long wing-type fences, the extremities of which were 1.6 to 3.2 kilometres apart. When the caribou met with these "hawk or wing-fences," they walked along them until they were "insensibly drawn into the pound as partridges are into a tunnel net."[76] Cartwright was of the opinion that this particular pound was not intended to trap large herds, because it was located in an area where the caribou travelled in companies of about a dozen head.

In 1768 the fences and sewels seen by the Cartwrights on either bank of the Exploits River, between Bishop's Falls and Badger, were thought to extend for more than fifteen kilometres.[77] In the early 1800s, Capt. David Buchan and William E. Cormack independently estimated the length of the fences at about fifty kilometres.[78] They were positioned on the upper course of the river, starting from Red Indian Lake. In some places trees were transformed into fenceworks; at Rushy Pond wisps of birchbark attached with salmon twine to bushes were placed so as to direct caribou for a long way through the marsh to the river.[79] Fences flanking the Exploits River three kilometres up from Badger Bay Brook were apparently used in combination with a third fence that extended in a westerly direction through an island in the river. Buchan also recorded an "apparatus for killing deer" (presumably caribou fences or a trap) at the southwestern end of Red Indian Lake, close to the junction with Lloyd's River.[80] Cormack, who examined Beothuk caribou fences on the Exploits River in 1827, said that they extended from Red Indian Lake for about forty-nine kilometres, "a gigantic effort ... forsaken and going to decay."[81] He noted two additional fences on the northern shore of Red Indian Lake. Built about one kilometre apart, they diverged for several kilometres from the water's edge into the forest in a northwesterly direction.

In the 1870s the geologist T.G.B. Lloyd found evidence of Beothuk fences off the northeastern arm of Red Indian Lake, running north-south across a wide marsh. They were said to have extended formerly from Red Indian Lake to the southeastern side of Grand Lake, a distance of over fifty kilometres. Micmac still used the fences, having repaired parts of them by putting the stakes back into the ground in a zig-zag line and placing grass sods on the tops about one metre above the ground. Lloyd also recorded remains of fences on the northeastern end of Grand Lake.[82] The surveyor and author J.P. Howley discovered what he believed to be a Beothuk lookout and two caribou traps on Lloyd's River, south of Red Indian Lake. The trap on the southern bank of the river was

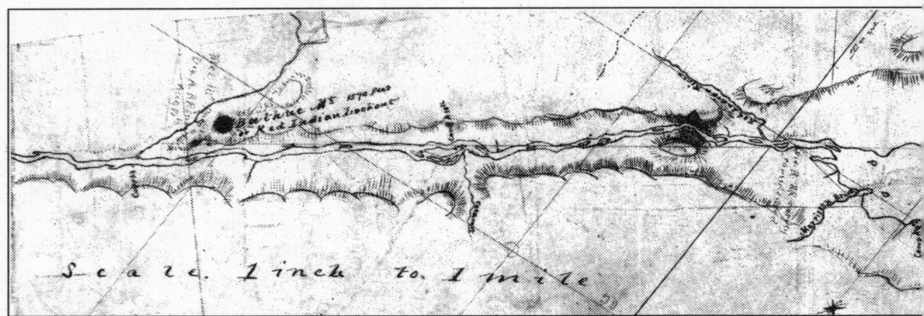

Fig.20.3 Map of lower part of Lloyd's River where it flows into Red Indian Lake with Beothuk looko area on the left) and caribou trap (dark areas on the right), by J.P. Howley, 1880s. (By permission of D Howley, St John's)

oblong and fully enclosed, that on the northern bank of a half-circular shape and open on its western end (Figs. 20.3, 20.4).

Remnants of fences on the Exploits River a few kilometres down from its junction with Red Indian Lake and two kilometres above Red Indian Falls were still visible in the early 1900s, when Frank Speck investigated these areas. He found "trunks of trees felled to form a line barrier leading obliquely from the water's edge to the wooded bank. This rough abattis, as it were, is said to have extended for some miles along the river."[83] In another location the fence was "formed of cross-pieces as high as one's head, with horizontal tree-trunks felled to fall into the crotches here and there."

It has yet to be determined how the building of the extensive fenceworks was accomplished. No stone axes large enough for the purpose have been found at Beothuk sites. Aboriginal Beothuk chopping and cutting implements were useful for trimming branches or cutting saplings but were not suitable for felling large trees. Native people traditionally brought down trees by using a technique known as girdling: tree trunks were tightly bound close to the ground to prevent the sap from rising, which eventually caused them to die. Combined with a judicious application of fire, the trees could be brought down without the use of large chopping tools. These techniques, however, are laborious and would not have been practicable on a large scale. The most plausible answer is that the Beothuk originally made fences out of sewels of the sort seen at a lake inland from Hare Bay in 1720 and later described by John and George Cartwright.[84] Solidly built tree fences, as recorded by the Cartwrights in 1768 and by Buchan and Cormack in the early 1800s, may not have been constructed until the Beothuk gained access to iron axes, enabling them to fell a large number of trees to make impenetrable and long-lasting obstructions.

John Cartwright records that caribou were killed with arrows. This was reiterated by Santu, who added that an arrow that had killed an animal was thrown away as a sacrifice.[85] W.E. Cormack and the furrier William Cull reported that the Beothuk attacked caribou with spears from their canoes while the animals were crossing a river or lake.[86] The Beothuk may also have set snares inside the pounds

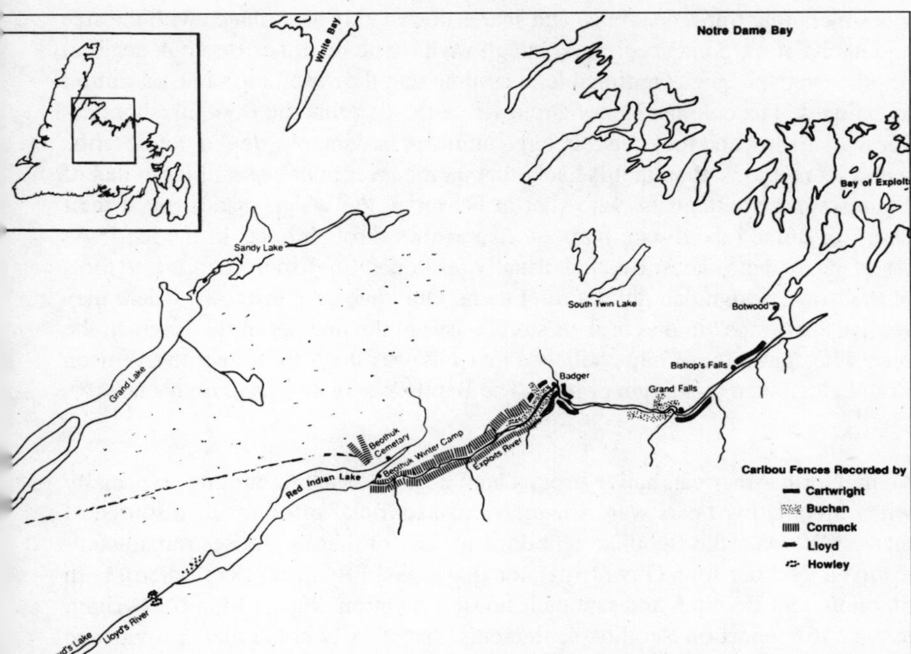

g.20.4 Map of caribou fences recorded between 1768 and the 1880s. (Provided by Cliff George, St John's)

or on known caribou paths, a technique that was widely applied by northern people; snaring was also referred to by Shanawdithit.[87] Cabot's crew had actually found "snares set to catch game" when they landed in Newfoundland in 1497.[88] Snares could be fastened to saplings, which, upon impact, would snap up, pull the noose tight, and lift the caribou off the ground. Naskapi from the Little Whale River "tied the free end of the [snare] line to a suitable tree and suspending the noose where the heads or antlers will become entangled. Some are placed so that when the foot is lifted the noose is carried along and tightens on it."[89]

If conditions were not suitable for building fences or setting snares, the Beothuk may have tracked down animals on foot, as other native groups did. Lescarbot, who described Micmac hunting methods, said the Micmac would "go off bow in hand, and quiver on back" and not give over until they had the animal down; they might follow the chase for three days, if necessary. Micmac considered winter, when the snow was deep, to be the fittest time for hunting animals on land, since the men wore snowshoes that prevented them from sinking into the snow, while the animals were impeded by it.[90]

Hunting Smaller Terrestrial Animals

Relatively little is known about the Beothuk's methods of hunting and trapping smaller terrestrial game. North American Indians generally used a variety of devices including traps, deadfalls, and snares designed in accordance with the size and habits of different species. Although we have no record of Beothuk deadfall or other traps, it seems reasonable to assume that they used the same or similar techniques. The colonist Henry Crout wrote in 1613 that the Beothuk shot beaver with arrows and took them in large numbers in winter.[91] He did not describe the exact methods, though it is likely that their beaver hunt was similar to that of Micmac and Montagnais, who shot at beaver in the water, or destroyed their dams, or hunted them with harpoon-like arrows through holes in the ice.[92] As far as the evidence goes, Beothuk usually fashioned English iron traps into tools of their own design and did not reset them. Only one case is known where they set five "cat-traps" in one of their storehouses in the manner of the English; the men who found these traps believed that this was done to protect the venison from being taken by marten or lynx. The Beothuk may also have used snares.[93]

Many North American native groups kept dogs to assist in hunting, especially when hibernating bears were sought, or as sacrificial offerings or a source of meat.[94] Whether the Beothuk kept dogs for any of these purposes remains unresolved. Neither John Guy (1612) nor Capt. David Buchan (1811, 1820), both of whom met Beothuk and saw their houses, mention dogs.[95] John Cartwright, in his 1768 report on Beothuk settlements, specifically noted that "providence has even denied them [the Beothuk] the pleasing services and companionship of the faithful dog."[96] His brother George corroborated this statement.[97] With one exception, none of the trappers, salmon catchers, or fishermen who described encounters with Beothuk refer to dogs, and John Peyton, Jr, when questioned by T.G.B. Lloyd, confirmed the absence of dogs.[98] A note in the Cormack Papers reads: "Whether the Beothuk had any dogs amongst them or domestic animals" "(No)." This note is interpreted to mean that Cormack had asked Shanawdithit whether her people kept dogs and she had replied that they did not.[99]

Archaeological evidence would agree with the majority of informants. While a Maritime Archaic Indian cemetery at Port au Choix contained skeletal bones of four dogs, no dog remains have ever been found in association with a Beothuk burial.[100] The faunal analyst who examined animal bones from a Beothuk midden at Boyd's Cove in Notre Dame Bay found no gnawing marks on the bones and concluded that dogs would not have been present.[101]

Shanawdithit's wordlist includes the term *mammasameet* or *mammasamit*, for dog; but knowing about dogs does not mean that the Beothuk actually kept them.[102] Thomas Peyton, John Peyton, Jr's son, told Howley that the fisherman Genge, "who lived alone at Indian Arm [in the 1820s] frequently saw the Red Indians, but never interfered with them, they in turn did not harm him … he always had a dog with him, of which the Indians were very much afraid."[103]

Only two persons have associated the Beothuk with dogs. One was Jehan Mallart, who cruised along Newfoundland's coast between 1545 and 1547 and later recorded that "in Teree Neufue from north to south there are men of fine bodies and arms and of high stature; fight with the black bestial men who have no faith and believe in nothing; they live on fruits, fish, meat, which they do not cook; have dogs."[104]

The second informant was E.S. (presumed to have been a member of the mercantile Slade family in Notre Dame Bay), who had been present at the capture of Demasduit in 1819. This man recorded that he saw a "bitch and her whelps, about two months old" in one of the Beothuk houses.[105] Since many details of the encounter supplied by E.S. were verified by others, his observation cannot be dismissed. However, the presence of a bitch in one Beothuk camp does not necessarily imply that the Beothuk were in the habit of keeping dogs. In this particular case they may have provided a home for a stray dog or may have taken a dog from settlers. The bitch could also have been a wolf with her litter. Whitbourne, in 1622, claimed that wolves in Newfoundland were not as "violent and devouring" as those in other countries; his mastiff had stayed with wolves in the woods for nine to ten days and had returned unharmed.[106]

Catching Marine Species and Fish

Seal. For the Beothuk, seal was second only to caribou as a source of meat, oil, and fur. Yet there are no eyewitness accounts of their methods of obtaining this mammal. According to Shanawdithit their harpoon was specifically designed for hunting seal; its detachable head was retrieved with the aid of a thong tied to it (Fig. 20.2). The Beothuk may have harpooned seals through holes in the ice or pursued them in their canoes when migrating herds swam close to the shore in December and January. Since the pull exerted by a diving seal could upset a canoe, seal hunting in the ocean required skillful handling of the vessel. The hogged sheer (upturned sides) of the canoes allowed for heeling (leaning sideways) without shipping water when a seal or other animals were being taken aboard.

In one case, recorded in the 1700s, Beothuk had converted a fishing net into one for catching seal by cutting out every second mesh.[107] They may have learned the technique of using nets from the settlers, who set net traps for catching seal around headlands and in narrow passages between islands.[108] Once harp and hooded seal commenced whelping on the ice in March and April, the pups may have been clubbed or shot with arrows; while adult seals may have been hunted while they were moulting on the ice in April or early May.

Harbour seals, which remain close to shore until fall and whelp on land, may have been taken in the same manner while on land, or harpooned once they had taken to the water. Crignon recorded in 1529 that the native people in Newfoundland hunted seal on islands; he may have referred to harbour seal, which haul out on the beaches.[109]

Porpoise and whale. According to the sixteenth-century chroniclers Crignon and Thevet, the native people in Newfoundland took "porpoise." Harbour porpoise as well as different species of dolphins move about in herds and often come close to shore to feed. They can, and often do, become trapped when ice floes close in on the coast; dolphins as well as pothead whales can also become stranded in shallow water, or they can be driven towards shore where it is possible to kill them with clubs or axes. Beothuk may also have hunted these animals with harpoons or arrows from their canoes.[110]

Whether and how Beothuk hunted whale is not recorded. One of the Beothuk's emblems of mythology, drawn by Shanawdithit, portrays a whale's tail (Fig. 24.1). Cormack noted that it represented the bottle-nosed whale and that "the Red Indians consider it the greatest good luck to kill one," suggesting that the whale's tail might have been important in relation to hunting whale.[111] Cormack also stated that these whales frequented the northern bays in great numbers and came into Clode Sound. However, bottle-nosed whales grow to a length of seven to seven and a half metres and usually stay in deep offshore waters; it is therefore questionable whether Shanawdithit actually referred to this particular species.[112]

Salmon and other fish. Many written accounts mention Beothuk consuming salmon and other fish, though their techniques of catching them have not been recorded. John Guy's party, which discovered a Beothuk camp by a salmon river in Placentia Bay in 1612, found a basket with many fish hooks (probably of European origin) but made no mention of fish spears, weirs, or nets.[113] Only one late-nineteenth-century source states that the Beothuk speared fish.[114] Archaeological evidence for this method of catching fish is scarce. Two-pronged, compound, iron (fish) spearheads have only been found on the Indian Point site. Several unilaterally and bilaterally barbed bone spearheads collected in Newfoundland are illustrated in Howley's *The Beothucks or Red Indians*, but the ethnic origin of these artifacts has not been ascertained.[115] The technique of spearing fish was widely employed by other native groups. Micmac often speared salmon from their canoes at night, attracting the fish with torches. In one night, a party could take 150 to 200 large salmon. Micmac also constructed wooden fish weirs fitted with a bag net behind a central opening, into which the salmon were funnelled.[116] There is no record of Beothuk trapping salmon in enclosures or weirs, although this technique was employed by English settlers. Stone enclosures, probably built by settlers in the early days, could still be seen in river mouths in Gander Bay and New Bay in the 1960s.[117]

Whether the Beothuk used fishing nets prior to contact is not known. Montagnais and Micmac are said to have made nets from reeds, rushes, root and bark cordage, or from twisted rawhide lines.[118] Since the Beothuk had access to these materials, it is reasonable to speculate that they made nets as well. An open-mesh bag made of spruce roots and found at a Beothuk burial site is clear indication that they knew how to make net-like receptacles.[119] Suggestive evidence is also provided by a short blunt bone implement resembling a thick sewing needle, found at another Beothuk burial site near Musgrave Harbour.[120] This needle has a large eye for threading fairly substantial materials such as root thongs, babiche, or European twine and may have been used as a netting tool (Plate 20.1c). "A needle for making nets" was also found by Cabot's crew when they landed on the Newfoundland coast in 1497.[121]

In the eighteenth and nineteenth centuries, as noted elsewhere, the Beothuk often took nets, hooks, and lines from European boats or premises and may have adopted European fishing techniques along with these tools. In one mamateek, settlers found English lines and hooks baited with squid and noted that Beothuk had split some sculpins in the manner of the English.[122]

In winter, the Beothuk are likely to have caught trout and landlocked salmon by fishing through holes in the ice. In 1811 Captain Buchan recorded a snow shovel, an implement that was traditionally included in native ice-fishing kits. However, the practice of ice fishing has not been recorded among the Beothuk, nor have ice-fishing tools been found on Beothuk sites.[123]

Bird Hunting. The Beothuk are known to have harvested quantities of seabirds such as gannet, murre, puffin, and razor bill whose nesting colonies were located on rocky cliffs or small offshore islands. They shot large birds with arrows hafted with a sharp point; for small birds they used blunt, knobbed arrows that killed or knocked down the bird upon impact.[124] The most sought-after species was the great auk, a flightless bird that could be clubbed on the ground. Henry Crout in 1613, said that the Beothuk drove these "penn gwynnes" from the shore into their boats.[125] The most prolific breeding colonies of the auk were on Funk Island, about sixty kilometres from the Newfoundland shore. Funk Island cannot be seen from the coast and contemporaries have marvelled how the Beothuk could find the island, particularly since they often made the journey in dense fog.[126] To catch waterfowl the Beothuk sometimes employed a decoy; this was done by attaching a seabird to a long line so as to tempt other fowl to alight close by, where they could be shot.[127] The Beothuk also took ptarmigan (locally known as partridge). This species is found in the barrens and in forests. During the winter season flocks of up to one hundred may congregate, and because they do not easily take flight in windy weather when temperatures are low, they can be knocked off the branches on which they roost. Micmac were said to have caught ptarmigan by slipping a noose at the end of a long pole over the birds' heads as they were tame as chickens.[128]

CHAPTER TWENTY-ONE

Appearance and Clothing

The first reliable accounts of Beothuk were given by John Guy and Henry Crout in 1612. No further information on Beothuk apparel and physiognomy was recorded until the second half of the eighteenth and early nineteenth centuries, by which time they had been encountered on numerous occasions, and several had been captured and had lived with the English. Not all accounts agree as to details of costume, hairstyle, and other features. The diversity of descriptions may be due to changes over time or to stylistic varieties among or within bands that accentuated individual differences or affiliation to a specific group; they may also have been the result of inaccurate observation.

PERSONAL APPEARANCE

Several sixteenth-century records state that the Beothuk were "tall," "of large stature," or simply "large," in contrast to other Indians who were of "our size." Guy and Crout thought that the Beothuk were "of a reasonable stature, of an ordinarie middle size," broad-breasted, with a bold and upright posture, and flat, broad faces.[1] In the late 1700s George Cartwright described the Beothuk as large and stout men; one individual whom he had seen through his telescope was "remarkably tall."[2] Fishermen in Notre Dame Bay claimed that some of the Beothuk were exceptionally huge, stout, or gigantic.[3] As J.P. Howley later commented, particularly large individuals would have been the exception rather than the rule. The more trustworthy evidence goes to prove that the Beothuk were of ordinary build.[4] As Captain Buchan wrote in 1811: "Report has famed these Indians as being of gigantic stature, this however is not the case as far as regards the tribe we saw, and must have originated from the bulkiness of their dress and partly from misrepresentation. They are well formed, and appear extremely healthy and athletic, and of the medium structure, probably from five feet eight to five feet nine inches."[5]

John Peyton, Jr, later described the Beothuk as healthy looking, of medium height, with a very active lithe build.[6] Beothuk women were said to have been tall or of medium height, that is, about five and a half feet. Demasduit and Shanawdithit were credited with "fine figures."[7]

As regards complexion, sixteenth-century sources compared the Indians (presumed to have been Beothuk) to dark-skinned people or Gypsies.[8] John Peyton, Jr, in whose household Shanawdithit lived for nearly five years, told Howley that the Beothuk were a better-looking people than the Micmac because they had a lighter complexion, regular features, and slightly aquiline noses.[9] In conversation with T.G.B. Lloyd, Peyton, Jr, said they resembled Spaniards or Gypsies.[10] Rev. John Leigh, who had cared for Demasduit, Rev. John Lewis, who had several interviews with her, and Captain Buchan, who had seen Demasduit as well as Shanawdithit and her family, agreed with Peyton that the complexion of the Beothuk was fairer than that of most Indians and close to that of Europeans. On a miniature portrait of Demasduit painted by Lady Hamilton in 1819 and said to be a striking likeness, she is depicted as a fair-skinned, attractive young woman with delicate features and black eyes (Plate 12.1).[11] However, several of Shanawdithit's contemporaries said that she looked "swarthy" like the Micmac, or was of mulatto colouring (Shanawdithit and Demasduit are more fully described in chapters 12 and 14).[12] Webber, author of a poem on the Beothuk, had seen a Beothuk man in a fishing boat who did not appear to be darker than the English fishermen he worked with but could be distinguished from them by "something peculiar about the eyes."[13]

With regard to the Beothuk's hairstyle, John Guy wrote that the Indians "goe bare headed, wearing theire haire somewhat long but rounded … Behind they have a great locke of haire platted with feathers like a hawke's lure, with a feather in yt standing uprighte by the crowne of the head, & a small locke platted before."[14] Perhaps this spectacular hairdo was worn only on special occasions or was peculiar to the Beothuk group in Trinity Bay: records describing Beothuk in other regions some 150 to 200 years later do not mention elaborate hairstyles. Most reports simply state that the Beothuk's hair was black and coarse and both sexes wore it straight; Captain Buchan told Dr Carson that it was "jet black rat-tailed."[15] Shanawdithit's dancer (Fig. 20.2) is depicted with straight, shoulder-length hair. Demasduit's hair, as portrayed by Lady Hamilton, was cropped short.[16] Beothuk men were said to have been beardless. This could have been the result of deliberate removal because many North American Indian groups considered facial hair unbecoming or even repulsive.[17] However, "chief" Nonosabasut, Demasduit's husband, had a bushy beard.[18]

The Application of Colouring Substances

John Guy and Henry Crout both noted the Beothuk's use of red ochre. Guy wrote of "their faces … red with okir, as all their apparel is & the rest of their bodie"; Croute recorded that "they do Reed all ther Faces with ockar and all ther skins."[19] Guy also said they were "full dyde of a black colour" but did not explain how the black was applied.[20] Among Micmac, for example, painting themselves black was a sign of mourning, which might also have been customary among the Beothuk.[21] Other sources confirm that the Beothuk painted their bodies and hair with ochre that was usually mixed with grease.[22] While clay-like ochre would have been the most effective and preferred colouring agent, the Beothuk also used reddish earth (probably soil with a high iron content) and reddish dye extracted from alder bark or from a "red root."[23] The application of reddish earth might explain why Guy thought the hair of some men was brown or even yellow, an observation that contradicts all other accounts.[24] The custom of painting the skin with various pigments was practised by many North American Indians and vividly portrayed by artists such as John White, Benjamin West, Karl Bodmer, George Catlin, and others.[25] It usually amounted to different patterns on face, hands, or body. The Beothuk appear to have been distinct in their custom of covering their bodies and all their belongings with a uniform layer of ochre. Some writers have suggested that the grease-and-ochre mixture would have protected the skin from insects in summer, made them less sensitive to the effects of intense cold in winter, or served as camouflage during the hunt.[26] While the mixture may well have had these functions, Santu, a woman of Beothuk-Micmac parentage, said that the Beothuk used ochre as a mark of tribal identity. The first coat, given to infants, was regarded as a sign of initiation.[27] The Beothuk also placed ochre with the dead.[28] To some native peoples, red ochre symbolized blood, life force, or power; the Beothuk's use of ochre could relate to this belief.[29]

Whether the Beothuk tattooed their skin is uncertain. Crignon, for example, describes the Indians on the Newfoundland south coast in 1529 as being marked "by certain lines made by applying fire to their faces, and are as if striped with a color between black and brown."[30] This description could have referred to tattoo, facial scarification, or markings made with charcoal. Facial markings were also noted on native people who were brought to Europe in 1501 and 1508 and who may have been Beothuk.[31] Since tattooing was popular among many Indian and Inuit groups it is possible that it was also practised by Beothuk, though descriptions from the seventeenth century onwards do not mention facial markings or tattoos.[32]

In the opinion of Europeans, the Beothuk's "exotic" appearance indicated that their nature and personality would have differed from their own. Thus, several documents include descriptions of the Beothuk's disposition as manifest both in individual and group behaviour. Cantino and Pasqualigo, who had seen and interacted with captives in 1501, thought they were gentle and given to laughter.[33] Cartier considered the Indians to be "wild" and "savage," Crignon found them "cruel and austere," and Thevet thought they were "inhuman and intractable."[34] Hayes, the surviving captain from Gilbert's voyage in 1584, called the natives "harmless"; John Guy and Henry Crout described them as personable, ready to laugh, trustworthy, and bold but given to revenge and distrustful of the English;

other colonists of that time thought they were gentle, subtle, and ingenious people who would neither hurt nor burn anything belonging to the English.[35]

It is noteworthy that Guy and Crout, who thought that the Beothuk were trustworthy, nevertheless believed that they were also revengeful. This characterization is significant for two reasons: first, the need for revenge appears to have been a prominent feature in Beothuk traditions (as indicated by later events and by Shanawdithit's testimony); second, Guy and Crout recognized hostile acts by Beothuk, such as when they took gear or cut loose fishing boats, as retaliation for wrongs done to them and not as expressions of evil-mindedness. It has been shown in Part One that by the 1700s, when relations with the English had deteriorated, the Beothuk were considered to be hostile, savage, and deceptive. However, fishermen who were kindly disposed said that they were inclined to play tricks and would sometimes spare the life of a person whom they could easily have killed.[36]

The disposition of particular Beothuk individuals was not recorded until the 1800s, when captives were brought to St John's. The first woman, whose name we do not know, was said to have been gentle, inoffensive, generally cheerful, and passionately fond of children. Governor Gower later wrote: "To judge of the disposition and manners of her tribe from … this woman … we should be inclined to think favourably of them."[37]

Demasduit, captured in 1819, was described as mild and delicate, of a gentle and interesting disposition, playful, astute, patient, and proud.[38] Her husband, Nonosabasut, showed courage and willingness to negotiate but when provoked by the refusal of the English to release his wife, he became enraged.[39]

Shanawdithit's mother was said to have been morose, while Shanawdithit herself was considered to be bland, affable, and affectionate, not the least abashed at anything.[40] The reader is again referred to Part One for fuller accounts of the Beothuk captives. But the general impression is conveyed in a comment by Dr William Carson, who cared for Shanawdithit throughout her illness: "My acquaintance with her and the still more interesting female Mary March [Demasduit] gave me a high opinion of the disposition and abilities of the Red Indians."[41]

THE MANUFACTURE OF CLOTHING

Throughout the centuries of contact the style and material of Beothuk clothing seems to have changed little. As far as we know, the Beothuk made their clothes largely from caribou skins. The hide, particularly in coats, was usually left intact and worn with the hair side against the body.[42] According to Samuel Hearne, who in 1771 lived with northern Indians for several months, it took the prime parts of eight to eleven caribou skins to make a complete suit of clothing for a grown person.[43] The hair of the skin could also be removed and the hide tanned on both sides, resulting in a supple leather that was made into a variety of garments and sometimes lined with other furs.[44] For collars, trim, or lining, or for the production of supplementary items of apparel, the Beothuk used beaver, marten, seal, and the skins of other small fur bearers.[45] They also possessed birdskins – one such skin was offered to Guy in trade – which were probably intended for making clothing.[46] While many Inuit groups made clothing from the feathered skins of birds, very few Indian groups other than the Beothuk are said to have used this light, waterproof material.[47]

We have little information about Beothuk hide-working techniques, but presumably they corresponded in general to North American Indian traditions and may have been similar to those of the Micmac and Montagnais. Several methods were used to skin an animal. Either the skin was cut with a skinning knife, or, as recorded by Henricksen from the Naskapi, an incision was made the length of the thorax and abdomen, starting at the lower jaw, after which the skin was punched off the carcass to avoid accidental cutting.[48] The residue of flesh and fat was then removed from the hide. Ethnographic observation and use-wear analysis have variously recorded the use of scapulae, stone scrapers, or longbones for this purpose. The latter were split in half and given a bevelled and sharpened edge.[49] Stone or iron axes could also have doubled as scrapers for the removal of subcutaneous fat and flesh.[50] For the removal of more resistant portions, scoop-shaped instruments of bone or brow plates from caribou antlers may have been used. If the skin was to be tanned on both sides, the hide was soaked for up to a week to loosen the hair, which was then removed with a bone beamer, a method still used among northern people.[51] The user would have stretched the hide over a log and grasped the beamer with both hands, drawing it towards himself or herself as a spokeshave might be used today by a carpenter.[52] After the skins had been thoroughly cleaned the Beothuk, like other Indians, would have tanned them with a mixture of putrefied animal livers, brains, urine, grease, wood-ash, or other tempering agents. In order to apply this mixture and then to allow the skins to dry properly, they were stretched on racks or frames formed from poles; many such frames were found at Beothuk sites.[53] In order to tie a skin onto a frame, holes were punched into the edges with an awl, then cordage was threaded through the holes. During the drying process, the skin had to be pounded or rubbed to prevent the leather from becoming hard. After tanning, the skins were smoked. In preparation for sewing, the edges of fur or leather were chewed to render them supple. The manufacture of clothing was usually the task of women, who were very skilled at this craft. For example, a young Beothuk woman who was captured in her camp and believed that she, her child, and another woman would be taken by their captors to an English village, "made two pair of Mogosans [moccasins] that night by y/e light of y/Fire for herself, two pair for the old Woman & a pair of arm sleeves for her Child all out of Deer skin … Instead of needles the Beothuk used awls for sewing."[54]

Mr Curtis, speaking of Shanawdithit, wrote, "I never saw her with a needle, but often saw her stitch by passing the thread through a hole made with a sharp point or awl."[55] Santu remembered that the Beothuk used bone awls. However, they also made awls from settlers' fish-hooks or from iron nails, indicating an innovative adaptation to a new material.[56] The thread used for sewing leather or fur was often made of sinew or perhaps of the sheathing of the muscles that run up either side of the spine; it comes off like a semitransparent membrane and when dried, splits along its length into threads.[57]

The Beothuk rubbed all items of clothing with a grease-and-ochre mixture.[58] This treatment of skins and leather goods helped to waterproof and preserve them, since ferrous oxides in the ochre destroy enzymes produced by bacteria that contaminate the skins.[59] Some native people believed that the colouring agent ensured personal protection or power.[60]

The Outer Robe

The Beothuk's major garment for both women and men was a robe or coat, often referred to as a "cassocke" or "cossack."[61] This robe has been described by different observers in varying detail. Guy said in 1612 that "a shorte gowne or cassocke made of stag skinnes, the furres innermost that came downe to the middle of their leg, with sleeves to the middle of their arme, & a beaver skinne about their necke, was all their apparell."[62] In the early 1800s, Captain Buchan and William E. Cormack gave similar descriptions of Beothuk coats but claimed that they had no sleeves.[63] Either Guy was mistaken, the sleeves having been formed from the corners of the robes when pulled over the shoulders and arms, or the garments he saw were of a different design from those used in the early nineteenth century. According to W.E. Cormack, whose information otherwise complements Guy's, the coats were made from two caribou skins sewn together to form a nearly square piece. This was thrown over the shoulders and came down to the middle of the legs, the upper corners being doubled over at the arms and chest. Experiments with caribou skins, however, have shown that two skins sewn together are not large enough to reach down over the legs if wrapped around the shoulders and chest.[64] It is therefore suggested that more than two skins were used for a coat. Buchan recorded that sometimes the coat was gathered in at the collar. Both he and Cormack said that a belt around the waist caused the coat to fall in a large fold over the abdomen, forming a triple layer. It constituted additional padding and protected the abdomen from injury and, as their English pursuers were later to discover, from small shot.[65] The fold might also have been used as a carrying device for small articles. When a man wanted to use his bow, he would disengage his right shoulder, or both shoulders, from the garment. A collar of marten, beaver, or other fur, or of alternating strips of otter and caribou fur, was sometimes attached to the coat and reached along its whole breadth such that it could cover the head and face.[66] Buchan said that the loose "cossack" was "fringed round with cutting of the same substance."[67] While this description could be interpreted to mean that the edge of the coat was cut into fringes, most likely the fringes were produced separately from tanned hide and sewn to the lower edge of the finished garment, since caribou fur is too thick to be cut into fringes.[68] Women's robes were augmented with a hood attached at the back in which to carry a baby.[69]

Micmac informants told anthropologist Frank Speck that Beothuk coats were either made from caribou furs with the hair turned inside, or from caribou leather (from which the hair had been removed) that was lined with otter, beaver, or other fur.[70] Nonosabasut's coat was of the latter type. It was "made of deer skin lined with beaver and other skins" and appears to have been a luxury variation of the ordinary caribou robe. Demasduit was said to have had "clothes of dressed deer-skins tastefully trimmed with Martin, but she would never put them on, or part with them."[71] Some researchers have interpreted the term deerskin (caribou) to mean leather. Since the coat appears to have been the only garment she wore on her upper torso (in the winter season), it is likely to have been made from caribou fur with the hair turned inside. The term "dressed" was used at that time for prepared skin with or without fur.[72]

An anecdote circulating among fishermen in the 1840s recounts how Beothuk had taken the sails of a fishing boat and were seen on the following day wearing cloaks made from these sails, which had been daubed with red ochre (see chapter 7).[73] However, considering all available information on Beothuk clothing the latter part of the tale is likely to be an embellishment. The Beothuk are otherwise not known to have adopted European-style clothing or to have used European materials for the manufacture of garments, even though among presents laid out for them blankets were occasionally included.[74] Contemporary observers accounts agree that, as late as the 1820s, when many Beothuk were starved and sick, those who were encountered wore clothes made of skins.[75]

In contrast to the garments of other Indian groups, sometimes described as colourful and stunning, Beothuk daily wear did not strike Europeans as spectacular or beautiful.[76] Captain Pulling alone, who collected data on the Beothuk in 1792, wrote that "on some of their skins they draw the shape of men & Women, on some, Fish, others fanciful scrawls."[77] Pulling did not specifically refer to garments and it is possible that the skins thus embellished were used for other purposes. No other contemporary observer corroborated Pulling's information with the exception of the Micmac John Paul, who claimed in the early 1900s that the Beothuk's hooded coats were frequently decorated with painting.[78]

In addition to their everyday robes, the Beothuk may have reserved certain garments for festive occasions. At least, Shanawdithit's sketch 8 portrays a dancer with a robe of a different style (Fig. 20.2).[79] Its upper section, wrapped snugly around the dancer's torso, goes over one shoulder and under the other, with a loose flap trailing at the back. It is girded at the waist, forming a heavy fold. The costume is decorated along the upper and the lower edges of the robe and on the edge of the flap with fringes that may have carvings or shells tied to them. The drawing shows a zig-zag pattern along the lower edge of the garment, and a border of geometrical configurations along the upper edge that is worked into, or sewn onto, the leather. Incised bone pendants and a necklace consisting of bone carvings with an animal tooth as a centrepiece, all found at Beothuk

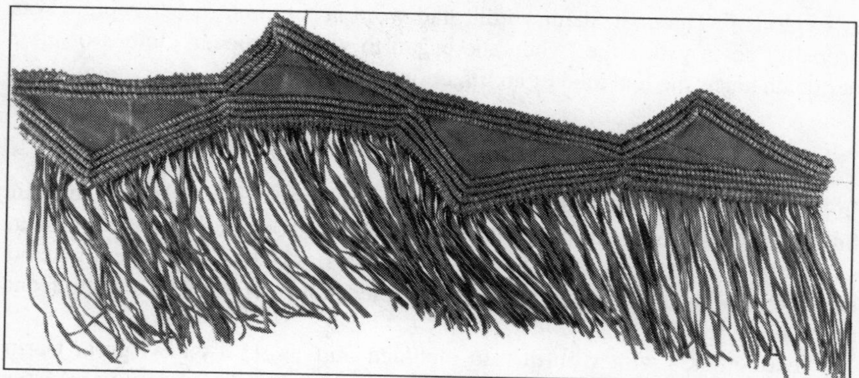

Plate 21.1 Coat fringe. (By permission of the British Museum, London, no.2583, neg.K 50762)

burial sites, could have been worn around the neck or tied to items of clothing. If one can extrapolate from customs among other Indians who ornamented their clothing, the Beothuk may have applied these decorations not only to make the garments look more attractive but to add to the status of the wearer and perhaps also to please supernatural entities, or to achieve protection.

An interesting Beothuk technique of decorative stitching can be found on a sample in the collection of the British Museum (Plate 21.1).[80] It consists of an elongated strip of caribou leather cut along the long axis to form four triangles, alternating apex up/apex down. The edges of the irregular zig-zag outline are accentuated, in raised relief, by small lengths of rolled up intestine (or possibly very large bird quills), which were laid on the leather and then tightly oversewn with sinew to produce a corrugated effect. A fringed leather section was sewn to the lower edge of this piece and the entire product was rubbed with a mixture of grease and red ochre.[81] Another decorative effect, seen on a Beothuk legging and on moccasins in the Newfoundland Museum collection, was achieved by stitching lengths of spruce root over the sinew used to sew the seams. When the bark is freshly peeled off, split root is shiny and white and would have contrasted nicely with the ochre-coloured leather.[82]

In 1965 descendants of Attorney General James Simms donated a painted, tailored leather coat to the Newfoundland Museum. It was believed that the coat had been made or worn by Shanawdithit, whom James Simms had taken into his home in 1828 or 1829.[83] However, it has since been identified as a typical Naskapi man's coat.[84] It is true that Shanawdithit had made "a dress of her tribe" in 1828 for W.E. Cormack, presumably to demonstrate Beothuk clothing, but Cormack probably took this dress to Scotland, along with other Beothuk artifacts he had acquired. The garments Shanawdithit and her mother and sister wore at the time of their capture were described as "deer-skin shawls" but not as coats.[85] While living with the English Shanawdithit wore European garments; at her transfer to St John's she was said to be in need of new clothes, which Cormack was to purchase for her in St John's where they were much cheaper than at Exploits.[86] The coat Shanawdithit had worn at the time of her capture was probably destroyed, either when she began to wear European clothes or after her death since she had died of an infectious disease.[87]

Sleeves and Mittens, Loincloths and Leggings

In cold weather the Beothuk wore sleeves or cuffs of caribou hide with the hair on the inside. They were not attached to the main robe and might have been similar to those used by Micmac and Montagnais, which covered the arms and shoulders and were tied together under the outer robe across the back and front of the body.[88]

The Beothuk's winter outfit also included mittens. In 1536 a "great warm mitten" was found on a deserted Beothuk campsite. About seventy years later John Guy was offered a mitten as a trade item. Guy also wrote that the Indian who "seemed to have command over the reste" wore mittens.[89] Since this type of garment was recorded at a relatively early date, it is likely to have been an item of aboriginal clothing and not one that was introduced by Europeans, as has been claimed for the Montagnais.[90]

Most North American Indians covered their lower torso with a loincloth or apron. It consisted of a soft piece of skin, either suspended from a hip string like an apron, or else drawn between the legs and kept in place by attaching it front and back to a string.[91] Records of the use of loincloths by Beothuk men or women are ambivalent. Several sixteenth-century observers claimed the inhabitants of "Terra Nova" went about naked in summer.[92] The Indians captured by Côrte Real were described as "quite naked except for their privy parts which they cover with a skin of the abovementioned deer."[93] A loincloth or breechcloth of some sort was also worn by the seven Indians brought to Rouen in 1508–09 by the crew of *Pensée*.[94] We cannot say with any certainty, however, that these sixteenth-century accounts refer to Beothuk.

In the early 1600s Richard Whitbourne wrote that the Beothuk went about "naked in summer and winter" and George Wells told Howley in the late 1800s that the Indians had worn "no clothes in summer."[95] However, the term "naked" cannot be taken literally because by European standards, Indians were often considered "naked" even when they wore rudimentary items of clothing.[96] It has therefore been concluded that even though loincloths were not described as part of the Beothuk's outfit from the seventeenth century onwards, it is nevertheless likely that they wore this article of clothing since it was used by most Indians and had been referred to in earlier records. There is also a Maliseet tradition that the "red people" of Newfoundland had loincloths.[97]

In winter, when the legs and lower torso needed protection from the cold, leggings, gaiters, or pants were worn. Some were made of caribou hide, usually worn with the hair next to the body, while others were made of tanned leather.[98] The standard Beothuk legging appears to have covered the leg and hip from the ankle to the waist. Three leggings of this type were included in the burial of a

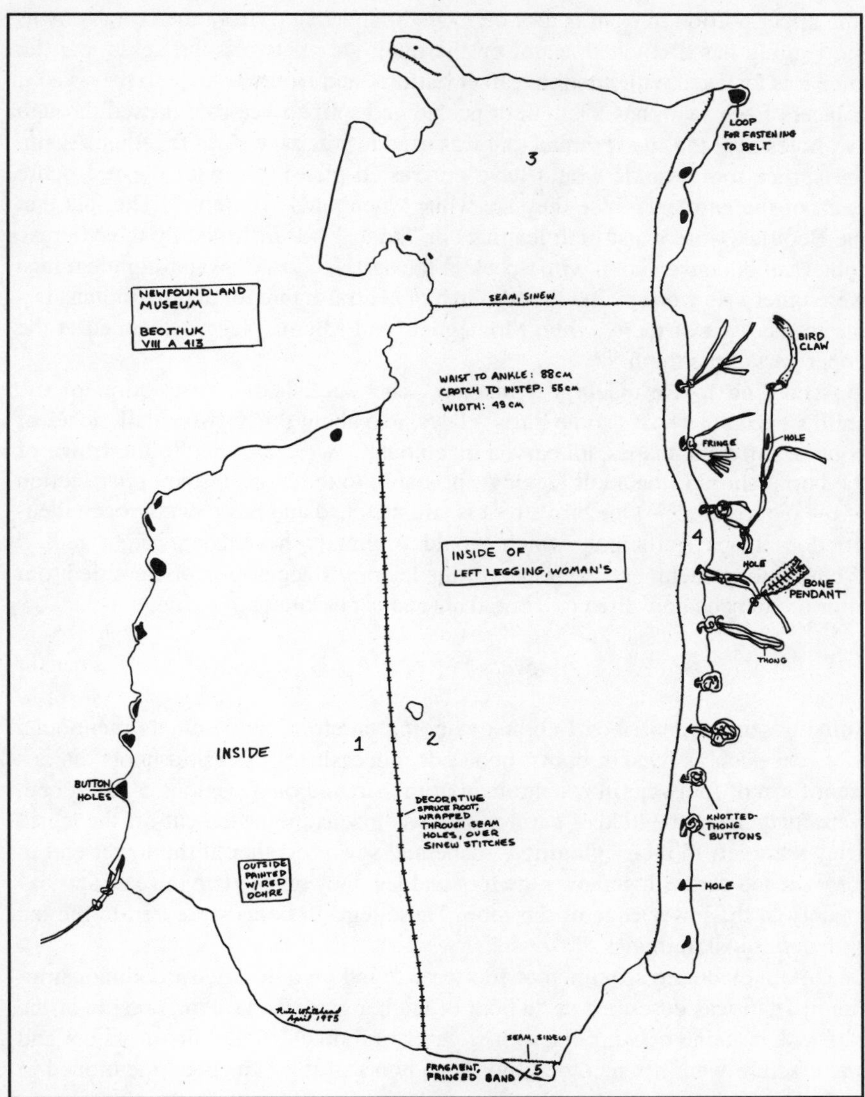

Fig.21.1 Adult pants used as burial shroud in grave of child on Big Island, Pilley's Tickle. (Illustration by Ruth Holmes Whitehead)

mummified Beothuk child, found in the 1880s, in which the body was "clothed with a sort of skin pants ... fringed at the sides with strips of skin cut into fine shreds."[99] The body was also encased in a burial shroud that has recently been identified as the left legging of an adult (Fig. 21.1). It is eighty-eight centimetres long; the upper section would have covered the left buttock of the wearer (the upper portion in front is torn off). On the inner side (from the crotch down) the legging has a stitched seam; on the outer side between the ankle and the knee it is fastened with knotted leather buttons, and from the knee to the waist it is laced. Each seam has a length of peeled and split spruce root passed through awl holes over the sinew thread that was used to stitch the sides together. Again, the spruce-root strands would have contrasted pleasingly with the red ochre paint of the garment, since they are white when newly peeled.[100] The fact that the Beothuk wore waist-high leggings or "pants" was affirmed by the Micmac John Paul in conversation with Speck in the early 1900s.[101] Waist-high leggings were otherwise worn by the Woods Cree of central Labrador and by Indians living to the west of them, while Montagnais and Micmac leggings ended at the upper part of the thigh.[102]

According to Rev. George Patterson, who published a description of the child's burial in 1891, "some birds' claws, and about thirty-two small pieces of bone of different shapes, all carved ingeniously" were fastened to the fringe of the burial shroud (the adult legging), probably to the loops in the upper section of the outer seam.[103] One bird's foot is still attached and has recently been identified as black guillemot, which would originally have been bright red.[104] Whether the attachments were part of the legging's decoration or were tied to it after it had been converted to a burial shroud is not known.

Footwear

Some observers described Beothuk as going barefoot, while others mentioned footwear such as legskin boots, boots, or moccasins.[105] Legskin boots, an ancient form of footwear in use throughout the circumboreal regions of the globe, were made from the hide of caribou shanks "just as they were cut off the legs." They were left in their cylindrical shape and sewn together at the lower end to form the toe part. Slipped over the foot and leg, they reached up the calf approximately to the lower edge of the robe. These legskin boots were tied to the leg with caribou-skin thongs.[106]

A more elaborate specimen of footwear found on a deserted Beothuk campsite in 1536 was described as "a boot of leather garnished on the outside of the calf with certaine brave trails, as it were of raw silke."[107] Details of its cut and manufacture were not recorded; nor have boots of this type been mentioned in any other document.

Moccasins, as referred to in archival documents, may have been ankle boots akin to those found in the burial of the Beothuk child mentioned earlier (Plate 21.2). Such boots were made from three pieces of caribou leather: sole, vamp (covering the upper front of the foot), and cuff (placed around the back of the heel), as illustrated in Fig. 21.2a and b. Vamp and sole were nearly rectangular and at the toes the sole was folded squarely over and sewn to the vamp, ungathered, in a straight seam. The sides of the sole were folded upwards and stitched to the vamp edges and to the cuff. The remaining length of vamp was

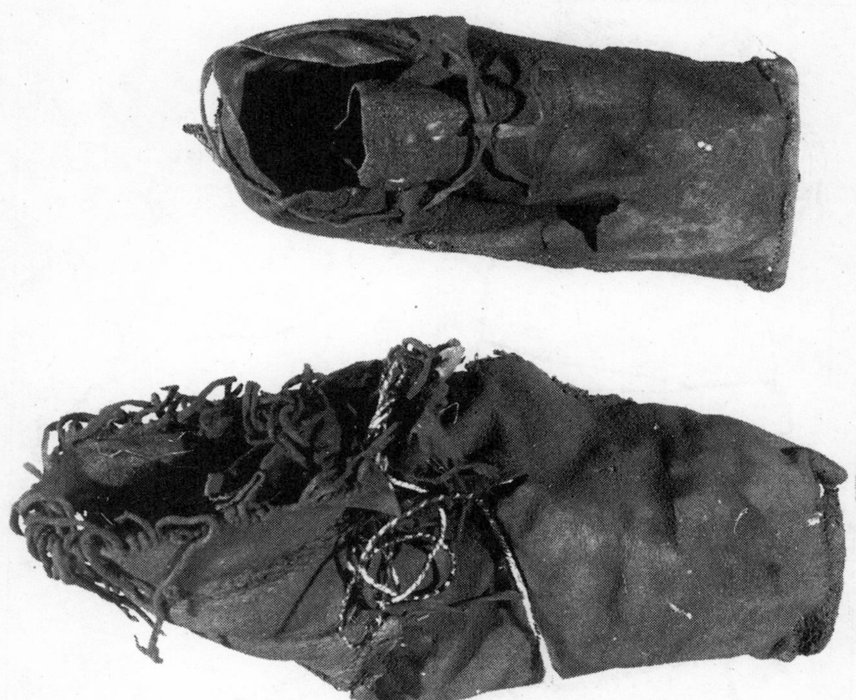

Plate 21.2 Two moccasins from the burial of a child on Big Island, Pilley's Tickle. (Collection of the Newfoundland Museum)

tucked in behind the cuff and acted as a tongue. The cuff itself reached up to cover the ankle. One of the moccasins from the burial had a finely fringed band sewn to its upper edge.[108] The footwear was secured by means of a drawstring thong or by a thong knotted through holes in the front of the cuff. This design, with the sole folded squarely over at the front, gives the toe an angular appearance that differs markedly from the forms made by other Indian groups, who would gather the width at the toes into a rounded shape. However, the Beothuk moccasins from the burial were intended for a child, and it is possible that the design of Beothuk footwear for adults was different. Among the Montagnais, young children often wore square-toed moccasins while adults wore round-toed boots.[109]

An unusual feature of the Beothuk moccasins from the child's grave is a cone-shaped projection at the base of the heel (Fig. 21.2b). It is formed by the edge of the fourth side of the sole, which was folded half way and sewn together vertically. This projection is not found on moccasins of other native groups, where the central part of the sole at the heel is cut away or laid double so that

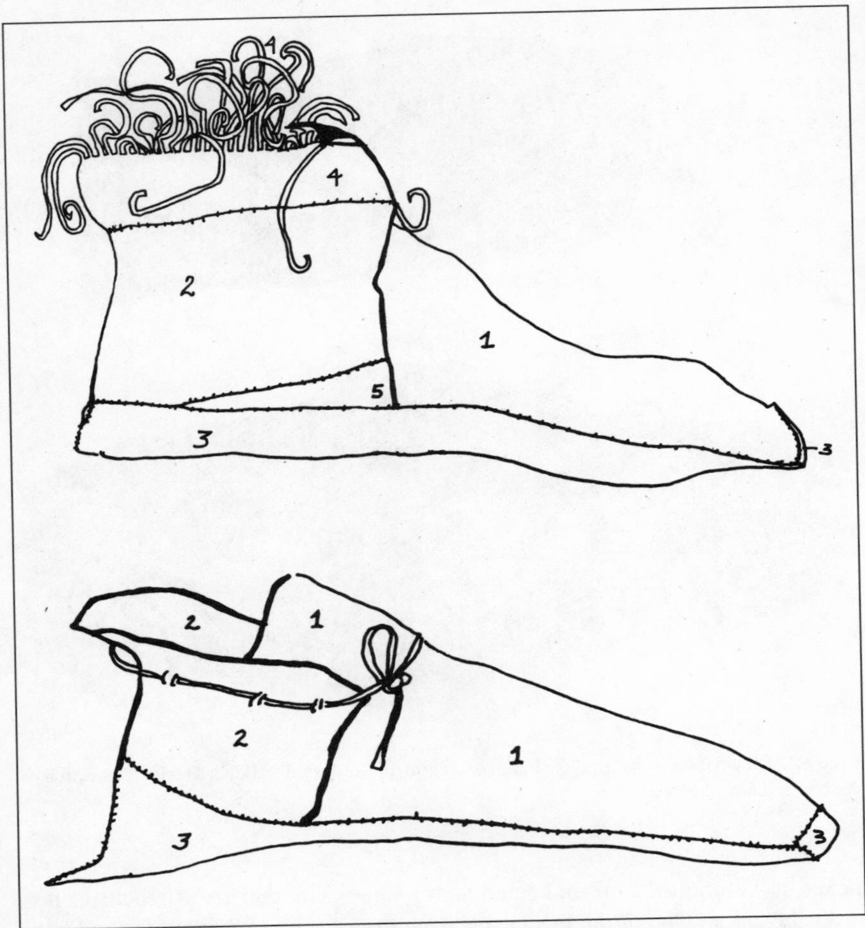

Fig.21.2a and b Two moccasins from child's burial on Big Island: (1) vamp; (2) cuff; (3) sole; (4) fringe border; (5) patch. (Illustration by Ruth Holmes Whitehead)

one seam runs horizontally along the bottom of the heel and another vertically in the centre, forming a T-shaped heel seam.

Gudmund Hatt, who has made a detailed study of the construction of moccasins, proposes that all variations of this footwear derive from a prototype that consists of a single piece of skin "gathered around the foot by means of a straight seam." One of the earliest innovations was to use two- or three-piece patterns that fitted the shape of the foot. A second innovation was to have a T-shaped heel construction where the sole at the back is folded in from the sides, avoiding the cone-shaped projection seen on the Beothuk moccasins.[110] Judging from the specimens at hand, the Beothuk incorporated only the three-piece pattern but continued to manufacture some of their moccasins without a

T-shaped heel seam, which rendered them technically and visually different from those of other tribes.

Headgear

In the early 1600s, English sailors shot muskets at a group of Beothuk in Trinity Bay so that "all ran away naked, without any apparell, but onely some of them had their hats on their heads, which were made of Seal skinnes, in fashions like our hats, sewed handsomely, with narrow bands about them, set round with fine white shels."[111] It is worth noting that the hats were styled "like our hats" and were probably not of native design. European hats seem to have intrigued Indians greatly. Le Jeune, who gave a detailed description of Montagnais clothing in the 1600s, thought that few of them had used hats before contact with Europeans. In fact, they seemed not to know how to make hats and bought them already made, or at least ready cut, from the French. LeClercq recorded a similar situation among the Micmac, saying that they did not make use of hats or caps "until the French had given them the use thereof."[112] Perhaps the hats worn by the Beothuk on this occasion were also derived from European designs, shells having been added to give them an emblematic or personal touch. Considering that it was summer and that Beothuk gowns had hoods and fur collars that could be pulled over head and face if such protection were required, the hats were probably not worn for warmth but may have had a symbolic or ceremonial significance.

Later descriptions of Beothuk apparel do not mention hats of this type. Instead, Captain Buchan recorded in 1811 that the headman of the group at Red Indian Lake wore a "high cap" that distinguished him from the others. This same Indian also owned a "mythological emblem" and seemed to have special status.[113] That ceremonial headgear existed can be deduced from a reference to a drawing by Shanawdithit of "Men singing to Ash-wa-meet [the name of a mythological emblem], with Eagles feathers and deers ears in cap," suggesting that decorated caps constituted part of the regalia required for a ceremony involving *Ash-wa-meet*.[114]

CHAPTER TWENTY-TWO

Mamateeks and Other Structures

Several sixteenth- and seventeenth-century documents mentioning Newfoundland's native people describe their summer dwellings on the coast. Beothuk winter camps in inland regions were seldom observed since Europeans rarely penetrated into the interior of the country and even then did not necessarily record their exploits. The first person to describe Beothuk structures in detail was Lieut. John Cartwright who was sent up the Exploits River by Governor Palliser in 1768 in search of Beothuk (see chapter 6). In the early 1800s Beothuk winter houses were described by Lieut. David Buchan, the explorer William E. Cormack, and others. Contemporary information also comes to us through Shanawdithit's sketches.

Since the 1960s Beothuk habitation sites have been surveyed and excavated by archaeologists. Their investigations not only confirm historic records but add measurements of the circumference of houses and of other features that contemporary observers failed to notice or record.

The accumulated data show that the Beothuk built a variety of mamateeks[1] for seasonal habitation. The different mamateek types are discussed here according to their shapes, in the sequence in which they were dated or recorded. They include conical, six-sided, square and rectangular, oval, eight-sided, and five-sided structures. Contemporary accounts are quoted first, followed by information from archaeological investigations.

CONICAL MAMATEEKS

The earliest description of a conical mamateek comes from John Guy, who saw many of these dwellings in Trinity Bay in 1612: "Theire housen theare weare nothing but poules set in a rownde forme, meeting all togeather alofte, wh[i]ch they cover w[i]th deere skinnes. They are about tenne foote broade, and in the middle they make theire fire. One of them was covered w[i]th a sayle, wh[i]ch they had gotten from some Christian." Guy's companion Henry Crout examined a dwelling of this type in 1613 and found it "covered with some skynnes and they lay one w[i]th Fine long green grasse for their pillow at their heades and some vnder them, but by all Imagination th[ey] could not be but a man and his wyffe and child."[2]

Beothuk dwellings seen in 1718 in the vicinity of Hare Bay on the Northern Peninsula were said to be like those of other Indians (presumably conical in shape) but sturdier because they were reinforced with horizontal cross poles or hoops.[3] On Shanawdithit's drawing of a conical summer mamateek (sketch 6, Fig. 22.3) two or possibly three horizontal lines could indicate such reinforcement.[4]

George Cartwright described conical houses seen in 1768 on the banks of the Exploits River thus: "The wigwams were constructed of poles in the form of a cone about six or seven feet in diameter at the base, eight or nine feet in height, covered with birch rind or skins, and often with sails, which they contrived to steal from the fishing rooms."[5] His brother John, who led this expedition, gave a more detailed description:

> The whigwham is a hut in form of a cone. The base of it is proportioned to the number of the family, and their beds form a circle around a fire that burns in the centre. The beds are only so many hollows in the earth, lined with the tender branches of fir and pine. Several straight sticks like hoop-poles, compose the frame of the whigwham, and covering is supplied by the rind of the Birch-tree. This is overlaid sheet upon sheet, in the manner of tiles and perfectly shelters the whole apartment except the fire place, over which there is left an opening to carry off the smoke. The birch rind is secured in its place by outside poles, whose weight from their inclined position is sufficient for that purpose. The central fire spreading its heat makes it quite warm; and notwithstanding one of these habitations where materials are plentiful, may be completed in less than an hour, yet they are extremely durable.[6] (See Figs. 6.2, 23.3).

Capt. David Buchan characterized conical houses as a few poles "supported by a fork" and similar to the wigwams of other North American Indians.[7]

The size of these dwellings varied. While Crout had come upon a house barely large enough for three persons, Captain Pulling in 1792 recorded one from Indian Cove in the Bay of Exploits with seven or eight sleeping hollows.[8] In the early 1800s, a settler said the conical houses measured about thirty to forty feet (nine to twelve metres) in circumference, which would have required a diameter of between three and four metres.[9] Generally, summer houses seem to have been cramped; as Pulling said, they were "so small that when the Holes which are round the Fire place are occupied they can have scarce room to stir."

Typically, native house builders used sheets of bark from birch or fir sewn together into lengths that fitted the circumference of the frame. These were laid on the poles from the bottom upwards, like shingles, terminating below the top to allow the passage of smoke.

The sleeping hollows in Beothuk mamateeks were relatively small, and observers conjectured that the Beothuk slept either in a sitting position or "curled up."[10] Certainly, the Beothuk captive Demasduit was entirely familiar with this position; when sleeping on a European bed she was said to have been "rolled up in a ball."[11] Sleeping hollows lined with grass or branches may have been peculiar to the Beothuk, although one unconfirmed source states that among the Athapaskan Ahtna the women dug nest-like hollows in the ground, which they lined with grass or branches.[12]

Archaeological excavations of circular housepits have shown that the living floor was lower than the level of the surrounding forest floor. This suggests that before erecting a mamateek the Beothuk first cleared the ground of any grass cover and then scraped loose soil into a circular earthen wall or berm. A housepit at Pope's Point that was archaeologically excavated was described as a circular depression surrounded by a mounded margin with large cobbles on its crest; the rocks were possibly used as anchorage for the covering of the structure.[13] At another archaeological site (Noel Paul's Brook-3) a berm up to twenty centimetres higher than the forest floor surrounded the house depression.[14] The depths of twenty-six housepits at the Wigwam Brook site were between fifteen and forty-six centimetres below ground level.[15] Of eighteen circular housepits on the Exploits River that were measured from the crest of the earthen wall to the bottom of the sleeping hollows, ten were fifteen to twenty-five centimetres deep and eight were thirty to sixty centimetres deep.[16]

The diameter of circular housepits varied. The depression at Pope's Point measured 3.7 metres across whereas a foundation at Wigwam Brook measured 4.25 metres.[17] Nine housepits on Aspen Island and twenty-five at North Angle had diameters of 2.75 to 6.10 metres, although not all these pits may have derived from conical mamateeks.[18] The diameter of the nineteen circular housepits seen by T.G.B. Lloyd on The Beaches site in 1876 averaged 3.7 metres.[19] The Exploits River housepits ranged from three to eight metres (averaging 5.2) when measured from crest to crest of the surrounding earthen wall.[20]

Some of the housepit depressions may have been the remains of multisided rather than conical houses – without excavation they are hard to differentiate. This cautionary note is based on Lloyd's report of a large "circular" housepit at Red Indian Lake, which his Micmac informant claimed to be the foundation of an octagonal structure. Two roughly round depressions on the Boyd's Cove site turned out, upon excavation, to be remains of multisided houses.[21]

Most circular houses had a central hearth that was either relatively flat or heavily mounded with ashes; others showed no evidence of a hearth.[22] Occupants of shelters of the latter type, which were presumably used only in summer, appear to have tended to their cooking and other activities requiring fire outside. Hearth features between housepits have been recorded at several sites on the Exploits River and at Red Indian Lake.[23]

Sleeping hollows were not always discernible archaeologically. Where they could be identified, they ranged in depth and outline from single "berths" to relatively marginal depressions that were no more than a shallow dip in the ground.[24]

Fig.22.1 Hexagonal housepit at the Indian Point site, Red Indian Lake, Locality B5, drawn by Roberta M. O'Brien (Devereux Ms.743, 1970: ii). (By permission of H. Devereux, Govt. of Newfoundland, Dept. of Tourism, Culture and Recreation, and the Canadian Museum of Civilization)

SIX-SIDED (HEXAGONAL) MAMATEEKS

We have no contemporary accounts of hexagonal houses, though some scholars believe that the winter mamateek drawn by Shanawdithit on sketch 6 (Fig. 22.3) is ambiguous with regard to its outline and could depict a hexagonal dwelling.[25] In the 1970s Helen Devereux excavated the foundation of such a structure at Indian Point, Red Indian Lake (Figs. 22.1, 22.2).[26] Six metres long and 7.5 metres wide, it was a semisubterranean dwelling whose floor had been dug out in places to a depth of 1.5 metres. The upper limit of the six earthen walls was flush with the surface of the surrounding forest floor and there was no mounding of earth around the perimeter of the structure. The six corners of the earthen walls showed signs of having been reinforced. Four walls were 3.3 metres long and two measured 3.6 metres; all walls sloped slightly inward and downward to lower, flat platforms made of soil. These platforms were present all around the perimeter, excepting the area of the entrance. They were between sixty-one and ninety-one centimetres wide. Since there was no evidence of studs or trunks along the walls, the roof – probably constructed of poles and covered with bark, sods, or both – may have reached down to the forest floor.[27] The house had a central hearth and a

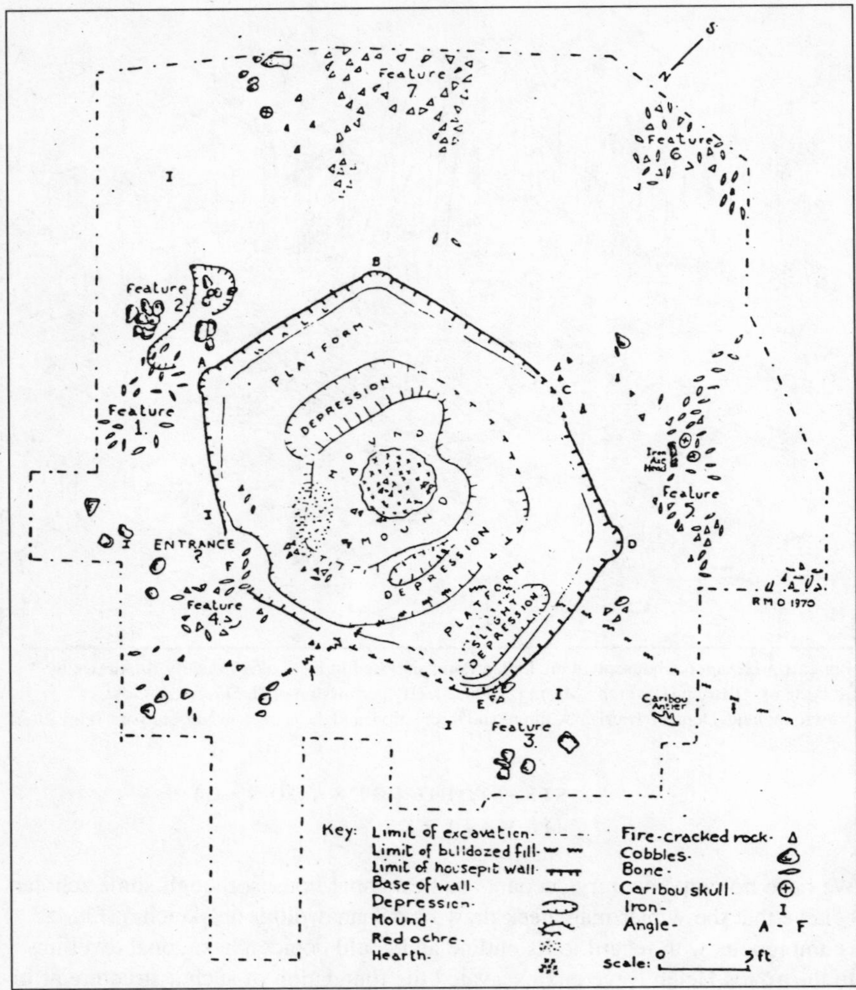

Fig.22.2 Preliminary plan of excavated hexagonal house at Indian Point site, Red Indian Lake, Locality B5 (Devereux Ms.743, 1970, Fig.5). (By permission of H. Devereux, Govt. of Newfoundland, Dept. of Tourism, Culture and Recreation, and the Canadian Museum of Civilization)

series of conjoined (sleeping?) hollows, each about forty-five centimetres deep, which were arranged between the platforms that ran alongside the house walls and the central hearth.[28] The latter consisted of an oblong mound about two by three metres across. A carbon sample from the upper occupation layer of the site, associated with the earth lodge, was dated 355 +/- 100 BP (ca. AD 1595).[29] Discrete but well represented features at the same level contained Little Passage-type tools, suggesting that the site had been used since prehistoric times.

Two housepits on the Beothuk site at Boyd's Cove in Notre Dame Bay were also roughly hexagonal in outline. One dwelling (House no. 11), with a maximum inner diameter of 4.7 metres, had a low earthen wall.[30] A more substantial structure (House no. 3) with an irregular hexagonal outline was about seven metres wide at its maximum, measured from crest to crest of the surrounding walls. The earthen walls were about twenty to thirty centimetres high; the roof is believed to have been supported by posts.[31] The interior had been dug out to an average depth of ten to twelve centimetres. Both houses had a mounded central hearth. While House no. 3 had no discernible sleeping hollows, House no. 11 had four or perhaps five oblong depressions around the outer perimeter. Pastore who excavated this site considered this house type to be intermediate between the Beothuk summer dwellings and the well-insulated winter houses described in early-nineteenth-century records.

SQUARE AND RECTANGULAR MAMATEEKS

John Guy was the first person to record a house "in a square forme w[i]th a small roofe."[32] At the time he explored Trinity Bay, in October/November 1612, this house, seen at Dildo Pond, was not completed and it is uncertain whether it was intended as a dwelling or a storehouse.

Two rectangular winter houses were noted by John Cartwright in 1768, one on the bank of the Exploits River close to Little Red Indian Pond, the second near Indian Point on Red Indian Lake. He described them as follows:

> They were … rectangle, framed nearly in the fashion of the English fishing houses, only that the studs were something apart, from which it was evident that they alone could not, in that state, form the shell … But about eighteen inches within this and parallel to it, there was another frame of slighter workmanship rising to the roof. From the hair which adhered to the studs, the interval appeared to have been filled with deer-skins; … This was the construction of only three sides, the fourth being raised by trees well squared and placed horizontally one upon another, having their seams caulked with moss. This inferior side of the dwelling bore a SE. aspect … The lodgement of the rafters on the beams and the necessary joints were as neatly executed as in the houses commonly inhabited by our fishers. The roof was a low pyramid, being encompassed at the distance of three feet from its vertex by a hoop tied to the rafters with thongs. Here the covering had terminated, and the space above the hoop had been left open as in the whigwham, for a passage for the smoke, the fire-place, according to custom, having been in the centre.[33]

John's brother George claimed the houses were approximately square with ten to twelve feet to a side; sleeping places were arranged around a central fireplace. He had seen "several" such houses.[34] At Indian Point the depression left by a rectangular dwelling 9.2 metres in length was still visible in the early 1900s. Its central area had been dug out to a depth of about sixty centimetres and would originally have been deeper. Allegedly the house that once stood on this spot had been the dwelling of a Beothuk "chief."[35] Four of the sixteen housepits partially excavated at Indian Point in the 1960s had rectangular outlines.[36]

OVAL MAMATEEKS

Dwellings with an oval outline are not recorded in contemporary accounts but have been identified archaeologically. One of two oval depressions at Boyd's Cove, assumed to have been inhabited between AD 1650 and 1730, enclosed a space 9.4 by 6.1 metres, measured from crest to crest of the surrounding wall; interior dimensions were 7 by 4.1 metres and the wall was twenty to thirty centimetres high (House no. 4).[37] The roof design is unknown, but either a gabled or an arched roof has been proposed.[38] One of the two entrances of this house had an overlapping wall that could have served as a wind baffle. Eleven shallow oval-shaped depressions between 3.5 and 7.5 centimetres deep were thought to have been sleeping hollows.

House no. 4 had a large, elongated hearth along its central axis with an extensive accumulation of caribou bone mash, covering an area of almost five by one metres. The large size and the particular configuration of this building, as well as the bone-mash residue, resemble those of the Montagnais/Naskapi *shaputan*, a multifamily dwelling used for communal feasts known as *mokoshan*. These feasts were celebrated in honour of the caribou spirit throughout the hunting season and involved the extraction, boiling, and consumption of substantial amounts of marrow from caribou leg bones. Considering the shape and size of the Beothuk structure and the massive residue of bone mash, Pastore suggests that the Beothuk at Boyd's Cove used the oval house for similar purposes.[39]

A large oval housepit at the Wigwam Brook site on the Exploits River measured 6.1 by 5.2 metres and was forty-six centimetres deep. Excavation revealed a central fireplace but no bone mash. Previous disturbance had removed possible signs of sleeping hollows.[40] This camp was believed to have been occupied between AD 1770 and 1820.

EIGHT-SIDED (OCTAGONAL) MAMATEEKS

There are no eyewitness accounts of octagonal dwellings prior to 1811, when Buchan visited a Beothuk camp on Red Indian Lake between Millertown and Indian Point. He wrote that the houses

> were of the octagonal structure, the diameter of the base being nearly 22 feet, and enclosed with studs of four feet above the surface. On these was affixed a wall plate [horizontal beam] from which were projected poles forming a conic roof and terminating in the top in a small circle sufficient for emitting the smoke and admitting light, this and the entrance being the only apertures. A right line being drawn to equal distances from each

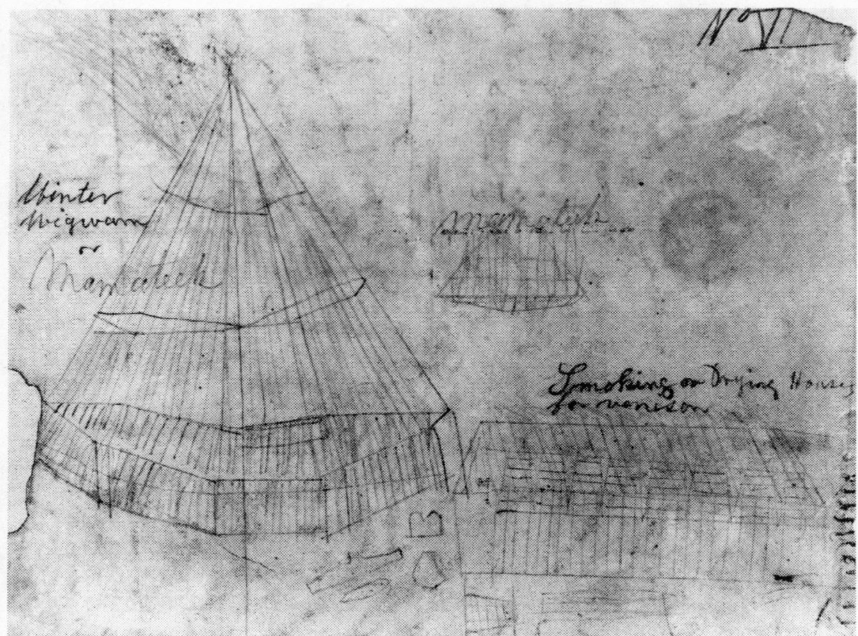

Fig.22.3 Shanawdithit's sketch 6: Winter and summer mamateek, smoking or drying house for venison, two small racks, and several unidentified items. (Collection of the Newfoundland Museum)

of the angular points, was fitted neatly with a kind of lattice work forming the points of so many recesses which were filled with neatly dressed deer skins. The fire was placed in the centre of the area around which was formed their place of repose, everyone lying with their feet towards the centre and their heads up to the lattice work somewhat elevated. The whole was covered in with birch bark, and banked on the outside with earth, as high as the studding, making these abodes with little fuel warm even in the inclemency of winter. Skins covered the entrance.[41]

It was later learned that each house was occupied by about twelve to fifteen people.[42] The construction features described by Buchan agree with Shanawdithit's drawing of a winter mamateek (Fig. 22.3), which shows the underlying structure of a house rather than its finished appearance. Her illustration depicts what is believed to be an eight-sided house (rather than a six-sided one) with a relatively low substructure made of upright sticks or poles, some corners having double uprights. It was covered with a high conical roof consisting of poles that were secured on the inside by two circular hoops. In the completed dwelling, part or all of the uprights would have been hidden behind an earthen berm, while the roof poles would have been covered with bark and moss, and possibly sods. Buchan spent several hours in one of these structures and concluded that it was "finished in a manner far superior to what might have been expected."[43]

In the 1870s, the geologist T.G.B. Lloyd found a "circular wigwam pit" nearly ten metres in diameter in the area where Buchan had seen the Beothuk winter camp in 1811. According to his Micmac guide, the house originally built over this pit had been an eight-sided structure "at the corners of which upright posts were driven to carry a bow frame for supporting the sides of the wigwam."[44]

One of the housepits at Boyd's Cove (House no. 1) was the remnant of what may have been an eight-sided dwelling; its inner diameter measured 6.1 metres. The living space had been dug out and the excavated soil used for a low earthen wall around the perimeter. Outer and inner post holes in this wall suggest two parallel rows of posts, perhaps similar to the double studding described by Cartwright from rectangular houses on the Exploits River, in which the space between the posts was insulated with furs. The house at Boyd's Cove had a central hearth. An oblong hollow some 1.7 metres long and five to seven centimetres deep and an area devoid of rocks may have served as sleeping places.[45]

FIVE-SIDED (PENTAGONAL) MAMATEEKS

Cormack stated in one of his notes that Beothuk houses had developed from "the simple circular to the angular and straight walled dwelling, from the octagonal to the five sided."[46] This statement suggests that he actually saw five-sided houses, probably at South Twin or Red Indian Lake, and believed them to be a recent innovation. However, neither Cormack himself nor other contemporary observers have recorded five-sided mamateeks from Beothuk camps. Cormack's opinion that this house type replaced other forms is difficult to substantiate with so little data at hand; it seems best to refrain from making any firm conclusions on this point.

However, there is archaeological evidence of a five-sided dwelling at the Wigwam Brook site on the Exploits River, believed to have been occupied by Beothuk between AD 1770 and 1820.[47] The housepit measured roughly 6.4 by 7.3 metres, the walls being 2.7, 3.4, 3.7, 3.7, and 4.6 metres long (Fig. 22.4). It had a mounded central hearth and slight depressions in the floor but no clearly defined sleeping hollows.

UNSPECIFIED HOUSE TYPES

In his 1792 report of a raid on a Beothuk camp on the Exploits River, Captain Pulling refers to winter houses but does not describe them in any detail. They must have been far more commodious than the ordinary conical hut, however, since four dwellings were said to have housed about a hundred people along with forty to fifty packs of preserved caribou meat, more than a hundred skins, and weapons and utensils of various kinds.[48] Pulling gathered that the Beothuk had covered the roofs with sails, which may have been used alone or placed over the traditional materials such as bark, moss, and sods.

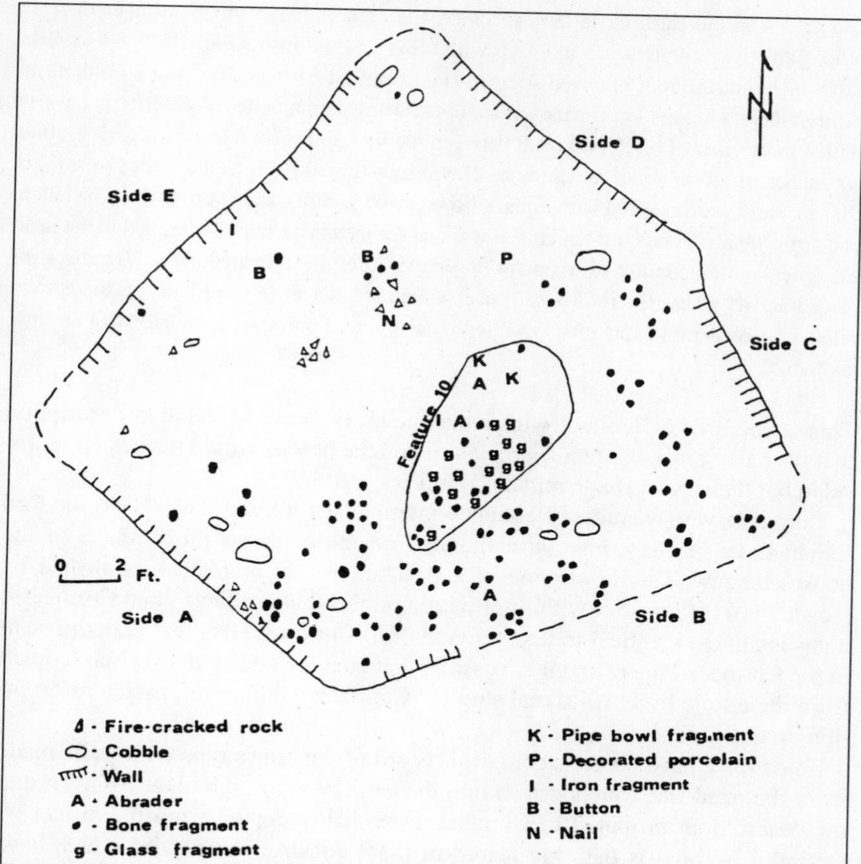

Fig.22.4 Plan of excavated pentagonal housepit at the Wigwam Brook site, (LeBlanc 1973, Fig.10). (By permission of Raymond J. LeBlanc)

In 1810, the furrier William Cull reported that he had "fallen in with a wigwam, sufficiently large to contain from fifty to sixty persons."[49] He gave no further information about the structure and measurements of this dwelling. Since no other record mentions a house of this size it has been concluded that Cull overestimated the capacity of the house he saw.

In a letter to the *Liverpool Mercury* published in September 1829, E.S. gave a lengthy description of Beothuk winter houses (as already noted, he had taken part in the expedition that led to the capture of Demasduit at Red Indian Lake in 1819). His account reads:

The houses of these Indians are very different to those of the other tribes of North America; they are built of straight pieces of fir about twelve feet high, flattened at the sides and driven in the earth close to each other; the corners being much stronger than the other parts. The crevices are filled up with moss and the inside entirely lined with the same material; the roof is raised so as to slant from all parts and meet in a point at the centre where a hole is left for the smoke to escape; the remainder of the roof is covered with a treble coat of birch bark, and between the first and second layers of bark is about six inches of moss; about the chimney clay is substituted for it ... The sides [inside] of the tenement were covered with arms, – bows, arrows, clubs, axes of iron ... stone hatchets, arrow heads, in fact implements of war and for the chase, but all arranged in the neatest order and apparently every mans' property carefully put together ... Beams were placed across where the roof began; over which smaller ones were laid; on these were piled a considerable quantity of dried venison and salmon, together with a little codfish.[50]

This account of a Beothuk winter mamateek is the most detailed description that we have. Since "corners" are mentioned the houses would have been multisided but their exact shape remains obscure.

Cormack, who examined Beothuk winter houses at South Twin Lake and Red Indian Lake in 1827, has not elaborated on the construction or shape of the houses he saw. The description of a Beothuk winter mamateek published by Howley (1915) together with information on Beothuk artifacts from Cormack's notes is almost identical to that given by E.S. Curiously, this text is not present in the Cormack Papers and it is possible that Howley added this section (copied from the article by E.S.) to make up for Cormack's failure to provide information on this topic.[51]

To date we have no archaeological record of the house type with walls made from flattened tree trunks driven into the earth next to each other.[52] Given that the description attributed to Cormack is probably copied from the article by E.S., this account is the only record of these construction details, which have since been widely quoted as the "norm" in nineteenth-century Beothuk house building. Perhaps these compact dwellings only existed in more permanent settlements, such as those on Red Indian and North Twin lakes, whose shores are now submerged under several feet of water due to dams and not accessible for archaeological excavations.

A note by Cormack reads: "Then in their style of adorning the posts or poles outside of their doors, we can evidently trace the corinthian a composite order in architecture, different countries producing animals with different kinds of horns, will cause variations in the capital."[53] J.P. Howley believed that Cormack was referring to carved doorposts of Beothuk dwellings, a detail which has not otherwise been reported.[54]

The claim by the surveyor J.B. Jukes's Micmac guides (in 1839–40) that Beothuk houses were raised on wooden platforms has not been recorded elsewhere, nor has it been substantiated archaeologically.[55] Equally abstruse is the story that Beothuk houses had twenty- to thirty-metre-long tunnels that led into the woods to allow the Beothuk to retire quickly in the face of danger.[56]

CHANGES IN THE USE OF CONICAL MAMATEEKS AND DEVELOPMENTS IN BEOTHUK HOUSE BUILDING

Circumstantial evidence shows that in the first two to three hundred years after contact with Europeans, the Beothuk used conical mamateeks not only as summer habitations but also during fall and winter. According to John Guy's diary, at the end of October Beothuk had moved to an inland hunting camp with conical houses of a design that he had seen on the coast.[57] Dwellings recorded in 1720 close to a caribou fence in the vicinity of Hare Bay also appear to have been of the conical type. They would have served as shelter for the duration of the caribou hunt in October and November; whether the Beothuk at Hare Bay remained in these houses throughout the winter cannot be said.[58]

Further evidence comes from John Cartwright, who explored the country along the Exploits River in August 1768. It was mentioned earlier that Cartwright counted eighty-six conical mamateeks on the river banks, particularly between Bishops Falls and Badger Brook. Some of them appear to have been quite spacious: a single house accomodated his party of fourteen men for a night.[59] Cartwright thought that these "extremely durable" mamateeks constituted the Beothuk's "principal winter settlements," particularly in view of the fact that they were surrounded by many bones and horns.[60] He also saw two rectangular dwellings that were built with three studded and insulated walls and one wall made of horizontally laid logs. These two houses would only have accommodated a few families; the remainder of the population in the Exploits River area, estimated at over two hundred people, appear to have wintered in the conical mamateeks.

Forty-odd years later, Captain Buchan and E.S. recorded separately that the Beothuk at Red Indian Lake all lived in solidly built winter quarters whose walls were constructed of studs or of shaped tree trunks. Although Buchan believed that the light, conical houses on ponds and rivers were occupied only during the summer, he later noted (in February 1820) that "wigwams" close to a large storehouse had been inhabited in the early part of winter; one in particular had "quite recently" had a fire in it.[61] One interpretation of this information would be that in the 1800s conical mamateeks were generally used between spring and fall but on occasion were inhabited in early winter as well and could serve as temporary shelters at any time of the year. At that time advances in house construction (and possibly the declining population) allowed all members of the group to move to well-insulated winter quarters for the coldest months of the year. This development, however, is only indicated for those Beothuk who wintered on the banks of the Exploits River and at Red Indian Lake.

The majority of houses in coastal camps, whether recorded contemporaneously or later by archaeologists, were typical summer dwellings, though some structures at Boyd's Cove had been winterized to some degree. The Beothuk from this camp probably spent the coldest months of the year in inland hunting camps, so that they would rarely have lived in their coastal dwellings in subzero temperatures.

There is some evidence that both the choice of building materials and building techniques were influenced by the availability of European tools and gear. The application of ships' sails as roof cover for conical mamateeks as well as for larger winter houses was only one of the results of contact with Europeans. Beothuk technology was more profoundly affected by metal axes, which facilitated the cutting of trees and would have encouraged their more extensive use in house building. Thus, in the late 1700s rectangular houses were constructed with walls made from squared, horizontally placed tree trunks, and a few decades later of 3.6-metre-high flattened trunks that were driven into the ground vertically and contiguously.[62] The incorporation of neatly shaped trunks is unlikely to have been traditional because the extensive wood cutting and shaping required would have been impractical with stone tools. In keeping with traditional techniques, however, houses continued to be bermed and the floors excavated to some degree.

A comparison of the shapes and floor plans of Beothuk dwellings with those built by other North American native groups shows that conical, oval, square, and rectangular houses were common.[63] Pentagonal, hexagonal and octagonal dwellings may be unique to the Beothuk; they are not recorded outside Newfoundland.[64] Semisubterranean winter lodges (though not hexagonal) were widely used by northwestern native groups, particularly the West Main Cree and Athapaskans.[65]

VAPOUR BATHS, STORAGE FACILITIES, AND OTHER STRUCTURES

At a Beothuk settlement at South Twin Lake Cormack noted the remains of a vapour bath, which he described as a hemispherical framework that would have been placed over a pile of previously heated stones, the whole closely covered with skins.[66] The user would creep underneath the cover with a birchbark bucket of water and a small cup. Steam was produced by pouring small quantities of water from the cup over the hot stones. Shanawdithit later said that vapour baths were chiefly taken by older people or by those who sought relief from rheumatic afflictions.[67] It seems, however, that they were also used to relieve other complaints; for instance, while Shanawdithit's sister was suffering from what was probably pulmonary tuberculosis, her mother prepared a vapour bath for her.[68]

The Beothuk stored their food in various ways. In winter houses items such as dried venison and fish were placed on beams that ran across the mamateek at roof level.[69] Food was also stored in "square mouthed or oblong pits, dug in the earth about four feet deep," and lined with birchbark. Cormack had seen such pits next to each of the winter houses at the settlement at South Twin Lake. Captain Buchan noted pits of this type close to a portage path on the Exploits River along the edge of the forest.[70] The above-ground storage facilities he recorded included a circular structure, smaller than a mamateek, that was covered with skins, and a square or rectangular building constructed in the manner of a log house, as well as larger storage houses consisting of a wooden frame that was covered with bark and skins; one of them had wall-plates.[71] William Cull saw two storehouses of the latter kind on the banks of the Exploits River. He examined the smaller of the two which was "forty to fifty feet" long and nearly as wide and held the meat of about a hundred caribou. The meat was stowed in bark boxes of birch or spruce, each containing up to two hundred pounds.[72] While Buchan did not elaborate on the roof construction of storehouses, those encountered by Cull were built with a ridge pole and had gable ends.[73] A storehouse drawn by Shanawdithit (sketch 8) measuring ten feet in length and four and a half feet in height was depicted with a gabled roof; it appears to have had two levels, each represented by cross-hatched squares alternating with solid ones. The former may represent lattice-work sections that allowed air to circulate. The title of this drawing reads: "Store house (10 feet long) in which they put their dried venison in birch rind boxes or packages to keep during Winter" (Fig. 20.2).

Shanawdithit also illustrated a structure labelled "smoking or drying house for venison" (sketch 6). Its walls appear to have been built of uprights surmounted by roof poles that were leaning onto a central ridge pole. The distinct pattern shown in the lower part of the roof could be racks or drying shelves. The walls may have been left uncovered so as to allow air to circulate freely (Fig. 22.3). Cormack found a building of this type on a campsite at Red Indian Lake "in still perfect condition."[74] The simple racks for drying salmon or skins as sketched by Shanawdithit were similar to one described by John Cartwright as "a slight frame made of sticks pricked into the ground and crossed with others … which gave it the appearance of a machine for drying salmon upon."[75]

A sturdier type of rack was left by the Beothuk at the east end of South Twin Lake, close to a portage path. It consisted of perpendicular posts that supported a few horizontal beams about sixty centimetres off the ground and served as a canoe rest.[76]

CHAPTER TWENTY-THREE

Birchbark Canoes and Other Means of Transportation

BIRCHBARK CANOES

The Beothuk, like other North American Indians, built birchbark canoes, which had an excellent carrying capacity and were reputed to be swifter than a ten-oared boat.[1] These canoes were the Beothuk's most important means of transportation, enabling them to travel long distances at speed and to portage with ease. A small canoe could be carried by one man on his head or shoulders and a larger one by two or three.[2] Portage paths on the Exploits River circumvented rapids and the waterfall at Grand Falls; other portage routes led from Trinity to Placentia Bay, from Winter Tickle to Southern Arm in New Bay, and from Badger Brook to Badger Bay.[3]

The Beothuk travelled in their canoes not only on lakes and river systems but also on the ocean. By sea they went as far as Funk Island, east of Cape Freels.[4] George Cartwright considered it almost incredible that the Beothuk should visit this island, which lies about sixty kilometres out into the Atlantic, well out of sight of the coast.[5] To travel such distances on the open sea, the Beothuk must have been skilled canoeists and excellent navigators. The naturalist Joseph Banks, when visiting Newfoundland in 1766, was so impressed with the Beothuk canoe that he asked Captain Wilkinson to obtain one and bring it back to Britain on HMS *Grenville*. Unfortunately, it was washed overboard and lost on the homeward journey.[6]

Sources of Information

Information on the shape and construction of Beothuk canoes comes from contemporary reports and illustrations and from miniature replicas. The earliest description of Beothuk birchbark canoes is given in John Guy's journal of 1612. Guy described and sketched a Beothuk canoe he had found at Trinity Bay as half-moon shaped in profile with a pointed, hogged (upturned) sheer (Fig. 23.1).[7] A canoe similar in outline because of the curved keel-line but with

Fig.23.1 "The picture of the savages canoa," by John Guy, 1612. (By permission of the Archbishop of Canterbury and the Trustees of Lambeth Palace Library, London, Ms.250, f.412)

Plate 23.1 Birchbark canoe replica 80 cm long collected in 1827 by W.E. Cormack from Nonosabasut's burial hut. (Copyright The Trustees of the National Museums of Scotland, 1996, neg.0418)

considerably more elevated bow and stern sections was drawn by John Cartwright in 1768 (Fig. 23.3).[8] In a second drawing dated 1773, Cartwright depicts a canoe that varies from the earlier one in that it has a straight rather than a curved keel-line and curved ends (Fig. 20.1).

Further information has been gleaned from four small canoe replicas. One was taken from the burial hut of Nonosabasut at Red Indian Lake in 1827 (Plate 23.1); two others come from the grave of a young child on Big Island in Pilley's Tickle, Notre Dame Bay (Plate 23.2).[9] The fourth, the only one to show most or all structural details, is a replica made by Shanawdithit while she lived with the Peyton family on Exploits Islands (Plates 23.3, 23.4). This replica was presented to Capt. William H. Jones of *HMS Orestes* in 1826 or 1827, when he called on the Peytons. It is now in the collection of the National Maritime Museum in London, UK.[10] Each one of the replicas has a straight rather than a curved bottom.

A thorough examination of the available material suggests that the Beothuk built two major canoe types: one with a straight bottom line, well suited for travel on rivers, lakes, and the ocean; the other with a strongly curved bottom probably designed specifically for ocean navigation. The former design was also the more versatile of the two. It persisted until the early nineteenth century, as exemplified by the replicas from Beothuk graves and by that made by Shanawdithit. The curved-bottom canoe, described and illustrated by Guy in 1612

Plate 23.2 Two birchbark canoe replicas from burial of a child on Big Island, Pilley's Tickle. (Collection of the Newfoundland Museum)

and by Cartwright in 1768, appears to have been a modification of the straight-bottom canoe and may have become obsolete in later years.[11]

The size of Beothuk canoes was seldom recorded, though observers often mentioned the number of occupants. This information, in combination with data collected by E.T. Adney on the size and carrying capacity of birchbark canoes built by other tribes, has been used to estimate the length of different Beothuk canoe types. Hunting canoes for one to two people were usually twelve to fourteen feet long.[12] Canoes for travel on lakes, rivers, and the ocean suitable for three to five persons (the most frequently quoted number of occupants) were between fourteen and twenty feet long. Cartwright described a canoe of fourteen feet in length and four in width. Ocean canoes, roomy enough for six, eight, or ten passengers, were about twenty to twenty-four feet long.[13] Guy recorded a twenty-foot canoe from Trinity Bay and in 1827 Cormack found an abandoned canoe at Red Indian Lake that measured twenty-two feet in length.[14]

The Construction of Beothuk Birchbark Canoes

While contemporary observers described the features of finished canoes, actual construction methods used by Beothuk have not been recorded. Thus, some of the methods given below have been inferred from those documented for other native groups, taking into account the technical problems that would have occurred in the building of Beothuk canoe types.[15] Despite some structural differences between the straight- and curved-bottom canoes, their construction would have been similar and the following description would apply to both types.

For the hull cover the Beothuk used bark from the paper birch (*Betula papyrifera*), which was plentiful in Newfoundland and of excellent quality.[16] The in-

Plate 23.3 Replica of a birchbark canoe made by Shanawdithit. (National Maritime Museum, London, neg.B-6075)

Plate 23.4 Replica of a birchbark canoe made by Shanawdithit, inside view. (National Maritime Museum, London, neg.C-5514 A)

ner frame would usually have been made from black spruce. Split roots from the same species served for lashing and sewing, while sinew was used for fine sewing or tying. From the seventeenth century onward, iron nails from fishing stages or boats may have superceded some of the lashings and wooden pegs.[17]

The building process began with the clearing of a flat piece of ground or "building bed" on which a large sheet of birchbark, often composed of smaller pieces stitched together, was rolled out. The outer bark surface was turned upward to form the inside of the canoe. On Beothuk canoes (not observed in other Indian canoes) a long, shaped pole that was to serve as keelson (longitudinal beam) was laid down along the centre line of the bark. On the straight-keelson canoe it was as long as the bottom line and rendered the bottom straight and without rocker, that is, without a curvature built into the ends. The bark was then folded upwards on either side of the keelson at an angle of approximately forty-five degrees, forming a deadrise, or V-shape in cross section, instead of the flat or rounded bottoms found on other northeastern bark canoes. The keelson with a deadrise gave the Beothuk canoe greater draft and thereby made it safer for open-water travel, since it helped prevent the canoe from being blown off course.

The major difference in the construction of the canoe form described thus far, when compared with the curved-keelson type, is found in the shape and length of the keelson and in the technique used for fitting the bark onto the hull. The keelson of the curved-bottom canoe was considerably longer and was bent into a half-moon shape, extending upwards on either end to the peaks of bow (front) and stern (back). Since the strong curvature of the keelson did not permit the bark cover to be folded up sharply on either of its sides without excessive crimping (wrinkling), the hull cover was said to have been made from two half-moon shaped bark sections that were sewn together along the centre line underneath the keelson.[18] Experts on birchbark-canoe building doubt whether the bark could have been sewn together along the bottom since the seam would have been vulnerable to abrasion. However, Cartwright, a naval officer who seems to have examined a Beothuk canoe, specifically described this feature. The curved end sections of the keelson, which extended into the stem (front) and stern sections, were lashed to the bark hull inside the canoe to add stiffness to stem and stern, replacing the "stem pieces" found on bark canoes of other tribes.

The next steps in the construction would have been similar for either canoe type. A flat, temporary building frame was usually employed to mark the outline of the craft when building a narrow-bottom canoe; Athapaskans, for example, used this technique. Although a frame was not recorded for the Beothuk they probably used one. It was first placed at the centre of the bark sheet from which it was later lifted onto posts to mark the appropriate height of the canoe sides. Having established the outline and height of the canoe in this manner, long wooden battens that constituted the gunwales were lashed along the sheer (upper edge) of the bark sides as marked by the frame, with over-and-over wrappings of spruce roots. The frame was then removed, and the thwarts, or cross pieces, which established the width of the craft and held the sides apart, were inserted.

To protect the bark hull inside, the canoe was lined with thin wooden boards or splints that were held in place by ribs, the latter being fashioned from wooden slats. They would have been treated with steam, as with other native canoe builders, before they could be bent sharply in the centre. The ribs were then inserted across over the keelson and over the lining splints, one end being pushed under the starboard (right) gunwale and the other end under the gunwale on the port (left) side. It was important to fit the ribs tightly so as to produce tension, because the shape of the bark hull was largely maintained by the pressure of the ribs. While many other maritime builders of bark canoes strengthened the end sections inside with stem pieces and headboards, the Beothuk appear to have secured the canoe ends by lashing sticks, which acted as seam battens, externally onto the seams of the bark hull at bow and stern; at least, that is how Shanawdithit constructed her replica.[19] On the ocean canoe, the keelson extensions, lashed to the end sections inside, served this purpose. To further stiffen the bark and to protect the seams from abrasion, another set of sticks was lashed to either side of the seams on the outside (Fig. 23.2).

The lashing along the sheer was protected by thin strips of wood or gunwale guards, probably tacked with wooden pegs, on top of the gunwales (not recorded for the ocean canoe). In the 1800s (and possibly earlier) the Beothuk used iron nails.[20] Slender saplings, fastened on the outside below the gunwales, acted as bumpers or fenders. To render the canoe watertight, all seams and weak spots were gummed inside and out with a mixture of spruce resin, charcoal, fat, and possibly other ingredients. The final touch would have been the application of a coat of ochre, which is likely to have called for special ritual and feasting.[21] Cormack found a canoe-rest daubed with red ochre on a Beothuk site at South Twin Lake; Helen Devereux recorded what could have been an ochring place for canoes at Indian Point.[22]

One disadvantage of bark canoes was their vulnerability to damage. The relatively frail hull tended to puncture on contact with rocks or logs and could be staved in by the battering of heavy waves. Constant vigilance and the repair and replacement of cracked caulking material were part of the daily routine. To avoid injury to the bottom, a canoe had to be loaded and unloaded in the water;

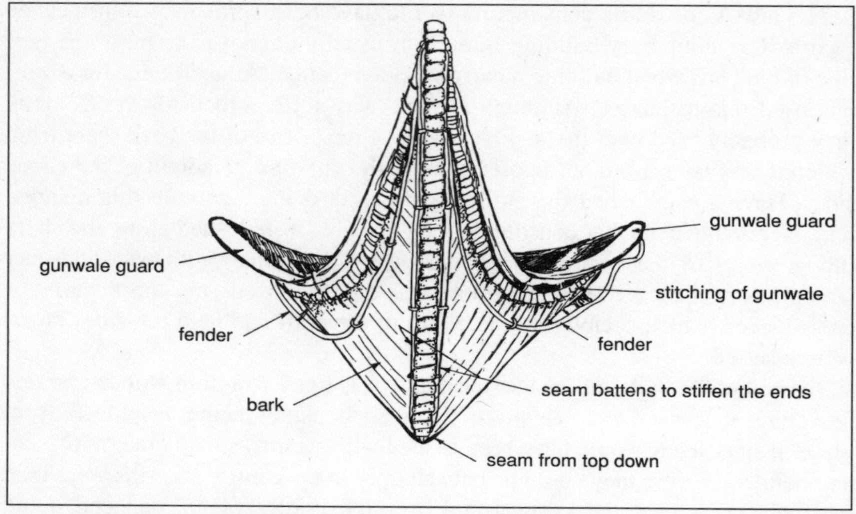

Fig.23.2 End profile of canoe replica made by Shanawdithit, showing structural parts. (Provided by Cliff George, St John's, reproduced by permission of the Canadian Museum of Civilization)

once a canoe was brought on shore, care had to be taken that it was not damaged by the wind.[23]

The claim that the Beothuk collapsed their canoes sideways for easier transport is probably erroneous.[24] Such a collapse would have required the removal and, later, the laborious resetting of the thwarts and of all the ribs. The account of folded canoes probably originated with the sighting of "a canoe half built," presumably before the thwarts had been inserted. At that stage it might indeed have looked "folded."[25]

On occasion, probably on temporary canoes, the Beothuk used skins as cover material, as was customary among many native people.[26] Santu, of Beothuk-Micmac parentage, remembered how her Beothuk father's skin canoe was decked on the front end, and how she and other members of her family, as well as dogs, were stowed away under this decking.[27] This may not have been a canoe in the Beothuk style since her father grew up among Micmac.

The Shape of Beothuk Canoes

Both canoe types, those with a straight bottom line and those with a curved bottom, had a keelson along the centre line and flaring sides that rendered the hull V-shaped in cross section (Fig. 23.2). They had high peaked end sections and a hogged sheer. A certain amount of hogging or upward buckling of the bark along the sheer can result from the manner in which the bark cover of a narrow-bottom canoe is folded upwards.[28] The Beothuk extended this upward curvature to a conspicuous height. It strengthened the sides, protected occupants from spray, and, most importantly, allowed for safer heeling (leaning sideways) when heavy objects such as seals were taken aboard.

The high bow and stern sections on Beothuk canoes may not have been introduced until after 1612; Guy's 1612 sketch depicts the canoe he had seen with a fairly low bow and stern. In his diary he explained that sticks about three feet long, fastened to these (low) end sections, were used to lift the boat in and out of the water. A high bow and stern prevented the shipping of water when running rapids, a skill in which the Beothuk were said to excel. The high prow was also said to have acted as a shield against arrows.[29] When the canoe was upturned on land and used as shelter, high ends would have increased the space underneath. Beyond their practical functions, the peaked end sections and the unusually high hogging of the sheer could have served as ethnic markers that visibly distinguished Beothuk canoes from those of other tribes. Differences in the shape of the hogged sheerline – on some rounded, on others pointed – may have signalled canoes from different Beothuk bands.[30]

The two types of keelson, one straight and running the length of the bottom and the other strongly curved and extending to the top of stem and stern, caused variations not only in construction techniques but also in several hull features. The canoe built with the shorter, straight keelson had a corresponding straight bottom line that turned up into bow and stern at an angle. No rocker (upward curvature) was built into the ends. In addition, the measurements of the replicas suggest that the greatest beam (width) of these straight-bottom canoes was placed slightly astern of the midpoint. These canoes were deeper in the aft section than in the bow, with a slightly greater height but shorter rake (projection beyond the keel-line) at the stern in comparison with the bow (Plate 23.4).

In contrast, the canoe with a curved bottom line was described as being symmetrical lengthwise, with the beam (greatest width) half way between bow and stern and the depth and draft alike fore and aft, as was the case on most northeastern bark canoes (Fig. 23.3). The extreme curvature of the Beothuk canoe at bow and stern was similar to the strong rocker on "crooked canoes" of the Eastern Cree and Montagnais/Naskapi. However, the canoes of these two tribes had a wide, rounded bottom.[31] The V-shape (in cross section) of Beothuk canoes rendered them bottomless, so to speak, since the sides flared out from the central keelson so that there was no flat floor area in the centre. The additional draft that was gained by the V-shape combined with rocker increased the canoe's capacity to keep on course in strong winds and made it more manoeuvrable. This gain seems to have offset the disadvantages of having a central seam in the bark cover, which would have been vulnerable to injury and abrasion, and of having to load and unload ballast. Ballast was needed to settle the canoe upright in the water to counteract its tendency to tip sideways when unloaded, and to keep the craft stable. The Beothuk were said to have used rocks that they covered with moss for this purpose.[32] The fact that the strong rocker in combination with a sharp keel added considerably to the canoe's lateral in-

Fig.23.3 Beothuk camp on "A Sketch of the River Exploits the East End of Lieutenants Lake and Parts Adiacent in Newfoundland taken on the spot by Lieutenant John Cartwright of His Majesty's Ship Guernsey, 1768." (Provincial Archives of Newfoundland and Labrador, Cartographic Section, MG 100, the Cartwright Collection)

stability was confirmed by the Micmac Long Joe, who once found a Beothuk canoe by the side of the Exploits River near Badger Brook. When he pushed off in it, he discovered that the craft was "develish crank" (unstable) and quickly made for shore again.[33] Experiments with full-sized canoe replicas built from plywood, one with a curved bottom and a second with a straight bottom line, have shown that the amount of rock ballast required to settle the curved canoe upright in the water is about twice that needed for a straight-bottom canoe.[34] It is possible that skilled canoeists would not have required rock ballast in the latter type if the canoe's occupants provided sufficient weight. In 1989, Lloyd Seaward, an experienced canoe builder from Bishops Falls, made a Beothuk-type birchbark canoe based on Shanawdithit's model. He tried it out on ponds and then took it down the Exploits River (Plate 23.5). Ballasted with twenty-five kilograms of rock, the canoe handled well. Seaward was most impressed by its performance when paddling against the wind or running into the tide because its unusual draft stopped it from being blown off course. On the shallow parts of the river Seaward tipped the canoe sideways by sitting on one side to bring the keel-line close to the surface so that it would pass over rocks without damage.[35]

Plate 23.5 Beothuk-type canoe made by Lloyd Seaward, Bishop's Falls. (Photograph by permission of Dennis Minty, St John's)

Development of Beothuk Canoe Types

A comparison of Beothuk birchbark canoes with native bark canoes from across North America shows that construction methods were similar among all tribes. All bark craft were built using the same general principle: a frame consisting of gunwales, ribs, thwarts, and stem and stern supports was built into a hull made from sheets of bark. But shapes and styles varied greatly from one native group to another. In part this diversity reflects different functional needs. The hull shape of a canoe intended for ocean travel would have differed from that of a canoe used on shallow inland ponds and streams. But the varieties in form also reflect stylistic features specific to different tribal groups.

A comparison of the shape of Beothuk canoe hulls with those of other canoes reveals some interesting affinities.[36] In form and construction, the straight-bottom Beothuk canoe most closely resembles the canoes of northwestern Athapaskans, which were used on interior waterways. Beothuk and Athapaskan canoes both had the straight bottoms with an angular upturn of the end sections (no curvature built into the ends), a hogged sheer, flaring sides, and the unequal proportions of stern to bow. In both, the greatest beam (width) was abaft midships and the depth of the canoe was greater aft than in the corresponding position to the fore, so that the canoe was not symmetrical fore and aft. Beothuk canoes, like Athapaskan ones, also lacked elaborate stem and stern pieces and headboards.

As a rule, Athapaskans traversed lakes and streams and the properties of their canoes were best suited for inland waterways. The Beothuk, in their quest for food, frequently travelled on the ocean. They made regular excursions to Funk Island and were also said to have visited and traded with native groups on the Labrador coast, which would have involved lengthy journeys on the open sea.[37] It is possible that Beothuk canoes originally had a narrow flat bottom and angular turns in the bow and stern similar to Athapaskan canoes but were modified to suit travel conditions on the ocean. The first step in this development would have been the introduction of a keelson and a deadrise to achieve the V-shape (in profile) recorded by Guy and Cartwright and demonstrated on the canoe replicas. The second step might have been the incorporation of a strong curvature in the bottom and at either end of the craft, perhaps modelled on the crooked canoes of the Montagnais/Naskapi. These two corrections of the hull would have resulted in the curved-bottom canoe type. With loss of access to many of their traditional coastal and island sites, the Beothuk's ocean travel decreased and with it, perhaps, the need for a specialized ocean canoe. Canoes with a curved bottom line were not recorded after 1768. The more versatile canoe type with a straight bottom, suitable for a variety of travel conditions, would have been the more practical type and it is this design that persisted into the nineteenth century.

Paddles, Oars, and Sails

To propel their canoes, the Beothuk employed single-headed paddles. They were approximately four feet long and had a narrow, pointed blade that merged into a plain handle with no cross grip (Figs. 20.1, 23.3).[38] Oars were also recorded; perhaps they were used to steer or propel a canoe. John Guy described a ten-foot-long oar "made of two peeces, one being as long, big & rownd as a halfe pike made of beeche wood, which by likelihood they made of a biskaine [Basque] oare, th'other is the blade of the oare, which is let into th'end of the long one slit, & whipped very stronglie."[39] An oar of this type was carried by the Beothuk "who seemed to have some command ouer the rest," it could have been a badge of office.

Canvas sails, appropriated from fishing vessels, were sometimes hoisted but not as a rule. Cartwright thought that the Beothuk's delicate and unsteady bark vessels were not designed for sailing and believed that the Beothuk did not use sails until after the arrival of Europeans.[40] For lack of evidence to the contrary, his opinion has generally been accepted.[41]

OTHER MEANS OF TRANSPORTATION

Rafts. The raft was another means of water transportation. John Cartwright saw a "large raft ... of indian construction ... lodged on the bank" of the Exploits River in 1768 and said it was "composed with strength and ingenuity."[42] About fifty years later Captain Buchan described a raft of about thirty feet in length and four and a half feet in width that he found on the banks of the same river. It "was formed of three logs of dry asp" eighteen inches in diameter and "secured together with much ingenuity."[43] The Beothuk may not have made rafts from trunks as thick as those seen by Buchan until they had access to metal tools. As a means of transportation, however, they are likely to have employed rafts since prehistoric times.

Snowshoes. For travel on foot in wintertime the Beothuk used snowshoes. In 1791 William Cull measured the tracks of Beothuk "rackets" and said that they were three and a half feet long and two feet wide.[44] Captain Buchan recorded in 1811 the total length of a snowshoe as four and a half feet; of this, the webbed section was three and a half feet and the tail one foot long; he gave the width as fifteen inches.[45] A third approximate set of measurements is taken from an 1876 sketch by the surveyor T.G.B. Lloyd, who obtained his information from John Peyton, Jr, of Exploits Islands. The drawing shows the snowshoe to be about 1.68 metres long with a webbed section of about sixty-six centimetres and a tail of roughly 1.02 metres; the width is about 0.46 of a metre.[46]

Both Buchan and Lloyd considered that the shape and construction of Beothuk snowshoes was different from the "ordinary North American type," which presumably meant those in use by the neighbouring Micmac and Montagnais.[47] According to Lloyd, Beothuk snowshoes were "broader in the nose and far longer and [had] more taper in the tail," and thus resembled "the racket of our English [tennis] game." The space within the frame was filled with a mesh supposedly composed of sealskin or cord or "babishe," a cordage made of rawhide. A Newfoundland "Indian" bone netting tool of unique design (presumed to be Beothuk), collected in Newfoundland prior to 1826, may have been used for the webbing of the mesh on snowshoes (Plate 20.1b).[48]

Based on what is known from other native groups we could expect a Beothuk snowshoe to have been made from one narrow strip of wood bent into a loop, with the ends lashed together to form the tail at the back. The mesh size would have varied according to the use for which the snowshoes were intended. A more open mesh lessens its weight, tends to prevent accumulation of snow on top, and is optimal for fast travel. A closer mesh helps to support and spread the weight of the wearer and his burdens and is better for snow travel when carrying loads.[49]

An important feature of Beothuk snowshoe design is the single support bar for the foot. Most snowshoe types have two bars across the webbed section, but both Cull and Lloyd said Beothuk snowshoes had only one board. According to Lloyd, this board "had a hole in it to receive the toes" and was "fixed across the middle of the racket bow." Buchan's description was not as clear, but he does mention only one cross piece and not two.[50] According to Davidson's comprehensive study, snowshoes evolved from a simple circle filled with mesh into circles with a single cross bar to support the foot, and later into a more advanced type with two or more bars.[51] In this sequence the one-bar Beothuk design would have been a relatively early type. One-bar snowshoes of the "bear paw" variety with an elongated frame and no tail were also used by the Northern Saulteaux, Eastern Cree, and Montagnais/Naskapi of Labrador.[52]

When travelling on soft, deep snow, maximal surface contact is desirable and is improved by a larger webbed section. To increase this section Montagnais/Naskapi made wide, rounded shapes such as the swallowtail or beaver-paw type.[53] Cree and Athapaskans achieved a large surface area by making narrow but very long snowshoes, sometimes as long as the wearer was high.[54] Both Lloyd and Buchan specifically remarked on the unusual overall length of Beothuk snowshoes, which were of the swallow-tail type but narrower and longer than those of the Montagnais/Naskapi; furthermore, the tail was longer than that on Micmac snowshoes. Buchan believed this length would be troublesome for walking in the woods. If the tail section was anywhere near as long as shown on Lloyd's sketch, it would certainly have been uniquely long.[55]

Buchan and Lloyd also reported that both end sections, that is, the toe and the tail end, were curved upwards.[56] Though Lloyd surmised that this was the result of the unusual length and breadth of the toe part of the snowshoes, which "caused the ends to bend upwards under the weight of the body," it is likelier that a raised toe part was built into the frame. This was a common feature on snowshoes used by Eastern Cree, Northern Ojibwa, Chipewayan, and tribes to the west of them and spread from the west to more easterly groups.[57] An elevation of the tail end has not been recorded elsewhere, and if Buchan's and Lloyd's observations were correct, it was a unique feature.

Thus, in concept and construction Beothuk snowshoes were similar to those of other tribes, although the use of only one toe board indicates an early version. The Beothuk appear to have created their own distinctive style by combining the swallowtail form with an unusually long and possibly elevated tail and a rounded, elevated toe section.

Sledges or Toboggans. Captain Buchan was the only person to mention the Beothuk's use of sledges. On his way up the Exploits River, "marks of sledges" in the snow showed that Beothuk had recently conveyed venison from a storehouse. Nearing their camp on Red Indian Lake, Buchan also noted a sledge being dragged across the lake. Later, tracks of sledges left tell-tale signs in the snow that the Beothuk had fled from him and taken their possessions with them.[58] Since Buchan did not elaborate on the size or construction of the sledges, it is not possible to determine whether they were flat-board toboggans or runner sleds. Both types, flat runnerless sleds as well as runner sleds, were used by native people throughout the Maritime Provinces and Labrador.[59]

An unusual carrying device used by Beothuk was the "*Bochmoot* or Seal skin sledge," illustrated in Shanawdithit's sketch 7 (Fig. 19.1). It consisted of a whole sealskin sewn up and used as storage vessel that could be dragged on snow like a sled. The property of fur would have allowed it to slide easily in a forward direction while preventing its slipping backwards.[60] J.P. Howley thought that this sealskin "sled" would have been lined with a wooden frame, but there is no indication of any such frame in Shanawdithit's sketch.[61]

CHAPTER TWENTY-FOUR

Beothuk World View and Belief-Related Practices

Seventeenth- and eighteenth-century English observers maintained either that the Beothuk had no religion, or that it "rose but little above ... harmless trifling observances." Beothuk cosmology as described by Shanawdithit, however, appears to have constituted a pervasive force in their lives, influencing individual as well as communal behaviour.[1] Outside of Shanawdithit's testimony, much of what is known on this topic has been deduced from contemporary accounts, linguistic evidence, comments made by other captives, and certain artifacts and practices demonstrated through archaeological excavation. These pieces of information are not sufficient to recreate the Beothuk's belief system. The best that can be done is to fit them into an approximate framework, and to validate their significance through comparisons with practices and belief systems of other native hunters, fishers, and gatherers who lived in a similar environment.

THE SPIRIT WORLD

The cosmology of North American Indians was generally based on the concept of a multiplicity of animate beings. Every conspicuous object in nature, such as the sun, the moon, water, and plants, was considered to be animate and had to be regarded with respect. Within this framework, the beliefs of different groups varied and called for different rituals and taboos. The animistic conception of northern Algonquians such as Montagnais/Naskapi and Cree, who were boreal forest hunters like the Beothuk, was of a parallel world of spirits that represented forces of nature as well as man-made objects. Spirits had their own separate world existing just beyond the world of humans, and a social organization analogous to human band-level society.[2] Other Algonquian speakers, such as Micmac, considered the "Great Spirit" or "Creator" to be the most powerful supernatural being; other beings – some benevolent, some not – acted as intercessors between the "Great Spirit" and the people.[3] Among Micmac this "Creator" and nurturer of all of nature was the sun, which, according to Father LeClercq, "had always been the constant object of their [Micmac] devotion, homage, and adoration." Maillard recorded that Micmac prayed to the sun and to the moon.[4] The sun was also revered by Montagnais.[5]

Reverence for sun and moon by natives in the northern region was recorded as early as the sixteenth century. On a map of "Terra Nova (of the Codfish)," the inhabitants were described as "idolators, some worship the sun, others the moon and many other kinds of idols."[6] This description probably goes back to reports by Sebastian Cabot, who met native people, possibly Beothuk, while in Newfoundland in 1508–09. A second sixteenth-century record, published in a collection of reports from North America (1511–55), may come from the same source: "The new lande of Baccalaos, is a colde region whose inhabitauntes are Idolatours and praye to the soone and moone and dyuers Idoles."[7]

According to the captive Demasduit, the Beothuk believed in a "Great Spirit." Captain Robinson, who recorded this information, added that "they seem to have no religious ceremonies."[8] Whether this "Great Spirit" personified the "Creator" and was a "superior being" in a hierarchy cannot be said.

The Beothuk are also said to have worshipped the sun and moon. Oubee, the young Beothuk girl who provided the earliest Beothuk wordlist, gave the term *dewis*, meaning sun or moon, to which Captain Pulling, who compiled the wordlist, added "which they worship."[9] Beothuk vocabularies obtained from Demasduit and Shanawdithit include the terms *kius*, *kuus*, *keeose*, and *keuse* for sun or moon, which may, according to linguistic evidence, be more correctly translated as "luminary"; once the prefix *washe* (or *washa*) is added, the word specifies moon while the prefix *magara* (or *maugero*) specifies sun.[10] A special position of these luminaries within the Beothuk belief system is also indicated by Shanawdithit's drawing of a mythological emblem, a half circle surmounting a slender staff, named *kuus* (Fig. 24.1). Cormack, who obtained his information from Shanawdithit, translated the word *kuus* as *moon*. In a mamateek in the Beothuk camp from which Demasduit was taken, the Beothuk had displayed an image of a human head rudely carved out of a block of wood. It had a European watch case hanging from its neck, which may have signified its relation to the sun or moon since in the Beothuk language the word for watch is *dewis*, or *kius*, or *keeose*, the same as that for the luminaries, sun and moon. When one of the English took down the "idol" and irreverently threw it aside, Demasduit, who later proved to be of a mild disposition, flew into a rage and was not pacified until the image was restored to its proper place.[11]

In another camp raided by furriers in 1790, the men saw a "figure of a Child made out of Birch rind and very well executed," but we have no explanation of what this figure represented.[12]

Cormack recorded that Shanawdithit differentiated between "good spirits" and "bad spirits."[13] "Her tribe believed that the aurora borealis [northern lights] consisted of happy messengers that came from the good spirit to watch over the Boeothics."[14] This interpretation of the northern lights is not associated with other tribes. Northern Inuit believed that they were created by "the good spirit"; the Naskapi thought that the souls of the dead, manifested in the form of stars, congregated in a dance and illuminated the night sky as the northern lights.[15] The Innu of Labrador today are taught that it is not good to stare at the northern lights.[16]

Good and bad spirits in Beothuk tradition could also work their power through people who interacted with the tribe. According to Shanawdithit: "A tradition of old times told that the first white men that came over the great lake were from the good spirit, and that those who came next were sent by the bad spirit; and that if the Boeothics made peace and talked with the white men which belonged to the bad spirit, or with the Mic-maks, who also belonged to the bad spirit, that they would not, after they died, go to the happy island."[17] Shanawdithit gave no further explanations. She also revealed the existence of "an invariable religious principle laid down by her people to sacrifice to the *munes* of the victims slain by the whites and Mik-maks any Boeothic who had been in contact with them."[18] Shanawdithit did not explain the concept of *munes*; the term was probably chosen by Cormack and may indicate "spirits" of the dead (*manes*) that needed to be avenged.[19] No comparable practice has been recorded for any other northern tribe, so far as I know. As noted in Part One, Shanawdithit was certainly afraid of being sacrificed to the *munes* and therefore consistently refused to accompany expeditions into Beothuk territory, saying "she would not go back to the Red Indian Lake, because she would be killed there."[20] The threat of being sacrificed may also have been the reason why Demasduit wanted only to retrieve her child and then to remain with the English.[21]

One malevolent counterpart to friendly spirits was called *Aich-mud-yim*, who had been sighted at the Great Lake (Red Indian Lake). Shanawdithit's drawing shows a short human figure with a beard and long hair(?), clad in a shapeless black robe (Fig. 20.2); Cormack labelled it "The Black Man or Red Indian Devil short and very thick, he dresses in Beaver skin, has a large beard & Beaver-skin gosset [in pencil]." Whether this "Black Man" could be compared with some of the fearsome and punishing creatures in southern Algonquian mythology, which could take on the shape of a man and were appeased by sacrificial offerings, cannot be determined.[22]

Greatly feared by the Beothuk was a "powerful monster, who could appear from the sea and punish the wicked."[23] It may be significant that this fearsome, evil creature was connected with the sea. A similar sea being recorded among the Netsilik Inuit was the woman called "Mother of Sea." She controlled the seal and was feared more than any other being.[24]

RITUALS AND TABOOS

Among hunters and gatherers, many rituals and taboos centred around the animals on which they depended for their subsistence. Some scholars consider that the relationship between native people and these animals was based on a "covenant" whereby the animals allowed themselves to be killed to feed the people and were honoured and respected in exchange.[25] Among the

Montagnais/Naskapi, who like the Beothuk were subarctic hunters, specific rituals and taboos were observed in the preparation for a hunt and in the killing and disposal of an animal. Frank Speck found that these rituals were generally performed in order to avoid offending the animal's "spirit," particularly the "Master [Spirit] of the Caribou."[26] Before an animal was hunted, the "hunter's soul-spirit" would try to gain control over the soul of the animal, often through the medium of dreams, in order to induce it to serve human needs.[27] Gratitude and respect for the animal spirit were shown by way of ceremonies, feasting, and sacrificial offerings that involved the hunter as well as the community. As an aside, it should be said that the terms "spirit" and "soul" are used here in keeping with anthropological convention. The underlying concepts of soul and spirit as held by native peoples overlap but do not coincide with English definitions.[28]

Given that the Beothuk's relationship to nature and to the animal world would likely have been similar to those of neighbouring hunter-fisher-gatherers, rituals and restrictions in connection with hunting were presumably observed. However, we have practically no information of this type. For example, in preparation for the hunt, particularly if black bear was the quarry, the Naskapi of Labrador made use of the "magic influence" of the sweat lodge, undergoing a bath rite before embarking on a hunt.[29] Although the Beothuk are known to have taken sweat baths, Shanawdithit claimed that they were taken only by the old or by individuals who sought relief from illness.[30]

Captain Buchan observed two practices that may relate to rituals honouring caribou. First, he noted that several caribou antlers had been placed on a projecting rock on the bank of the Exploits River.[31] This observation fits with LeBlanc's reports of excavations at the Wigwam Brook site on the Exploits River, where antlers appeared to have been "purposefully removed" from the camp.[32] These circumstances recall the Mistassini Cree ritual of displaying caribou antlers to honour the animals.[33] It is tempting to conclude that accumulation of antlers on a rock by the river, as observed by Buchan, had a similar purpose.

Captain Buchan also described a decorated tree on a site inland from Badger Bay. About 40 feet high, it was located on a projecting point of land on the shore of a lake where there was a wigwam. The bark had been stripped off, leaving only a small tuft of branches at the top. From this tuft downward, the trunk was painted with alternate circles of red and white "resembling wide hoops."[34] To Buchan, the whole had the appearance of a place of observation.

In native rites and myth, a tree standing alone was a potential means of communication between man and the supernatural world. The Saulteaux would create a tree of this type when they consumed a bear. Only a tuft of branches was left at the top, while below it, foot-wide sections were peeled at three-foot intervals and rubbed with ochre. The skull and other parts of the bear were fastened to the tree together with offerings to the spirit of the dead animal.[35] Tufted and decorated trees were also created by the Mistassini Cree, who called them *mistikuan*, meaning "made trees"; they would hang various animal bones on these as offerings.[36] *Mistikuan* were preferably located between a campsite and a body of water overlooking the dwellings. Most likely the marked tree seen by Buchan inland from Badger Bay was of the same general type.

In the early 1900s, Speck saw a large white spruce with its lower branches lopped off at Indian Point overlooking Red Indian Lake.[37] It is notable that among the Beothuk (as among Mistassini Cree), trees with possible ceremonial significance as well as sites used for ritual observances were usually located near a body of water. The Beothuk held their annual ochring ceremony at Red Indian Lake, where they also celebrated the death of the two marines.[38] However, the significance of proximity to water is not known, and given the abundance of lakes in Newfoundland and the obvious convenience of living near water, one should not make too much of this.

Periodically throughout the winter months, Montagnais/Naskapi celebrated the feast of *mokoshan* to honour the caribou spirit and to ensure good luck in hunting. In an elaborate ritual, caribou longbones – sometimes several hundred of them – were crushed and boiled to extract the marrow, which was then consumed. All members of the community participated in this feast with its drumming, singing, and dancing.[39] Although we have no eyewitness account of Beothuk ritual in honour of caribou, large amounts of caribou bone mash (the residue left after the marrow has been extracted) have been found in excavated sites at Indian Point, Wigwam Brook, and Boyd's Cove.[40] At Boyd's Cove considerable amounts of bone mash were accumulated around an elongated fireplace within a large oval-shaped mamateek pit, similar in size and shape to the wigwams used by Naskapi for the *mokoshan*; the bone-mash residue in the Beothuk housepit may be tangible evidence of similar feasts.[41]

In the Beothuk camp that Buchan visited at Red Indian Lake, "each wigwam had a quantity of deer's [caribou] leg bones ranged on poles (in all three hundred)."[42] The Beothuk man who was with Buchan at the time "used the marrow of some of these" and then replaced the used bones with others, which he signified were his. Evidently this was some sort of store or display and bones that were removed had to be accounted for, presumably because of their significance in ceremonial feasts.

Festivities of various kinds usually included the singing of songs, of which the Beothuk had a large repertoire. Many songs centred on natural phenomena such as darkness, mountains, marshes, ponds, water, brooks, ice, snow, deer [caribou], bears, birds, eggs, seals, salmon, fishes, shells, fire, firestone, wood or sticks, and birch rind.[43] Shanawdithit, who listed these topics, did not explain the content of the songs but the titles suggest they celebrated different aspects (or spirits) of nature.

It is not known whether the Beothuk smoked in ceremonies in honour of dead game as the Montagnais/Naskapi did, or during other ceremonial events.[44] John Peyton, Jr, stated that "he never had any knowledge of their using tobacco or any other narcotics nor had he ever seen any pipes belonging to them."[45] J.P. Howley and A.S. Brown have argued that the Beothuk, who would not have had easy access to tobacco, could well have smoked indigenous dried plant material such as the dried inner bark of the Red Willow, known among Micmac as *kinnikanik*, or dried roots of the Michaelmas daisy.[46] As for pipes, Howley knew that the Micmac would twist strips of birchbark into the form of a pipe, "which after being once used was so burnt as to be useless and consequently cast aside."[47] If the Beothuk had used bark pipes no traces of them would have been left.

Santu claimed that the Beothuk smoked a certain species of leaf in stone pipes, though she did not say whether this was done as a pastime or for ceremonial purposes.[48] Pipes of unquestionably Beothuk origin have not been found. The two soapstone pipe bowls that were picked up in Newfoundland, one at Pipestone Pond and one at Fleur de Lys or on an island in White Bay, are believed to have been produced by Micmac.[49]

Shanawdithit used the word *nechwa* for tobacco, which some have taken as evidence that the Beothuk smoked. However, as John Hewson points out, it is not at all clear whether *nechwa* denoted chewing or smoking tobacco, nor whether it was applied to tobacco derived from the tobacco plant or from indigenous substances;[50] hence the presence of this term in the Beothuk vocabulary does not necessarily imply that Beothuk smoked.

PERSONAL GUARDIAN SPIRITS

Among many native groups, men and women acquired personal guardian spirits (or allies) through a vision quest.[51] This quest was a period of isolation and starvation culminating in the appearance of an animal or bird that would become the guardian spirit or ally of the questor.[52] Usually the vision quest was undertaken at puberty and a token of the guardian spirit – a claw, a tooth, a bill – was henceforth kept on the person. A tutelary spirit was thought to give protection and to increase personal power; dreaming about this spirit was connected with future luck in hunting or the successful completion of other tasks.

Though there is no direct evidence of Beothuk guardian spirits, several Beothuk graves contained birds' feet and skulls as well as perforated animal teeth and tusks, which are traditionally tokens of guardian spirits or personal charms in other cultures.[53] In one grave, two birds' feet were tied to the burial shroud of a young child.[54] A broken seal bone that was in Cormack's possession may have had a similar significance.[55]

The importance to Shanawdithit of a rounded piece of granite and a piece of quartz that she presented to Cormack as keepsakes is not known.[56] Pebbles of this type long appear to have been considered important in many parts of the world. Micmac valued stone objects as tokens of good luck and they kept them on their person or in the house.[57] Among the Koryak of northeast Asia pebbles were used as divining stones.[58] Going back in time, pebbles or stones of an unusual shape were one of the most numerous grave goods in the Maritime Archaic cemetery in Port au Choix.[59]

ORIGIN MYTH AND BELIEF IN AN AFTERLIFE

Native people including the Beothuk explain the origin of their ancestors through myths and legends. Shanawdithit said of her people that "the Voice told them that they sprang or came from an arrow stuck in the ground."[60] A similar creation myth circulated among the Etchemin and Montagnais, whose *sagamo* (elder) told Champlain: "After God had made all things he took a number of arrows and did stick them into the ground from whence men and women grew."[61]

North American Indians usually subscribed to the idea of a human soul (or souls) that survived after death, though there are variations with respect to details.[62] Some tribes thought the souls of those who had died eventually passed to the land of the dead. Others believed in two souls, one of which would linger on and influence the living.[63]

In the Beothuk language, as in Naskapi, the term death has the same derivation as the term denoting sleep, and Shanawdithit said that death was regarded as a form of sleep.[64] The Beothuk did not expect the soul (or one of two souls?) to abandon the sphere of the living entirely. Shanawdithit told Cormack of the existence of "burying places near Exploits Burnt Island and Caves where numerous large human skulls" were lying and that "they [the Beothuk] have an idea that those were spirits" that remained there after physical burial.[65] In another context she said that "the spirits of the dead came … back to watch over the actions of their living friends," indicating that these were friendly spirits.[66] It is not clear whether these spirits came back from the grave or from the land of the dead. While Shanawdithit lived with the Peyton family, she claimed to have communicated with her dead mother and sister, sometimes while walking in the woods but more often whilst in her room. On such occasions she talked aloud apparently to herself but explained afterwards, "A yes, they here, me see them and talk to them."[67]

Shanawdithit also revealed that life after death was spent "in the country of the good spirit," on a happy island where one could hunt and fish and feast. It "was far away, where the sun went down behind the mountains."[68] The Beothuk's belief that an afterlife was similar to life on earth and the practice of placing tools and utensils used in ordinary life, or miniature versions thereof, in their graves were shared by many other native tribes. Nor were the Beothuk alone in thinking that the land of the dead lay in a westerly direction.[69]

It is noteworthy that entitlement to a happy afterlife depended on moral conduct. As Shanawdithit explained to Cormack: "If the Boeothics made peace and talked with the white men which belonged to the bad spirit, or with the Mic-maks, who also belonged to the bad spirit, they would not, after they died, go to the happy island."[70] The idea that compliance with prescribed social behaviour was a prerequisite for a happy afterlife was also subscribed to by other tribes. Among the Narragansett, for example, only the good souls were admitted to the "house" of the creator spirit (the symbolic place where life after death continued), while murderers, liars, and other wrongdoers were punished by having to wander restlessly. It is of interest here that moral conduct among the Beothuk in the early 1800s included shunning white men and Micmac, a rule that was probably not introduced into their moral code before the 1700s.

Shanawdithit also told Cormack that "her father and her lover and her mother were with the good spirit, and that she would go there too."[71] Even though she had stayed with the whites, which was said by her elders to bar a person after death from entering the "country of the good spirit," she was apparently confident that she would join them. Perhaps this was because she had not chosen to live among whites.

When Shanawdithit expressed her fear that if she visited her people, she would be sacrificed to the *munes* of victims of white men and Micmac, she assured Cormack that she would not, with such a death, "be buried with the things she should want for her journey" into the land of the dead. We can infer that some grave goods in Beothuk burials were to assist on the way to the "happy island."[72]

APPLICATION OF RED OCHRE

As noted before, a characteristic practice of the Beothuk was to cover their faces, hair, and entire bodies, as well as their clothing, utensils, weapons, and canoes with red ochre (said to have been mixed with grease) or with other reddish colouring substances.[73] In 1792 Pulling wrote that "they rub Oaker over every thing they make use of as well as over themselves at least evry thing that I saw which had belong'd to them had Oaker on it."[74] The Beothuk also placed ochre in burials, either in small packages or by mixing it into the soil covering the remains of the dead. Occasionally, ochre was rubbed onto the bones of secondary burials after the flesh had decomposed.[75]

Red ochre, which is a mudstone with a clay texture that gives excellent stain, occurs most often in tertiary deposits that are comparatively rare in Newfoundland.[76] Given the scarcity of genuine ochre, the Beothuk had to use substitutes such as soil with a high iron content (five to ten percent), which produces an inferior stain but is nevertheless effective. Governor Gower described the woman who had been captured in 1803 as having been smeared with a "composition of grease and red earth or oker." Captain Buchan thought some of the Beothuk he saw had smeared their faces and hair with "red earth."[77] A Micmac tradition told by Mary Doucet Newell describes how a Beothuk woman, taken captive, used "soft red stones … mixed … with grease and put the red paint on her face and hands and all over her body."[78] John Paul, Speck's Micmac informant, knew that the Beothuk coloured themselves with "red clay."[79]

In the eighteenth century, the Beothuk were said to procure ochre not only from Ochre Pit Cove, south of Bay de Verde in Conception Bay, but also from an unnamed place probably in Bonavista Bay and to visit Ochre Pit Island in the Bay of Exploits.[80] An ochre deposit was found by Cormack between Barrasway

River and Flat Bay, close to St George's Bay. According to the Micmac John Paul, "red clay" abounded at the Exploits River and Red Indian Lake.[81] One might expect that extraction of the ochre would be accompanied by a ritual in honour of the spirits controlling the resource; the Kutchin, for example, who used red colouring (haematite) as face and body paint, would leave offerings at the places where they obtained it.[82] But there is no record of any such ritual among the Beothuk.

It was earlier mentioned that in the early 1800s, according to Santu, the Beothuk gathered for the ochring of every member of the tribe at Red Indian Lake and that the event called for a ceremony.[83] The red colour was considered to be a mark of tribal identity and the first coat, applied in infancy, was regarded as a sign of initiation. Santu claimed her father was the last infant to be treated in this manner and that the colouring agent was obtained from a "red root." She also recalled that being ordered to wash off the dye was a form of punishment.[84]

The origin of the Beothuk's custom of applying ochre may be found in a prehistoric "red paint" culture, which flourished in the North American northeast after 3200 BP. Graves of this prehistoric culture included large amounts of red ochre together with mortuary offerings.[85] Maritime Archaic Indian burial places found in Newfoundland and Labrador featured these characteristics and the Beothuk practice of using ochre and of burying the dead with grave goods fits well into this cultural tradition; these practices have also been observed by Micmac.[86] The application of red colouring substances to the face was recorded among Montagnais, Saulteaux, Illinois (who painted the face and parts of the body with ochre), and others.[87] Among a number of Athapaskan tribes who used ochre as face paint, the Kutchin, who also painted their garments with red ochre, attributed "a degree of supernatural power" to the red mineral *caih* (probably haematite).[88] Although we have no proof that to the Beothuk the ochre represented such power, the inclusion of ochre in burials suggests that it was not only used as a tribal marker but had belief-related connotations.

MYTHOLOGICAL EMBLEMS

In 1828 Cormack wrote to Bishop Inglis: "I have lately discovered the key to the Mythology of her [Shanawdithit's] tribe which must be considered one of the most interesting subjects to enquire into."[89] This tantalizing reference and Shanawdithit's drawing of six "Emblems of the Red Indians Mythology" are the only tangible evidence of Cormack's discovery (sketch 9, Fig. 24.1). If he obtained from Shanawdithit more than the shapes and names of the emblems, the information has not survived.[90]

The six emblems are staves about three metres long, surmounted by different configurations; three appear to be of an abstract nature while the others are renderings of recognizable objects. On Shanawdithit's illustrations, the abstract staves and the handles of the remaining ones are shaded in pencil, consistent with the notion that the dark parts indicate a coating of ochre. This interpretation

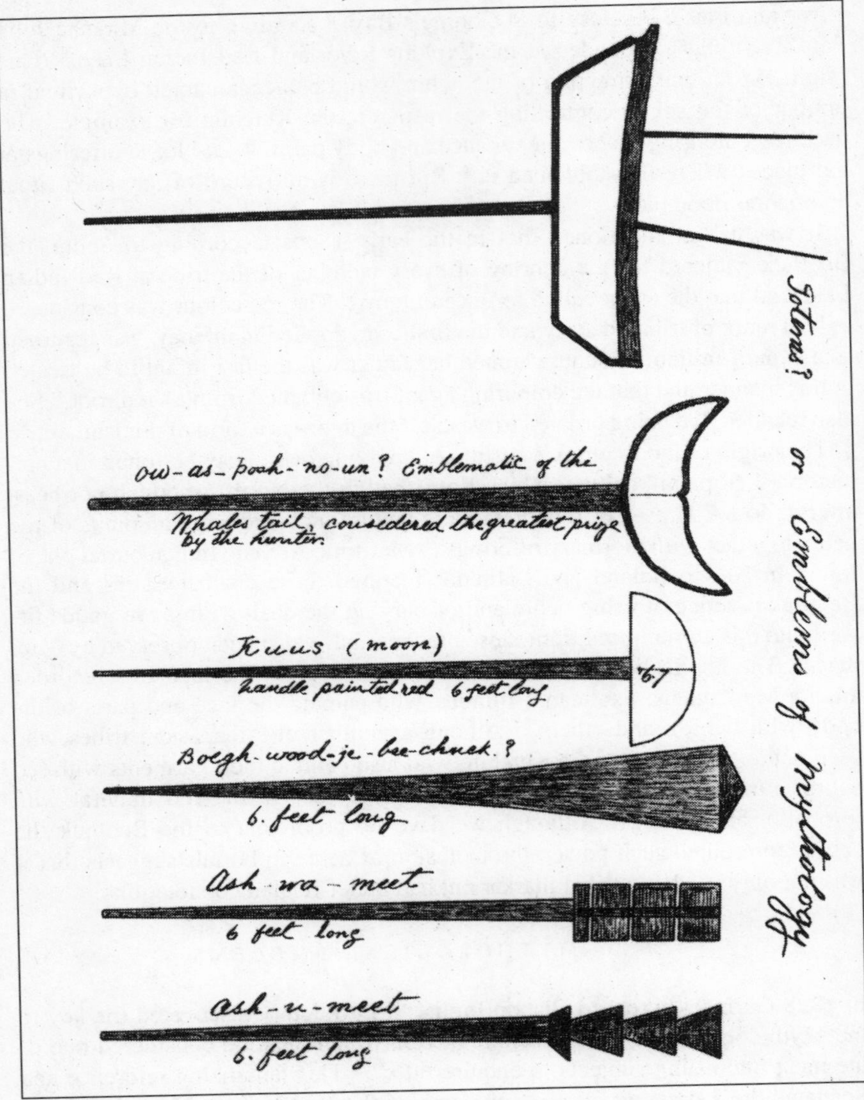

Fig.24.1 Shanawdithit's sketch 9: "Emblems of Mythology." (Howley 1915,249)

is supported by the notation "handle painted red" next to the stave named *Kuus*; it is also confirmed by Captain Buchan's description of a staff he saw in a Beothuk mamateek, which was entirely stained red.[91]

One staff from the abstract group labelled *Ash-wa-meet* bears at its upper end three cubes over a smaller rectangular box-like piece. Its name is referred to in a note recording information from Shanawdithit: "Men singing to Ash-wa-meet, with Eagle feathers and deers ears in cap"; this suggests that the staff may have been used in a ritual involving special regalia and songs.[92] A similar staff with what may have been pyramidal shapes at the top is called *Ash-u-meet* and answers the description of the staff seen by Captain Buchan at Red Indian Lake. A third staff, labelled *Boegh-wood-je-bee-chuk,* is pyramidal at the top and tapers gradually towards the lower end. The significance of the staves remains obscure.[93]

Whether these three symbols represent the entire abstract repertoire or whether some Beothuk groups may have used additional or different symbols cannot be ascertained. In the 1790s it was commonly believed among the settlers that "the Indians had a singular veneration for the Cross," and that by erecting "a cruciform figure upon their winter houses, furriers saved them from being destroyed during their absence in summer."[94] It is possible, of course, that the Beothuk simply respected this symbol because they understood it to be powerful in the European tradition, and not because they used the cruciform shape themselves. However, in the 1700s, native people in Labrador were seen with red crosses painted on their faces and canoes.[95] Veneration of the cross was also recorded among the Micmac of Miramichi, to whom it had become a sacred symbol.[96]

Of the three Beothuk staves with realistic representations, one already referred to as *kuus* (moon) displays a light-coloured half-moon shape at its upper end and may have been a symbol for (one of) the luminaries.[97] Another staff called *ow-as-posh-no-un* portrays a whale's tail, which, as Cormack noted, was "considered the greatest prize by the hunter … The Bottle Nosed Whale which they represent by the fishes tail, frequents in great numbers, the northern bays … and the Indians consider it the greatest good luck to kill one."[98] The figure on the sixth staff is particularly intriguing; it is a two-masted Newfoundland fishing boat, faithfully rendered "down to the rake of the second mast, familiar to all acquainted with this type of craft."[99] Although some researchers have interpreted this staff as commemorating a successful raid on such a fishing boat, it is suggested here that, if ranked as a mythological emblem, it might have had a more complex meaning. Its importance would more appropriately be defined by its function rather than by its possible origin; unfortunately, this function remains unknown.

CARVED BONE PIECES

Among Beothuk artifacts that have survived to this day perhaps the most striking items are carved and decorated bone pieces, often referred to as pendants. These carvings mostly conform to a general pattern but each one is unique and unlike any other. About 470 of these carvings have been collected.[100] They were mostly found in burials, sometimes in bundles of about thirty wrapped in bark or skin. On occasion carvings or fragments thereof have also turned up in excavations of Beothuk houses.[101] The only contemporary reference to carved bone pieces is included in John Cartwright's report. They were "neatly carved into four prongs; the two middle ones being parallel and almost close together, while the outer ones spread like a swallow's tail. In the few that I have seen the same form was invariably preserved though the ornamental carving has been diversified according to fancy. And everyone of them being furnished with a thong, seemingly to suspend them from some part of the indians dress. I have therefore imagined them to have been worn as amulets or sacred charms."[102] It is one of the many frustrations of Beothuk studies that the significance of these interesting carvings was not explained by any of the Beothuk captives. One can only compare them with similar items in other cultures and speculate about their meaning and purpose.

The carvings vary in length from two and a half to seventeen centimetres and are narrow, flat, and well polished. They are referred to as pendants because of a suspension hole at one end that has been gouged out biconically (i.e., there is no evidence of the use of a drill). At the lower ends they are cut obliquely or transversely, or else they end in a swallow's tail or a fork with two, three, or four prongs. Both faces are usually decorated with the same geometric patterns, which are scratched or carved into the surface and rubbed with ochre so that the designs stand out prominently against the lighter, polished bone (Plates 24.1, 24.2). The quality of workmanship in bundles of thirty or more pieces found together varies considerably and suggests that more than one person had carved them. Though the general shape of the carvings conforms to a definite stylistic tradition, no two pieces are alike. The ever-changing combination of different shapes, with their varying notches, curvatures, "shoulders," and "necks," and decorative motifs gives each piece an individual appearance. Favoured motifs are an incised line following the outer edge, vertical ladder effects, short lines extending from a solid line, small triangles, and zigzags. From an artistic point of view, the shape of each carving and the geometrical design on it are conceptualized as a harmonious whole. Some carvings are stylistically simple, featuring a plain outline and only a few basic patterns. Others have livelier and more diverse shapes with patterns that are cut more deeply into the surface or with circular or longitudinal sections that are entirely carved out.

A small number of the sculptured, three-dimensional pieces shown in Plate 24.2 (bottom row) are potentially interpretable. Four of them are fairly realistic renderings of skeletal fingers or claws, while three others seem to be partially stylized derivations of the same theme. Following this interpretation, it is possible to arrange some of the stylized, flat carvings in derivative stages and to identify them tentatively as abstractions of skeletal limbs. A similar line of interpretation for other carvings suggests that vertical ladder-like markings running down the centre of the piece, interrupted by one or two transverse patterns, may denote the vertebral column of a mammalian figure with the shoulder girdle and pelvis expressed by the transverse patterns (Plate 24.1, two upper rows). Some carvings with prongs are reminiscent of birds' feet (Plate 24.1, bottom row); others cannot be so easily identified. However, the diversity of shapes and patterns suggests that many different subjects may be represented.

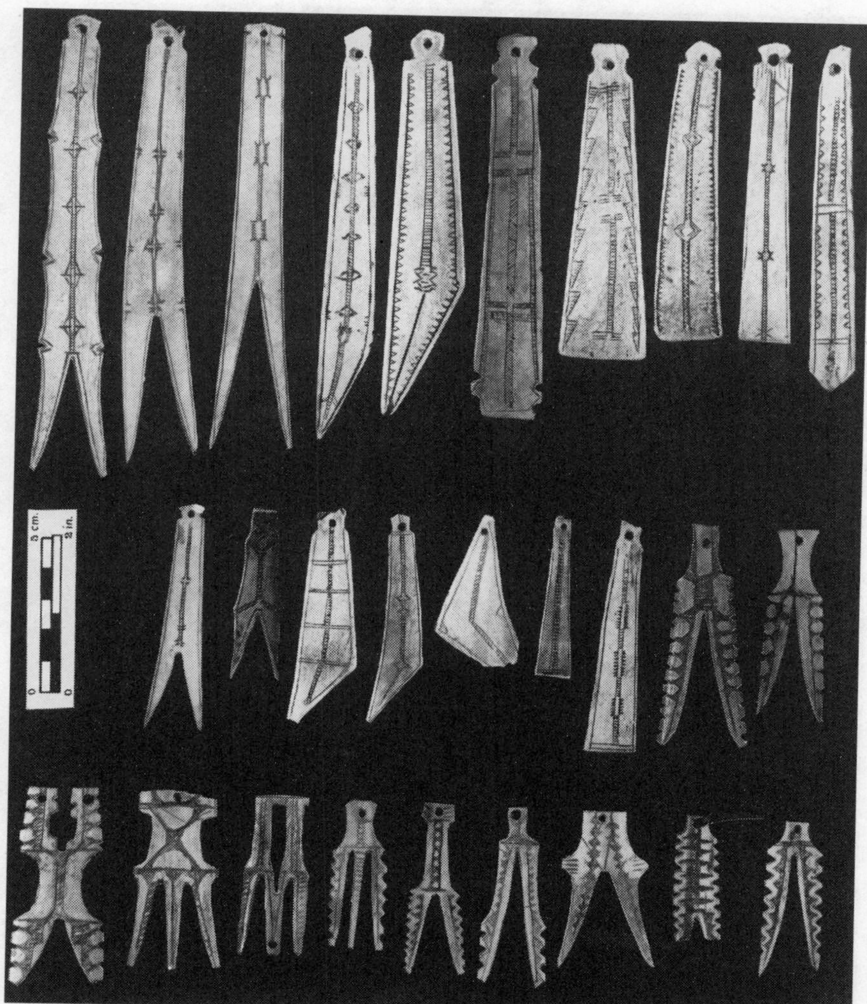

Plate 24.1 Carved bone pendants, plain style with incised patterns; pronged style with carved-out patterns. (Collection of the Newfoundland Museum)

The carvings are likely to have formed only part of a larger complex of artifacts, many of which, being of perishable material, disintegrated while these more durable objects survived.[103] Items in this proposed complex may have assisted in personal magic; in amulet form they may have been relied on for safety and good fortune by the wearer. Where large numbers of carvings were placed in burial sites, they may have served as symbolic tokens for the benefit of the community rather than for individuals.

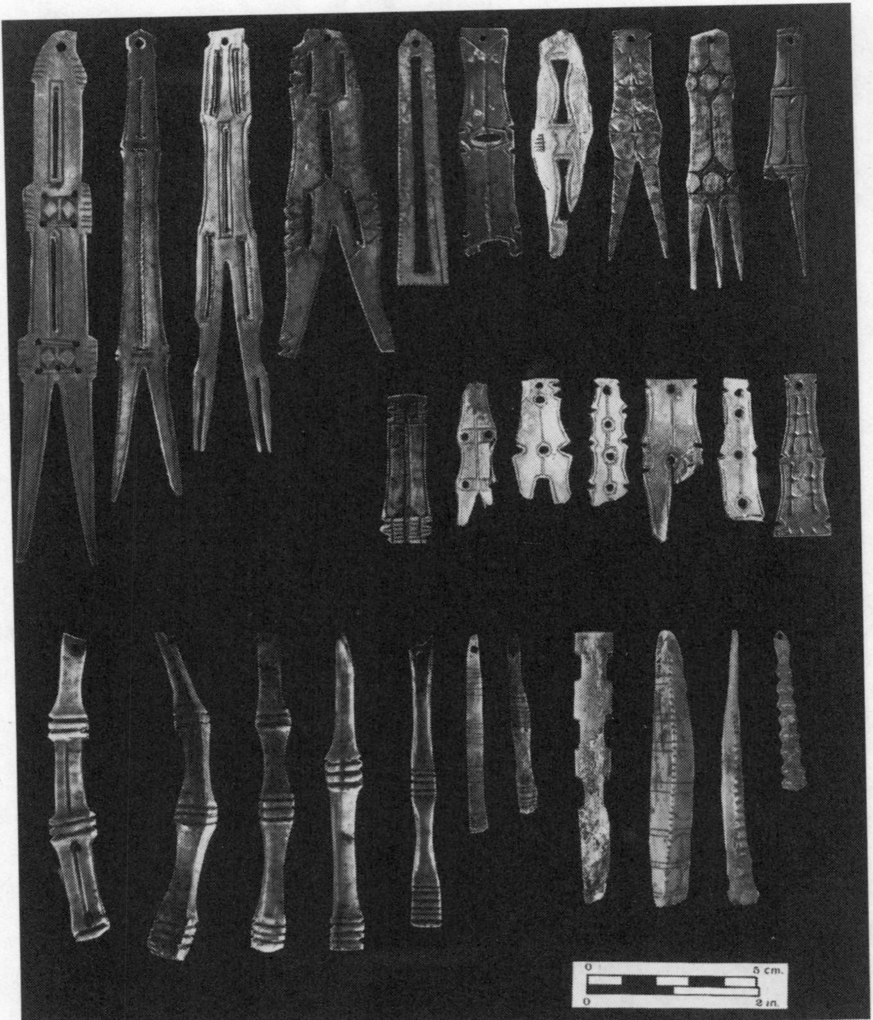

Plate 24.2 Carved bone pendants. Rows one and two: divers shapes; row three: phalange-shaped. (Private collections and collections of the Newfoundland Museum and the Canadian Museum of Civilization)

Why the Beothuk would carve representations of skeletal finger bones or claws remains puzzling, though comparisons with rituals of other native groups provide clues.[104] In the belief pattern of Montagnais/Naskapi in Labrador and Quebec, for instance, the spirit of the bear was one of the most powerful among the animal spirits.[105] Bear bones were disposed of with the greatest care and some bones, claws, and skin pieces were kept as hunting charms.[106] The possibility that the Beothuk revered bears or other animals with phalanges of this type should thus be considered. Whitehead, who concluded that the carvings more closely resemble human phalanges than bear claws (Plate 24.2, bottom row), has pointed out that among native groups, fingers and finger joints are used for counting, in games as well as in genealogical reckonings of the family, clan, and tribe.[107] The carvings of phalanges may therefore have been significant in this respect.

The Dorset Eskimo, who inhabited Newfoundland contemporaneously with the prehistoric ancestors of the Beothuk (the Little Passage Indians), produced bone carvings of animal and human forms. Unlike the realistic renderings found in Dorset carvings from more northerly regions, many of the carvings found in Newfoundland are to some degree stylized.[108] Since this was a unique development within the Dorset culture, it is possible that the carving traditions of the Newfoundland Dorset and the Little Passage Indians influenced each other. Judging from the context in which the Dorset carvings were found and from the ethnographic records of Inuit people, Harp suggested that they were used as "personal amulets denoting an intimate relationship between individuals and the several species of game animals that were important to their survival."[109] The Beothuk bone carvings may have had a similar purpose.

Going back in time, it is noteworthy that bone pieces of pendant-like character portraying birds' heads, a bear, and a human effigy were also found in burial sites of Maritime Archaic Indians in Newfoundland, most plentifully at Port au Choix.[110] The carvings were found together with bills, skulls, and feet of birds as well as the teeth and bones of many terrestrial species, and it has been concluded that they functioned as amulets or charms.

Farther afield, incised bone pendants similar to those made by the Beothuk were part of what is believed to be a mid-nineteenth-century shaman's neck-ring from the Athapaskan Tutchone of the Yukon Plateau. These carvings have been interpreted as embodying the spirit power of the shaman's "zoomorphic assistants."[111] A second neck-ring with carved pieces that strikingly resemble Beothuk pendants was collected from a Tlingit shaman but is thought to have been of Athapaskan origin.[112] It is possible that the necklace made up of six carved pendants with a large animal tooth as a centrepiece that was found in a Beothuk grave (Plate 24.3) belonged to a shaman. These examples show that the carving of pendant-shaped objects from bone was not, as many have thought, unique to the Beothuk.

GAMES

Santu Toney told the anthropologist Frank G. Speck that dancing, feasting, and playing two different types of dice-and-bowl games accompanied the Beothuk's springtime ochring ceremony. "One of these [games] was [played] with seven dice discs and a bowl, and seventeen counters – four square ones and a crooked one called the 'chief.' The other form of the game was played with one large die, about two inches across, and six small ones, which were thrown upon a

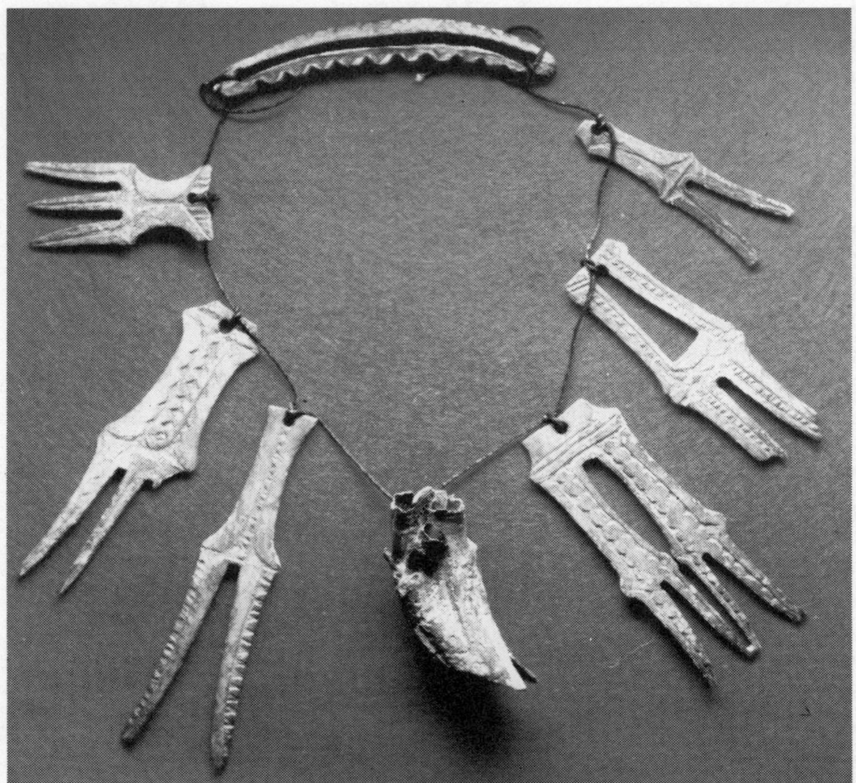

Plate 24.3 Necklace of six carved pendants and an animal tooth. (Collection of the Newfoundland Museum)

blanket or a hide and struck sideways with the hand. Men only played the latter."[113] Rectangular and diamond-shaped bone and ivory carvings that have been found in Beothuk graves seem to confirm Santu's information. Altogether, sixteen carvings of this type have been documented (Plate 24.4).[114] Seven pieces in the collection of the Newfoundland Museum are rectangular, about three centimetres long, two and a half centimetres wide, and one centimetre thick; five dice are diamond shaped and slightly longer but thinner than the rectangular ones; one piece is of a triangular shape. All the pieces have been incised with lines or patterns on one face and left plain on the other. Two of the rectangular pieces are incised with criss-cross lines, while the remaining five have intricate geometric patterns, including double or triple triangles and ladder effects. The incised lines on the diamond-shaped pieces include ladder effects, chevron patterns, and other geometrical forms. Most of the patterns consist of mirror-image designs. One of the rectangular pieces (not illustrated) has notches and few line patterns and thus differs visually from the rest, as does the

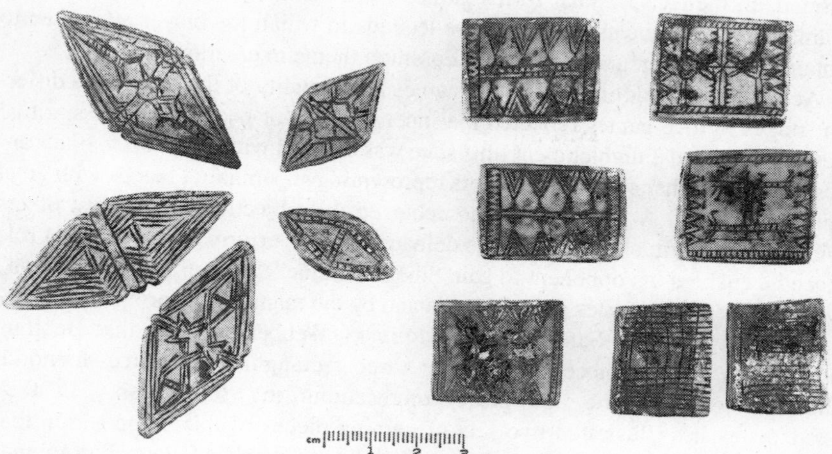

Plate 24.4 Diamond-shaped and rectangular gaming pieces. (Collection of the Newfoundland Museum)

triangular piece, which has a blunt apex and criss-cross lines. All carvings show traces of ochre. They are assumed to have been used as gaming dice. Unfortunately, nothing further is known about the dice or about the Beothuk gaming complex.

In order to form an idea of the purpose of bowl-and-dice games among North American native people and how they were played, it may be appropriate to outline Alika Podolinsky Webber's study of the gaming complex.[115] The essential implements of all dice games were the dice, or gaming pieces, which usually had two faces distinguished by colours or markings and instruments for keeping count. The latter were either sticks, leaves, or beads that could be passed from hand to hand, or counting boards. The number of counters varied, but there were often ten or multiples of ten up to 160. Generally, throwing only marked sides up on the dice counted highest; throwing no marked sides up scored second highest; the more mixed the dice were, the lower the count. Counting methods for keeping score could be very complex; the game ended when one player won all the counters.

Games were not only played for entertainment but could also have implicit or hidden aspects. They were commonly played at fixed seasons, at festivals, or at special rites. Usually men and women of all ages played, but not children. Preparation for a game could include dreaming, fasting, and sacrifices not only by the players but also by the spectators. Games could be a means of personal initiation and regeneration, or they could concentrate on a much desired goal such as securing fertility, causing rain, curing illness, or assisting recently departed souls to reach the other world safely. They could also be closely related to divination practices. Games were sometimes seen as sacred and were played on hallowed ground. In their ceremonial forms games were distinctly the preserve of men. Games were also the subject of native legends in which the player attempted to obtain magic power, and they were a common theme in creation myths.

According to Podolinsky Webber, games had a reality of their own; the different stages in dice games reflected the inner struggle of people towards spiritual development and enlightenment; this state was equated with a "return to one's ancestors on the other side, the ancestors representing supernatural beings with great spiritual power." A person who had achieved this objective could assist others who were in spiritual transition. The defeated player performed an important role since he enabled his opponent to gain "the other side." Ancestral "participation" was indicated by complex paraphernalia and by the manner of scoring.

In agreement with Santu's tale, Podolinsky Webber suggests that Beothuk used seven gaming pieces in a game: three rectangular and three diamond-shaped ones plus one odd piece, representing the "Old Man." In fact, J.P. Howley has illustrated two sets of gaming pieces of this composition that may have been found together, though Podolinsky Webber favours a combination of different pieces to a set.[116] She has also advanced some speculative interpretations for the different shapes and patterns on Beothuk gaming pieces. Since dice can often be divided into male and female shapes, she believes that among the Beothuk the rectangular shapes represented female and the diamond shapes represented male aspects. She considered it possible that the line patterns were of a symbolic character similar to the line patterns on Beothuk pendants. The criss-cross lines on the three dice without a distinctive pattern, fourteen on one, twenty-eight on the two others, may have represented an extended family or a genealogical count; the significance of twenty-eight is that ancestors were often counted on finger joints, of which there are twenty-eight altogether on a person's two hands. Twenty-eight is also the number of days in the lunar month, and this too may have been significant.[117] The designs on most of the dice are drawn as mirror-image patterns and thus could have represented two complementary aspects such as male and female or present and past generations; triangles may stand for mamateeks, which could have been a way of counting families.[118]

Since there is no evidence that the Beothuk used counting boards, they are thought to have employed sticks, leaves, or perhaps strings of discoidal beads for scoring games, as several other native tribes did (Plate 24.5).[119] The Beothuk burial cave on Swan Island contained not only the majority of the gaming pieces that have been preserved but also strings with such beads.[120] Of the two strings that are intact, one has eighty-three the other 157 beads. Whether these numbers would fit into the Beothuk's scheme of counting games is not known.[121]

Tribes to the west of the Beothuk, among them Micmac, Maliseet, and Pasaquamoddy, also played bowl-and-dice games. Santu claimed that they had learned this game originally from her people (the Beothuk).[122] A Micmac game called *waltes* was played with six round caribou-bone dice (or *waltestaqn*) and

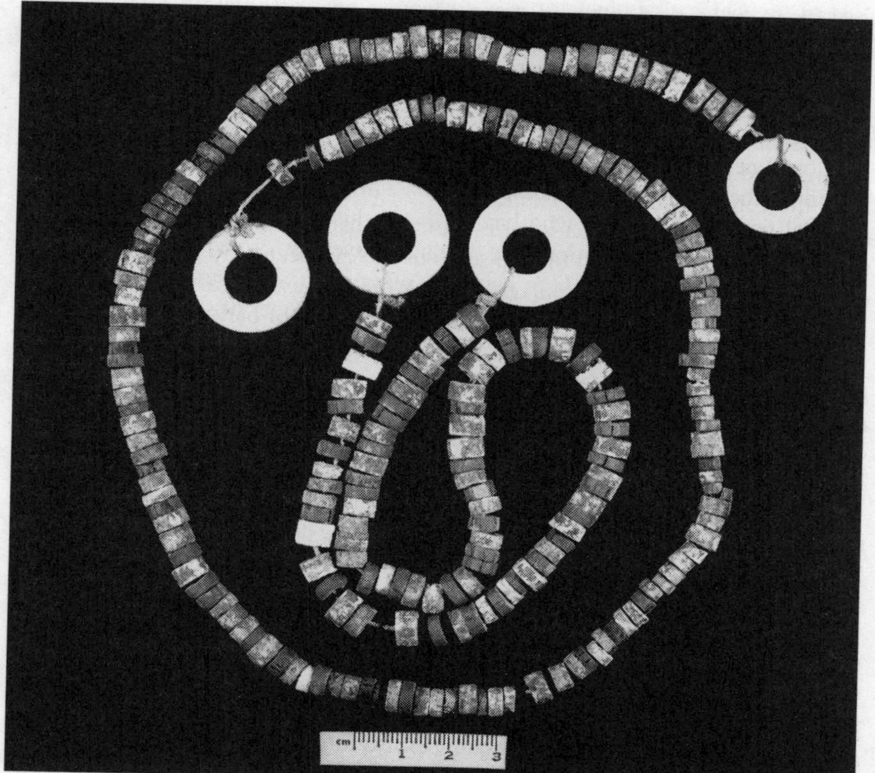

Plate 24.5 Two strings of discoidal beads, tied to rings made of bone and shell. (Collection of the Newfoundland Museum)

fifty-five counting sticks.[123] The dice were thrown up into the air from a bowl – here a wooden dish. The highest count was scored when all pieces fell down with the marked faces up; overall scoring was complex.[124] A second Micmac dice game called *wapnaqnk* was played with eight dice but no bowl.[125]

In view of the evidence, it is assumed that the Beothuk carvings that resemble gaming pieces were used as such; the Beothuk may have played their games in a manner similar to that of their Micmac neighbours, or they may have had their own rules. Although we do not know whether their gaming complex had the functions described here, the presence of gaming pieces in graves suggests that dice games were an important part of their culture.

DIFFERENT TYPES OF BEADS

The Beothuk produced beads and discs from a variety of materials including small univalve shells and winkles.[126] Some beads were placed on a string and could have been used either as game counters or as decorative objects. They could also have served as ritual objects. For example, John Guy, who traded with Beothuk in Trinity Bay in 1612, recorded that he and his companions were presented with chains of "leather full of small perwincle shells" before trade was commenced.[127]

Two bead strings in the collection of the Newfoundland Museum, probably from the cemetery on Swan Island (Plate 24.5), are 39.2 and 59.5 centimetres long; the diameter of the beads varies from one half to one centimetre.[128] Those on the longer string consist of thin sections of European clay pipestems, small circles of sheet lead, and circular sections of the inner bark of birch; beads on the shorter string were made of pipestem sections and of bark or wood.[129] They are strung on a very fine twisted thong; the ends are tied either to flat bone rings or to discoidal shell beads. "Strings of wampum" or "small beads" were also among the grave goods in burial sites at Comfort Cove and on Tilt Island, Placentia Bay; bone rings were found in burial sites on Long Island, in the Bay of Exploits, and at North China Head.[130]

Other discoidal beads were made from flat shell discs that were perforated in the centre. Twenty-five finished and two unfinished discs of this type, recovered from a burial site at Rencontre, are now in the collection of the McCord Museum in Montreal (Fig. 24.2).[131] Others were retrieved from burial sites on Tilt Island, at Fox Bar, Spirit Cove, Comfort Cove, and in two caves on Swan Island, including the cemetery mentioned above, and from a beach near Musgrave Harbour.[132] The shell discs from the Swan Island cemetery may have been made from the shells of clams, *Mya truncata* and *Saxicava rugosa*, and those from Rencontre Island from the shells of "the large *Mactra*, probably *M. solidissima*."[133] Some of these discs are between three and four centimetres in diameter and less than 0.25 centimetres thick, others are considerably smaller. Chute, who examined them, believes that the perforations had been drilled rather than gouged out.[134]

Among other northeastern tribes, shell beads were widely used for adornment and were often considered personal property.[135] This may also have been the case among the Beothuk; it was recorded in 1612 that the Beothuk in a camp close to Heart's Ease wore sealskin hats that were decorated with "fine white shels."[136]

According to Speck, the production and use of shell-disc beads (or wampum) was a prehistoric phenomenon. They were found in abundance on archaeological sites over the entire eastern part of the continent, particular'y in Iroquoian and Algonquian regions.[137] During the late prehistoric and early historic period, the mainland tribes replaced shell-disc beads with smaller, finer cylindrical or tubular beads. However, there is no evidence that the Beothuk produced or trades these new types of beads. An exception would be the cylindrical beads found in a burial site on the Labrador side of the Strait of Belle Isle, which W.J. Wintemberg believed to be of Beothuk origin.[138] The evidence suggests that, rather than adopting cylindrical or tubular types, the Beothuk ex-

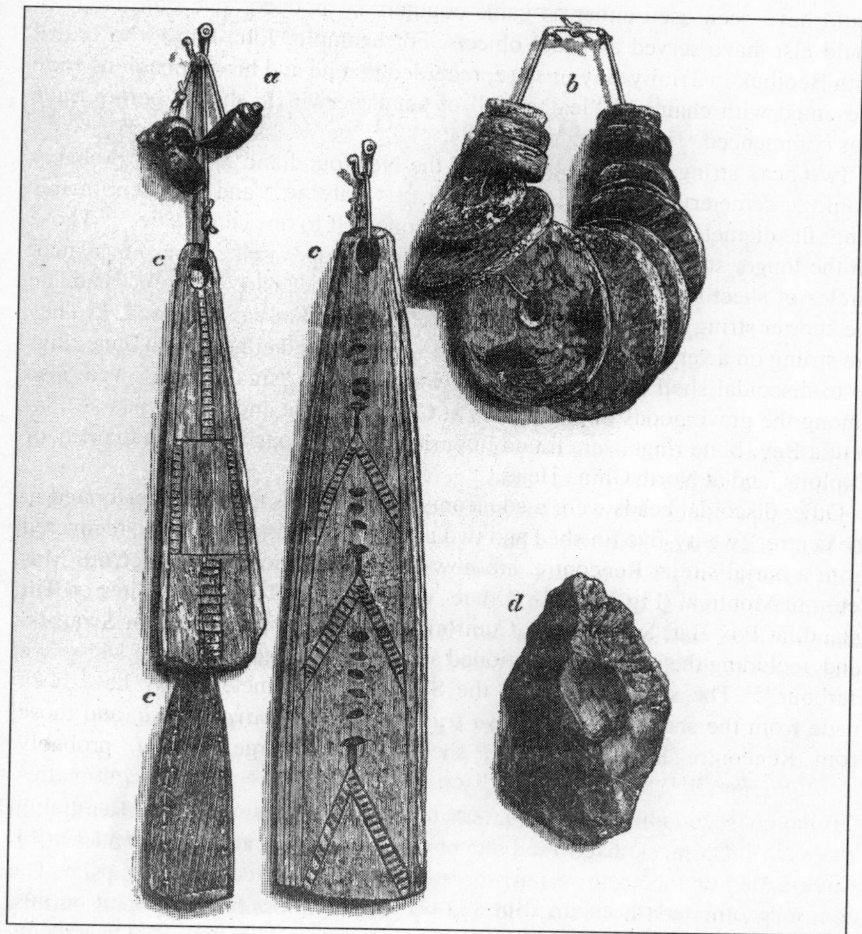

Fig.24.2 Grave goods from burial on Rencontre Island: a) pierced shells of purpura lapillus; b) discoidal shell beads of mactra; c) pendants; d) stone tool. (Dawson 1880, Fig.5)

tended their bead production by including new materials, such as pipestem pieces and sheet lead.

CHAPTER TWENTY-FIVE

Burial Places and Mortuary Practices

The Beothuk, like other native people, took great care in the disposal of their dead. Since there are no eyewitness accounts of actual burial, information on mortuary practices derives from historic documents written by people such as W.E. Cormack who discovered burial sites many years ago, from archaeological excavations, and from study of grave goods in museum collections[1]. To give an idea of the kind of information that is available from well-documented graves, the following section describes two burial places along with type of burial, placement of the dead, and the deposition of grave goods.

A BURIAL HUT AND THE BURIAL OF A CHILD

During his second unsuccessful attempt at making contact with the Beothuk in 1827, W.E. Cormack discovered one of their cemeteries at Red Indian Lake.[2] It was situated on the northwestern shore close to a large, deserted campsite. The cemetery contained both scaffold and box burials, possibly in-ground burials, and also a wooden hut "in the most perfect state of preservation."[3] On opening this hut, the curiosity of Cormack and his party was "raised to the highest pitch." Inside, as recounted in chapter 13 they were surprised to find a pine coffin with a "skeleton neatly shrouded in muslin." It was soon understood to be that of the captive Demasduit, called Mary March by the settlers, whose coffined remains had been returned to the Indian camp in 1820.[4] The burial hut also housed the remains of her husband, chief Nonosabasut, who was killed at during Demasduit's capture, another adult, and the bodies of children, one of whom was believed to be Nonosabasut and Demasduit's child. Except for Demasduit, the bodies of the adults had been wrapped in caribou skins and laid out on the floor. Deposited with them was a variety of articles:

> in some instances the property, in others the representation of the property … two small wooden images of a man and woman … a small doll … several small models of their ca-

noes; two small models of boats; an iron axe; a bow and quiver of arrows were placed by the side of *Mary March's* husband; and two fire-stones (radiated iron pyrites from which they produce fire by striking them together) lay at his head; there were also various kinds of culinary utensils neatly made, of birch rind and ornamented, and many other things some of which we did not know the use or meaning.[5]

Cormack purloined the skulls of Demasduit and her husband, the pelisse (a garment made of fur) of what was believed to be their child, a large canoe replica, the two images of a man and woman, a carved bird, and birchbark dishes. Some of these artifacts are now in the collections of the British Museum in London and the Royal Museum of Scotland in Edinburgh.[6] The male skull was said to have borne "the marks of several wounds, one of which had cleaved the lower jaw; it, however, reconnected in healing; another wound was evidently caused by a shot."[7]

The child's burial was found on Big Island (formerly Burnt Island) in Pilley's Tickle, Notre Dame Bay. It consisted of a shallow pit roofed over with branches, a birchbark canopy and then loose stones, gravel, and soil. It was discovered accidentally in the 1880s by berry pickers, one of whom trod on the canopy and fell through. Howley described the contents of the grave: "The body itself was enshrouded in its natural skin, now dried and shrunken and resembling Chamois leather, and was almost perfect."[8] It was lying on its left side with its legs bent up and was clothed in "a sort of skin pants" and moccasins, all having been smeared with red ochre.[9] The whole was encased in a fringed skin cover to which thirty-two carved bone ornaments and several birds' feet had been fastened.[10] The remains are considered to be those of a four- or five-year-old child.[11] While sexing the skeletons of young individuals is difficult, a small wooden image of a male figurine found in the grave may indicate the gender of the child (Plate 25.1). Other articles arranged around the corpse included miniature bows and arrows, three miniature birchbark canoes and paddles, three pairs of moccasins, packages of red ochre tied up in birchbark, and dried or smoked salmon and trout in a neat parcel of bark, which was held together by a network of rootlets like a crude basket. The bulk of the grave goods is now in the collection of the Newfoundland Museum. The burial shroud has recently been identified as a single adult-size legging (Fig. 21.1).[12] Only one bone ornament (pendant) and one foot of a southern black guillemot (*Cepphus grylle atlantis*) are still tied to the garment.[13]

Other Beothuk Burials

A further thirty-seven burials may also be Beothuk. However, paucity of information makes it difficult to decide whether they are all authentic. Using information from the child's burial on Big Island and from the cemetery at Red Indian Lake, I have established several diagnostic features by which to determine whether burials are of Beothuk origin. The criteria include location,

Plate 25.1 Wooden male figurine from the burial of a child on Big Island, Pilley's Tickle. (Collection of the Newfoundland Museum) Inset: Figurine wrapped in skin clothing as originally found. (By permission of David Howley, St John's)

placement of the deceased, types of grave goods, and the presence or absence of ochre.[14] Following these criteria, twenty-five burial sites, including the two described above, are considered to be Beothuk. A grave recorded by the anthropologist W.J. Wintemberg in 1928 on the north shore of the Strait of Belle Isle is tentatively included in this list (List 1A).[15] Fourteen others are left undetermined because of insufficient documentation (List 1B).

Plate 25.2 Cobble beach burial at Spirit Cove, New World Island.

Of the twenty-five Beothuk burial sites given in List 1A and Table 25.1, at least three contained the remains of more than three individuals and are classified as cemeteries. Two were located in Notre Dame Bay, in a cluster of rock shelters on Comfort Island in Comfort Cove, and in a large cave on Swan Island in the Bay of Exploits (Plate 25.4). The third cemetery is the one found by Cormack on the northwest shore of Red Indian Lake.[16] This last burial ground, by far the largest of the three, was evidently in use during the last years of Beothuk existence and may have originated with the interment in 1819 of Nonosabasut, whose burial hut was constructed on the foundation of his mamateek.[17] At this time the Beothuk no longer had easy access to the coast, which appears to have been the preferred location for burial.

Of the remaining twenty-two burial sites, sixteen contained one to three individuals (ten single, five with two people, and one with three), three were too disturbed to judge how many had been interred, and three cave burials contained carved pendants but no skeletal material.

With the exception of the cemetery at Red Indian Lake, all known burials were located within sight of the sea, the majority of them in caves or rock shelters. Six sites were found directly on the coast (Plates 25.2, 25.3) while eighteen

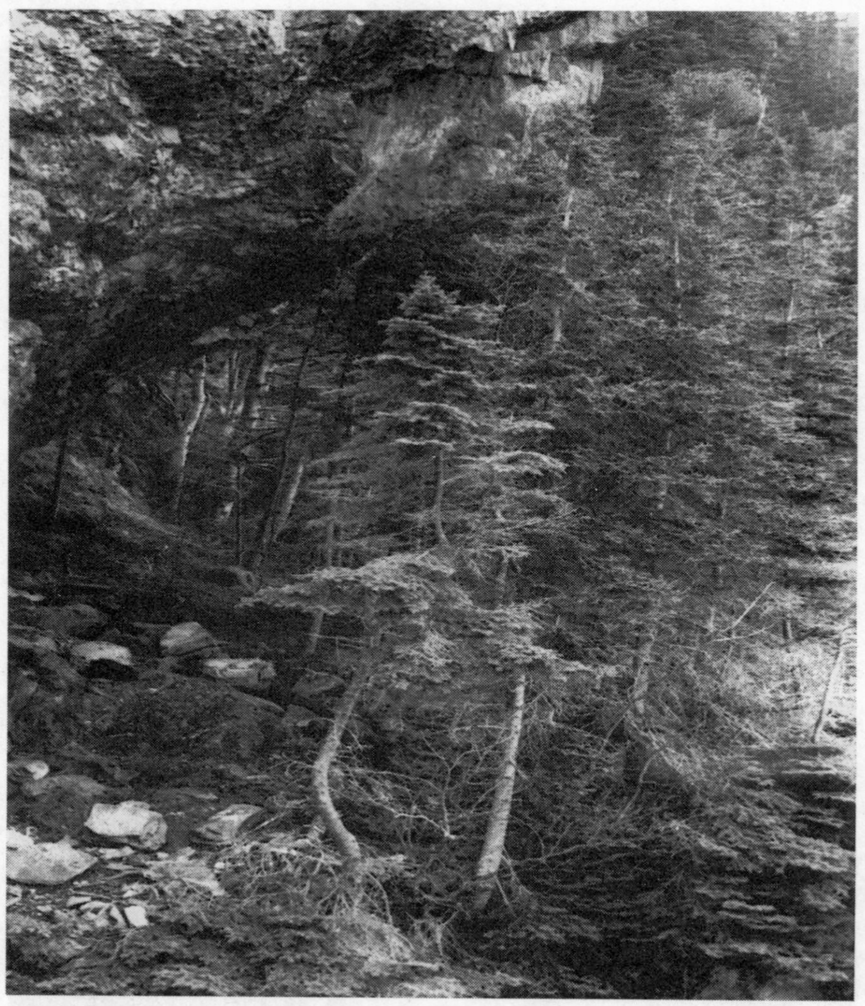

Plate 25.3 Burial under rock overhang, Fox Bar, Bonavista Bay.

others were situated on offshore islands (Plates 25.4, 25.5, 25.6). The frequency of coastal burials reflects the Beothuk custom, recorded by Cormack, of "carrying their dead from a distance to the seacoast to bury them there".[18] In many cases this would have required temporary storage of the body, perhaps in a tree or on a scaffold, before actual burial. The custom of depositing a corpse temporarily before final burial, referred to as secondary burial, is also known among Montagnais, Micmac, and other Indian peoples.[19]

The Micmac, who preferred islands or small narrow peninsulas for their burial places as the Beothuk appear to have done, believed that the spirits of the dead survived and were something to fear. Because they thought that these spir-

Plate 25.4 Burial cave, Swan Island, Bay of Exploits. Entrance is to the right of the rock formation.

Plate 25.5 Pendant burial cave Launch I, Long Island, Green Bay. (Provided by Gerry Penney, St John's)

Plate 25.6 Disturbed burial on the point of a small island off Western Indian Island, locally known as Phillip's Island. (Provided by Marianne Stopp, St John's)

its could not cross water, Micmac saw to it that burials were separated from their habitations by a body of water. Whether the Beothuk practice of burying their dead close to the sea was based on the same belief is not known. Shanawdithit told Cormack that the Beothuk believed the bones of the dead either were spirits or housed spirits and "that the spirits of the dead came … back to watch over the actions of their living friends."[20]

PREPARATION OF THE DEAD FOR BURIAL

Whether the Beothuk prepared their dead for burial by washing, dressing, and painting the body prior to interment has not been recorded. Shanawdithit said only that a surviving spouse would have to wash in hot water treated with shavings of dogwood (bark or wood), which may have been a cleansing ritual.[21] Beothuk do not seem to have embalmed corpses; no such treatment has been noted on any of the remains. The mummified body of the remarkably well preserved young Beothuk child from the Big Island burial showed no discernible incisions or seams that might have been left by preservation treatments, such as the removal of organs or of flesh. However, the corpse may have been dried in the sun prior to interment, a method occasionally employed by Micmac.[22]

As a rule, the remains of the dead were wrapped in skins or in birchbark. Ochre was also applied, traces of which were found in nearly every burial, either in the soil, on the skeletal remains, or on the grave goods. In some cases the ochre may have been applied directly to the bones after the flesh had decayed; this could have been done in the course of reburial or during a later visit to the grave.[23] A burial at Fox Bar in Bonavista Bay included a bed of ochre-coloured earth some 1.50 metres by 0.60 of a metre wide and up to 0.10 of a metre thick. In this instance the ochre in the soil could have caused the staining of the bones that were embedded in the coloured layer (Plate 25.3).[24]

Burial positions varied. Some skeletal remains were found fully extended lying on the back, others were flexed and placed on the side (either right or left). In one case the corpse had been tied into a sitting posture with a grass rope.[25]

TYPES OF BURIALS

W.E. Cormack wrote a graphic account of the different ways the Beothuk interred their dead. He described scaffold and box burials, a burial hut, and in-ground burials.[26] It is unclear, though, whether Cormack's descriptions refer exclusively to what he saw at the Red Indian Lake cemetery or included information on burial sites he had seen elsewhere.

Scaffold burial. Wooden scaffolds were constructed of four two-metre-high posts that were driven into the ground. These posts supported a crib that was suspended 1.40 metres off the ground and measured about 1.70 by 1.20 metres; its floor was made of small squared beams. It contained the body, which was wrapped in birchbark and accompanied by grave goods.[27] The scaffold could have served as a temporary repository until the bones of the deceased were transported to a final resting place; alternately, the scaffold together with the corpse might have been left untouched until the body decayed and the scaffold collapsed. According to T.G.B. Lloyd's Micmac guide, the "Red Indians" placed (and presumably left) their dead on scaffolds, a burial method that was prevalent among many Indian tribes.[28]

Box burial. In this type of burial, the flexed body of the deceased was wrapped in birchbark and placed in a box lined with birchbark. The box was about 1.20 metres long, 0.90 of a metre wide, and 0.75 of a metre deep. It was constructed of small squared posts laid horizontally on each other and notched at the corners for a close join. The box was set on the ground in such a manner that the body lay on its right side.[29] Burial boxes have also been recorded among Micmac at Restigouche and among Inuit of Lower Yukon, the latter tying the body together with a cord before placing it in the box.[30]

Burial hut. The most conspicuous repository at the Red Indian Lake cemetery was the burial hut built on the foundation of, and with materials from, Nonosabasut's mamateek.[31] It was about three metres long, 2.50 to 2.70 metres wide, and 1.20 to 1.50 metres high in the centre. The floor was made of squared poles, the roof, possibly gabled, was covered with bark, and the hut was well secured against the elements. The remains of Nonosabasut, wrapped in caribou skins, were laid out full length on the floor. Demasduit's remains were shrouded in muslin and encased in the pine box in which they had been delivered by Captain Buchan. The position of the others, including the children, was not recorded. The hut also contained a large variety of grave goods. The custom of placing the remains of persons of high status, such as chiefs and shamans, into mortuary houses has also been recorded among Algonkians and Iroquoians.[32]

In-ground burial. According to Cormack, the most common manner of disposal was to wrap the body in bark, place it in a shallow grave or on the ground, and cover it with soil and rocks.[33]

One of the burials in List 1A was discovered on a sandy beach on the Straight Shore.[34] Twenty-three other graves, most of them found in rock shelters or caves, had been placed in or on the ground and covered with soil and rocks (it should be remembered that some of the twenty-five listed burial places had more than one grave). However, in some cases there was an additional structure. In five burials, the body was surrounded by a low rock wall that was covered with large flat rocks; in two of these there was a bark canopy cover. Four other graves either had a rock wall or a slab cover.[35] A structure of walls and slabs discovered in Seal Cove on Fogo Island was described as roughly six to seven feet long and thirty inches deep, the sides having been constructed of flat stones of almost uniform thickness. The cover consisted of large flagstones that rested on the walls. Birchbark sheets, neatly sewn together, had been placed above the flagstones to form a tight cover.[36]

Rock walls were also erected on flat open ground. A grave on Phillip's Island, off Western Indian Island, for example, was said to have had stones piled

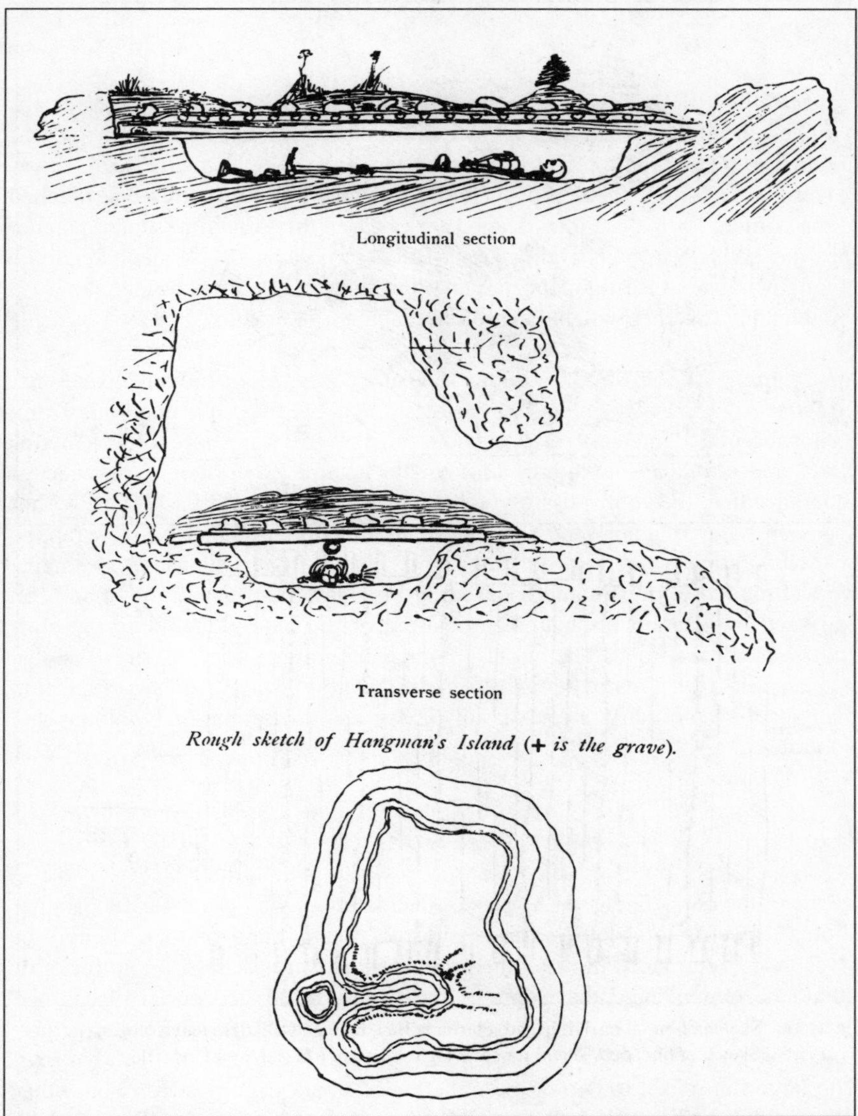

Fig.25.1 Sketch of burial on Hangman's Island, Placentia Bay, by R.S. Dahl. (Howley 1915,292)

up like a low dry-stone wall about "grave size"; the wall was surmounted by larger flat stone slabs (Plate 25.6).[37] A variation on this theme was a rock-wall burial on a cobble beach at Spirit Cove, New World Island. It was placed about one metre below the surface of the cobble beach and had a heavy rock structure on one end; remnants of poles about five centimetres thick that were embedded

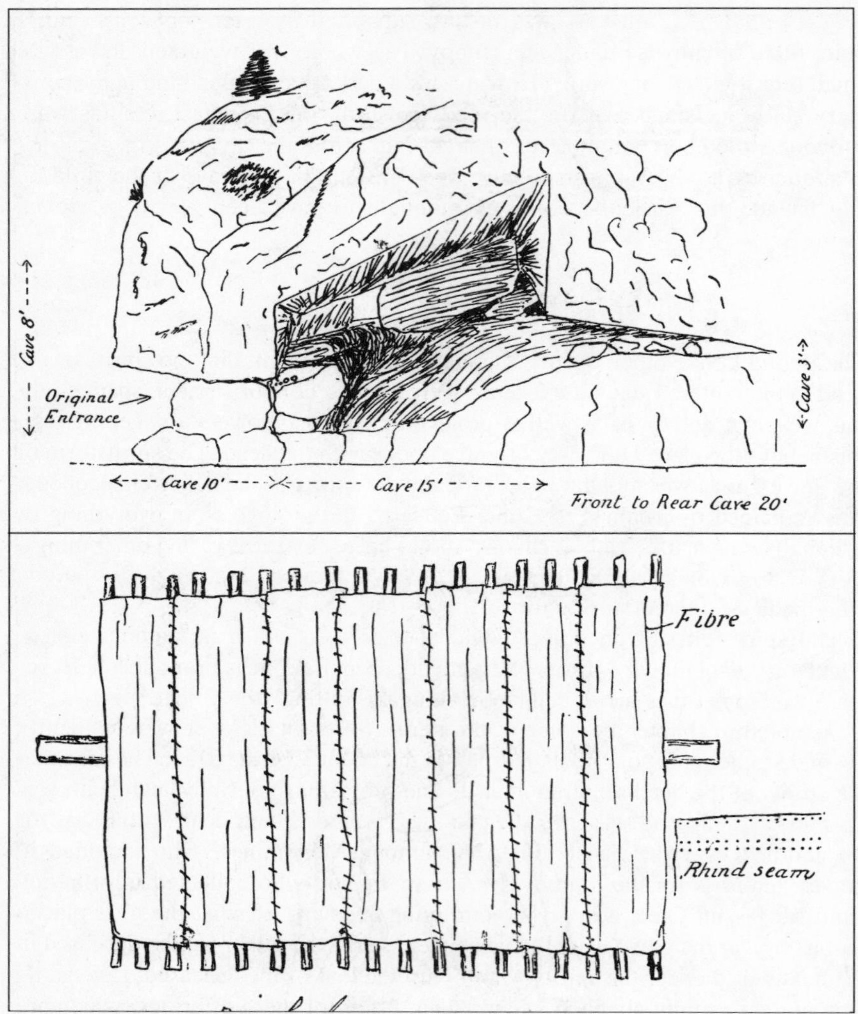

Fig.25.2a Sketch of burial on Tilt Island, Placentia Bay, by R.S. Dahl. (Howley 1915,294)
Fig.25.2b Sketch of birchbark shield for covering remains in a burial, by J.P. Howley. (Howley 1915,291)

in one of the side walls suggest that poles had originally supported a bark cover, on which the cobbles had been piled up (Plate 25.2).[38]

A birchbark "shield" or canopy placed over the body before soil or rocks were piled on top was described by R.S. Dahl, a surveyor, who discovered a burial on Hangman's Island.[39] It was made of ten- and twelve-inch-wide strips of bark neatly sewn together and then fastened to eighteen sticks, seven feet long, that were placed crosswise underneath the bark about four inches apart

(Fig. 25.1). This framework was in turn supported by a ten-foot-long central pole, fitted lengthwise under the canopy. The whole was weighted down with small rocks, gravel, and soil.[40] Howley saw a bark cover of this kind in the cemetery at Swan Island, where "the rocks covering the [skeletal] remains were supported upon horizontal pieces of sticks laid across the cavity" (Fig. 25.2b).[41] A similar bark cover appears to have been present on the grave of the child on Big Island; this particular cover was thought to have been part of a broken canoe.[42]

GRAVE FURNISHINGS

The Beothuk, like other North American Indians, thought that the spirits of the dead in their altered state of existence were in need of nourishment, spare clothing, weapons, and tools, as well as protection from evil powers. In keeping with this belief they placed a variety of grave goods with the dead. The spirit-form of the grave goods was thought to accompany the spirits of the dead. This concept was explained by Micmac to Father LeClercq in the 1670s. "In everything of which they make use, such as canoes, snow shoes, bow, arrows and other things, there is a particular spirit which would always accompany after death the one who made use thereof during life."[43]

The spirit-form of an object could also derive from a miniature version, which may explain why graves often included small replicas or models.[44] Its release was sometimes facilitated by breaking or "killing" the object.[45]

As noted in chapter 25, some of the items in Beothuk graves were evidently destined to help the soul on its journey to the country of the dead. The idea that the spirits of the dead required utensils and provisions after physical death was also prevalent among Western Abenaki, who provided their dead with food "for the journey over the ghost trail," and among Menominee, who included in graves "utensils for the journey."[46] Adrian Tanner, who collected information from Mistassini Cree, was given conflicting accounts of what the gifts placed in, on, or near the grave were for. They were said to be either for the deceased in the next world or for the spirits who mourn the loss of the deceased. Like game animals, they might abandon an area were it not for these offerings, which are inducements for them to stay and to become attached to new human patrons.[47]

Nearly all graves recorded in List 1A contained some grave goods (see Table 25.1). However, detailed information on quantity and type is sketchy because many burials had been disturbed before they were properly documented. Ten of the twenty-eight actual graves (as mentioned, some burial sites had more than one grave) contained only objects of native origin; one burial had no grave goods; three contained only metal objects or broken glass, and fourteen contained both native and European materials. While the burials in the last two categories were clearly effected after the arrival of Europeans, the absence of contact material in the first category is not necessarily proof that these graves were prehistoric.

Items of daily use found in graves included iron pyrites for starting fire (in five graves), full-sized and miniature bark containers (in six graves), and moccasins and combs (in one grave each). With the exception of a bone needle, which may have been used for netting (in one grave), tools and raw materials were mostly of European origin. These included iron axeheads (in seven graves), metal knife, blade, or chisel (in four graves), pieces of metal (in nine graves), nails (in three graves), broken glass (in three graves), kaolin tobacco-pipe fragments (in three graves), and musket shot (in two graves). Full-sized, miniature, or broken hunting weapons (in nine graves) included a bow, arrows, a quiver, arrow and spear shafts, one bone spearhead, one bone harpoon head, and one whaling harpoon.[48] Stone tools were present in seven graves. Two burials contained strings of beads consisting of circular sections of kaolin pipestems, birchbark, and sheet lead tied to bone rings.[49] Discoidal shell beads were found adjacent to the skeleton(s) in eight graves, bone rings in four graves, small perforated shells in two graves, glass beads in one (or two) graves, and unspecified types of beads in two graves.[50] Whether in some instances the beads had originally been tied or sewn to clothing cannot be determined. Tubular beads only turned up in a burial on the Labrador side of the Strait of Belle Isle.[51]

It was earlier observed that two human images, one male and one female, and a "doll" had been placed into the burial hut of Nonosabasut, Demasduit, and their child, while a male figurine was found in the child's burial on Big Island. Since the gender of the figurines in the burial hut corresponded to that of the interred, the images may have been representations of the dead. Though other Indian groups are not known to have placed human figurines in burials, it was customary among Algonquians to mount a carved representation of the deceased on a wooden upright to mark the grave.[52]

Organic objects in Beothuk burials that may have served as amulets or charms included bird skulls and feet (in three graves) and animal teeth: beaver incisors – which could also have served as tools – (in three graves), perforated animal teeth (in three graves), and seal or unspecified tusks (in three graves).[53] Carved pendant-like bone pieces were recovered from a total of eighteen graves. Single graves contained up to thirty-five of these pieces.[54]

Red ochre either packaged, mixed in the soil, or smeared on objects (recorded in twenty-one graves) and the frequent inclusion of a variety of animal tokens (in ten graves) and carved bone pieces (in eighteen graves) indicate the Beothuk's practice of enlisting supernatural assistance and protection.

The large number and variety of grave goods in chief Nonosabasut's burial hut suggest that a person of high esteem was more lavishly equipped than others. The similar array of objects in the burial of the young child on Big Island may indicate that he was the child of or otherwise related to a person of high status. However, these two burials are exceptional with regard to preservation. In most Beothuk burials, factors determining which grave goods were included with the body of a particular individual cannot be inferred from the archaeological record, due to extensive disturbance of the graves. The poor quality of the skeletal material, moreover, precludes determinations as to gender and age in many cases. Given the practices of other native groups, it is doubtful whether Cormack's statement that "with their women" the Beothuk "bury only their clothes" is correct.[55] Certain items that were included in burials may have been individual belongings such as a "medicine bundle" or tools. Other objects could reflect the status and property of the giver rather than of the deceased. For example, Denys, a Frenchman who lived among Micmac in the seventeenth century, recorded that mourners "competed as to who would make the most beautiful gift."[56]

LIST 1A
AUTHENTICATED BEOTHUK BURIALS

South Coast Including Placentia Bay (Area 1)

1 Rencontre Island, Lower Burgeo group (CjBj-2): remains of one individual found either by Smith McKay, prospector, as recorded by Dawson 1860,462, or found by the Reverend M. Blackmore in 1847, as recorded by Patterson 1892,157 and Howley 1915,334.

2 Hangman's Island, Ragged Islands, Placentia Bay:* remains of one individual found by Benjamin Warren and R.S. Dahl, surveyor, recorded by Howley 1915,292–3 (Fig.25.1).

3 Tilt Island, Ragged Islands, Placentia Bay:* remains of one individual found by Benjamin Warren and R.S. Dahl, recorded by Howley 1915,293–4 (Fig.25.2a).

Bonavista Bay (Area 3)

4 Fox Bar, Bonavista Bay (DeAk-2): remains of three or more individuals, recorded by Carignan 1973,12 (Plate 25.3).

Notre Dame Bay East, Straight Shore, Atlantic Islands (Area 4)

5 Straight Shore (?), opp. Indian Islds., Hamilton Sound:* remains of one individual found by a fisherman and confirmed by Dr Winter of Greenspond in 1834, recorded by Lloyd 1876a,227; Howley 1915,334 (omitted opp. Indian Islds., Hamilton Sound).

6 Musgrave Harbour, ocean beach close to Saltwater Pond:* remains of one individual found in the 1940s by Joseph Mouland; informant Walter Mouland; investigated by Anna Sawicki in 1978 (pers. com.).

7 Phillips Isld, off Western Indian Isld., facing Indian Isld. Tickle (DjAn-1): remains of one individual found by Roland Hoddinott in 1948, recorded by MacLeod 1966, App.II (Plate 25.6).

8 Seal Cove on Fogo Island:* remains of one individual found by Thomas Farrel in 1887, recorded in the article "Discovery of the Red Indian Remains at Fogo," 2 November 1887,4.

9 Spirit Cove, Farmer's Head, New World Island (DiAr-3): remains of one individual found by Scott Wheeler and Lloyd Watkins in 1936–37, recorded by Marshall 1973, ibid. 1974b, Sect.8 (Plate 25.2).

Bay of Exploits (Area 5)

10 Comfort Island, Comfort Cove, cemetery (DiAr-1): a) remains of one individual; b), c) and possibly other places, disturbed bones; found by M.C. Hodder and Jas. Templeton in 1888; recorded in the article "Relict of a Red

* No Borden number has been allocated.

Indian," 22 September 1888; MacDougall 1891,102; Howley 1915,332–3; Locke 1974,14, 21, 28, 29, 30–4, 41.

11 Musslebed Island, Comfort Cove (also called Cranberry Isld.):* remains of one individual found by Kayward Manuels in 1973–74, recorded by James A. Tuck and Sonja Jercik (pers. com.); Marshall 1974b,7.

12 Yellow Fox Island:* remains of several individuals found by J.P. Howley in 1886; recorded in Howley n.d., 7 August 1886, and Howley 1915,291.

13 Swan Island, cemetery (DiAs-9): remains of several individuals found by J.P. Howley in 1886; recorded in Howley n.d., 7 and 16 August 1886, and Howley 1915,289–90; MacLeod 1966, App.IV (Plate 25.4).

14 Swan Island II, about a hundred metres down the coast from the above (DiAs-1): remains of several individuals, found and recorded by Locke 1974,14,29; MacLean 1990a.

15 Long Island:* remains of three individuals found by Diamond Jenness 1927; recorded by Jenness 1929,36–7; Archaeological Survey, Museum of Civilization, Ms. 80–1766 (post 1927); Old System's Catalogue, NF.VIII A No. 126–62.

16 High Greco Island (DiAt-3): remains of one individual found by Jordan Haynes 1925–30; recorded by Devereux 1965b, Ms.735.

Red Indian Lake and Other Lakes (Area 7)

17 Red Indian Lake, northwestern shore, cemetery:* a) burial hut with remains of Nonosabasut, his wife Demasduit, and their child, one other adult, and several children; b) box burial(s); c) scaffold burial(s); found by W.E. Cormack in 1827; recorded by Cormack 1829,323–4 (in Howley 1915,193–4).

Notre Dame Bay West, Incl. New, Seal, Badger, Halls, and Green Bays (Area 8)

18 Charles Arm, eastern shore, a hundred metres from mouth (DiAt-2): remains of one adult and one child under an overhanging rockface in a natural niche in sunken area, found and recorded by Devereux 1966, Ms.740/2.

19 Big (formerly Burnt) Island, Pilley's Tickle: a) remains of one child (DjAw-17); b) remains of one adult (DjAw-18); found by berry pickers, removed by S. Coffin in 1886 and handed over to Jabez Tilley; recorded by Patterson 1892,156; Howley 1915,331–2, Plates XIIb, XXXI, XXXIII, XXXIV, and n.d. chapter 1886,3.

20 Triton Island:* remains of two individuals found by residents around 1875; recorded by Jenness 1934,26, 28; Archaeological Survey, Museum of Civilization, Old System's Catalogue, NF.VIII A No. 90–4.

21 Devil's or Charley's Cove, Indian Head, near Robert's Arm (DjAw-16): remains of two individuals found by B. Anthony and Andrew Burton in the 1960s, recorded by Taylor 1964b; LeBlanc 1973,44.

22 Long Island, Green Bay, The Launch I (DiAv-2): cave burial of carved bone pieces (no skeletal material), found by Winsor and Budgell 1912; Howley 1915, Plate XXXVI, 341; Marshall 1974b,50 (Plate 25.5).

23 Long Island, Green Bay:* cave burial of carved bone pieces (no skeletal material), found and recorded by Jenness, Archaeological Survey, Museum of Civilization, Old System's Catalogue, NF.VIII A No. 95–124.

24 Long Island, Green Bay, North China Head (DjAw-1): cave burial of carved bone pieces (no skeletal material), found by D.W.S. Ryan and the Reverend Mr Rowsell in 1941; recorded by Ryan 1948,41–4; Marshall 1973, 1974a; 1974b, Sect.5.

Northern Peninsula, Strait of Belle Isle, Newfoundland West Coast (Area 9)

25 Indian Cliff, between Bradore and Blanc Sablon, Quebec coast:* remains of two individuals, found by Edward Jones in 1888; recorded by Wintemberg 1928, 1936,25.

LIST IB
RECORDED BURIALS WHOSE BEOTHUK ORIGIN HAS NOT BEEN AUTHENTICATED

South Coast, Including Placentia Bay (Area 1)

1 Sugar Loaf near Salmonier, Placentia Bay: remains of one individual in a rock shelter; found by Mr Curtis; recorded by Lloyd 1875,33.

Bay of Exploits (Area 5)

2 Winter Tickle, NW of Thwart Island: remains of one individual; found by residents; recorded by Jenness 1934,30.

3 Little Black Island: remains of one individual in a ravine; found by residents; recorded by Howley n.d., 13 July 1877.

4 Ochre Pit Island: remains of two individuals; reported by Douglas Ball of Little Burnt Bay; recorded by Devereux 1965b, Ms.735, who found no remains.

5 Pigeon Island, SE of Long Island: found by residents; recorded by Jenness, Old System's Catalogue, NF.VIII A No.169 (piece of sewn birchbark).

Exploits River (Area 6)

6 Red Cliff near Grand Falls, overlooking Exploits River: remains of one individual; found by a resident; reported by anthropologist Zelda Cohen, 1986 (pers. com.).

7 North shore of river, opp. Quesawetquek Brook (prob. Joe Brook), below rock cliff, close to several wigwam hollows: found by J.P. Howley in 1871 and recorded in Howley Papers, CNS Archive, Box 4, file 280.

Red Indian Lake and Other Lakes (Area 7)

8 Millertown: two Indian graves found by Miller's workmen while levelling ground near the bank of the river. William Keilly(?), who saved the graves

from destruction, notified Constable Dawe. Dawe reported the graves to Archbishop Howley in a letter of 31 May 1901 (Howley Papers).

9 Island in Red Indian Lake: Indian burial hut; found by a man known by the name of Old Tom who had lived in Exploits Bay for more than sixty years; recorded by J.G. Bourinot 1868,93.

Notre Dame Bay West, Incl. New, Seal, Badger, Halls, and Green Bays (Area 8)

10 Seal Bay, western shore, 1.5 kilometres SW of Gull Isld.: pieces of birchbark, one with a crimped edge, in a small crevice between rock layers, which was divided by a loose rubble wall into two chambers; found by U. Linnamae; recorded by Devereux 1966, Ms.740/2.

11 Woodward's Cabin Site, Western Arm, New Bay (DiAs-1): this site consisted of a pit 3.96 by 0.91 metres large, filled with an admixture of soil and ochre, no skeletal bones, at one end slabs of rock, charcoal, tuff flakes, and tools; found and recorded by Devereux 1969, vol.I.

12 Kelly Cove, Haywards Island, Green Bay: remains of one individual; found by Mr Ryan's grandfather; recorded by Brenda Rowsell (Canada 1972).

13 Wards Harbour, Long Island, Green Bay: remains of one individual found by residents in 1841; viewed by Methodist minister John S. Addy, 9 November 1841, and recorded by him in his letter to the Wesleyan Missionary Committee, 9 November 1841, MMS: LR, North America, Newfoundland, 1841–42, Box 102, file 12g, no.23; Addy said that several burials of this type had been found previously in this area.

Northern Peninsula, Strait of Belle Isle, Newfoundland West Coast (Area 9)

14 McGrath Island, Hare Bay, close to Little Springs: remains of one individual; found by men who removed gravel for the building of the hospital in St Anthony in the 1930s; the bones were examined by the hospital's Dr Curtis and pronounced to be of Indian origin; Isabel and Mary Pilgrim of Main Brook, Hare Bay, 1987 (pers. com.).

Table 25.1 Beothuk Graves and Grave Goods

Areas: 1 South Coast incl. Placentia Bay; 2 Avalon Peninsula, Conception Bay and Trinity Bay; 3 Bonavista Bay; 4 Notre Dame Bay East, Straight Shore, Atlantic Islands; 5 Bay of Exploits; 6 Exploits River; 7 Red Indian Lake and Other Lakes; 8 Notre Dame Bay West, incl. New, Seal, Badger, Halls, and Green Bays; 9 Northern Peninsula, Strait of Belle Isle, Newfoundland West Coast.

burial number	*1*	*2*	*3*	*4*	*5*	*6*	*7*	*8*	*9*	*10a*	*/b*	*/c*	*11*	*12*	*13*	*14*	*15*	*16*	*17a*	*/b*	*/c*	*18*	*19a*	*/b*	*20*	*21*	*22*	*23*	*24*	*25*
area no.	1	1	1	3	4	4	4	4	4	5	5	5	5	5	5	5	5	5	7	7	7	8	8	8	8	8	8	8	8	9
located on coast				x	x	x																x				x				x
on island	x	x	x				x	x	x	x	x	x	x	x	x	x	x	x					x	x	x		x	x	x	
on lakeshore																			x	x	x									
by a river																														
burial disturbed	x		x	x	x	x	x		x		x	x	x	x	x	x	x	x				x		x	x	x				x
cave/rockshelter	x	x	x	x				x		x	x	x	x	x	x	x	x	x				x	x	x	x	x	x	x	x	x
in/on open ground						x	x																							
on cobble beach									x																					
birchbark canopy	x	x						x	x?						x		x?						x							
hut structure																			x											
box on ground																				x										
scaffold																					x									
stone walls							x	x	x									x				x	x							

burial number	*1*	*2*	*3*	*4*	*5*	*6*	*7*	*8*	*9*	*10a*	*/b*	*/c*	*11*	*12*	*13*	*14*	*15*	*16*	*17a*	*/b*	*/c*	*18*	*19a*	*/b*	*20*	*21*	*22*	*23*	*24*	*25*
rock-slab cover				x			x	x	x									x												x
posit: extended		x							x?									x	x											
flexed										x										x			x							
sitting					x																									
1 individual	x	x	x		x	x	x	x	x	x			x					x		x	x		x	x						
2 individuals				2+																		x			x	x				x
3 individuals																	x													
cemetery										x					x				x											
disturbed remains				x							x	x		x	x	x														
no human remains																											x	x	x	
adult(s)	x	x		x?	x		x		x	x					x		3	x	x			1		x						
adult m/f	m				x?		f?			m							m/f		m/f+					m?						
child															x?		x		1+			1?	1							
wrapped in bark	x						x			x								x		x	x									
in skin								x		x									x				x							
ochre present	x			x		x	x		x	x		x			x	x	x						x	x						
on bones				x						x									x			x								x
on objects				x	x				x		x	x			x	x			x				x	x		x	x	x	x	

Table 25.1 Beothuk Graves and Grave Goods *(cont'd)*

burial number	*1*	*2*	*3*	*4*	*5*	*6*	*7*	*8*	*9*	*10a*	*/b*	*/c*	*11*	*12*	*13*	*14*	*15*	*16*	*17a*	*/b*	*/c*	*18*	*19a*	*/b*	*20*	*21*	*22*	*23*	*24*	*25*
birchbark present	x	x	x		x	x	x	x	x	x	x	x			x	x	x	x		x	x	x	x				x		x	x
grave goods	x	x	x	x	x	x	x	x	x	x	x	x	x	x	x	x	x	x	x		x		x	x	x	x	x	x	x	x
of native origin	x	x	x	x	x	x			x	x	x	x		x	x	x	x	x	x				x	x	x	x	x	x	x	x
(a)rrow/(s)pear	a				s					a					a		a		a											
shafts (b)roken										b					b		b													
quiver w. arrows										x									x											
(b)ow/(b)roken															b/b				b											
miniat. bow & arrows																							x							
bone spearhead	x																													
harpoon head											x																			
stone tool(s)	x		x		x				x							x								2+					x	
utensils																			x											
bone needle						x																								
gaming pieces				x											x															
iron pyrite					2					1					x		1		2											
mocassins																							6							
combs															x															

burial number	*1*	*2*	*3*	*4*	*5*	*6*	*7*	*8*	*9*	*10a*	*/b*	*/c*	*11*	*12*	*13*	*14*	*15*	*16*	*17a*	*/b*	*/c*	*18*	*19a*	*/b*	*20*	*21*	*22*	*23*	*24*	*25*
packaged food																							x							
bead strings										3					x															
disc. shell beads	x		x	x		x			x		x				x	x														
tubular beads																														x
sm. perf. shells	x	x																												
bone rings															x	1	2												1	
unident. beads			x							x																				
ochre package																1?							2							
"medicine bag"										x																				
bird skulls										x							1													
bird feet																							2+							
bone pendants	3+	24		27		3				10+	1	5		1	x	13	15	12					32		5	7+	30	30	35	
beaver incisor				x																							x		x	
tusk	x														x		x													
perf. animal tooth															x	x										x				
seal tooth															x															
birchbark cont.												2					2		3+					16 (in a+b)					2+	

Table 25.1 Beothuk Graves and Grave Goods *(cont'd)*

burial number	*1*	*2*	*3*	*4*	*5*	*6*	*7*	*8*	*9*	*10a*	*/b*	*/c*	*11*	*12*	*13*	*14*	*15*	*16*	*17a*	*/b*	*/c*	*18*	*19a*	*/b*	*20*	*21*	*22*	*23*	*24*	*25*
miniat. canoe replica																			2+				3							
miniature paddles																							x							
miniat. boat replica																			2											
small human image																			3				1							
contact material	x			x	x	x	x	x	x	x	x	x	x	x	x	x	x		x					x		x			x	
knife/blade/chisel	x						x	2																x						
axe/hatchet head	2			1		1	1												1					1		1				
whaling harpoon													x																	
broken glass															x	x													x	
pieces of metal				x			x		x		x			x	x	x	x							x						
kaolin pipe frag.				x											x	x														
nails				x						x					x															
shot/(i)n skull					si							x																		
glass beads	x?																									x				

CHAPTER TWENTY-SIX

Fighting Methods and Peace Tokens

WEAPONS AND SHIELDS

The Beothuk's main weapons in skirmishes were the bow and arrow, which were powerful tools in their hands.[1] They were said to be "Extreemly Dextrous in the use of their Bows & arrows & will when Pressd by an Enemy take 4 arrows 3 between the Fingers of their Left hand with which they hold the Bow & the fourth notchd in the string & Discharge them as quick as they Can draw the bow & with great Certainty."[2] Darts, slings, and wooden clubs, referred to in the record of Sebastian Cabot's voyage in 1508, may also have been employed.[3] Clubs were also seen in a Beothuk mamateek in 1819.[4] Spears were probably reserved for hunting since they were never mentioned in connection with fighting. Once the Beothuk had access to iron tools, axes may have served in hand-to-hand combat. According to John Peyton, Jr's account of Demasduit's capture, Nonosabasut, when trying to wrest his wife from the furriers, brandished an axe and later a dirk.[5]

Unlike the majority of native tribes, the Beothuk never used firearms. It has repeatedly been recorded that the report of a gun alone frightened them into flight.[6] This response was also documented for other native people on the Atlantic coast; Indians in Maine, for example, fell flat on their faces at the sound of gunshot, and the Meherin of New England ran into the woods when visitors fired a gun.[7] But while other native people eventually added firearms to their repertoire of weapons, the Beothuk never overcame their aversion to guns. The captive Demasduit frequently responded to plans for sending out parties to look for Beothuk by saying, "Guns no good." She may have been expressing her conviction that conciliating the Beothuk would not be possible if the English were equipped with guns.[8] Why the Beothuk rejected firearms remains a matter of guesswork. Some writers suggest they simply had no access to guns, though one can argue that, had the Beothuk been determined, they could have traded for guns as other native people did, or taken guns from trappers' cabins or boats; when firearms came into their possession, the Beothuk actually destroyed them.[9]

To protect themselves against missiles or arrows the Beothuk used shields, as was customary among northeastern native people.[10] They were described by Guy and Whitbourne as "wooden targets"; the term target designated "a small round shield."[11] Once their adversaries were equipped with guns the Beothuk probably dispensed with these protective devices, which would have been ineffective against bullets and an encumbrance when swift escape was necessary. At any rate, shields are not mentioned in the records after 1622. In skirmishes on water with native opponents the Beothuk ducked behind the high stem and stern sections of their canoes, which were intended to protect them from arrows.[12] To avoid being shot by whites when travelling on the sea, the Beothuk were said to lie flat on the bottom of their craft.[13]

There is no evidence that the Beothuk used body armour, as depicted in the Newfoundland armorial bearings assigned by letters patent in 1638. Charles Martijn, who has investigated the authenticity of the native attire in that drawing, concluded that the artist may have copied the illustration of Huron in armour that was published by Champlain in 1619.[14]

Whether the Beothuk applied war paint cannot be ascertained. Over and above their routine use of a red ochre mixture (and possibly a black colouring agent), it is not known whether they observed special painting rituals prior to fighting as did tribes on the mainland.[15] The chronicler Thevet wrote in the 1500s that the leader of a war party was carried on the shoulders of his men into battle; however, it is uncertain whether Thevet's description applies to Beothuk.[16]

FIGHTING METHODS WITH OTHER NATIVE GROUPS

Thevet also claimed that the Newfoundland natives were "not warlike but defend themselves when attacked," suggesting that they were not particularly aggressive.[17] Nevertheless, as detailed in Part One, they came into conflict with Inuit who crossed the Strait of Belle Isle from Labrador and with Micmac who came to fish and hunt in southern and western Newfoundland. Inuit started to come over to Newfoundland from the mid-sixteenth century onward. By 1768, John Cartwright recorded that formerly the Beothuk had been embroiled in hostilities with this people. Ranging southward Inuit had "fallen in with Red Indian canoes and … treated all they met as enemies. The Esquimaux in harassing them kept to their own element the water; where their superior canoes [kayaks or umiaks] and missile weapons, provided for killing whales, made them terrible enemies to encounter."[18] This description would imply that the Inuit largely confronted Beothuk on the sea and were able to beat them into retreat. Most likely their victories were due not only to the manoeuvrability of their kayaks and their skills in sea-mammal hunting but also to the size of their groups: sometimes numbering a hundred or more, they would have been far larger than Beothuk hunting or trading parties.[19] In Cartwright's time Inuit no longer came to the northern part of Newfoundland since by then, the region had been settled by the English.

There were hostile encounters between the Beothuk and Micmac as well. Alphonse de Saintonge's description from 1544 leaves it open whether clashes took place on the sea or on land saying that natives from "Cape Breton [Micmac] make war against those from Newfoundland when they go fishing and never grant life to anyone whom they capture unless it be an infant or a young girl."[20] The Beothuk appear to have retaliated in kind and to have been more successful in their fights with Micmac than they were with Inuit. According to Micmac traditions recorded in the 1820s, "in former times, when the several tribes [Micmac and Beothuk] were upon an equality in respect of weapons, the red Indians were considered invincible and frequently waged war upon the rest."[21] The reputation of the Beothuk as fierce fighters prevailed among Micmac until the Beothuk had disappeared from the island. However, once Micmac acquired firearms the Beothuk's superiority in warfare came to an end. According to Micmac lore, hostilities arose in the area of St George's Bay (probably around 1720) when Micmac killed and decapitated some Beothuk. In revenge, the Beothuk fell upon the Micmac at a feast; at a prearranged sign every Beothuk killed his Micmac neighbour.[22] In the ensuing confrontation, in which the Micmac were said to have used firearms while the Beothuk had only bows and arrows, the latter were beaten into retreat. Micmac tradition has it that twenty or thirty years later, Beothuk and Micmac fought at the northern end of Grand Lake and that all Beothuk men, women, and children were massacred.[23] The Beothuk were subsequently excluded from Newfoundland's south and west coasts and from the territory inland from these coasts. Shanawdithit, who was captured in the 1820s, confirmed the Micmac tradition and stated that their enmity was implacable and deadly.[24] She also disclosed that, from infancy, Beothuk were taught to hate Micmac and to crave revenge. If a Beothuk were to make peace with Micmac, he or she would not enjoy a happy afterlife.[25] The Beothuk continued to feed their enmity up to the time of their demise.

STRATEGIES IN CONFLICTS WITH EUROPEANS

In conflicts with Europeans the Beothuk generally acted defensively. The small size of Beothuk bands and their tendency to disperse, aided by the relative independence of individual groups, was not compatible with action in unison on a large scale. No attacks by a sizeable group have been recorded. In chance encounters or when taking revenge, the Beothuk often resorted to ambush or hit-and-run attacks.

In the early period of contact, Beothuk responded to European transgressions by cutting fishing boats from their moorings and by taking away fishing gear or other goods. For example, in 1594 natives, presumably Beothuk, cut the mooring ropes of the two pinnaces and the ship's boat of the *Grace*, an English fishing vessel, which fished in "Pesmark" (probably Presque), Placentia Bay.[26] The boat's crew took the Beothuk's hostile gesture as a warning that worse acts might follow. Fearful "of a shrewder turne of the Savages," they elected to leave.[27] But within a relatively short time neither fishing crews nor settlers could be intimidated or frightened off by such tactics.[28] Thus, in the 1620s, sailors in Trinity Bay who had been robbed of equipment chased Beothuk away from their camp by shooting off their guns. They then carried away the Beothuk's canoes, provisions, and furs.

The Beothuk nevertheless continued to take sails, tools, and other gear from fishermen presumably in retaliation for wrongs they had suffered, including intrusion into their territory. Before launching a raid, the Beothuk carefully observed the object of their offensive from a hiding place and timed their attack in such a way that they were able to slip away before they were discovered.[29] Their most publicized coup was the cutting loose of a large boat owned by John Peyton, Jr. Loaded with produce and ready to proceed to market, it had been tied up for the night at the Peytons' wharf at Sandy Point. The Beothuk hid under this same wharf and, when darkness fell, cut the ropes of the boat under the very noses of the guards. They then brought the boat to a creek down the bay, where they stripped it and allowed it to founder on the rocky shore.[30]

Another strategy was to shoot "dumb arrows," which fell short of their aim, so as to entice the English to come within reach of their deadly projectiles. The Beothuk also employed decoys. For example, they placed a decoy pigeon at the entrance to Shoal Bay and when a group of fishermen passed it without shooting, the Beothuk correctly assumed that they had no guns.[31] As soon as the men rowed ashore, Beothuk who were hiding behind the cliffs discharged a volley of arrows and wounded five of the men. On occasion Beothuk killed or wounded one or two men when they were at work and unarmed.[32] They did not attack furriers on their traplines or in their tilts, although these men often worked alone and remained inland for weeks or months at a time. A Micmac informant later remarked to Howley that if the Beothuk had wished to do so, they could have killed every fishermen (or trapper) without letting themselves be seen, a statement that supports the idea that the Beothuk were not overly aggressive.[33] Unfortunately, the injuries and killings inflicted by the Beothuk increased their reputation as a hostile and dangerous people and provided settlers and furriers with reasons for staging punitive raids. Thus, the Beothuk's cunning surprise attacks ultimately led to further bloodshed as the enraged settlers, equipped with guns, retaliated by shooting at Beothuk while travelling in their canoes and by raiding their camps inland. These attacks caused heavy losses among the Beothuk, while the settlers rarely sustained an injury.[34]

As already noted, when confronted with firearms the Beothuk usually fled. The only precaution to have been recorded was the stringing of a piece of salmon twine from one house to another to raise the alarm.[35] The claim by Micmac that the Beothuk excavated thirty-metre-long tunnels from their wigwams into the forest to allow them to escape unobserved has not been verified.[36]

Though one may assume that the Beothuk developed some strategy for their defence and security, the records lead us to believe that such strategies were not effective. Presumably, their success depended on a complex set of circumstances involving the power of persuasion and inventiveness of "chiefs" and beliefs concerning supernatural support. For example, Shanawdithit disclosed that Beothuk children were told that both Micmac and white men belonged to the "bad spirit" and that making peace with either deprived Beothuk of the benevolence of the "good spirit."[37] If these beliefs resembled those of other native groups, the approval and support of well-disposed supernatural beings would have been an essential ingredient for scoring a victory. A defeat by either Micmac or whites could have been blamed on the superior power of an adverse spirit rather than on adverse conditions. There was also the injunction ("laid down by her people") that those Beothuk who had been in contact with the whites or with Micmac were sacrificed (or threatened with being sacrificed?) to the *munes* (spirits) of the victims slain by either of these groups.[38] This injunction would indicate that securing the good will of supernatural beings was an important ingredient in the Beothuk's defence strategy, and that Beothuk leaders were prepared to resort to severe measures to enforce revenge.

SIGNALS OF PEACE

Although the Beothuk did not acquire guns, they were quick to adopt European tokens of peace. When John Guy hoisted a white flag on his excursion to Trinity Bay in 1612, the Beothuk seem to have understood the sign and waved a white wolfskin in response. They later exchanged the skin for Guy's flag.[39]

Presumably the Beothuk also adopted the "shaking of hands" from Europeans who, on meeting Beothuk, routinely used this gesture to show their peaceful intentions. Thus, in the 1760s the shipmaster Scott, the first settler in the Bay of Exploits, is said to have gone unarmed among a group of Beothuk and to have shaken hands with them to alleviate their fears. On this occasion the Beothuk either did not understand the meaning of this gesture or were unwilling to heed it.[40] About fifty years later, when Capt. David Buchan surprised Beothuk in their camp, he shook hands to make them feel at ease. John Peyton, Jr, and his men, coming upon Beothuk at Red Indian Lake, proceeded in the same manner.[41] In turn, chief Nonosabasut shook hands with many of the men, having first made a lengthy oration.[42]

Beothuk peace tokens as recorded by Guy included loud and forceful speeches, singing and dancing, and the presentation of strings of shells. The highlight of Guy's amiable meeting was the sharing of a meal, which seems to have been an important feature in the process of establishing friendly relations before trade could ensue. The Beothuk contributed dried or smoked meat and a root, and Guy brought bread, butter, raisins, beer, and aqua vitae. A food offering was also recorded by the colonist Henry Crout, who returned to Trinity Bay a year later. On entering a mamateek he found that pieces of roasted meat had been left for him by the fire, though the occupants had disappeared. Crout left "bisket" and cheese, a linen cap, and a napkin in return.[43]

Other signs of peace were the display of bows without strings, together with goods for barter, the display of arrows without points, the placing of bows and arrows on the ground, the holding up of a green spruce or fir branch, and the presentation of a feather taken from the hair of the Beothuk making the offer.[44] Cormack, who set out to search for remnants of the Beothuk in 1827, was said to have been provided with "[Beothuk] hieroglyphics and emblems of peace." Unfortunately, Cormack did not give any details about these peace tokens.[45]

HEAD TROPHIES

Upon killing one of their English enemies, the Beothuk would remove the head so it could be used in a victory feast and possibly also be preserved in the form of a "shrunken head." The best-authenticated incident, mentioned earlier, is that in which the two Royal Navy marines left as hostages with the Beothuk at Red Indian Lake were killed and decapitated. Shanawdithit later related that her mother had done the beheading, and that the Beothuk had celebrated the event immediately after their flight from the scene by impaling one of the heads on a pole and dancing and singing around it. The second head, left in a different location, was the occasion of another feast the following spring. In her sketch of these events she depicted the heads on poles, and drew double circles around them (Plate 10.1); among some native people the drawing of a circle was the first step in a magical ceremony.[46] Accounts of the killing of the first Englishmen to settle in Halls Bay relate that their heads were found stuck on poles.[47] Another head, carried off by the Beothuk "as was their usual custom," was that of the "Indian killer" Rowsell of New Bay. Michael Turpin, an Irishman from Fogo, was beheaded in 1809 and two boys from Twillingate Island suffered the same fate. Two fishermen from Western Bay were ambushed and killed on a beach and their bodies were said to have been found "mutilated in a shocking manner"; possibly they too were found headless.[48] Ben Jore's grandfather was shot and decapitated by Beothuk who subsequently placed the head on a pole and danced around it.[49] Whether the Beothuk also beheaded Micmac is not entirely certain. Of two stories (both describing the same event) that dealt with a Micmac hunter who was killed by Beothuk when he approached a mamateek, only one claims that he was beheaded.[50]

The custom of decapitating their victims was not peculiar to the Beothuk. Friederici, an authority on this topic, concluded that, at the time the Americas were discovered, the taking of head trophies was widely practised by Indians but not by Inuit. Although the custom predominated in Middle and South America, it was also practised by Algonquians in New England and the eastern part of New York. Other Algonquian groups tended to scalp victims and only occasionally cut off heads. Those Northwestern Athapaskans who had not adopted the Inuit custom of mutilating slain enemies also took heads.[51] Eyewitness reports of head-hunting Algonquians include those by Poutrincourt and Champlain. The latter described how in 1603, a victory feast of Algonquians, Montagnais, and Etchemins entailed a warrior's dance around the heads of their slain Iroquoian foes.[52] Closer to home, the taking of Beothuk heads by Micmac was mentioned in Micmac traditions as one of the factors that precipitated hostilities between the two tribes.[53]

Taking the head of an enemy was the first step in the practice of producing "shrunken heads." Since the preparation of these trophies was too difficult and time consuming to be done at the scene of death, and since they required the entire head, the latter were usually carried away to be processed later. Friederici convincingly argues that the taking of heads preceded the practice of scalping.[54] Early Indian pictographs often show slain enemies headless, while the survival of the word "head" as a designation for "scalp" in some native languages is similarly suggestive. Scalping eventually replaced the taking of heads among most Indians of North America, except among the Beothuk.[55] Among some Indian groups scalps not only were visible proof of a warrier's valour but represented a persons soul or spirit. By taking the scalp the power and identity of the scalped person was transferred into the hands of the victor; the preparation and display of scalps was connected with considerable ritual.[56]

Thevet, whose writing may not necessarily refer to the Beothuk, recorded in the 1550s that the inhabitants of Newfoundland removed the facial skin as well as the hair from their enemies' heads and dried them on a circular frame.[57] About two hundred years later, in 1766, Joseph Banks on a visit to Newfoundland was told that the Beothuk were not content with taking their enemies' hair but skinned "the whole face … as far as the upper lip."[58] Banks even received a "scalp of this kind" removed from the head of a Newfoundland fisherman, Sam Frye. Frye had been killed by Beothuk who had subsequently prepared his head in the manner described. A year later, when this trophy fell into the hands of men who knew Frye, they immediately recognized his well-preserved facial features.

The earliest reference to cannibalism among Newfoundland natives is found in reports of Sebastian Cabot's explorations, according to which the natives were said to have consumed human flesh but to have concealed this activity from their "chief." Half a century later, Thevet recorded that the native people in Newfoundland had formerly been cannibals.[59] While there is no record of this practice among Beothuk from the seventeenth century onwards, a Micmac informant told Cormack in the 1820s that the Beothuk devoured each other.[60] The informant did not say whether they had done so in times of starvation like several other native tribes, or whether it was a traditional practice. The consumption of human flesh in rituals connected with war has been recorded among Inuit as well as Montagnais, Eastern Cree, and Abenaki, and it is possible that at some point the Beothuk observed a similar custom.[61]

CHAPTER TWENTY-SEVEN

The Beothuk Language

Wordlists obtained from three Beothuk captives who lived in the Exploits River region represent all that is known of the Beothuk language. The first list was compiled in 1792, others were collected in the early 1800s. The varied histories of the informants and their contributions are presented in the first sections of this chapter. Generally, Beothuk terms for everyday objects and phrases were recorded by untrained listeners using improvised English phonetic spelling. Since the compilers of the lists were not familiar with Beothuk pronunciation, their interpretations of what they heard have resulted in rather unreliable renditions of the words.[1] The wordlists are therefore of uncertain quality. They also represent only a rudimentary and unbalanced portion of the Beothuk language, since few verb forms and little grammatical and structural information are included in the lists. This deficiency led to considerable controversy among nineteenth-century linguists with regard to the linguistic affinities of the Beothuk tongue. Linguists today tend to agree that Beothuk would be of Algonquian origin.

Considering that Newfoundland fishermen and settlers lived alongside the Beothuk for more than three hundred years, it is unfortunate that so little has been recorded of their language. Quite singular is the case of a man of unknown nationality who had learned to speak Beothuk "very well." Henry Crout from the English colony in Cupids recorded in 1613 that this man had once lived with the Beothuk for five years, but nothing further is known about him.[2]

In 1768 Governor Hugh Palliser advocated the capture of a Beothuk because he wished to become acquainted with Beothuk customs and language. In response to his offer of a reward, furriers brought a four-year-old boy (known as John August) to him. But Palliser lamented that this child was too young to give any information about his people, not even "a word of their language."[3]

In the early 1800s several people reportedly learned Beothuk words from captives. Among them were the fisherman/furrier William Cull, his wife, and possibly one of his sons, who were taught by the Beothuk woman Cull had captured in Gander Bay in 1803.[4] This woman, whose name has not been recorded, lived in the Cull household for an entire winter while waiting to be brought back to her people. The Cull family's knowledge of Beothuk was neither put to paper nor utilized in any other way. When Captain Buchan required guides to take him to the Beothuk settlement at Red Indian Lake in 1810–11, he hired Cull and two other furriers. But there was no mention in his report that Cull could speak Beothuk; Buchan merely expressed his regret at being entirely ignorant of the Beothuk language.[5] He later commented: "To me their tongue was a complete jargon uttered with much rapidity, and vehemence, and differing from all other Indian tribes that I had heard, whose language, generally, flows in soft melodious sounds."[6]

Another person to learn Beothuk words was Mrs Jure, a servant in the Peyton household when Shanawdithit lived there. When questioned by Howley in 1886, Mrs Jure, then about seventy-five years old, was able to recall twenty-one Beothuk terms and said that Shanawdithit had complimented her for the purity of her pronunciation.[7] Mrs Jure corrected several misspelt words in a vocabulary shown to her by Howley and gave the pronunciation of others, affording Howley a clue to the phonetics of the language.

Cormack, who had ample opportunity to do so, never mentioned whether he had acquired any skills in speaking Beothuk from Shanawdithit. He noted that the language abounded with diphthongs such as "sh" and "th" and included the letter "r," which is not found in Micmac and Montagnais. He claimed that the Beothuk had no characters to serve as hieroglyphics or letters but had "a few symbols or signatures." These, however, have not been preserved.[8]

THE OUBEE WORDLIST

In the summer of 1791 a party of fishermen raided a Beothuk camp near Charles Brook, Bay of Exploits, and captured a young girl. Her Beothuk name was Oubee. She was taken into the home of Thomas Stone of Trinity and in 1793 moved with him and his family to England, where she died within one or two years.[9] While Oubee was living with the Stones in the community of Trinity, Capt. G.C. Pulling, then stationed in Trinity Harbour, was an occasional guest in their house and was thus able to meet and talk to Oubee.[10] Pulling used the opportunity to collect a list of 111 Beothuk words from her because he hoped to be entrusted with a peace mission to the Beothuk, the success of which would depend on his ability to communicate with them. In his 1792 report about settler/Beothuk relations, Pulling mentioned that "I know a few words in their language w/ch I mean to Pen down." The first entry in his list reads "Ou=bee – The name of y/e Indian girl who lives w/th Mr Stone."[11] Pulling attached the wordlist to his report on settler/Beothuk relations which he submitted to authorities in England in the spring of 1793. Both documents were filed among the papers of the Earl of Liverpool (now in the collection of the British Library) and did not come to the attention of researchers until the 1960s.[12]

While Pulling was still stationed in Trinity Harbour, he gave a copy of a preliminary version of his report, presumably with the vocabulary attached to it, to Dr G.C. Jenner, medical practitioner in the community and partner of the Reverend John Clinch.[13] In 1797 Jenner sent the report on relations between settlers and Beothuk to Governor William Waldegrave in response to Waldegrave's proclamation advocating the protection of the native population.[14] Three years later Clinch submitted a copy of Pulling's wordlist (received either from Pulling himself or through Jenner) to Governor Charles Morris Pole. The list was subsequently entered into the Colonial Secretary's Correspondence as "The Rev. John Clinch of Trinity's Vocabulary of the Language of the Native Indians residing in the Island of Newfoundland."[15] Linguists who found Clinch's vocabulary in the government records but were not aware of Pulling's wordlist believed Clinch to have been the compiler. However, the evidence shows that Captain Pulling was the original recorder, and his spellings of Beothuk words, as pronounced by Oubee, would be more accurate than those in Clinch's list, divergences being the result of copy errors. Oubee's vocabulary, copied from Clinch's listing, was published in the *Harbour Grace Standard* in 1888 and a few years later by the Reverend George Patterson, who used the *Standard* as his source.[16] The linguist Albert S. Gatschet examined and published the Oubee vocabulary in the *Transactions of the Royal Society of Canada* in 1890; the original wordlist as collected by Pulling was published by Hewson in 1978.[17]

A VOCABULARY OBTAINED FROM DEMASDUIT

Demasduit, known among the settlers as Mary March, was captured in March 1819 at Red Indian Lake by the John Peytons, father and son, and men employed by them.[18] For a short period she was placed under the care of the Reverend John Leigh, episcopal minister in Twillingate, then briefly taken to St John's, and subsequently returned to Twillingate. According to Leigh, Demasduit had a remarkable gift for mimicry, which enabled her to learn the language she heard quickly. Before she could properly express herself, her signs and "dumb Crumbo were curiously significant."[19] Once she had achieved a reasonable understanding of English, Leigh compiled a list of about 180 Beothuk words. He gave a copy of this vocabulary to John Peyton, Jr, of Exploits Islands and there is circumstantial evidence that Peyton gave a copy of it in 1827 to W.E. Cormack.[20] In the late 1800s, this version of Demasduit's vocabulary was published, with varying degrees of accuracy, by T.G.B. Lloyd (1875), J. Hatton and M. Harvey (1883), Albert S. Gatschet (1885), and the Reverend George Patterson (1893); in 1950 it was included in an article on the Beothuk in the *Twillingate Sun*.[21] The original has since been lost.

Leigh also presented a copy of the vocabulary to the Society for the Propagation of the Gospel in London, together with a covering letter dated 30 July 1819.[22] Unfortunately, the wordlist as well as Leigh's letters from 1819 are no longer among the institution's papers. However, a copy of the vocabulary was preserved by Capt. Hercules Robinson of *HMS Favorite*, who visited Leigh after the minister had been transferred to Harbour Grace in 1820.

Robinson was greatly intrigued by the story of Demasduit and wrote down what Leigh had told him about her. He also copied the wordlist and published it in 1834.[23] It includes twenty-four terms from the Oubee vocabulary, which Leigh had apparently added to his Demasduit wordlist during a visit with the Reverend Mr Clinch in Trinity in August 1819.[24] Robinson noted that Mary March's native name was Waunathoake, information that has not been recorded elsewhere.[25]

Leigh's own copy of the extended Demasduit wordlist, that is, the list that contained items from the Oubee vocabulary, found its way into the Provincial Archives of Newfoundland and Labrador in 1957. The title page of this copy reads: "A Vocabulary of The Native Red Indians' Language, Newfoundland, from Mary March, a female red Indian, who was caught by Mr John Peyton of the Exploits on the fifth March, 1819, and presented to the Society for propagating the Gospel in foreign parts by the Rev'd. John Leigh, Episcopal Missionary, Twillingate."[26] Pages of English glosses starting with the letters C, D, H, M, N, and W are missing; fortunately, the missing words can be reconstructed from the vocabulary copied and published by Robinson, which contains 203 terms and ten numerals. Hewson has identified 120 that are new or substantially different from the terms given by Oubee.[27]

Rev. John Leigh was not the only person to collect Beothuk words from Demasduit. In a letter to the Methodist Committee in London dated 10 July 1819, John Pickavant, Methodist clergyman in Carbonear, tells of his attempts to elicit some words from the captive before she could understand English. During several interviews with Demasduit, Pickavant "used various methods (for no one here understands their language) with a design of finding out what views she had of a Supreme being. I was sorry to find she could not enter into my design – with difficulty I got her to count numbers as far as 10 in her own language – and likewise to name several other things which I presented to her."[28] This account is followed by the terms for the numbers one to ten and for boy, girl, fire, and dog, which do not substantially differ from those of the other known vocabularies.[29]

WORDS AND PHRASES SUPPLIED BY SHANAWDITHIT

In 1823 Shanawdithit, together with her mother and sister, surrendered to furriers who found them in the woods. They were sick and starved and two of the women died shortly thereafter; Shanawdithit survived and was taken into the household of John Peyton, Jr, on Exploits Islands. In October 1827, before setting out on his second expedition to make contact with the Beothuk, W.E. Cormack briefly stayed with the Peytons.[30] His equipment for the expedition appears to have included a "vocabulary," and after his return, Cormack reported to the Boeothick Institution that he had obtained a vocabulary "consisting of 200–300 words."[31] Though Shanawdithit was then living with the Peytons, Cormack was their guest only for a short time and could not have elicited a long wordlist from her. It is therefore assumed that this vocabulary was a copy of the Demasduit vocabulary that John Peyton, Jr, had received from Rev. John Leigh.[32]

When Cormack returned from his unsuccessful expedition, he arranged for Shanawdithit to be transferred to St John's under the auspices of the Boeothick Institution.[33] She remained under Cormack's tutelage until the end of January 1829 and stayed for part or all of this time in his house.[34] When she arrived in St John's, Shanawdithit spoke "so little English that only those who were accustomed to her gibberish, could understand her." But under Cormack's instruction she acquired confidence and became an invaluable source of information through her stories and drawings alike.[35]

On 10 January 1829, in response to his election as member of the Natural History Society in Montreal, Cormack sent to the society "a list of words and phrases of the Boeothic or Red Indian language gathered from a female of that tribe at present residing in my house here."[36] This vocabulary is no longer among the society's papers. That Cormack had collected Beothuk words from Shanawdithit is confirmed by Mr Sweetland, who had known both Cormack and Shanawdithit. In an article published in 1862 under the pen-name Avalonus, Sweetland mentions that "Cormack had formed a pretty large vocabulary during Shanawdithit's residence with him."[37]

When Cormack left for England at the end of January 1829, he took all or most of his notes as well as Shanawdithit's drawings and wordlists with him. At a later date he appears to have given the wordlists to an acquaintance. A note in his papers dated 24 June 1851 states that "the vocabulary of the Red Indians is (I think) in Dr Yates' possession," along with drawings by Shanawdithit and a variety of artifacts.[38] This man could have been Dr James Yates, antiquarian, fellow of the Geological, Linnean, and Royal Societies, and secretary to the council of the British Association (appointed in 1831), whom Cormack may have known from his university days in Glasgow in 1811.[39] It is assumed that Dr Yates forwarded the vocabulary to Dr Richard King, member of the council of the British Association and secretary of the Ethnological Society, who, in turn, gave it to his friend, Professor Robert G. Latham, at the time a distinguished scholar in the field of comparative linguistics. After examining this Beothuk vocabulary, Latham published his conclusions in 1850 and thereby became the first linguist to comment on the Beothuk language.[40]

In the 1880s, J.P. Howley enquired with Latham about Cormack's vocabulary. When Latham searched through his (old) papers he discovered two wordlists, one of which – the list of words collected from Shanawdithit – Latham called the "King Vocabulary." He sent copies of both lists to Howley, Albert S. Gatschet, the Bureau of American Ethnology, and the linguists John Powell and John Campbell.[41] In the King Vocabulary, which contains previously unknown words and phrases, the entries are made under alphabetical headings. The list concludes with the Beothuk terms for "don't be afraid," "not hurt you," and "we come to be friends," which were presumably intended for use in a hoped-for encounter.[42] Hewson deduced from the phrases "Shinadonthit is alive & well lives with the English," and "Doodebewshet [Shanawdithit's mother] is alive" that they were obtained from Shanawdithit. He also believes that the term Moomeshduck is the name of Doodebewshet's father (Shanawdithit's grandfather).[43]

Latham considered the second set to be a copy of the Demasduit vocabulary, which in his opinion was "both like and unlike" the King Vocabulary. He addedd: "It is a very queer one besides the Beothuck it gives us a fair amount of Micmac words, Banikee [Abenaki], fewer of the Mountain Indians and about half a dozen of Eskimo, and finally three columns of Norwegian."[44] A note in Cormack's papers suggests that he had compared Beothuk words with those from other native languages and concluded that they were entirely different.[45] Cormack had also considered it possible that Beothuk derived from northern European languages, such as "Greenland, Iceland, Lapland etc." If this had been the case, the relationship could have thrown "some light upon the course of peopling the Northern Hemisphere."[46]

In the early 1880s, probably before Latham discovered the King Vocabulary among his papers, J.P. Howley provided the linguist Albert S. Gatschet with a list of 245 Beothuk terms and a reference to a Beothuk song, the latter taken from a scribbled note by Cormack.[47] Most of the words came from the Demasduit vocabulary to which Howley had added Beothuk numerals, names of months, terms corresponding to English glosses with the initials A and B, and words from Shanawdithit's drawings.[48] Howley also sent a copy of this list to Sir William Dawson, principal of McGill University in Montreal. Dawson sent what was believed to have been a copy of this list to the Reverend Silas T. Rand, who subsequently made a copy available to Gatschet. Gatschet considered that Rand's list was a previously unknown Cormack vocabulary and called it the "Montreal Copy."[49] Though it contained obvious copy errors, he argued that in many instances, the words appeared "to have a more original form preferable to the one copied by Mr Howley" from Cormack's notes.[50] One may speculate that this copy, which had come to Gatchet in such a roundabout way, contained material from the vocabulary that Cormack had sent to the Natural History Society in Montreal in January 1829.

Hewson, who compared the Beothuk terms Cormack had collected from Shanawdithit with the vocabularies obtained from Oubee and Demasduit, notes that about 120 words or phrases in Shanawdithit's vocabulary are new or distinct from previously known ones, and that there are eleven new numerals as well as the names of months.[51] In his definitive work on the Beothuk language, Hewson has integrated the vocabularies collected from Oubee, Demasduit, Shanawdithit, and Mrs Jure into one master wordlist of 325 English glosses plus twenty-one numerals and the names of the months.[52]

BEOTHUK SONGS

In 1912, when Speck questioned Santu, daughter of a Beothuk man and his Micmac wife, she was seventy-five years old and unable to recall more than a few Beothuk words. She alleged that in conversation, the Beothuk used their hands a great deal. The words she remembered, listed here in the notes, differ considerably from terms in the Beothuk wordlists.[53] Santu also knew a Beothuk song of which Speck made a wax phonograph. He transcribed the tune of the song and published it in 1922, but the syllables, which Santu was "unable to explain because they had no sequence of meaning to her," were too inarticulate to be taken down.[54] This record is now in the collection of Smithsonian Institution in Washington DC.[55]

A note in the Cormack Papers refers to Beothuk song(s), though it is not clear whether the words are part of a song or concern subjects of songs. They are very difficult to decipher.[56]

THE TERM BEOTHUK

Until the 1820s, the Beothuk were commonly known as "savages," "aborigines," "natural inhabitants," "Indians," "red men," "red or wild Indians," or were referred to by similarly nonspecific terms.[57] Not until 1819, when a Beothuk wordlist was obtained from Demasduit, was the term "beathook – Red Indian" disclosed, though it was not applied at that time.

The name Beothuc or Boeothic was first recorded by Bishop Inglis in his diary of a tour around Newfoundland in 1827. After his encounter with Shanawdithit and John Peyton, Jr, he noted that the tribe was called "the Boeothic Indians, such is their own name."[58] It is assumed that the bishop heard this name from John Peyton, Jr, who had learned it from Shanawdithit. Three months later, William E. Cormack proposed the name Boeothick Institution for a society formed for the purpose of opening communication with the aborigines of Newfoundland.[59] Since the formation of the society preceded his visit to the Peytons, and since there is no evidence that Cormack had already met Shanawdithit, it is probable that he too had heard the name Boeothick from John Peyton, Jr.[60] In his subsequent correspondence with members of the institution, Cormack spelled the name Boeothuck, Beothuck, Boeothic, and Boeothick(s).[61] In a letter to John Stark he noted: "Boeothuck is the pronunciation of the word in question – or Boethuck, or Boethick, the emphasis being on the diphthong oe and almost dropping the o."[62] The wordlists collected from Demasduit and Shanawdithit give "beathook," "behathook," "beothuck," "beothuk," "beothick," and "boeothuc."[63] Hewson advocates "Beothuk" since it adequately expresses the short "u" sound in the second syllable; the term most likely denotes a plural (k being the animate plural ending), although among English speakers Beothuk is generally used to denote both singular and plural.[64] In his *Etymology of "Beothuk"*, Hewson demonstrates a linguistic relationship between components of the word Beothuk with words in other Algonquian languages denoting man or human being to which an animate plural ending has been attached.[65] Gatschet had also concluded that Beothuk stood for man, though his argumentation differs from Hewson's because he did not consider Beothuk an Algonquian language.[66]

Alphonse de Saintonge, who travelled with Jean-François de la Rocque de Roberval along the Newfoundland coast in 1542–43 and briefly described Newfoundland's native population, claimed that they were called "Tabios." This name has not been verified.[67]

Santu remembered that her father Kop had mentioned the name "Osa yan a" (by modern orthography Osaqana) as that of "a Beothuk tribe"; according to Speck this name was known among the Micmac.[68]

IS BEOTHUK AN ALGONQUIAN LANGUAGE?

The question whether or not Beothuk is part of the Algonquian phylum has not been resolved entirely, although there is now a tendency to believe in an Algonquian affinity. Nineteenth-century linguists were divided between those who thought Beothuk to be of Algonquian origin and those who believed that it constituted an altogether separate linguistic group.[69] The most prominent defender of the latter view was Albert S. Gatschet, from the American Bureau of Ethnology in Washington, who investigated the extant Beothuk wordlists, examined Beothuk phonetics, morphology, and the different parts of speech, and compared Beothuk with the Inuit, Tinné (Dene), Iroquoian, and Algonquian languages. Although he determined some Algonquian word similarities, Gatschet concluded that the Beothuk phonetic system, as well as some grammatical forms and much of the basic vocabulary, differed so completely that an Algonquian affinity could not be suggested.[70] Brinton (1891) essentially agreed, suggesting that words that were similar to Algonquian forms could have been borrowed. While there were slight coincidences with Inuit dialects, he thought "the main body of the idiom stands alone, without affinities."[71]

Among the linguists who believed that Beothuk was an Algonquian language, however obscurely related, were Robert G. Latham (1850), John Powell (1891), and Rev. John Campbell (1893).[72] Powell, however, was doubtful and Latham, in his second publication (1862), became more cautious, saying that Beothuk was "Algonkin rather than aught else."[73] Latham adduced some parallels between Beothuk and Tinné, or Dene, dialects, especially Taculli (Carrier) but did not consider them proof of an affinity.[74] Dr S.M. Dawson thought the little Beothuk had in common with other American languages would "point to Tinné or Chippewan affinities," but he would not insist on it.[75] Sir William Dawson of Montreal, in his book *Fossil Men and Their Modern Representatives* (1880), also suggested that the Beothuk were of Tinné or Chippewayan (Athapaskan) stock. This opinion was based on his theory that the Tinné had at one time "extended quite to the Atlantic coast" and on his examination (in Edinburgh) of two Beothuk skulls, but not on linguistic evidence.[76]

Differing opinions concerning the affiliation of Beothuk have been carried over into the twentieth century. The linguists Sapir (1949), Greenberg (1953), and Gursky (1964) consider an Algonquian relationship probable, although of a fairly distant or divergent type.[77] Voegelin and Voegelin (1946, 1963) support Gatschet's argument and explain Algonquian elements in Beothuk as the result of borrowing.[78] Gursky argues against such a possibility on the grounds that Algonquian words in Beothuk are part of the basic vocabulary, and he asserts that such words are rarely borrowed.[79] Goddard, specialist in Algonquian languages at the Smithsonian Institution, is of the opinion that "the long conjectured relationship with the extinct and poorly documented Beothuk language of Newfoundland must continue to be regarded with serious reservation as long as the phonology and morphology remain so completely unknown as to make impossible an objective evaluation of the forms recorded."[80] In the *Handbook of North American Indians* (1978) he cautiously states that the Beothuk language "does not look Algonquian on its face, and if it is related to Algonquian it can only be on a very deep time level."[81]

An extensive study of the Beothuk language has since been undertaken by John Hewson of Memorial University, St John's. Hewson has traced and collated the wordlists from Oubee, Demasduit, and Shanawdithit and has compared Beothuk terms with word forms of the hypothetical Algonquian protolanguage (see below).[82] This research tool was not available to nineteenth-century linguists, whose evidence for relationships was based on word similarities. Hewson's method made use of regular sound correspondences or reflexes, applying them to the data of the Proto-Algonquian lexicon and demonstrating grammatical or structural resemblances where the sound correspondences also correlate.[83] Since he was working with poorly transmitted words, Hewson has found the full operation of this comparative method difficult, though he was able to trace coherent reflexes of the Proto-Algonquian consonants in almost sixty Beothuk words. Analysis of the structure of the few verb forms of Beothuk that were available also revealed that, in several cases, whole words could be interpreted in terms of an Algonquian base or formative when using the conjunct forms of the verbs.[84]

John Hewson points out that if Beothuk is an Algonquian language, it is markedly divergent in its vocabulary. He nevertheless maintains, and is supported in this view by several other linguists, that there is sufficient evidence to consider Beothuk as related to the Algonquian family of languages. However, neither the time depth nor the exact nature of this relationship can be established.[85]

All Algonquian languages are presumed to be derived from a single precursor. This hypothetical language, Proto-Algonquian, has been recreated by a collaborating group of linguists from studies of today's Algonquian languages. It is estimated that Proto-Algonquian was spoken about 2,500 to 3,000 years ago.

The homeland of this parent language is believed to have been the area between Georgian Bay and Lake Ontario.[86] According to Goddard, linguistic evidence suggests that when the original Proto-Algonquian-speaking nucleus expanded, it became fragmented into ten or so distinct and decreasingly interacting Algonquian speech communities, which were the forerunners of the three Plains Algonquian languages, six Central Algonquian languages including Cree, Montagnais/Naskapi, and Ojibwa, and Proto-Eastern Algonquian.[87] This last language continued to develop for a time before breaking up into Micmac, Maliseet, and Abenaki, with the result that languages of the eastern group differ less among themselves than the languages of the entire Algonquian family taken together. The extent of their differences nevertheless suggests that they diverged about 2,000 years ago. Central and Plains Algonquian languages do not share innovations that set them apart from the rest of the family. This means that they diverged into separate entities earlier than the three Eastern Algonquian languages; their time depth is thought to be equivalent to the time depth of the Algonquian family as a whole, that is, about 2,500 to 3,000 years. A similar time depth would apply, as a minimum, to the Beothuk language, given its divergence from the other languages in the Algonquian speech community to which it may belong.

CHAPTER TWENTY-EIGHT

Concluding Discussion

The information on Beothuk culture presented in the foregoing chapters gives a general idea of the Beothuk's appearance, way of life and daily activities, their tools and techniques for procuring subsistence, some belief-related practices, and the dramatic changes in population size and distribution that occurred after contact with Europeans. The information is multidisciplinary in that it comes from historic records, archaeological excavations and surveys, linguistic investigations, folklore, and, to an extent, from recent biological studies of large mammal populations. While many cultural aspects are obscure and many questions remain unanswered, the accumulated data allow for some new syntheses.

For some time it has been generally accepted that, as a cultural unit, the Beothuk did not differ significantly from other northeastern Indian groups, with whom they shared cultural traits involving all aspects of life and death. However, their origin and affiliation remained a matter of speculation until the 1970s. As shown in the last chapter, several nineteenth-century linguists, notably Albert S. Gatschet, believed that the Beothuk language was entirely different from that of other North American tribes and belonged to a separate linguistic family.[1] This view, taken with the mystery surrounding the Beothuk, opened the door to unrestrained speculation about their origin: the Beothuk's sun worship, burial customs, and use of ochre, also known from ancient Egypt, inspired the proposal that Beothuk religious practices and those of the ancient Egyptians derived from a common source; another theory placed the Beothuk as descendants of the Tartars of Asia.[2]

Linguistic investigations by John Hewson in the 1970s have laid these speculations to rest. Hewson has argued convincingly that an Algonquian affiliation is more than likely, though the available evidence was not sufficient to decide whether Beothuk belongs to the Central or Eastern Algonquian type.[3] That Hewson expected it to be Central agrees with more recent archaeological research that points to a prehistoric Beothuk affiliation with Central Algonquians rather than with an eastern group such as Micmac.

Also in the 1970s, another approach was taken by Janet E. Chute, who compared Beothuk practices and bone, hide, and wooden artifacts with those of Montagnais/Naskapi and Micmac to see whether the Beothuk were culturally distinct from their Algonquian neighbours. She also examined Beothuk cultural traits to see whether they could be traced to the Maritime Archaic Indian tradition.[4] As a result of her comparisons, Chute postulated that the Beothuk had maintained a separate cultural existence from the surrounding Algonquian-speaking tribes. According to her model, prehistoric interior-oriented Algonquian (or Proto-Algonquian) speakers moved eastward and assimilated the small, already established coastal Maritime Archaic Indian population or their descendants, so that the Beothuk culture represents an admixture of two traditions. The interior-oriented component is represented by the shapes of the Beothuk canoe, snowshoes, and moccasins, while the maritime component, which is the larger one, is represented by a marine-oriented subsistence economy and symbolism, an extensive use of red ochre in burials, a sophisticated bone-and-antler carving and incising industry, eyed needles, bone awls, long-bone beamers, and barbed and toggling harpoons. Chute noted that ancient maritime-culture traits have survived longest in the greatest number in Newfoundland, though she did not imply that the Beothuk were direct descendants of the Maritime Archaic Indians.

Over the last two decades extensive archaeological investigations have firmly established the Beothuk's descent from the prehistoric Little Passage Indians, who directly followed the earlier Beaches population. The line of descent of the Beaches complex from the immediately preceding Cow Head complex is less clear. At the present state of knowledge a continuity is proposed, based on chronological and geographical considerations and on the style of some of the Cow Head tools, which is believed to represent a link with the Beaches material. Tracing ancestral populations further back in time becomes more difficult due to a gap in the archaeological record in Newfoundland for the millennium between the end of the Maritime Archaic Indian occupation and the earliest Cow Head complex sites. Although certain resemblances between stone tools might be leads, any interpretation of these observations can only be speculative. James A. Tuck offers two possible alternatives or a combination of these alternatives: The Cow Head people might represent descendants of a remnant of the Maritime Archaic people who had been "archaeologically invisible" in Newfoundland for a millennium and then re-emerged in the archaeological record around AD 1 (1950 BP); some of the flaked-stone material of both groups, such as the large bifaces, is similar enough to consider a cultural relationship. An alternative would be an expansion at that time of an Indian population from southern Labrador across the Strait of Belle Isle. Evidence for this second scenario consists of considerable similarities that had developed by the end of the first millennium AD (1000 BP) among Recent Indian complexes in southern and central Labrador (Point Revenge complex) and those in Newfoundland (Beaches complex); this evidence includes use of Ramah chert, style of projectile points, and location of campsites in inner coastal regions.

A possible combination of these two scenarios would be the persistence of an Archaic Indian people in Newfoundland – not yet recorded archaeologically – who, during the latter half of the first millennium AD, began to make contact or increased already existing contact with Recent Indians in Labrador, resulting in trade for Ramah chert and the production of similar tool types. Other possible interpretations by Tuck and others are at the discussion stage. Robbins and Loring have come to favour an expansion hypothesis and propose the reoccupation of Newfoundland by a new Indian population from Labrador around AD 1.[5]

Although the Beothuk shared many cultural traits with other native groups, certain traits clearly reflect Beothuk modifications; the Beothuk may also have imbued some practices with new significance. Many modifications were relatively minor, but a few resulted in notable new functions or styles that are considered typically Beothuk. One should remember, though, that our idea of what is characteristic of the Beothuk is based on comparisons with traits of other native people and is unlikely to coincide with the Beothuk's own perception of their identity. It should also be noted here that all so-called typical Beothuk traits or features were based on generally known elements. Objects or practices that had no equivalent, however rudimentary, in other native cultures have not been identified.

The modifications that have been detected display much ingenuity and inventiveness. For example, Beothuk caribou fences were often made from large trees and were thus almost impenetrable; they were also more extensive than those of other northern hunters. This gave the Beothuk greater control over the movement of migrating caribou herds and enabled them to kill large numbers of animals. They stockpiled the surplus meat in special-purpose storehouses for the winter. The Beothuk also achieved a high level of sophistication in the construction of winter dwellings. The walls of some of their early-nineteenth-century multisided winter mamateeks were built from trunks of trees that had been flattened on the sides and placed vertically and contiguously into the ground. The mamateeks were then bermed on the outside. Typically Beothuk were the pentagonal, hexagonal, and octagonal house shapes and the single and conjoined sleeping hollows placed inside around the central fireplace.

Among the artifacts that have become symbols of Beothuk uniqueness, the most prominent is the half-moon-shaped birchbark canoe. Although Beothuk methods of canoe construction generally conformed to those of other North American native people, the Beothuk incorporated a keelson into the bottom of the craft, accompanied by sharply flaring sides. They also extended the end sections to an unprecedented height and had the upward-curving sheer (known as hogging) come to a point in the centre. These new features not only upgraded the performance of the canoe but set it apart visually from those of other tribes. While the straight-bottom canoe design is thought to have been the standard type, the version with a strong curvature to the bottom, which gave the canoe a half-moon shape in profile, is the one that caught the eye of Europeans and has since become a hallmark of Beothuk culture.

The practice of coating face, body, and belongings with red ochre distinguished the Beothuk visibly from other groups and was a mark of tribal identity. Maritime Archaic Indians had used ochre, and it figured among neighbouring Algonquian tribes in the early historic period; but the extent to which the Beothuk applied this colouring agent and the significance it held for them is believed to have been peculiar to their tribe.

Other typically Beothuk features were their mythological emblems, which remain unexplained, and their creation of spectacular, pendant-like carvings. Their burial context and resemblance to animals or parts thereof indicate symbolic representation and a belief-related function; but illuminating details elude us. Although Athapaskans and, in the more distant past, Palaeo-Eskimos and Maritime Archaic Indians produced carvings of a comparable type, the style and variety of the Beothuk pieces are considered to be characteristic of their culture group.

Some cultural traits exhibited by the Beothuk in the eighteenth and early nineteenth centuries had formerly been common among a number of native groups who had since abandoned them, indicating that the Beothuk adhered to traditions more rigorously and for a longer time. A striking example is their continued use of bows and arrows, which other native groups had exchanged for guns. The Beothuk also continued to subsist through traditional means and made their clothing exclusively from skins, in contrast to neighbouring groups who adopted European foodstuffs such as flour, dried peas, beans, and prunes and used blanket material for the production of their apparel. As late as the nineteenth century, the Beothuk decapitated slain enemies and danced around their heads in victory feasts, a custom that other tribes had long since relinquished.

The Beothuk's tendency to preserve traditional traits would have been enhanced by their relative isolation in an island habitat. Contact with mainland tribes was probably sporadic and exposure to outside influences limited. During the historic period the Beothuk were only marginally involved in conflicts between native groups on the mainland and seem not to have had native allies. The considerable size of the island and the projected smallness of the tribe enabled the Beothuk to retreat to less-accessible harbours and coves, away from the cod-fishing grounds, where they continued with their traditional way of life for nearly two hundred years after explorers first came to the island. Since the cod-fishing fleets returned to Europe for the winter, the Beothuk were able to secure European implements by scavenging beaches and stages for items that had been discarded; this opportunity, combined with the fact that they did not acquire guns and so did not require ammunition, diminished their need to engage in trade. As a result, the Beothuk's experience of European intrusion differed substantially from that of mainland groups, which were unable to defend their land against European settlers who wanted to farm. In addition, in the process of living alongside Europeans, mainland Indians were introduced at an early stage of colonization to alcohol and several deadly diseases.

However, the strategy of retreat and isolation, which allowed the Beothuk to retain their independence at first, began to work against them once English settlers moved into Notre Dame Bay and encroached on major resources. From the 1760s onward, competition for subsistence and animosity and the Beothuk's need for revenge led to a vicious cycle of violence and retaliation. Although these conflicts would have contributed to a reduction of the Beothuk population, their eventual extinction was due to a combination of circumstances ranging from environmental to cultural, historical, and biological factors.[6] The seasonal, migratory nature of the Beothuk's resource base was salient. Theoretically, resource procurement fitted neatly into a pattern of overlapping periods of plenty, ensuring that food, fresh or stored, was available all year round. One model of Beothuk extinction queries this deceptively seamless arrangement with the argument that biological factors or local weather or ice conditions could have led to the consecutive failure, in the annual cycle, of one or more pivotal staple species such as caribou or seal. Such circumstances could have had fatal consequences for the Beothuk. Indeed, resource fluctuations are thought to have contributed to the extinction of several prehistoric native groups in Newfoundland.[7] In the post-contact period such fluctuations, aggravated by European encroachment on resource-based campsite locations such as those along salmon rivers, are likely to have led to starvation among the Beothuk.

Among the cultural factors contributing to the demise of the Beothuk was the Europeans' belief in the superiority of their civilization and of the Christian religion. On the strength of this belief they aggressively pursued expansionist political and economic policies without regard to the rights and needs of the aboriginal population. With their highly effective weaponry, the Europeans were invincible opponents to those possessed only of bows and arrows.

As for the Beothuk, cultural factors may have determined their conspicuous restraint – which seems to have been exercised by all bands – from aggressive acts against non-native encroachment during the first two centuries following contact. This reticence contrasts sharply with their reputation as fierce warriors among other native groups such as the Micmac. However, over time, the Beothuk's restraint and self-confidence towards Europeans such as Guy and Crout were tempered by suspicion and anger. By the 1760s, if not earlier, they had come to reject the whites and their culture and were intent on avenging a long experience of persecution by the English, who mercilessly killed their people in a succession of reprisals. The Beothuk's independence of the usual ties with Europeans and their proud nature (if Shanawdithit was typical of her tribe) impelled them to choose revenge over subjugation. When English authorities belatedly tried to make peace, their commitment to this course of action forestalled any change in relations.

Among the historical events that contributed to the demise of the tribe was the increasing European encroachment on Beothuk territory and resources, which dovetailed with resource competition and led to open hostilities. While the seasonal fishing industry, centring on the catching and processing of cod, did not directly interfere with Beothuk food collection (although it would have barred them from many favoured beaches), the English salmon and seal fisheries, birding expeditions, and hunting and trapping practices did. The English not only pre-empted Beothuk access to the most productive hunting, fishing, and birding areas but also caused a heavy reduction in food species, particulary fur bearers, salmon, harbour seal, and birds such as the great auk. As early as the 1600s, the Beothuk had been pushed away from the south coast and from Placentia and Trinity bays. This pattern was repeated in the 1700s, when European settlement prevented access to the west coast and to parts of Bonavista and Notre Dame bays, and when Micmac hostilities deprived the Beothuk of large tracts of territory on the west and south coasts. Eventually, the westerly portion of Notre Dame Bay became the Beothuk's last refuge.

As Pastore has argued, Indian agents, missionaries, and traders, who elsewhere provided a link between native groups and Europeans and might have promoted peaceful relations, were not present in Newfoundland.[8] Government was not interested in employing agents to woo the Beothuk to the English side in their frequent conflicts with the French. Missionaries made no attempt to convert Beothuk to the Christian faith. Funds – and clerics willing to serve in Newfoundland outports – were in short supply at the best of times, and because the elusive Beothuk were not integrated into English communities, no effort was made to seek them out. Since the Beothuk did not engage in the regular exchange of furs, they had no contact with traders. The settlers who trapped and cured their own furs came to perceive the Beothuk as a hindrance rather than as a potential source of profit through trade. Thus, the absence of intermediaries such as agents and traders isolated the Beothuk and deprived them of a voice through English or French interest groups.[9]

Finally, there was disease. An investigation into the contagious diseases that could have been transferred to the Beothuk suggests that bubonic plague, carried by rodents and transmitted by a vector flea to humans after the rodent has died, could not have been sustained in Newfoundland because of the severe winters.[10] Smallpox, which has decimated many native populations (among them Innu and Inuit in Quebec and Labrador), may have reached isolated Beothuk camps by means of Montagnais visitors. Because of the manner in which it spreads and its incubation period, it is unlikely to have caused many deaths among the Beothuk since the various bands were too isolated from one another.[11] The likelihood that Beothuk were infected with measles, which is one of the most contagious of viral infections, is small.[12]

Tuberculosis, thought to have been a major cause of death among North American native people in the last century, may also have been significant in the decimation of the Beothuk.[13] It is contracted through an invasion of tubercle bacilli borne, like the measles virus, in respiratory droplets from one active case, but with an extended incubation period. Sickness and death may follow within a few weeks or months of infection. However, the development of chronic pulmonary tuberculosis, in which the patient's condition deteriorates slowly, is more common. During this period the patient may continually cough up tubercle bacilli that can remain virulent for several weeks and infect other people. Inhaling the bacilli alone does not necessarily result in the disease; the susceptibility of an individual or a population are important factors, as are unhygienic conditions, overcrowding, and starvation. The status of the Beothuk as a population that was previously unexposed or underexposed to certain viruses and bacteria, taken with their crowded living quarters, would have optimized the spread of this disease.

Whether tuberculosis reached the Beothuk in the eighteenth century through contacts with English raiding parties that stayed overnight in Beothuk mamateeks, or by way of Beothuk captives who visited their kin, is not known. In 1811, Lieut. David Buchan described the Beothuk as a vigorous people, free of the "pestilences of civil society" and from "disease brought on by intemperance." The thirty or so children in the camp struck him as remarkably healthy.[14] Yet within one or two years twenty-two out of the seventy-two Beothuk who were still alive in 1811 had died, which suggests the possibility of transmission of disease as a result of contact with Buchan's party.[15] In an 1830 report on the health of the native population in Newfoundland, Dr William Carson attributed the deaths of the four women taken captive in and after 1819 to "pulmonary consumption." One of the women had been in an advanced state of the disease when taken and the health of two others had been precarious, indicating that tuberculosis was by that time prevalent among the Beothuk and contributed to their rapid decline.[16] There is also Shanawdithit's testimony that her tribe (estimated to number about 345 people in 1768) had decreased to seventy-two members in 1811, and to twelve or thirteen by the spring of 1823.[17] Diminished numbers and the inability of those afflicted with disease to help with food gathering would have impaired the Beothuk's ability to maintain adequate subsistence levels. Malnutrition reduces resistance to infection and raises infant mortality, which creates a vicious cycle of sickness and starvation and thereby accelerates population decline.

In Canada, the Beothuk are the only tribe whose extinction is popularly linked to persecution by Europeans.[18] They have therefore received more posthumous attention than any other native groups, and their extinction has led to more recrimination.[19] Although certain factors, such as the Beothuk's isolation and ability to secure iron goods without having to trade, were probably peculiar to them, their fate parallels that of other tribes on the Atlantic Seaboard, where Europeans claimed harbours and land at an early date. Mooney, who compared population figures for North American native groups from around AD 1600 with those from 1907, concluded that of the twenty-four tribes enumerated for New England, New York, New Jersey, and Pennsylvania in about 1600, fourteen tribes (with an estimated original population of 20,600) had become extinct by 1907; six others had been reduced to fewer than fifty members each. The decreases were primarily caused by epidemics, including smallpox, followed by destructive wars by the English against the Indians, accompanied by intertribal fighting. Mooney reckoned that the subjugation of tribes by Europeans brought about their final disintegration.[20] His estimates for the size of tribes in the South Atlantic region show a population decrease of close to ninety-six percent. More recent population estimates tend to be higher than Mooney's, but they show similar rates of decline.[21] Thus, history has shown that other native people in the Atlantic region, through a combination of adverse factors, met the same fate as the Beothuk.

In conclusion, the evidence presented in this volume indicates that several factors that led to the Beothuk's demise resulted from prejudice, a total disregard for the rights and needs of the native population, and ruthlessness and brutality on the side of the English, and from the Beothuk's withdrawal and their commitment to revenge. Other factors were beyond the control of either people.

Though prejudice and cruelty played an important role in the history of relations, the Beothuk's response indicates that they made choices and were not helpless victims who allowed circumstances to rule their lives. In my view, they were a heroic people who valued their independence and traditions above all and were prepared to face hostilities and possible annihilation rather than be subjugated. They therefore rank alongside those North American native groups who are renown for their courage in the defence of their territory and cultural integrity.

Newfoundlanders have generally shown much interest in the history and culture of the Beothuk and are anxious to preserve and honour their memory. Two projects presently underway are designed to accomplish this. At Boyd's Cove, where a large Beothuk camp site has been excavated, an extensive Beothuk interpretation centre is about to open to the public and Newfoundland artist, Gerry Squires, is planning to sculpt a large bronze statue of Shanawdithit to be placed on an island in the Bay of Exploits where her spirit resides.

Even though research on the Beothuk has cast a very wide net, many features of their culture remain obscure, and it is unlikely that the gaps in our knowledge will be filled. As-yet-unknown contemporary documents may surface here and there, but they are not expected to change our present interpretations to a great extent. The most promising source of new information is archaeological investigation. Excavations in areas with high potential, such as western Notre Dame Bay and the lake-and-river system connecting Badger and New bays with the Exploits River, could throw new light on Beothuk culture; the discovery of Maritime Archaic Indian remains in Newfoundland dating from between 3200 and 2000 BP could disclose a relationship between these ancient Indians and the Beothuk's ancestors; archaeological research in Labrador may confirm the proposed affiliation between Beothuk and Central Algonquian groups; comparative studies with culture traits of other native groups could lead to new insights; and if techniques for DNA analysis become more refined, some genetic information may be obtained.

APPENDIX THREE

Beothuk Namefile

BEOTHUK The wordlist obtained from Demasduit in 1819 includes the word *beathook* – Red Indian, a term that was never used by the English.[1] The first person to record the name the Newfoundland Indians applied to themselves was Bishop John Inglis in his diary of his trip around Newfoundland in June-July 1827. Inglis probably obtained this name from Shanawdithit through John Peyton, Jr. He spelt it Beothuc, Beothic, Beothick, Boeothic, and Boeothick (the letters o and e drawn together into one letter).[2] In his correspondence with W.E. Cormack, Inglis spelled the tribal name Boeothick (transcribed by Howley into Boeothuck[s]).[3]

On 2 October 1827 Cormack founded a society formed for the benefit of the aboriginal Indians of Newfoundland. In his draft of the address to the institution, Cormack spelt the name of the tribe Boeothuck(s) and the name of the institution Boeothuck Institution.[4] In his notes on the resolutions made during the meeting Cormack spelt the name Boeothick Institution with the e drawn closely into the first o as one letter (transcribed by Howley as Boeothick Institution).[5] A report of the meeting, as published in the *Royal Gazette*, refers to Boeothick(s) and the Boeothick Institution. (Howley, in his transcription of the article, changed the names to Beothuck(s) and Beothuck Institution).[6]

The published version of Cormack's report on his expedition in search of the Beothuk in 1827 has Boeothick(s) and Boeothick Institution (transcribed by Howley as Beothuck(s), Boeothick(s), and Beothuck Institution).[7] In his handwritten draft of a history of the Beothuk Cormack refers to the Boeothick Institution (transcribed by Howley as Beothuck Institution).[8] In subsequent correspondence with John Stark, Cormack spelled the name Boeothick(s), (transcribed by Howley as Boeothuck and Boethuck).[9] When John Stark wrote in December 1827: "If the word 'Boothick' is wrong and should be 'Boothuck,'" Cormack answered, "*Boeothuck* is the pronunciation of the word in question – or *Boethuck*, or *Boethick*, the emphasis being on the diphthong oe and almost dropping the o." Stark adopted Boeothick (transcribed by Howley as Boeothuck).[10]

The wordlists that Cormack accumulated with the help of Shanawdithit and to which he added words from the Demasduit vocabulary give *beathook*, *behathook*, *beothuck*, *beothuk*, *boeothuc*, and *beothick*.[11] John McGregor, a close friend with whom Cormack stayed after he had left Newfoundland in 1829, spelled the name Boeothic(s).[12] Howley

(1915) adopted the spelling Beothuck(s) in his text and in transcriptions. John Hewson, research professor in the Department of Linguistics at Memorial University of Newfoundland, advocates *Beothuk*; he suggests that the term denotes both singular and plural.[13] The spelling Beothuk has been adopted in this work.

TABIOS Alphonse de Saintonge, who is said to have travelled to Newfoundland with Jean-François de la Rocque de Roberval in 1542–43, claimed that Newfoundland's native population was called "Tabios".[14] This name has not been verified.

OSA YAN A (OSAQANA) The name of a Beothuk "tribe" of which Santu's father Kop (a Beothuk) was a member; this name was also known to the Micmac. By modern orthography the name would be spelled "Osaqana".[15]

DEMASDUIT Demasduit was captured in 1819 and died ten months later on *HMS Grasshopper* while under the care of Capt. David Buchan. In a handwritten note Cormack spelled her name Demasduit.[16] In his draft of a history of the Beothuk, he spelled the name Demasdoweet.[17] Surveyor General Joseph Noad, who had access to Cormack's papers, spelled the name Demasdoweet.[18] Howley mostly used the spelling Demasduit and it is this spelling that is now generally used.[19] Hewson added a "w," writing Demasduwit to indicate that the name had four syllables.[20] The settlers called Demasduit Mary March because she had been captured in the month of March.[21]

WAUNATHOAKE Capt. Hercules Robinson of *HMS Favorite*, in his "History of Mary March" (1820), recorded that her native name was Waunathoake.[22] In the published version of his history, the name is spelled *Waunathoke*. Howley transcribed the name Waunathoake and Waunatoake.[23] No other person has recorded this name.

SHENDORETH This name was used in a letter from the governor's secretary to Rev. John Leigh, dated 3 June 1819, with reference to Demasduit.[24] It has not been recorded elsewhere and may have been applied to her in error.

DOODEBEWSHET Listed at the end of a vocabulary collected by Cormack from Shanawdithit is the phrase "Doodebewshet is alive"; Hewsen suggests that it refers to Shanawdithit's mother.[25] Among the settlers, Shanawdithit's mother was known as Betty Decker because the party who captured her was engaged at the time in decking a vessel. She was also referred to as Old Smut because people thought her to be capable of wicked deeds.[26]

LONGNON One of Demasduit's brothers, who was among the few survivors of the Beothuk group at the time of Shanawdithit's capture, was called Longnon; this information comes from Shanawdithit's sketch 4 (Fig.14.1).

MOOMESHDUCK A phrase in the vocabulary collected by Cormack from Shanawdithit reads: "wawashemet o-owin moom meshduck." Hewson suggests that this phrase corresponds to two English glosses; the first two terms mean "we give you a knife" and "moom meshduck" (*moomeshduck*) stands for "Doodebewshet's father."[27]

NONOSABASUT Nonosabasut was a Beothuk chief and the husband of Demasduit. In one of his notes Cormack spelled the name Nonosabasut.[28] In a draft of his history of the Beothuk Cormack spelled it Nonosbawsut.[29] Joseph Noad used the spelling Nonosbawsut. Howley and Hewson adopted the spelling Nonosabasut, which is now generally used.[30]

OUBEE The young girl Oubee was captured by furriers in the summer of 1791. She was the informant of the earliest Beothuk vocabulary collected by Capt. G.C. Pulling. The first entry in this vocabulary reads: "Ou=bee ... the name of y/e Indian Girl who lives w/th Mr Stone."[31]

SHANAWDITHIT Shanawdithit was taken, together with her mother and sister, in the spring of 1823. She died in St John's in 1829. In his manuscript "Of the Red Indians" and in other notes, Cormack spelled the name Shawnawdithit.[32] J.P. Howley used the same spelling in the transcription of some of Cormack's notes and stated, in a footnote, that "Cormack always spelled her name like this and he should be considered the authority."[33] However, in his transcript of Cormack's history, Howley spelled the name Shanawdithit.[34] Cormack, in his correspondence with Bishop John Inglis, spelled the name Shannadithit and Shawnadithit. Howley, in his transcription of these letters, adjusted the spelling to Shawnawdithit.[35]

On Shanawdithit's sketches the spelling of her name, as inserted by Cormack, varies: sketch 1, Shannadithit (Plate 10.1); sketches 4 and 10, Shawnawdithit (Figs. 14.1, 14.2a); sketch 5, Shanawdithit (Fig. 10.2). The phrase "Shinadonthit is alive and well lives with the English," contained in Shanawdithit's wordlist, collected by Cormack (as copied by Robert G. Latham), is believed to refer to Shanawdithit.[36]

Bishop John Inglis, in his diary from July 1827, spelled the name Shanadithit, Shanandithit, and Shannandithit; in the copy of this diary sent to the USPG: Shanawdithit.[37] In his correspondence with Cormack, Inglis spelled the name Shannawdithit, transcribed by Howley as Shawnawdithit.[38] John Stark used Shawnawdithit.[39]

On her burial certificate the name is spelt *Shanadithi*, which Howley transcribed as Shanadithe.[40] Joseph Noad spelled Shawnadithit; Howley transcribed it as Shawnawdithit.[41] In his text, Howley used Shanawdithit, an exception being Shawnawdithit on page 79.[42] He generally transcribed the name from other sources also as Shanawdithit.[43] In his book *British America*, John McGregor spelled the name Shanandithit. In the article "Sketches of savage life," which he published anonymously, McGregor wrote: "Her name in her own language was pronounced *Shaa-naan-dithit*."[44]

The corruption of the name to Shananditti, used by Winter, is not found in any contemporary document.[45] The most widely adopted version is Shanawdithit. The settlers usually referred to Shanawdithit as Nance, Nancy, Nance April, or Indian Nance.[46]

KOP The name of a Beothuk man who was captured as a child and brought up by Micmac. He subsequently married a Micmac girl. The name Kop was probably given to him by Micmac. His daughter, Santu, said *kop* is the name of a "red root found in the lake" (Red Indian Lake).[47]

SANTU Kop's daughter was called Santu, which is the Micmac name for Saguenay River. Santu was born ca. 1837 and in 1910 told Frank G. Speck what she remembered of her father's tales about the Beothuk.[48]

BEOTHUK PERSONS WHOSE NATIVE NAMES ARE NOT KNOWN. *Easter Eve* is the name settlers gave to Shanawdithit's sister, who was taken together with her on Easter eve, in 1823. She died shortly thereafter.[49] *Tom June*, also known as June, was a Beothuk boy who was captured in 1758, when he was nine years old.[50] June was reared and employed in Fogo, in the fishery; he drowned sometime before 1788.[51] *August*, also referred to as *John August*, was a Beothuk boy who was captured in 1768 at the age of four.[52] August was employed in the fishery in Catalina and Trinity and died in 1788.[53] *Gabriel* is said to have been a Beothuk man who joined a Micmac group and married a Micmac girl.[54]

APPENDIX FOUR

Beothuk Artifact Collections

NEWFOUNDLAND MUSEUM, ST JOHN'S, NEWFOUNDLAND

The largest collection of Beothuk artifacts is housed in the Newfoundland Museum. It includes several hundred lithic and iron tools, a few bone tools, close to three hundred pendant-like bone carvings, a wooden male figurine, birchbark canoe replicas, birchbark containers, combs, gaming pieces, discoidal beads, a wooden bowl, moccasins, a burial shroud (made from the legging of an adult), and skeletal remains. The Newfoundland Museum also owns ten of Shanawdithit's sketches.

IN PRIVATE HANDS IN NEWFOUNDLAND

About forty pendant-like bone carvings, discoidal shell beads, one bone needle, and other miscellany.

CANADIAN MUSEUM OF CIVILIZATION, HULL, QUEBEC

Lithic, bone, and iron tools from archaeological excavations, a small number of organic artifacts collected from caves, and ca. sixty pendant-like bone carvings.

MCCORD MUSEUM, MONTREAL, QUEBEC

Grave goods from a Beothuk burial at Rencontre Island, including ca. twenty-five discoidal shell beads, three pendant-like bone carvings, pieces of walrus tusk, and miscellaneous items.

NOVA SCOTIA MUSEUM, HALIFAX, NOVA SCOTIA

One pendant-like bone carving.

MUSEUM OF MANKIND, ETHNOGRAPHIC DEPARTMENT OF BRITISH MUSEUM, LONDON, UK

Two pendant-like bone carvings, one leather coat fringe, two birchbark containers, harpoon head, and one netting needle of "Newfoundland Indian" origin.

NATIONAL MARITIME MUSEUM, GREENWICH, UK

One birchbark canoe replica made by Shanawdithit.

NATIONAL MUSEUMS OF SCOTLAND, EDINBURGH, UK
One birchbark canoe replica, four birchbark baskets, two skulls.

ETHNOGRAPHIC MUSEUM OF THE UNIVERSITY OF OSLO, OSLO, NORWAY
One bone harpoon head with incised pattern.

APPENDIX FIVE

Institutions Contacted in Search of Beothuk Artifacts and Documentary Source Material

NEWFOUNDLAND

Mary March Museum, Grand Falls.

Memorial University of Newfoundland, St John's:

Queen Elizabeth II Library, Centre for Newfoundland Studies and Centre for Newfoundland Studies Archive; Maritime History Archive.

Methodist Archive, St John's.

Newfoundland Museum, St John's.

Provincial Archives of Newfoundland and Labrador, St John's

Provincial Reference and Resource Library, St John's.

ELSEWHERE IN CANADA

Blacker-Wood Library, McGill University, Montreal.

Canadian Museum of Civilization, Hull.

McCord Museum, Montreal.

National Archives of Canada, Ottawa.

New Westminster Historic Centre and Museum, New Westminster.

Province of British Columbia Archives, Victoria.

UNITED STATES

American Museum of Natural History, New York.

Hudson River Museum, New York.

Museum of the American Indian, Heye Foundation, New York.

Peabody Museum of Archaeology and Ethnology, Harvard University, Cambridge.

Smithsonian Institution, Washington.

Thomas Gilcrease Institute of American History and Art, Tulsa.

William L. Clemens Library, University of Michigan, Ann Arbor.

GREATER LONDON, UK

Archives of the United Society for the Propagation of the Gospel in Foreign Parts.

Archives of the Methodist Missionary Society, School of Oriental and African Studies Library, University of London.

British Library, Department of Manuscripts.
British Library of Political and Economic Science.
Commonwealth Institute.
Greater London Record Office.
Guildhall Library.
Hampstead Borough Archives.
Horniman Museum.
House of Lords Record Office.
Lambeth Palace Library.
Museum of Mankind, Ethnographic Department of the British Museum.
National Register of Archives.
National Maritime Museum.
Public Record Office.
Religious Society of Friends Library.
Royal Anthropological Institute of Great Britain and Ireland.
Royal College of Physicians of London.
Royal Commission on Historical Manuscripts.
Royal Commonwealth Society Library.
St Paul's Cathedral Library.
Society of Antiquaries.
Trinity House Corporation.
University of London Library.
Wellcome Institute for the History of Medicine Library.
Westminster Diocesan Archives.

ELSEWHERE IN THE UK

Borough of Poole, Guildhall Museum, Poole.
City of Liverpool Library, Liverpool.
Cornwall County Record Office, Truro.
County Record Office, Gloucester.
County Record Office, Nottingham.
County Records Office, Plymouth.
Devon Record Office, Exeter.
Dorset County Archives, Dorchester.
Edinburgh City Library, Edinburgh.
Edinburgh University, Manuscript Division, Edinburgh.
Exeter Maritime Musem, Exeter.
Glasgow University Archives, Glasgow.
Glasgow University Library, Reference Section, Glasgow.
Lincolnshire Archives, Lincoln.
Merseyside Maritime Museum, Liverpool.
Ministry of Defence, Hydrographic Department, Taunton.
Mitchell Library, Manuscript Section, Glasgow.
National Library of Scotland, Manuscript and Map Divisions, Edinburgh.

National Register of Archives, Register House, Edinburgh.
National Scottish Museums, Royal Scottish Museum, Edinburgh;
Northamptonshire Record Office, Northampton.
Nottingham County Library, Local Study Centre, Nottingham.
Nottingham District Probate Registry, Nottingham.
Nottingham University, Manuscript Division, Nottingham.
Pitt Rivers Museum, University of Oxford, Oxford.
Poole Historical Trust, Bournemouth.
Rhodes House Library, Oxford.
Royal Society of Edinburgh, Edinburgh.
Sheffield City Library, Department of Local History, Sheffield.
West Register House, Edinburgh.
West Sussex Record Office, Chichester.

AUSTRIA

Völkerkundliches Museum, Vienna.

GERMANY

Hamburgisches Museum für Völkerkunde, Hamburg.
Linden Museum, Stuttgart.
Pelizaeus Museum, Hildesheim.
Provinzial Archiv, Hannover.
Stadtarchiv, Bremen.
Stadtarchiv, Hamburg.
Völkerkundliches Museum, Berlin-Dahlem.
Völkerkundliches Museum, Munich.

NORWAY

Ethnographic Museum of the University of Oslo, Oslo.

Notes

ABBREVIATIONS

ADM Admiralty Records, Public Record Office, Kew, UK
BL British Library, Department of Manuscripts, London, UK
BM British Museum, London, UK
BWL Blacker-Wood Library, McGill University, Montreal
CMC Canadian Museum of Civilization, Hull
CNS Centre for Newfoundland Studies, Queen Elizabeth II Library, Memorial University of Newfoundland, St John's
CO Colonial Office (Record Series), Public Record Office, Kew, UK
COED *The Compact Edition of the Oxford English Dictionary*
CSOC Colonial Secretary's Outgoing Correspondence, Provincial Archives of Newfoundland and Labrador, St John's
CSPC *Calendar of State Papers, Colonial Series, America and West Indies*
DCRO Dorset County Record Office, Dorchester, UK
DCB *Dictionary of Canadian Biography*
DNB *Dictionary of National Biography*
DNE *Dictionary of Newfoundland English*
DNLB *Dictionary of Newfoundland and Labrador Biography*
HoE Head of Enquiries on the Newfoundland Fishery, sent by the Board of Trade in Britain to Newfoundland governors
LPL Lambeth Palace Library, London, UK
MDHyD Ministry of Defence, Hydrographic Department, Taunton, UK
MHA Maritime History Archive, Memorial University of Newfoundland, St John's
MMS:LR Methodist Missionary Society Archive, Letters and Reports from North America, School of African and Oriental Studies, University of London, London, UK

MMss Willoughby Papers, Middleton Manuscripts, University of Nottingham, Nottingham, UK, transcript by Dr Robert Barakat, deposited in the CNS; transcript of Mix 1/24 by Gillian Cell
MUN Memorial University of Newfoundland, St John's
NAC National Archives of Canada, Ottawa
NJHA Newfoundland, *Journal of the House of Assembly*
NM Newfoundland Museum, St John's
NMM National Maritime Museum, Greenwich, London, UK
PANL Provincial Archives of Newfoundland and Labrador, St John's
PC Privy Council (Records), Public Record Office, Kew, UK
PRO Public Record Office, Kew, UK
PRRL Provincial Reference and Resource Library, St John's
RN Royal Navy
SPG Society for the Propagation of the Gospel in Foreign Parts, London, UK
USPG United Societies for the Propagation of the Gospel in Foreign Parts, London, UK
WLCL William L. Clemens Library, University of Michigan, Ann Arbor, Michigan, US
WO War Office (Records), Public Record Office, Kew, UK

INTRODUCTION

1 Horwood 1963, 9.
2 Dalton 1992; Budgel 1992.
3 John McGregor (1797–1857), statistician and historian, was born in Scotland but settled in Prince Edward Island, where he became a member of the House of Assembly and, in 1823, high sheriff. He returned to Britain, where he had a distinguished career. In 1840 he was secretary of the Board of Trade, entered Parliament in 1847 as the member for Glasgow, and later was chairman of the Royal British Bank. In 1832 McGregor published *British America*, followed by a large number of publications on history and commercial statistics. See DNB, vol.12, 540–2.
4 Fisher 1992, 44.

CHAPTER ONE

1 Quinn 1977,116. The exact location of Cabot's landfall is uncertain; Quinn favours Cape Breton but also considers Cape Bauld, Cape Race, and Cape Bonavista; Morison 1971,78, argues it was Cape Dégrat.
2 "Diarii di Sanuto," cited in Quinn 1981,11 (reprinted in Italian and English in Biggar 1911,13–15). According to the letter from John Day to the Lord Grand Admiral,

written in winter 1497–98, cited in Quinn 1981,11 (reprinted in English in Williamson 1962,212), Cabot found a fireplace and a stick half a yard long pierced at both ends, carved and painted red. Williamson and Quinn believed the Lord Grand Admiral to have been Christopher Columbus; Sauer 1968, 32 argues convincingly that the recipient of the letter would have been Don Fadrique Hernándes, Marqués of Tarifa, senior grandee of Castile.

3 The three natives were described in an "old chronicle" by Robert Fabian, reprinted by Hakluyt in 1582 (Hakluyt 1967,17); Quinn 1981,12–13, believes that Fabian's description refers to Indians brought to England by Bristol merchants in 1501, and not to captives taken by Cabot; see also Williamson 1962,220.

4 *Bacallaos* was the term used for codfish; Pietro Martiere d'Anghiera (Peter Martyr) 1530, cited in Quinn 1981,13 (reprinted in English by Williamson 1962,266–70). The eighth legend on the Sebastian Cabot World Map of 1544 contains a summary of reports from the Cabot voyages, cited in Quinn 1979,1:95, doc.54. The accounts on Cabot's third voyage are considered to be unreliable; details are likely to have been changed or confused with reports from other explorations.

5 Fabian, reprinted in Hakluyt 1967,17.

6 Seal were frequently referred to as "fish"; see Quinn 1979,1:95, doc.54.

7 Latten is a mixed metal of yellow colour, either identical with or similar to brass; copper had previously been used by Maritime Archaic Indians (Tuck 1976a, 64); according to Purchas 1906,18:219–20, 224–5, Champlain was told in 1603 that Indians further inland mined copper and a silverlike metal, which they may have traded.

8 Alberto Cantino to Duke of Ferrara, 17October 1501, cited in Quinn 1979,1:148–9, doc.116 (translated into English in Biggar 1911,61–5); Pietro Pasqualigo to the Signory of Venice, 18 October 1501, cited in Quinn, ibid. 149–51, doc.118, (translated into English in Biggar 1911,65–7.) The Cantino letter enumerates fifty captives, the Pasqualigo letter seven; Quinn, ibid., suggests that the figure in the Pasqualigo letter was probably an "L" that was erroneously transcribed into the figure 7.

9 Damiao Goes 1566–67, reprinted in Quinn 1979,4:152, doc.121.

10 Quinn 1981,13; Williamson 1962,216.

11 Eusebius 1518, reprinted with French translation in Harrisse, 1900,162–3; also published by Henri Estienne, cited in Quinn 1981,14; Howley 1915,7, gives a different text for Eusebius. An account of a voyage to the New World and Sumatra, probably made by Jean and Raoul Parmentier, is ascribed to Crignon and was first published by Ramusio in 1556, translated from Italian with notes and comments by Hoffman 1963,1–79. The account by Pietro Bembo Della Istoria Viniziana, was first printed in Latin in Venice, 1551, and translated into Italian in 1809, cited in Quinn 1981,14.

12 Sturtevant 1980,47, mentions a Labrador Inuit woman and her daughter, kidnapped in 1566, who had tattoo marks on their faces; Hoffman 1955,210, Micmac; Skinner 1911,13, Eastern Cree (scarification); Feest 1978,260, Virginia Algonquian.

13 John Rastell, ca. 1519, cited in Quinn 1981,14.

14 Ramusio, "Viaggi et navigatione," cited in Quinn 1979,1:281–7, doc.201.

15 Wroth 1970,89.

16 Quinn 1979,1:273, 275, docs.192, 195, 196. Three records describe Gomes's explorations, but it is not certain whether he landed in Newfoundland.
17 Morison 1971,331, thought that the Indians were captured in Newport, RI; Biggar 1911,194 and Ganong 1964,176–7,188–9, suggest that they came from the Penobscot River; McNutt 1912,2:260, 418, believed that they were captured in Virginia or Carolina.
18 Quinn 1979,1:192, 193, docs.145, 146. One document states that the ship came to explore Newfoundland and found fifty fishing vessels; when they tried to land to open communications, the Indians killed their pilot. The second document records that the ship, ordered to explore a passage between Newfoundland and Labrador, sailed north of fifty degrees latitude; certain persons died of cold and the pilot died as well.
19 Quinn 1979,1:293–4, doc.203.
20 Hoffmann 1963,54.
21 Howley 1915,10.
22 Champlain met Algonquins, Etchemins, and Montagnais, who painted themselves with a tawny colouring substance in the area of Tadousac, Purchas 1906,18:199; Gosnold met a shallop east of the New England coast that was manned by eight "savages" who painted their bodies (ibid., 304).
23 Rogers and Leacock 1981,171.
24 Hoffman 1963,54.
25 Martijn 1990b,49.
26 Biggar 1930,449–54; Quinn 1981,26.
27 Biggar 1930,459–64.
28 Tuck 1985,233.
29 Chapdelaine and Kennedy 1990,42.
30 Quinn 1979,1:207, doc.148.
31 Funk Island, located north-east of Bonavista Bay, housed the largest breeding colony of the great auk (*Pinguinus impennis*), locally called penguin; it was traditionally visited by European crews to replenish provisions and fresh water. Penguin Island is located north-east of Cape Breton, south of Cape Lahune, on the southern Newfoundland coast, around forty-seven degrees latitude.
32 Quinn 1979,1:207, doc.148. The ship was becalmed for a lengthy period, and when the crew ran out of food, some members of the party resorted to cannibalism.
33 Hoffman 1963,1–79.
34 The COED (1979) defines cruel as being indifferent to suffering or inflicting pain, but it can also mean savage, severely, hard or intensifying, i.e., "very".
35 Hoffman 1963,54, fn.29; Charles A. Martijn, 1980s, pers. com.
36 Quinn 1979,4:64, doc.560; Cell 1982,70–7,83–4.
37 Hoffman 1963,14.
38 Cartier's report was published in 1534 (Quinn 1981,18); Crignon's report was published in 1539 (Hoffman 1963).
39 Ganong 1964,274–5.
40 Quinn 1981,32.

41 Thevet 1557, cited in Quinn 1981, 33; Thevet 1568; Hoffman 1961, 177–8.
42 Hoffman 1961,177; Quinn 1981,34, translated "deer bone fleusters" as "flutes made from deer shanks."
43 Hoffman 1961,178; according to Quinn's translation (1981,34), they "honored" the leader rather than "obeyed" him.
44 Quinn 1981,34.
45 Innes 1978,23.
46 Ibid.
47 Selma Barkham, 1980s, pers. com.; in 1594, for instance, two wrecks of Basque fishing ships were recorded in St George's Bay (Quinn 1979,4:64, doc.560).
48 In 1586 there were four hundred sails just on the Banks and some of these ships were as large as three to four hundred tons (Quinn 1979,3:128, doc.364).
49 Selma Barkham, 1980s, pers. com.
50 In 1594 about one hundred English ships fished on the Newfoundland coast and the fleets of other European countries were, at times, larger than those of the English (Cell 1969,25).
51 Quinn 1979,4:23, doc.536.
52 Ibid.,33, doc.536.
53 Cell 1982,72.
54 Quinn 1979,4:7–10, doc.526, letter to Hakluyt written in 1578; Cell 1982,112,117, report by Whitbourne published in 1622; Isasti 1850,154, written in 1625.
55 Quinn 1979,4:64, doc.560.
56 Charles A. Martijn, 1980s, pers.com.
57 Cell 1982,117.
58 Speck 1922,28,122.
59 Simpson 1984,128–30, the Port au Port site.
60 Prowse 1972,160, Dudley's map of 1647 showing "di Piemarke" in this area.
61 A pinnace is a small light vessel, generally two-masted and schooner-rigged, often in attendance on a larger vessel as a tender or scout; or a double-banked boat (usually with eight oars).

CHAPTER TWO

1 Quinn 1979,4:5, doc.525; other promoters were Edward Hayes, Sir Humphrey Gilbert, and Sir George Peckham.
2 Cell 1982,149.
3 Ibid.,39, 229.
4 Quinn 1979,4:23–42, doc.536, Hakluyt.
5 Ibid, 3:34–60, doc.358, Peckham.
6 Ibid.
7 Eburne 1962.
8 Ibid., 137.
9 Quinn 1979,3:64–9, doc.360, Richard Hakluyt the Elder.

10 Ibid., 3:239–45, doc.401. Quinn suggests that Sir George Peckham, Martin Frobisher, Sir Humphry Gilbert, and one or both of the Hakluyts may have participated in the plan.
11 Quinn 1979,4:131, doc.628. The petition is dated February 1610.
12 Purchas 1906,19:406, Royal Charter of the Newfoundland Company, May 1610.
13 Quinn 1979,4:140, doc.632, Instructions to John Guy.
14 Cell 1982,60, letter from John Guy, 6 October 1610.
15 Henry Crout to Sir Percival Willoughby, 7 August 1612, MMSS. Mix 1/10.
16 Quinn 1979,1:300, doc.203.
17 Ibid, 4:306, doc.682.
18 Biggar 1930,453.
19 Quinn 1979,4:119, doc.615. In the 1600s the term "to truc" meant to exchange one thing for another with another person (COED).
20 Quinn 1979,4:5–7, doc.525.
21 Ibid, 1:140–4, docs.110, 111.
22 Ibid, 4:61, doc.557.
23 Crout to Willoughby, 7 August 1612, and 8 September 1612, MMSS. Mix 1/10, Mix 1/20.
24 Cell 1982,68–78. Since in England the Gregorian calendar was not adopted until 1752, the exact dates – here given according to the Julian calendar – would be ten days ahead by today's reckoning. This means that the exploration started on 17 October and Bull Arm froze over on 18 rather than 8 November 1612. Guy's voyage is also described in Kirke 1908, 140–2.
25 Cell 1982,79–89. According to Crout's letter to Willoughby, 7 August 1612, MMSS. Mix 1/10, the presence of the pirate Peter Easton had kept them from going on this exploration earlier in the year.
26 Cell 1982,70.
27 Ibid.,70, fn.3, 83, fn.9. The identification of this harbour is based on Crout's description, according to which there were three islands outside the harbour.
28 Crout's journal, 1 September 1612 to 31 April 1613, in Quinn 1979,4:157–78, doc.642; Crout mentions two or three fires on the lakeshore (Cell 1982,71,84).
29 Bisket refers to a kind of crisp, dry bread, more or less hard.
30 Cell 1982,83–8; Quinn 1979,4:157–78, doc.642; Cell (1982,71) believed that they moored on the night of 30 October at Bull Island; Gilbert (1990,156) argued that they returned to one of the islands in Dildo Arm.
31 Seary (1971,59) thought this was Rantem Cove; Cell (1982,72) suggested Great Mosquito Cove; Gilbert (1990,156) thought Collier Bay, which is most likely the correct location.
32 Cell 1982,72; Quinn 1979,4:157, doc.642. Both Guy and Crout mention two rocks well before the entrance of the first of the two coves, which would be the Shag Islands, identifying this harbour as Stock Cove.
33 Passage Harbour would be Come by Chance (Cell 1982,72, fn.1). See also Seary 1971,59.
34 Cell 1982,84; Quinn 1979,4:162, doc.642.

35 On the return voyage Guy was overtaken by a severe storm and, on approaching Perlican, was forced to abandon the canoe he had taken earlier (Cell 1982,72–3, 84).

36 Master: one having direction or control over the action of another or others, a director, leader, chief, commander; a ruler, governor; the captain of a merchant vessel (COED).

37 Cell 1982,73–4, John Guy; ibid.,84–5, Henry Crout.

38 Ibid.,74,85. Crout recorded that the Indians liked the aquavitae but disliked the beer.

39 Ibid.,75.

40 Ibid.,74, 86.

41 Ibid.,75. In his "Journall of the voiadge of discoverie ... ," LPL, Ms. No.250, f.421, Guy has drawn a Beothuk canoe; see chapter 23, Fig.23.1.

42 John Cartwright, "Remarks ... 1768," PRRL, 971.8 C24 (in Howley 1915,31–2).

43 Cell 1982,70–7, 85; Quinn 1979,4:157–78, doc. 642. An (English) halbert or holbert is a kind of combination of spear and battleaxe, consisting of a sharp-edged blade ending in a point and a spearhead, mounted on a handle five to seven feet long (COED).

44 Cell 1982,84; "A Reply to the answeare of the description of Newfoundland," Archbishop Laud, 29 September 1639, PRO, CO 1/10, f.97–115 (abbreviated in Howley 1915,23.)

45 This is a small neck of land connected by a tombolo beach to the southwest side of Sunnyside harbour. At high tide this beach is awash; an archaeological site was excavated there by Evans in 1981–82.

46 Cell 1982,75–6.

47 Ibid.,85; Pastore 1984,99 was the first to call it silent barter.

48 Quinn and Skelton 1965,558. Ingram described another method, which was to "hang your wares upon a long poles end and so put more or less on it, until you have agreed on the bargin"; presumably this was done in the presence of the trading partner.

49 Stefansson 1938,1:14–23, and 2:58–72, cited in Quinn 1981,37–9; Kupp and Hart 1976,8; Wilson and Miller 1973,5; Edey 1974,65. In Europe silent barter, also known as "dumb barter," was described in the fifth century BC by Herodotus, writing about the trading practices of the Phoenicians in Africa.

50 Cell 1982,76. Guy had already reinvented this form of barter when he left articles in exchange for moccasins and beaver meat in a Beothuk dwelling at Dildo Pond.

51 Cell 1982,76. Crout said it was the harbour in which they had anchored on 4 November (Quinn 1979,4:162–3, doc.642).

52 Cell 1982,86.

53 Gilbert (1992,8–9) suggests that Guy, while in Bristol in ca. 1620, employed Whittington to go again to Trinity Bay to barter with the Beothuk, because Kirke's letter, written in 1639, claims that a meeting with the Indians happened about twenty, rather than twenty-seven, years before. However, in his diary of 1612, Guy recorded many details of the encounter described by Kirke, for example that Whittington was master of the ship and was the first to land, that the Indians had to ford a river when they approached him, that food was brought ashore by both parties, that the colonists shared a meal with the Indians, and that they traded for furs by

silent barter. Kirke also describes how Whittington had indicated to the Beothuk that they should meet the following year – a description that is not in Guy's or Crout's notes, though Guy had his men build a trading post, and Crout mentioned that Guy intended to return to have "a parlaye" with the Indians. Kirke's letter does not state that Guy was not present; it just claims that it was Whittington who was in command of the party and not just of the ship. Because details of the meeting described in both records are so similar, it is my view that Kirke's letter refers to Guy's first and only meeting with the Beothuk. In addition, Guy became disillusioned with the colony and left Newfoundland in 1612, and he is unlikely to have sent a trading vessel all the way from England to Trinity Bay eight years later when no one had been able to establish proper communication or trade with the Beothuk.

54 William Gilbert, 1994 and 1995, pers. com.

55 Evans 1981,89; Robbins 1982; ibid.,1985.

56 Cell 1982,84.

57 Quinn 1979,4:168, doc. 642.

58 Letters from Crout to Willoughby, 7 August 1612, MMss. Mix 1/10, 20 August 1612, Mix 1/13, 27 August 1612, Mix 1/15, 8 September 1612, Mix 1/20, August 1613, Mix 1/24; all references to Mix 1/24 in this and subsequent chapters refer to the transcript by Gillian Cell; see also Appendix 1.

59 Crout to Willoughby, August 1613, MMss. Mix 1/24; this could have been Hopeall Island, which has fresh water and good pasture land; Gilbert suggests that it was Dildo Island (1995, pers. com.).

60 Crout to Willoughby, August 1613, MMss. Mix 1/24 (Appendix 1).

61 Crout recorded that after the incident on the island, the party went to the bottom of "Mounteagle Bay," but the Indians whom they had seen the previous winter had all gone away. According to the record of the exploration, the party had visited Mounteagle Bay, probably Hopeall, on 22 October 1612 (Cell 1982,83) but had not met Indians. Since Crout in 1613 desired to see the Indians by the freshwater lake, he would have been referring to those in Dildo Arm. Crout seems to have confused the names given to places in 1612 and mistakenly said, in 1613, that they went to Mounteagle Bay when they were actually looking for the Indians in Savage Harbour, today's Dildo South.

62 Cell 1982,212. Information about these islands comes from Whitbourne; according to the *English Pilot* (1967), Baccalieu Island was also known for its bird population.

63 Crout to Willoughby, August 1613, MMss, Mix 1/24 (Appendix 1).

64 Ibid.

65 Crout to Willoughby, 8 September 1612, MMss, Mix 1/20.

66 Lahey 1977,501, letter to Father Simon Stock.

67 Cell 1982,137. In contrast, Richard Whitbourne found that European fishing crews committed many thefts and acts of destruction, such as stealing boats and removing the ownership marks, or destroying them so as to make use of the wood, ripping apart or burning fishing stages and rooms, stealing bait from the nets or out of the fishing boats at night, or setting the woods on fire (ibid., 159–61).

68 Crout to Willoughby, 7 August 1612, MMSS, Mix 1/10, 27 August 1612, Mix 1/15, August 1613, Mix 1/24 (Appendix 1).

69 Ibid.

70 Ibid.

71 Richard Holworthy to John Slaney, 8 August 1612, cited in Quinn 1979,4:151, doc.639; Cell 1969,67.

72 Cell 1982,12. Crout left in 1613, but Willoughby sent him back to Newfoundland in 1616, only to dismiss him a year later.

73 Cell 1982,71, 72, 74, 84, 86; Quinn 1979,4:157–78, doc.642.

74 Cell 1982,11.

75 Dean 1967,133. The letter was addressed "To the right worshipfull Mr John Scot of Scottisterbatt, in Scotland, Director to His Majesties Court of Chancery."

76 Cell 1982,12–13, 96, 99; ibid.,91. Mason produced the first map of Newfoundland that showed the Avalon as a peninsula rather than a group of islands.

77 Cell 1982,96.

78 Thomas Rowley to Willoughby, 13 September 1619, MMSS, Mix 1/51.

79 Rowley to Willoughby, 1618–19, MMSS, Mix 1/60; "Inventory of provisions requested for Newfoundland," 1619, and "A note of such provisions as are fitting for our intended Plantation in Trinity Bay," 1619, MMSS. Mix 1/61, Mix 1/62.

80 Cell 1969,61–80; ibid. 1982,15. In 1995 Gilbert excavated what may be remains of the company's settlement in Cupids; among early seventeenth-century items was one black-and-white trade bead (Gilbert, 1995, pers.com.).

81 Cell 1982,15–19. Most Bristol members of the original Newfoundland Company belonged to the Bristol Society of Merchant Venturers.

82 Cell 1982,22–4, 211–12.

83 Ibid.,45–55.

84 Ibid.,56; see also Kirke 1908.

85 Ibid.,244. This idea coincides with, or may actually have come from, Richard Eburne (1962,25), who suggested that the natives should be influenced and converted through their children.

86 North Falkland did not include Bull Arm, where the Beothuk were known to live, and Falkland may have confused Bull Arm with Random Sound (north of Bull Arm), which was the most southwesterly part of "North Falkland."

87 Cell 1982,22–4.

88 Ibid.,34.

89 Ibid.,101–92; see also Whitbourne 1622.

90 Cell 1982,117.

91 Ibid.,109, 119, 146, 147, 192.

92 Tuck 1989b,301; ibid. 1993,299. James A. Tuck, 1995, pers. com.

93 John Downing, 7 November 1676, CSPC, 1675–76:486, doc.1120 (in Howley 1915,24); Cell 1982,110, 125, 119.

94 Ibid.,162.

95 Eburne 1962,8.

96 Lahey 1977,501.

97 Prowse 1972, Supplement: 1; Smith 1961,163, memorandum to Board of Trade requesting a chaplain on the convoy ships to help the people in Newfoundland to live in Christianity.

98 USPG, C/Can. Nfld: files on Newfoundland clergy; LPL, Fulham Papers, letters from Newfoundland clergy, vols.1–17; MMS: LR, Methodist Archives, letters from missionaries in Newfoundland, series North America, Newfoundland. "Jealousy" between denominations was another problem (Parsons 1964,44).

99 Cell 1982,212.

100 Cell 1969,75. In a case that was brought before the Privy Council in 1620, it is said that the English fishery in Newfoundland employed three hundred ships and ten thousand seamen annually; in addition, some two hundred French, Basque, and Portuguese ships frequented the island.

101 Newfoundland Census 1699, PRO, CO 195/1, f.322.

102 Cell 1982,192–4; Cell suggests that this was *Topsham*.

103 Ibid.,118.

104 "A Reply to the answeare ..." Archbishop Laud, 29 September 1639, PRO, CO 1/10, f.97–115 (abbreviated in Howley 1915,23.)

105 In addition to creating annoyance, mischief can mean doing injury or physical harm.

106 Crout to Willoughby, August 1613, MMSS, Mix 1/24.

107 Hart 1959,13–14.

108 Contract between C. Melyn and A. Delsaurdy for fishing and trading in Canada, 30 January 1637, NAC, Kupp Collection, vol.3, doc. 89; Declaration of skipper and mate of *Fortuyn*, 14 December 1637, ibid., doc.118.

109 Captain Wheeler of *HMS Tiger* to William Blathwayt, 27 October 1684, PRO, CO 1/55, f.242b (in Howley 1915,24.)

110 Commander Graydon's answer to Head of Enquiries (HOE) about the Fishery, 16 October 1701, PRO, CO 195/3, f.13.

111 Morandière 1962,1:19–20.

112 Morandière 1962,1:22. There are no seventeenth- or eighteenth- century records of native people burning the boats of the English.

113 Governor de Brouilan to the Minister of Marine, 25 October 1694, NAC, MG 1, Archives des Colonies, Série C"C, vol.2, f.20.

114 Report by the Captain of *Tryfall Merchantman*, 9 June 1697, PRO, CO 194/1, f.271a.

115 Pastore 1985,324–5; ibid. 1987,56–7.

116 Burd Journal, 1726, PANL, MG 231. Supercargo is the title of the officer on a merchant ship who is in charge of the cargo.

117 Report by William Taverner, 8 December 1727, PRO, CO 194/8, f.283.

118 Lysaght 1971,132.

CHAPTER THREE

1 Speck 1922,123–4.

2 Linnamae 1975; Penney 1984a, 1985a, 1986; Simpson 1984; Tuck 1984b.

3 Hoffman 1963,13–79; Thevet 1568,133–6; de Laet 1640,36; Purchas 1906,18:304; see also chapter 1.
4 Bishop John Inglis, Diary, 2 July 1827, NAC, microfilm A 713.
5 Adney and Chapelle 1964,20,26.
6 Thwaites 1959,3:82–4; Denys 1968,119, 138, 198, 214–15, 420–2; Lescarbot 1968,3:192.
7 Jukes 1969,1:151.
8 Ibid.; Speck 1922,119–20.
9 Champlain 1933,5:160.
10 Quinn 1979,3:347, 352, docs.459, 460.
11 Bourque and Whitehead 1985,327–41.
12 Campeau 1967,208, letter by Biard, 1 July 1612; the name "Presentic" was most likely taken over by the Micmac from the Spanish or French (Hewson 1981,11).
13 Denys 1968,186–7.
14 Testification by John Mathews, 28 January 1670, BL, Egerton Ms. 2395, f.471.
15 Order in Council, upon Report of the Committee for Foreign Plantations, 15 April 1675, CSPC, 1675–76:226, doc.550; Observations in the year 1675 by me [Sir John Berry] then commanding *HMS Bristol*, in relations to the trade and inhabitants of Newfoundland, CSPC, 1675–76:329, doc.769. In this context "Beaver trade" meant trapping for beaver.
16 In "A Brief Narrative concerning Newfoundland," 24 November 1676, PRO, CO 1/38, f.175, John Downing recorded the testimony of one John Aylred, who had been in Newfoundland in 1661. It reads: "Some Canida Indians [usually believed to refer to Micmac] are coming from the Forts of Canida in french Shalloways with French fowling pieces all spared them by the French of Canida." Since Aylred did not give the location that was visited, the Indians could also have been Montagnais who came to the west coast, or Maliseet, or Abenaki.
17 In 1695 a family of eleven and possibly others had settled near the fort (Judgement du council de guerre, 15 October 1695, NAC, MG 1, F.3, vol.54, ptie 2, cited in O'Reilly and Grodinsky 1982,28).
18 Report by Christian Pollard, who had fishing establishments in Ferryland and Caplin Bay, Newfoundland, dated 1697, CSPC, 1696–97:444, doc.922.
19 "Deposition of Frances Andrews and John Evans, St John's," 29 July 1704, PRO, CO 194/22, f.44; Lieutenant Moody to Governor Dudley, April 1705, CSPC, 1704–05:501, doc.1056; Colin Campbell to Council of Trade and Plantations, 15 June 1705, ibid.,538, doc.1185; S. de Sourdeval, 30 June 1707, NAC, MG 1, Series B, vol.29, pt.2, pp. 429–30, and M. de Costebelle, 10 November 1707, NAC, MG 1, C"C, vol.5, p. 164–8, cited in O'Reilly and Grodinsky 1982, Annex 1:10–11.
20 M. de Costebelle, 28 August 1705, NAC, MG 1, C"C, vol.4, p. 261, and M. de Subercase, 22 October 1705, ibid., p. 321, de Costebelle, 22 May 1706, NAC, MG 1, Series B, vol.27, pt.4, p. 695, cited in O'Reilly and Grodinsky 1982, Annex 1:5,8.
21 De Costebelle, 30 June 1707, NAC, MG 1, Series B, vol.29, pt.2, pp. 388–9; de Sourdeval, 30 June 1707, NAC, MG 1, Series B, vol.29, pt.2, p. 429–30; ibid., 18 October 1707, NAC, MG 1, C"C, vol.5, p. 242–4, de Costebelle, 10 November 1707, NAC,

MG I, Series B, vol.29, pt.2, p. 164–8, cited in O'Reilly and Grodinsky 1982, Annex 1,11–12.

22 Letters to de Costebelle, 6 June 1708, NAC, MG I, Series B, vol.29, pt.5, pp. 1136–40, and 10 August 1709, vol.30, pt.3, pp. 723–4, cited in O'Reilly and Grodinsky 1982, Annex 1,12, 14.

23 Report by de Brouillan, 25 October 1694, cited in Morandière 1962,1:20.

24 Howley 1915,292–4, 333–4; Patterson 1892,157; Dawson 1860,462.

25 Bartels 1978, cited in O'Reilly and Grodinsky 1982,9; Pastore 1978,9, 16, and 1989a,69, fn.54; Upton 1977a,150; Marshall 1988a,58.

26 William Taverner's Report to Mr Popple (written in 1715, included with papers dated 1718), PRO, CO 195/6, f.238, 241.

27 "Declaration et autres procédures du Sr Estienne Mousnier," capitaine du navire le St Antoine de Québec 23 May 1711, NAC, MG I, Archives des Colonies, Série G 3, Notariat-Isle Royale, No provisoire 8/176, Notariat non/classé (Terre-Neuve), pièce no.26.

28 Jukes 1969,2:126, 129–30 (in Howley 1915,25, 26), as told by John Peyton, Jr; Cormack Papers 12/84 (in Howley 1915,183) contains the note "two heads"; Inglis, Diary, 2 July 1827, mentions "two heads" NAC, microfilm A 713; "Sketches of savage life," 1836,316–17, "two heads."

29 Jukes 1969,2:126, 129–30 (in Howley 1915,25, 26); Hans Rollmann (1994, pers. com.) supplied me with a reference to Archbishop H.F. Howley, who recorded the tradition as told by Adelaide Moat (née Benoit) probably in the 1870s; Adelaide Moat died at Sandy Point aged ninety-six; in her version it was the Micmac who invited Red Indians to a feast and when they were arranged in a circle for a war dance, Red Indian and Micmac alternating, the Micmac drew their knives at a given signal and plunged them into the Beothuk next to them.

30 Cormack Papers 12/84 (in Howley 1915,25, 183).

31 "Sketches of savage life," 1836,316, 322.

32 Jukes 1969,1:172, and 2:130, fn.

33 Speck 1922,28,121–2.

34 Trigger 1985,167.

35 Thompson 1956,4:340.

36 Speck 1922,28.

37 Lieut. John Cartwright, "Remarks on the situation of the Red Indians … 1768," PRRL, 971.8 C24 (in Howley 1915,35); Cartwright to Governor Hugh Palliser, 19 September 1768, PRRL, 971.8 C24, (in Howley 1915,44).

38 Inglis, Diary, 2 July 1827, NAC, microfilm A 713. The entries in this diary are more detailed than those in the diary that Inglis sent to the SPG (USPG, C/can/NS9, doc.57–8). The Exploits Islands, also called Exploits Burnt Islands, are two small islands connected by a bridge and are often referred to as "Exploits Island."

39 Jukes 1969,2:130; Howley (1915,270) spelled the name "Shannock"; Lloyd (1875,29, fn.) spelled the term "Shonack."

40 Howley 1915,176.

41 Ibid.,181; Cormack Papers 35/84 (in Howley 1915,230) note that Shanawdithit was also fired at by a white man who wounded her in the palm of her hand and in the leg.

42 Howley 1915,176.

43 "Sketches of savage life," 1836,316, 322.

44 Speck 1922,65.

45 "Affidavit from Philip Roberts, Richard Selman and Samuel May, stated before two Justices of the Peace," 10 January 1696–97, PRO, CO 194/1, f.50.

46 Earl of Sunderland to Commissioners for Trade and Plantations, 24 May 1709, CSPC, 1708–09, doc.533: "Great indignation too, had been aroused by the action of the French in paying a reward of 5 pound sterling to their Indians for the head of every English subject brought in by them which the savages cannot challenge without shewing the scalps"; Governor Dudley of Massachusett Bay and New Hampshire to Council of Trade and Plantations, 1 March 1709, CSPC, 1708–09, doc.391. In 1708 scalps from English subjects obtained by French Indians in New Hampshire were carried to Canada for rewards (Commissioners for Trade and Plantations to Governor Dudley, 8 July 1708, PRO, CO 5/912, f.448–51).

47 O'Callaghan and Fernow 1858,10:174–5. In the 1750s bounties were offered and given to a Cape Breton Indian by the French at Louisbourg (Dickason 1976, 99). "A Plan of the Bay of 3 Islands in Newfoundland … 1764" (NAC, Cartogr. Div. H 3/140/1764) has the notation that the information on inland features was gathered from "Cape Breton Indians."

48 Jukes 1969,2:129. The information comes from Peyton, Jr (in Howley 1915,26). Jukes (1969,1:172) states, "at the beginning of the last century"; Howley (1915,269), who quoted Jukes's report, changed the wording to "at the beginning of the seventeenth century."

49 Harrisse (1900,153–4), as translated by Charles A. Martijn (1980s, pers. com.).

50 Howley 1915,152, W.E. Cormack published a shortened version of the report of his walk across Newfoundland in 1822 in the *Edinburgh Philosophical Journal*, 1824; his unabridged report *Narrative of a Journey* … was first published in 1856 under the auspices of government upon the instigation of Governor Darling (Darling to Henry Labouchere MP, 11 October 1856, PRO, CO 194/148, f.406–7); Darling had received the manuscript from the Honourable Joseph Noad, Surveyor General of Newfoundland, who left the province in 1855. The *Narrative* was reprinted in 1873 by Rev. Moses Harvey, and later by J.P. Howley (1915,130–68); in this work all references to Cormack's *Narrative* refer to the Howley version.

51 Such 1973; Winter 1975; Whitelaw 1978,187.

52 Jukes 1969,1:172, and 2:130; Millais 1907,217; Cormack Papers 12/84 (in Howley 1915,183.)

53 Speck 1922,28.

54 Morandière 1962,1:22.

55 Lack of good anchorage was reported by Basque fishing crews Selma Barkham (1980s, pers. com.).

56 There were no French fishing stations in this part of White Bay (Head 1976,12,15).

57 Jukes (1969,1:172) said "70 years ago."

58 Cape Ray: Extract of representation of the Board of Trade to His Majesty upon the State of Newfoundland, 29 February 1715/16, PRO, CO 194/26, ff. 209–10; Governor Graves to Lords Commissioners of Trade and Plantation, 20 October 1763, NAC, Graves Papers, microfilm A 133. Port aux Basques: Lieutenant Governor Armstrong to Duke of Newcastle, 17 November 1727, CSPC, 1726–27:402, doc.789 XV. Codroy: Log of *HMS Pearl*, 4–5 August 1768, MDHYD, Misc. Series I, vol.21, p. 308. Anguille: Taverner's survey of the French coast, 1718, PRO, CO 194/6, f.241; Graves to Lords Commissioners, 20 October 1763, PRO, CO 194/15, f.102. St George's Bay: Captain Reynolds's Report of Native and Foreign Indians to Governor Elliot, 1788, PRO, CO 194/21, vol.1, f.172; Capt. Ambrose Crofton to Governor Waldegrave, 10 January 1798, PRO, CO 194/40, f.19; Major Thorne to Henry Dundas, 30 June 1793, PRO, WO 1/15, f.84–6; Bay of Islands: ibid.; William Parker, Chart of the Isle of Newfoundland, 1770, MDHYD, 346/Ahl. Pointe Riche: Palliser to Earl of Shelbourne, 15 December 1767, PRO, CO 194/27, p. 320–1. Port au Choix, Ferolle, St John Bay: Palliser to Lieutenant Stanford, 16 August 1767, PRO, ADM 50/19; Reynolds's Report of native foreign Indians to Elliot, 1788, PRO, CO 194/21, vol.1, f.172.

59 "A Plan of the Bay of 3 Islands in Newfoundland ... 1764," NAC, Cartogr. Div. H 3/140/1764; John Cartwright, "A Map of the Island of Newfoundland," NAC, NMC 14033; Parker, "Chart of the Isle of Newfoundland," 1770, MDHYD, 346/Ahl.

60 Palliser to Admiralty, 25 August 1766, PRO, CO 194/27, f.257; Griffith Williams 1765,34.

61 Palliser to John Broom, 29 July 1764, PANL, CSOC, GN 2/1/A, vol.3, f.235, and Palliser to Lieutenant Colonel Pringle, 22 October 1765, ibid., f.345–6. This policy was introduced by Governor Hugh Palliser in 1765 to confine the Micmac to "their own side of the Gulph" since in the eyes of the English the Micmac were still "foreign" Indians; Palliser to Hon. M. Franklin, 16 October 1766, PANL, CSOC, GN 2/1/A, vol.4, f.9–10.

62 Cartwright, "Remarks ... 1768," PRRL, 971.8 C24, (in Howley 1915,35, 44); Cartwright 1792,1:12 (in Howley 1915,48.)

63 Cartwright to Palliser, 19 September 1768, PRRL, 971.8 C24 (in Howley 1915,44).

64 Best described by William E. Cormack (Howley 1915,152); Reynolds's Report of Native and Foreign Indians to Elliot, 1788, PRO, CO 194/21, f.172. Earlier records are not as detailed but refer to the Micmac's practice of living on the coast during the winter season; Crofton to Waldegrave, 10 January 1798, PRO, CO 194/40, f.26–7; Capt. H.F. Edgell to Governor Charles Morris Pole, 28 August 1801, PANL, Pole Papers, MG 205; Rev. John Chapman, USPG, C/CAN/NF 3, doc.107, p. 367.

65 Jukes 1969,2:130; Howley 1915,26, 270.

66 Martijn 1980a, 105–25; ibid. 1980b, 77–104; Taylor 1980, 18–124; On Saddle Island, Red Bay, Inuit remains that were found mixed with Basque material were thought to originate from the second half of the sixteenth century (Tuck 1985, 227–32).

67 Morandière 1962, 1:385; in contrast to the designation of "Petit Nord" for this limited area, many seventeenth- and early-eighteenth-century maps mark the entire Northern Peninsula as "Petit Nord."

68 Captain Wheeler to William Blathwayt, 27 October 1684, PRO, CO 1/55, f.242b; Captain Deprès-Lefévre was attacked by Inuit in Boutitou (Hilliers Harbour) in 1693 (Morandière 1962, 1:21); see also de Brouague, 6 September 1719, NAC, MG 1 Archives des Colonies, Série C"A Correspondance générale, Canada, vol.109, pp. 155–74 (transcript).

69 Cited in Morandière 1962, 1:18–19; ibid., 19, deposition by Vice Admiral Théve-nard, 1785, who had himself seen the results of such attacks in 1753–54 and knew that the natives were "Esquimaux" from Labrador; Martijn 1980a, 107; Champlain 1933, 5:168–9.

70 Morandière 1962, 1:19–20, 387; Michelant and Ramé (1867, 34) cite "délibérations des habitants de St Malo," 26 October 1610.

71 Captain Francis Wheeler of HMS *Tiger* to William Blathwayt, 27 October 1684, PRO, CO 1/55, f.242b, also in CSPC 1681–85:707, doc.1907.

72 "A Reply to the answeare of the description of Newfoundland," Archbishop Laud, 29 September 1639, PRO, CO 1/10, f.97–115 (abbreviated in Howley 1915, 23); summarized in CSPC, 1574–1660:303, 1639.

73 This sequence of events was also suggested by Howley (1915, 23 fn.2); Nicholas Frottet Landelle related that French fishermen were killed by the "sauvaiges de Terre neuffve" in 1609 (in Michelant and Ramé 1867, Documents sur le Canada:35).

74 De Brouague, 6 September 1719, mentions the large size of Inuit groups that came to the Newfoundland coast (NAC, MG 1 Archives des Colonies, Série C"A Correspondance générale, Canada, vol.109, pp.155–74, transcript). Charles A. Martijn (1980s, pers. com.) has suggested that the attackers may simply have dressed themselves in looted clothing without intending to use the garments as disguise; there are numerous examples of native people (not Beothuk) who adopted the apparel of Europeans, for example the natives Gosnold met in 1602 (Quinn 1979, 3:352, doc.460).

75 Deputation to the Lords Commissioners of Trade and Plantations, 1714, PRO, CO 194/6, f.4; Biggar 1930,449–53; Rogers & Leacock 1981,171; Quinn 1981,18, 25, 26; Williams 1987,179.

76 Fay 1961, 19. Several places at Petit Nord bear Channel Island names (Le Messurier 1916, 449–53.)

77 Morandière 1962, 1:21–2; Papers of Abraham Hill, Commissioner of Trade and Plantations, 1698, BL, Sloane MSS. 2902,197–202; Trudel (1978, 115) lists many incidents of Inuit robbing fishing stations on the Labrador coast.

78 Morandière 1962, 1:22; Lahontan 1905, 1:308; Commodore Graydon's answer to Head of Enquiries on the Newfoundland Fishery, 16 October 1701, PRO, CO 195/3, f.11, 13; William Taverner's Report to Lords Commissioners 1713–17 (PRO, CO 194/6, f.241) cites Captain Dehalldy's testimony.

79 Letters from Courtmanche cited in Trudel 1978, 107, 109; Morandiére 1962, 1:19; Representation by Governor Hugh Palliser, 16 April 1765, PRO, CO 194/27, f.44; Board of Trade report, 15 March 1763, PRO, PC 1/52, vol.6:354; report from HMS *Solebay*, 20 August 1763 to 30 November 1764, MDHYD, Misc. Papers Series I, S (II), vol.26; Report on the State of the Newfoundland Fisheries, 1761, by Thomas Cole, WLCL, Townsend Papers, box 34.

80 Richard Master to Lords Commissioners of Trade and Plantations, 29 November 1762, PRO, CO 194/15, f.45; Proposals for Encouraging the Fisheries in Labrador by Governor Hugh Palliser, 13 April 1766, BL, Add. Ms. 33030, Newcastle Papers, vol.CCCXLV, f.220.

81 Palliser to Lord Egmont, 31 March 1766, PRO, CO 194/27, f.178–9.

82 Palliser to Earl of Halifax, 11 September 1765, PRO, CO 194/27, f.99–104; "Journal of the two Brethren Jens Haven and C.A. Schloezer," 23 July to 3 September 1765, PRO, CO 194/16, f.240–5; Lysaght 1971, 199–200; Palliser's Journal 1767–68, 26 July 1767, PRO, ADM 50/19; Palliser believed that the Inuit were essentially enterprising and "timorous" people who had become enraged by the barbarous treatment they received and acted in a spirit of revenge (Palliser, 31 October 1768, PRO, PC 1/52, unbound handwritten notes). Palliser's representation to the Board of Trade, concerning the State of the Newfoundland and Labrador Fishery, 31 March 1766, PRO, PC 1/52; Palliser's report on the Labrador Fishery, 1 August 1766, PRO, CO 194/27, f.283.

83 Palliser's proclamation, 28 August 1765, PRO, CO 194/27, f.211–13; "Short Account of the Territory of Labrador," by Officer Roger Curtis, 1772, PRO, CO 194/30, f.156–91.

84 Governor John Elliot, "Report on Foreign and Native Indians, 1786," PRO, CO 194/21, f.51; Capt. Ambrose Crofton to Governor William Waldegrave, Report on the State of the Indians, 3 February 1798, PRO, CO 194/40, F.17–34.

85 Commodore William Elliot on trade with natives in Labrador, 4 October 1810, PRO, CO 194/49, f.117a-118; Report by Lieutenant Adams, 1824, MDHyD, Misc. Papers, Series II, Ab4 vol.35:221. In 1824 only a few Inuit stragglers journeyed down the Labrador coast.

86 Graydon's answer to HOE, 16 October 1701, PRO, CO 195/3, f.11, 13.

87 Cartwright, "Remarks … 1768," PRRL, 971.8 C24 (in Howley 1915, 29–41; information on Beothuk/Inuit relations, 35).

88 Lysaght 1971, 196: according to an account by Moravian missionaries who had been sent to Labrador in 1765, Governor Palliser believed that a large number "of the Esquimaux Tribes" lived in Newfoundland close to Fogo Island. Palliser sought the missionaries' help in meeting and coming to an agreement with them. Taking all factors into account, the natives would have been Beothuk rather than Inuit.

89 Forster (1788, 143, ref.77) mentions hostilities between inland Newfoundland Indians and the northern Esquimaux but does not quote a primary source.

90 Charlevoix (1962, 144) does not disclose his source.

91 Shuldham's report on Labrador missions, written by Officer Curtis, 5 September 1773, PRO, CO 194/31, f.52–75; Graydon's answer to HOE, 16 October 1701, PRO, CO 195/3, f.11, 13; William Taverner's Report to Lords Commissioners, PRO, CO 194/6, f.241.

92 John Bland to Governor Waldegrave, 20 October 1797, GN 2/1/A, vol.14, f.90–4 (in Howley 1915, 58).

93 Jukes 1969, 2:130.

94 "His Excellency Sir John Thomas Duckworth … to the Micmacs, the Esquimaux and other American Indians frequenting [Newfoundland]," August 1810, PRO, ADM 80/122, f.29 (in Howley 1915, 70); Howley 1915, 108; a similar proclamation was issued by Governor Hamilton in 1819.

95 Howley 1915, 104–5.

96 Lieut. David Buchan's "Sketch of the River Exploits as explor'd in Jan.y and March 1811, Newfoundland," PRO. CO 194/50 MPG 589, see Fig.10.1.

97 Inglis, Diary, 3 July 1827, USPG, C/Can/NS 9, doc.57–8.

98 Cell 1982, 112, 117; De Laet (1625) repeated Whitbourne's tale that the assistants of the whalers were Newfoundland Indians, but he added that they covered themselves and their clothes with ochre; his description of the Newfoundland Indians was based on the reports by Petri Martyris, Richard Hakluyt, Samuel Purchas, Richard Whitbourne, and probably John Guy (though he did not acknowledge Guy). Although some of these writers described the Beothuk as using ochre, none of them said that the assistants of the whalers were covered with ochre; this piece of information seems to have been added by de Laet. Dickason (1984, 102) claims that the Indian helpers of the Basques were Micmac and cites de Laet and Whitbourne as her sources, neither of whom, however, identify the native people who assisted the Basques as Micmac.

99 Isasti 1850, 154. The pertinent section reads: "*Otros se llaman montaneses o canaleses* …," translated by Selma Barkham (1980s, pers. com.) as "The others are called people of the mountains *or* of the channel."

100 Trudel 1978:100–01; Packard 1891:246,259.

101 See also Tuck 1987, 64.

102 In 1675 Sieur de Courcelle came to the Bay of Islands where Spanish boats had moored; native people there agreed to supply venison and partridges for his crew; it took them three days to return from their hunting trip. These native hunters, who seemed to be familiar with the country thereabout, could have been Montagnais or possibly Micmac (Harisse 1900, 317–8, Sieur de Courcelle, 1675, Manuscript Chart of Newfoundland and Labrador).

103 Trudel 1978, 105–6; Martijn 1990a, 231.

104 De Brouague, 6 September 1719, NAC, MG 1, Archives des Colonies, Série C"A Correspondance générale, Canada, vol.109, 155–74 (transcript).

105 Martijn 1990a, 233.

106 Commander Percy's Report relating to the Fishery and Trade of Newfoundland, 13 October 1720, PRO, CO 194/7, f.7.

107 Report relating to the Fishery and Trade of Newfoundland for 1722, rec. in Britain, 12 November 1722, PRO, CO 194/7, f.99.

108 Taverner to Commissioners of Trade and Plantations, 12 February 1733/34, PRO, CO 194/23, f.184.

109 Morandière 1962, 1:21, recorded in 1720.

110 Ibid., 21–2, recorded in 1719.

111 Ibid.; Martijn 1990a, 233.

112 In 1642 Jesuits reported that "sundry contagious disease consumed the greater part of the Montagnais and Algonquins who are neighbours to us," and while formerly about 1,200 to 1,500 people – including Montagnais – used to assemble at Tadoussac, disease had by then nearly exterminated this group (Thwaites 1959, 24:271; ibid., 29:123); Dobyn (1983, 15, 17) identified these diseases as smallpox and measles; see also Marshall 1992, 143.
113 Howley 1915, 26, 270; Cartwright to Palliser, 19 September 1768, postscript 8 November 1769, PRRL, 971.8 C24 (in Howley 1915, 44–5).
114 Palliser, 19 March 1766, answer to HOE, PRO, PC 1/52, copy no.15.
115 Curtis to Shuldham, probably 1772, PRO, CO 194/30, f.158–61.
116 Captain George Lumsdain's report on the French Fisheries between Cape St John and Cape Ray, 25 November 1785, PRO, CO 194/36, f.65.
117 Ibid.; Elliot's Answer to HOE on Foreign and Native Indians, 1786, PRO, CO 194/21, f.51.
118 Officer R.C. Reynolds's Report of Native and Foreign Indians for 1788, PRO, CO 194/21, f.172.
119 Record kept by Captain Reynolds of HMS *Echo*, 17 April 1787 to 13 February 1788, entry "Griquet Bay, Nfld," MDHYD, Misc. Papers Ab3, vol.34:568–9.
120 Log of HMS *Winchelsea*, 1787, NMM, N/W/1. Two French fishermen from Hawke's Harbour on a shooting excursion inland were robbed of their arms and stripped almost naked by a group of Montagnais (Cartwright 1792,3:206).
121 Inglis, Diary, 4 July 1827, USPG, C/Can/NS 9, doc.57–8.
122 Jukes 1969, 2:130–1; Howley (1915, 270) paraphrased Juke's words.
123 Robbins 1989, 23, 29.

CHAPTER FOUR

1 To the Lords Commissioners for Trade and Plantations from the Newfoundland Merchants, 1 December 1703, PRO, CO 195/3, f.258; Capt. Wm. Taverner to Lord Stanhope, 1718, PRO, CO 194/6, f.227.
2 The Beothuk term mamateek for house is only known in the singular; since it has been incorporated into English (DNE 1982;322) the plural is expressed by the addition of the letter "s". Pipestem pieces found on the Beothuk site at Frenchman's Island were dated to about AD 1650 (Evans 1981,90); Answer to Heads of Enquiry, 1 March 1702/3, PRO, CO 195/3, f.175; census figures for Bonavista Bay: Bonavista: 290; Fox Isle near Greenspond: 125 (Report by Captain Crone, 31 October 1711, PRO, CO 194/24, f.31a).
3 Howley 1915,269.
4 Report by Commander Percy, 13 October 1720, PRO, CO 194/7 f.7.
5 Carbon samples collected during excavations in 1990 by archaeologists Laurie MacLean and William Gilbert yielded four dates between AD 1490 and 1630 (1991, pers. com.); artifacts unearthed in 1991 suggest a Beothuk presence until the end of the eighteenth century (Laurie MacLean, 1992, pers. com.).
6 Answer to HOE by Captain Falkingham, 4 October 1732, PRO, CO 194/9, f.215: "New settlements have been started at Fogo and Twillingate this year."

7 John Masters, a Principal Trader to Newfoundland and Agent to the Inhabitants there, Silly Cove [Winterton], to the Office of Lord High Admiral of Great Britain, rec. 6 September 1740, PRO, CO 194/12, f.1–3.
8 Morandière 1962,1:22. See Pastore 1989,58–71 on contraction of Beothuk world.
9 For more details see chapter 19.
10 Henry Crout (Crout to Sir Percival Willoughby, 8 September 1612 and August 1613, MMSS, Mix 1/20 and Mix 1/24 [Appendix 1]) requested a salmon net from the company and in 1613 sent a barrel of pickled salmon to England; Cell 1982,94,200; Poynter 1963,55; Answer to HOE, 11 January 1705/6, PRO, CO 195/4, f.85, refers to a "noble salmon fishery" in Salmon Cove, Bonavista Bay.
11 Petition by George Skeffington, 23 February 1720, PRO, CO 194/6, f.332.
12 Instructions by A. Popple, 12 April 1722, PRO, CO 194/7, f.122–39; NJHA 1884,757–60, cited in Taylor 1985,24.
13 Prowse 1972,283.
14 Commander Ogle to A. Popple, 13 October 1719, PRO, CO 194/6, f.312; Wm. Keen, 26 December 1720, CSPC, 1719–20, doc.347. A tierce was originally a measurement for wine, about forty-two gallons; a tierce of salmon as used in Newfoundland records is usually converted to 360 lb. [162 kg] round weight (Taylor 1985, 9).
15 Captain Scott to A. Popple, 16 November 1718, CSPC, 1717–18, doc.751.
16 Report on the Newfoundland Fishery, 1759, WLCL, Townsend Papers, box 46. The anonymous author, who was then commander of a ship, claimed that the form letters for the "Report on the Fishery" were usually written ahead of time and the figures hastily filled in by the magistrate when the naval officer came to collect them; he personally checked the figures given for cod in the form letter for Conception Bay by going into every creek and cove and found that the total, based on his own figures, was about three times that of the official one.
17 Figures between 1717 and 1722 are quoted from: CSPC, 1717–18, doc.751, ibid., 1719–20, doc.414; ibid., 1722–23, doc.337. Beginning with 1723, the figures for salmon catches are taken from Taylor 1985,52–8, Table A3.
18 Captain Reynolds's "Enquiry into the State of the Newfoundland Salmon Fishery" 24 November 1786 (PRO, CO 194/21, f.43), lists the names of men or firms that held a salmon licence and the brook(s) their licences were issued for.
19 Head 1976,75.
20 Taylor 1985,7. Stake nets were gill nets strung on posts or stakes that had been driven into the river bottom; the first reference found to floating gill nets comes from the 1760s, at which time gill nets were used in the Bay of Exploits; Peyton (1987,7), describes the "rack works" as weirs or dams consisting of stakes driven into the river bed like a fence; these stakes were intertwined with brushwood and diverted the main stream and school of salmon to the narrow opening, where "a rack" or "toothed bar" allowed the flow of water through but blocked the passage of the salmon; the salmon could be dipped out in the dammed shallow pool.
21 Answer to the HOE by Commander Bowler, 20 April 1725, PRO, CO 194/8, f.14.
22 Answer to HOE, rec. 12 November 1722, PRO, CO 194/7, f.115.
23 Ibid.
24 Wm. Keen, 26 December 1720, CSPC, 1719–20, doc.335.

25 Answer to HOE by Commodore Bowler, 9 October 1724, PRO, CO 194/7, f.240.
26 Governor Ph. Vanbrugh's report on the Newfoundland fishery, 6 November 1738 (PRO, CO 194/4, f.142), states that there was no obstruction to the salmon fishery but that complaints had been received about thieving, presumably by local inhabitants.
27 Burd Journal, 1726, PANL, MG 231.
28 Answer to HOE, 14 October 1729, PRO, CO 194/8, f.276; Prowse (1972,283) claims that as early as the 1720s salmon catchers from Fogo and Twillingate occupied several rivers in Notre Dame Bay, including the Exploits River, but he did not cite his source.
29 Letter Book from an officer of *HMS Drake*, 1732, NMM, LBK/12; Answer to HOE by Captain Lee, 29 September 1735, PRO, CO 194/10, f.1–22.
30 John Cartwright, "Remarks … 1768," PRRL, 971.8 C24, (in Howley 1915,33).
31 Cartwright 1792,1:14 (in Howley 1915,49).
32 R.P. Rice's Report on the limits of the estuaries of salmon rivers for netting purposes, for the year 1884, NJHA 1885,425, App.
33 Report on the Salmon Fishery in Fogo and Bonavista, 1800, PANL, Pole Papers, MG 205. The Terra Nova River, which flows into Alexander Bay close to The Beaches site, was not commercially exploited until 1829 (Taylor 1985,9).
34 Reynolds's Report on the Salmon Fishery, 24 November 1786, PRO, CO 194/21, f.43.
35 Governor Byron's Proclamation concerning the salmon fishery, 29 July 1769, PRO, CO 194/28, f.123.
36 Commodore Duff's Enquiry into the State of the Salmon Fishery, 1775, NMM, DUF/13; Duff also prohibited the granting of exclusive rights to salmon rivers.
37 Annual Report of the Newfoundland Fisheries Commission, 1889, 18–25, cited in Taylor 1985,25; Taylor 1985,52–8, Table A3; Bishop John Inglis recorded in his diary, 2 July 1827 (NAC, microfilm A 713), that "Mr Peyton has the right of the Salmon fisheries [on the Exploits River] which employ a dozen men who fish at various points many miles asunder for 30 miles. He now seldom takes more than 150 tierces of 3 Cwt in the year worth from 12 to 16 dollars." Howley (n.d., chapt. 1886) notes: "Tues. June 29th, Salmon are very scarce this season in fact hardly any at all in this bay [Exploits]. Like everything else they are almost destroyed."
38 Reynolds's Report on the Salmon Fishery, 1786, PRO, CO 194/21, f.43.
39 Marshall 1989,123, 130, 133, 135, 138, 139.
40 Ibid.,140.
41 Ibid.,130.
42 Howley 1915,267, 270, 282.
43 Ibid.,283; Peyton 1987,8.
44 Ibid.,10; Howley 1915,267.
45 Crout to Willoughby, August 1613, MMss, Mix 1/24 (Appendix 1).
46 Cartwright, "Remarks … 1768," PRRL, 971.8 C24 (in Howley 1915,33).
47 Ibid.; Cartwright 1792,1:10 (in Howley 1915,48); Cell 1982,194; Marshall 1989,127, 131–2.

48 Ibid.,127.

49 Cartwright 1792,1:10 (in Howley 1915,48); Lysaght 1971,133. In 1766 Banks commented on the Beothuk's visits to Funk Island.

50 Biggar 1924,6.

51 Answer to HOE by Commodore Aldred, 26 November 1710, PRO, CO 194/4, f.554.

52 Cartwright 1792,1:6 (in Howley 1915,47).

53 Marshall 1989,120; now called Gannet Islands.

54 Ibid.,128.

55 Peters and Burleigh 1951,246–9.

56 The great auk was extinct in Newfoundland by about 1800, and extinct in the world by 1844 (Encyclopedia of Newfoundland and Labrador 1981,1:89).

CHAPTER FIVE

1 For details see chapter 19.

2 Cumbaa 1984, analysis of faunal remains excavated at the Beothuk site at Boyd's Cove.

3 Quinn 1979,4:140, doc.632, and 4:146, doc.636. Henry Crout's diary from 1 September 1612 to 1 April 1613, cited in Quinn 1979,4:158–74, doc.642; Crout to Sir Percival Willoughby, 8 September 1612, and B. Pearson to Willoughby, April 1613, MMSS, Mix 1/20, Mix 1/21.

4 Answer to HOE by Captain Story, 1681, PRO, CO 1/47, f.52.

5 Williams 1987,190. In the light of information on trapping by the English from other sources, the claim that more than two hundred of the English trapped in winter would have been an exaggeration.

6 Answer to HOE by Commander Graydon, 16 October 1701, PRO, CO 195/3, f.75; Wm. Taverner, 1712, CSPC. 1712–14, vol.22, doc.206.

7 The extent and details of the answers differ; presumably it was not always possible to obtain accurate data for all of Newfoundland, and between 1677 and 1720, few answers to the HOE cite figures; those that are given probably include seal pelts. After 1720 the reports regularly cite figures for furs that were sold; they usually did not include seal takes.

8 After the Treaty of Utrecht (1713), efforts were made to transfer trade for furs with Indians from the French to the English; see Instructions to Wm. Taverner, 22 July 1713, PRO, CO 324/33, f.4; Wm. Taverner (Taverner to Commissioners for Trade and Plantations, 22 October 1714, PRO, CO 194/5, f.254), agreed to this task without saying which native group he intended to approach; Report by Taverner to Commissioners for Trade and Plantations, 10 May 1715, PRO, CO 194/23, f.69.

9 See chapter 3.

10 Answer to HOE by Commander Bowler, 1726, PRO, CO 194/8, f.88; ibid., 1727, CO 194/8, f.151–66; see also CSPC 1726–27, doc.743.

11 Answer to HOE by Commander Vere Beauclerk, 14 October 1729, PRO, CO 194/8, f.270.

12 Answer to HOE by Commander Falkingham, 4 October 1732, PRO, CO 194/9, f.211–46, and CO 194/24, f.118.
13 Letter Book from an officer of *HMS Drake*, 1732, NMM, LBK/12.
14 Answer to HOE by Captain Lee, 29 September 1735, PRO, CO 194/10, f.1–22.
15 Howley 1915,265. This information comes from Mr H.C. Watts, who received it from Thomas Pike, who died in 1843, aged 103.
16 Lieut. John Cartwright "Remarks on the situation of the Red Indians … 1768," PRRL, 971.8 C24, (in Howley 1915,29); Cartwright 1792,1:6 (in Howley 1915,47.)
17 George Cartwright 1792,1:6–7; Howley 1915,50–1.
18 Locke 1974,15, South Exploits site, opposite Rushy Pond; Don Locke, 1970s, pers. com., Red Indian Falls site; Devereux 1965a, 15–16, Ms. 261, Pope's Point site, at Badger Brook; Pastore 1983,137 (kIIa12: circular translucent oyster white and kIIa56: circular transparent bright navy), and 1985,325, MacLean 1990c, 172, Boyd's Cove site. Taylor (1964, Ms.744,2) found blue, white, and black trade beads in Devil's Cove; Patterson (1892,157) mentioned glass beads in the burial on Rencontre Island though the grave goods that are now in the McCord Museum do not include such beads. Burials found on Tilt Island and Comfort Island contained "beads" whose origin was not defined (Howley 1915, 293, 333).
19 Howley 1915,67.
20 Buchan's report, 1811, PRO, CO 194/50, f.153–88, list of articles, 8 August 1819, PANL, CSOC, GN 2/1/A, vol. 30, f.262 (in Howley 1915,78,117).
21 Pastore 1987,57–8.
22 Report by Captain Norris, 24 May 1698, PRO, CO 194/1, f.267.
23 Pastore 1987,48.
24 Hoffman 1963,13; Crout to Willoughby, August 1613, MMSS, Mix 1/24 (Appendix 1); report by Captain Norris, 24 May 1698, PRO, CO 194/1, f.271a.
25 Pastore 1987,57; Morandière 1962,1:22.
26 Buchan's report, 1811, PRO, CO 194/50, f.153–88 (in Howley 1915,86). One exception was cooking pots, which replaced bark vessels; mamateek, the Beothuk term for house, is only known in the singular; since it has been absorbed into English (DNE 1982,322) the plural is expressed by adding the letter "s".
27 Hearne 1958,50.
28 Report on the Newfoundland Fisheries for 1773, PRO, CO 194/31, f. 92.
29 Answer to HOE by John Ruthven, 29 September 1763, NAC, Graves Papers, microfilm A-133. Since the merchants provided hunters with winter provisions, the hunters had to give them first offer on furs and rarely received proper value for the furs; Murray 1968,133.
30 Governor Graves's answer to HOE, 1763, NAC, Graves Papers, microfilm A-133, and Graves Papers, 1763, NMM, GRV/105. Three hundred pounds sterling were received for 300 beaver (at five shillings per pound), 53 fox (silver fox, one guinea; patch fox, ten shillings; red fox, 2.6 shillings), 67 otter (ten shillings each), 96 marten (nine shillings a pair), and 167 catts (probably ermine, also known as pole cat).

The sale value of the different species and the percentage they represent within the total of £300 sterling are calculated as follows: 53 fox (33 red, 16 patch, 4 silver),

£16, or five percent of the total; 67 otter, £34, eleven percent of the total; 96 marten, £21, seven percent of the total; 300 beaver, £150, fifty percent of the total; 167 catt, £79, twenty-seven percent of the total.

By prorating the catch recorded from Croque, based on an annual average of £1,500 sterling in furs for all of Newfoundland (the average between 1755 and 1800), the number of animals trapped in Newfoundland in that year and monies received are estimated as follows: fox £80, 265 pelts; otter £170, 335 pelts; marten £105, 480 pelts; beaver £750, 1500 pelts; "catts" (presumably ermine) £395, 835 pelts, a total of 3,415 pelts. (Beaver pelts are estimated at an average weight of two pounds. George Scott of the Hudson's Bay Company, St John's, explained that beaver pelts are usually sorted into seven sizes, weighing between half a pound and three pounds each.) The given ratio of fox pelts is based on catches in Newfoundland between 1963 and 1993, where on average, red fox accounted for sixty-two percent, patch fox for thirty percent, and silver fox for four percent, (Shane Mahoney, 1995, pers. com.). The price for "catts" (ermine) has been guessed at about nine shillings apiece.

On 16 April 1985 Oscar Forsey, regional biologist with the Wildlife Division, Gander (1985, pers. com.), stated that, based on figures from 1975 to 1984, the average yearly harvest in Newfoundland (of the species listed in 1763 except for marten, now protected) is 5,342 pelts. The ratio is as follows: beaver, 2,675 pelts, fifty percent; red fox, 1,221 pelts, twenty-three percent; otter 660 pelts, twelve percent; ermine, 786 pelts, fifteen percent. Added to this is the annual average of species that were not listed in 1763 from Croque Harbour but that are accounted for in Forsey's listing. They are: black bear, 25; lynx, 306; arctic fox, 3; wild mink, 3,631; muskrat, 1,926; squirrel, 257 (recently introduced).

31 Cumbaa 1984,18; the faunal analysis of bones from a midden at the Beothuk campsite at Boyd's Cove has shown that the Beothuk used to occupy this coastal camp from April to November, consuming black and polar bear, beaver, otter, marten, and seal in addition to caribou.

32 George Cartwright 1792,1:6 (in Howley 1915,47.)

33 John Cartwright, "A Sketch of the River Exploits and the East End of Lieutenants Lake in Newfoundland," NAC, NMC27.

34 Ibid.

35 Peyton 1987,7: Dicks had carved "T.D.1778" into the trunk of a pine tree; it was still clearly visible in 1908.

36 Wm. Parker, "A Chart of the Isle of Newfoundland," 1770, MDHYD, 346/Ahl.

37 Marshall 1989,132, 133.

38 Peyton 1987,7; "Report on the Fishery in Croque and Grandsway," 10 August 1801, PANL, Pole Papers, MG 205.

39 Marshall 1989, 132.

40 Ibid.,127, 137.

41 Answer to HOE by Captain Story, 1681, PRO, CO 1/47, f.52.

42 Cartwright, "Remarks ... 1768," PRRL, 971.8 C24, (in Howley 1915,30–1); Buchan's report, 1811, PRO, CO 194/50, f.153–88, (in Howley 1915,74, 75, 87); Howley 1915,124, 152; Cormack 1824,161.

43 Cell 1982,112; Report on the Newfoundland Fishery for 1681 by Captain Story, PRO, CO 1/47, f.52; Answer to HOE for 1691, PRO, CO 1/68, f.259; Answer to HOE for 1698, 7 March 1700, PRO, CO 195/2, f. 403; Answer to HOE by Captain Crone 31 October 1711, PRO, CO 194/4, f.22, and CO 195/5, f.234.

44 Account of the State of the Fishery in Newfoundland by Commander J.E. Percy, 13 October 1720, PRO, CO 194/7, f.7; Answer to HOE by Captain Osborne, 14 October 1729, PRO, CO 194/8, f.228. According to George Cartwright (n.d., 23), taking into account eighteenth-century methods of producing oil from seal carcasses, one thousand medium-sized animals would yield twenty-eight tons of oil. Though in 1742 the export of seal oil netted £12,550 sterling, this bumper crop was an exception (Chafe 1923,18).

45 The greatest number of seal was caught on the east coast of the Great Northern Peninsula and in White Bay (Head 1976,77).

46 Burd Journal, 1726, PANL, MG 231: "The inhabitants in winter catch seal of which they make very good oil; they catch them in nets set in the manner of herring nets." Governor Falkingham to A. Popple, 4 October 1732, PRO, CO 194/9, f.211–46; Banks described how nets were set to block narrow passages between islands (Lysaght 1971,144–6); Head (1976,76) gives a detailed description of how seal were caught in nets.

47 Chafe 1923,15.

48 Report on the Newfoundland Fishery for 1794, by Governor James Wallace, PRO, CO 194/23, f.497; Sanger 1977,147.

49 The Beaches: Carignan 1975,138, and MacLean and Gilbert, 1991, pers. com.; Boyd's Cove: Cumbaa 1984,18; Howley (n.d., chapter 1871) states that "Harbour Seal were very plentyful" in the island area around New World Island; Penney (1985,54) identified seal bones at L'Anse a Flamme; Wigwam Brook: LeBlanc 1973, App.I: 4–5; see also chapter 19 of this work. Bishop Inglis (Diary, 3 July 1827, NAC, microfilm A713) who was taken on a tour of the Exploits River in July 1827 noted that four seals had been taken that day in salmon nets and that many seals were basking in the sun at "The Falls" [Bishops Falls]; in the 1980s seals could be seen sunning themselves by the dozen there ("Seals and Salmon," 1984, 3).

50 Boulva and McLaren 1979,1; Mansfield 1964,4.

51 In a survey by Boulva and McLaren (1979,3), about 2,010 animals were counted.

CHAPTER SIX

1 By an Order in Council of 1729, the naval commander of the warships that escorted the fishing fleet to Newfoundland was given a commission to be governor and commander-in-chief in Newfoundland during the fishing season (Matthews 1988,101).

2 Governor Hugh Palliser to the Earl of Halifax, 11 September 1765, PRO, CO 194/27, f.99–104; Proclamation by Palliser, 28 August 1765, PRO, CO 194/27, f.211–14; see also chapter 3.

3 George Cartwright probably discussed the matter with Palliser in 1766, while travelling to Newfoundland as a passenger on *HMS Guernsey* under Palliser's command; Cartwright 1792,1:11 (in Howley 1915:48); DCB 1983,5:166.

4 Palliser to the Earl of Hillsborough, 20 October 1768, PRO, CO 194/28, f.26; Lieut. John Cartwright, "Remarks on the situation of the Red Indians ... 1768," PRRL, 971.8 C24, (in Howley 1915,29–41). Cartwright's report together with an "Extract of the Letter to Governor Palliser, 19 September 1768" (in Howley 1915,41–4) and a "Postscript, 8 November 1769" (ibid.,44–5) are bound in hard cover; the volume is entitled "An Account of the Red Indians of Newfoundland by John Cartwright Esq 1768," PRRL, 971.8 C24. Howley (1915,29–45) reprinted these documents, but shortened the text and occasionally changed the spelling.

5 Prowse 1972,324; Log of *HMS Guernsey*, 10 September 1767, PRO, ADM 50/19.

6 A shallop is a boat propelled by oars or a sail, for use in shallow waters or as a means of effecting communication between, or landings from, vessels of a large size. John Cartwright was lieutenant on *HMS Guernsey*, whose log for 1767–68 (PRO, ADM 51/4210) says that Lieutenant Walters set off in *Guernsey*'s shallop on 1 August 1768 to patrol Cape Ray and returned on 9 October; Cartwright set out on 6 August 1768 and returned to the ship on 15 September; Cartwright probably used the shallop of *HMS Liverpool*, which the seamen of *Guernsey* had cleaned and repaired on 5 August; on 6 August the crew "got her [the shallop] alongside, employed getting her ready for sea. 11 am. Lieut. Cartwright sailed in her to the N'ward." Howley (1915,29) included in the title *"by Lieutenant John Cartwright of HMS. Weymouth,"* but the reference to *Weymouth* is not explained since it appears neither on the original report in the collection of the PRRL nor in the printed version of the report in Cartwright 1826,2: App.2:307. The title on Cartwright's 1768 map and on a copy of this map in Cartwright 1826,33, include the notation "Taken on the spot by Lieutenant Jn. Cartwright of His Majesty's ship Guernsey 1768."

7 According to the Thomas Peyton correspondence (CNS Archive, Peyton Family Collection,), John Cousens was a resident of Fogo, Newfoundland, and a close associate and friend of John Peyton, Sr; Cousens originally induced Peyton to come to Newfoundland; both men came from Wimbourne, UK; John Cousens died in Wimbourne on 2 January 1790 (MHA, Keith Matthews's namefile "Cousens").

8 Cartwright to Palliser, 19 September 1768, PRRL, 971.8 C24 (in Howley 1915,43). Since June was employed in the fishery in Fogo where Cousens resided, June was probably in Cousens's employ (Howley 1915,273, 283, 288).

9 Cartwright to Palliser, 19 September 1768, PRRL, 971.8 C24 (in Howley 1915,41–5). The place names used by Cartwright have been converted to today's nomenclature; see also Marshall 1977a, and Handcock 1987.

10 Cartwright to Palliser, 19 September 1768, PRRL, 971.8 C24 (in Howley 1915,43); see also Fig. 6.2. Howley thought that June's Cove was in the area of Millertown.

11 Cartwright to Palliser, 19 September 1768, PRRL, 971.8 C24 (in Howley 1915, 44).

12 Devereux 1970: David Buchan "Sketch of the River Exploits," 1811, Fig. 10.1; "Capt. David Buchan's Track ... 1820," Fig. 12.2; Shanawdithit's sketches 1–3, Plates 10.1, 10.2, 12.2; mamateek is the Beothuk term for house that has been incorporated into English (DNE 1982,322), the plural is expressed by an added "s."

13 Cartwright, "A Sketch of the River Exploits ... 1768," PANL, MG 100, Cartwright Collection. For a section of the map see Fig. 23.3. A note on the map gives details about the river banks, and the water level at different times of the year.

14 Ibid. Cartwright thought that Cousens's information was "remarkably accurate and judicious."

15 John Cartwright, "Remarks ... 1768," PRRL, 971.8 C24 (in Howley 1915,29–41).

16 Cartwright 1826,1:33, 2:307–25. The map included in this publication shows caribou fences and Beothuk dwellings that are not marked on the 1768 map sent to Palliser but are drawn on the map that John Cartwright submitted to the earl of Dartmouth in 1773 (Fig.6.2). According to correspondence in the Cartwright family papers, South Africa, F.D. Cartwright corresponded with Bishop Feild, St John's, about the erection of a memorial to the Cartwright brothers in Cartwright, Labrador, in the 1850s; in June 1858 she referred to the manuscript of Cartwright's report in a letter to her nephew George Cartwright; Lloyd (1875,23) mentioned that the manuscript was in possession of the "Protestant Bishop" in St John's, presumably Bishop Feild. It has been concluded that F.D. Cartwright sent the manuscript to the bishop in the course of her correspondence with him in the 1850s.

17 Instructions to Governor John Byron, 3 May 1769, PRO, PC 5/12, f.219.

18 Proclamation by Byron, 8 July 1769, PRO, ADM 80/121, f.57 (in Howley 1915,45.)

19 Cartwright to Dartmouth, 13 January 1773, NAC, Dartmouth Papers, MG 23 A 1, series 1, vol.16.

20 The position and configuration of Grand Lake and Red Indian Lake, drawn as one body of water, were apparently taken from Capt. James Cook's map of Newfoundland, reprinted in Prowse 1972,317.

21 NAC, NMC 14032; in the following text the presently used "St John" will be applied.

22 Cook charted the south and west coasts from the tip of the Northern Peninsula via Cape Ray to Placentia between 1763 and 1767; Lieutenant Michael Lane charted the east coast between 1768 and 1775.

23 Cartwright, "A Sketch," NAC, NMC 27.

24 See chapter 3.

25 Chapters 20, 22, 23.

26 Cartwright, "Remarks ... 1768," PRRL, 971.8 C24 (in Howley 1915,33).

27 Ibid.; Cartwright 1792,1:5 (in Howley 1915,46).

28 Cartwright to Dartmouth, 13 January 1773, NAC, Dartmouth Papers, MG 23, A1, series 1, vol.16, f.29.

29 Cartwright to Dartmouth, 13 January 1773, NAC, Dartmouth Papers, MG 23, A 1, series 1, vol.16, f.46.

30 Ibid, 44–5.

31 Cartwright, "Remarks ... 1768," PRRL, 971.8 C24 (this part of the report is not reprinted in Howley).
32 The map is torn here.
33 Cartwright "Remarks ... 1768," PRRL, 971.8 C24, (in Howley 1915,38).
34 Marshall 1977a, 233; see also Part Two, chapter 17, section on contemporary estimates of the size of the Beothuk population.
35 Described in more detail in Part Two, chapter 20, section on hunting caribou.
36 The wing-type extensions of fences as described by George Cartwright (1792,1:9) are not marked on John Cartwright's maps.
37 Cartwright, "Remarks ... 1768," PRRL, 971.8 C24 (in Howley 1915,34.)
38 Ibid.; Palliser to Lord Egmont, 31 March 1766, PRO, CO 194/27, f.178. The killing of a pregnant woman was also claimed to have occurred in Labrador, but no trophy was mentioned: George Cartwright (1784, PRO, CO 194/35, f.338–42) had heard of three men who found a wigwam in the woods; all three fired and killed all its occupants. A pregnant woman begged for mercy but the men shot her and brutally exposed the unborn. It remains unresolved whether two separate killings in Labrador and Newfoundland occurred under similar circumstances, or whether the same story erroneously acquired two locations.
39 Cartwright, "Remarks ... 1768," PRRL, 971.8 C24 (in Howley 1915,34.)
40 Ibid. (in Howley 1915,36).
41 Ibid.
42 Ibid. (in Howley 1915,33); George Cartwright 1792,1:6 (in Howley 1915,47).
43 Palliser to Hillsborough, 20 October 1768, PRO, CO 194/28, f.26.
44 Cartwright, "Remarks ... 1768," PRRL, 971.8 C24 (in Howley 1915:35).
45 The log of *HMS Guernsey* (1768, PRO, ADM 51/4210) records: "15. Sept. 6 pm. Arrived our shallop from the N'ward; 16. Sept. got the Shallop alongside to get her ready for sea; 17. Sept. 6 am. Sailed hence our Shallop Tender to the northwd. 22. Oct. p.m. arrived our Shallop from the Northward." Cartwright to Palliser, 19 September 1768, PRRL, 971.8 C24 (in Howley 1915,41).
46 Cartwright 1792,3:49 (in Howley 1915,49); Howley 1915,59, 288, 299, 318; Marshall 1989,140, 154; see also chapter 9.
47 Instructions to Byron, 3 May 1769, PRO, PC 5/12:219 (in Howley 1915,45).
48 Proclamation by Byron, 8 July 1769, PRO, ADM 80/121, f.57, (in Howley 1915,45). The proclamation was reissued by Governor Molineux Shuldham in 1772 (PANL, GN 2/1/A vol.5, f.56), by Governor Robert Duff in 1775, and by Governor John Montague in 1776 (Howley 1915,45); instructions to issue a proclamation were also given to Governor John Elliott, 2 June 1786 (PRO, PC 5/14:401) and to Governor Mark Milbanke, 1 June 1789 (ibid.,507).
49 Lieutenant Governor Otho Hamilton of Placentia to the Duke of Newcastle, 9 June 1748, PRO, CO 194/25, f.10a; Answer to HOE by Captain Lee, 25 September 1736, CSPC, 1735–36, doc.389.
50 English (1990,103) has argued that even before 1750 the order was ignored, and one could therefore postulate that the threat of being sent to England was not serious. Governor Mark Milbanke's Report on the Judicature of Newfoundland to the Lords

of the Committee of Privy Council for Trade and Plantation, 31 December 1789 (PRO, CO 194/21, f.275) includes the request that "something be done to reconcile to vulgar minds the seeming contradiction … between the Commission [of Oyer and Terminer, which permitted the trial of capital offences in Newfoundland] and the Act of Parliament," which required that such offences be tried in England.

51 Instructions to Byron, 3 May 1769, PRO, PC 5/12:219, and to Elliott, 2 June 1786, PRO, PC 5/14:401, and to Milbanke, 1 June 1789, PRO, PC 5/14:507; Routh, St John's Customs House, to Elliot, 11 August 1787, enquiring which type of rum the Beothuk would prefer, PRO, CO 194/37, f.30.

52 Cartwright, "Postscript," 8 November 1769, PRRL, 971.8 C24 (in Howley 1915,44). According to Byron's log of *HMS Antelope*, 3 June 1769 to 25 November 1769 (PRO, ADM 50/2), Cartwright was sent northward in July in the shallop, manned by two petty officers and fifteen seamen, "as my surrogate for Trinity and Conception Bay."

53 Cartwright to Dartmouth, 13 January 1773, "Postscript," 1770, NAC, Dartmouth Papers, MG 23 A 1, series 1, vol.16, f.76–83.

54 Ibid.; Cartwright's "Postscript," 1769, PRRL, 971.8 C24 (in Howley 1915,45). This incident may have been the one referred to as "a flattering prospect at one juncture" that, due to ill fortune, failed.

55 Cartwright to Dartmouth, 13 January 1773, "Postscript," 1770, NAC, Dartmouth Papers, MG 23 A 1, series 1, vol.16, f.76–83.

56 Byron to Phil. Stephens, 17 November 1770, PRO, ADM 1/470.

57 Cartwright 1792,1:4, 5; George Cartwright operated seal and fishing stations in Labrador; a cooper is a cask-and-barrel maker; such containers were used to store saltfish, salmon, seal oil, and other products.

58 "Sketches of savage life," 1836,322.

CHAPTER SEVEN

1 Anspach 1819,181; John McGregor (1832,1:254), who probably had this information from Cormack, claims that it occurred in 1750.

2 Howley 1915,27; Peyton 1987,7.

3 Lysaght 1971,133.

4 Diary of Benjamin Lester, 11 August 1789, DCRO, D 365/F6.

5 Marshall 1989,128, 130, 132–3, 136–9, 140; Howley 1915,271, 275.

6 Locke 1974,14–28; LeBlanc 1973,244; Pastore 1984,100; Devereux 1970,57–60.

7 Marshall 1989,120–1.

8 Ibid,121–2. The men had one gun in the schooner but left it behind when they rowed ashore in their punt. A story recalled by Inspector Grimes in the late 1800s may be an embellished version of this incident; according to this tradition, a party of fishermen was attacked in their boat by the Indians and all were killed except one man, who managed to escape with an arrow sticking in his neck (Howley 1915,273). The same incident may also have been the basis of a story described to Howley by John Wells, a native of Joe Batt's Arm, which contains all elements of the tale reported by Pulling (ibid., 283).

9 Marshall 1989,139.
10 Howley 1915,265.
11 Ibid.,275.
12 Ibid.
13 Ibid., 274; Marshall 1989,130. Since there is no other record of a man with the name of Cooper, it is possible that the tradition originated with the death of William Hooper's father (perhaps erroneously remembered as Cooper), which death, according to Pulling, was avenged by his son.
14 Tocque 1846,285.
15 Howley 1915,283.
16 Ibid., and 270. Rowsell told a similar story of the Beothuk's ability to take aim.
17 Howley 1915,283. This could have been Kiar's Cove, Black Island.
18 Ibid.,273.
19 Ibid.,282.
20 Ibid.,51.
21 Marshall 1989,128.
22 Howley 1915,27.
23 Marshall 1989,138; Howley 1915,50, 271.
24 For example, in a murder trial before a Newfoundland court of a mistress who beat her Irish servant, Mildred Bevil, to death, evidence was produced that she had frequently called the servant an "Indian bitch" and had expressed her belief that killing an Indian was not a crime. Record of Court Proceedings, St John's, 1752, PANL, CSOC, GN 2/1/A, 1752, vol.2, f.9.
25 Marshall 1989,137.
26 Ibid., 133, 134, 139.
27 Ibid.,138.
28 Ibid.,141.
29 Ibid.,129.
30 Ibid.,151; as the crow flies, the distance between Beaver Cove/Cape Farewell and Indian Arm is about sixty to seventy kilometres.
31 Ibid., 134–5.
32 Ibid.,123.
33 Ibid.,140.
34 Howley 1915,268. The name could have been Tracy.
35 Ibid.,269. The fishermen wanted to exhibit the huge Beothuk man to the others and towed him along, but when a northeasterly breeze sprang up, they were obliged to cut the corpse adrift; it came ashore at Lance Cove Head, and all through the summer people went there to inspect the body.
36 Ibid,269.
37 Bloody Bay is marked on "A General Map of the Northern British Colonies …" by Major Holland, 1776, BL, Map No.69917(59); Harold Horwood (1959,42), for example, has claimed that the waters of this bay "once ran red with the blood of Indians slain there by white men."
38 Wilson 1866,308.

39 Stroud (1976,9) collected the information from Mr Fred Stroud, Glovertown South.
40 Lane 1976,3.
41 Howley 1915,273.
42 Ibid.,97, 273; Dobie to Cockburn, 10 September 1823, PRO, CO 194/66, f.326. The Reverend Mr Langharne, a minister at Twillingate, was probably talking about the same man when he informed the surgeon of *HMS Egeria*, James Dobie, that some years earlier a man (from Twillingate?) claimed that he had killed ninety-seven "Red Indians" and wished to make it one hundred.
43 Howley 1915,181.
44 Baughman 1966,424: item X955d concerns a woman who was said to have killed thirty-seven Indians with a broomstick.
45 Marshall 1989,124, 126.
46 Ibid.123.
47 G.C. Pulling record that the men had travelled "between 80 and 100 miles" ("Facts relating to the Native Indians of Newfoundland collected from the Salmon Catchers and Furriers, who reside near those parts frequented by the Indians" 1792, PRO, CO 194/39, f.221–9).
48 Marshall 1989,127.
49 Ibid.,124, 126.
50 Samson Busby, Methodist preacher in Carbonear to the Wesleyan Missionary Committee in London, 16 January 1816, MMS: LR, North America, Newfoundland, 1805–16, Box No.1, file 1d, no.33: included in Busby's story of the raid were descriptions of a Beothuk building a canoe (it should be noted that, for technical reasons, canoes are not built in mid-winter), the killing of two Beothuk passing them on their return trip, the killing of a pregnant woman, and the killing of more Beothuk who were seen "buried to the neck in snow" (Marshall 1986,22).
51 Howley 1915,274. In the two nineteenth-century traditions, the Beothuk were led by a powerful "chief" who, shot by the furriers, died a heroic death; while it is quite possible that shots were fired, it is questionable whether there was a "chief" who was killed.
52 Pulling, "Facts relating to the Native Indians ..." 1792, PRO, CO 194/39, f.226b. They travelled up the Exploits River "about thirty Miles"; assuming that the party started from Miller's house at Upper Sandy Point, the Beothuk camp that they raided would have been in the area of Grand Falls or Rushy Pond.
53 Marshall 1989,135–7.
54 Ibid.,137, Pulling spelled the name Pitman.
55 Ibid.,153, note 73.
56 George Cartwright's proposal, probably submitted in 1784, PRO, CO 194/35, f.338–42. Cartwright's claim that the camp was located at Red Indian Lake is not confirmed by the eyewitness account of Thomas Taylor, who said they travelled three days up the Exploits River and mentions "Indian tracks" on an island and wigwams that were a "very little way from the side of the Brook" (Marshall 1989,137).
57 Howley 1915,50.

58 Howley (1915,268) was told in the late 1800s that fishermen or furriers in Notre Dame Bay, having suffered thefts by Beothuk, determined to kill them all; when they found Beothuk asleep in a wigwam, they surrounded it, set it on fire, and shot down the fleeing Beothuk as they emerged; it is possible that this tale is another version of the Peyton raid.

59 Ibid., 50.

60 Marshall 1989,123.

61 Ibid.,121, 130, 138; Howley 1915,280.

62 Marshall 1989,122.

63 Howley 1915,267; Pulling was told that both Rowsells had been on friendly terms with Beothuk "comparatively speaking," but this does not seem to have been the case (Marshall 1989, 130).

64 Marshall 1989,123.

65 Howley 1915,267.

66 Peyton 1987,10.

67 Admiral Milbanke's Report on Judicature of Newfoundland to the Lords of the Committee of Privy Council for Trade and Plantation, 31 December 1789, PRO, CO 194/21, f.275–326; Governor William Waldegrave to Duke of Portland, 25 October 1797, PRO, CO 194/39, f.233.

68 English 1990,100.

69 A whipping boy is a person who is made to bear the blame for another's mistake; formerly a boy educated along with a young prince or nobleman and taking punishment for him.

70 Log of *HMS Salisbury*, 1786–88, Capt. Edw. Riou, NMM, RUSI/MN, ER/2/2. Some of these offences were insolence to an officer, drunkenness, and neglect of duty; for example, in 1786, seaman John Murphy received a dozen lashes on each 9 September, 20 September, and 6 October, two dozen on 21 September, and one and a half dozen on 13 October 1786.

71 Answer to HOE by Commander Bowler, 20 April 1725, PRO, CO 194/8, f.14; ibid., 13 October 1726, CO 194/8, f.39.

72 English 1990,108–10; Prowse 1972,355.

73 Proceedings of the Court of Oyer and Terminer in the Court of General Assize, 17 November 1789, PRO, CO 194/38, f.178; the items were a table cloth, a hat, a shirt, and a great coat.

74 Court House, St John's, Examination of Convicts from Ireland, 22 July 1789, PRO, CO 194/38, f.91–4.

75 D. Gardner's report on Newfoundland, 1784–85, BL, Add. Mss. 15493, f.26–8. (in Prowse 1972,355). Clark from Greenspond, who had lost all his property during his imprisonment (it was sold by the order of the judge of the Admiralty), was so shocked that he shortly afterwards "died with grief."

76 Cited in Dickason 1984,126–7.

77 Waldegrave to Duke of Portland, 30 October 1798, PRO, CO 194/40, f.135.

78 Wm. Keen, 3 October 1728, PRO, CO 194/8, f.181; the Reverend Mr Balfour (29 October 1768, USPG, Minutes of the SPG, vol.18, 1768:2) states "that there being

no magistrate [in Trinity] the place is [the] most lawless of any and the poor most wretched."

79 Report on the Newfoundland Fishery, 1759, WLCL, Townsend Papers, Buccleuth Muniments, Box 46.

80 John Reeves to Right Hon. Henry Dundas, "State of the Wild Indians in the Interior Parts of Newfoundland," 5 December 1792, BL, Add. Ms. 38351, f.339 (reprinted with small changes in Howley 1915,55).

81 MHA Keith Matthews's namefile "Peyton": as a young man, in 1770, John Peyton, Sr, had travelled with George Cartwright from England to Fogo and from there to the Labrador coast; Peyton subsequently carried on a cod fishery in Fogo; he later engaged in the salmon fishery on the Exploits River and at Charles Brook in partnership with Harry Miller.

82 Marshall 1989,127.

83 John Bland to J.P. Rance, Governor Waldegrave's Secretary, 1 September 1797, PRO, CO 194/39, f.218; Howley (1915,56) mistakenly gives the date as 1 September 1790. Shanawdithit's sketch 5, Plate 10.3 "Peyton Sr killed a Beothuk woman on the Exploits River" in the winter of 1814–15.

84 Howley 1915,51, 53.

85 Ibid.,50.

86 Ibid.,51.

87 Answer to HOE by Commander Falkingham, 4 October 1732, PRO, CO 194/9, f.211–46.

88 "An Account of the number of Indians Foreign and Native who frequent the following places upon the coast of the Island of Newfoundland the nature and Patent of the Commerce they carry on with the inhabitants, Year 1786," PRO, CO 194/21, f.51.

89 Proposal [by G.C. Pulling, 1786] in the Papers of the Earl of Liverpool, then President of the Council for Trade and Plantation (1786–1804), BL, Add. Ms. 38347, f.348–9.

90 Edw. Parkenham, Commander, *HMS Mulin*, Log: 15 March to 30 September 1787, MDHYD, Misc. Papers Ab3, vol.34:326.

91 Answer to HOE by Richard Edwards, 2 April 1779, PRO, CO 194/34, f.90a.

92 Instructions to Governor John Byron, 3 May 1769, PRO, PC 5/12, f.219.

93 Answer to HOE by Richard Edwards, 1758, PRO, CO 194/14, f.5; Howley 1915,54; Edwards to Wm. Keen, 11 August 1758, PANL, CSOC, GN 2/1/A, vol.2, f.429. Two different men with the name Richard Edwards served as governor in Newfoundland, both were vice admirals; one Richard Edwards was governor from 1757 to 1759, and from 1789 to 1790; the second was governor during the years 1779–81 (Prowse 1972,294, 349, and Howley 1915,56).

94 Quinn 1981,19, Cartier; ibid.,43, Bellanger; ibid.,45, John Davis; ibid.,49, Gabriel Archer.

95 Cell 1982,193–4.

96 "A Reply to the answeare of the description of Newfoundland," Archbishop Laud, 29 September 1639, PRO, CO 1/10, f.97–115.

97 Morandière 1962,1:22; Howley 1915,50.

98 "Sketches of savage life," 1836,322.
99 Thwaites 1959,5:243.
100 Howley 1915,13; Marshall 1989,138; Peyton 1987,34.
101 Howley 1915,230.

CHAPTER EIGHT

1 George Cartwright, "The Case of the Wild or Red Indians," probably submitted in 1784, PRO, CO 194/35, 1780–84 miscell., f.338–42. A handwritten ms. of Cartwright's proposal is in the collection of the Thomas Gilcrease Institute of American History and Art, Tulsa, Oklahoma, US; neither of the two manuscripts include the sketch-map of the reserve that Cartwright proposed.
2 Ibid.
3 See chapter 7.
4 Cartwright, "The Case …," 1784, PRO, CO 194/35, miscell., f.338–42.
5 George Cartwright also mentions his financial misfortunes, brought about by the confiscation of his possessions in Labrador by privateers, the loss of three vessels, and debts left by his father, all of which left him in a precarious financial situation and anxious to secure the post.
6 Captain Robertson's Log of *HMS Thisbe*, February 1785 to January 1786, PRO, ADM 51/988: *Thisbe* moored in Trinity Harbour from 5 September to 9 October; Muster roll of *Thisbe*, entries for 18 March 1785, September-October 1785, November-December 1785, PRO, ADM 36/10276.
7 "To His Majesty's Government," submitted 1786 (written in G.C. Pulling's hand), BL, Liverpool Papers, Add. Ms.38347, f.348–9 (in Marshall 1989,45–50.)
8 Pulling's service record, PRO, ADM 9/2, f.247; Diary of Benjamin Lester 1792–93, DCRO, D 365/F9: *Trinity* was Lester's new brig.
9 Pulling to Admiralty Office, 4 November 1793, PRO, ADM 1/3062, f.99: "I request you will be pleased to acquaint their Lordship of my arrival in England from Marsailles in France after being captured in the Merchant Ship Trinity on her voyage from Newfoundland for which I had their Lordships Leave of absence dated 5th March 1792."
10 Pulling to Chief Justice John Reeves, 1792–93, BL, Add. Ms. 38352, f.48–9.
11 A boat master is a captain of an inshore fishing craft, or skipper.
12 The original of the ms. has not been located, but a transcription is in the Colonial Record Office Correspondence, PRO, CO 194/39, f.221b–229.
13 See also Marshall 1989.
14 BL, Liverpool Papers, Add. Ms.38352, f.18–47 (in Marshall 1989, Apps.6, 7). The final report is thirty-four typed pages compared to nineteen pages of the preliminary report; circumstantial evidence suggests that Pulling compiled the final report on-board ship.
15 Marshall 1989,123.
16 Rev. John Clinch to the SPG, 5 December 1793, USPG, Minutes, 1793, vol.26, p.208: when the Stone family removed to England, Oubee accompanied them and

died there in or before 1795; John Bland to J.P. Rance, Governor's Secretary, 1 September 1797, PRO, CO 194/39, f.218–19 (in Howley 1915,56.)

17 BL, Liverpool Papers, Add. Ms.38352, f.45–7. For a discussion of the vocabulary see chapter 27; Marshall 1989,26, 114, 141; Hewson 1978.

18 John Clinch, Trinity, 12 September 1800, PANL, Pole Papers, MG 205; "The Rev. John Clinch of Trinity's Vocabulary of the Language of the Native Indians residing in the Island of Newfoundland" [September 1800], PANL, CSOC, GN 2/1/A, vol.15, f.433–4.

19 Marshall 1989,26–30.

20 BL, Liverpool Papers, Add. Ms.38352, f.48–49b (in Marshall 1989,51–60.)

21 Marshall 1989,58.

22 Great Britain, First Series Reports, 1785–1808,10:392–504.

23 Pulling's report was subsequently filed in the private papers of the earl of Liverpool.

24 BL, Liverpool Papers, Add. Ms. 38352, f.49b (in Marshall 1989, 60).

25 A note in G.C. Pulling's hand, dated by the record keeper 1793, PRO, CO 194/23, f.397.

26 Prowse 1972,359.

27 Reeves's report "State of the Wild Indians in the Interior Parts of Newfoundland" to the Right Honourable Henry Dundas, 5 December 1792, BL, Add. Ms.38351, f.338–41 (in Howley 1915,54.)

28 Ibid.

29 Routh to Lord Hawkesbury, 6 February 1793, PRO, CO 194/21, f.406b.

30 Reeves to Dundas, 5 December 1792, BL, Add. Ms.38351, f.339, (in Howley 1915,54.)

31 Ibid.

32 This refers to Palliser and George Cartwright's appeasement of the reputedly hostile Inuit; see also chapter 6.

33 Reeves to Dundas, 5 December 1792, BL, Add. Ms.38351, f.339 (in Howley 1915,54); Moravians were missionaries of the Moravian church, or Unitas Fratrum, the *Herrnhuter Brüdergemeinde*, whose headquarters were at Herrnhut, Czechoslovakia.

34 Reeves to Ed. Cooke Esq. (also spelled D'Ewes Coke), 10 April 1808, PRO, CO 194/47, f.111.

35 Proclamation by Waldegrave, 28 July 1797, PRO, CO 194/39, f. 216.

36 Bland to Rance, 16 August 1797, PRO, CO 194/39, f.217.

37 Bland to Rance, 1 September 1797, PRO, CO 194/39, f.218 (Howley 1915,56–8 mistakenly gives 11 September 1790). Waldegrave had sent Bland's letters to the Duke of Portland and had no doubt that "his Grace must have perused them with no less pleasure and satisfaction than I did myself" (Waldegrave to Bland, 27 September 1798, PANL, CSOC, GN 2/1/A, vol.14, f.274).

38 Bland to Rance, 1 September 1797 [given as 1790 in Howley 1915, 56–8], PRO, CO 194/39, f.221.

39 Waldegrave to Bland, 20 September 1797, PANL, CSOC, GN 2/1/A, vol.13, f.228.

40 G.C. Jenner came to Trinity in 1789 to work as a medical practitioner but probably was not able to make a living in his profession; he was ordained in England in 1794

and appointed minister in Harbour Grace by the SPG in 1795. Jenner left Newfoundland between 1798 and 1800 (Marshall 1989, 21; see also Davies 1970,558–60).

41 Jenner to Waldegrave, 28 September 1797 (PANL, CSOC, GN 2/1/A, vol.13, f.298) includes a note by the scribe that reads: "The notes alluded to in the above letter were so exceedingly voluminous as to prevent their being inserted in the [governor's letter] book."

42 Waldegrave to Duke of Portland, 25 October 1797, PRO, CO 194/39, f.214–229.

43 Waldegrave to Portland, 3 February 1798, PRO, CO 194/40, f.15; Capt. Ambrose Crofton's Report to Waldegrave, 10 January 1798, PRO, CO 194/40, f.17.

44 Ibid.,f.26–8.

45 A similar claim was made in a petition to Sir Richard King, 30 October 1792 (PRO, WO 1/15, f.24), in which merchants stated that "more than one half of the Isld. is nearly if not quite the whole season without any effective Justice whatever."

46 Crofton to Waldegrave, 10 January 1798, PRO, CO 194/40, f.17.

47 "Extracts from a letter by Governor Waldegrave to the Duke of Portland, 25 October 1797," PRO, CO 194/23, f.420b-21. The volume CO 194/23 is a collection of miscellaneous documents dated between 1711 and 1805; it includes the extracts mentioned above together with information from Crofton's report, 9 January 1798, and "Minutes relative to proposed alterations for the benefits of the Island of Newfoundland," in which Waldegrave promotes an Indian reserve and the employment of a vessel in the Bay of Exploits, as suggested by Crofton, f.420–5; the file bears no date, but the documents would have been collected after 3 February 1798, the date on which Waldegrave had forwarded Crofton's report to Britain.

48 Waldegrave to Portland, probably 3 February 1798, PRO, CO 194/23, f.424a-25.

49 Referring to the French revolutionary war (1793–1802); Waldegrave to the Earl of Liverpool, 1814 (BL, Liverpool Papers, Add. Ms.38257, f.288d), refers to the duke of Portland's negative response.

50 Bland to Waldegrave, 19 August 1799, PANL, Pole Papers, MG 205.

CHAPTER NINE

1 Instructions by the Council of the Newfoundland Company to John Guy, 1610, in Quinn 1979,4:140, doc.632; Prowse (1971,96), citing BL, Ms.Otto. E, VIII.5, said Guy was asked to [capture] one of the Indians; the word "capture" was not legible and was apparently supplied by Prowse.

2 Henry Crout to Sir Percival Willoughby, August 1613, MMSS, Mix 1/24 (Appendix 1).

3 Cited in Dickason 1976,21; Quinn 1979,1:334, doc.207; ibid.,4:316–17, 338, doc.694.

4 Crout to Willoughby, August 1613, MMSS, Mix 1/24 (Appendix 1); Unfortunately Crout failed to say who the person was, under what circumstances he had joined the Beothuk, and what his experiences had been.

5 Ibid.

6 Wm. Taverner to Mr Popple, Board of Trade, 8 October 1729, PRO, CO 194/8, f.283–4. Taverner said they are settled in a part of the country by themselves "between y English & French."

7 Howley 1915,54.

8 Governor Richard Edwards to Wm. Keen, Justice of the Peace at Bonavista, 11 August 1758, PANL, CSOC, GN 2/1/A, 1758, vol.2, f.429.

9 Howley 1915,54.

10 Edwards to Rt Hon. Gentlemen, 5 January 1759, PRO, CO 194/14, f.5.

11 Lieut. John Cartwright to Governor Hugh Palliser, 19 September 1768, PRRL, 971.8 C24 (in Howley 1915,43); Howley 1915,54.

12 Lieut. John Cartwright, "Remarks on the situation of the Red Indians … 1768," and Cartwright to Palliser, 19 September 1768, PRRL, 971.8 C24 (in Howley 1915,29,43–4); Cartwright's "Sketch of the River Exploits … 1768," PANL, Cartogr. Sect. MG 100, and "Sketch," submitted in 1773, NAC, Cartogr. Div., NMC 27.

13 John Bland to Governor William Waldegrave, 20 October 1797, PANL, CSOC, GN 2/1/A, vol.14, f.90–4 (in Howley 1915,59); Howley 1915,277.

14 Avalonus (pen-name of William Sweetland, magistrate of Bonavista) 1862,1–2 (in Howley 1915,288).

15 Bland to Waldegrave, 20 October 1797, PANL, CSOC, GN 2/1/A, vol.14, f.90–4 (in Howley 1915,58); Howley 1915,58 fn.1, 273.

16 Cartwright, "Remarks … 1768," PRRL, 971.8 C24 (in Howley 1915,34).

17 Palliser to Earl of Hillsborough, 20 October 1768, PRO, CO 194/28, f.26; see also chapter 6.

18 Cartwright, "Remarks … 1768," PRRL, 971.8 C24 (in Howley 1915,35.)

19 Cartwright 1792,3:49 (in Howley 1915,49 and fn.1).

20 Church of England Records, St Paul's, Trinity, 1753–1857,43, PANL, microfilm 31. Thomas Street was the agent of John Jeffrey, a Pool merchant; the two men were partners from 1771–89. Captain Pulling records that August died as a "middle aged man" (Marshall 1989,140).

21 Bland to Waldegrave, 20 October 1797, PANL, CSOC, GN 2/1/A, vol.14, f.90–4 (in Howley 1915,59).

22 Avalonus 1862,1–2.

23 Cartwright 1792,3:5, 34–5, 46–9.

24 Marshall 1989,59, 128–30.

25 Ibid.; Bland to J.P. Rance, Gov. Secretary, 1 September 1797 (given mistakenly as 1790 in Howley 1915,56), PRO, CO 194/39, f.218b.

26 Bland to J.P. Rance, 16 August 1797, PRO, CO 194/39, f.217.

27 Marshall 1989,141, 154 note 86; see also chapter 27.

28 Bland to Waldegrave, 20 October 1797, PANL, CSOC, GN 2/1/A, vol.14, f.90–4 (in Howley 1915,59).

29 Marshall 1989,136.

30 Ibid.,135–7.

31 Ibid.,125, 127.

32 Ibid.,137.

33 "Sketches of savage life," 1836,322.

34 Bland to J.P. Rance, 1 September 1797 (given mistakenly as 1790 in Howley 1915,56), PRO, CO 194/39, f.218b; Whitelaw 1978, 114.

35 James Hutton to Lord Dartmouth, 5 January 1773, NAC, Dartmouth Papers, GM 23 A 1, Series 1, vol.2 (VIII) 2400–25.

36 Officer Curtis, Report on Labrador to Governor Shuldham, 1772, PRO, CO 194/30, f.182–4.

37 Hutton to Dartmouth 5 January 1773, NAC, Dartmouth Papers, GM 23 A 1, Series 1, vol.2 (VIII) 2400–25; George Cartwright (1792,1:269) recorded that, when asked how they would describe what they had seen to their countrymen, the five Inuit he brought to London replied that they should not mention it lest they should be called liars.

38 Hutton to Dartmouth, 5 January 1773, NAC, Dartmouth Papers, GM 23 A 1, Series 1, vol.2 (VIII) 2400–25.

39 Cartwright 1792,1:262; Taylor 1974,8, see also Dickason 1976;22.

40 Capt. David Buchan's report on his second expedition to Red Indian Lake to Governor Hamilton, 10 March 1820, PRO, CO 194/63, f.64–5 (in Howley 1915,121); Cormack's address to the Boeothick Institution, Cormack Papers, 12/84 (in Howley 1915,184); Cormack Papers 20/84 (in Howley 1915,221); Howley 1915,108.

41 "Sketches of Savage Life," 1836, 323.

42 Bland to Governor Pole, 25 August 1800, PANL, CSOC, GN 2/1/A, vol.15, f.402–4 (in Howley 1915:60); Pole to Duke of Portland, 25 October 1800, PRO, CO 194/42, f.213–17; John Slade to Pole, 30 September 1800, and Bland to Pole, 9 October 1800, PANL, CSOC, GN 2/1/A, vol.16, f.9–10.

43 Pole to Bland, and Pole to Moses Cheater, 16 August 1800, PANL, CSOC GN 2/1/A, vol.15, f.392–3. Bland to Pole, 25 August 1800, PANL, CSOC, GN 2/1/A, vol.15, f.402–4: Rowsell and Miller were furriers who lived in the area; Captain Larkham concurred with Bland's opinion that without intervention by government, friendly interactions could not be effected, Return on Fishery in Trepassy by Capt. Robert Larkham of *HMS Camilla*, 22 September 1800, PANL, Pole Papers, MG 205.

44 Pole to Portland, 25 October 1800, PRO, CO 194/42 f.213–17; no public announcement of the reward has been found in the documents, but Governor Gower, in his "Observations on the Return of the Fishery for 1804" (18 March 1806, PRO, CO 194/45, f.29–30), mentions that Governor Pole offered such a reward.

45 "The Indians were at one time on tolerable good terms until some of them were caught on an Island by Three Boats Crews. The poor creatures did not attempt to resist or Fly when they were immediately murdered and in the sight of many observing Indians Stakes were driven through the bodies of the Women. To that and similar acts of Barbary may be attributed in great measure their present Inveteracy. That the practice still continues of Firing at them whenever seen, by the People employed in the River Exploits and Gander Bay, I have no doubt, and that they are actually hunted in the Winter and plundered of their Furs. Thus the unfortunate Indian is surrounded by Enemies" (Report by Harry Folkes Edgell, captain of *HMS Pluto*, Supreme Surrogate

for the Island of Newfoundland, 28 August 1801, from Twillingate, PANL, Pole Papers, MG 205).

46 Ibid.

47 Governor James Gambier to Lord Hobart, 21 November 1802, PRO, CO 194/43, f. 94.

48 Gambier to Hobart, 23 November 1803 (PRO, CO 194/43, f.169–70), does not say the money was a reward that had been promised; Statement by Gambier for William Cull, 17 September 1803, PRO, CO 194/43, f.166, and PANL, CSOC, GN 2/1/A, vol.17, f.154–5 (in Howley 1915,63).

49 James Dobie, surgeon on *HMS Egeria*, to Sir G. Cockburn, 10 September 1823, PRO, CO 194/66, f.326.

50 Anspach 1819,245–6. Among several native tribes items of personal clothing were considered to be an extension of the person and imbued with soul-spirit; they should therefore not be loaned to others. Clothing could also be manipulated to bring its owner harm, Thompson 1987,148–9.

51 Gower's "Observations ... for 1804," 18 March 1806, PRO, CO 194/45, f.29–30.

52 Chappell 1818,182–3.

53 Statement by Gambier for Cull, 17 September 1803, PANL, CSOC, GN 2/1/A, vol.17, f.154.

54 Gambier to Hobart, 23 November 1803, PRO, CO 194/43, f.169–70.

55 Howley 1915,64; Dobie to Cockburn, 10 September 1823, PRO, CO 194/66, f.324–6. William Cull's receipt for fifteen pounds for board and lodging for a Beothuk from 20 September 1803 to 15 August 1804, dated 15 August 1804, PANL, CSOC, GN 2/1/A, vol.17, f.347.

56 Gower to Andrew Pearce, Fogo, 11 August 1804, PANL, CSOC, GN 2/1/A, vol.17, f.334; Gower's "Observations ... for 1804," 18 March 1806, PRO, CO 194/45, f.29–30.

57 Instructions to Erasmus Gower, 1804, PRO, PC 1/16, f.285.

58 Cull to Secretary M. Trounsell, 27 September 1804, PANL, CSOC, GN 2/1/A, vol.18, f.47; Account of expenditures bringing the Indian woman back into the country, 5 October 1804, PRO, CO 194/44, f.174, and PANL, CSOC, GN 2/1/A, vol.18, f.288–9; Gower to Earl Camden, 22 August 1805, PRO, CO 194/44, f.170.

59 Chappell 1818,184; McGregor 1832,1:256; "Sketches of savage life," 1836,317.

60 Gower's "Observations ... for 1804," 18 March 1806, PRO, CO 194/45, f.29–30.

61 McGregor 1832,1:256.

62 Bland to Holloway, 22 September 1807, PANL, CSOC, GN 2/1/A, vol.19, f.135–6 (in Howley 1915,65); Holloway to Magistrate Thomas Coote, 1 September 1807, PANL, CSOC, GN 2/1/A, vol.19, f.192–3; Holloway to Bland, 5 October 1807, PANL, CSOC, GN 2/1/A, vol.19, f.214 (in Howley 1915,66); Holloway to Lieutenant McKillop, 19 September 1807, PRO, ADM 50/48.

63 Tocque 1846,284; ibid,1878,504: Wiltshear, who told Tocque that he was one of the men taken to court, claimed that this incident had occurred in 1810 and that he and his companions had brought the canoe to St John's to present it to the governor.

64 Proclamation by Holloway, 30 July 1807, PANL, CSOC, GN 2/1/A, vol.19, f.171–2, (in Howley 1915,64–5); Holloway's answer to Instructions to His Excellency, 4 August 1807, PRO, CO 194/46, App.B, f.82–101. There is no record that Holloway was authorized to offer a reward.

65 Ibid.,f.94, Article 11.

66 Holloway to Viscount Castlereagh, 20 May 1808, PANL, CSOC, GN 2/1/A, vol.20, f.8; also PRO, CO 194/47, f.33 (in Howley 1915,66); Holloway to Sir T. Cottrell, 3 June 1808, PRO, CO 194/47, f.119 (in Howley 1915,67). Holloway thought that the persistence of the Indians' inveteracy may have been due to the flawed execution of previous efforts to win their trust by way of presents.

67 Chief Justice John Reeves to Ed. Cooke, Esq. (usually D'Ewes Coke), 10 April 1808, PRO, CO 194/47, f.111; Holloway to Wm. Fawkener, Committee of Privy Council for Trade, 13 June 1808, and ibid., 14 June 1808, PANL, CSOC, GN 2/1/A, vol.20, f.14 (in Howley 1915,67).

68 Fawkener to Cooke, 8 June 1808, PRO, CO 194/47, f.117; Amount for Presents purchased for the Indians, 8 June 1808, PRO, CO 194/47, f.76 (in Howley 1915,67).

69 Holloway to Lieut. J.W. Sprott, commander of *HMS Herring*, 26 July 1808, PRO, CO 194/47, f.69–71; Holloway to Sprott, 30 July 1808, PRO, CO 194/47, f.71a-72.

70 Holloway to Viscount Castlereagh, 18 November 1808, PRO, CO 194/47, f.65–6.

71 Faulkner [Fawkener] to Holloway, 2 December 1808, cited in Howley 1915,68. First Lord Redesdale (J.A.B.F. Mitford) wrote to Earl Bathurst, 31 December 1808 (Bathurst 1923,79–80), that "I am not surprized at their [the Beothuk's] perseverance because I well remember my unfortunate nephew [Capt. Henry Mitford, lost at sea in 1803] who was several times on the Newfoundland station, represented the Newfoundland traders as treating the Indians very much as we treat a mad dog – shooting them without mercy whenever they found them."

72 Holloway to Sprott, 22 October 1808, PRO, CO 194/47, f.72a.

73 Holloway to Castlereagh, 25 November 1809, PRO, CO 194/48, f.59, claimed that "the Indians keep in the Interior of the Island … from a Dread of the Micmacs who come over from Cape Breton."

74 Smith 1890,44; Rev. John Clinch, Trinity, writing to the SPG, 18 December 1809 (PANL, USPG Papers, MG 598, Series A 164/64 [A/17], f.218), assumed the unlikely scenario that "government at home" had contacted Dr Coke from the Wesleyan Missionary Committee and asked him to send a missionary to convert the Beothuk to Christianity.

75 Cull to Trounsell, 27 September 1804, PANL, CSOC, GN 2/1/A, vol.18, f.47 (in Howley 1915,64).

76 Rimmington [Remmington] et al. 1810,86.

77 John Remmington to the Wesleyan Missionary Committee, August 23, 1810, MMS: LR, North America, Newfoundland 1805–16, Box 1, file 1d, no.4.

78 Ellis and McDowell 1811,275–6.

79 Crout to Willoughby, August 1613, MMSS, Mix 1/24 (Appendix 1).

80 Howley 1915,271–2, 284.

81 Webber 1978,37 n.5.

82 Cyril J. Byrne collected this information in the 1960s (1980s, pers. com.); Furey had also heard that Beothuk lived in the watershed area of Bay St George into the 1840s and 1850s and intermarried with the whites; this last information might refer to the Beothuk Gabriel who married a Micmac girl and whose son married a white woman (Cuff 1966,25).

83 Howley 1915,265; PANL file Shortis, MG 282.

84 Buchan's report of his expedition to Red Indian Lake, 1811, PRO, CO 194/50, f.153/88 (in Howley 1915,86).

85 Cormack Papers, 23/84 (in Howley 1915,220, and fn.220).

86 Speck 1922, 58–60, 64–6.

87 I have received a letter from a person in Ontario who was told by her grandfather that she was descended from the "last blond Indian of Newfoundland," whose offspring was brought to England by a sea captain; but I have not been able to verify this.

88 Marshall 1989, 139.

89 Cartwright, "Remarks ... 1768," PRRL, 971.8 C24 (in Howley 1915,35); Howley 1915,54; Marshall 1989,125–7, 129, 137.

90 Marshall 1989,126.

91 Chappell 1818, 182.

92 Upton 1978,153; Rowe (1977,157) believed that "miscegenation" was likely.

CHAPTER TEN

1 Lieut. David Buchan's report of his expedition to Red Indian Lake, 1811, PRO, CO 194/50, f.153–88 (in Howley 1915,72–90, shortened version; reference here: ibid., 88–9). A handwritten manuscript copy of the report is in the collection of the PRRL, 917.18 B 85.

2 Reports by Capt. Robert Larkham, 22 September 1800, and by Capt. H.F. Edgell, 28 August 1801, PANL, Pole Papers, MG 205; Tocque 1878,504.

3 Howley 1915,268, 283.

4 Tocque 1846,285; John Bland to J.P. Rance, Gov. Secretary, 1 September 1797 (given mistakenly as 1790 in Howley 1915, 56–8), PRO, CO 194/39, f.218b-221; Report by Edgell, 28 August 1801, PRO, Pole Papers, MG 205; Buchan's report, 1811, PRO, CO 194/50, f.153–88 (in Howley 1915,88–9); J. Dobie, surgeon on *HMS Egeria*, to Sir G.Cockburn, 10 September 1823, PRO, CO 194/66, f.324.

5 Buchan's report, 1811, PRO, CO 194/50, f.153–88 (in Howley 1915,89); Marshall 1989,120; Buchan to Governor Duckworth, 25 July 1812, NAC, Duckworth Papers, MG 24 A 45, f.5032–5.

6 Marshall 1989,127; Report by Edgell, 28 August 1801, NAC, Pole Papers, MG 205.

7 Buchan's report, 1811, PRO, CO 194/50, f.153–88 (in Howley 1915,88).

8 Survey by Don Locke, recorded in Marshall 1980,41–3; Thomson 1982,35.

9 LeBlanc 1973,154; ibid.,App.I, 25; Rowley-Convy 1990,24–25. Conclusions about the time of year when a camp was occupied are based on analysis of animal bones found in middens that indicate the age of the animals at the time they were killed.

10 Cormack 1829,319 (in Howley 1915,190).

11 Morandière 1962,1:22; Webber 1978,97, n.3; Ingstad 1985,2:472. Sixty-year-old Mr Decker told Helge Ingstad in the 1960s that in his great-grandfather's day Beothuk lived near L'Anse aux Meadows, and that this area was their last refuge.

12 Governor Holloway to Lieutenant Sprott, 30 July 1808, PRO, CO 194/47, f.71a-72: Holloway's request to enquire for "the man who took the Indian Woman round from hence last year" and to hire him as a guide probably referred to William Cull; since Cull took the woman back in 1804, the reference to "last year" would have been made in error.

13 "Substance of the narrative of William Cull of Fogo, who was employed by Governor Holloway to obtain information of the native Indians of Newfoundland," 22 July 1810, PANL, CSOC, GN 2/1/A, vol.21, f.27–30; also PRO, CO 194/49, f.116–17 (in Howley 1915,69–70). For details on fences and houses see chapters 20 and 22.

14 Buchan to Duckworth, 2 August 1810, NAC, Duckworth Papers, MG 24 A 45, f.4644–9.

15 Bourinot 1868,91.

16 Instructions to Duckworth, 5 June 1810, NAC, Duckworth Papers, MG 24 A 45, f.11–84; Duckworth's proclamations to the Micmac Indians, 10 August 1810, PRO, ADM 80/122, f.29, and to the inhabitants of Newfoundland, 24 July and 1 August 1810, PRO, CO 194/49, f.26 (in Howley 1915,70, 71).

17 Duckworth to "my Lord" (probably earl of Liverpool), 24 July 1810, PRO, CO 194/49, f.24.

18 Rev. Edmund Violet to Duckworth, 6 August 1810, NAC, Duckworth Papers, MG 24 A 45, f.1274–80.

19 Violet to Duckworth, 8 September 1810, NAC, Duckworth Papers, MG 24 A 45, f.1301–7.

20 Violet to Duckworth, 24 September 1810, NAC, Duckworth Papers, MG 24 A 45, f.1335–40.

21 DNB 1949–50,6:95; writing to the SPG, Rev. John Clinch described Duckworth as a man of "great discernment and penetration." (28 December 1810, USPG, Minutes vol.30:141).

22 Although the Colonial Records and the Duckworth Papers contain many letters and orders pertaining to this expedition, nothing has been found to indicate that Duckworth requested or received authorization from the Privy Council or another government agency in Britain.

23 Prowse 1972,384.

24 Duckworth's Observations in response to his Instructions, October 1810, PRO, CO 194/49, f.87.

25 Duckworth to Buchan, 26 July 1810, NAC, Duckworth Papers, MG 24 A 45, f.5543; Duckworth to Buchan, 26 August 1810, PANL, CSOC, GN 2/1/A, vol.21, f.29; Commander William Elliott to Duckworth, 4 October 1810, PRO, CO 194/49, f.117–19, containing a list of articles that had been traded with natives in Labrador; presumably Duckworth forwarded this list to Buchan.

26 Duckworth to Buchan, 1 October 1810, PRO, CO 194/49, f.114–15.

27 "Most secret order" from Duckworth to Buchan, 25 October 1810, NMM, DUC/7.

28 Buchan's report, 1811, PRO, CO 194/50, f.153–88 (in Howley 1915,72).
29 Ibid. (in Howley 1915,77).
30 Ibid. The emphasis is added; the wording in Howley differs from Buchan's original report.
31 Thomas Taylor later claimed that, knowing the Beothuk's habit, he warned Buchan not to leave the men behind because he thought they would not see them again (Peyton 1987,4).
32 Although Buchan called this man a "chief," this term tends to be associated with a formal power position – since we are not certain about the extent of authority of Beothuk leaders the term chief is set here in quotation marks and used with the proviso that it indicates an unspecified leadership position; see also chapter 18.
33 Buchan's report, 1811, PRO, CO 194/50, f.153–88 (in Howley 1915,80). In his testimony in 1836 to the Select Committee on Aborigines ([1836] 1968,1:476), Buchan said that the arrows stuck in the men's clothes.
34 Buchan's report, 1811, PRO, CO 194/50, f.153–88 (in Howley 1915, 83–5).
35 Cormack Papers 20/84 (in Howley 1915,226–7); Wm. Avalonus 1862,1; Bishop John Inglis, Diary, 2 July 1827, NAC, microfilm A 713. Inglis probably recorded what Peyton, Jr, told him and did not receive the information directly from Shanawdithit.
36 Cormack Papers 20/84 (in Howley 1915,227, fn.1, 229).
37 The notes on sketch 1 read (starting at the right-hand side): "(42 men with Capt. B – 2 killed) [Buchan said his party counted 28]
Luggage left here by Captn. Buchan untill his return from the Great Lake
One of the two Red Indians desert Capt. B here
(2 of the 4 Red Indians return from Capt. B. here)
Capt. B' party returning for presents with six of the Indians [only four Indians accompanied him]
Capt. Buchan's party going on the ice to surprise the Indians
the 3 wigwams taken by Capt. B
Nancy's Fathers wigwam
Mary March's Fathers wigwam
killing marines
Red Indians retreating after killing marines
Mary March's cemetery
Nancy's uncle running from Capt. B after returning to the Lake and witnessing what had happened
Trousers thrown away during his flight
First night of retreat reach this, stop 2 hours untill joined by 5 men and four women; 3 boys and 4 girls, who occupied these two wigwams
Reach this before day-light and remain one day and a half waiting for Nancy's uncle who remained with Capt. B and who escaped and joined them here
They reach this at night and camp in the woods set-off early next morning across the lake
half a days march across

Indians crossing the Lake
Small party that were encamped here remove and join the main body of the Tribe
The whole tribe encamped here and remain the winter
Marine's Head stuck on a pole around which the Indians danced and sang two hours in the woods at A, they having carried the head with them the other marines head they left at B and on their return there in the spring they danced and sang round it in like manner."

The inscription on the back reads: "Capt. Buchan's visit to the Great Lake when the two hostages were killed."

38 Buchan's "Sketch of the River Exploits as explor'd in Jan.y and March 1811," PRO, MPG589, CO 194/50.

39 Cormack 1829,323 (in Howley 1915,193); Cormack Papers 20/84 (in Howley 1915,228); Buchan's report of his second expedition up the Exploits River to Governor Hamilton, 10 March 1820, PRO, CO 194/63, f.64–77 (in Howley 1915,123).

40 Buchan's report, 1811, PRO, CO 194/50, f.153–88 (in Howley 1915,89).

41 Ibid. (in Howley 1915,88).

42 Ibid. (in Howley 1915,88).

43 Ibid. (in Howley 1915,87). Dr William Carson's Answers to Questions by the Royal College of Physicians of Great Britain, 1830, Governor Cochrane to Viscount Goderich, 7 February 1831, PRO, CO 194/81, f.59a;

44 Buchan's report, 1811, PRO, CO 194/50, f.153–88 (in Howley 1915,88).

45 Carson, 1830, PRO, CO 194/81, f.59a; Select Committee on Aborigines [1836], 1968:1:475.

46 Duckworth to the Earl of Liverpool, 27 October 1811, PRO, CO 194/50, f.152.

47 Noad 1859,42.

48 Buchan's report, 1811, PRO, CO 194/50, f.168a.

49 Ibid. (in Howley 1915,89).

50 Ibid.

51 Select Committee on Aborigines [1836] 1968,1:479.

52 Duckworth to Liverpool, 27 October 1811, PRO, CO 194/50, f.151; Letter from Downing Street (probably from the earl of Liverpool) to Duckworth, 6 June 1812, PRO, CO 194/50, f.22a.

53 "Memorandum of the Cruize of HM Schr. Adonis from Augt. 13th to 19th Octr. 1811," Commander Buchan, NAC, Duckworth Papers, MG 24 A 45, f.4918–20.

54 Buchan to R.C. Sconce, Esq., 29 September 1811, NAC, Duckworth Papers MG 24 A 45, f.1960–63; Duckworth to Liverpool, 27 October 1811, PRO, CO 194/50, f.151, stating that Buchan's health had been impaired as a result of the excessive hardships he underwent on the expedition.

55 Buchan to Sconce, 29 September 1811, NAC, Duckworth Papers MG 24 A 45, f.1960–3.

56 Buchan to Duckworth, 18 October 1811, NAC, Duckworth Papers MG 24 A 45, f.4914–17.

57 Duckworth to Liverpool, 27 October 1811, PRO, CO 194/50, f.152.

58 Buchan to Duckworth, 9 February 1812, NAC, Duckworth Papers, MG 24 A 45, f.4973–6.

59 Duckworth to M. Tucker, 11 April 1812, NMM, DUC/16, no.18; Duckworth's instructions upon his appointment as governor included the request for such a survey; Governor Keats (29 December 1814, PRO, CO 194/55, f.95) reported that the first six leagues north of Bonavista had been surveyed.

60 Ice conditions could be severe even as late as July; see also Captain Hamilton from *HMS Vesuvius* to Sir Alexander Milne, Halifax, 29 July 1863, PRO, CO 194/171, f.205.

61 Buchan to Duckworth, 27 June 1812, NAC, Duckworth Papers, MG 24 A 45, f.5003–6.

62 Buchan to Duckworth, from Morton's Harbour, 10 July 1812, NAC, Duckworth Papers, MG 24 A 45, f.5013–15; Buchan to Duckworth, 17 July 1812, NAC, Duckworth Papers MG 24 A 45, f.5021–3. Buchan wrote that Laole Tickle "is formed by many islands opposite to the mainland extending from New Bay to Badger Bay"; the northernmost of these islands is Wards Island.

63 Buchan to Duckworth, 17 July 1812, NAC, Duckworth Papers, MG 24 A 45, f.5021–3.

64 Buchan to Duckworth, 25 July 1812, NAC, Duckworth Papers, MG 24 A 45, f.5032–5: Winter Tickle, located at the beginning of a portage path to Southern Arm/New Bay, was favoured by Beothuk for repairing and building canoes.

65 Buchan to Duckworth, 31 July 1812, NAC, Duckworth Papers MG 24 A 45, f.5040–2.

66 Buchan to Duckworth, 23 August 1812, NAC, Duckworth Papers MG 24 A 45, f.5080–1.

67 Proclamation by Keats, 10 August 1813, PANL, CSOC, GN 2/1/A, vol.24, f.373–4 (in Howley 1915,91); Keats's Observations on the King's Instructions to Earl Bathurst, 15 April 1816, PRO, CO 194/57, f.34.

68 Cormack Papers 20/84 (in Howley 1915,223). In 1813 Buchan was still serving on *Adonis* and not on *Pike*.

69 The inhabitants presented Buchan with a silver serving dish and cover that was engraved with the text "From the Inhabitants of St John's Newfoundland to Capt. David Buchan RN in recognition of his valuable and important service while administering the Government of that Colony and more especially in testimony of their appreciation of his humane and judicious conduct during the winter of great distress and difficulty, 1815–16." This dish is treasured by Buchan's descendants in Britain (Correspondence with Mrs L.H. Baxter, Westbury/Wilts., UK); Howley 1915,179.

70 Prowse 1972,408; Captain's Log, *HMS Pike*, Capt. David Buchan, 18 April–31 October 1816, PRO, ADM 51/2654.

71 *HMS Pike* left Twillingate on 12 October 1816 and returned to Cape Freels by 19 October; E.S. (presumed to have been Slade), who referred to Buchan's trek up the Exploits River and the killing of two marines, erroneously believed that this occurred in 1815 or 1816 (Howley 1915, 97). These dates are also cited by McGregor (1832,1:257, and 2d ed., 1833,1:229); McGregor seems to have received

this information from W.E. Cormack (Cormack Papers 20/84). Cormack may have gathered it from Slade's article; hence the incorrect date.

72 Howley 1915,97.

73 "Sketches of savage life," 1836,323.

74 John Gale to Governor Hamilton, 1819, PANL, CSOC GN 2/1/A, vol.30, f.342. One of the silver spoons taken by Beothuk was found in a mamateek at Red Indian Lake at the time of Demasduit's capture in 1819 (Howley 1915, 280).

75 Jukes 1969,2:128.

76 James Dobie to Sir G. Cockburn, 10 September 1823, PRO, CO 194/66, f.326.

CHAPTER ELEVEN

1 Captain Crofton to Governor Waldegrave, 10 January 1798, PRO, CO 194/40, f.26–7; Captain Edgell to Governor Pole, 28 August 1801, PANL, Pole Papers, MG 205.

2 A Micmac from the St George's Bay band told Chappell (1818, 76) in 1817 that the land was given to a "Sachem" (Sacmow), which meant "elder" or "chief."

3 Howley 1915,151–2.

4 Captain Parker to Governor Duckworth, 28 September 1810, NAC, Duckworth Papers, MG 24 A 45, f.4684–7.

5 Crofton to Waldegrave, 10 January 1798, PRO, CO 194/40, f.17–34; Edgell to Pole, 28 August 1801, NAC, Pole Papers, MG 205.

6 Governor Holloway to Viscount Castlereagh, 18 November 1808, PRO, CO 194/47, f.61–9; Holloway to Castlereagh, 19 November 1808, PANL, CSOC, GN 2/1/A, vol.20, f.118; Holloway to Castlereagh, 25 November 1809, PRO, CO 194/48, f.59.

7 Proclamations by Governor Duckworth, 1 August 1810, PRO, CO 194/49, f.113–14 (in Howley 1915, 71). Governor Hamilton to the Reverend Mr Leigh, 31 May 1819, PANL, CSOC, GN 2/1/A, vol.30, f.149 (in Howley 1915,108).

8 Parker to Duckworth, 28 September 1810, NAC, Duckworth Papers, MG 24 A 45, f.4684–7; Parker also described the Micmac's wasteful slaughter of birds for feathers and the destruction of excessive numbers of caribou, often taken out of season and left to rot.

9 Lieut. David Buchan's report of his expedition to Red Indian Lake, 1811, PRO, CO 194/50, f.153–88 (in Howley 1915,72–85); Howley 1915,226; Select Committee on Aborigines [1836] 1968,1:475–9.

10 Buchan to Duckworth, 17 July 1812, NAC, Duckworth Papers MG 24 A 45, f.5021–3; Cormack 1824,160.

11 Report by Governor Richard Keats, 10 November 1815, PRO, CO 194/56, f.110, and 15 April 1816, CO 194/57, f.34–5.

12 Howley 1915,108; Marshall 1989,135, Peyton, Sr, had been involved in killing Beothuk in the 1780s; according to Shanawdithit's sketch 5, Plate 10.3, he also killed a Beothuk in 1814–15.

13 Robinson 1834,216 (in Howley 1915,127).

14 James Dobie to Sir G. Cockburn, 10 September 1823, PRO, CO 194/66, f.324–9.

15 Howley 1915,151–2; Cormack 1824,160; Newfoundland 1858, Abstract Census 1857, gives broad confirmation to Cormack's estimate as it enumerates a total Micmac population of 157: fifty-five in Bay D'Espoir, twenty-six in Grandy's Brook, fifty-two in Cod Roy, twenty-three in Exploits Bay and one in Brigus/Conception Bay.

16 Deposition by the Rev. Thomas G. Langharne of Twillingate, 1 October 1822, USPG, C/Can/NF 3, doc.367. Langharne made oath that he went to the house of Henry Knight in Moreton's Harbour to see an Indian who was in Knight's house. In the course of the conversation Knight had said that Langharne was as much "of an Indian as the Indian was." Langharne was so infuriated by this comment that it came to a scuffle and he subsequently took Knight to court.

17 Rev. John Chapman to Rev. Anthony Hamilton, 28 October 1826, USPG, C/Can/NF 3, doc.107, pp. 101–15.

18 Johnston 1960,1:360; Howley 1915,152.

19 Cormack 1824,160; Howley 1915,148–9, 152.

20 Cormack 1824,160.

21 Buchan's report, 1811, PRO, CO 194/50, f.153–88 (in Howley 1915,73).

22 Howley 1915,152.

23 Speck 1922,48.

24 Cormack Papers 20/84 (in Howley 1915,176; also 176 fn.1, and 224); Cormack 1824,161.

25 Chappell 1818,71.

26 Cormack 1824,161

27 Cormack Papers 20/84 (in Howley 1915,224, 229); Howley 1915, 176.

28 Howley 1915,279. Less convincing traditions have not been included here; see Marshall 1988a,79–80.

29 Speck 1922,51.

30 Howley 1915,285, citing letter from Silas Rand, 1887.

31 Parsons 1925,100.

32 The information comes from one of Gabriel's descendants, Mrs Richard White of Stephenville, who has produced a complete family tree in which Gabriel and his Micmac wife are shown to be her great-grandparents (Cuff 1966,25).

33 The anthropologist Speck (1922,58–60, 64–6) devoted much time and effort to investigating the authenticity of Santu's ancestry and was satisfied that her claim was genuine.

34 Ibid., 69.

35 This information was given to me by Cyril Byrne, St Mary's University, Halifax, whose grandfather worked with Charlie Brake when Brake was a section foreman on the railroad; it was originally taken down in 1958, when Brake was about sixty-eight years old.

36 Wetzel et al. 1980,8.

37 Thwaites 1959,56:77; Taylor 1980,188. Already in the seventeenth century Montagnais from Tadoussac and the Middle Quebec coast intermarried with Gaspé Micmac immigrants (Charles A. Martijn, 1980s, pers. com.).

38 Speck 1922,126.
39 Howley 1915,149.
40 Cormack Papers 20/84 (in Howley 1915,216).
41 Jukes 1969,1:172, and 2:126.
42 "Sketches of savage life," 1836,322.
43 Ibid.
44 Howley 1915,280.
45 Howley 1915,280 fn.1.
46 Cormack 1829,325–6 (in Howley 1915,194–5); Howley 1915, 152; Chappell 1818,71; Speck 1922,28–9.
47 Howley 1915,27.
48 Jukes 1969,1:171; Noad 1859,43.
49 Speck 1922,47–8.
50 Wetzel et al. 1980,4, 41.

CHAPTER TWELVE

1 Deposition by John Peyton, Jr, 30 September 1818, PANL, CSOC, GN 2/1/A, vol.29, f.148–51; Peyton, Jr, to Governor Hamilton, 27 May 1819, PANL, CSOC, GN 2/1/A, vol.30, f.127–37 (in Howley 1915,105–8).
2 Peyton, Jr, to Governor Hamilton, 27 May 1819, PANL, CSOC, GN 2/1/A, vol.30, f.127–37 (in Howley 1915, 105–8).
3 Howley 1915,91 fn.1.
4 Ibid.,91 fn.1, 92–3.
5 Ibid.,96.
6 Peyton, Jr, to Hamilton, 27 May 1819, PANL, CSOC, GN 2/1/A, vol.30, f.127–37 (in Howley 1915,105–8); Hamilton to Earl Bathurst, 27 September 1819, PANL, CSOC, GN 2/1/A, vol.30, f.304, and PRO, CO 194/62, f.61–4 (in Howley 1915,119).
7 Peyton, Jr, to Hamilton, 27 May 1819, PANL, CSOC, GN 2/1/A, vol.30, f.127–37 (in Howley 1915,105–8); Howley 1915,93.
8 Cormack Papers 20/84 (in Howley 1915,223). A statement by Thomas Peyton (Twillingate, 12 March 1910 [transcript], MHA, Keith Matthews's namefile "Peyton") reads, "A reward was offered by the Imperial Government of one thousand pounds to any person who would capture an Indian and bring about such a measure [a friendly intercourse]. My father [John Peyton, Jr] with such intention in view, in the month of March 1819, fitted out a party of men."
9 Proclamation by Governor Richard Keats, 10 August 1813, PANL, CSOC, GN 2/1/A, vol.24, f.373 (in Howley 1915,91).
10 Although Amy Peyton (1987,49) claims that Peyton, Jr, has been unjustly maligned with regard to the outcome of his expedition to Red Indian Lake, there can be no question that he deliberately refused to hand over the captive to her husband Nonosabasut, who asked that she be released.
11 Peyton, Jr, to Hamilton, 27 May 1819, PANL, CSOC, GN 2/1/A, vol.30, f.127–37 (in Howley 1915,105–8); Peyton 1987,41.

12 Ibid. Thomas Peyton's "grandfather, John Peyton the elder, was not among the party which captured Mary March as has often been reported" (Thomas Peyton, 12 March 1910, MHA, Matthews's namefile "Peyton"); Howley (1915,272) cites a description by "Carey or Kierly," who was a member of Peyton's party.

13 Hamilton to Bathurst, 27 September 1819, PANL, CSOC, GN 2/1/A, vol.30, f.304–8, and PRO, CO 194/62, f.61–4 (in Howley 1915,119).

14 Howley 1915,91–3.

15 Ibid.,281–2.

16 Ibid.,96–101.

17 Ibid.,101.

18 One mamateek housed thirteen persons including three married couples, the second twelve persons including three married couples, and the third six persons including one married couple. (Cormack Papers 20/84, in Howley 1915,227–8) .

19 The time period given by Shanawdithit to Cormack would have placed the birth of the child into the year 1820; hence Cormack placed question marks behind the years (Cormack Papers 20/84). Presumably for the same reason, Howley (1915,227) changed "five years" into "two years"; a note in the Cormack Papers 20/84 (in Howley 1915,228) states that Demasduit was married for four years before she had "children"; in the context of the child's death, Cormack referred to "her only child, an infant."

20 Shanawdithit's sketch 2, Plate 10.2, upper part; one of the mamateeks is coloured red, one is outlined in red, and one is outlined in black pencil; Howley (1915,94, 241) interpreted the colours as indicating the type of roof cover used, because Peyton, Jr, had said that two mamateeks were covered with birchbark, the third with a sail.

21 Reference to the date of Demasduit's capture: "A Vocabulary of the Native Red Indians' Language, Newfoundland, from Mary March, a female red Indian, who was caught by Mr John Peyton of the Exploits on the fifth March, 1819," PANL, MG 57; Newfoundland Museum catalogue entry for a wooden bowl: "Taken from a Red Indian wigwam at Lake Bathurst [Red Indian Lake] on the 5th of March 1819 at the capture of a Red Indian woman, after named Mary March."

22 Howley 1915,94. Lloyd (1876a,288) recorded that Demasduit became fond of Peyton, Jr, and placed his snowshoes under her pillow; presumably he had heard this from Peyton.

23 Howley 1915,261.

24 Robinson 1834,215–16 (in Howley 1915,127).

25 Peyton, Jr, to Hamilton, 27 May 1819, PANL, CSOC, GN 2/1/A, vol.30, f.127–37 (in Howley 1915,105–8).

26 Grand Jury Room, 25 May 1819, PANL, CSOC, GN 2/1/A, vol.30, f.125 (in Howley 1915,105).

27 Hamilton to Captain Glascock, 3 June 1819, PANL, CSOC, GN 2/1/A, vol.30, f.160–1, (in Howley 1915,111).

28 Hamilton to Chief Justice Forbes, 26 June 1819, PANL, CSOC, GN 2/1/A, vol.30, f.180; Forbes to Hamilton, 29 June 1819, PANL, CSOC, GN 2/1/A, vol.30, f.181;

Hamilton to Bathurst, 27 September 1819, PANL, CSOC, GN 2/1/A, vol.30, f.304–8, and PRO, CO 194/62, f.61–4 (in Howley 1915,120).

29 Noad 1859,21.

30 Rev. John Leigh to the SPG, 17 April 1817, USPG, C/Can/NF 3, file Leigh, doc.239. The Reverend Mr Clinch travelled on *HMS Pike* from St John's as far as Trinity.

31 Ibid. Leigh thought it would be expensive to feed the captives since they ate nothing salted, while the winter diet of the English was principally salt fish and salt meat.

32 General Meeting of the Society [SPG], 19 November 1819, USPG, Minutes 1819–20, vol. 32, pp. 141–3, discussion about Leigh's letters of 12 and 30 July 1819 from Twillingate, and one dated 9 September 1819 from Harbour Grace.

33 Ibid.

34 SPG to Leigh, November 1819, USPG, Secretary's Letter Books, 1814–25, X 148.

35 Howley 1915,270, 274, 282; see also chapters 4 and 7.

36 Following the correspondence cited above, the Reverend Mr Leigh asked the SPG for permission to move to Harbour Grace; he received permission and remained in Harbour Grace until his death in August 1823.

37 Howley 1915,179.

38 Ibid.,283.

39 Robinson 1834,215–20, (in Howley 1915,127–9).

40 See note 50, chapter 9.

41 Robinson, "History of Mary March," BL, Add. Ms.19350 (in Howley 1915,127).

42 Leigh to the SPG, 30 July 1819, USPG, Minutes, 1819–20, vol.32, p. 141–3; SPG to Leigh, November 1819, USPG, Secretary's Letter Books, 1814–25, X 148; according to Lloyd (1875,37), Leigh also gave a copy of the vocabulary to Peyton, Jr.

43 Robinson 1834,216 (in Howley 1915,128).

44 Ibid.; Pedley (1863,339) claimed that Demasduit spent several months in St John's, but that is not the case; she was brought to St John's in May, and according to a letter from Chief Justice Forbes to Governor Hamilton from 31 May 1819 (PANL, CSOC, GN 2/1/A, vol.30, f.151–4, in Howley 1915,109), Hamilton had already asked Leigh to take her back to Twillingate by that date.

45 Hamilton to Bathurst, 27 September 1819, PANL, CSOC, GN 2/1/A, vol.30, f.304–8, and PRO, CO 194/62, f.61–4, (in Howley 1915,120); Robinson (1834,217, in Howley 1915,129) said she was twenty-four years old.

46 Howley 1915,179; Bonnycastle's description (1842,276) of Demasduit was identical to that given by Anspach (1819,245) for the woman captured in 1803 by Cull, including the claim that she was fifty years old; Tocque (1846,373) copied this description, believing that it pertained to Demasduit; Pedley (1863,339) evidently based his description of Demasduit on the report from Hamilton to Bathurst, PRO, CO 194/62, f.61–4 (in Howley 1915,120).

47 On the back of the miniature, now in the NAC (Picture Div., neg. C87698), is the inscription: "Mary March, A Female Native Indian of the Red Indians who inhabit Newfoundland painted by Lady Hamilton 18 …"; Lady Hamilton presented the painting to Mrs Dunscombe, wife of the Honourable John Dunscombe, one of the principal merchants in St John's, aide-de-camp to Governor Cochrane from 1825 on-

wards, and later vice president of the Boeothick Institution. One branch of the Dunscombe family moved to New York and it was in New York that the miniature eventually turned up in an auction in 1976 (Marshall 1977b, 5–6).

48 William Gosse made two copies of the miniature on which he changed the facial features; one of the copies was later published by the SPG in *The Mission Field*, 1856, and claimed to portray Shanawdithit; Howley (1915, Plate IX, 231) published a copy of this picture as a portrait of Shanawdithit; the second Gosse miniature has not been copied or published. Tocque (1893) writes that the (house) painter Trenair, "who was quite good at drawing," also copied the miniature by Lady Hamilton; this drawing of Mary March was published by Tocque in 1845. A copy of Trenair's drawing was published (as an etching) in the "Garland Tinto-Gravure Series" of Newfoundland postcards, no. 20 (printed in Belgium), with the inscription "Demasduit (Mary March) The Last of the Red Indians of NFLD." This version was reprinted in Howley (1915, Plate VI, 91) as a portrait of Mary March; see also Hardy and Marshall 1980,25–8.

49 John Lewis to the Missionary Committee of the Wesleyan Society, begun 17 May, cont. 5 June 1819, MMS: LR, North America, Newfoundland 1819–20, Box 2, file 2d, no.5.

50 Ibid.; John Pickavant, Methodist minister in Carbonear, made a similar observation (Pickavant to the Wesleyan Society in London, 10 July 1819, MMS: LR, North America, Newfoundland 1819–20, Box 2, file 2d, no. 10).

51 Smith (1986,126) suggests this interpretation.

52 Pedley 1863,339; Howley (1915,94) added that she was allowed to go into the shops and select whatever she fancied – a description taken from Pedley (1863,227) that actually pertained to the woman captured by Cull in 1803.

53 Cormack Papers 12/84 (in Howley 1915,184); "Sketches of savage life," 1836,323.

54 Peyton, Jr, to Hamilton, 27 May 1819, PANL, CSOC, GN 2/1/A, vol.30, f.127–37 (in Howley 1915,105–8); Captain Buchan's report of his second expedition up the Exploits River to Governor Hamilton, 10 March 1820, PRO, CO 194/63, f.64–77 (in Howley 1915,121–6).

55 *Mercantile Journal*, 27 May 1819,2.

56 *Mercantile Journal*, 3 June 1819,2. John Pickavant described the meeting in a letter to the Missionary Committee of the Wesleyan Society (10 July 1819, MMS: LR, North America, Newfoundland 1819–20, Box 2, file 2d, no.10); his information comes from an article in the *Royal Gazette* and is of particular interest since copies of the *Gazette* for 1819 have not survived.

57 *Mercantile Journal*, 3 June 1819,2.

58 Forbes to Hamilton, 31 May 1819, PANL, CSOC, GN 2/1/A, vol.30, f.151–4 (in Howley 1915,109–10).

59 Hamilton to Forbes, 5 June 1819, PANL, CSOC, GN 2/1/A, vol.30, f.163 (in Howley 1915,113). Hamilton to Captain Glascock, 3 June 1819, PANL, CSOC, GN 2/1/A, vol.30, f.156–9 (in Howley 1915,110).

60 List of Articles for the Beothuk Delivered to Glascock, no. 1, PANL, CSOC, GN 2/1/A, vol.30, f.160 (in Howley 1915,112); List no. 2 (in ibid.).

61 Hamilton to Glascock, 3 June 1819, PANL, CSOC, GN 2/1/A, vol.30, f.156–9 (in Howley 1915,110–11).
62 Glascock to Hamilton, 20 July 1819, PANL, CSOC, GN 2/1/A, vol.30, f.201–9 (in Howley 1915,113–16).
63 Ibid.
64 Master Jno. Trivick to Hamilton, 28 May 1820, PANL, CSOC, GN 2/1/A, vol.31, f.162, and PRO, CO 194/63, f.81 (in Howley 1915,126).
65 Peyton 1987,54.
66 Hamilton to Glascock, 15 July 1819, PRO, ADM 80/125 X/M00232, f.70; Glascock to Hamilton, 20 July 1819, PANL, CSOC, GN 2/1/A, vol.30, f.201–9 (in Howley 1915,113–16); Account from Mr William Burge, Twillingate, board and lodging for Indian Woman, 17 August to 5 November 1819, PRO, CO 194/63, f. 127, for 81 days, £6.1.6.
67 Glascock to Hamilton, 20 July 1819, PANL, CSOC, GN 2/1/A, vol.30, f.201–9 (in Howley 1915,113–16); see also *Mercantile Journal*, 19 August 1819,2.
68 The aim of the expedition had been to discover a northwest passage to the Bering Strait. Hamilton's instructions to Buchan, 8 August 1819, PANL, CSOC, GN 2/1/A, VOL.30, f.260–1, AND PRO, ADM 80/126, f.211 (in Howley 1915,116); Hamilton to Bathurst, 27 September 1819, PANL, CSOC, GN 2/1/A, vol.30, f.304, and PRO, CO 194/62, f.61–4 (in Howley 1915,120).
69 List of Articles delivered to Captain Buchan for distribution among the Native Indians, 8 August 1819, PANL, CSOC, GN 2/1/A, vol.30, f.262 (in Howley 1915,117). According to a note from Hamilton to Stabb and Co. (26 October 1819, PRO, CO 194/62, f.121), £265 sterling worth of tools, implements, and articles of clothing, including 120 sealskins, were delivered to *HMS Grasshopper* after the sloop had moored in Peter's Arm; some of these items may have been destined for Buchan's search party.
70 Hamilton to Buchan, 22 September 1819, PANL, CSOC, GN 2/1/A, vol.30, f.299–302, and PRO, CO 194/62, f.66–8 (in Howley 1915,117); Hamilton to Buchan, 10 November 1819, PRO, ADM 80/125, X/M00232.
71 Hamilton to Bathurst, 27 September 1819, PANL, CSOC, GN 2/1/A, vol.30, f.304–8, and PRO, CO 194/62, f.61–4 (in Howley 1915,119). In his testimony to the Select Committee on Aborigines ([1836] 1968,1:476), Buchan said that when he received orders to bring Demasduit back to her people, he conveyed her to the northern part of the island and left her under the charge of the Reverend Mr Leigh until November 1819. This information does not agree with the report by Glascock, who returned her to Twillingate when he called off his search in Notre Dame Bay in July 1819. There is no indication that Demasduit was brought to St John's a second time between July and November 1819.
72 Captain's Log, *HMS Grasshopper*, 27 November 1819, PRO, ADM 51/3193, X/M01416; Peyton 1987,61.
73 Since Buchan did not leave St John's until 25 September, he may have visited Demasduit in Twillingate on his return trip from England to Newfoundland in August. According to Glascock, Demasduit had been in Twillingate since July.

74 Buchan to Hamilton, 10 March 1820, PRO, CO 194/63, f.64–77 (in Howley 1915,121–6).

75 Dr William Carson, 1830, Answers to questions by the Royal College of Physicians of Great Britain, attached to Governor Cochrane's letter to Viscount Goderich, 7 February 1831, PRO, CO 194/81, f.59a.

76 Ibid.; Hamilton to Bathurst, 26 May 1820, PRO, CO 194/63, f.53.

77 In his published journal, Robinson (1834,215) mentioned that Demasduit took "a ring from her finger and beg[ged] it might be sent to John Peyton"; this detail is likely to have been an embellishment of the story of her death since in his original manuscript Robinson does not refer to a ring; the only eyewitness of her death who recorded the event was Buchan, who did not mention "a ring for John Peyton" (Buchan to Hamilton, 10 March 1820, PRO, CO 194/63, f.64–77 in Howley 1915,121).

78 Buchan to Hamilton, 10 March 1820, PRO, CO 194/63, f.64–77 (in Howley 1915, 121).

79 For the convenience of the reader, the English units as given in the original document have been converted to decimal ones in the text. According to the captain's log of *HMS Grasshopper* for 21 January 1819 (PRO, ADM 51/3193, X/MO1416), Buchan took the following provisions: "Bread 1477 lbs, Beef 74 pieces of 8 lbs each, Pork 480 pieces of 4 lbs each, Flour 677 lbs, Cocoa 146 lbs, sugar 330 lbs, Tea 15 lbs, Rum 151 1/4Gallons, Tongues 13 lbs, Fresh Beef 180 lbs."

80 Catamarans are usually floating devices. Since the Exploits River was frozen, Buchan seems to have used catamaran-type sledges; he does not explain how they were constructed.

81 Captain's Log, *HMS Grasshopper*, 29 November to 28 December 1819, PRO, ADM 51/3193, X/MO1416.

82 Ibid., 21 January 1820.

83 Buchan to Hamilton, 10 March 1820, PRO, CO 194/63, f.64–77 (in Howley 121–6); Peyton, Jr, said that twenty men were sent back in the first instance, and as the loads to be carried grew lighter and as more men became unwell, more men returned (Howley 1915,95).

84 See also Howley 1915,241–2; Shanawdithit related that when Buchan passed up the Exploits River the Beothuk were camped at "Badger Bay waters," that is, Badger Brook and the chain of lakes leading towards Badger Bay (Cormack Papers 20/84, in Howley 1915,228).

85 Howley 1915,95, 103; Noad 1859,22.

86 Buchan to Hamilton, 10 March 1820, PRO, CO 194/63, f.64–77 (in Howley 1915,121–6).

87 The information on the wooden dolls comes from Peyton, Jr (Howley 1915,95).

88 Ibid. According to Peyton, Jr, the spears and arrowheads were stamped with "the broad arrow" and were modelled after the Beothuk's own spears but were not as well made.

89 Buchan to Hamilton, 10 March 1820, PRO, CO 194/63, f.64–77 (in Howley 1915,121–6); report on Buchan's expedition in the *London Times*, 10 July 1820, cited in Howley 1915,104.

90 Captain's Log, *HMS Grasshopper*, 19 March 1820, PRO, ADM 51/3193, X/MO1416; Buchan to Hamilton, 10 March 1820, PRO, CO 194/63, f.64–77 (in Howley 1915,121–6); Buchan to Hamilton, 4 June 1820, PRO, CO 194/63, f.79.
91 Alexander Murray 1881, cited in Peyton 1987,71.
92 Buchan to Hamilton, 10 March 1820, PRO, CO 194/63, f.64–77 (in Howley 1915,21–6).
93 Buchan's manuscript maps, BL, Mss. 51222, Add. 57703f.1, and Add. 57703.f2; Jukes 1969,2:150. Peyton, Jr, had kept a journal that Buchan later asked for; he had also helped in drawing a map (Peyton 1987, 68). The original is probably item CO 700/13 "anonymous" in the PRO.
94 Hamilton to Bathurst, 28 June 1820, PANL, CSOC, GN 2/1/A, vol.32, f.209, and PRO, CO 194/63, f.62–3 (considerably shortened in Howley 1915,120).
95 Hamilton to Bathurst, 3 December 1821, PRO, CO 194/64, f.159.
96 Tocque 1878,504; see also chapter 9, Governor Holloway's attempt to lure the Beothuk with a painting.
97 Whitelaw 1978,187.
98 See chapter 13.

CHAPTER THIRTEEN

1 Howley 1915,233–7.
2 Howley (ibid., 237) spelled the name Joseph Silvester.
3 Cormack Papers 1/84 and 2/84, diary of the trial walk.
4 Howley 1915,134.
5 Charles Fox Bennett was aide-de-camp to Governor Hamilton at the time.
6 Howley 1915,130.
7 The following description is taken from Cormack's *Narrative*, published by him in an abbreviated form in 1824,156–62; his full account was first published in 1856,1–63, under the auspices of government, instigated by Governor Darling (Darling to Henry Labouchere MP, 11 October 1856, PRO, CO 194/148, f.406–7); it was edited and reprinted by Harvey (1873,5–83) and republished by Howley (1915,130–68). In this work the text printed by Howley is cited.
8 Howley 1915,135.
9 Ibid.,234.
10 Ibid.,137.
11 In a note for Sylvester dated 14 September 1822, Cormack promised additional rewards if he delivered Cormack safely on the west coast; Sylvester was to receive food and passage in one of Cormack's vessels to Portugal, Spain, or England; while in St John's he could live in Cormack's house. In his account (entry for 10 October) Cormack mentions that he had sometimes to encourage Sylvester with promises of additional rewards; evidently he made his first promise on 14 September and repeated and extended it from time to time (Cormack Papers 4/84, in Howley 1915, 237).
12 Howley 1915,149.

13 Ibid., 151.

14 Ibid., 158.

15 Cormack and Sylvester seem not to have parted altogether amicably; the Cormack Papers (7/84) include a lengthy note that was to be left in Cormack's house in St John's for any native people who might have come in his absence. The note reads, in part: "Englishmen say, why Joe Sylvester no come to England. I say, Joe hunt well, walk well, better than two Englishmen: long time in country, Joe wants to go home, he grumble, and because he grumble he no like to ask me to go to England: I sorry I no like to ask him to go to England for he angry because he grumble … But because Joe grumble and fall out a little with me."

16 Cormack Papers 20/84 (in Howley 1915,224); ibid., 169, 174; Shanawdithit's sketch 4, chapter 14, Fig. 14.1; Session in the Supreme Court, 23 June 1823, PRO, CO 194/66, f.73.

17 Session in the Supreme Court, 20, 21, 23 June 1823, PRO, CO 194/66, f.73–7. Heavy ice kept Adams from travelling to St John's; hence he was unable to appear in court. Affidavit by Wm. Davey, 20 March 1823, Cormack Papers 74/84; McGregor (1832,1:237) and Howley (1915,169) erroneously record that the killing occurred in New Bay.

18 McGregor 1832,1:259. In his diary entry of 23 June 1828, Wilson (1866,312–13) claimed that only a Beothuk man was shot when he attacked furriers with a club. In his testimony to the Select Committee on Aborigines ([1836] 1968,1:477), Buchan said: "When the Indians came within a short distance of the furriers they stopped; after some conversation between them, one Indian advanced a little holding a knife and at last made a run towards the furriers; a gun was fired, but because the man fell down, the ball killed the woman behind him; the Indian man then rushed upon the two furriers and was shot in the ensuing scuffle."

19 Session in the Supreme Court, 23 June 1823, PRO, CO 194/66, f.74.

20 A man named Carey had accompanied Peyton on the excursion to Red Indian Lake when Demasduit was captured and her husband killed (Howley 1915,272); whether this was the same man cannot be ascertained. The names of the furriers who accompanied Buchan in 1820 are not recorded.

21 Session in the Supreme Court, 23 June 1823, PRO, CO 194/66, f.75a.

22 Ibid., f.76.

23 Ibid., f.76a-77. In a rape trial in the Court of Oyer and Terminer, St John's, 12–14 September 1751, no such indulgence was shown; one of the accused was sentenced to be hanged (PRO, CO 194/25, f.111a-14, 119a).

24 Session in the Supreme Court, 23 June 1823, PRO, CO 194/66, f.77.

25 "Sketches of savage life," 1836,318; McGregor (1832,1:259) states that the man was first shot and "the woman in despair remained calmly to be fired at … the mind is slow to believe that so brutal an act as this could have been committed …
Mr Cormack was told this by the very white barbarian who shot her." This version is also recorded in Cormack Papers 20/84 (in Howley 1915,229 fn.1). Howley (ibid., 272) stated that a man named Carey who had "killed the Indians in New Bay [should be Badger Bay] boasted of it as a deed to be proud of."

26 Cormack Papers 20/84 (in Howley 1915,227 fn.1, 229).
27 Howley 1915,277.
28 Session in the Supreme Court, 23 June 1823, PRO, CO 196/66, f.75.
29 Bishop John Inglis, Diary, 2 July 1827, NAC, microfilm A 713.
30 Cormack Papers 20/84 (in Howley 1915,229); Shanawdithit's sketch 4, chapter 14, Fig.14.1.
31 Cormack Papers 20/84 (in Howley 1915,224); Howley 1915, 174; Inglis (Diary, 2 July 1827, NAC, microfilm A 713) recorded the same story but did not mention "others"; Inglis (ibid., 4 July 1827) received a memorandum from Peyton, Jr, in which the events were described in similar terms, though it included passages referring to Peyton's well-known wish to have friendly intercourse with the Beothuk.
32 Cormack Papers 20/84 (in Howley 1915,229); in "Sketches of savage life," 1836,323, the author states that Shanawdithit's mother was shot in the summer before Nonosabasut's death while paddling in a canoe, and that her father died some moons "after."
33 "Sketches of savage life," 1836,323.
34 Peyton, Jr, to P.C. Legeyt, Secretary, 18 June 1823, PRO, CO 194/66 f.68–9 (in Howley 1915,170–2).
35 Wilson had recently been assigned to Grand Bank, Ellis came from Burin; Wilson 1866,314–15; The Reverend Mr Wilson to Methodist Missionary Society, 12 August 1823, MMS: LR, North America, Newfoundland 1823–24, Box 4, file 4f, no.14; Wilson 1839,469–70.
36 Wilson 1866,313.
37 Wilson to the Methodist Missionary Society, 12 August 1823, MMS: LR, North America, Newfoundland 1823–24, Box 4, file 4f, no.14.
38 Buchan to Hamilton, 28 June 1823, PRO, CO 194/66, f.66 (in Howley 1915,172).
39 Wilson 1866,313.
40 Buchan to Hamilton, 28 June 1823, PRO, CO 194/66, f.66 (in Howley 1915,172); Wilson to the Methodist Missionary Society, 12 August 1823, MMS: LR, North America, Newfoundland 1823–24, Box 4, file 4f, no.14.
41 Inglis to Cormack, 10 August 1827, Cormack Papers 72/84–1 (in Howley 1915,206); Howley 1915, 182.
42 Wilson 1866,313.
43 Ibid.; in a letter to the Methodist Missionary Society (12 August 1823, MMS: LR, North America, Newfoundland 1823–24, Box 4, file 4f, no.14), Wilson wrote that she was of "Mulatto colour."
44 Wilson to Methodist Missionary Society, 12 August 1823, MMS: LR, North America, Newfoundland 1823–24, Box 4, file 4f, no.14.
45 Howley 1915,174.
46 Buchan to Peyton, Jr, 28 June 1823, PRO, CO 194/66, f.70 (in Howley 1915,172–3).
47 Howley 1915, 175, Peyton, Jr's version; Wilson (1866,314) claimed that the women went ashore with great reluctance and screamed and rushed into the water when the boat left. The captain thought it would be cruel to leave them and took them to the person "who brought them away." Since this information was not entered in

Wilson's original journal, it is presumably an embellishment that became attached to the story during the intervening four decades.

48 The name Easter Eve was chosen because she was taken on that day (Howley 1915,181).

49 Howley 1915, 180; Dr William Carson, 1830, Answer to questions … PRO, CO 194/81, f.59a.

50 Howley 1915, 180, 181. Mr Gill, whose mother had been a servant in Peyton's household when the three women were captured, told Howley the name Betty Decker was bestowed because the men who captured her were at the time engaged in decking a vessel.

51 Ibid.,175; Bishop Inglis's diary (3 July 1827, NAC, microfilm A 713) records that Peyton returned the women to their wigwam and that the older daughter died as soon as they landed; the mother died at one of Peyton's stations.

52 Howley 1915,282.

53 Ibid.,175.

54 Ibid.,180, presumably Gills Point.

55 Ibid.,180; since Curtis said that Nance came back to "Burnt Island" (One of the two Exploits Islands) and "lived with Peyton and myself," it is assumed that the hut (or tent) was erected outside Peyton's door on Exploits Island; on a visit to the island, former residents repeated to me the tradition that Shanawdithit had lived on Exploits Islands in a wigwam close to the water's edge; a note in the Howley Papers about Howley's interview with Curtis states, "They lived in a *tent* outside our door" (emphasis added).

56 Howley 1915,180.

57 Peyton 1987,6. John and Eleanor Peyton were married in February 1823.

58 Cormack papers 25/84.

59 "Statement of Expenses for the maintenance and attendances of three native female Indians under the care of John Peyton, from 28 June to 12 July, passages to and from the Exploits for 4 persons, a man in attendance, supply of bread, pork and butter when left at Charles Brook, board and lodging for Nancy from 1 August to 16 October 1823, 51–15–4 pound sterling" (PRO, CO 194/66, f.142–3).

60 Howley 1915,175.

61 Ibid.,180, 181; in ibid.n.d. (chapter 1871,2–3) Howley records that he met John Peyton, Jr, and his wife. While Peyton was full of stories about the Beothuk, his wife was more reticent and declined to talk; she was, however, able to pronounce Beothuk words that she had learned from Shanawdithit.

62 Howley 1915,175, 181, 260, 270.

63 Ibid.,180, 181.

64 Ibid.,181; Inglis, Diary, 4 July 1827, USPG, C/Can/NS9, doc.57–8.

65 Howley 1915,175, 181.

66 Ibid.,181.

67 Ibid.

68 Ibid.,175.

69 Ibid.,176, 181, 182.

70 Ibid.,176, 181. Cormack Papers 35/84 (in Howley 1915,230).
71 Howley 1915,175.
72 Ibid.,181 (Mr Gill); a memo in the Howley Papers about his 1886 visit with Mrs Jure at Kite Cove states that Mrs Jure told him Shanawdithit was a married woman and had one child, and that her husband was shot.
73 Cormack Papers 20/84 (in Howley 1915,229); Shanawdithit's sketch 4, Fig.14.1; "Sketches of savage life," 1836,323.
74 R.A. Tucker, Adm. to the Govt. of Newfoundland, to R.W. Horton, 29 June 1825, PRO, CO 194/71, f. 11–14 (in Howley 1915,174) includes the comment that "a gentleman of talent and learning" has conjectured that the Beothuk were "the remains of an Icelandic Colony"; Howley (1915,174 fn.2) believed this gentleman to have been Cormack; it is also possible that he was David Macpherson (1805,1:280); see also chapter 27; or he could have been an acquaintance of Governor Waldegrave on whose behalf Waldegrave made enquiries to this effect with John Bland in a memo attached to his letter of 27 September 1798 (PANL, CSOC, GN 2/1/A, vol.14, f.276).
75 Handwritten note on back of Tucker's letter, PRO, CO 194/71 f.14a; Horton to Tucker, 6 August 1825, PRO, CO 324/37, f.95.
76 Captain's Log, *HMS Orestes*, May 1827 to July 1827, PRO, ADM 53/940.
77 Inglis to Cormack, 10 August 1827, Cormack Papers 72/84–1 (in Howley 1915,206); Inglis, Diary, 5 June 1827, NAC, microfilm A 713.
78 Ibid., 3 July 1827.
79 Ibid.; Inglis's Report on Newfoundland, Part I, sent to the SPG on 17 December 1827, is no longer extant. Part II, 5 January 1828, is in the papers of the USPG, C/Can/NS9, doc.57–8; Minutes 1826–28, vol.37, p. 342.
80 Inglis, Diary, 4 July 1827, USPG, C/Can/NS9, doc.57–8.
81 This canoe model is now in the National Maritime Museum, Greenwich, UK; the entry in the 1869 museum catalogue reads: "Canoe made from the bark of a birch tree by Shanawdithit an Indian woman, the last of the Beothic or Red tribe of Newfoundland, and presented by her to Captain Jones HMS Orestes."
82 See also chapter 3, Shanawdithit's information on Montagnais, and chapters 24 and 25.
83 Inglis, Diary, 2 July 1827, NAC, microfilm A 713; ibid., 4 July 1827, USPG, C/Can/NS9, doc.57–8; discussed in chapters 3, 10, 11, 13.
84 Howley 1915,180.
85 Inglis, Diary, 4 July 1827, NAC, microfilm A 713.
86 Rev. John Chapman to the Reverend Anthony Hamilton, 28 October 1826, USPG, C/Can./NF 3, doc.107.
87 Peyton 1987,66.
88 Cormack Papers 5/84 include a note saying that the party should surround the Beothuk, securing all ways against escape by land and water, and should advance upon them "as friends or as their determined captors"; the party should then convince the Beothuk by signs and drawings of their friendly intention and persuade them to come to the coast; in Cormack Papers 6/84, the list of equipment intended

for this expedition includes "mineral test apparatus, a seamless canoe-skin, a brass pocket compass with quadrant attached, pocket spy glass, pocket theodelite," and other items.

89 Ibid.

90 Cormack Papers 23/84; Cormack to Inglis, 26 October 1828, Cormack Papers 62/84 (in Howley 1915,208). When requested to report on inland resources, Governor Cochrane nevertheless submitted Cormack's map to Viscount Goderich, secretary of state (9 October 1827, PANL, GN 1/1/3 (3) f.69).

91 Howley 1915,159.

92 Inglis to Cormack, 10 August 1827, Cormack Papers 72/84–1, (in Howley 1915,205–6); Thomas Slade offered to join Cormack and Peyton on such a trip (Cormack to John Peyton, Twillingate 5 October 1827, PANL, C.F. Rowe Collection, MG 134).

93 "Sketches of savage life," 1836,322.

94 Wm. Crud to Cormack, Galtois, 30 August 1827, Cormack Papers 51/84; Cormack spelled the name Louis or Lewis, Howley spelled it Lewis; Mr Curtis told Howley that John Lewis was a Mohawk "Metis"; elsewhere Howley said that John Lewis was a Micmac Indian (Howley 1915, 203, 301, 323). Cormack to Peyton, 29 September 1827, CNS Archive, Peyton Collection.

95 Cormack Papers 17/84; Cormack 1829,319 (in Howley 1915,189); Inglis, Diary, 3 July 1827, USPG, C/Can/NS9, doc.57–8.

96 Judge A.W. Des Barres to Cormack, 6 August 1827, Cormack Papers 71/84 (in Howley 1915,205).

97 A draft of Cormack's address to the second meeting of the Boeothick Institution includes the following paragraph: "The original idea of founding such an institution emanated from our worthy Vice Patron when at Twillingate in Sept. last; I was then on my way to the ancient territory of the Boeothicks to search for some of the remaining of that mistreated and singularly ancient tribe'' (Cormack papers 10/84).

98 The name Boeothic(k) first appears in the word list collected from Shanawdithit; it is assumed, that Cormack had heard the name Boeothick from Peyton, Jr, before he met Shanawdithit; this assumption is supported by the fact that Bishop Inglis, who had stayed with the Peytons in July of that year, used the term Boeothick in his diary, he was the first person to record this name in writing (Inglis, Diary, 3 July 1827, USPG, C/Can/NS9 doc.57–8; see also Part Two, Appendix 4, "Beothuk Namefile").

99 "Boeothick Institution." *Royal Gazette*, 13 November 1827 (in Howley 1915,189).

100 Cormack Papers 12/84 (in Howley 1915,183–4); "Boeothick Institution." *Royal Gazette*, 13 November 1827; McGregor 1832, I:260–2; parts of Cormack's address are also reprinted in "Sketches of Savage Life," 1836,316–7.

101 Proceedings of the meeting on 2 October 1827, Cormack Papers 48/84 (in Howley 1915,186).

102 Ibid; Howley (1915,218) records that half a year later William Thomas took over as treasurer. Other officers of the institution, according to Cormack Papers 48/84 (Howley 1915,185–6), were John Dunscombe, aide-de-camp to Governor

Cochrane, vice president; and John Stark, clerk and registrar of the Northern Circuit Court in Harbour Grace, secretary; Dr John Barrow, secretary to the Admiralty in London, and Professor Robert Jameson, president of the Wernerian Society, Edinburgh, were voted honorary vice patrons. (According to the *Edinburgh New Philosophical Journal* 20, no.6,1829, Robert Jameson was regius professor of Natural History, lecturer on Mineralogy, keeper of the museum at the University of Edinburgh, fellow of the Royal Societies of London and Edinburgh, the Antiquarian, Wernerian, and Horticultural Societies, and the Linnean and Geological Societies of London, and an honorary member of about twenty-five other societies in England, Germany, France, Russia, Asia, and North America.)

John Peyton, Jr, was named resident agent and corresponding member; other corresponding members were Attorney General Charles Simms, St John's (previously a member of the Citizen's Committee); the Reverend Mr Sinnott, Roman Catholic minister at King's Cove, Bonavista Bay; Dr Tremlett, MD; Rev. John Chapman, Church of England minister, Twillingate; Joseph Simms, chairman of the grand jury in Twillingate; Andrew Pearce, formerly justice of the peace at Fogo; James Slade and Thomas Lyte, from Twillingate; Thomas and David Slade, merchants at Fogo; Benjamin Scott of Harbour Grace; Capt. Hugh Clapperton RN, "traveller in Africa," probably an acquaintance of Cormack; (Clapperton lived in Edinburgh in 1820 and in 1822–25 took part in two excursions through Central Africa, where he died in April 1827; the only survivor of this expedition did not return to England until 1828, so that Cormack could not have known that Clapperton was no longer alive in October 1827; see DNB, vol.4, p. 372).

103 Cormack Papers 49/84; on a draft copy of the proceedings Cormack had listed (but later crossed out) the following names: "Honorary Patrons: Earl Aberdeen, Viscount Goderich; Honorary Vice Patrons: Sir Thomas Cochrane, R.W. Horton, Esq., R.W. Hay, Esq., Hon. A. Tucker, Hon. Judge Brenton, Hon. Judge Paterson, Hon. A.H. Brooking, Doctor Carson, Charles Cogan, Esq., Rev. Knight."

104 Cormack to Stark, 26 October 1827, Cormack Papers 63/84 (in Howley 1915,197); Stark to Cormack, 21 December 1827 (given as 1828 in Howley 1915, 200), Cormack Papers 70/84–1, informing Cormack that he had not yet tried to gain public subscription and was waiting for Cormack's advice; in his letter to Peyton from Twillingate (5 October 1827, PANL, C.F. Rowe Collection, MG 134), Cormack said funds were to be raised in 1828.

105 Cormack to Stark, 26 October 1827, Cormack Papers 63/84 (in Howley 1915,197); "Boeothick Institution," 13 November 1827 (in Howley 1915,182); "Boeothic Institution," 26 February 1828,281; in Cormack to Stark, 20 May 1828 (Cormack Papers 59/84, in Howley 1915,199), notices were published in two "Liverpool papers" and "several other English and Scotch papers"; part of the proceedings were printed in McGregor 1832,1:260–2.

106 Cormack to Peyton, 5 October 1827, PANL C.F. Rowe Collection, MG 134.

107 Circuit Court Record, Twillingate, Presentment of the Grand Jury, 2 October 1827, PANL, GN 5/2/B/1, box 2, f.25.

108 Morris 1827,7.

109 Cormack to Peyton from Twillingate, 5 October 1827, PANL, C.F. Rowe Collection, MG 134.

110 Ibid.; Cormack Papers 6/84; Cormack to Peyton from Exploits, 27 November (should be October) 1827, transcript in Howley Papers.

111 In Cormack to Peyton from Twillingate, 5 October 1827 (PANL, C.F. Rowe Collection, MG 134), Cormack thanked Peyton for his letter with "enclosures." Cormack to Peyton from London, 18 October 1829, PANL, C.F. Rowe Collection, MG 134: "I have it not in my power yet, to make you a return for your civility to me when at Exploits, but hope some time to have the pleasure to do so."

112 Cormack 1829,319–29 (in Howley 1915,189–97); the departure date was 31 October *1827*, not 31 October *1828* as printed in the *Edinburgh New Philosophical Journal* and in Howley 1915,190.

113 Cormack 1829,327 (in Howley 1915,196).

114 The equipment list in Cormack Papers 6/84 includes a "vocabulary"; Cormack 1829,327 (in Howley 1915,196); Lloyd 1875,37.

115 Inglis, Diary, 3 July 1827, USPG, C/Can/NS9, doc.57–8.

116 Cormack Papers 20/84 (in Howley 1915,176 fn.1, 224): in the spring of 1826 "recent" traces of Beothuk had been seen by Micmac at South Twin Lake.

117 According to Cormack to Stark, 24 December 1827, Cormack Papers 58/84 (in Howley 1915,198), the Beothuk seemed to have deserted the lake five or six years earlier; Rev. John Chapman, in his letter to the SPG, 15 December 1827 (USPG, C/Can/NF 4 doc.252), noted that Cormack thought the Beothuk had removed from the lake two or three years before.

118 Cormack 1829,326 (in Howley 1915,194).

119 University Museum, Edinburgh, day-record book, "Addition to College Museum, 1827, 1828:15 March 1828, Mr Cormack brought from Newfoundland 1) Skull of male Red Indian, [rubbed with red ochre, marked in ink: 'Newfoundland chief Mr Cormack 1827'], 2) Skull of female Red Indian [no signs of red ochre, marked in ink: 'Red Indian Newfoundland'], 3) Model of a canoe made by Red Indians, 4+5) small wooden human figure found in the chief's cemetery, 6+7) meat dish of bark, 8) point of spear, 9) model of a bird found in the chief's cemetery, 10) drinking cup of bark, 11) fire stones (Iron pyrites), 12) [blank]"; ibid., week record book: "15 March 1828: Presented by Mr Cormack from Newfoundland 12 listed (see daybook), No. 12) Pelisse [dress] of the chief's infant daughter." The Wernerian Society Record Book, vol.1, p. 285: "College, 22nd March 1828, Two skulls, male and female, of the Red Indians or native Inhabitants of Newfoundland sent home by Mr Cormack were also exhibited to the meeting"; McGregor 1832,1:278.

120 "Sketches of savage life," 1836,321. This finding was confirmed by Maureen Barrie, National Museums of Scotland, 29 October 1992, who said in a letter to me: "There are indeed several marks of wounds, one of which does appear to have cleaved the lower jaw. There is also a perforation of the maxillary bone (right side) which might have been caused by a shot but we cannot confirm this."

121 Cormack 1829,327 (in Howley 1915,195).

122 Ibid.

123 Cormack 1829,327–9 (in Howley 1915,195–6); Howley 1915,196 fn.1, 234; Cormack to Peyton, 27 November (should be October) 1827, transcript in Howley Papers.

124 Howley 1915,195–6 fn.1, 234; Cormack left Twillingate on 9 December 1827; Rev. John Chapman to the SPG, 15 December 1827 (USPG, C/Can/NF 4 doc.252) gave a brief account of Cormack's expedition; Howley 1915,186 fn.2.

125 Cormack 1829,318–29 (in Howley 1915,189–97); preliminary announcements appeared in the *Edinburgh New Philosophical Journal*, December 1827,205–6, cited in Howley 1915:187, and January 1828,408–10 (in Howley 1915, 188. Reports of Cormack's expedition were probably also published in Newfoundland newspapers but issues from that time are not preserved. John McGregor incorporated Cormack's report in his *British America*, 1832,1:256–77.

126 Bonnycastle 1842.

127 Cormack 1829,318–29 (in Howley 1915,189–97).

128 Cormack 1829,329 (in Howley 1915,196); Cormack Papers 8/84 (in Howley 1915,215); Cormack wrote to Peyton (27 November [should be October] 1827, transcript in Howley Papers) that he had hired John Louis for this purpose before his expedition. Crud wrote to Cormack (30 August 1827, Cormack Papers 51/84) that "I will inform John you will provide for him the Winter, besides handsomely rewarding him otherwise." According to Cormack Papers 17/84 (in Howley 1915,228–9), John Louis and John Stevens had seen a Beothuk party at Red Indian Lake in 1822.

129 *Public Ledger*, 15 January 1828,2–3: Cormack sailed on the brigantine *Geo Canning*, which left St John's 14 January 1828; Cormack 1829,329 (in Howley 1915,197).

130 Cormack Papers 67/84; "Boeothick Institution," 19 February 1828,3 (in Howley 1915,215).

131 Cormack Papers 27/84–1 and 2 (in Howley 1915,216).

132 Crud to Cormack, from Galtois, 15 April 1828, Cormack Papers 51/84.

133 "Boeothic Institution," 26 June 1828,2 (in Howley 1915,217–18).

134 Ibid.; Cormack to Stark, 21 June 1828, Cormack Papers 61/84 (in Howley 1915,200); Cormack to Le Commandant Administrateur pour Sa Majesté Le Roi de France À Terre Neuve, 26 June 1828, Cormack Papers 53/84 (in Howley 1915,218).

135 The following list of subscribers (and the amounts they contributed) was published under "Boeothick Institution," 24 June 1828,2: "His Honor the President, Hon. Chief Judge Brenton, Hon. Judge Des Barres, Hon. Capt. Paterson, C.B., Hon. Judge Cochrane, Hon. and Right Rev. the Lord Bishop of N.-Scotia, Rt. Rev. Bishop Scallan, D.D., Hon. A.H. Brooking, W.A. Clarke, Secty, Messrs. W. & H.Thomas, Colonel Burke, C.B., Colonel Dunscomb, Jas. Simms, Atty. Genl., George Bayly, Comptroller of Customs, Geo. T. Hayward, Doctor Carson, Charles Simms, G.W. Rusteed, Robert Job, W.E. Cormack, Joseph Templeman, Charles Cook, Robert R. Wakeham, J.M. Gibbon, Wm. Vallance, Thomas Bennett, C.F. Bennett, Stephen Lawler, William Stewart, James Stewart, Patrick Morris,

J.B. Bishop?, John Jen ...?" Additional subscribers were to be announced in the next issue, which is no longer extant.

136 Cormack Papers 27/84–3 (in Howley 1915,219); Cormack 1828,2.

137 Howley 1915,219–20.

138 Ibid.

139 Cormack to Peyton, 28 October 1828, PRRL, 917.18 C 81 NRV; *Public Ledger*, 2 September 1828,2.

140 *Royal Gazette*, 2 September 1828, cited in Noad 1859,43, reported that three weeks earlier Beothuk had shot an arrow at Nippers Harbour; Robert Tremlett, MD wrote to Cormack, 22 June 1828, that "John Gale a furrier living in White Bay states he has seen some late traces of the Boethicks in his vicinity" (Cormack Papers 80/84); Stark to Cormack, 16 September 1828, Cormack Papers 70/84–6 (in Howley 1915,202): Mr Dale (Gale?) of Exploits claimed to have seen "the smoke of the Red Indians' wigwams" the previous winter; Cormack to Inglis, 26 October 1828, Cormack Papers 62/84 (in Howley 1915,208).

141 T.H. Brooking to John Peyton, 28 October 1828, PANL, C.F. Rowe Collection, MG 134; Howley 1915,225.

142 Select Committee on Aborigines [1836] 1968,1:477; it is unlikely that Governor Cochrane had accompanied Buchan on his patrols along the coast every year.

143 Inglis to Cormack, 13 November 1828, Cormack Papers 72/84–5 (in Howley 1915,209); Stark to Cormack, 12 September 1828, Cormack Papers 70/84–4 (in Howley 1915,201).

CHAPTER FOURTEEN

1 Cormack Papers 48/84 (in Howley 1915,186).

2 Cormack 1829,318 (in Howley 1915,198).

3 Select Committee on Aborigines [1836] 1968,1:477; Howley 1915,225; T.H. Brooking to John Peyton, 28 October 1828, PANL, MG 134, C.F. Rowe Collection.

4 W.E. Cormack to Peyton, 28 October 1828, PRRL, 917.18 C81 NRV.

5 T.H. Brooking to Peyton, 21 September 1828, PANL, MG 134, C.F. Rowe Collection: Mrs Peyton informed her husband of the events (he had gone to Stag Harbour Tickle south of Fogo Island); John Stark to Cormack, 16 September 1828, Cormack Papers 70/84–6 (in Howley 1915,202); Mr Abbot, who took Shanawdithit to St John's, agreed to have his charge for her passage credited towards his subscription for the Boeothick Institution.

6 Cormack to Peyton, 28 October 1828, PRRL, 917.18 C81 NRV; Howley 1915,225.

7 Stark to Cormack, 16 September 1828, Cormack Papers 70/84–6 (in Howley 1915,202); Stark repeated the request to have her vaccinated in a separate note, which Shanawdithit personally delivered to Cormack (Stark to Cormack, 16 September 1828, Cormack Papers 70/84–5, in Howley 1915,203).

8 Though an article in the *Royal Gazette*, 21 October 1828,2, mentioned that there were at Mr Cormack's house "accessible at all times to those who feel an interest" Indians from three tribes, "a Mountaineer from Labrador, two of the Banakee

[Abenaki] nation from Canada and a Boeothick from Newfoundland," there is no indication that Shanawdithit became a "public spectacle" as claimed by Peyton (1987,96).

9 Stark to Cormack, 16 September 1828, Cormack Papers 70/84–6 (in Howley 1915,202): Stark had shown an "arrow point" to Shanawdithit, who commented that it "never could have been made by an Indian;" Stark did not mention where the point came from and what material was used; it could well have been a Dorset Eskimo point since Dorset remains are abundant in Newfoundland.

10 Brooking (governor's secretary) to Peyton, 28 October 1828, PANL, MG 134, C.F. Rowe Collection; Upton (1978,154) includes an innuendo about illicit sexual relations between Beothuk and the English based on a note in Cormack's hand, which mentions J.(?)H. Brooking. Upton, who believed that Brooking was a Fogo settler, claimed that Cormack thought he might have been responsible for Shanawdithit's being whisked away by Peyton in 1823. Upton quotes Cormack's note as follows: "This man was one of her Tribe taken at a mature age & *familiarized* [original italics] among us before her and merely that itself is worth any man's consideration and investigation." This note, which is in the Cormack Papers, file 25/84, is difficult to decipher; I have transcribed the entire text of the note as follows: "J.(?)H. Brooking Esq. in the first(?) effort of the Inst.(?) for 4 years(?) part(?): She is here now and let us keep her and be kind to her. This woman [see note below] was one of her tribe taken at a mature age and familiarized among us before him(?) and merely that itself is worth any man's consideration and investigation." The word transcribed here as "woman" is spelled "wom" (Cormack often used abbreviations – his own shorthand) and is unlikely to stand for "man" as transcribed by Upton; the phrase "familiarized" is taken to mean "become familiar with our culture" and the phrase "before him" to express that this transpired before his eyes, i.e., that Brooking was able to observe the transformation. The reference to Brooking's connection with the (Boeothic) Inst. suggests that the initial should be T.H. and not J.H (although it does look like J.H.); in the light of these explanations, the note does not seem to indicate improper relations and should remove any innuendo from J.(?) or T.H. Brooking.

11 Cormack Papers 19/84 (in Howley 1915,210); Cormack Papers 25/84.

12 Howley 1915,180, 181; Bishop Inglis, Diary, 4 July 1827, USPG, C/Can/NS9, doc.57–8.

13 Cormack Papers 20/84 (in Howley 1915,225).

14 Cormack to Peyton, 28 October 1828, PRRL, 917.18 C81 NRV.

15 Cormack to Inglis, 26 October 1828, Cormack Papers 62/84 (in Howley 1915, 208–9).

16 Cormack Papers 24/84: this paragraph was included in Cormack's draft of his address at the formation of the Boeothick Institution but was eliminated from the actual speech.

17 Cormack Papers 12/84 (in Howley 1915,183).

18 Lord Bathurst to Dr Barrow, n.d., Cormack Papers 73/84 (in Howley 1915,205): Professor Jameson sent a copy of Bathurst's letter to Cormack.

19 Cormack Papers 20/84 (in Howley 1915,225); Cormack Papers 29/84: this note reads: "From Nancy living in my house I have been enabled with pains to elucidate these and many other facts from her."
20 Cormack Papers 20/84 (in Howley 1915,225).
21 "Sketches of savage life," 1836,322.
22 Ibid.,323.
23 Dr William Carson, MD, Answers to questions by the Royal College of Physicians of Great Britain, 1830, attached to Governor Cochrane's letter to Viscount Goderich, 7 February 1831, PRO, CO 194/81, f.59a-60.
24 Carson to Govt Secr. Ayre, 17 November 1830, PANL, CSOC, GN 2/2 1830, Box 43/T/4, f.325–8; Carson had originally written "suspicious" but then replaced it with "cautious."
25 Cormack 1829,318 (in Howley 1915,196).
26 The miniature by W. Gosse, frontispiece, turned up in an auction in 1992; the inscription on the back of the actual portrait is pencilled over writing that has been erased; the inscription on the wooden backing of the frame, written in a different hand, reads: "A Female Red Indian Nfl 'Mary March' that was captured in the month of March 1819 painted by W. Goss of St Johns Nfd. July '41 from an originall by Lady Hamilton May 1821 [should be 1819]." The miniature by W. Gosse, Plate 14.1, came to light in 1987; it is now in the collection of the Newfoundland Museum, on exhibit in the Mary March Museum in Grand Falls.
27 Crewe 1968,3; Prowse 1972, x; Gosse 1890,20.
28 Bonnycastle 1842,2:264.
29 In St John's Shanawdithit wore European-style garments, and Gosse may have copied the clothing from the Hamilton miniature to present the woman in her "native attire."
30 "Sketches of savage life," 1836,322.
31 William Gosse was a well known miniature painter; a portrait of his friend William Charles St John of Harbour Grace, 1837, is in the collection of Memorial University; a portrait of his brother Philip H. Gosse, 1839, is in the National Portrait Gallery, London; see also Foskett 1972,1:292; ibid., 2, Plate 130, No.344.
32 Barbara Hilton-Smith, Witt Library, Courtauld Institute of Art, London, wrote to me in 1993 that Dickes was a well-known mid-nineteenth-century English engraver. McLean (1972,197–200) notes that he excelled in wood and copper engraving and also used the process of chromolithography; Dickes illustrated some of Philip Henry Gosse's books on shoreline wildlife.
33 Cited in Howley 1915,295.
34 Inglis, Diary, 4 July 1827, USPG, C/Can/NS9, doc.57–8. Howley (1915;295 fn.1), who was not aware of the existence of Gosse's portraits, suggested that the one in the SPG publication was "probably a copy of a … portrait referred to by W.E. Cormack, and seen by Bonnycastle."
35 Cormack Papers 20/84 (in Howley 1915,226–9).
36 Ibid.; according to the Inglis diary, 2 July 1827 (NAC, microfilm A 713), Shanawdithit claimed Buchan fell in with all the remaining Beothuk who lived in three

wigwams. One was that of her father's family, with ten individuals; another had nine, and the last sixteen occupants. Inglis added: "Buchan thought there were more but she seems to be very clear." This information does not tally with what Shanawdithit told Cormack.

37 "Sketches of savage life," 1836,323.

38 Ibid.; Cormack seems not to have asked Shanawdithit about what appears to have been two sets of parents.

39 Cormack Papers 20/84 (in Howley 1915,228); some of Shanawdithit's figures do not fit (particularly since Cormack gave 1816 as the date for Buchan's first trip to Red Indian Lake) and Howley has changed them in his transcription.

40 Morandière 1962,1:22; Webber 1978,98 note 5.

41 Cormack Papers 20/84 (in Howley 1915,229).

42 Mr Scott James from Grand Falls has identified the lakes and brooks on Shanawdithit's sketch 4 as follows: the first lake to the north of the Exploits River is Joe's Lake, followed by Paul's Lake and Crooked Lake. Two large lakes flow into Crooked Lake by way of Rocky Pond: North Twin Lake on the left when proceeding upstream and South Twin Lake on the right. Two portage routes are shown to Badger Bay, to the north of North Twin Lake, the westernmost by way of Tommy's Arm River and Crescent Lake, the other primarily by Sop's Arm Brook and Sop's Lake. Two portage routes to Badger Bay are also shown from South Twin Lake (called Badger Bay Great Lake by Cormack), the westernmost by way of Penny's Brook and the other on a series of small ponds and unnamed brooks. The large lake with many islands to the east of Crooked Lake is most likely Frozen Ocean Lake. The large islands to the east of Seal Bay are Cull's Island and Burnt Island at Leading Tickles.

43 Cormack Papers 20/84 (in Howley 1915,229).

44 Ibid. (in Howley 1915,224, 229).

45 Ibid. (in Howley 1915,229).

46 Ibid. (in Howley 1915,228–9).

47 On Shanawdithit's sketch 4, a note under (enlarged) A 2 reads, "8 died before Nancy's Uncle & Cousin shot at Badger Bay by Carey &."

48 According to another version of the story, her father drowned while avoiding his wife Doodebewshet's captors (Cormack Papers 20/84, in Howley 1915,224).

49 The notations on sketch 4, particularly with regard to the chronology of the events, are confusing. They read (from left down – to right): "We may suppose those left in the country amounted to 12 people
1. 5 men, 4 women, 1 lad, 2 children = 12
2. 1 mother 1 father 1 sister 3 women = 6 (+) 1 Nancy = 7, 8 died before Nancy's Uncle and Cousin shot at Badger Bay [should be New Bay] by Carey ec.
Nancy's uncle who was married to one of them Mary Ms sister, 1 Mary Marchs mother, 1 Longnons wife, 1 Nancy's cousin her uncles daughter
Mary March's brothers 2, 1 Longnon, Nancy's brother 1, son of Longnon = 5 men, 4 women, 1 lad (Mary Marchs sisters son), 2 children (Nancys brothers boy and girl)
Nancys Uncle & Cousin went to Badger Bay 6 weeks before she and her family went & Uncle & Cousin shot a month before they were taken

Want of food forced them to the sea coast. Total number The 12 or 13 left in the country returned in a N S circuitous route to the Great Lake
The surviving part of the Tribe went in this direction and are all that remain by Shanawdithit's account
[camp with four mamateeks] Shanawdithits Fathers 5 [second mamateek] 9 – 1 dead leaves 8 which with the 4 = 12 left in the country after Shanawdithit [third mamateek] 7 Nancys uncle and his daughter shot by Carew & Adams – 3 died & killed as above & 2 died afterward at C [fourth mamateek] 6 (2 of them died 4 alive at C) C – 4
Track by which Shanawdithit's uncle & and her mother sister and herself went to Badger Bay to obtain shelfish in March and April 1823
Shanawdithit's mother sister & herself taken here in April 1823
General statement April 1823, Nancy's uncle's family, living: 8,4 = 12, dead: 1,2,3,2,2, = 10 + 5 = 15 + 12 = 27."

50 Cormack Papers 20/84 (in Howley 1915,229).
51 Ibid. The discrepancy between information from sketch 4 and from Shanawdithit's report to Cormack, claiming twelve and thirteen survivors respectively, has not been resolved. According to R.A. Tucker's letter to R.W. Horton, 29 June 1825 (PRO, CO 194/71, f.11–14, in Howley 1915,174), Shanawdithit told Peyton that in the winter of 1823 only fifteen people were left alive; of these, two were shot by settlers, one drowned, and three fell into the hands of furriers, so that by late spring of 1823 only nine remained.
52 "Sketches of savage life," 1836,323.
53 Cormack Papers 20/84 (in Howley 1915,229).
54 Carson, Answers to questions ... 1830, PRO, CO 194/81, f.59a.
55 A full description of these drawings is given by Howley 1915,238–51.
56 Cormack to Inglis, 10 January 1829, Cormack Papers 57/84 (in Howley 1915, 210).
57 Capt. David Buchan to Horton, 24 November 1824, PRO, CO 194/68, f.249–50.
58 Upton (1977b,44) published this drawing together with Buchan's letter.
59 Howley 1915,181.
60 Upton 1977b, 44; Fardy 1983,64.
61 Cormack Papers 15/84; the drawing has not been published in the *Edinburgh New Philosophical Journal*.
62 Howley 1915,230. An original note by Cormack with this text is not in the Cormack Papers.
63 "Sketches of savage life," 1836,322.
64 Searches for the papers of John McGregor have been unsuccessful. According to correspondence with the Royal Commission on Historical Manuscripts, London, 6 August 1992, "McGregor absconded to France at the end of life to escape prosecution for fraud and it is possible that he destroyed his papers before doing so."
65 Cormack Papers 13/84 (in Howley 1915,220).
66 Minutes of the Natural History Society of Montreal, 23 February 1829, BWL, the vocabulary is no longer among the society's papers.

67 Cormack Papers 47/84 (in Howley 1915,230–2): Cormack gave a set of his Beothuk wordlist to Dr Yates, presumably Dr James Yates, antiquarian, fellow of the Geological, Linnean, and Royal Societies and secretary of the British Association, who attended Glasgow University at the same time as Cormack (DNB 1920–21, 16; 121); James Yates's papers have not been located. Dr Yates seems to have forwarded the vocabulary to Dr Richard King, member of the council of the British Association and secretary of the Ethnological Society, who in turn gave it to Professor Robert G. Latham, at the time a distinguished scholar in the field of comparative linguistics (Latham 1850, 330; Latham to Howley 25 December 1882, Howley Papers); see also chapter 27, section on wordlists collected from Shanawdithit.

68 Hewson 1978,122–4, plates 56–8, Ms. 881; ibid., 127–9, plates 61–3, Ms. 1449; ibid., 125–6, plates 59–60, Ms. 881; ibid.,130–1, plates 64–5, Ms. 1449.

69 Cormack to Inglis, 10 January 1829, Cormack Papers 57/84 (in Howley 1915, 210); two bark containers and a coat fringe are in the British Museum, London.

70 Alika Podolinski Webber, 1974, pers. com.; Burnham 1991,238–9; since a member of the Simms family spent several years in Labrador in the 1800s, it is possible that the coat was collected by him from a Naskapi (Paul Carignan, 1974, pers. com.). The coat is discussed in chapter 21, section on the outer robe.

71 Cormack Papers 13/84, 16/84; Howley 1915, 200–1.

72 Questions in Cormack's notes 13/84 and 16/84 for which answers have not been found are: "Ask her what her old people say were the greatest number of her tribe in former times?" "Have they any exterior form of worship?" "Their Government." "Ascertain their mode of counting." "If any of the party John Louis and Stevens saw in 1822 [at Red Indian Lake] were with the New Bay party in 1823?"

73 "Sketches of savage life," 1836,322.

74 Ibid.,322. *Munes*, or *manes*: spirit "shades" of deceased demanding revenge, COED.

75 Ibid.,322–3.

76 Cormack Papers 8/84, 19/84 (in Howley 1915,211).

77 Cormack Papers 13/84.

78 Ibid.,9/84, draft of an address to the Boeothick Institution.

79 Ibid.,8/84.

80 Ibid.,39/84.

81 Cormack to Peyton, Jr, 28 October 1828, PRRL, 917.18 C81 NRV; Cormack to Inglis, 26 October 1828, Cormack Papers 62/84 (in Howley 1915,209).

82 Mrs Regina O'Keefe (August 1988, and 1995, pers. com.) writes that Dr Charles Renouf had studied medicine with Dr Carson's son in Scotland and may have received from him mementos of Shanawdithit. According to the family tradition, Dr Carson, who cared for Shanawdithit until her death, was frequently called to the home of Mr Simms on her behalf and Cormack often visited Shanawdithit in the Simms home.

83 Minutes of the Natural History Society of Montreal, 23 February 1829, BWL; McGregor 1832,1:276–7; "Sketches of savage life," 1836,323; Howley 1915,231.

84 Peyton, Jr, to Legeyt, Secr. 18 June 1823, PRO, CO 194/66, f.68–9, (in Howley 1915,174); Carson, Answers to questions ... 1830, PRO, CO 194/81, f.59a.

85 "Sketches of savage life," 1836,322.
86 Ibid.
87 Cormack Papers 20/84 (in Howley 1915,225).
88 Cormack to Inglis, 26 October 1828, Cormack Papers 62/84 (in Howley 1915,208); Inglis to Cormack, 13 November 1828, Cormack Papers 72/84–5 (in Howley 1915,209).
89 Cormack to Inglis, 10 January 1829, Cormack Papers 57/84 (in Howley 1915,210).
90 Stark to Cormack, 16 September 1828, Cormack Papers 70/84–6 (in Howley 1915,203).
91 Noad 1859,34–5.
92 Lloyd 1876a,31 wrote: "A small lock of her [Shanawdithit's] hair in my possession is of a black colour"; Mrs O'Keefe suggests that Shanawdithit gave the items to Dr William Carson, who had cared for her since her arrival in St John's, and that his son, Dr Samuel Carson, who had studied medicine with Dr Charles Hugh Renouf in Edinburgh, might have given them to Dr Renouf (Regina O'Keefe, August 1988, and 1995, pers. com.).
93 Carson, Answers to questions ... 1830, PRO, CO 194/81, f.59a.
94 Shanawdithit's obituary in the *Public Ledger*, St John's, 12 June 1829, cited in the *Conception Bay Mercury*, 19 June 1829,3.
95 *London Times*, 14 September 1829, cited in Howley 1915,231–2; Cormack to Peyton from London, 18 October 1829, PANL, MG 134, C.F. Rowe Collection; Cormack's claim that Mary March's husband, the "chief" of the tribe, was *accidentally* killed is clearly uncalled for; presumably the remark was intended to appease Peyton.
96 Carson, Answers to questions ... 1830 PRO, CO 194/81, f.60: "Her Scull exhibited a peculiarity, the pareital bones were divided in the middle by sutures running parallel with the sagittal suture and extending from the lamdoidal to the coronal suture. An experienced anatomist would in all probability have discovered other peculiarities."
97 Ibid.; Carson to Secretary Ayre, 17 November 1830, PANL, GN 2/2 1830, f.325–8.
98 Royal College of Surgeons to J. Laws Esq. London, 29 January 1953 CNS, file Shanawdithit.
99 Cited in Howley 1915,231; the burial certificate, in the Howley Papers, reads: "Burial in the Parish of St John's, in the Diocese of Newfoundland in the year One Thousand Eight Hundred and Twenty Nine, Nancy Shanadithi, Abode: South Side, When Buried: October [*sic*] 23rd, Age not known, By whom the ceremony was performed: Frederic H. Carrington A.B. Rector, St John's."
100 M.F. Howley 1903,4.
101 Cormack's obituary of Shanawdithit, *London Times*, 14 September 1829, cited in Howley 1915,231. As with other matters concerning Shanawdithit, her exact age is not known. Buchan, writing to Governor Hamilton (28 June 1823, PRO, CO 194/66, f.66, in Howley 1915,172), said he thought she was twenty years old at the time of her capture; Wilson to the Methodist Missionary Society, 12 August 1823, MMS: LR, North America, Newfoundland 1823/24, Box 4, file 4f, no.14 believed her to be twenty-three years old at the time; according to "Sketches of savage life," 1836,323, Shanawdithit was about twenty at the time of her capture; Howley

1915,231: the Cathedral register entry for Shanawdithit's burial gives her age as twenty-three at the time of her death, which would make her seventeen at the time of her capture.

CHAPTER FIFTEEN

1 Kirke 1908,143 (in Howley 1915,229); Wix 1836,90: Micmac, who talked to Archdeacon Wix on his tour of communities in rural Newfoundland in 1835, agreed with this assessment.
2 Jukes 1969,1:171; Webber 1978,98 n.9.
3 Speck 1922,54.
4 *Conception Bay Mercury*, Harbour Grace, 12 September 1834,2, and *Star and Conception Bay Journal*, Carbonear, 17 September 1834,3, both cited in MacLeod 1966,3; John E. Bishop (1993, pers. com.), who had been a school teacher in the 1930s on Eastern Indian Island (south of Fogo), was told at the time by a man in his sixties that the Indians used to come to the island for the summer and set up wigwams there; they took gear from his father at night and he sometimes left things out for them to take, implying that Beothuk still came to Eastern Indian Island in the 1850s. Most likely these Indians were Micmac (from Exploits Bay?); see Newfoundland Census 1858.
5 John S. Addy to the Wesleyan Mission House, 9 November 1841, no.2, MMS: LR, North America, Newfoundland 1841, Box 102, file 12g, doc.23.
6 Commodore Shott(?) of *HMS Hyacinth* to Governor Sir John Harvey, 26 October 1845, PANL, CSOC, GN 2/2 f.470; Harvey also asked John Stark, as the former secretary of the Boeothick Institution, for information on Beothuk history, language, and habits (Des Barres to Stark, 29 October 1844, Cormack Papers 77/84).
7 Howley n.d., chapter 1886,53; Howley 1915,271.
8 Cyril J. Byrne, St Mary's University, Halifax, 1982, pers. com.
9 Webber 1978,98n.5.
10 Howley 1915,256; presumably this information comes from John Peyton, Jr.
11 Ingstad 1985,2:472.
12 Noad 1859,43; Speck (1922;69) had heard of a Micmac named McCloud who was said to know where descendants of Beothuk could be found in Labrador.
13 Bonnycastle 1842,2:251.
14 Lloyd 1875,31, 36.
15 Howley 1915,266.
16 Ibid. The fishermen thought the Naskapi and Inuit had killed them all off. Mullock (1860,11) mentions tales of strange natives "of a large race," clothed in long robes or cassocks of skin, who fled from Montagnais and were believed to have been Beothuk.
17 Jukes 1969,2:131; ibid. 1847,114.
18 Speck 1922,15, 16, 18, 126.
19 Speck (1931,588) reported "a noteworthy prevalence of red coloration" on specimens collected from the St Augustin Montagnais band on the Lower North Shore.

Also, the name of one of the families (Poker=Pok-ue) meant "stranger coming into a strange country"; other villagers considered the members of this family to be different looking; cf. Martijn 1990a,236.

20 Speck 1922,65.

21 Howley 1915,284.

22 Shanawdithit's sketch 4, Fig.14.1.

23 "The Aborigines of Newfoundland, from Blackwood's Magazine," 18 September 1832,1, and 25 September 1832, supplement. This article is based on a review entitled "McGregor's *British America*," published in Blackwood's Edinburgh Magazine, June 1832,907–17; McGregor, who had provided the basis for the author's assessment of the history of Newfoundland's aboriginal population, had been informed and influenced by his friend W.E. Cormack.

24 "The Aborigines of Newfoundland, from Blackwood's Magazine," 18 September 1832,1, and 25 September 1832, supplement.

25 Select Committee on Aborigines [1836] 1968,1:475–9.

26 Ibid.,478.

APPENDIX TWO

1 Church of England Parish Records, St Paul's Church, Trinity, PANL, microfilm 31: "Baptized Sept. 25th 1813 daughter to David Buchan Esqr., Commander of HMS Adonis, by his spouse Maria [Adye]; Privy named Sophia Maria, Born 25 Aug 1813, Puby 14 Sept. 1814."

2 DCB 1988,7:114–16; Howley 1915,176–9; Fardy 1983; Gazetteer of Canada 1968,30; Peyton 1987,71.

3 DCB 1979,5:165–7.

4 Lieut. John Cartwright, "Remarks on the situation of the Red Indians … 1768," PRRL, 971.8 C24 (in Howley 1915,29–41).

5 George Cartwright: "The Case of the Wild or Red Indians of Newfoundland," 1784, PRO, CO 194/35, f.336–42.

6 George Cartwright 1792.

7 Cartwright Papers, in private hands.

8 Great Britain, First Series Reports, 1785–1808,10:392 (in Howley 1915, 50–4).

9 Gazetteer of Canada 1968,38.

10 Gerry Penney, 1990s, pers. com.

11 DNB 1949–50,3:1133–34; Townsend 1911: xxii; F.D. Cartwright 1826.

12 Townsend 1911: xxii.

13 Cartwright "Remarks … 1768," PRRL, 971.8 C24 (in Howley 1915:29–41); Cartwright to Governor Hugh Palliser, 19 September 1768, PRRL, 971.8 C24 (in Howley 1915,41–4); Cartwright's submission to the earl of Dartmouth, 13 January 1773, NAC, Dartmouth Papers, MG 23 A 1, series 1, vol.16; Cartwright, "A Sketch of the River Exploits … 1768," PANL, MG 100, Cartwright Collection; Lieut. John Cartwright, "A Sketch of the River Exploits and the East End of Lieutenants

Lake in Newfoundland," NAC, Cartographic Div., NMC 27; Cartwright, "A Map of the Island of Newfoundland," NAC, NMC 14033.

14 Cartwright to Dartmouth, 13 January 1773, "Postcript," 1770, NAC, Dartmouth Papers, MG23 A1, series 1, vol. 16, f.76–83.

15 Osborne 1972,153.

16 Census for St John's/NF 1794–75, PANL, GN 2/39/A; Graham 1868,3 (in Howley 1915, 234); DCB 1976,9:158–62; the name Eppes was often shortened to Epps.

17 Cormack 1824, an abbreviated account. Cormack's full account was first published in 1856 under the auspices of government, instigated by Governor Darling (Darling to Henry Labouchere MP, 11 October 1856, PRO, CO 194/148, f.406–7); it was edited and reprinted by Harvey (1873) and re-published by Howley in 1915.

18 Cormack Papers 10–12/84, 48, 49/84; Howley 1915,182–7.

19 Cormack Papers 15,20,29,30–5/84; Howley 1915,210–51; Shanawdithit's sketches 1–10,12 and vocabulary.

20 Minutes of the Natural History Society of Montreal, 23 February 1829 and 27 December 1852, BWL.

21 Fardy 1985.

22 Graham 1868,3; Fardy 1985.

23 Gazetteer of Canada 1968,47.

24 DCB 1966,1:240–1; Cell 1982,12, 79–89.

25 Cell 1982,5, 68–78; Purchas 1905–07,19:405.

26 DCB 1966,1:349–51; Cell 1969,71.

27 Encyclopedia of Newfoundland and Labrador 1984,2:1093–95; Howley 1915.

28 Gazetteer of Canada 1968,105.

29 DCB 1987,6:580–1; Peyton 1987.

30 Keith Matthews, namefile Peyton, MHA.

31 Howley n.d., chapter 1886, 29 June, 4 July, 15 July: information from Winsor and Alfred Beaton, Exploits.

32 DCB 1987,6:580–1; Peyton 1987.

33 Howley 1915,105–9.

34 Gazetteer of Canada 1968,172.

35 Marshall 1989, 9–11.

36 Speck 1922,24, 55–67, 79.

37 DCB 1966,1:668–9; Cell 1982,24–34.

38 Gazetteer of Canada 1968,144.

CHAPTER SIXTEEN

1 Tuck 1976a; 1976b, 16–60; 1982,206.

2 The technique of carbon dating is based on measuring the minute quantities of radioactive C14 isotopes, resulting from cosmic radiation, which are a component of the ordinary C12 in all organic matter. The proportions of C12 to C14 are identical in all organic matter, which continuously absorbs the isotopes as long as it is alive. Once it dies, C14 is no longer absorbed. After death the radioactive C14 dwindles by

decay, turning into ordinary C12. Since the rate of decay of C14 is known, a scientist can calculate, by measuring the proportion of C14 to C12 in a sample, the time that has elapsed since death. Statistical errors in counting are expressed in +/- figures to give a range of years rather than a specific date. For example 2000 +/- 100 BP expresses the range from 2100 to 1900 BP. Archaeological specimens used for carbon dating are often charcoal from fireplaces. Bones, bark, or other organic matter can also be tested, though it has been found that sea-mammal bones tend to yield dates that are too old.

3 Tuck 1992.

4 Tuck and Fitzhugh 1986,161–7, have redefined the nomenclature for prehistoric Eskimo groups in northeastern Canada and broadly divided them into Early and Late Palaeo-Eskimo. Early Palaeo-Eskimo in Labrador include the previous designations of Independence I, Early and Late Pre-Dorset, and Transitional Pre-Dorset/Groswater Dorset. In Newfoundland the designation of Early Palaeo-Eskimo refers to Groswater Dorset. The term tradition refers to a way of life of a people in a specific area over an extended period of time.

5 Tuck 1982,213, Cow Head; Renouf 1987, Phillips Garden East; Auger 1984, Factory Cove; Krol 1986, Broom Point; Pastore 1986a, 13, Boyd's Cove; Penney 1987a, n.p., and Archaeological Site Record Form, Newfoundland Museum: Grand Bruit.

6 Tuck 1982,213; Tuck and Fitzhugh 1986,163–4.

7 Ibid.,161–7. Late Palaeo-Eskimo, as defined by Tuck and Fitzhugh, were previously referred to as Dorset in Labrador and as Middle Dorset in Newfoundland.

8 Pastore 1986b, 126; Robbins 1986,122.

9 MacLean 1990a.

10 Port au Choix: Harp 1964, and Renouf 1991; Cape Ray Light Site and Pittman Site: Linnamae 1975; Stock Cove: Robbins 1985.

11 Tuck and Fitzhugh 1986,164–5.

12 Robbins 1986,122.

13 McGhee 1978,107.

14 Relations between Beothuk and Inuit are discussed in chapter 3.

15 John Cabot discovered Newfoundland in 1497. Quinn 1979,1:95–6, docs. 53–8.

16 Austin 1984,117, reviewed by Loring 1989,62, and by Robbins 1989,22–3. The term "type site" indicates the archaeological site on which a particular tool type or series of tools that represents a previously unknown tradition or phase within a tradition was first excavated.

17 Tuck 1978c; Renouf 1992,101; Austin 1984,119; Carignan 1977; Gerry Penney, 1993, pers. com.; Tuck 1992.

18 Tuck 1992.

19 Carignan 1975a, Plate 36a-k; Pastore 1985,323; Penney 1989a, 13.

20 Tuck 1992; Pastore 1985,323, Boyd's Cove 960 +/- 50 BP (Beta 10235); two carbon dates from Cape Cove, 1815 +/- 55 BP and 1865 +/- 110 BP, obtained by Austin (1984,117) are too early to fit into the time frame as it is presently understood and will have to be verified through further excavations. A date of 760 +/- 110 BP

from The Beaches (MacLean 1991,11) is not considered reliable because the carbon sample may have been contaminated (Laurie MacLean, 1992, pers. com.).

21 Pastore 1985,323. Artifact typology is a method by which specimens of a particular artifact type from one culture, such as projectile points, are examined to determine changes in shape, size, or hafting elements over a lengthy time period. For example, early Little Passage projectile points were side-notched for hafting while the points from a later time were notched at the corners, showing that the hafting element changed from the side to the corner.

22 Fitzhugh 1972,123. An artifact is considered "diagnostic" if it is unique to a specific Indian or Eskimo group and allows archaeologists to establish the ethnic origin of a particular set of tools or of a site. Projectile points are often diagnostic because their size, shape, and hafting elements tend to differ from one culture to another.

23 Tuck 1992; Loring 1992,344. Fitzhugh 1978,166, 325 +/- 80 B.P. (Lab.No.SI-1276).

24 Carignan 1975a,201 l-n; Pastore 1983,139.

25 Fitzhugh 1972,193; Loring 1985,134; Pastore 1986a,223.

26 Fitzhugh 1977,14; Rogers and Leacock 1981,169, 175; Loring 1983,45–6; 1985,134; 1988,164; 1992. Perhaps these were the Indians described by Brouage, 6 September 1719 (NAC, MG I Archives des Colonies, Série C"A Correspondence générale, Canada, vol.109, f.155–74, transcript), as people who live to the north, fear Europeans, and make their arrows from stone and bone; Cranz 1816,170: as late as 1799, the Moravian missionaries mentioned "fearful" Indians in Labrador's interior who used bows and arrows because they had no guns; these Indians could have been Naskapi.

27 Howley 1915,297. Relations between Beothuk and Montagnais are discussed in chapter 3.

28 Tuck 1992.

29 Carignan 1977; Austin 1984.

30 Devereux 1969; Carignan 1975a; MacLean 1990b; 1991; 1993; Penney 1988,40.

31 McGhee and Tuck 1975,88,241; Tuck 1976a,24.

32 Tuck 1976a, 54.

33 Magnusson and Palsson 1976,65 (Graenlendinga Saga), 98 (Eirik's Saga).

34 Ibid.,67–70, 100.

35 Ibid.,65, 98–100. The "scraelings" are described as evil-looking men with coarse hair, large eyes, and broad cheekbones; one of the Norse was killed with a flintstone. Although skin boats and war slings have primarily been associated with Inuit people, they are not unknown among Algonquians.

36 Ingstad 1985,1:65–71, 119, 241–50; Schonback, Wallace, et al. 1976,20–1; Wallace 1977. The lithics (other than Palaeo-Eskimo ones) were originally thought to be "most closely related to Martime Archaic Indian artifacts" (Tuck 1976c); more recent excavations at Cow Head have shown them to be identical with regard to type and raw material to those of the Cow Head complex (James A. Tuck, 1993, pers. com.). One isolated projectile point, illustrated in Ingstad 1985,1, Fig.8, belongs to the Beaches complex (James A. Tuck, 1993, pers. com.).

37 Magnusson and Palsson 1976,60, 65–7, 95, 98–101. The sagas mention (wooden) ships propelled by sails, red cloth, domesticated cattle/livestock, metal tools, and arms. Ingstad 1985,1:92, Fig.48a, 97–103, 145; Schonback et al. 1976,5–6, 13–17; Wallace 1977,6: archaeological remains show that the Norse used a spinning whorl, extracted bog iron, and forged iron in a smithy.

38 Pastore 1985,323.

39 Schwarz 1984,51–2.

CHAPTER SEVENTEEN

1 Penney 1984,19, 64, 166; 1989a,14, Boat Hole Brook, Couteau Bay, 450 +/- 60 BP Beta-17854; Upper Burgeo, 350 +/- 60 BP Beta 3357, Gerry Penney, 1990s, pers. com. Burials: see chapter 25, List 1A, nos.1–3.

2 Hoffman 1963,13.

3 Quinn 1979,4:64, doc.560 (in Howley 1915,12); Cell 1982,72, 84.

4 Hart 1959,14.

5 De Brouillan, Governor of Placentia, 25 October 1694, cited in Morandière 1962,1:20.

6 Tuck 1989b,301.

7 Cell 1982,149.

8 *English Pilot* 1967,15.

9 Howley 1915,265.

10 Robbins 1982,199; Evans 1981,215.

11 Cell 1982,74.

12 Ibid., 70–6,83–7,193; Henry Crout to Percival Willoughly, August 1613, MMSS.Mix 1/24 (Appendix 1).

13 Howley 1915,269.

14 Devereux 1965b, Ms.735; 1969; Carignan 1975a; 1977,27, 264–6; MacLean 1991; 1993.

15 Carignan 1973,12.

16 MacLean 1991,31.

17 Carignan 1975b,38, Cary Cove; 1977,268–71, Bloody Bay Cove; Schwarz 1992a,37, 43, 47, Gambo Pond; Tuck 1983,31, 42, Shambler's Cove; see also Table 16.1.

18 Carignan 1975a; 1977,28, 148–50, 214–16; Devereux 1969; Austin 1980, 168–9.

19 Quinn 1979,1:207, doc.148 (in Howley 1915,10).

20 Cell 1982,118.

21 Comm. Percy, Account of the State of the Fishery in Newfoundland, 13 October 1720, PRO, CO 194/7, f.7.

22 Cartwright 1792,1:7; Cormack Papers 34/84 (in Howley 1915,230); Howley 1915, 267, 269; MacLean 1991; 1993.

23 Pastore 1984,98, 102, 107; 1985,323; 1986a,218; 1989a,57.

24 See chapter 25, List 1A, nos.5–11.

25 Lysaght 1971,132; Lieut. David Buchan's report of his expedition to Red Indian Lake, 1811, PRO, CO 194/50, f.153–88, (in Howley 1915,88–9); Howley 1915, 268, 273, 283; Marshall 1989,120, 121, 128.
26 Lescarbot 1968,2:28: in 1534 Jacques Cartier loaded his ships with birds.
27 Buchan to Governor Duckworth, 25 July 1812, NAC, Duckworth Papers, MG 24, A 45, f.5032–5.
28 Buchan's report, 1811, PRO, CO 194/50, f.153–88 (in Howley 1915,89); Howley 1915, 28, 268, 273, 283; Marshall 1989,120, 121, 129, 138, 140.
29 Marshall 1989,122, 140; Tocque 1846,285–6; Tocque's informant was Mr Whiltshear, who had lived in the area since 1817 and had himself seen these mamateeks.
30 Governor James Gambier to Lord Hobart, 23 November 1803, PRO, CO 194/43, f.169.
31 Thomson 1982,167; MacLean 1990a; stone tools and flakes have been found on several other sites on the Exploits River but it has not been possible to identify which population produced them.
32 Devereux 1970, Ms. 743, Carbon Dates 1982,109, 355 +/- 100 BP (Lab.No.I 6502).
33 See chapter 25, List 1A, nos.12–16.
34 Lieut. John Cartwright, "Remarks on the situation of the Red Indians ... 1768," PRRL, 971.8 C24 (in Howley 1915,29–44); Cartwright, "A Sketch of the River Exploits ... 1768," PANL, MG 100, Cartwright Collection; Buchan's report, 1811, PRO, CO 194/50, f.153–88 (Howley 1915,74–6, 83–5); Buchan's report on his second expedition to Red Indian Lake to Governor Hamilton, 10 March 1820, PRO, CO 194/63, f.64–77 (in Howley 1915,122–4); Cormack 1829,326–7 (in Howley 1915,195); Lloyd 1876a,222–4; Speck 1922,19–25; MacLean 1990a,4–10; Marshall 1980,41–3; Thomson 1982,35; see also Tables 15.1 and 16.1.
35 Marshall 1977a,225. Since publication of this paper the original Cartwright map has been examined and it is thought that only eighty-six circular markings represent conical mamateeks plus one square one; because the map is faded, even this number may not be accurate. The term mamateek for house is only known in the singular; since it has been absorbed into English (DNE 1982, 322) the plural is expressed by the letter "s."
36 Marshall 1989,123–7, 135–7.
37 Buchan's report, 1811, PRO, CO 194/50, f.153–88 (in Howley 1915,72–90); Buchan's report to Hamilton, 10 March 1820, PRO, CO 194/63, f.64–77 (in Howley 1915,123–4); Cormack 1829,323–25 (in Howley 1915,189–97).
38 Devereux 1965a, Ms.261; 1966, Ms.740; Marshall 1973; 1974b; Pastore 1981; Penney 1988.
39 See chapter 25, List 1A, nos.18–24.
40 Howley 1915,267, 271, 282, 283.
41 Ibid.,267, 270, 272, 274, 282; Marshall 1989,130, 140.
42 Buchan's report to Hamilton, 10 March 1820, PRO, CO 194/63, f.64–77 (in Howley 1915,123–6); Cormack 1829,320 (in Howley 1915,190); "Substance of the narrative of William Cull, of Fogo ... ," 22 July 1810, PRO, CO 194/49, f.116–17 (in Howley

1915,69–70); Captain Glascock to Hamilton, 20 July 1820, PANL, CSOC, GN 2/1/A, vol.30, f.201–9 (in Howley 1915,114–15); Cormack Papers 20/84 (in Howley 1915,224–7); Shanawdithit's sketch 4, Fig.14.1.

43 Ingstad 1985,1:244.

44 Little Passage tools, Eddies Cove: Geologist Dan Bragg, 1991, pers. com.; Little Passage and Beaches-type tools, Port au Choix: Renouf 1993,73–4, and 1995 (pers. com.).

45 Howley (1915,257) cites French charts and the *English Pilot*, 1755; James Cook, "A Chart of the Straights of Belle Isle ...," 1766, shows an "Indian path" along the coast from St Barbe to Open Bay.

46 Cell 1982,149.

47 Morandière 1962,1:21–2.

48 Webber 1978,97n.3.

49 Jukes 1969,1:173, 2:131; Lloyd 1875,31; Howley 1915,256, 257, 266; Speck 1922,65.

50 Penney 1989b: 12; Simpson 1984,128–30; Renouf 1993,73–4.

51 Quinn 1979,4:64, doc.560 (in Howley 1915,12).

52 Jukes 1969,1:151; 2:129; Cormack Papers 12/84 (in Howley 1915,183).

53 Morandière 1962,1:21–2.

54 Quinn 1979,4:64, doc.560 (in Howley 1915,12–13).

55 Cell 1982, 84.

56 Henry Crout to Sir Percival Willoughby, August 1613, MMSS, Mix 1/24 (Appendix 1).

57 Cell 1982,70: at Dildo Pond only two of the three houses seen by Guy had "lately" been occupied; Cartwright ("Remarks ... 1768," PRRL, 971.8 C24, in Howley 1915,38) commented that of the Beothuk wigwams he saw on the banks of the Exploits River, many were no longer in use.

58 Crout to Willoughby, August 1613, MMSS, Mix 1/24; Marshall 1989,128.

59 Schwarz 1984,39–40.

60 Pastore 1986a,223.

61 Cell 1982,96, 117.

62 Cartwright, "Remarks ... 1768," PRRL, 971.8 C24 (in Howley 1915,36).

63 Ibid. (in Howley 1915,38).

64 Lysaght 1971,132; Marshall 1989,127; W. Sherrett to Lord Pelham, 22 September 1801, PRO, CO 194/43, f.196.

65 Observations on certain parts of His Majesty's Instructions to the Governor of Newfoundland by J. Holloway, 4 August 1807, PRO, CO 194/46, f.94; ibid. by J.T. Duckworth, October 1810, PRO, CO 194/49, f.89; ibid. by R.G. Keats, 10 November 1815, PRO, CO 194/56, f.110; Chief Justice John Reeves to Ed. Cooke, 10 April 1808, PRO, CO 194/47, f.111.

66 Buchan's report, 1811, PRO, CO 194/50, f.153–88 (in Howley 1915,87–8); Dr William Carson, MD, Answer to questions by the Royal College of Physicians, Great Britain, 1830, Governor Cochrane to Viscount Goderich, 7 February 1831, PRO, CO 194/81, f.59a; Select Committee on Aborigines [1836] 1968,1:475–9.

67 Duckworth to Earl of Liverpool, 27 October 1811, PRO, CO 194/50, f.152.
68 Cormack Papers 20/84 (in Howley 1915,226).
69 Howley 1915,94.
70 Ibid.,96, 100.
71 Hercules Robinson, "History of Mary March-Waunathoake ..." 1820, BL, Add. Mss.19350 (in Howley 1915,128).
72 Cormack Papers 20/84 (in Howley 1915,224, 226, 228); Howley 1915,227 fn.1; Shanawdithit's sketch 4, Fig.14.1 – figures in the text differ from those on the drawing; Shanawdithit's sketches 1, 2, Plates 10.1, 10.2.
73 Noad 1859,17.
74 Mooney 1928,23–4; in his bibliography Mooney cites Patterson (1892), who in turn cites Cartwright; Patterson (1892,128, 139) thought that the Beothuk would not have exceeded 4,000 people.
75 Marshall 1977a,235: after examining the original, the figures have been adjusted to eighty-six conical mamateeks plus one square one.
76 Jenness 1955,266.
77 Kroeber 1963,141, Table 7, no.15; ibid.,171, Table 15, no.15.
78 Ibid.,97, 141.
79 The entire island of Newfoundland encompasses 112,299 square kilometres.
80 Kroeber 1963,169, 171.
81 Ibid.,169. The "Northern Area" included Montagnais, Beothuk, Cree, Khnaia-Khotana of Cook Inlet, Alaska, and Caribou-eaters (for the latter, an area but no population figure is tabulated).
82 Eggan 1968,181.
83 Upton 1977a,134.
84 Winter 1975,1; English 1960,11–13.
85 Tuck 1991,116; Ralph Pastore, 1994, pers. com.

CHAPTER EIGHTEEN

1 Trelease 1960,2–3.
2 Rogers 1963,24.
3 For details see chapter 17, section "Estimates of Band Size."
4 Lieut. John Cartwright, "Remarks on the situation of the Red Indians ... 1768," PRRL, 971.8 C24 (in Howley 1915,29–41, population estimates: 37–8). See also Capt. David Buchan's report, 1811, PRO, CO 194/50 f.153–88 (in Howley 1915, 89). Chapter 17 for contemporary estimates of the size of the Beothuk population.
5 Cormack Papers 20/84 (in Howley 1915,226).
6 Cartwright to the Earl of Dartmouth, 13 January 1773, NAC, Dartmouth Papers, MG 23 A 1, series 1, vol.16, f.29.
7 Cartwright "Sketch of the River Exploits and the East End of Lieutenants Lake ...," to Dartmouth, 13 January 1773, NAC, NMC 27.
8 Tanner (1979,212) observed that when Mistassini bands found animals to be scarce during the winter, as they were between 1925 and 1940, they broke up into very

small groups, often single families, but located themselves within easy reach of one another on lakes dependable for fish. Food was distributed between a number of these small groups within a district. With the return of beaver and larger game, the pattern of independent multifamily groups for the winter re-emerged.

9 This topic is discussed at length in chapter 5, section on factors that prevented a regular fur trade.

10 Howley 1915,91 fn.1,92, 106.

11 Santu said that a good coating of the colouring agent lasted for six months (Speck 1922,62–4).

12 Cormack Papers 32/84 (in Howley 1915,230).

13 *English Pilot* 1967,9.

14 Cormack 1829,320 (in Howley 1915,190–1).

15 Devereux (1970, Ms.743, locality B4) says the eastern line was ca. 671 centimetres long and 41 centimetres wide and the western line ca. 244 centimetres long and 46 centimetres wide; she suggests that this configuration may have been caused either by an upturned, ochred canoe left to disintegrate on this site or by the painting of a canoe in this location.

16 Shanawdithit's sketch 1, Plate 10.1. The text, written by Cormack, reads: "Marines Head stuck on a pole around which the Indians danced and sang 2 hours in the woods at A they having carried the head with them, the other Marines head they left at B and on their return there in the Spring they danced and sang round it in like manner."

17 Bishop John Inglis, Diary, 2 July 1827, NAC, microfilm A 713.

18 Howley 1915,27, 267, 268, 273; Speck 1922,53.

19 "Sketches of savage life," 1836,322.

20 Erickson 1978,132: among the Maliseet, for example, there existed a taboo against telling tales in summer.

21 Cormack Papers 29/84 (Howley 1915,230, did not list all titles from Cormack's notes).

22 Howley 1915,106.

23 Thomas Rowley, Percival Willoughby's agent in the colony at Cupids, listed a drum among the items he requested for bartering with the Beothuk in 1619 (MMss, Mix 1/62).

24 Speck 1940,49; Turner 1979,260–4.

25 Avalonus (pen-name of Wm. Sweetland, magistrate in Bonavista Bay, who conversed with Shanawdithit when she resided with W.E. Cormack in St John's and who was acquainted with Captain Buchan) 1862,1 (in Howley 1915,252).

26 Service 1966,49–53; Rogers 1963,62.

27 Thwaites (1959,1:75) recorded that the Micmac leader Membertou was exempt from subsistence activities.

28 The COED defines civil as orderly, civilized, refined, polite, seemly in behaviour.

29 Cell 1982,74.

30 Howley 1915,274; Samson Busby (Busby to the Wesleyan Missionary Committee, 16 January 1816, MMS: LR, North America, Newfoundland 1805–16, Box no.1, file 1d, no.33) recorded this tale in a very distorted form.
31 Marshall 1989,123–7. It is possible that this story was an embellished version of the raid recorded by Capt. G.C. Pulling in 1792, in which a "chief" is not mentioned.
32 Avalonus 1862:1 (in Howley 1915,287).
33 Howley 1915:92–3,99–101.
34 Cormack Papers 20/84 (in Howley 1915,228); Howley 1915, 92–93, 99–100.
35 "Sketches of savage life," 1836,323.
36 Cormack 1829,323 (in Howley 1915,194).
37 Ibid., 323–5 (in Howley 1915,193–4).
38 Shanawdithit's sketch 1, Plate 10.1; of the three mamateeks depicted on this sketch that of "her uncle" was the largest, the others being owned by her father and Demasduit's father.
39 Buchan 1811 (in Howley 1915,77); Speck 1922,22; Thomson 1983,167, 168–9.
40 Robinson 1834,215 (in Howley 1915,127).
41 Ibid.,216 (in Howley 1915:128); Howley 1915,261.
42 Barbara Neis, 1994, pers. com.
43 Howley 1915,262.
44 Robinson 1834,215–16 (in Howley 1915:128); Howley 1915,180, 181, 261; Marshall 1989,126.
45 Cartwright, "Remarks … 1768," PRRL, 971.8 C24 (in Howley 1915,34); Howley 1915, 99; Marshall 1989,124, 129, 140.
46 Cormack Papers 20/84 (in Howley 1915,228); Driver 1975,236.
47 Robinson 1834,216 (in Howley 1915,128).
48 Howley 1915,214.
49 Ibid.
50 Ibid.,181.
51 Table 25.1, burials 13,15. Use of tusks: Bock 1978,116, Micmac; Erickson 1978,132, Maliseet-Passaquamoddy; Feest 1978,279, North Carolina Algonquians.
52 Cormack Papers 31/84 (in Howley 1915,214); Shanawdithit told Cormack that the Beothuk used a "decoction of the rind of the dogwood for pains in the stomach; for sore head, neck &c pounded sulphuret of iron mixed with oil was rubbed over the part affected … for sore eyes, woman's milk as wash" (Howley 1915, 214).
53 Howley 1915,180, 181. This daughter, who was captured in 1823, was called Easter Eve by the settlers; she died within a few weeks of her capture.
54 Ibid., 180.
55 See listing of Beothuk graves and grave goods: chapter 25, List 1A and Table 25.1; a photograph of the tooth was examined by Darlene Balkwill, Acting Head, Zooarchaeological Identification Centre, National Museum of Natural Sciences, May 1987; Balkwill said that it could be a horse upper molar or a pig canine tusk, although there are problems with either of these interpretations; John Maunder, Curator of Natural History, Newfoundland Museum, 1987, pers. com.

56 Thompson 1987,142; Jonaitis 1978,62; Fitzhugh and Crowell 1988,273.
57 McDougall 1891,2:102; Howley (1915, Plate XXXV) identified the bird skulls in the collection of the Newfoundland Museum that are likely to have come from this burial place as arctic tern [*Sterna hirundo*], probably meaning common northern tern [*Sterna hirundo hirundo*]. A marten-skin pouch with silver coins was found in one of the mamateeks that had housed Nonosabasut and his group; what else it contained and who owned it has not been recorded (ibid.,273).
58 LeClercq 1968,222; a dew claw is an animal's rudimentary inner toe or hallux.
59 Parsons 1925,101.

CHAPTER NINETEEN

1 To date, no pollen cores from Beothuk sites have been taken for analysis.
2 Arber 1971,344–5 (in Howley 1915,2): information from Sebastian Cabot as recorded by Peter Martyr and translated by Richard Eden in 1555.
3 Hoffman 1963,14.
4 Ibid; Quinn 1979,1:207, doc.148; Ganong 1964,274–5; Quinn 1981,27, 32.
5 Thevet before 1559, cited in Quinn 1981,34.
6 Quinn 1979,4:64–5, doc.560 (in Howley 1915,12).
7 Hoffman 1963,14.
8 Quinn 1981,33.
9 Cell 1982,70–4, 83–6.
10 Ibid.,194.
11 Henry Crout to Sir Percival Willoughby, August 1613, MMss, Mix 1/24 (Appendix 1).
12 Lysaght 1971,133; Cartwright 1792,1:10 (in Howley 1915,46); Funk Island was still visited by Beothuk in 1792 (Marshall 1989,120, 128).
13 Lieut. John Cartwright, "Remarks on the situation of the Red Indians … 1768," PRRL, 971.8 C24 (in Howley 1915,33, 40). LeClercq (1968,281) recorded that the Micmac caught partridge by slipping a noose at the end of a long pole over the birds' heads as they were as tame as chickens.
14 Morandière 1962,1:22–3.
15 Cartwright 1792,1:9; Cartwright, "Remarks … 1768," PRRL, 971.8 C24 (in Howley 1915,33, 38); Lieut. David Buchan's report of his expedition to Red Indian Lake, 1811, PRO, CO 194/50, f.153–88 (in Howley 1915, 87).
16 Cartwright, "Remarks … 1768, PRRL, 971.8 C24 (in Howley 1915, 33).
17 Cartwright to the Earl of Dartmouth, 13 January 1773, NAC, Dartmouth Papers MG 23, A 1, series 1, vol.16, f.19.
18 Cormack 1829,319–23 (in Howley 1915,190, 192); Cell 1982,74.
19 Marshall 1989,131–2; Cell 1982,193; Thevet cited in Quinn 1981,34; seal oil was also applied to the hair and, mixed with ochre, it was used as body paint and on artifacts.
20 Cell 1982,85. It has been said that the taste for hard liquor is an acquired one, which would suggest that the Beothuk in Trinity Bay were familiar with this type of alcoholic beverage.

21 Robinson 1834,216 (in Howley 1915,128).

22 "Substance of the narrative of William Cull ... ," 22 July 1810, PANL, CSOC, GN 2/1/A, vol.21, f.27–30 (in Howley 1915,69); Buchan's report 1811, PRO, CO 194/50, f.153–88 (in Howley 1915,75–7); Marshall 1989,125, 131, 132; Cell 1982,74, 76, 85, 194; Shanawdithit's sketch 7.

23 Cell 1982,71, 74; Crout to Willoughby August 1613, MMSS, Mix 1/24 (Appendix 1).

24 Marshall 1989,125.

25 Penney 1985a,50.

26 Devereux 1969, App.I, cited in Schwarz 1984,31; according to Carignan (1975a,138), many bones were those of adult and juvenile harp seal; Lloyd 1876a,223.

27 Austin 1980,71–85; Locke 1974,36.

28 Pastore 1985,326–7, App.II: 332.

29 Cumbaa 1984,12, 18; Cumbaa calculated that the edible meat weight provided by polar and black bear, caribou, and seal constituted 92 to 95 percent of the total meat intake; in this calculation whale was excluded.

30 Ibid.,11–18.

31 LeBlanc 1973, App.I: 4–5, Table I.

32 Locke 1974,14, 31, 36; Don Locke (1980s, pers. com.)

33 Simpson 1986,203.

34 Cormack Papers 29/84 (in Howley 1915,230).

35 Cell 1982,74, 194.

36 Ibid.,74.

37 Cartwright 1792,1:10 (in Howley 1915,48); Cormack 1824,161.

38 "Substance of the narrative ...," 22 July 1810, PANL, CSOC, GN 2/1/A, vol.21, f.27–30 (in Howley 1915,69); Buchan's report, 1811, PRO, CO 194/50, f.153–88 (in Howley 1915,79, 84, 87); Marshall 1989,125.

39 Cartwright, "Remarks ... 1768," PRRL, 971.8 C24 (in Howley 1915,39).

40 Buchan's report, 1811, PRO, CO 194/50, f.153–88 (in Howley 1915,79, 84, 87); Cormack 1829,320 (in Howley 1915,190); Marshall 1989,125; Howley 1915, 100.

41 Buchan's report, 1811, PRO, CO 194/50, f.153–88 (in Howley 1915,79).

42 Quinn 1979,4:64–5, doc.560 (in Howley 1915,12); Marshall 1989,127, 131.

43 Cartwright, "Remarks ... 1768," PRRL, 971.8 C24 (in Howley 1915,41).

44 Shanawdithit's sketch 7, Fig.19.1; Howley (1915, opp.246) omitted the phrase "in the sun"; Cell 1982,194.

45 Marshall 1989,132; Lysaght 1971,132: Banks was told in 1766 that the Beothuk mixed eggs with caribou hair to make them hang together before drying them in the sun; cruncheons, or scrunchins, are pieces of fatback pork cut into cubes and fried (DNE).

46 Cartwright, "Remarks ... 1768," PRRL, 971.8 C24 (in Howley 1915,33); Cartwright 1792,1:10 (in Howley 1915,48).

47 LeClercq 1968,119.

48 Cormack 1829,323–6 (in Howley 1915,193–4); Howley 1915,215, 230, 291, 333, 335; Lloyd 1876a,225; Devereux 1970,19, Ms.743 (Indian Point site); Jenness 1929,36.
49 Chute 1976,60–1; Thwaites 1959,6:217; Slobodin 1981,517: also recorded from the Kutchin.
50 Quinn 1979,4:64–5, doc.560 (in Howley 1915,12).
51 Crout to Willoughby, August 1613, MMss, Mix 1/24 (Appendix 1); Marshall 1989,132.
52 Buchan's report, 1811, PRO, CO 194/50, f.153–88 (in Howley 1915,79).
53 Speck 1922,24. In 1914 Frank Speck recovered a "stone hammer or bone cracker" from a Beothuk housepit at Badger Brook (Pope's Point site), which he believed to have been used for cracking bones.
54 Marshall 1989,132.
55 Cell 1982,193.
56 Ibid.,71, 72, 118.
57 Howley 1915,50; Marshall 1989,127, 136.
58 Buchan's report, 1811, PRO, CO 194/50, f.153–88 (in Howley 1915,86).
59 Speck 1922,62.
60 This number is an approximation because in some cases, identification of a site as being of Little Passage origin was based on survey results that have not been confirmed by excavation; also, new camps are continuously added to the list and details of some sites have not been released; see Table 16.1.
61 Schwarz 1984,39–40. The coastal sites included in this study are Upper Burgeo, Furby's Cove II, Isle Galet, Sot's Hole, L'Anse à Flamme, Tack's Beach, Frenchman's Island, Stock Cove, The Beaches, Shambler's Cove, Cape Cove, Boyd's Cove, Inspector Island, Southwest Harbour, Swan Island, Oil Islands, Port au Port; the inland site is Indian Point at Red Indian Lake.
62 The artifact classes are: projectile points (high frequency), scrapers, linear and retouched flakes, triangular bifaces, large bifaces, biface preforms, abraders, gravers, hammer stones, and cores.
63 Schwarz 1984,29–31, 44.
64 Schwarz 1984,46, based on Fitzhugh's "modified-interior" model (Fitzhugh 1972,158–9) in which both coastal and interior adaptation are generalized; in general terms this adaptation is also described in Tuck 1976b,69, and Tuck and Pastore 1985,77.
65 Cumbaa 1984,16–17: the occupation period of coastal camps is deduced from Cumbaa's faunal analysis of material found at the Boyd's Cove site. Information on seasonality: presence of medullary bone of Canada goose indicates March-May; presence of polar bear suggests April-May; smelt suggests April-June; the bird species suggest summer; tooth eruption and wear at death on remains of three caribou suggests that one of the animals was killed in late summer, one in fall, and one in late winter or early spring; Rowley-Conwy (1990,14–16) deduced possible occupation between February and November.
66 Schwarz (1984,44) proposed that prehistorically Frenchman's Island would have been a basecamp; in 1612 Guy did not record native habitations on this island; he chose this locality to build a trading post.

67 Ibid.,28–9.

68 Howley 1915,151; Bergerud 1958, map 2; 1971,14, 52; wildlife biologist E. Mercer, 1980s, pers. com.; Rowley-Conwy (1990,20) surmised that the Beothuk who procured seal at The Beaches would not have gone as far as Red Indian Lake to hunt caribou.

69 Bergerud 1971,51; Cell 1982,86–7.

70 Cartwright to Dartmouth, 13 January 1773, NAC, Dartmouth Papers, MG 23, A 1, series 1, vol.16, f.43.

71 Cell 1982,70–5, 83–6; Quinn 1979,4:64–5, doc.560 (in Howley 1915,12).

72 Gilbert and Reynolds 1989,6–7; William Gilbert, who excavated the Little Passage site at Russel Point close to the Trinity Bay coast, tentatively concluded that this was a caribou slaughtering site (1994, pers. com.). Plate 2.1 is on page xxii.

73 Cell 1982,70–5, 83–6, 194; Crout to Willoughby, 8 September 1612, MMss, Mix 1/20; ibid., August 1613, MMss, Mix 1/24 (Appendix 1).

74 Cell 1982,72; Robbins (1985,114), who excavated the Stock Cove site, suggests that caribou, harbour seal, and grey seal would have been procured here since harp seal, at least in modern times, do not come to the bottom of Trinity Bay.

75 Boulva and McLaren 1979,2.

76 Cell 1982,193.

77 Ibid., 194; other feasts celebrated in coastal camps would have been those accompanying the application of red ochre; for example, the *English Pilot* (1967,15) records that this substance was procured and applied by the Beothuk at a cove south of Bay Verde; Speck 1922,62–4.

78 Crout to Willoughby, August 1613, MMss, Mix 1/24.

79 Quinn 1979,4:64–5, doc.560 (in Howley 1915,12).

80 John Lien, 1995, pers. com.

81 William Taverner's survey of the Newfoundland south and southwest coasts, made in 1715, dated 1718, PRO, CO 194/6, f.240; Bergerud 1971,7: to this day the "La Poile herd" grazes and winters south of St George's Bay; Mahoney 1980,26.

82 Simpson 1984,128–30; Cormack 1824,158.

83 Cartwright "Remarks … 1768," PRRL, 971.8 C24 (in Howley 1915,33–6); Marshall 1977b,226.

84 Caribou migration routes and feeding grounds have since been disturbed by logging, hunting, and the spread of settlements, so that today's distribution and migration routes only partially reflect the situation that prevailed several hundred years ago. Of the ten discrete Newfoundland herds that are accounted for at the present time, seven feed all year round south of the Trans-Canada Highway. The Avalon herd remains on the Avalon Peninsula and may have done this for centuries. The Humber River and Northern Peninsula herds no longer cross the Exploits River but migrate and winter in northerly regions. While the herds that formerly crossed Sandy and Birchy lakes and the Exploits River travelled long distances, herds today in other locations often wander no more than forty-five to seventy kilometres from their summer range (Bergerud 1971, 14, 52; ibid.,1958, Map 2). Wildlife biologists Shane Mahoney and E. Mercer, Provincial Wildlife Department (1992, pers. com.), have found that

not all caribou follow the migratory instinct; a small percentage of animals may remain all year in the same locality, occasionally shifting their ground on account of weather conditions, or to find new supplies of food. Consequently, few if any districts on the island become completely devoid of caribou during the winter season. Mahoney has also pointed out that caribou are incredibly complex creatures so that there are many variations on the general theme of seasonal behaviour.

85 See chapter 20, section on hunting caribou, for details on fence building.

86 Cartwright, "Remarks … 1768," PRRL, 971.8 C24 (in Howley 1915,30, 31, 38); Extract of letter from Lieut. John Cartwright to Governor Hugh Palliser, 19 September 1768, PRRL, 971.8 C24, (in Howley 1915,42). Cartwright drew two maps of the Exploits River; one is now in the PANL, MG 100, Cartwright Collection (in Marshall 1977a,230), the other is in the NAC, NMC 27 (in Marshall 1977a,225). I counted ninety-four conical mamateeks on the banks of the Exploits River, using a copy of the map (Marshall 1977a, 235); after consulting the original this figure was revised to eighty-six plus one square house.

87 Buchan's report, 1811, PRO, CO 194/50, f.153–88 (shortened version in Howley 1915,72–90); see Fig.10.1, Buchan's "Sketch of the River Exploits as explor'd in Jan. and March 1811 Newfoundland," PRO, CO 194/50, HPG 589; Figs.12.1 and 12.2, "Capt. David Buchan's Track into the Interior of Newfoundland … 1820" (two maps) BL, Ms.51222, Ad.57703. 1+2; Cormack 1829 (in Howley 1915,189–97); Howley's ms. map of the upper part of Lloyd's River, Fig.20.3.

88 Lloyd 1875,24; ibid. 1876a,223; Devereux 1970, Ms.743; Marshall 1980; Sproull Thomson 1981,174; Thomson 1982; 1983; MacLean 1990a; Locke 1974; Don Locke, 1980s, pers. com.

89 Tuck and Pastore (1985,77) concluded that the Beothuk's relatively sophisticated techniques for preserving and storing food imply that food resources were not reliable.

90 Thwaites 1959,32:41; 25:61; Lescarbot 1928,269.

91 Marshall 1989,127.

92 Shanawdithit's sketch 1, Plate 10.1; Speck 1922,62–4; Cormack 1829,323 (in Howley 1915,192).

93 Cartwright to Palliser, 19 September 1768, PRRL, 971.8 C24 (in Howley 1915,43): Red Indian Lake abounded with fish and fowl; Cartwright's opinion was reiterated by Buchan in his report, 1811, PRO, CO 194/50, f.153–88 (in Howley 1915,75–6, 87); Howley 1915,142: Cormack recorded geese and ducks on ponds and lakes in great numbers; see also Colonial Secretary Clark's report about the natural resources in the interior of Newfoundland, 9 March 1829, PRO, CO 194/74, f.203.

94 Marshall 1989,127.

95 Cormack Papers 34/84 (in Howley 1915,230).

96 Cartwright to Dartmouth, 13 January 1773, NAC, Dartmouth Papers, MG 23, A 1, series 1, vol.16, f.29.

97 Ibid.; Marshall 1989,128, 129; Cartwright 1792,1:4, 17 (in Howley 1915,46, 49); Howley 1915,284.

98 Reynolds (1978,102) and other scholars advocate the same subsistence pattern for all Beothuk groups.

99 Preston 1981, 196; Loring 1988,163.

100 Devereux 1964, Ms.260; 1965a, Ms.261; 1970, Ms.743, Carbon Dates 1982,109, Lab.No.I-6562; Locke 1974,32–4; MacLean 1990a; Thomson 1982,167.

101 Cumbaa 1984,18.

102 Cartwright to Palliser, 19 September 1768, PRRL, 971.8 C24 (in Howley 1915,43); Cartwright, "A Sketch of the River Exploits ...," NAC, NMC 27, (in Marshall 1977b,225).

103 Suggested by Rowley-Conwy 1990,24–5. An important variable with respect to the availability of the animals is the size of the herds and of the caribou population as a whole. Accurate figures for earlier times are not available, but estimates and census figures (collected in the early 1900s) suggest extreme fluctuations. At the beginning of this century the Newfoundland caribou population was estimated at forty thousand head. By 1930, it had diminished greatly, reputedly to one to two thousand head. By 1966, herds had increased again to around 8,800 head, and by the mid 1980s to the original size of forty thousand (Bergerud 1971, 15, 18–9, 52). A similarly spectacular decline and recovery of caribou herds has been observed in Labrador (Bergerud 1963,1, 6, 8–9). In the 1930s, it was believed that the reduction of herds resulted from overhunting or from environmental factors. Investigations in the 1970s and 1980s, however, have shown that the variability in herd size is a natural phenomenon and that caribou populations decline and recover cyclically. Based on historical, statistical, and game-biological sources from the last 250 years, Meldgaard (1986, 59) has been able to show a similar cyclic pattern for barren-ground caribou in Greenland. The cyclical decreases and increases of herds there lasted between sixty-five and 115 years with the population maxima spanning a period of ten to twenty-five years, and the population minima thirty-five to seventy years. The differences in cycle length were evidently due primarily to different lengths of the minimum phase. Shane Mahoney (1992, pers. com.) has pointed out that severe fluctuations not only affect the number of animals available: when herd sizes are extremely low or extremely high, their movements are restricted, and these variations influence the herds' migration patterns, routes, and distribution. Notable fluctuations in the caribou population would, therefore, have been reflected in native hunting patterns and would have been a factor in their subsistence economies.

104 Rowley-Conwy (1990,23) who examined faunal remains from several Beothuk sites on the coast and inland, has concluded that the settlement pattern in the last few decades of the Beothuk's existence was not different from that of the preceding century or so.

105 Cormack 1829,319–20 (in Howley 1915,190); Buchan's report, 1811, PRO, CO 194/50, f.153–88 (in Howley 1915,72–90).

106 "Sketches of savage life," 1836,323.

CHAPTER TWENTY

1 Hearne 1958,62–3.

2 MacLean 1991; Pastore 1982,158; Simpson 1984,17, 128–30.

3 Tuck 1982,211; Pastore 1983,139; 1985,323; Penney 1985,165.

4 Speck 1922,25, 34, 60; Howley 1915,180; Marshall 1989,131; Locke 1974,40; MacLean (1991,11) records two bone awls from The Beaches site.

5 The bone needle was found in a burial on a beach close to Musgrave Harbour (Anna Sawicki, 1980s, pers. com.); the netting tool is in the Ethnographic Collection of the British Museum (Beasley Collection); it was presented by G.Bayly to the Portsmouth Philosophical Institute on 13December 1826 (corresp. with Jonathan King, Keeper of the Ethnogr. Coll., BM, 1988). Presumably this was George Bayly, comptroller of customs in Newfoundland, who made a financial contribution to the Boeothick Institution in 1828, as recorded in "Boeothick Institution," 24 June 1828,2.

6 Jenness 1934,26, 28; CMC, Archaeol. Survey, Old Systems Cat. NF VIII-A, 29; this piece is similar to the bone points illustrated in Howley 1915, Plate XXIV, nos.23–8.

7 Cell 1982,71, 74, 76, 85–6; Henry Crout to Sir Percival Willoughby, August 1613, MMss, Mix 1/24 (App. 1).

8 Cell 1982,118; Morandière 1962,1:22.

9 Marshall 1977a,238.

10 Ibid. 1989:127, 132, 137.

11 Pastore 1985,324; Thomson 1983,167–9; MacLean 1991, Devereux 1970, Ms.743.

12 Howley 1915,271.

13 Lloyd 1876a,226, Plate VII; Locke 1974,26–7; Howley 1915,341, Plate XXX; there are several specimens of this type in the Newfoundland Museum collection.

14 Pastore 1983,137; 1985,325, 1987,56.

15 MacLean 1990b,169, 173.

16 Howley 1915,100.

17 John Cartwright, "Remarks on the situation of the Red Indians … 1768," PRRL, 971.8 C24 (in Howley 1915,33); Cormack Papers 30/84 (in Howley 1915,212, 229–30); Micmac had told Howley (1915, 212, fn.1) that the Beothuk also used a "species of fir called boxy fir, a hard grown, tough springy wood." The term boxy fir is descriptive of its tough or gnarled nature, grown under harsh conditions; it does not designate a separate species.

18 Cartwright, "Remarks… 1768," PRRL, 971.8 C24 (in Howley 1915,33).

19 Howley 1915,271. There are discrepancies in the different descriptions of the Beothuk bow; John Cartwright specifically described the inward side of the bow as the flattened portion; George Cartwright (1792,1:9) stated that the inner side of the bow was flat and that one edge was thicker than the other; George Wells described the bow as being flattened on the outside with the ends thinned.

20 Howley 1915,271; Lysaght 1971,132.

21 Lieut. David Buchan's report of his expedition to Red Indian Lake, 1811, PRO, CO 194/50, f.153–88 (in Howley 1915,86).

22 Cartwright, "Remarks … 1768," PRRL, 971.8 C24 (in Howley 1915,33); Cormack Papers 30/84 (in Howley 1915,212, 230); Cartwright (1792,1:9–10) said they were made of "Weymouth pine" *sharpened like a barbed lance*.

23 Hoffman 1963,14; it is possible that "fish bone" stands for seal bone, because in the early historic records seal were sometimes referred to as "fish."
24 Cormack Papers 30/84 (in Howley 1915,212); Pastore 1985,325.
25 Cartwright 1792,1:10.
26 Chute 1976,80; Pastore 1987,56.
27 Buchan's report, 1811, PRO, CO 194/50, f.153–88 (in Howley 1915,86); Howley 1915,271; Marshall 1989,121; Lysaght 1971,132.
28 Cormack Papers 30/84 (in Howley 1915,212, 230); the blunt knob at the end of the arrow may have been added to the shaft or carved from it.
29 Cartwright's sketch; 1773, NAC, NMC 27, Fig. 20.1; quivers are mentioned in Buchan's report to Governor Hamilton, 10 March 1820, PRO, CO 194/63, f.64–77 (in Howley 1915,125); Cormack 1829,324 (in Howley 1915,193).
30 Buchan's report, 1811, PRO, CO 194/50, f.153–88 (in Howley 1915,86); Marshall 1989,127.
31 Ibid., 127, 132; Comack Papers 30/84 (in Howley 1915,212).
32 In ibid. the spear is said to be twelve feet long, the harpoon fourteen feet; on Shanawdithit's sketch 8, Fig.20.2, the harpoon is twelve feet, the spear is shorter; the word "Iron" seems to indicate that the point was made of iron. The name "*amina* Deer Spear" as given on Howley's copy is not on the original.
33 Chute 1976,81–2; Locke 1974,24–5, the shape of some of these points is quite similar to the spear point drawn by Shanawdithit; Ruth Holmes Whitehead, ethnologist with the Nova Scotia Museum (1992, pers. com.), has pointed out that the iron spearhead found by Devereux at the Indian Point site is identical to those traded to Micmac by Basques between 1580 and 1600.
34 Morison 1971,70.
35 Shanawdithit's sketch 8, Fig.20.2; Howley 1915,248: this copy of Shanawdithit's drawing is not quite accurate; on the original sketch the harpoon line leads from the toggle point straight back through the notch at the end of the shaft and is then curled up in a spiral; Cormack Papers 30/84 (in Howley 1915,212).
36 Lloyd 1876a,229; Lloyd owned a Beothuk harpoon bone socket, taken from one of the mamateeks at Red Indian Lake at the capture of Demasduit in 1819, which he donated to the BM, Ethnogr. Dept. The naturalist Stuwitz collected a "Red Indian" harpoon bone socket in Newfoundland while "excavating for remnants of the extinct bird *Alca impennis* [great auk]" (corresp. with the Ethnogr. Museum, Univ. of Oslo, 1986–87); see also Tompkins 1986,9.
37 Chute 1976,89–90.
38 Jenness 1929,38–9, illustrations of two self-pointed harpoon head sockets; Jenness, who collected these sockets in western Notre Dame Bay, suggested that they were of Beothuk origin. Since the area was also frequented by Palaeo-Eskimos, and since their shape is similar to that of Palaeo-Eskimo harpoon heads it is quite possible that these harpoons were made by Palaeo-Eskimos.
39 Quinn 1979 vol.1,95, doc.54; Howley 1915,100.
40 Adney stated that stone tools were unsuitable for whittling wood (Adney and Chapelle 1964,18).

41 Chute 1976,47; Marshall 1974a, Plate II.

42 Howley 1915,341, Plates XXX, XXXIII; Chute 1976,41, 47: a second knife in the Newfoundland Museum collection is closer to crooked knives used by natives on the mainland, but its origin is not documented.

43 Chute 1976,51, 228: having examined the Beothuk shell discs in the McCord Museum, Chute thought that the central perforation was drilled.

44 Adney and Chapelle 1964,16–25; Ritzenthaler 1950.

45 Quinn 1979,4:64–5, doc.560 (in Howley 1915,12); Howley 1915, Plate XXXIII: roasting sticks were also recoverd from old Beothuk campsites and burial caves in Notre Dame Bay.

46 Newfoundland Museum catalogue entry: "Taken from a Red Indian wigwam at Lake Bathurst [Red Indian Lake] on the 5th of March 1819 at the capture of a Red Indian woman, after named Mary March."

47 Howley 1915, Plates XXXI, XXXIV.

48 Quinn 1979,4:64–5, doc.560 (in Howley 1915,12).

49 Cell 1982,70, 193.

50 Ibid.

51 Buchan's report, 1811, PRO, CO 194/50, f.153–88 (in Howley 1915,86); Marshall 1989,131–2.

52 Sproull Thomson 1984,17.

53 Entry in the day-record book of the Edinburgh University Museum (forerunner of the Royal Scottish Museum), 15 March 1828: "two meat dishes of bark" and "drinking cup of bark" are listed together with other items, some of which are entered with the comment "found in the chief's cemetery."

54 This description comes from Chute (1976,132) who has examined the specimens in the Newfoundland Museum.

55 Podolinski Webber 1980,5.

56 Corresp. with Dale Idiens, Keeper, National Scottish Museums, 1987: the bark dish in Plate 20.5b has two separate pieces of bark stitched over the seams inside the dish.

57 The full inscription reads: "Red Indian Meat Dish for Deer's flesh found in the Chief's tomb at Rd I Lake 1827 by W.E.C.." The place is Red Indian Lake, and the "chief" was Nonosabasut; this dish as well as the cup-shaped one were presented to the British Museum by the Royal Institution, which presumably received them from Cormack either directly or through another person.

58 Corresp. with Dale Idiens, Keeper, National Scottish Museums, 1987: the meat dish in Plate 20.6 has flaps that are bent up inside over the seams.

59 On Plate 20.6 one of the thongs is shown as a loop; a later photograph shows all thongs broken so that they look like fringes.

60 These features are present on Athapaskan netted bags made from babiche (a cordage made from rawhide); see Rogers and Smith 1981,145; Thompson 1987,157, Fig.42; McClellan and Denniston 1981,383, Fig.14.

61 Podolinsky Webber 1980,9, 14: a mug-shaped bark container whose upper edge, rather than being pinked, is reinforced with a strip of wood was collected in 1970

from Carrier Indians of British Columbia; for a larger container of this shape see McClellan and Denniston 1981,383, Fig.13.

62 Speck 1937, Plate XVIII: d, g; Plate XIX: d, Plate XX: e; Skinner 1911,134; Chute (1976,149) examined a variety of bark containers from different native groups but found no observable parallels between Beothuk and other Maritime baskets. A close comparison of the different vessels shows that some types are similar in concept while others are clearly different.

63 Speck 1937,74.

64 Howley 1915, 175, 181.

65 Specks 1937, 77.

66 Ibid.,79.

67 Marshall 1989,131; Speck 1922,43.

68 Howley 1915,298, Plates XXVII, XXIX.

69 Marshall 1989,126, 131.

70 Howley 1915,175, 181.

71 Cartwright, "Remarks … 1768," PRRL, 971.8 C24 (in Howley 1915,30, 31); Bergerud 1971.

72 Ibid.

73 Howley 1915,155.

74 Cartwright, "Remarks … 1768," PRRL, 971.8 C24 (in Howley 1915,30–1); Cartwright 1792,1:8–10 (in Howley 1915,47–8).

75 Cartwright 1792,1:8–10 (in Howley 1915, 47–8).

76 Cartwright 1792, 1:8–10.

77 Cartwright, "A Sketch of the River Exploits …" submitted in 1773, NAC, NMC 27 (in Marshall 1977b,225); the given length of fifteen km of fences is an approximation based on measurements on a current map.

78 Buchan's report, 1811, PRO, CO 194/50, f.153–88 (in Howley 1915,74–6); Howley 1915,152; Cormack 1829,326–7 (in Howley 1915,194, 195); Select Committee on Aborigines [1836], 1968,1:478; "Substance of the narrative of William Cull of Fogo …," 22 July 1810, PANL, CSOC, GN 2/1/A, vol.21, f.27–30 (in Howley 1915,69–70).

79 Buchan's report, 1811, PRO, CO 194/50, f.153–88 (in Howley 1915,74–5).

80 Buchan to Hamilton, 10 March 1820, PRO, CO 194/63, f.64–77 (in Howley 1915,124).

81 Cormack 1829,327 (in Howley 1915,195).

82 Lloyd 1876a,224.

83 Speck 1922,19–20.

84 Morandière 1962,1:21–22; Cartwright, "Remarks … 1768," PRRL, 971.8 C24 (in Howley 1915,31); Cartwright 1792, 1:8–10 (in Howley 1915,47–8).

85 Cartwright, "Remarks … 1768," PRRL, 971.8 C24 (in Howley 1915, 31); Speck 1922,62.

86 Cormack 1829,326–27 (in Howley 1915,194–5); Cormack Papers 30/84 (in Howley 1915,212); "Substance of the narrative … ," 22 July 1810, PANL, CSOC, GN 2/1/A, vol.21, f.27–30, (in Howley 1915,70).

87 Tanner 1947,618; Turner 1979,151; Champlain 1971,3:85; "Sketches of savage life, 1836,322.

88 Quinn 1981,11; Howley 1915,1.

89 Tanner 1947,618.

90 Lescarbot 1928,270, described in 1609; Cormack also described Micmac hunters pursuing a caribou for several days (Howley 1915,152).

91 Cell 1982,88; Crout to Willoughby, 8 September 1612, MMSS, Mix 1/20.

92 Denys 1968,429, 431; Chute 1976,84; Thwaites 1959,5:61; 6:301; Rogers 1967, 44.

93 Howley 1915,106; "Sketches of Savage Life," 1836,322.

94 Dogs used to assist in hunting: Feest 1978,258, for Virginia Algonquians; Clifton 1978,734, for Potawatoni; Rogers 1978,764, Ojibwa. Dogs used as sacrificial offering: Fenton 1978,316, Iroquois; Sturtevant 1978,541, Seneca-Cayuga (symbolizing flesh of captives); Callender 1978,686, Miami; Clifton 1978,735, Potawatoni (eaten for ritual purposes); Rogers 1978,764, Ojibwa. Dogs used as source of meat: Heidenreich 1978,368, Huron; Day and Trigger 1978,795, Algonquin.

95 Cell 1982,76; Buchan's report, 1811, PRO, CO 194/50, f.153–88 (in Howley 1915,77–90); Buchan to Hamilton, 10 March 1820, PRO, CO 194/63, f.64–77 (in Howley 1915,121–6).

96 Cartwright, "Remarks ... 1768," PRRL, 971.824, C24 (in Howley 1915,35).

97 Cartwright 1792,1:5–6 (in Howley 1915,46).

98 Marshall 1989,120–41; Lloyd 1875,30; Howley 1915,322.

99 Cormack Papers 13/84 (in Howley 1915,220–1); among the fifteen questions and notes that Cormack listed, two others have "(No)" marked next to them.

100 Tuck 1976a,77, 202, Plate 10. The burial was dated ca. 3500 BP.

101 Cumbaa 1984,18.

102 Hewson 1978,153.

103 Howley 1915,267.

104 Quinn 1981,33.

105 Howley 1915,100, 101 fn.1.

106 Cell 1982,192; Whitbourne had also been told that the natives "in the north" were said to keep wolves, which they marked in the ears with several markers as was done in England with sheep; indeed, he had heard that these people would avenge any wrongs done to "their wolves"; this information probably did not pertain to Beothuk.

107 Howley 1915,271.

108 Head 1976,76.

109 Hoffman 1963,14.

110 Burrage (1967,392) gives a description of a whale chase from small boats by Penobscot in New England in 1605.

111 Cormack Papers 34/84 (in Howley 1915,230, 249–50); Cormack's note reads "bottle-nosed whale"; Howley believed that Shanawdithit would have meant the "Common Porpoise," which is considerably smaller.

112 According to John Lien (1995, pers. com.), bottle-nosed whales usually remain in deep water; he considered it unlikely that they would have come into any of the bays in great numbers.
113 Cell 1982,84.
114 Howley 1915,268.
115 Devereux 1970,58, Ms.743; Howley 1915, Plate XXIV.
116 Denys 1968,436–7.
117 Devereux 1969, vol.2, plates 3–7, showing a stone configuration in the river close to the Woodward site, West Arm, New Bay. The use of weirs by the English is remembered by Saunders 1986,128.
118 Whitehead 1980,51–3; Rogers 1967,85; Skinner 1911,27; Speck 1926,278.
119 Howley 1915,341, Plates XXXI, XXXIV.
120 Anna Sawicki, 1980s, pers. com.
121 Quinn 1979,1:95–6, doc.56.
122 Howley 1915,92–3, 97; Marshall 1989,133, 135, 138, 139, 140.
123 Buchan's report, PRO, 1811, CO 194/50, f.153–88 (in Howley 1915,76); Chute 1976,67: ice-fishing kits used by Montagnais included a snow shovel, an ice chisel made from a pole with a sharp conical bone or metal point, and a gill net of twisted babiche lines.
124 Cormack Papers 30/84 (in Howley 1915,212, 230).
125 Crout to Willoughby, August 1613, MMss. Mix 1/24 (Appendix 1).
126 Cartwright 1792,1:10 (in Howley 1915, 48); Lysaght 1971,133.
127 Howley 1915, 270.
128 Cell 1982,87; Peters and Burleigh 1951,154; LeClercq 1968,281.

CHAPTER TWENTY-ONE

1 Cell 1982,75, 86; Hoffman 1963; cited in Quinn 1981,12,32.
2 Cartwright 1792,1:4 (in Howley 1915,46); Howley 1915,51.
3 Ibid.,257, 261, 266; Marshall 1989,121, 122, 131, 140; the COED defines stout as strong in body and powerfully built, robust, brave, undaunted, fierce and intractable.
4 Howley 1915,258.
5 David Buchan's report of his expedition to Red Indian Lake, 1811, PRO, CO 194/50, f.153–88 (in Howley 1915,75,86).
6 Howley 1915,261.
7 Buchan's report, 1811, PRO, CO 194/50, f.153–88 (in Howley 1915,86); Howley 1915,175, 181, 260; Noad 1859,34; Wilson (1866,313) said that Shanawdithit was up to six feet tall; Cormack Papers 30/84 (in Howley 1915,225): Cormack noted that Shanawdithit had become stout during captivity.
8 Sebastian Cabot, cited in Quinn 1981,13; Cantino and Pasqualigo, 1501, cited in Quinn 1981,12; Saintonge, 1559, cited in Quinn 1981,27.
9 Howley 1915,261.
10 Lloyd 1876a,230.

11 Buchan's report, 1811, PRO, CO 194/50, f.153–88 (in Howley 1915,86); Robinson 1834,216 (in Howley 1915,127); Howley 1915,261; Rev. John Lewis to the Wesleyan Society, begun 17 May, cont. 5 June 1819, MMS: LR, North America, Newfoundland 1819–20, Box 2, file 2d, no.5.

12 Howley 1915,260, Mrs Jure and Mr Gill; Wilson 1866,313; Rev. William Wilson to Methodist Missionary Society, 12 August 1823, "Extracts from my Journal," MMS: LR, North America, Newfoundland 1823–24, Box 4, file 4f, no.14.

13 Webber 1978,98 fn.4.

14 Cell 1982,75.

15 Buchan's report, 1811, PRO, CO 194/50, f.153–88 (in Howley 1915,86); Dr William Carson, MD, Answers to questions by the Royal College of Physicians of Great Britain, 1830, Governor Cochrane to Viscount Goderich, 7 February 1831, PRO, CO 194/81, f.59a; Robinson 1834,216 (in Howley 1915,127); Howley 1915,181; Marshall 1989,131.

16 Shanawdithit's sketch 8, Fig.20.2; in the reproduction of this drawing in Howley's book the dancing person is called "dancing woman, Thub-wed-gie"; on the original the caption reads "dancing"; the remainder may have faded; Marshall 1977b,4; Cormack Papers 20/84 (in Howley 1915,228): Demasduit's short hair may have signified mourning, as was the custom among other groups such as the Western Abenaki (Day 1978,156).

17 Cell 1982,75; Whitehead 1984,10; Quinn 1979,3:370, doc.464; Lescarbot 1928,191; Burrage 1967,368.

18 Howley 1915,99.

19 Cell 1982,75, 86.

20 Ibid.,75.

21 LeClercq 1968,97; Howley 1915,154, Micmac used *Salix vulgaris* root to produce black dye.

22 Cell 1982,75, 85; Lieut. John Cartwright, "Remarks on the situation of the Red Indians ... 1768," PRRL, 971.8 C24 (in Howley 1915,29); Cartwright 1792,1:6 (in Howley 1915,46); Marshall 1989,126, 131; Governor Gambier to Lord Hobart, 23 November 1803, PRO, CO 194/43, f.169–70; Buchan's report, 1811, PRO, CO 194/50, f.152–88 (in Howley 1915,86); Robinson 1834,216 (in Howley 1915,127).

23 Cell 1982,75; Buchan's report, 1811 (PRO, CO 194/50, f.153–88) mentions red earth (in Howley 1915,86); Chappell (1818,183) refers to alder juice; Speck 1922,51, 63, red clay and root juice; Rogers and Taylor 1981,237: the Northern Ojibwa used boiled alder to stain birchbark red.

24 Cell 1982,75.

25 Feest 1978,277; Benjamin West illustrated in Tooker 1978,434; Wied and Bodmer 1976; Catlin 1965; Miller 1973; Thwaites 1959,1:279, Micmac; Purchas 1906,199, Algonquin, Etchemin, Montagnais; Skinner 1911,21, Eastern Cree.

26 Howley 1915,262; Lloyd 1875,23; Thwaites 1959,1:279; Champlain 1971,4: 168.

27 Speck 1922,58, 62–3.

28 Howley 1915,262, 331; see also chapter 25, Table 25.1.

29 Hoffman 1891,181, 222: among Ojibwa vermilion stood for the blood of an animal to be hunted; Slobodin 1981,517: the Kutchin, who painted their bodies as well as their garments with red ochre or other colouring agents, attributed "a degree of supernatural power" to the red mineral caih (which was probably hematite); Cordwell 1979,49: some native people associated red with blood, fire, and life.
30 Hoffman 1963,13.
31 Cantino and Pasqualigo, 1501, cited in Quinn 1981,12; Eusebius, 1518, cited in Quinn 1981,14.
32 Skinner 1911,21, Eastern Cree; Sturtevant 1980,47, Inuit; Quinn 1981,38, Central Eskimo; Brasser 1978,202, Mahican; Goddard 1978,229, Delaware; Feest 1978,260, Virginia Algonquian; Kalm 1964,1:472, Huron; Hoffman 1955,210–11, Micmac, citing Diereville and Maillard.
33 Cantino and Pasqualigo, 1501, cited in Quinn 1981,12.
34 Cartier, cited in Quinn 1981,18; Crignon, cited in Hoffman 1963,13; Thevet, cited in Quinn 1981,33.
35 Quinn 1979,4:23, doc.536; Cell 1982,75, 85, 119, 137; Henry Crout to Sir Percival Willoughby, August 1613, MMSS, Mix 1/24 (App. 1).
36 Marshall 1989,123; Howley 1915,51.
37 Anspach 1819,245; Governor Gower's Observations on the Return of the Fishery for the year 1804, 18 March 1806, PRO, CO 194/45, f.29–30.
38 Robinson 1834,216 (in Howley 1915,128); Lewis to Wesleyan Society, 17 May and 5 June 1819, MMS: LR, North America, Newfoundland 1819–20, Box 2, file 2d, no.5; Governor Hamilton to Earl Bathurst, 27 September 1819, PANL, CSOC, GN 2/1/A, vol.32, f.209; Buchan's report of his second expedition to Red Indian Lake to Hamilton, 10 March 1820, PRO, CO 194/63, f.64–77 (in Howley 1915,121); *Mercantile Journal*, 27 May 1819,2.
39 Howley 1915,99.
40 Wilson 1866,313; Howley 1915,174.
41 Carson, Answers to questions ..., 1830, PRO, CO 194/81, f.59a-60.
42 Buchan's report, 1811, PRO, CO 194/50, f.153–88 (in Howley 1915:86); Howley 1915,212; Cell 1982,75; Marshall 1989,131; Speck 1922,43.
43 Hearne 1958,32.
44 Howley 1915,100; Speck 1922,43.
45 Robinson 1834,216 (in Howley 1915,127–8); Howley 1915,212; Cell 1982,75.
46 Cell 1982,76.
47 Tuck (1976a,54) found birdskins in graves of Maritime Archaic Indians in Port au Choix.
48 George Henricksen, quoted in Tuck 1976a,39; George Cartwright, in "Addition to the Labrador the Companion," Cartwright Papers, described the method used by Montagnais women to skin an otter as follows: "They are provided with a sort of chizzel, made out of the long bone in the fore-leg of a white bear, with the corners rounded off. They begin at the mouth, and work with a sharp knife until they have turned a sufficient part of the skin over the head; they then hang the carcass on a strong stake or tree, fixed in a perpendicular direction, and drive the skin off by

striking the bone-chizzel very forcibly between the skin and the fat. By this process, the work will be completed in about half an hour and there will be little need to scrape it when dry; in contrast it generally takes three hours to skin an otter with a knife and it requires as long a time to scrape it afterwards."

49 Chute 1976,54.

50 Rogers 1967,42.

51 Jenness 1935,115. The only preserved hide-working instrument that might be of Beothuk origin was unearthed by the anthropologist Speck at a campsite on Red Indian Lake (Speck 1922,25, Plate XXV, 34); it was made from a longitudinal section of a split caribou longbone and sharpened slightly on the beaming edge and Speck considered it to be a "perfect bone implement for removing hair from caribou skins." Since some Beothuk campsites at Red Indian Lake were later reused by Micmac, the Beothuk origin of the beamer is questioned. Chute (1976,60) who examined this and other bone beamers, wrote: "In form and technique of manufacture the tool [the beamer found at Red Indian Lake] was indistinguishable from most of the caribou bone beamers acquired by Speck from the Badger's Brook Micmac settlement the same year."

52 Skinner 1911,126.

53 Marshall 1989,128, 131–2.

54 Ibid.,125.

55 Howley 1915,180.

56 Speck 1922,60; Marshall 1989,131; Chute 1976,51.

57 Ruth Holmes Whitehead, 1980s, pers. com.

58 Cell 1982,75, 86; Marshall 1989,131; Buchan's report, 1811, PRO, CO 194/50, f.153–88 (in Howley 1915,86); Howley 1915,100, 212; Speck 1922,43.

59 According to Cordwell (1979,48), ferrous oxides act as a preservative; McClellan 1981,498: the Tutchone use the red ochre and grease mixture to waterproof clothing.

60 Slobodin 1981,517, Kutchin.

61 Cell 1982,75; Marshall 1989,138, 140; Buchan's report, 1811, PRO, CO 194/50, f.153–88 (in Howley 1915,86); Howley 1915,100; a cassock was a long loose coat or gown worn by rustics and sailors (DNE).

62 Cell 1982,75.

63 Buchan's report, 1811, PRO, CO 194/50, f.153–88 (in Howley 1915,86); Howley 1915,212, 271.

64 Costume Designer Peggy Hogan, 1994, pers. com.

65 Buchan's report, 1811, PRO, CO 194/50, f.153–88 (in Howley 1915,86); Howley 1915,212; Marshall 1989,140.

66 Robinson 1834,216 (in Howley 1915,128); Howley 1915,212; Cell 1982,75.

67 Buchan's report, 1811, PRO, CO 194/50, f.153–88 (in Howley 1915,86).

68 This is suggested by costume designer Peggy Hogan, who has worked with different types of furs to reconstruct Beothuk clothing (1994, pers. com.)

69 Buchan's report, 1811, PRO, CO 194/50, f.153–88 (in Howley 1915,86).

70 Speck 1922,43.

71 Robinson 1834,216 (in Howley 1915,128).

72 COED.

73 Wilson 1866,308; Tocque 1846,285.

74 Buchan's report, 1811, PRO, CO 194/50, f.153–88 (in Howley 1915,80); List of articles delivered to Capt. Glascock for the Indians, 3 June 1819, PANL, CSOC, GN 2/1/A, vol.30, f.160; Howley 1915,112, 152: in the 1820s Micmac told Cormack that they had seen blankets in Beothuk wigwams.

75 Gower's Observations …, 18 March 1806, PRO, CO 194/45, f.30; Robinson 1834,216 (in Howley 1915,128); Record of the Supreme Court, St John's, 20 June 1823, PRO, CO 194/66, f.73; Wilson 1866,313.

76 Thompson 1987,147–55.

77 Marshall 1989,131.

78 Speck 1922,43.

79 The word "woman" and the Beothuk term *Thub-wed-gie* as given on Howley's copy are not on the original.

80 The fringe, together with the two bark containers now in the British Museum, were part of the "Christie Collection," which came to the British Museum in the 1860s or in 1870. Since the two bark containers were collected by Cormack from Nonosabasut's burial hut in 1827, it is likely that the coat fringe came from the same burial.

81 Whitehead 1987b,15; Orchard (1984,7–8, 64–5) describes raised line work in which porcupine or bird quills are used as fillers; Ruth Holmes Whitehead, who has examined the piece, believes that rolled intestines were used (1991, pers. com.).

82 Whitehead 1987a,26–7.

83 Fraser 1965,34: the coat was donated by Mr V. Simms of Quebec.

84 Burnham 1992,238–9.

85 Cormack to Inglis, 10 January 1829, Cormack Papers 57/84 (in Howley 1915,210) Wilson 1866,313.

86 John Stark to W.E. Cormack, 16 September 1828, Cormack Papers 70–6/84 (in Howley 1915,202).

87 In the early 1970s Helen Devereux enquired with the Simms family about the coat and was told that a member of the Simms family had lived for several years in Labrador; it is therefore possible that this person collected the coat and that, in the Simms family tradition, it later became associated with Shanawdithit (Paul Carignan, 1974, pers. com.).

88 Marshall 1989,125, 126; Buchan's report, 1811, PRO, CO 194/50, f.153–88 (in Howley 1915,86); Howley 1915,212, 271; Whitehead 1980,10, Micmac; Grant 1967,55, Micmac; Thwaites 1959,7:13, 15, Montagnais; Wissler (1915,71–82) described the cultural trait of sleeves separate from the garment as characteristic of an "intermediate zone," that is, an interim solution between that in which sleeves were entirely lacking and that of "true sleeves."

89 Quinn 1979,1:207, doc.148; Cell 1982,74, 76, 86.

90 Rogers 1967,60.

91 Burrage 1967,333, 348, 368 (citing Brereton, 1602, Pring, 1603, and Rosier, 1605).

92 Ganong 1964,274–5; Howley 1915,12 (map by Mattioli).

93 Cantino, 1501, cited in Quinn 1981,12.

94 Hoffman 1963,45.

95 Cell 1982,195; Howley 1915,271.

96 Kuppermann 1980,39; some native people were truly naked, as recorded by the anthropologist Morice (1907,2:30), who found that several Athapaskan tribes that had lived in relative isolation used no loincloth of any sort until the nineteenth century.

97 Mechling 1914,65.

98 Buchan's report, 1811, PRO, CO 194/50, f.153–88 (in Howley 1915,86); Howley 1915,212, 331; Patterson 1892,156; Whitehead 1987a,27.

99 Howley 1915,331; the child's pants are now missing; a photograph of the child and some of the grave goods by J.P. Howley depicts a long piece of thickly fringed leather.

100 Whitehead 1987a,27; Ruth Holmes Whitehead (1991, pers. com.) has suggested that a short piece of fringe in the collection of the Newfoundland Museum would originally have been attached to the lower edge of the legging since it measures the length of this edge.

101 Speck 1922,43, 76.

102 Speck 1922,43; Thwaites 1959,7:11, Montagnais; Denys 1968,412, Micmac; Skinner 1911,15, Woods Cree; Hatt 1914,79; Ruth Holmes Whitehead, 1991, pers. com.: no Micmac leggings from before 1780 have been preserved. Leggings worn after 1780 had a narrow extension on the outer side of the legging that reached up to the waist and was attached to a belt-like strip of leather.

103 Patterson 1892,156; Thwaites 1959,7:13–15: Le Jeune described Montagnais leggings as being fringed and decorated with shells and beads.

104 John Maunder, Curator of Natural History, Newfoundland Museum, 1980s, pers. com.

105 Quinn 1979,1:207, doc.148; Cell 1982,75,86; Howley 1915,212, 331–2; Speck 1922,43.

106 Chute 1976,198; Howley 1915,271.

107 Quinn 1979,1:207, doc.148.

108 Whitehead 1987b,13; Cell 1982,71: Guy saw footwear made from caribou and sealskin.

109 Turner 1979,120–1.

110 Hatt 1964,175.

111 Cell 1982,194.

112 Thwaites 1959,2:75–7; 7:11; LeClercq 1968,98.

113 Buchan's report, 1811, PRO, CO 194/50, f.153–88 (in Howley 1915,79).

114 Howley 1915,230; this drawing is now lost; Shanawdithit's sketch 9, Fig.24.1; LeClercq (1968,98) described Micmac ceremonial headdress made from two bird wings; Turner (1979,286) mentions Montagnais ceremonial headdress.

CHAPTER TWENTY-TWO

1 The Beothuk term for house, mamateek, is only known in the singular. Since the term has been absorbed into English (DNE 1982,322), the plural is expressed by adding an "s."

2 Cell 1982,71; Henry Crout to Sir Percival Willoughby, August 1613, MMSS, Mix 1/24 (Appendix 1).
3 Morandière 1962,1:22.
4 Speck 1922,31: hoops were also used by Micmac and Montagnais.
5 Cartwright 1792,1:9 (in Howley 1915,48).
6 Lieut. John Cartwright, "Remarks on the situation of the Red Indians … 1768," PRRL, 971.8 C24 (in Howley 1915,29–30).
7 Lieut. David Buchan's report of his expedition to Red Indian Lake, 1811, PRO, CO 194/50, f.153–88 (in Howley 1915,85).
8 Marshall 1989,128, 132.
9 Howley 1915,277.
10 Cormack 1829,322 (in Howley 1915,192); Morandière 1962,1:22.
11 Robinson 1834,216 (in Howley 1915,128).
12 Blake (1888,912) did not quote her source.
13 Devereux 1964,4–6, Ms.260. 1969:1: Two roughly circular house depressions at The Beaches site (which may not have been remains of conical mamateeks) were thirty-seven and sixty-one centimetres deep respectively.
14 Thomson 1983,163.
15 LeBlanc 1973,106; Locke 1975, n.p., North Angle site.
16 Thomson 1982,14–34; the depressions left by two larger houses had a depth of 82 and 100 centimetres respectively; they would not have derived from conical summer dwellings.
17 Devereux 1964,5–6, Ms.260; LeBlanc 1973,106, feature 16.
18 Locke 1975, n.p., Aspen Island and Wigwam Brook.
19 Lloyd 1876a,223; two of these house depressions, excavated by Devereux (1969,1), had diameters of 2.1 and 3.7 metres. Carignan (1975a,139) measured four depressions with diameters of between 3.65 and 7 metres.
20 Thomson 1982,13–34.
21 Lloyd 1876a,223; Pastore 1983,134–6; 1984,104; 1985,324.
22 Devereux 1969,1; LeBlanc 1973,106; Sproull Thomson 1982,180–1; Carignan 1975a,139.
23 Devereux 1970,35, 59, Ms.743, Indian Point; LeBlanc 1973,67, Wigwam Brook; Locke 1975, n.p., Indian Point.
24 Sproull Thomson 1982,180–1; LeBlanc 1973,109; Thomson 1982,14–34.
25 Devereux 1970,62, Ms.743.
26 Ibid.,16–17.
27 The site was vandalized at the close of the season and it is possible that some evidence of construction details was destroyed (corresp. with Devereux, 1995).
28 Devereux now steers clear of the interpretation that they were sleeping hollows (corresp., 1995).
29 Carbon Dates 1982,109, Lab. No.I-6562.
30 Pastore 1984,106.
31 Ibid.,104–6; 1985,324.
32 Cell 1982,71.

33 Cartwright, "Remarks … 1768," and Cartwright to Governor Hugh Palliser, 19 September 1768, PRRL, 971.8 C24 (in Howley 1915,30, 43).
34 Cartwright 1792,1:9 (in Howley 1915,48).
35 Speck 1922,21–2, 24.
36 Locke 1975, n.p., Indian Point.
37 Pastore 1986a,219–24; 1992,40–3.
38 Gabled roofs have been seen on Beothuk storehouses; arched roofs were widely used among other Indian groups but have not, on the evidence, among Beothuk.
39 Henricksen 1973,10, 53–7; Turner 1979,322–3; Pastore, 1992,40–3.
40 LeBlanc 1973,103.
41 Buchan's report, 1811, PRO, CO 194/50, f.153–88 (in Howley 1915,77, 79, 85): Buchan described the large house in which the party stayed overnight as circular.
42 Cormack Papers 30/84 (in Howley 1915,226).
43 Buchan's report, 1811, PRO, CO 194/50, f.153–88 (in Howley 1915,77, 85).
44 The Micmac trapper had received this information from his father, also a long-time trapper in that area (Lloyd 1876a,223).
45 Pastore 1983,136–9; 1984,102–3; it was eight-sided, or an irregular circle.
46 Cormack Papers 19/84 (in Howley 1915,211 line 16–25). The paper Cormack used for this note bears the watermark 1833, which indicates that he wrote it down after he left Newfoundland.
47 LeBlanc 1973,99–104.
48 Marshall 1989,124, 125, 127.
49 Buchan to Governor Duckworth, 2 August 1810, PANL, CSOC, GN 2/1/A, vol.21, f.27–30.
50 Howley 1915,100.
51 Howley (1915,211) attributed the following description to Cormack (there is no note with this text in the Cormack Papers):

"They were in general built of straight pieces of fir about twelve feet high, flattened at the sides, and driven in the earth close to each other; the corners being made stronger than the other parts. The crevices were filled up with moss, and the inside lined with the same material; the roof was raised so as to stand from all parts and meet in a point in the centre, where a hole was left for the smoke to escape. The remainder of the roof was covered with a treble coat of birch bark, and between the first and the second layers of bark was placed about six inches of moss, about the chimney clay was substituted for the moss. The sides of these mamateeks were covered with arms, that is, bows, arrows, clubs, stone hatchets, arrow heads, &. and all these were arranged in the neatest manner. Beams were placed across where the roof began, over which smaller ones were laid; and on the latter were piled their provisions – dried salmon, venison &c"

52 Ralph Pastore, 1995, pers. com.
53 Cormack Papers 19/84 (in Howley 1915,211); Howley transcribed "composite" as "complete." In his transcription Howley omitted: "Qu.Is the rectangular the most convenient for all houses & streets etc." Again, the paper on which this note was written bears the watemark 1833.

54 Howley 1915,211 fn.1.
55 Jukes 1969,2:126.
56 Millais 1907,27.
57 Cell 1982,70.
58 Morandière 1962,1:22.
59 Cartwright to Palliser, 19 September 1768, PRRL, 971.8 C24 (in Howley 1915, 41).
60 Cartwright, "Remarks … 1768," PRRL, 971.8 C24 (in Howley 1915,30, 33); Marshall 1977a,233; Cartwright's submission to the Earl of Dartmouth, 13 January 1773, NAC, Dartmouth Papers, MG 23 A1, series 1, vol.16, f.42, 46.
61 Buchan's report, 1811, PRO, CO 194/50, f.153–88 (in Howley 1915,85); Buchan's report of his second expedition to Red Indian Lake to Governor Hamilton, 10 March 1820, PRO, CO 194/63, f.64–77 (in Howley 1915, 123).
62 Cartwright, "Remarks … 1768," PRRL, 971.8 C24 (in Howley 1915,30); Howley 1915, 100.
63 Speck (1922,32) records rectangular-based winter wigwams built of logs with a pyramidical bark superstructure from Abenaki; Tanner 1979,73–83: square houses were used by Mistassini Cree; Townsend 1981,627–28: rectangular, semisubterranean communal houses are known among Athapaskan Tanaina.
64 Jochelson (1975,71, 453) recorded that some semisubterranean winter houses of the Eastern Siberian Koryak were of an octagonal shape.
65 Honigman 1981,220, West Main Cree; Crow and Obley 1981,507, Han; Slobodin 1981,518, 525, Kutchin; Hosley 1981,539, peoples of the Alaskan Plateau; McKennan 1981,569, Tanana; Clark McFadyen 1981,588, 596, Koyukon; Snow 1981,605, 513, Ingalik; Hosley 1981,618, Kolchan; Townsend 1981,627, Tanaina.
66 Cormack 1829,319–20 (in Howley 1915,190).
67 Cormack 1829,319–20, 320 fn.1 (in Howley 1915,190–1, 191 fn.1).
68 Howley 1915,175.
69 Ibid., 100; see also chapter 19, section on preservation of food.
70 Cormack 1829,319–20 (in Howley 1915,190); Buchan's report, 1811, PRO, CO 194/50, f.153–88 (in Howley 1915,84).
71 Ibid., (in Howley 1915,75, 82, 84); Buchan to Hamilton, 10 March 1920, PRO, CO 194/63, f.64–77 (in Howley 1915,123); Cormack 1829,320–2 (in Howley 1915,192).
72 "Substance of the narrative of William Cull of Fogo …," 22 July 1810, PANL, CSOC, GN 2/1/A, vol.21, f.27–30 (in Howley 1915,69–70).
73 Buchan's report, 1811, PRO, CO 194/50, f.153–88 (in Howley 1915,85).
74 Cormack 1829,322–3 (in Howley 1915,192).
75 Cartwright to Palliser, 19 September 1768, PRRL, 971.8 C24 (in Howley 1915,41); Marshall 1989,125.
76 Cormack 1829,319–20 (in Howley 1915,190).

CHAPTER TWENTY-THREE

1 Burd Journal, 1726, PANL, MG 231.

2 Denys (1968,421) observed Micmac portaging their canoes.

3 Cell 1982,72, 84; Lieut. John Cartwright to Governor Palliser, 19 September 1768, PRRL, 971.8 C24 (in Howley 1915,41–4); Lieut. David Buchan's report of his expedition to Red Indian Lake, 1811, PRO, CO 194/50, f.153–188 (a shortened version in Howley 1915,72–90); Buchan to Governor Duckworth, 25 July 1812, NAC, Duckworth Papers, MG 24 A 45, f.5032–35; Shanawdithit's sketch 4, Fig.14.1.

4 Lysaght 1971,133; Howley 1915,57, 268, 270; Marshall 1989,120.

5 Cartwright 1792,1:10 (in Howley 1915,48).

6 Cook 1965, 18.

7 John Guy's *Journal*, "The picture of the Savages canoa," LPL, Ms.No.250, f.412; Cell 1982,75.

8 Lieut. John Cartwright, "Remarks on the situation of the Red Indians ... 1768," PRRL, 971.8 C24 (in Howley 1915,29–41); Cartwright, "A Sketch of the River Exploits ... 1768," PANL, MG 100, Cartwright Collection (in Marshall 1977a,230); Cartwright, "A Sketch of the River Exploits and the East End of Lieutenants Lake ...," submitted to the Earl of Dartmouth, 13 January 1773, NAC, NMC 27, in Marshall 1977a,225). The drawing in Howley 1915,32 entitled "Section of Beothuk canoe Cartwright" is not applicable; it was produced by the surveyor Alexander Murray and is based on the canoe replica in the Royal Museum of Scotland, Edinburgh (note and drawing in Howley Papers).

9 Cormack 1829,328 (in Howley 1915,196); Howley 1915 331, Plate XXXI; the replica that Cormack took from Nonosabasut's burial at Red Indian Lake is now in the Royal Museum of Scotland at Edinburgh.

10 Logs of *HMS Orestes*, PRO, Captain's Log 1826–28, ADM 51/3332, Ship's Log 1826–27, ADM 53/940; Marshall 1985,47.

11 See also Marshall 1985; information reproduced here by permission of the CMC.

12 Adney and Chapelle 1964; canoes were originally measured in fathoms, which Adney converted into feet.

13 Cartwright, "Remarks ... 1768," PRRL, 971.8 C24 (in Howley 1915,33); Marshall 1985,23–8; ibid., 1989, 128.

14 Cell 1982,75; Cormack 1829,322–23 (in Howley 1915,192).

15 Adney and Chapelle 1964,27–57, 94–8; in his attempt to reconcile conflicting evidence about Beothuk canoe forms and construction, Adney, who accepted Howley's drawing (1915,32) as accurate, proposed a composite Beothuk canoe combining features of the two designs.

16 Hosie 1979,160.

17 Morandière 1962,1:21: the Beothuk on the Northern Peninsula procured iron nails by burning fishermen's boats as early as 1720; Marshall 1989,132, 137; Cormack 1829,322–3 (in Howley 1915,192): not until 1827, when Cormack found the wreck of a birchbark canoe on the shore of Red Indian Lake with iron nails still in place, was the use of nails specifically associated with Beothuk canoes; Le Blanc

(1973,144), Devereux (1965, Ms.261, and 1970, Ms.743), and Pastore (1987,56) provide archaeological evidence for the use of metal.

18 Cartwright, "Remarks ... 1768," PRRL, 971.8 C24 (in Howley 1915,31–2).

19 Marshall 1985,55: on the replica made by Shanawdithit the seam batten consists of extensions of the gunwales that were carried over the stem and stern as one piece and then lashed into the end seams outside. Fenton (1949,185) observed this technique on a Seneca elmbark canoe model; it may have been a convention in model making.

20 Cormack 1829,323 (in Howley 1915,192).

21 Cell 1982,193; Cartwright, "Remarks ... 1768," PRRL, 971.8 C24 (in Howley 1915,29).

22 Cormack 1829,319 (in Howley 1915,190); Devereux 1970,40, Ms.743, locality B4.

23 Ritzenthaler 1950,62; Adney and Chapelle 1964,8.

24 Lysaght 1971,133; Howley 1915,114; Lloyd 1875,27; Lloyd (1876a,225) records that Peyton said the joint of the two canoe sides underneath the keelson was made of deerskin, which acted as a flexible hinge.

25 Cartwright, "Remarks ... 1768," PRRL, 971.8 C24 (in Howley 1915,42).

26 Cormack Papers 33/84 (in Howley 1915,213); Howley 1915,152; Speck 1940,66; Parsons 1925,100.

27 Speck 1922,61; Adney and Chapelle 1964,219: Athapaskan canoes often had partial decking.

28 Adney and Chapelle 1964,162: hogging or buckling of a bark sheet, which produces an upward curvature in the bottom and sheer, occurs in the process of building kayak-type canoes, though such hogging disappears when afloat and loaded. Hearne 1958,62, Plate III: hogging is often evident on Athapaskan canoes, which have a very narrow bottom; hogging was also present on some Micmac canoes and may have been copied from Beothuk canoes or those of other tribes for its usefulness in open-water travel. Alternatively, Micmac might formerly have built narrow-bottom canoes that had a hogged sheer on account of the buckling of the bark when folded; in the eighteenth century and thereafter, Micmac canoes had a wide flat bottom, the sides being tumble-home (turning inward), a shape that does not naturally result in hogging.

29 Cell 1982, 75. Patterson 1892,161: Micmac claimed that the Beothuk were unusually skilled in running rapids; Cormack Papers 16/84: Shanawdithit appears to have been questioned about the high end sections; their use as shields is mentioned in "Sketches of savage life," 1836,331.

30 See Steward, J.M., and F.M. Setzler 1938:10 on style as a stable ethnic marker.

31 Adney and Chapelle 1964,99–106.

32 Cartwright, "Remarks… 1768," PRRL, 971.8 C24 (in Howley 1915,32).

33 Howley 1915,282.

34 These experimental canoes were constructed by Scott James of Grand Falls. See also Marshall 1985,132–5.

35 Lloyd Seaward, 1994, pers. com.

36 Marshall 1985,93–122.

37 Lysaght 1971,133; George Cartwright 1792,1:10 (in Howley 1915,48); Howley 1915,57, 268, 270; Marshall 1989,120.

38 Cell 1982,71; John Cartwright's maps PANL, MG100, Cartwright collection, and NAC, NMC 27.

39 Cell 1982,71.

40 Cartwright, "Remarks ... 1768," PRRL, 971.8 C24 (in Howley 1915,33).

41 Adney and Chapelle 1964,65–7; Friederici 1907.

42 Cartwright to Palliser, 19 September 1768, PRRL, 971.8 C24 (in Howley 1915,42).

43 Buchan's report of his second expedition to Red Indian Lake to Governor Hamilton, 10 March 1820, PRO, CO 194/63, f.64–77 (in Howley 1915,123).

44 Marshall 1989,134.

45 Buchan's report, 1811, PRO, CO 194/50, f.153–188 (in Howley 1915,86, 87).

46 Lloyd 1876a,225, the measurement are taken from the sketch and are prorated.

47 Ibid; Buchan's report, 1811, PRO, CO 194/50, f.153–88 (in Howley 1915,86).

48 The tool is part of the Beasley collection and was presented to the Portsmouth Philosophical Institute on 13 December 1826 by G. Bayly (see note 5, chapter 20).

49 Whitehead 1984,27.

50 Lloyd 1876a,225; Buchan's report, 1811, PRO, CO 194/50, f.153–88 (in Howley 1915,87); the drawing of a Beothuk snowshoe "according to Lieut. Buchan's description" showing two support bars was Howley's and not Buchan's and is inaccurate. This error has unfortunately been incorporated, through copying, into the excellent study of snowshoes by Davidson 1937,164.

51 Davidson 1937,16–20.

52 Rogers 1962,58; Skinner 1911,44–5, 145. The bear-paw type was among the earliest and simplest snowshoes.

53 Rogers 1962,58, 59, 61, 63.

54 Helm 1981,308, Dogrib; Ash 1981,341, Slavey; McClellan and Denniston 1981,382, Kutchin.

55 A pair of snowshoes allegedly made by Shanawdithit and given by John Peyton, Jr, to a couple in Moreton's Harbour, New World Island, as a wedding gift is still in possession of this family. A photograph of the snowshoes has been examined by Rogers, who said they look in all respects like Montagnais swallowtail snowshoes (Carignan, 1974, pers. com.).

56 Buchan's report, 1811, PRO, CO 194/50, f.153–88 (in Howley 1915,87); Buchan thought the elevation at the toes would prevent quantities of snow from collecting in front of the foot and theorized that the elevation at the tail end would help to accelerate the wearer's movements.

57 Lloyd 1876a,225; Rogers 1967,93; Rogers and Smith 1981,139; on an unpublished drawing of a Montagnais/Naskapi snowshoe by George Cartwright the pointed toe section is bent upward (Cartwright Papers). McClellan and Denniston 1981,382: the snowshoes of the Kutchin are regarded as typical of the western subarctic type; their elevation at the toe is rounded as is described from the snowshoes of the Beothuk.

58 Buchan's report, 1811, PRO, CO 194/50, f.153–88 (in Howley 1915,76, 79); Buchan to Hamilton, 10 March 1820, PRO, CO 194/63, f.64–77 (in Howley 1915,123, 125).

59 Chute 1976,146–8.
60 Rogers 1967,105.
61 Howley 1915,246.

CHAPTER TWENTY-FOUR

1 Lieut. John Cartwright, "Remarks on the situation of the Red Indians … 1768," PRRL, 971.8 C24 (in Howley 1915,39); "Sketches of savage life," 1836,323.
2 Speck 1977,27; Tanner 1979,136; Adrian Tanner, 1993, pers. com.
3 LeClercq 1968,84–5; Maillard 1758,22, 25, 47–8, cited in Whitehead 1988,7–8, Micmac; Hoffman 1955,381–2; Bock 1978,117. Belief in a "Great Spirit" recorded from other groups: Hoffman 1891,154, Ojibwa; Simmons 1978,192, Narragansett; Feest 1978,262, Virginia Algonquians, and 1978,278, North Carolina Algonquians; Heidenreich 1978,373, Huron; Callender 1978,628, Shawnee; Feest and Feest 1978,777, Ottawa.
4 LeClercq 1968,143; Maillard 1758, cited in Whitehead 1988,17.
5 Lescarbot 1928,158.
6 Map published in 1547–48 by Mattioli, cited in Howley 1915,11.
7 Arber 1971,344–5.
8 Robinson 1834,216 (in Howley 1915,128).
9 Marshall 1989,141.
10 Hewson 1978,53, 163, no.281.
11 Howley 1915,100.
12 Marshall 1989,131.
13 Since Cormack, who recorded this information, would have had little insight into how the Beothuk related to the supernatural, the term "spirits" may not be appropriate, but it is the one he used.
14 "Sketches of savage life," 1836,323.
15 Washburne and Anauta 1940,28; Speck 1977,45.
16 Anthropologist Peter Armitage, 1994, pers. com.
17 "Sketches of savage life," 1836,322.
18 Ibid.,322.
19 COED: *Manes* (the term *munes* is not listed) are the deified souls of departed ancestors (as beneficent spirits); also the spirit "shade" of a departed person, considered as an object of homage or reverence, or as demanding to be propitiated through vengeance.
20 "Sketches of savage life," 1836,322.
21 Capt. David Buchan's report of his second expedition to Red Indian Lake to Governor Hamilton, 10 March 1820, PRO, CO 194/63, f.64–77 (in Howley 1915,121).
22 Goddard 1978,215, Delaware; Feest 1978,253, Virginia Algonquians, and 1978,278, North Carolina Algonquians. Ruth Holmes Whitehead (1980s, pers. com.) suggests that the Beothuk monster may have been a "European monster personification" because no Algonquian creatures had beards.

23 Bishop John Inglis, Diary, 4 July 1827, USPG, C/Can/N.S.9, doc.57–8 (in Howley 1915,297).
24 Rasmussen 1931,225.
25 Ruth Holmes Whitehead, 1980s, pers. com.
26 Speck 1977,73, 80.
27 Ibid.,50, 73.
28 Ibid.,33. The soul or soul-spirit of a person, referred to by Naskapi as "Great Man," gives guidance, provides the means of overcoming the spirits of animals in the search for food, and reveals himself in dreams. The closest definition for "soul" in English usage as given in the COED may be "the vital sensitive or rational principle in plants, animals, or human beings."
29 Speck 1977,98.
30 Cormack Papers 20/84 (in Howley 1915,190, 191 fn.1).
31 Lieut. David Buchan's report of his expedition to Red Indian Lake, 1811, PRO, CO 194/50, f.153–88 (in Howley 1915,75).
32 LeBlanc 1973,25.
33 Tanner 1979,171; Speck (1977,90) records that the Naskapi placed caribou antlers on frozen lakes so that they would sink when the ice broke up and not be gnawed by animals.
34 Buchan to Hamilton, 10 March 1819, PRO, CO 194/63, f.64–77 (in Howley 1915,125).
35 Skinner 1911,162.
36 Tanner 1979,92–3.
37 Speck 1922,12, Plates I–IV.
38 Buchan to Hamilton, 10 March 1819, PRO, CO 194/63, f.64–77 (in Howley 1915,125); Shanawdithit's sketch I, Plate 10.1; Speck 1922,25.
39 Henricksen 1973,10, 35–7; Turner (1979,158–9) called it "feast of furs."
40 Devereux 1970,67, Ms.743; Locke 1975, n.p., Indian Point site; LeBlanc 1973,83; Pastore 1986a,218.
41 Pastore 1986a,218, 221; see also chapter 22, section on oval mamateeks.
42 Buchan's report, 1811, PRO, CO 194/50, f.153–88 (in Howley 1915,79).
43 Cormack Papers 29/84 (in Howley 1915,230).
44 Roger and Leacock 1981,185, Montagnais/Naskapi; McClellan 1981,488: the Tagish smoked to assist ancestors and newly dead; Lurie 1978,693: among Winnebago smoking was associated with efforts to maintain peace; Callender 1978,643: Fox smoked to signify participation in war; Ritzenthaler 1978,754: Southwestern Chippewa smoked in religious ceremonies.
45 Lloyd 1875,35.
46 Brown 1923,29; Howley 1915,339; Howley himself had occasionally smoked these substitutes.
47 Howley 1915,339, fn.1.
48 Speck 1922,62, 63: in some of her descriptions the old woman's memory was so hazy that she could not distinguish between her Beothuk father's tales and what had been the custom among Micmac.

49 Chute 1976,272: the pipe picked up near Pipestone Pond where Micmac and Montagnais are known to have collected stones for pipes (Howley 1915,339, Plate XXII) is similar to nineteenth-century keeled-based Micmac pipes from Nova Scotia. Howley 1915,339 fn.1: the second soapstone pipe had an animal carved on the outside with its head projecting over the bowl, as is often seen on Micmac pipes; Gatschet 1892,2.

50 Hewson 1978,112.

51 Ruth Holmes Whitehead (1991, pers. com.) suggests that "ally" is more in keeping with native beliefs than "guardian spirit."

52 Day 1978,157, Western Abenaki; Goddard 1978,220, Delaware; Callender 1979,642, Fox; Spindler 1978,718, Menominee.

53 For example: Day 1978,157, Western Abenaki; Goddard 1978,220, Delaware; Rasmussen 1931,167, Netsilik Eskimo.

54 See chapter 25, List 1A; Howley 1915,289; Patterson 1892,156; physical anthropologist Sony Jerkic has recently established that the child, probably a boy, would have been four to five years old. Whitehead (1987a,27) has identified the burial shroud as a legging of an adult; it has now only one foot from a southern black guillemot (*Cepphus grylle atlantis*) attached to it. The feet of this bird are red when fresh.

55 Cormack Papers 47/84 (in Howley 1915,230).

56 Noad 1859,34–5.

57 Wallis and Wallis 1955,36, 117; Speck 1922, Plate XXXI.

58 Jochelson 1975,44.

59 Tuck 1976a,70.

60 Avalonus (pen-name for Wm. Sweetman, Magistrate in Bonavista) 1862,1; John Steckley, 1980s, pers. com.: the term "the Voice" was also recorded from the Huron and translated by the Jesuits into "Master."

61 Lescarbot 1928,158.

62 According to the COED, soul can mean "the spiritual part of man regarded as surviving after death and capable of happiness or misery in a future state." This English usage for the term "soul" may cover part of the soul concept of native people.

63 Belief in an afterlife: Speck 1977,35, Naskapi; Thwaites 1959,6:175–81, Montagnais; LeClerq 1968,207–9, Micmac; Goddard 1978,231, Delaware; Feest 1978,271, North Carolina Algonquians; Fenton 1978,296, Northern Iroquoian; Spindler 1978,717, Menominee. Belief in two souls: Simmons 1978,192, Narragansett; Feest 1978,253, Virginia Algonquians; Heidenreich 1978,368, Huron; Feest and Feest 1978,783, Ottawa. Belief that one soul would linger on and influence the living: Goddard 1978,231, Delaware; Feest 1978,253, Virginia Algonquians; Spindler 1978,717, Menominee.

64 Inglis, Diary, 4 July 1827, USPG, C/Can/N.S.9, doc.57–8; Hewson 1978,153; Speck 1977,74.

65 Cormack Papers 13/84 (in Howley 1915,221).

66 "Sketches of savage life," 1836,322.

67 Howley 1915,181.

68 "Sketches of savage life," 1836,322.

69 Afterlife was assumed to be similar to life on earth: Simmons 1978,191, Narragansett; Feest 1978,278, North Carolina Algonquians; Heidenreich 1978,375, Huron; Callender 1978,676, Illinois; Spindler 1978,717, Menominee. Examples of the practice of placing grave goods with the dead: Day 1978,156, Western Abenaki; Heidenreich 1978,374, Huron; Callender 1978,639, Fox; Callender, Pope, and Pope 1978,659, Kickapoo; Callender 1978,676, Illinois; Spindler 1978,717, Menominee. The land of the dead thought to be located in a westerly direction: Ritzenthaler 1978,752, Southwestern Chippawa; the land of the dead was to the west or the east: Feest and Feest 1978,777, Ottawa; the land of the dead was to the west or south: Goddard 1978,220, Delaware.

70 "Sketches of savage life," 1836,322.

71 Ibid.,323.

72 Day 1978,156: Western Abenaki placed food items in the grave for the journey over the ghost trail; Spindler 1978,717: Menominee provided the dead with utensils for the journey; see also Fenton 1978,319, Northern Iroquoian.

73 Cell 1982,193; Cartwright, "Remarks … 1768," PRRL, 971.8 C24 (in Howley 1915,29); Buchan's report, 1811, PRO, CO 194/50, f.153–88 (in Howley 1915,86); Cormack 1829,319 (in Howley 1915,190); Cartwright 1792,1:5 (in Howley 1915,47); Marshall 1989,126, 131.

74 Marshall 1989, 131.

75 See chapter 25, Table 25.1; Howley 1915,262, 331.

76 Doug Vandeveer and Baxter Kean, Dept. of Mines and Energy, Govt. of Nfld., 1980s, pers. com.

77 Governor Gower's Observations on the Return of the Fishery for 1804, 18 March 1806, PRO, CO 194/45, f.30; Buchan's report, 1811, PRO, CO 194/50, f.153–88 (in Howley 1915,86).

78 Parsons 1925,38, 55.

79 Speck 1922,51.

80 Conception Bay: Ochre Pit Cove, *English Pilot* 1967,9; Howley 1915,265; Bonavista Bay: Com. Bowler, Answer to HOES, 9 October 1724, PRO, CO 194/7, f.240; Bay of Exploits: Ochre Pit Island, Howley 1915,262, 266; Devereux (1965b, Ms.735) has surveyed this island and reported a layer of inaccessible brownish earth but no ochre deposit.

81 Cormack 1824,158; Speck 1922,51.

82 Slobodin 1981,517.

83 Speck 1922,58, 62–3.

84 Ibid.,64.

85 Tuck 1978a,42.

86 Denys 1968,423, Micmac. Harper (1957,4) found a leather pouch with trade vermilion in one of two seventeenth-century Micmac "Copper Kettle" burials; one of the skins in this burial was painted entirely red; Grant 1967,61, Micmac; Blant and Baudry 1967,104, Micmac; LeClerq 1968,97, Micmac; Thwaites 1959,1:297, Micmac; Kupp and Hart 1976,19, Montagnais.

87 Kupp and Hart 1976,19, Montagnais; Goddard 1978,229, Delaware; Callender 1978,677, Illinois; Steinbring 1981,250, Saulteaux; Hoffman 1891,181, 222, Ojibwa, for whom vermilion stood for the blood of the animal to be hunted.

88 Lane 1981,403, Chilcotin; McClellan 1981,498, Tuchtone; Crow and Obley 1981,509, Han; Slobodin 1981,517, Kutchin.

89 Cormack to Inglis, 26 October 1828, Cormack Papers 26/84 (in Howley 1915,209).

90 Howley (1915, opp.249) has given this drawing the title "Totems? or Emblems of Mythology"; in his commentary (ibid.), he referred to the drawing as "Emblems of Red Indian Mythology," which is the title on the original. The names on the drawing as printed by Howley are not on the original; presumably they have faded or have otherwise been removed.

91 Buchan's report, 1811, PRO, CO 194/50, f.153–88 (in Howley 1915,79).

92 Howley 1915,230.

93 Ruth Holmes Whitehead, 1980s, pers. com.: some of the counting sticks used by Micmac in their *waltes* game have designs at the top that resemble those of the Beothuk's mythological emblems; to the Micmac they represent animate beings, such as "grandfather," "loon," and others.

94 John Bland to Governor Wm. Waldegrave, 20 October 1797, PANL, CSOC, GN 2/1/A, vol.14, f.90–4 (in Howley 1915,59).

95 Kupp and Hart 1976,19.

96 LeClercq 1968,144–54; Podolinsky Webber (1986,33–4) points out the symbolism of the cross with respect to zones and stages in Indian games; for this reason the cross recurs on many gambling instruments. Nietfeld 1981,416: among the Micmac each band had a specific symbol that could, for example, be a cross, a salmon, a sturgeon, or a beaver; the symbol was painted inside and outside of wigwams and canoes, or embroidered on clothes, and was displayed at council meetings to invoke protection.

97 The Cormack Papers (29/84) contain a note in Cormack's hand with a drawing of this stave and the term "Ke-u-us or moon." The handle of the stave is marked A, the semicircular part B. The note continues under A: "woman" which is crossed out, "handle painted red"; under B: "death to her" which is crossed out and above it "& other Red," followed by "painted red?" Cormack seems to have attempted here to understand and write down what Shanawdithit tried to convey about the emblems.

98 Howley (1915,230 fn.5) added "This is the common Dolphin (*Delphinus*)." Presumably he believed that it would not have been the northern bottle-nosed whale (*Hyperoodon ampullatus)*; John Lien also doubted whether this would have been a bottle-nosed whale since these animals usually live in deep water and are not known to come close to shore; in Cormack Papers 29/84, a note reads: "Ow-as-bosh-xx-xx or emblematic of the [mode? shade? is the? crossed out] slain? of the whole? tribe? mode? I made is one Hunter?" – presumably another attempt at understanding and jotting down what Shanawdithit said about the drawing.

99 Howley 1915,249.

100 Marshall 1978b,141; 1975.

101 Pastore (1985,325) found broken pieces of bone carving in house walls at Boyd's Cove; MacLean (1990a,7) records that Locke found ten bone carvings at the North Angle/Wigwam Brook site; fragments have also been found at The Beaches (Laurie MacLean, 1993, pers. com.).

102 Cartwright to the Earl of Dartmouth, 13 January 1773, NAC, Dartmouth Papers, MG 23 A 1, series 1, vol.16, f.54.

103 Rasmussen 1931,167: among the Netsilik Eskimos not only were animal teeth and bones used as amulets or tokens of good luck but also more perishable objects such as sea scorpions, a small cod, a shrimp, a louse, which were sewn into the coat of an individual. Rasmussen records one case in which a boy had more than eighty tokens of this type fastened to his coat.

104 George Swinton (1970s, pers. com.) has pointed out the similarity of these carvings to finger bones and bear claws.

105 Speck 1977,92–8.

106 Skinner 1911,69, 72.

107 Ruth Holmes Whitehead, 1980s, pers. com.; Podolinsky Webber 1986,50.

108 Harp 1970,109–24.

109 Ibid,112.

110 Tuck 1976a,60; Fitzhugh 1985,93–5: soapstone pendants with geometric markings have been found on several sites in Labrador assigned to the Nuttiak Phase of the Late Maritime Archaic Indians.

111 Thompson 1987,142; LeBlanc (1984,370) recorded incised pendant-like carvings rubbed with ochre from the Rat Indian Creek site, a late prehistoric Athapaskan site in the interior of northern Yukon.

112 Fitzhugh and Cromwell 1988,273.

113 Speck 1922,63.

114 According to the Newfoundland Museum catalogue the collection included at one time sixteen gaming pieces; see also Podolinsky Webber 1986,47.

115 Podolinsky Webber 1986; in the following section reference is made to pp. 3, 6, 10–13, 16–18, 23, 35–6, 38.

116 Howley 1915, Plate XXVII, no.28–34, Plate XXVIII, no.1–7.

117 Podolinsky Webber 1986,54, 63.

118 Ibid., 55–6; Podolinsky Webber pointed out that on Shanawdithit's sketches 1 and 2, Plates 10.1 and 10.2, the floor of the Beothuk mamateeks is drawn towards the water, like mirror images, instead of parallel to the bottom of the page.

119 Podolinsky Webber 1986,17.

120 Howley 1915,289.

121 Podolinsky Webber 1986,11; Howley (1915, Plate XXXV) illustrates strings of beads or counters; the thin twisted thong is very slack and it is possible that some beads have disintegrated and fallen off; Podolinsky Webber (1986,53, 71) states that she counted eighty and 160 beads respectively.

122 Podolinsky Webber 1986,14–18; Speck 1922,63.

123 Ruth Holmes Whitehead, 1980s, pers. com.: *Waltestaqn* translates into "implements for doing *waltes*."

124 Podolinsky Webber 1986,17; the counters consisted of fifty-one plain ones, a king pin (the Old Man), and three notched sticks (the three wives of the Old Man).
125 Ruth Holmes Whitehead, 1980s, pers. com.
126 Dawson 1860,462; Howley 1915,293.
127 Cell 1982,74; see also grave goods in burials list 1A, No. 1 and 2, Table 25.1.
128 Howley 1915,289–90, Plate XXXV.
129 Evans 1981,89: that Beothuk collected broken pipestems is shown by a cache of some 250 pipestem pieces on the Beothuk site at Frenchman's Island, Trinity Bay.
130 MacDougall 1891,102; Howley 1915,293, 333; Jenness 1934,32; Marshall 1974a; Plate II.
131 Dawson (1860,462) recorded that the burial at Rencontre included "shell wampum finished and in various stages of manufacture"; Patterson 1892,157, and Howley 1915,293, 334, described the same burial contents, recording "glass beads"; this may be a misunderstanding, since there are no glass beads among the grave goods from Rencontre in the McCord Museum.
132 Carignan 1973,12; Marshall 1974b,8; information on the grave near Musgrave Harbour comes from anthropologist Anna Sawicki (1980s, pers. com.); Howley 1915,289, 333; Locke 1974,29.
133 Howley 1915,289; Dawson 1860,462.
134 Chute 1976,228; Wintemberg (1936,24) described the same discoidal beads as being up to one inch in diameter.
135 Speck 1964,19–22.
136 Cell 1982,194.
137 Speck 1964,4–7, Speck found that wampum only figured in the mythology of tribes south of the St Lawrence and concluded that bead making derived from the Iroquois.
138 Wintemberg 1928; 1936,25: those beads, now lost, were said to resemble beads found in pre- and post-European sites of Iroquois and other cultures farther to the south.

CHAPTER TWENTY-FIVE

1 The term "burial" is used for the burying place, the grave, and the act of burying, according to the COED.
2 Cormack 1829,323 (in Howley 1915,192).
3 Cormack 1829,323–5 (in Howley 1915,193–4). In his report of his second expedition to Red Indian Lake to Governor Hamilton, 10 March 1820 (PRO, CO 194/63, f.64–77, in Howley 1915,123), Capt. David Buchan mentions that he had seen this burial hut when he brought the remains of Demasduit back to the Beothuk camp.
4 See chapter 12, section on Capt. David Buchan's final attempt to meet Beothuk.
5 Cormack 1829,324–5 (in Howley 1915,193–4).
6 Day and week record books of the Edinburgh University Museum, (forerunner of the Royal Museum of Scotland), entries 15.3.1828: "Additions to College Museum 1827, 1828:25. Two skulls of the Aborigines of Newfoundland, presented by

Mr Cormack to Professor Jameson & by him to the Museum. 39. Model of a Red Indian Canoe, also two Models of Human figures found in the cemetry of the 'chief' of the country of the Red Indians: likewise model in wood of a bird found in the chief's cemetry, presented to Professor Jameson & by him to the Museum. 40. Fire Stones from Newfoundland, presented by Mr Cormack to Professor Jameson, & by him to the Museum. 41. Pelisse of the daughter of the 'chief' of the Red Indians by Professor Jameson to the Museum." For illustrations see Plates 20.5a and b, 20.6, 20.7a and b and Plate 23.1.

7 "Sketches of savage life," 1836,321; this information was confirmed in correspondence with Maureen Barrie, National Museums of Scotland, Edinburgh, 1992; Busk (1876,230–3) described the two craniums: "The outline of the two skulls, starting from the vertex backwards, is very nearly alike in the two. The chief difference between them is the more upright forehead in the female skull."

8 Howley (1915,331) believed that this child was a boy approximately ten to twelve years old.

9 See chapter 21, Figs. 21.2a and b, Plate 21.2.

10 Howley (1915,331–2) mentions "a couple of bird's feet" and "several carved bone pieces"; Patterson (1892,156) records "several" bird's feet and "32 pieces of bone differently shaped."

11 Jerkic et al. (1995) estimated the age of the child at five to six years on account of dental eruption and the degree of skeletal ossification and fusion observed on X-ray. No pathology or external trauma was observed. Absence of Harris lines on the long-bones was interpreted to mean that either there was no nutritional or other health stress, or that there was continued stress, i.e., unrelieved poor nutrition that precluded the resumption of normal growth.

12 Whitehead 1987a,27.

13 John Maunder, Curator of Natural History, Newfoundland Museum, 1980s, pers. com.

14 Features of the child's burial on Big Island, Pilley's Tickle, and of the cemetery at Red Indian Lake were listed and used as baseline data. Scoring for over seventy separate items, a nucleus of Beothuk burial features was identified. They were then checked against information from other burials. If they matched listed features, the burials were provisionally considered Beothuk. This procedure is somewhat arbitrary but it provided a workable definition of diagnostic features of Beothuk burials. To be considered Beothuk, a burial had to be located in an area known to have been occupied by Beothuk, and all native artifacts had to be consistent with Beothuk technology. In addition, at least two of the following criteria had to be met: 1) presence of ochre in the soil, on skeletal remains, or on grave goods; 2) presence of carved bone pieces of the type generally associated with the Beothuk; 3) presence of grave goods of native origin clearly identified as Beothuk, such as carved game pieces, human representations, miniature Beothuk canoes, Beothuk-style moccasins, harpoon heads or birchbark vessels, iron pyrites, discoidal shell beads, perforated animal teeth, tusks, bird legs, or skulls; 4) location of the burial in a cave or rock shelter; 5) presence of a surrounding rock wall and a birchbark canopy or rock slabs as covering, or

close association with graves that were clearly Beothuk. With regard to the grave found on Musslebed Island, less than five hundred metres distant from the Comfort Cove cemetery, the physical anthropologist Jerkic concluded that there were enough physical resemblances between the skeletal remains from these two burial places to consider them of the same physical type. Evidence for the Beothuk origin of the burial at Charles Arm, recorded by Devereux, is marginal but was considered admissible because of the faint ochre stain on the skeletal bones and because it was located in an area that was much used by Beothuk.

15 This burial was located under an overhanging cliff. The skeletal remains had been covered with slabs of local rock; the bones were covered with a "reddish substance"; pieces of birchbark were mixed with the bones; there were also a few cylindrical beads, not otherwise recorded among Beothuk, see also chapter 24, section on different types of beads. Wintemberg, who believed that this burial was of Beothuk origin, surmised that it was less than a hundred years old on account of the excellent preservation of the birchbark; however, birchbark, when undisturbed, can preserve extremely well and cannot therefore serve as a tell-tale sign of the antiquity of a site; Howley (n.d., chapter 1886,19), for example, said that the Swan Island burial contained "a lot of bark and most of it was as sound as the day it was placed there."

16 Cormack 1829,323 (in Howley 1915,192); Howley 1915,288–9, 332.

17 Buchan to Hamilton, 10 March 1820, PRO, CO 194/63, f.64–77 (in Howley 1915,123); Cormack Papers 20/84 (in Howley 1915,228).

18 Cormack 1829,325 (in Howley 1915,194).

19 Remains from primary burials differ from secondary ones in that they have been placed into their final resting place directly after death, when soft tissue connects all or most of the skeleton, so that the bones remain in correct anatomical position; skeletal material from secondary burials that has been stored and transported is usually out of position and smaller bones are often missing. Secondary burials were also recorded: Thwaites 1959,5:129, Montagnais; Harper 1957,2, Micmac; Denys 1968,438–40, Micmac; LeClercq 1968,302, Micmac; Goddard 1978,219, Delaware; Feest 1978,245, Nanticoke and neighbouring tribes; Feest 1978,262, Virginia Algonquians; Callender 1978,626, Shawnee.

20 Cormack papers 13/84 (in Howley 1915,221); "Sketches of savage life," 1836,323.

21 Cormack Papers 32/84: Cormack's original note reads: "shavings" of "dogwood" and not "shrimps" of the "dogberry tree" as transcribed by Howley (1915, 230).

22 Signs of incision on the mummified child cannot be discerned, though the skin is torn around the abdomen and back in several places. Many North American tribes used preservation methods. Feest 1978,262, and 1978,279: Virginia and North Carolina Algonquians removed the flesh of the deceased; Feest 1978,245, Nanticoke; LeClercq (1968,302) described the preservation treatment used by Micmac and Denys (1968,439–40) said that the Micmac wrapped the body in birchbark and placed it on a scaffold for about a year to dry out; Wallis and Wallis (1955,260) recorded that Micmac preserved corpses by drying and smoking them.

23 Howley 1915,262, 333.

24 Carignan 1973,12.

25 Cormack 1829,324–5 (in Howley 1915,193–4); Howley 1915, 293, 331, 333; according to Hind (1973,1:170), Montagnais and Naskapi sometimes buried their dead in a sitting posture.
26 Cormack 1829,323–5 (in Howley 1915,192–4).
27 Cormack 1829,325 (in Howley 1915,194): Cormack's original note reads: "The deceased … was placed on a sort of scaffold about four feet and a half *from* the ground." Howley transcribed "on the ground."
28 Lloyd 1875,32–3. Use of scaffolds has also been recorded by Bock 1978,114, Micmac; Day 1978,156, Western Abenaki (until burial was possible); Feest 1978,245, Conoy; ibid., 262, Virginia Algonquians; Heidenreich 1978,375, Huron; White 1978,410, Neutral; Spindler 1978,717, Menominee.
29 Cormack 1829,325 (in Howley 1915,194).
30 LeClercq 1968,303, Micmac; Nelson 1971,314, Unalit Eskimo.
31 Buchan to Hamilton, 10 March 1819, PRO, CO 194/63, f.64–77 (in Howley 1915,123); Cormack Papers 20/84 (in Howley 1915,228). Turner 1979,108, Skinner 1911,167: this practice is also known among the Northern Naskapi and Saulteaux, who buried a distinguished hunter inside his tent.
32 Boyce 1978,285, Iroquois; Day and Trigger 1978,789, Algonquians.
33 Cormack 1829,325 (in Howley 1915,194); Howley 1915,214.
34 Anthropologist Anna Sawicki, 1980s, pers. com.
35 These structures are reminiscent of the "stone coffins" built by Inuit in western Greenland recorded by Kleivan 1984,614; McGhee 1984b, 372: Thule Eskimo in the Central Arctic often set rocks around the corpse.
36 "Discovery of the Red Indian Remains at Fogo," 1887,4.
37 MacLeod 1966, App II:11.
38 Marshall 1973; 1974b,8.
39 Howley 1915,293.
40 Ibid.; Jenness (1929,37) suggests that the presence of birchbark and thick sticks in a burial on Long Island, Bay of Exploits (List 1A, no.15), which contained the remains of a man, woman, and child, indicated that the grave was placed on the foundation of a wigwam; since this grave was located in a rock shelter, it is more likely that the debris stemmed from a canopy; Thwaites (1959,3:129–31) recorded that Micmac used arched sticks to prevent earth from falling onto the remains.
41 Howley n.d., chapter 1886,19.
42 Howley 1915,332.
43 LeClercq 1968,209, 212–14; Denys 1968,439–40: Micmac explained that the disrepair of a kettle in an old grave indicated that its spirit had abandoned it to be of use in the other world.
44 LeClercq (1968,217) recorded that the medicine bundle of one Micmac shaman contained miniature bow and arrows; according to Rand (1971,5, 70, 272, 321), in Micmac mythology miniature objects either represent the actual artifact or else metamorphose into the full-sized counterpart; Rasmussen 1929,199: Iglulik Eskimo buried their dead with full-sized as well as miniature implements and believed that the dead person's soul passed with those objects to the land of the dead.

45 Sagard-Théodat (1939,172), a Recollect missionary, recorded in 1632 that the Huron deliberately broke some of the grave goods so as to release their souls/spirits.
46 Day 1978,156, Western Abenaki; Spindler 1978,717, Menominee.
47 Adrian Tanner, 1993, pers. com.
48 The provenance of two harpoon heads mentioned by Jenness, (1929, Plate I) is not recorded.
49 See chapter 24, section on beads; only one string had beads made of sheet bad.
50 Dawson (1860,462), who recorded that the burial at Rencontre was discovered by the prospector Smith McKay, listed only shell beads; some of these grave goods, illustrated in Dawson 1880, Fig.5, are now in the McCord Museum (Fig.24.2). Patterson (1892,157) and Howley (1915,330) claim that the grave had been found by the Reverend Mr Blackmore in 1847 and listed glass beads among the grave goods.
51 Wintemberg 1936,25.
52 Day and Trigger 1978,796; Champlain 1971,4:178.
53 Howley (1915, Plate XXXV) identified the bird skulls as those from the "Common Arctic Tern (*Sterna hirunda*)," (probably meaning northern common tern); John Maunder, curator of Natural History in the Newfoundland Museum, has identified the single bird foot that is still attached to the burial shroud of a Beothuk child as southern black guillemot (1980s, pers. com.).
54 For details see chapter 24, section on carved bone pieces.
55 Cormack 1829,325.
56 Denys 1968,439–40.

CHAPTER TWENTY-SIX

1 Thevet 1568,136; Lieut. John Cartwright, "Remarks on the situation of the Red Indians … 1768," PRRL, 971.8 C24 (in Howley 1915,29, 33); Cartwright 1792,1:12 (in Howley 1915,49); Howley 1915,99, 271; for details see chapter 20, section on bows, arrows, and quivers.
2 Lysaght 1971,132–3.
3 Quinn 1981,13.
4 Howley 1915,100; Cormack Papers 30/84: the note on "Beothuck Arms" did not include the word "clubs"; Howley (1915,212) in his transcript appears to have inserted it.
5 Howley 1915,93, 99; a dirk is a kind of dagger.
6 De Brouillon, Governor of Placentia, 25 October 1694, NAC, MG 1, Archives de Colonies, Série C"C, vol.2, f.20; Cell 1982,194; Account of the State of the Fishery in Newfoundland by Commander Percy, 13 October 1720, PRO, CO 194/7, f.7.
7 Quinn 1979,3:370, doc.464, recorded by Rosier (1603); Binford 1967,133; Quinn 1979,4:344, doc.694, Champlain; 62, doc.558; Morice (1905,62) reports a similar reaction from the Carrier Athapaskans.
8 Capt. David Buchan's report on his second expedition to Red Indian Lake to Governor Hamilton, 10 March 1820, PRO, CO 194/63, f.64–77 (in Howley 1915,121).

9 Howley 1915,93; see also chapter 5, section on factors that prevented the establishment of a regular fur trade.
10 Thwaites 1959,5:95; Champlain 1971,44, Plate III; Wallis and Wallis 1955,33; Biggar 1930,460–4.
11 Cell 1982,70, 72, 194 COED 1979:2:3237:93.
12 "Sketches of savage life," 1836,321.
13 Marshall 1989,122.
14 Martijn 1981a, 315; Marshall 1988b, 50.
15 Quinn 1981,61; Thwaites 1959,1:279; Champlain 1971,4:168.
16 Thevet 1568,133–6; Stefansson (1938,2:14–23) describes a similar custom among Inuit in Frobisher Bay.
17 Quinn 1981,33–4; Thevet 1568,133–6.
18 Cartwright, "Remarks ... 1768," PRRL, 971.8 C24 (in Howley 1915,35).
19 Brouage, 6 September 1719, NAC, MG 1, Archives des Colonies, Série C"A Correspondance générale, Canada, vol.109, f.155–174 (transcript).
20 Harisse 1900,153–4.
21 Howley 1915,152.
22 Cormack Papers 12/84; Jukes 1969,2:126, 129–30; Bishop John Inglis, Diary, 2 July 1827, NAC, microfilm A 713; "Sketches of savage life," 1836,316–17, 322–3; see also chapter 3, section on Micmac traditions about relations with Beothuk.
23 Jukes 1969,1:151, 172; Howley 1915,26, 183, 270.
24 Inglis, Diary, 2 July 1827, NAC, microfilm A 713.
25 "Sketches of savage life," 1836,322–3.
26 COED: a pinnace is defined as a small, light vessel, generally two-masted and schooner-rigged, often in attendance of a larger vessel as a tender; or a double-banked boat (usually eight-oared.)
27 Quinn 1979,4:64, doc.560.
28 Howley 1915,105, 106; Marshall 1989,123, 132, 133, 138, 139; author Gary Saunders, who has collected traditions about the Beothuk in Bonavista Bay, was told that on one occasion the Beothuk cut every boat from their moorings in an island community, leaving the fishermen stranded (1980s, pers. com.).
29 Howley 1915,96; Marshall 1989,122, 128.
30 Howley 1915,92, 106.
31 Marshall 1989,121–2.
32 Howley 1915,268, 270, 273, 274; Marshall 1989,121, 130, 138, 140.
33 Howley 1915,27.
34 Ibid., 268, 269; Marshall 1989,122–4, 127, 128, 130, 134, 136–8.
35 Howley 1915,273.
36 Millais 1907,27.
37 "Sketches of savage life," 1836,322.
38 Ibid. The underlining is mine. For *munes*, see note 19, chapter 24.
39 Cell 1982,73, 84, 85.
40 Howley 1915,27; Peyton 1987,7.

41 Lieut. David Buchan's report of his expedition to Red Indian Lake, 1811, PRO, CO 194/50, f.153–88 (in Howley 1915,77); Marshall 1989,135–6; Howley 1915,99.
42 Howley 1915, 99.
43 Cell 1982,74, 85; Henry Crout to Sir Percival Willoughby, August 1613, MMss, Mix 1/24 (Appendix 1).
44 Cell 1982,75; Howley 1915,99; Buchan to Governor Duckworth, 2 August 1810, NAC, Duckworth Papers, MG 24 A 45, f.4644–9.
45 Inglis, Diary, 3 July 1827, USPG, C/Can/N.S.9, doc. 57–8 (in Howley 1915,296).
46 Howley 1915,180; Buckland 1876,440, cited in Podolinski Webber 1986,153.
47 Howley 1915,27.
48 Ibid.,267, 268, 273, 281.
49 Speck 1922,53.
50 Howley 1915,280.
51 Friederici 1906,171.
52 Purchas 1906,18:193, quoting Champlain; Lescarbot 1928,314–15: Poutrincourt observed victorious Etchemin warriors in Passaquamoddy Bay who danced with three heads of dead enemies prior to burying one of their own men (Etchemin were Maliseet-Passaquamoddy).
53 Cormack Papers 12/84; Inglis, Diary, 2 July 1827, NAC, microfilm A 713; Jukes 1969,2:129; "Sketches of savage life," 1836,317, 323.
54 Friederici 1906,16–18; Axtell 1981, 30–1.
55 Friederici (1906,22) described an incident that illustrates the gradual changeover from one practice to the other: a party of native people near the Caddo River returned from a victorious expedition; the men only brought scalps while the women, used to carrying heavy loads, bore entire heads.
56 Axtell 1981,28, 213–14.
57 Thevet 1568,136.
58 Lysaght 1971,133.
59 Arber 1971,344–5; Howley 1915,11–12: the text on the map of Terra Nova published in 1547–48 by Mattioli is thought to be based on Sebastian Cabot's reports; Quinn 1981,34.
60 Cormack 1824,161.
61 Sturtevant 1980,48; Quinn 1981,38–9; Kupp and Hart 1976,8; Skinner 1911,79; Quinn 1981,61; Bailey 1969,55; LeClercq 1968,113, 220; Speck 1977,37, 38; McClellan and Denniston (1981,377) report that among the Kaska, Tahltan, Han, and Kutchin in western Canada, warriors ritually ate parts of their slain enemies.

CHAPTER TWENTY-SEVEN

1 Hewson 1978,135.
2 Henry Crout to Sir Percival Willoughby, August 1613, MMss, Mix 1/24 (App.1).
3 Governor Hugh Palliser to the Earl of Hillsborough, 20 October 1768, PRO, CO 194/28, f.26.

4 James Dobie, surgeon on *HMS Egeria*, to Sir G. Cockburn, 10 September 1823, PRO, CO 194/66, f.326b.
5 Lieut. David Buchan's report of his expedition to Red Indian Lake, 1811, PRO, CO 194/50, f.153–88 (in Howley 1915,77).
6 Ibid. (in Howley 1915,89).
7 Howley 1915, vi, 182.
8 Cormack Papers 28/84, 29/84 (in Howley 1915,213).
9 Marshall 1989,128; John Bland to J.P. Rance, Gov. Secretary, 1 September 1797, PRO, CO 194/39, f.218–21 (in Howley 1915,54, the year 1790 is incorrect); John Clinch to the SPG, 5 December 1793, USPG, Minutes 1792–95, vol.26, f.208.
10 Marshall 1989,139.
11 Ibid.,27–31, 132.
12 Ibid.,141–3; for a full account and facsimile of Pulling's report and wordlist see ibid.,62–143.
13 Davies 1970,960; transcription of Pulling's preliminary report, PRO, CO 194/39, f.221b-229.
14 G.C. Jenner to Waldegrave, 28 September 1797, PANL, CSOC, GN 2/1/A, vol.13, f.298.
15 September 1800, PANL, CSOC, GN 2/1/A, vol.15, f.433–4.
16 "The Reverend John Clinch of Trinity Vocabulary," 1888, and Patterson 1893,19: both versions include numerous misspellings.
17 Gatschet 1890; Hewson 1978,15–21, 25–9; in his amalgamated Beothuk vocabulary (pp. 149–67) Hewson included the Clinch rather than the Pulling version.
18 Howley 1915,91–108; Cormack Papers 37/84: in a note Cormack spelled the name *Demasduit*; Cormack Papers 20/84 (in Howley 1915,227): in his draft of a history of the Beothuk, Cormack spelled the name *Demasdoweet*; see also Beothuk Namefile, App.3.
19 Robinson 1834,216 (in Howley 1915,128).
20 Lloyd 1875,37; Cormack Papers 6/84 contains an equipment list for his expedition in 1827 that included a vocabulary; Cormack 1829,327 (in Howley 1915,196) mentions in his report of the expedition that he obtained a Beothuk vocabulary of two to three hundred words.
21 Lloyd 1875,37–9; Hatton and Harvey 1883,218–21; Gatschet 1885,415–24; Patterson 1893,20–6; "Beothic Vocabulary," 29 July 1950, 3; Hewson (1978,36–8) has traced the publications of the Leigh vocabulary as described here.
22 Rev. John Leigh to the SPG, 30 July 1819, USPG, Minutes of the SPG, 1819–20, vol.32,141–3; this entry proves that the SPG received the vocabulary.
23 Robinson 1834,218–20; the handwritten original is entitled "Vocabulary of the Language of the Natives of Newfoundland procured by the Rev. J. Leigh from Mary March, a Native Woman taken up the Exploits by Mr Peyton in March 1818" (the date should be 1819), BL, Add. Mss. 19350; Hewson 1978,38–53, 74–9.
24 Leigh to the SPG, 4 November 1819, USPG, Minutes of the SPG, 1819–20, vol.32,172.

25 Robinson's "History of Mary March – Waunathoake (her native name)," BL, Add. Ms. 19350 (in Howley 1915,127–9); Howley 1915,103.
26 Rev. John Leigh's Vocabulary, PANL, MG 257, donated to the PANL by Mr F. Lunnen of Twillingate in 1957. The title page suggests that it is a copy of the vocabulary that was sent to the SPG, which included words from the Oubee list. Presumably Leigh added these words in August 1819, when visiting Rev. John Clinch in Trinity, and dispatched his letter dated July 30 after this visit.
27 Hewson 1978,38–53, 57–73.
28 Rev. John Pickavant to the Wesleyan Society in London, cited in Smith 1986,129.
29 Illegible or missing syllables are indicated by [].“One. Yath-thee. – Two. O-de-sike. – Three. Sin-dic. – Four. Ta[]. – Five. Nene-ic. – Six. Besh-re-dic. – Seven. Oth-ro-dice. – Eight. An-de-zu[]. Nine. Ya-tho-dutt. – Ten. Dun-now. – Boy. Bo-she-mish. – Girl. Emom[]. – Fire. Wood-rith. – Dog. Mo-me-smitt."
30 For the different spellings of Beothuk names see Beothuk Namefile, Appendix 3.
31 Cormack Papers 6/84; Cormack 1829,327 (in Howley 1915,196).
32 Hewson 1978,36; R.G. Latham to J.P. Howley, 25 December 1882, Howley Papers.
33 Resolution at the meeting of the Boeothick Institution, St John's, 12 January 1828, cited in Howley 1915,197; John Stark to Cormack, 16 September 1828, Cormack Papers 70/84–6 (in Howley 1915,203).
34 In his letters to the Bishop of Nova Scotia, 26 October 1828, Cormack Papers 62/84 (in Howley 1915,209), and to John Peyton, Jr, 28 October 1828, PRRL, 917.18 C81 NRV, Cormack wrote that Shanawdithit was to leave him in a week or two to live with Mr Simms; McGregor 1832,1:276 stated that Shanawdithit had lived with Mr Cormack until he left Newfoundland in January 1829.
35 Cormack Papers 20/84, (Howley 1915:225.)
36 Minutes of the Natural History Society of Montreal, 23 February 1829, BWL.
37 Avalonus 1862,1.
38 Cormack Papers 47/84 (in Howley 1915,230–1).
39 DNB 1920–21,16:121: James Yates "went to Edinburgh University (1810), and thence to Glasgow University (1811)"; Addison 1913,8281: "1811 Glasgow University, Guliemus [William] Cormack f.n.max. Alexandri [eldest son of Alexander Cormack]."
40 DNB 1920–21,11:152, Richard King; Latham 1850,330.
41 R.G. Latham to J.P. Howley, 25 December 1882, Howley Papers; the sets sent to Gatschet and the Bureau of American Ethnology are now in the Archive of the Smithsonian Institution; it is not known where Latham deposited the original.
42 Hewson 1978,122–4, Ms. 881; 127–9, Ms. 1449, part I; 125–6, Ms. 881; 130–1, Ms. 1449, part II.
43 Hewson 1978,106, 126, 131.
44 Latham to Howley, 25 December 1882, Howley Papers: "Then there is on the (very dirty cover): 1) I gave Dr M. Vin? 56 by words by Mr Wilson [possibly Prof. Andrew Wilson LLD., FRGS. University of Toronto, mentioned in Howley 1915,298], 2) D V

[?] Dmatry[?] m = nt to m,n H.S. July 1830"; Latham added: "Make what you can of this." These notes have not been decoded.

45 Cormack Papers 28/84 (in Howley 1915,213).

46 Cormack Papers 28/84.

47 Hewson (1978,117–20, Ms. 1449) published a facsimile of Howley's list as sent to Gatschet. Gatschet (1890,424) mentions "The subject of a Beothuck song."

48 Gatschet 1885,414. Cormack noted on the back of Shanawdithit's sketch 10: "months of the year of the Red Indians, 13 moons"; the names for every month of the year are written underneath, there are only twelve names and those for April, June, and September are the same; to quote: "1 Nov. goda bon *yeesh*, 2 Dec. Odasweet *ee* shamut, 3 Jan. cob shun *ee* samut, 4 Feb. Thos tha Bo*nong* Be wa jo wite, 5 March Ma na miss, (7 summer months) 6 April Wa*sum* a wee *seek*, 7 May Be de ja*mish* = Be ja jo wite, 8 June Wasum a wee seek, [9 July goda ben yea crossed out], 9 [10 Aug. crossed out] July Cow a ya *seek*, 11 Sept. Wa sum a wee seek, 10 Aug. Wa da whegh, a summer month 12 or 13 Goda bon yegh" (all are included in Hewson 1978,167). A note in the Cormack Papers 37/84 reads: "6 months winter & 6 months summer."

49 Howley 1915,301; Gatschet 1890,8; Hewson 1978,101–2.

50 Hewson (1978,101) believed that it was a garbled copy of Howley's list sent to Sir Wm. Dawson; Hewson (1978,102–4) transcribed only those terms that he ascribed to Cormack to which he added Beothuk words from Howley 1915,230, 246, 248, 249. This list could be extended by three names for mythological emblems that Cormack did not translate: *Boegh-woodje-be-chuck*, *Ash-wa-meet*, and *Ash-u-meet*, cited in Howley 1915,249.

51 Hewson 1978,102–13.

52 Hewson 1978,149–67; there may be two additional words: Lescarbot (1968,28) records two words from Cartier (1534), which may have been Beothuk terms for species of birds that his crew collected on Funk Island – *apponath*, for great auk, and *godeth*, for murre or razor bill (Whitehead, 1980s, pers. com.).

53 Speck 1922,66–7: *be'nam* – woman; *gu'wa* – fat person; *gau* – rain; *hag* – baby cradle or cradle board; *tub* – baby blanket; *se'ko* – prayer; *si kane's u* – whale; Hewson does not believe that these terms are Beothuk.

54 Speck 1922,67, 68.

55 It was tracked down by George Draskoy of Parks Canada, St John's, who had a copy of it made for use at Memorial University of Newfoundland; John Hewson, research professor in the Department of Linguistics, Memorial University of Newfoundland, has a copy of the song on tape.

56 Cormack Papers 29/84. The note reads: "*Red Indian Song* Subject of: "basn Bath staonosheen Babashet Sierhodabanyish Edabanser boradooosh – Edabanseek."

57 Cell 1982,73, 83, 109, 117, 152; Howley 1915,28, 55, 63, 72, 91 fn.1, 93, 174; Lieut. John Cartwright, "Remarks on the situation of the Red Indians … 1768," PRRL, 971.8 C24 (in Howley 1915,29–41); Lieut. David Buchan's report of his expedition to Red Indian Lake, 1811, PRO, CO 194/50, f.153–88 (in Howley 1915,72–90);

George Cartwright, 1784 Memo to the Colonial Office, PRO, CO 194/35, f.338; Marshall 1989,120–40.

58 Inglis, Diary, 2 July 1827, NAC, microfilm A 713; in the diary sent to the SPG, Inglis refers to the newly founded Boeothick Institution and records more details about the "Boeothick" (USPG, C/Can/N.S.9, doc.57–8; see also Beothuk Namefile, App.3).

59 Cormack Papers 48,49/84 (in Howley 1915,184).

60 Cormack to Peyton, Exploits 27 November (should be October) 1827, transcript in Howley Papers.

61 Cormack 1829,318, 328 (in Howley 1915,189, 196); Howley 1915,198, 199.

62 Cormack to Stark, 24 December 1827, Cormack Papers 58/84 (in Howley 1915,198).

63 Hewson 1978,117, Ms.1449: boeothuc; 118, Ms.1449: beathook; 122,123, Ms.881: beothuck; 125, Ms.881: beothick; 127, Ms.1449: behathook; 131, Ms.1449: beothuk.

64 John Hewson, 1993, pers. com.; Hewson 1978, vii: the spelling Beothuk is used throughout this study; In *The Beothucks or Red Indians*, Howley used Beothuck and Beothucks.

65 Hewson 1968,13–16.

66 According to Gatschet (1885,410), the term "Beothuk" means "red Indian," as recorded by Leigh and Cormack, but also comprises the word *haddabothic*– body – and was the Beothuk's generic expression for Indians. Just as many native groups refer to themselves with the term "the people," Gatschet suggested the Beothuk did the same; Latham, as recorded by Lloyd 1875,229, thought that the tribe should be named the "Good Night Indians," *betheok* being the term for "good night" in the Demasduit vocabulary as published by Lloyd. Hewson (1968,13) states that in the original manuscript this term reads *betheoate*, a form of the verb *baetha*, "to go home," and thus the real meaning of this term would be "I am now going home."

67 Quinn 1981,27.

68 Speck 1922,59, 79.

69 Perhaps the first person to investigate the Beothuk language was David Macpherson. In the *Annals of Commerce, Manufacture, Fisheries and Navigation* ..., vol.1, 1805,280, he suggests that the interior natives (as opposed to the coastal Esquimaux) may be the remains of the Icelandic (Norse) colony. To determine whether this was the case, Macpherson thought that a qualified person could compare their language to Norwegian and said, "Such an inquiry I have myself set on foot, but hitherto without success." Presumably he was unable to find a qualified person, or had hoped to investigate the language by conversing with some of the natives, only to find that they lived in seclusion away from English settlements. Though the Oubee vocabulary collected by Pulling would have been available, Macpherson was probably unaware of its existence. The reference to David Macpherson's work comes from Alan Macpherson, Memorial University of Newfoundland, Dept. of Geography.

70 Gatschet 1886,417–27.

71 Brinton 1970,67–8.

72 Latham 1850,330; Powell 1891,57; Campbell 1893,2:26–30.

73 Cited in Hewson 1978,139.

74 Quoted in Gatschet 1886,424; Fiedel (1991,9–32) and Shevoroshkin (1990,24) suggest that Dene (Athapaskan) and Algonquian belong to the same phylum.

75 Cited in Howley 1915,313.

76 Dawson 1880,19–20, 48–9; Sir William Dawson to J.P. Howley, 18 July 1880, Howley Papers, states that he had not as yet seen a word of the Beothuk language.

77 Sapir 1949,171; Greenberg 1953,283; Gursky 1964,4.

78 Voegelin and Voegelin 1946, and 1963,82, cited in Hewson 1978,139.

79 Gursky 1964,4.

80 In Goddard 1979,106–7.

81 In Goddard 1978,70, 77.

82 Hewson 1978,149–67.

83 For details about Algonquian phonology, voicing, and grammar see Hewson 1978,140–4; 1982,183–4.

84 Hewson (1978,144) states that the conjunct order is normally used for subordinate or imbedded verbs – it translates English participles and subordinate clauses, for example – and in most Algonquian languages the normal form for main clauses is the so-called independent order, which is plainly distinguished from the conjunct order by the use of personal prefixes. It is not unusual for the participial forms of the verb to supplant, in linguistic evolution, the normal independent forms of the verb. For instance Micmac has lost the old independent indicative, replacing it completely with conjunct forms; a development of this kind has taken place independently in Arapaho.

85 Hewson 1978,146; 1982,183–4.

86 Goddard 1978,586; Fiedel (1991,26) sees the northern Plateau region as the possible home of the Proto-Algic language, which he considers to be the common ancestor of Ritwans and Algonquians.

87 Goddard 1978,70; 583–7.

CHAPTER TWENTY-EIGHT

1 Gatschet 1886; Brinton 1891.

2 Noad 1859, 3; Horwood 1959, Pt.2; Avalonis 1862, Pt.2.

3 Hewson 1978, 146.

4 Chute 1976, 367–9.

5 James A. Tuck, chairman of the Archaeology Unit at Memorial University, 1995, pers. com., and Tuck 1992, 14–16; Robbins 1989, 23; Loring 1992, 451.

6 Regrettably, Saunders (1988, 277) in the *Handbook of North American Indians*, vol.4, devotes a single sentence to Beothuk/English relations: "The Beothuk Indian population of Newfoundland had been slaughtered by British settlers in the eighteenth and nineteenth centuries."

7 Tuck and Pastore 1985.

8 Upton 1977, 153; Pastore 1987.

9 Ibid.

10 Marshall 1992, 138–49.

11 Ibid.; Dobyn 1983, 15, Table I.

12 Dobyn (1983, 17, Table II) lists a measles epidemic among the Naskapi in 1633–34. Kleivan 1966, 146; Bishop John Inglis (Diary, 30 June 1827, USPG, C/can/NS9, doc.57–8) describes his arrival at Twillingate on his tour around Newfoundland: "We found at least half of the inhabitants here confined with Measles, and those who have escaped are afraid to venture from their homes lest they should take the infection."

13 Marshall 1992, 145–7; Wherrett 1977, 98; Moore 1961, 1,012–14.

14 Lieut. David Buchan's report, 1811, PRO, CO 194/50, f.153–88, (in Howley 1915, 87–8); Dr William Carson, MD, Answers to questions ... 1830, attached to letter by Viscount Goderich, 7 February 1831, PRO, CO 194/81, f.59a; Buchan had suggested that the Beothuk's good health could have resulted from the continuous exercise involved in the process of procuring food. Cormack, who was familiar with this way of life as practised by Micmac, denied that a hunting existence was conducive to good health (Howley 1915, 153): "Most Indians [Micmac] when they would otherwise be in the prime of life, have broken constitutions by over-exertions, casualties, and exposure to weather. Their perilous mode of life also leads them to be more subject to some kinds of bodily infirmities than men in more dense societies."

15 Cormack Papers 20/84 (in Howley 1915, 226–9).

16 Carson, Answers to Questions ..., 1830, PRO, CO 194/81, f.59a; John Peyton, Jr, to P.C. Legeyt, Secretary, 18 June 1823, PRO, CO 194/66, f.68–9 (in Howley 1915, 170).

17 Cormack Papers 20/84 (in Howley 1915, 226–9); see also chapter 6, section on information on the Beothuk, and chapter 14, Shanawdithit's story of her people.

18 Horwood 1959; Winter 1975, 7–8.

19 Moores 1986, 18–19; "Beothuck Memorial Update," 3 January 1987, 18.

20 Mooney 1928, 2–6: in Maryland, Virginia, and North and South Carolina (except Cherokee country), of thirty-five tribes, twenty, counting 21,400 members, had become extinct during the same period; others were decimated. Some of the "tribes" Mooney listed may represent bands or villages that were referred to by the names of the place where they lived; Salwen 1978, 169–74; Conkey et al. 1978, 178.

21 According to Ubelaker (1988, 289–91), Mooney's figure for the North American indigenous population of 1,150,000 (in ca. AD 1600) is close to estimates for an early historic native population by Rivet (1924), Wilcox (1931), Rosenblat (1945), and Steward (1945, 1948) but falls short of Sapper's estimate (1924) of 2,000,000 to 3,500,000 and that given by Dobyn of 9,800,000 (1966) – all cited in Ubelaker 1988. Mooney's estimate was the only one that was based on a tribe-by-tribe approach; the others relied on various projection techniques, utilizing generalized assumptions about human adaptation and depopulation. Dobyn's work in particular has indicated to many that the estimates should be revised upwards. Ubelaker, using his own estimates and those given in the new *Handbook of North American Indians* (1978–86), has calculated larger populations than Mooney; according to Ubelaker the population in the Northeast was reduced by seventy-three percent, the highest rate occurring between AD 1600 and 1700. Ubelaker also investigated Mooney's original notes and found that he sometimes deliberately reduced the figures that were suggested by

available documents, but he has not found fault with Mooney's listing of tribal groups (Ubelaker 1976).

APPENDIX THREE

1 Hewson 1978,44.
2 Bishop John Inglis, Diary, 1827, NAC, microfilm A 713. He sent a copy of this diary to the SPG, USPG, C/Can/N.S.9, doc.57–8.
3 Cormack papers 70/84 (in Howley 1915,206–9).
4 Cormack Papers 12/84.
5 Cormack Papers 48/84, 49/84; Howley 1915,184. Reference to the Cormack Papers and Howley 1915 are given separately in this appendix; although the text is alike, Howley has not always transcribed the spelling of names as given in Cormack's notes and correspondence so that both sources have to be considered.
6 "Boeothick Institution." *Royal Gazette*, 13 November 1827, Howley 1915, 182–4.
7 Cormack 1829,318, 320, 322, 328; Howley 1915, 189–97.
8 Cormack Papers 20/84; Howley 1915,225.
9 Cormack Papers 58/84, 59/84, 61/84, 63/84; Howley 1915,197–200.
10 Cormack Papers 58/84, 70/84; Howley 1915,198, 200–1.
11 Hewson 1978, Mss.881:122, 123, 125; Mss.1449: 117, 118, 127, 131.
12 McGregor 1832,1:254–78; "Sketches of savage life," 1836,322–3.
13 John Hewson, 1993, pers. com.
14 Quinn 1981,27.
15 Speck 1922,59; John Hewson, 1993, pers. com.
16 Cormack Papers 29/84.
17 Cormack Papers 20/84; Howley 1915,227, 228.
18 Noad 1859,21 (in Howley 1915,103).
19 Howley 1915,91, opp.91, 103, 239, 259, 299.
20 Hewson 1978,6, 33, 35, 54, 145, 171; John Hewson, 1980s, pers. com.
21 Howley 1915,283.
22 Hercules Robinson, "History of Mary March – Waunathoake (her native name) …," 1820, BL, Add. Ms.19350; Robinson published a shortened version in 1834 (in Howley 1915,127–9).
23 Robinson 1834,215 (in Howley 1915,127); Howley 1915,91, 103, 127.
24 Governor's Secretary to Rev. John Leigh, 3 June 1819, PANL, CSOC, GN 2/1/A, vol.30, f.162 (in Howley 1915,112).
25 Hewson 1978,106, 126.
26 Howley 1915,180, 181.
27 Hewson 1978,106, 131.
28 Cormack Papers 29/84.
29 Cormack Papers 20/84; Howley 1915,227.
30 Noad 1859,21; Howley 1915,261; Hewson 1978,145.
31 Marshall 1989,114, 128.
32 Cormack Papers 9/84, 20/84, 35/84.

33 Howley 1915,184, 186, 191, 196, 197, 201, 208, 209, 210, 213, 215, 224; 186 fn.1.
34 Howley 1915,225–9.
35 Cormack Papers 57/84, 62/84; Howley 1915, 208, 210.
36 Hewson 1978,126.
37 Inglis, Diary, 1827, NAC, microfilm A 713; ibid., USPG, C/Can/NS9, doc.57–8.
38 Cormack Papers 72/84; Howley 1915,206–9.
39 Cormack Papers 70/84; Howley 1915,201–3.
40 Parish Register 1829, entry Oct.23, Fredric H. Carrington A.B. Rector, St John's, copy in Howley Papers; Howley 1915,231, 231 fn.
41 Noad 1859,33, 34, 35, 36; Howley 1915,221.
42 Howley 1915; viii, 96, 101, 103, 173 fn.1, 174–6, 220 fn.1, 221 fn.1, 229 fn.1, 238, 239, 240, 243, 244, 245, 247, 250, 251, 252, 270, 271, 295, 300, 340, 342, 343.
43 Howley 1915,96, 172, 254, 256, 260, 261, 287, 295–7, 303.
44 McGregor 1832,1:276; "Sketches of savage life," 1836,322.
45 Winter 1975.
46 Howley 1915, vi, 180, 181.
47 Speck 1922,58, 64.
48 Ruth Holmes-Whitehead (1991, pers. com.). Speck 1922,58.
49 Howley 1915,181.
50 Marshall 1989,140, 154.
51 Lieut. John Cartwright to Governor Hugh Palliser, 19 September 1768, PRRL, 971.8 C24 (in Howley 1915,43, 44); John Bland to Governor Waldegrave, 20 October 1797, PANL, CSOC, GN 2/1/A, vol.14, f.90–4 (in Howley 1915,59); Avalonus (pen-name of Wm. Sweetland, Magistrate at Bonavista) 1862,1 (in Howley 1915,288); Howley 1915, 54, 58 fn.1, 273.
52 Marshall 1989,140, 154; Lieut. John Cartwright, "Remarks on the situation of the Red Indians … 1768," PRRL, 971.8 C24 (in Howley 1915,34, 35).
53 Bland to Waldegrave, 20 October 1797, PANL, CSOC, GN 2/1/A, vol.14, f.90–4 (in Howley 1915,59); Avalonus 1862,1 (in Howley 1915,288).
54 Cuff 1966,25: Informant Mrs White, Stephenville, descendant of Gabriel.

Bibliography

DOCUMENT COLLECTIONS

Great Britain

PUBLIC RECORD OFFICE (PRO)

CO 194. Newfoundland, original correspondence, 1696 onwards, eighty volumes up to 1830. This series includes despatches and their enclosures sent to the Board of Trade and to the secretary of state from the governors of Newfoundland. They are the basic primary manuscript sources used for this study.

CO 195. Newfoundland, original correspondence, partly duplicating the above series with some additional material. Selected volumes were searched.

CO 1. Colonial Papers, General Series. References to Newfoundland are scattered through these papers. Material from volumes 10, 38, 47, and 55 has been used.

CO 5. Correspondence of Secretary of State and the Board of Trade, America and the West Indies, volume 912.

CO 199. Newfoundland Miscellany (some of it duplicates CO 1). Volume 63.

CO 324. Entry Books, Series 1, 1662–1872, of commissions, instructions, petitions, grants etc. Volume 33.

PC 1. Privy Council Papers, vols. 16, 52.

PC 5. Privy Council Papers, vols. 9, 12, 14.

Admiralty Papers

ADM 1. vol. 470, John Byron correspondence, 1770.
vol.3062, Admiralty Office, 1793.

ADM 9. vol. 2, G.C. Pulling's service record, 1800s.

ADM 36. vol.10276, Muster roll of *HMS Thisbe*, 1785.

ADM 50. vol.2, Log of *HMS Antelope*, 1769.
vol.19, Hugh Palliser's Journal, 1767.
vol.48, John Holloway correspondence, 1807.

ADM 51. Captain's Logs
vol.4210, Log of *HMS Guernsey*, Captain Chad, 1767–68.
vol. 988, Log of *HMS Thisbe*, Captain Robertson, 1785.
vol.2654, Log of *HMS Pike*, Capt. David Buchan, 1816.
vol.3193, Log of *HMS Grasshopper*, Capt. David Buchan, 1819.
vol.3332, Log of *HMS Orestes*, Capt. Will. Jones, 1826–27.
ADM 53. Ship's Logs, similar to ADM 51
vol. 940, Log of *HMS Orestes*, Capt. Will. Jones, 1826–27.
ADM 80. vol.121, John Byron correspondence, 1769.
vol.122, John Duckworth correspondence, 1810.
vol.125, Charles Hamilton correspondence, 1819.
vol.126, Charles Hamilton correspondence, 1819.

War Office Records
WO 1 Volume 15

Map Collection
MPG.589. CO 194/50. Lieut. David Buchan's "Sketch of the River Exploits as explor'd in Jan.y and March 1811, Newfoundland."

BRITISH LIBRARY (BL), MANUSCRIPT DEPARTMENT

Document Collection
Egerton Mss. 2395, f.471, Testification by John Mathewes, 1670.
Sloane Mss. 2902, f.197–202, Papers of Abraham Hill, Commissioner of Trade and Plantations, 1698.
ADD.MS. 15493, f.26–8, D. Gardner's report on Newfoundland, 1784–85.
ADD.MS. 19350, Hercules Robinson, "History of Mary March – Waunathoake …," 1820.
ADD.MS. 33030, Newcastle Papers, vol.CCCXLV, f.220. Proposals for Encouraging the Fisheries in Labrador, 1766.
ADD.MS. 38257, f.288, Liverpool Papers. Waldegrave to Liverpool, 1814.
ADD.MS. 38347, f.348–9, Liverpool Papers. Proposal [by G.C. Pulling, 1786.]
ADD.MS. 38351, f.338–41, Liverpool Papers. Reeves to Dundas, "State of the Wild Indians in the Interior Parts of Newfoundland," 1792.
ADD.MS. 38352, f.18–47, Liverpool Papers. "A few facts by G.C. Pulling respecting the native Indians of the Isle of newfoundland, anno Domini 1792."
Ibid. f.48–9, Pulling to Reeves, 1792–93.

Map Collection
MS. Map No. 69917(59), "A General Map of the Northern British Colonies …," Major Holland, 1776.
MSS. 51222, ADD. 57703f.1 and 57703f.2. "Capt. David Buchan's Track into the Interior of Newfoundland, 1820."

National Maritime Museum (NMM)
LBK/12. Letter Book, *HMS Drake*, 1732.
GRV/105. Graves Papers, 1763.
DUF/13. Duff Letter Books, 1775.
RUSI/MN, ER/2/2, Log of *HMS Salisbury*, 1786–88.
N/W/1. Log of *HMS Winchelsea*, 1787.
DUC/7, DUC/16. Duckworth Papers, 1810, 1812.

Archive of the United Society for the Propagation of the Gospel in Foreign Parts (formerly SPG)
Collection of letters from missionaries in Newfoundland to the secretaries of the society in London.
C/Can/NF 3, doc.239. Rev. John Leigh, 1817.
C/Can/NF 3, doc.367. Rev. Thomas G. Langharne, 1822.
C/Can/NF 3, doc.107. Rev. John Chapman, 1826.
C/Can/NF 4, doc.252. Rev. John Chapman, 1827.
C/Can/N.S.9, doc.57–8. Bishop John Inglis, Diary, 1827.
X 148. Secretaries Letter Book, 1814–25.
Minutes of the General Meetings of the Society (SPG)
vol.18 (1768–71), vol.26 (1793), vol.30 (1810–11),
vol.32 (1819–20), vol.37 (1826–27).

Archive of the Methodist Missionary Society (MMS: LR), School of African and Oriental Studies, University of London.
Collection of letters from missionaries in Newfoundland to the secretaries of the Wesleyan Society in London.
North America, Newfoundland:
1805–16 Box 1, file 1d, no. 4. John Remmington, 1810.
Box 1, file 1d, no.33. Samson Busby, 1816.
1819–20 Box 2, file 2d, no. 5. John Lewis, 1819.
Box 2, file 2d, no.10. John Pickavant, 1819.
1823–24 Box 4, file 4f, no.14. William Wilson, 1823.
1841–42 Box 102, file 12g, no.23. John S. Addy, 1841.
Methodist Magazine, vol.33 (1810), vol.34 (1811).

Lambeth Palace Library (LPL)
Ms. No. 250, f.406–12, John Guy's *Journal*, 1612.
Fulham Papers. Letters from Newfoundland, vol. I-XVII.

Ministry of Defence, Hydrographic Office (MDHyD)
Misc. Papers, Series I, vol.21. Log of *HMS Pearl*, 1768.
Misc. Papers, Series I, S (II), vol.26. Report from *HMS Solebay*, 1763–64.
Misc. Papers, Ab3, vol.34. Log of *HMS Mulin*, 1787.
Misc. Papers, Ab3, vol.34. Capt. R.C. Reynolds of *HMS Echo*, 1787–88.

Misc. Papers, Series II, Ab4, vol.35. Report by Lieut. Adams, 1824.
346/Ah1. Map of Newfoundland, Wm. Parker, 1770.

Dorset Record Office (DCRO)
D365/F6. Diary of Benjamin Lester, 1789.
D365/F9. Diary of Benjamin Lester, 1792–93.

National Scottish Museums, Royal Scottish Museum
Old University Museum records: Additions to College Museum, 1827, 1828.
Day record book, March 1828.
Week record book, March 1828.
The Wernerian Society Record Book, volume I.

Canada

ST JOHN'S, NEWFOUNDLAND

Public Archives of Newfoundland and Labrador (PANL)
GN 1/1/3. Letter Books of Despatches to Colonial Office, London, vol.3, 1827.
GN 2/1/A. Colonial Secretary's Outgoing Correspondence (CSOC). This series starts in 1749.
GN 2/2. Incoming Correspondence of the Colonial Secretary's Office. Box 43/T/4, 1830; 1845 f.470.
GN 2/39/A. Misc. Census Materials, Census for St John's, Newfoundland 1794–95.
GN 5/2/B/1. Supreme Court, Northern Circuit, Box 2, f.5, 1827.
MG 100 Cartwright Collection; "A Sketch of the River Exploits the East End of Lieutenants Lake, 1768" by Lieut. John Cartwright.
MG 134. C.F. Rowe Collection, 1827–29.
MG 205. Pole Papers, 1800s.
MG 231. Burd Journal, 1726.
MG 257. Rev. John Leigh's Vocabulary of the Beothuk Language.
MG 282. Shortis – History of Carbonear.
MG 598. USPG. Papers, microfilm Series A 163/64, John Clinch correspondence, 1809.
Microfilm 31. Church of England Records, St Paul's Church, Trinity, 1753–1857.

Queen Elizabeth II Library, Centre for Newfoundland Studies (CNS), Memorial University of Newfoundland
File Shanawdithit. E99 B4 S45, File 2.
CNS Archive
Willoughby Papers, Middleton Manuscripts (MMSS). Transcripts by Robert Barakat, Mix 1/10,1/13,1/15,1/20,1/21,1/51, 1/60, 1/61, 1/62;
(Mix 1/24: transcript by Dr Gillian Cell).
Peyton Family Collection.

Maritime History Archive (MHA), Memorial University of Newfoundland

Keith Matthews's Namefile "Cousens."

Keith Matthews's Namefile "Peyton."

Provincial Reference and Resource Library (PRRL)

971.8 C24. "An Account of the Red Indians of Newfoundland by John Cartwright Esq. 1768." This volume, bound in hardcover, contains "Remarks on the situation of the Red Indians ... 1768"; "Extract of letter from Lieut. John Cartwright to Governor Hugh Palliser, 19 September 1768"; and "Postscript 8 November 1769."

917.18 B85. "Diary of David Buchan on HMS Pike, 1811 [should be HMS Adonis]; Journal 12-29 January 1811. Concluding Remarks by David Buchan after the expedition in 1811."

917.18 C81 NRV. W.E. Cormack to John Peyton, 28 October 1828.

Newfoundland Museum

Miniature portrait entitled "A female Red Indian named Mary March painted by W. Gosse July 1841, from an original by Lady Hamilton, May 1821."

Newfoundland and Labrador Archaeological Site Inventory.

OTTAWA AND HULL

National Archives of Canada (NAC)

MG 1. Archives des Colonies, série C"A, Correspondance générale, Canada, vol.109 (transcript); série C"C, Ministère de la France autre Mer, vol.2, 1694; série G 3, Notariat, No. provisoire 8/176, Notariat non/classe (Terre-Neuve).

MG 23. A 1 series 1, vols. 2(VIII),16, Dartmouth Papers, 1772–83.

MG 24. A 45 Duckworth Papers, 1810–12.

Kupp Collection. vol.3, docs.89, 118, from 1637.

A 133 Microfilm. Graves Papers, 1763.

A 713 Microfilm. Bishop John Inglis, Diary, 1827.

Cartographic Division

H3/140/1764. "A Plan of the Bay of 3 Islands in Newfoundland" 1764.

NMC 27. Lieut. John Cartwright, "A Sketch of the River Exploits and the East End of Lieutenants Lake in Newfoundland," submitted 1773.

NMC 14032. Lieut. John Cartwright, "Bay of Notre Dame," 1773.

NMC 14033. Lieut. John Cartwright, "A map of the Island of Newfoundland," 1773.

Picture Division

Miniature portrait of Mary March by Lady Hamilton, neg.C87698.

Canadian Museum of Civilization (CMC)

Archaeological Survey, Old Systems Catalogue, Newfoundland, VIII-A.

MONTREAL

Blacker-Wood Library (BWL), McGill University

Minutes of the Natural History Society of Montreal, 23 February 1829 and 27 December 1852.

UNITED STATES

William L. Clemens Library (WLCL), University of Michigan

Townsend Papers, Buccleuth Muniments, Box 46. "Report on the Newfoundland Fishery," 1759.

Ibid., Box 34. "Report on the State of the Newfoundland Fisheries, 1761," by Thomas Cole.

Thomas Gilcrease Institute for American History and Art

"The Case of the Wild or Red Indians" [1784], by George Cartwright.

Harvard University, Peabody Museum of Archaeology and Ethnology

File 06-30 Owen Bryant report, 1906.

PRIVATE COLLECTIONS

David Buchan Papers

The papers of the Buchan family are in the possession of the descendants of Capt. David Buchan. Correspondence with Mrs L.H. Baxter, Westbury/Wilts., UK, a member of the Buchan family, has established that they do not include material specifically related to Buchan's involvement with Beothuk. Buchan's maps of his two expeditions into the interior of the country are in the map collections of the Public Record Office, Kew (1811), and of the British Library, London (1820). His reports are in the Public Record Office, Colonial Series, CO 194, volumes 50 and 63. A handwritten diary of Buchan's 1811 expedition to Red Indian Lake and his concluding remarks are in the collection of the Public Reference and Resource Library, St John's.

Cartwright Papers

The papers of John and George Cartwright and of other members of the Cartwright family are in the possession of the Cartwright descendants in Johannesburg, South Africa. A large number of documents in this collection are family and property certificates. Eighteenth- and early-nineteenth-century material related to Newfoundland and Labrador that has been used for this study are as follows:

George Cartwright's *Journal of Transactions and Events during a Residence of nearly sixteen years on the Coast of Labrador.* 3 vols., with handwritten notes and sketches. Newark: Allin and Ridge, 1792.

An undated notebook in George Cartwright's hand entitled "Addition to the Labrador Companion," with practical suggestions about various aspects of life in Labrador (no "Labrador Companion" has been located).

A drawing of a Montagnais/Naskapi snowshoe;

F.D. Cartwright's correspondence from the 1850s, concerning the erection of a Cartwright memorial in Labrador.

The papers do not include new information on the Beothuk.

William Epps Cormack Papers

Cormack's papers have been widely dispersed; only some of them are still extant. For the fate of the wordlists collected by Cormack, see chapter 27. While in Britain, Cormack seems to have left some notes with information obtained from Shanawdithit with his friend John McGregor, who published them anonymously in the article "Sketches of savage life," in 1836. McGregor's papers could not be traced. Part of the remaining papers found their way back to Newfoundland in the early 1850s through the efforts of the surveyor general of Newfoundland, the Honourable Joseph Noad. Noad subsequently used information that Cormack obtained from Shanawdithit in a lecture on the Beothuk that he delivered in 1852–53. These papers largely consisted of notes and correspondence and probably included the ten sketches by Shanawdithit, which are now in the collection of the Newfoundland Museum, St John's.

The correspondence and notes have come into the hands of J.P. Howley. I have transcribed and sorted them into files numbered 1/84 to 81/84. In the end notes of this study, documents are referenced according to the file number and, where transcribed by Howley, to the page number in Howley's *Beothucks*. The correspondence consists largely of letters exchanged with members of the Boeothick Institution. The notes cover Cormack's preparations for his trek across Newfoundland in 1822, ideas for his second search for Beothuk survivors, a draft copy of his address to the Boeothick Institution, beginings of a history of the aborigines of Newfoundland, and information on Beothuk history and culture elicited from Shanawdithit. Most of this material has been published in J.P. Howley's *The Beothucks or Red Indians*. However, Howley excluded notes reflecting Cormack's opinion about the Beothuk people and his criticism of government; there is also a sketch of the interior of a room presumed to have been drawn by Shanawdithit. This material is included in the present study.

Among the papers brought to St John's in the 1850s was Cormack's "Narrative of a Journey across Newfoundland," undertaken in 1822. He had published only a shortened version of this report in the *Edinburgh Philosophical Journal* in 1824. Noad gave the manuscript of the complete narrative to Governor Darling, who subsequently published it under the auspices of government in 1856. It was later edited and republished by Rev. Moses Harvey in 1873. Harvey mentioned that he had compared the text with the original, indicating that he was in possession of Cormack's manuscript. However, it is no longer extant; presumably it was destroyed, together with Harvey's own papers, in one of the fires in St John's. In the 1820s or 1830s Cormack also sent a manuscript of his "Narrative of a Journey across Newfoundland" to the Natural History Society in Montreal. This copy is deposited in the Archive of the McCord Museum, Montreal.

J.P. Howley Papers

When I approached the late David Howley, St John's, in 1973, the J.P. Howley Papers were in his possession. They contained proof pages from J.P. Howley's *The Beothucks or*

Red Indians, lengthy notes and lectures on the history of Newfoundland, J.P. Howley's correspondence with scholars and informants about the Beothuk, books, photographs, and miscellaneous items.

Among this collection were J.P. Howley's handwritten diaries of various years between 1868 an 1910, in which he recorded activities during his career as surveyor in Newfoundland, and a typescript entitled "Reminiscences," prepared by J.P. Howley from these diaries. As I considered this typescript to be an important historic document, David Howley agreed to offer it to the late G.M. Story for publication. A copy of the typescript is in the process of being annotated and edited for publication by William J. Kirwin and Patrick O. Flaherty. John Howley, a descendent of J.P. Howley, donated the original diaries, and selected papers from the Howley collection in 1993 and the typescript "Reminiscences" in 1994 to the Centre for Newfoundland Studies Archive, Memorial University of Newfoundland.

The following notes and letters from the Howley Papers are referred to in the end notes of this study:

The typescript of "Reminiscences" is referenced J.P. Howley n.d., and year of diary entry.

Notebook n.p: A 1871, in CNS Archive, Howley Papers Box 4, file 280.

W.E. Cormack to John Peyton, Jr, Exploits, 27 November 1827, transcript.

Burial Certificate, "Nancy Shanadithi," 23 October 1829.

A map of the lower part of Lloyd's River on which the location of a Beothuk lookout and a caribou trap are marked, produced by J.P. Howley in the 1880s.

Sir William Dawson to J.P. Howley, Montreal, 18 July 1880.

Robert G. Latham to J.P. Howley, Putney SW, 25 December 1882.

Philip Tocque, Toronto, to J.P. Howley, 28 April 1886.

Philip Tocque, Toronto, to J.P. Howley, 28 May 1886.

Constable Dawe to Archbishop Howley, 31 May 1901.

George Hodder, Mortons Harbour, to J.P. Howley, 1 February 1907.

Note: "22 March 19__ Removed from Mr Samuel Coffin … remains" from the burial on Big Island, Pilley's Tickle.

A note about the Beothuk canoe replica in the National Scottish Museums and a drawing of the same by Alexander Murray.

Section of a photograph of Beothuk artifacts.

PRINTED MATERIAL, THESES, PAPERS

"Aborigines of Newfoundland from Blackwood's Magazine." 1832. *Royal Gazette*. St John's, 18 September, 1. and 25 September, Supplement.

Addison, W. Innes. 1913. *The Matriculate Albums of the University of Glasgow from 1728–1858*. Glasgow: J. Maclehose and Sons.

Adney, Edwin T., and Howard I. Chapelle. 1964. *The Bark Canoes and Skin Boats of North America*. Washington, DC: Smithsonian Inst.

Andrews, C. W. N.d. *The Origin, Growth and Decline of the Newfoundland Seal Fishery*. Harbour Grace: National Exhibition Centre, Conception Bay Museum.

Anspach, Lewis Amadeus. 1819. *A History of the Island of Newfoundland*. London: T. and J. Allman and J.M. Richardson.

Arber, Edwin, ed. 1885. *The First Three English Books on America (1511)-1555 AD.* Chiefly trans. and comp. by Richard Eden. Birmingham. Reprint, New York: Kraus, 1971.

Ash, Michael I. 1981. "Slavey." In *Subarctic*, ed. June Helm, 338–49. Vol. 6 of *Handbook of North American Indians*. Ed. William C. Sturtevant. Washington, DC: Smithsonian Inst.

Auger, Reginald. 1984. "Factory Cove: Recognition and Definition of the Early Palaeo-Eskimo Period in Newfoundland." Master's thesis, Memorial Univ. of Newfoundland, St John's.

Austin, Shaun. 1980. "Cape Cove Beach (DhAi-5,6,7) Newfoundland Prehistoric Cultures." Master's thesis, Memorial Univ. of Newfoundland, St John's.

– 1984. "Maritime Archaic and Recent Indian Evidence from Cape Cove Beach, Newfoundland." *Canadian Journal of Archaeology* 8, no.2: 115–26.

Avalonus, W. [William Sweetman]. 1862. "Aborigines of Newfoundland." *Royal Gazette*, St John's, 7, 14 January.

Axtell, James. 1981. *The European and the Indian*. Oxford and New York: Oxford Univ. Press.

Bailey, A.G. 1969. *The Conflict of European and Eastern Algonkian Cultures 1504–1700*. 2d ed. Toronto: Univ. of Toronto Press.

Bakker, Peter, and Lynn Drapeau. 1994. "Adventures with the Beothuks in 1787: A Testimony from Jean Conan's Autobiography." In *Actes du vingt-cinquième congrès des Algonquinistes*, ed. William Cowan, 32–45: Ottawa: Carleton University.

Barkham, Selma de L. 1980. "A Note on the Strait of Belle Isle during the Period of Basque Contact with Indians and Inuit." *Études/Inuit/Studies* 4, nos.1–2: 51–8.

Bartels, Denis. 1979. "Time Immemorial? A Research Note on Micmacs in Newfoundland." *Newfoundland Quarterly* 75, no.3: 6–9.

Bathurst, Seymour Henry. 1923. *Report on the Manuscripts of Earl Bathurst, Preserved at Cirencester Park*. Historic Manuscripts Commission No.76. London: His Majesty's Stationery Office.

Baughman, Ernest. 1966. *Type and Motif Index of the Folktales of England and North America*. Indiana Univ. Folklore Series No.20; The Hague: Mouton.

"Beothic Vocabulary." 1950. *Twillingate Sun*, vol. 70, no.30, 29 July.

"Beothuck Memorial Update." 1987. *Newfoundland Herald*, St John's, 3 January.

Bergerud, Arthur T. 1958. "Distribution, Movement, and Population Dynamics of Newfoundland Caribou, March 1957–1958." Ts. CNS.

– 1963. "Preliminary Report on the Caribou Herds of Northern and Southern Labrador." Ts. St John's: Wildlife Division, Mines, Agriculture, and Resources and CNS.

– 1971. *The Population Dynamics of Newfoundland Caribou*. Wildlife Monograph, no.25. Washington, DC: Wildlife Society.

Bergman, Sten. 1927. *Through Kamchatka by Dog-Sled and Skis*. London: Seeley, Service and Co.

Biggar, Henry P. 1911. *The Precursors of Jacques Cartier, 1497–1534*. A collection of documents relating to the early history of the Dominion of Canada. Ottawa: Publ. of the Canadian Archives, no.5.

– 1924. *The Voyages of Jacques Cartier*. Ottawa: Publ. of the Archives of Canada, no.11.

– 1930. *A Collection of Documents Relating to Jacques Cartier and Roberval*. Ottawa: Publ. of the Archives of Canada, no. 14.

Binford, Lewis R. 1967. "An Ethnohistory of the Nottoway, Meherrin, and Weanock Indians of Southeastern Virginia." *Ethnohistory* 14, nos.3–4:103–218.

Blake, Edith. 1888. "The Beothuks of Newfoundland." *Nineteenth Century* 24:899–918.

Blant, Robert le, et René Baudry. 1967. "Observations de Peiresc sur les curiositées rapportées d'Acadie par Pierre du Gua, Sieur de Monts." *Nouveaux documents sur Champlain et son époque*, vol.1 (1560–1622). Ottawa: Publ. des Archives Publiques du Canada, no.15:102–4.

Bock, Philip K. 1978. "Micmac." In *Northeast*, ed. Bruce G. Trigger, 109–22. Vol. 15 of *Handbook of North American Indians*. Ed. William C. Sturtevant. Washington DC: Smithsonian Inst.

"Boeothic Institution." 1828. *Newfoundlander*, St John's, 26 June.

"Boeothick Institution." 1827. *Royal Gazette*. St John's, 13 November.

"Boeothick Institution." 1828. *Kaleidoscope; or Literary and Scientific Mirror*. no.400, vol. 8. London, 26 February.

"Boeothick Institution." 1828. *Royal Gazette*, St John's, 19 February, 24 June.

Bogoras, W. 1909. *The Chukchee*. The Jesup North Pacific Expedition. Memoir of the American Museum of Natural History, vol. 11. Ed. Franz Boas. New York: Johnson Reprint Corp.

Bonnycastle, Sir R.H. 1842. *Newfoundland in 1842*. 2 vols. London: Henry Colburne.

Boulva, J., and I.A. McLaren. 1979. *Biology of the Harbor Seal, Phoca vitulina, in Eastern Canada*. Bulletin 200. Ottawa: Fisheries and Oceans Canada.

Bourinot, J.G. 1868. "Some Stories of a Lost Tribe." *New Dominion Monthly* 3, no.2. 91–4.

Bourque, Bruce J., ed. 1984. *12.000 Years of Maine Native History*. Augusta: Maine State Museum.

Bourque, Bruce J., and Ruth Holmes Whitehead. 1985. "Tarrantines and the Introduction of European Trade Goods in the Gulf of Maine." *Ethnohistory* 32, no.4: 327–41.

Boyce, Douglas W. 1978. "Iroquoian Tribes of the Virginia-North Carolina Coastal Plain."In *Northeast*, ed. Bruce G. Trigger, 282–9. Vol. 15 of *Handbook of North American Indians*. Ed. William C. Sturtevant. Washington, DC: Smithsonian Inst.

Brasser, T.J. 1978. "Mahican." In *Northeast*, ed. Bruce G. Trigger, 198–212. Vol.15 of *Handbook of North American Indians*. Ed. William C. Sturtevant. Washington DC: Smithsonian Inst.

Brice-Bennett, Carol, ed. 1977. *Our Footprints Are Everywhere: Inuit Land Use and Occupancy in Labrador*. Nain: Labrador Inuit Assoc.

Brinton, Daniel G. 1891. *The American Race*. New York: D.C. Hodges. Reprint. Johnson Reprint, 1970.

Brouage, François Martel de. 1922–23. "Divers memoirs de M. de Brouage au Conseil de Marine, 1718–1744." In *Rapport de l'Archiviste de la Province de Quebec*, 356–406. Quebec: Ls.-A. Proulx.

Brown, A.S. 1923. "Smoking among the Beothics." *Newfoundland Quarterly* 23, no.3:29–34.

Brown, George W., Ramsay Cook, Frances G. Halpenny, and David M. Hayne, eds. 1966–90. *Dictionary of Canadian Biography.* 12 vols. Toronto: Univ. of Toronto Press.

Budgel, Richard. 1992. "The Beothuks and the Newfoundland Mind." *Newfoundland Studies* 8, no.1: 15–33.

Burnham, Dorothy K. 1992. *To Please the Caribou: Painted Caribou-Skin Coats Worn by the Naskapi, Montagnais, and Cree hunters of the Quebec-Labrador Peninsula*. Toronto: Royal Ontario Museum.

Burrage, Henry S., ed. 1967. *Early English and French Voyages, Chiefly from Hakluyt 1534–1608*. 2d ed. New York: Barnes and Noble.

Busk, Geo. 1876. "Description of Two Beothuc Skulls." *Royal Anthropological Institute of Great Britain and Ireland Journal* 5:230–3.

Calendar of State Papers, Colonial Series, of the Reign of Charles II. "America and West Indies, 1675–1676." Ed. W. Noel Sainsbury. London: Eyre and Spottiswoode for Her Majesty's Stationery Office, 1893.

Calendar of State Papers, Colonial Series, of the Reign of William III. "America and West Indies, 1696–1697." Ed. J.W. Fortescue. London: Mackie and Co. for His Majesty's Stationery Office, 1904.

Calendar of State Papers, Colonial Series, of the Reign of Queen Anne. "America and West Indies," Jan.-Dec. 1702, 1704–1705, 1706–1708, 1708–1709, 1712–1714. Ed. Cecil Headlam, MA. London: His Majesty's Stationery Office, 1912, 1916, 1922.

Calendar of State Papers, Colonial Series, of the Reign of George I. "America and West Indies," Jan. 1716-July 1717, 1717–1718, 1719–1720, 1720–1721, 1722–1723, 1726–1727. Ed. Cecil Headlam, MA. London: His Majesty's Stationery Office, 1930, 1933, 1934, 1936.

Calendar of State Papers, Colonial Series, of the Reign of George II. "America and West Indies," 1728–1729, 1733, 1734–1735, 1735–1736. Ed. Cecil Headlam, MA. London: His Majesty's Stationery Office, 1937, 1939, 1953.

Callender, Charles. 1978. "Fox," "Miami," "Shawnee," and "Illinois." In *Northeast*, ed. Bruce G. Trigger, 636–47, 681–9, 622–35, 673–80. Vol. 15 of *Handbook of North American Indians*. Ed. William C. Sturtevant. Washington, DC: Smithsonian Inst.

Callender, Charles, Richard K. Pope, and Susan M. Pope. 1978. "Kickapoo." In *Northeast*, ed. Bruce G. Trigger, 656–67. Vol. 15 of *Handbook of North American Indians.* Ed. William C. Sturtevant. Washington, DC: Smithsonian Inst.

Campbell, John. 1893. "Remarks on Preceding Vocabularies." *Transactions of the Royal Society of Canada, 1892* Sect. 2: 26–30.

Campbell, Lyle, and Marianne Mithun, eds. 1979. *The Languages of Native America, Historical and Comparative Assessments*. Austin and London: Univ. of Texas Press.

Campeau, Lucien. 1967. *La première mission d'Acadie (1602–1616).* Quebec: Les Presses de L'Université Laval.

Canada. Department of the Secretary of State, 1972. "Archaeological Survey of Green Bay." Opportunities for Youth Program. Prepared by Brenela Rowsell, MS.

Canadian Encyclopedia. 1988. 4 vols. 2d ed. Edmonton: Hurtig.

"Carbon Dates, Newfoundland and Labrador." 1982. File, Archaeology Unit, Memorial Univ. of Newfoundland, St John's.

Carignan, Paul. 197_. "Preliminary Report on Archaeological Investigation of the Beaches Site, Bonavista Bay, Newfoundland." Ts. Newfoundland Museum, St John's.

– 1973. "Archaeology of Bonavista Bay Salvage Report." Ts. Newfoundland Museum, St John's.

– 1975a. *The Beaches: A Multi-Component Habitation Site in Bonavista Bay.* Ottawa: National Museum of Man, Mercury Series, Archaeological Survey of Canada, Paper No.39.

– 1975b. "Archaeological Survey, 1975." Ts. Newfoundland Museum, St John's.

– 1977. *Beothuck Archaeology in Bonavista Bay.* Ottawa: National Museum of Man, Mercury Series, Archaeological Survey of Canada, Paper No. 69.

Cartwright, F.D., ed. 1826. *The Life and Correspondence of Major Cartwright*. 2 vols. London: Colburn.

Cartwright, George. 1792. *A Journal of Transactions and Events during a Residence of Nearly Sixteen Years on the Coast of Labrador.* 3 vols. Newark: Allin and Ridge.

– "Addition to the Labrador Companion." N.d. Cartwright Papers.

Catlin, George. 1841. *Letters and Notes on the Manners, Customs and Conditions of the North American Indians*. 2 vols. Reprint. Minneapolis: Ross and Haines, 1965.

Cell, Gillian T. 1969. *English Enterprise in Newfoundland 1577–1660.* Toronto: Univ. of Toronto Press.

– *Newfoundland Discovered*. 1982. London: Hakluyt Society Publication, 2d ser., vol.160.

Chafe, Levi George. 1923. *Chafe's Sealing Book*. Ed. H.M. Mosdell. 3d. ed. St John's: Trade Printers and Publishers.

Champlain, Samuel. 1922–36. *The Works of Samuel Champlain*. 6 vols. Trans. and annot. by Henry P. Biggar, Toronto: Publ. of the Champlain Society. Reprint. Toronto: Univ. of Toronto Press, 1971.

Chapdelaine, Claude, and Gregory G. Kennedy. 1990. "The Origin of the Iroquoian Rim Sherd from Red Bay." *Man in the Northeast* 40, no.1:41–3.

Chappell, Edw. R.N. 1818. *Voyage of His Majesty's Ship "Rosamond" to Newfoundland and the Southern Coast of Labrador*. London: J. Mawman.

Charlevoix, Pierre François-Xavier de. 1870. *History and General Description of New France*. Trans. with notes by John Gilmory Shea. 6 vols. New York. Reprint. Chicago: Loyola Univ. Press, 1962.

Chiapelli, F., ed. 1976. *First Images of America*. Berkeley, CA: Univ. of California Press.

Chute, Janet E. 1976. "A Comparative Study of the Bark, Bone, Wood, and Hide Items Made by the Historic Micmac, Montagnais/Naskapi and Beothuck Indians." Master's thesis, Memorial Univ. of Newfoundland, St John's.

Clark, Donald. 1987 *Archaeological Reconnaissance at Great Bear Lake*. Ottawa: National Museum of Civilization, Mercury Series, Archaeological Survey of Canada, Paper No. 136.

Clark McFadyen, Annette. 1981. "Koyukon." In *Subarctic*, ed. June Helm, 582–601. Vol. 6 of *Handbook of North American Indians*. Ed. William C. Sturtevant. Washington, DC: Smithsonian Inst.

Clifton, James A. 1978. "Potawatomi." In *Northeast*, ed. Bruce G. Trigger, 725–42. Vol. 15 of *Handbook of North American Indians*. Ed. William C. Sturtevant. Washington, DC: Smithsonian Inst.

Compact Edition of the Oxford English Dictionary (The). 1971. 2 vols. Oxford: Oxford Univ. Press. Reprint. 1979.

Conception Bay Mercury (The). 1829. Harbour Grace: 19 June.

Conkey, Laura E., Ethel Boissevain, and Ives Goddard. 1978. "Indians of Southern New England and Long Island, Late Period." In *Northeast*, ed. Bruce G. Trigger, 177–89. Vol. 15 of *Handbook of North American Indians*. Ed. William C. Sturtevant. Washington, DC: Smithsonian Inst.

Cook, James. 1766. *Strait of Belle Isle with Part of the Coast of Newfoundland.* Chart. London: I. Mount and T. Page.

– 1965. *James Cook Surveyor of Newfoundland*. San Francisco: David Magee.

Cordwell, Justine M. 1979. "The Very Human Acts of Transformation." In *The Fabrics of Culture: The Anthropology of Clothing and Adornment*, eds. Justine M. Cordwell and Ronald A. Schwarz, 47–75. New York: Mouton.

Cordwell, Justine M., and Ronald A. Schwarz, eds. 1979. *The Fabrics of Culture: The Anthropology of Clothing and Adornment*. New York: Mouton.

Cormack, William E. 1824. "Account of a journey across the Island of Newfoundland, by W.E. Cormack, Esq. in a letter addressed to the Right Hon. Earl Bathurst, Secretary of State for the Colonies, && – with a map of Mr Cormack's journey across the Island of Newfoundland." *Edinburgh Philosophical Journal* 10, no.19:156–62.

– 1827–28. "Mr Cormack's journey in search of the Red Indians." *Edinburgh New Philosophical Journal* 18, no.4:205–6, 408–10.

– 1828. "Instructions given to John Louis, John Stephens and Peter John ..., 26 June 1828." *Public Ledger*, St John's, 5 September.

– 1829. "Report of Mr W.E. Cormack's journey in search of the Red Indians in Newfoundland. Read before the Boeothick Institution at St John's, Newfoundland. Communicated by Mr Cormack." *Edinburgh New Philosophical Journal* 20, no.6:318–29.

– 1856. *Narrative of a Journey across the Island of Newfoundland, the Only Ever Performed by a European.* St John's: Morning Post and Commercial Journal.

– 1873. *Narrative of a Journey across the Island of Newfoundland.* Ed. M. Harvey, Saint John's: Morning Chronicle.

Cowan, William, ed. 1990. *Papers of the Twenty-First Algonquian Conference*. Ottawa: Carleton Univ. Press.

Cranz, David. 1816. *Fortsetzung von David Cranzens Brüder Historie 4*. Abschnitt vom Synodo 1789 bis zum Synodo 1801. Gnadau.

Crewe, Nimshi. 1968. "The Gosse family of Carbonear produced novelists, painters, naturalists." *Evening Telegram*, St John's, 8 March.

Crow, John R., and Philip R. Obley. 1981. "Han." In *Subarctic*, ed. June Helm, 506–13. Vol. 6 of *Handbook of the North American Indians*. Ed. William C. Sturtevant. Washington, DC: Smithsonian Inst.

Cuff, Harry. 1966. "I interviewed the great-grandchild of a Beothuck." *Newfoundland Quarterly* 65, no.2: 25.

Cuff, R.H., M. Baker, and R.W.D. Pitt, eds. 1990. *Dictionary of Newfoundland and Labrador Biography.* St John's: Harry Cuff Publ.

Cumbaa, Stephen L. 1984. "'Divers furres and deeres flesh' – Animal Use by a 17th Century Beothuk Population at Boyd's Cove, Notre Dame Bay, Newfoundland." Ts. Zooarchaeological Identification Centre, National Museum of Natural Sciences, National Museum of Canada, Ottawa, and CNS.

Dalton, Mary. 1992. "Shadow Indians: The Beothuk motif in Newfoundland Literature." *Newfoundland Studies* 8, no.2:135–46.

Damas, David, ed. 1984. *Arctic*. vol. 5 of *Handbook of North American Indians*, ed. William C. Sturtevant. 20 vols. Washington, DC: Smithsonian Inst.

Davidson, D.S. 1937. *Snowshoes*. Memoirs of the American Philosophical Society, vol. 6, Philadelphia.

Davies, John W. 1970. "A Historical Note on the Reverend John Clinch, First Canadian Vaccinator." *Canadian Medical Association Journal* 102, no.9: 957–61.

Dawson, J.W. 1860. "Notes on the Relics of the Red Indians of Newfoundland Collected by M. Smith McKay and Exhibited to the Natural History Society." *The Canadian Naturalist and Quarterly Journal of Sciences* 5: 462.

– 1880. *Fossil Men and Their Modern Representatives*. Montreal: Dawson Brothers.

Day, Gordon M. 1978. "Western Abenaki." In *Northeast*, ed. Bruce G. Trigger, 148–59. Vol. 15 of *Handbook of North American Indians*. Ed. William C. Sturtevant. Washington, DC: Smithsonian Inst.

Day, Gordon M., and Bruce G. Trigger. 1978. "Algonquin." In *Northeast*, ed. Bruce G. Trigger, 792–97. Vol. 15 of *Handbook of North American Indians*. Ed. William C. Sturtevant. Washington, DC: Smithsonian Inst.

Dean, John Ward, ed. 1967. *Capt. John Mason*. New York: Burt Franklin.

Denevan, W.M., ed. *The Native Population of the Americas in 1492*. Madison, WI: Univ. of Wisconsin Press.

Denys, Nicolas. 1908. *The Description and Natural History of the Coasts of North America (Acadia)*. Trans. Wm. F. Ganong. Toronto: Publ. of the Champlain Society 12. Reprint. New York: Greenwood Press, 1968

Devereux, Helen. 1964. "Archaeological Survey and Investigation in Central Newfoundland." Ms. 260, Newfoundland Museum, St John's.

– 1965a. "The Pope's Point Site, Newfoundland (DfBa-1)." Ms.261, Newfoundland Museum, St John's.

– 1965b. "Preliminary Report on the Archaeological Survey in Newfoundland July-August, 1965."Ms.735, Ts. Newfoundland Museum, St John's.

– 1966. "Beothuk Project Field Notes: Miscellaneous." Ms.740/2, Ts. Newfoundland Museum, St John's.

– 1969. "Five Archaeological Sites in Newfoundland: A Description." 2 vols. Ms. Newfoundland Museum, St John's.

– 1970. "A Preliminary Report on the Indian Point Site, Newfoundland (DeBd-1)." Ms.743, Newfoundland Museum, St John's.

Dickason, Olive Patricia. 1976. "Louisbourg and the Indians: A Study in Imperial Race Relations, 1713–1760." *History and Archaeology*, 3–206. Ottawa: National Historic Parks and Sites Branch, Parks Canada, Indian Affairs Canada.

– 1984. *The Myth of the Savage and the Beginnings of French Colonialism*. Edmonton: Univ. of Alberta Press.

Dictionary of Canadian Biography. 1966–90. George Brown, W., Ramsay Cook, Frances G. Halpenny, and David M. Hayne, eds. 12 vols. Toronto: Univ. of Toronto Press.

Dictionary of National Biography. 1921–22. L. Stephen, and S. Lee, eds. 22 vols. London: Oxford Univ. Press. Reprint. 1949–50.

Dictionary of Newfoundland English. 1982. George Story, W.J. Kirwin, and J.D.A. Widdowson, comps. Toronto: Univ. of Toronto Press.

Dictionary of Newfoundland and Labrador Biography. 1990. R.H. Cuff, M. Baker, and R.W.D. Pitt, eds. St John's: Harry Cuff Publ.

"Discovery of the Red Indian Remains at Fogo." 1887. *Evening Mercury*, St John's, 2 November.

Dobyn, Henry F. 1983. *Their Numbers Become Thinned.* Knoxville: Univ. of Tennessee Press.

Driver, Harold E. 1975. *Indians of North America*. 2d rev. ed. Chicago: Univ. of Chicago Press.

Eburne, Richard. 1624. *A Plain Pathway to Plantations. (1624)*. Ed. L.B. Wright. Ithaca, NY: Cornell Univ. Press, 1962.

Edey, Maitland A. 1974. *The Sea Traders*. New York: Time-Life Books.

Eggan, Fred. 1968. "Indians, North American." In *International Encyclopedia of the Social Sciences*, ed. David L. Sills, 180–200. Vol. 7. Macmillan Co. and The Free Press.

Ellis, William, and Samuel McDowell. 1810. "Extract of a Letter from Messrs William Ellis and Samuel McDowell to the Rev. Dr Coke and the Missionary Committee." *Methodist Magazine* 34 (1811): 275–6.

Encyclopedia of Newfoundland and Labrador. 1981–91. 3 vols. Ed. Joseph Smallwood. St John's: Newfoundland Publ. (1967).

Engelbrecht, W.E., and Donald K. Grayson, eds. 1978. *Essays in Northeastern Anthropology in Memory of Marian E. White*. Rindge, NH: Franklin Pierce College.

English, Christopher. 1990. "The Development of the Newfoundland Legal System to 1815." *Acadiensis* 20, no.1: 89–119.

English, Leo F. 1960. "Some Aspects of Beothuk Culture." *Newfoundland Quarterly* 59, no.2: 11–13.

English Pilot, (The) The Fourth Book. [1689]. London. Reprint. Chicago: Rand McNally, 1967.

Erickson, Vincent O. 1978. "Maliseet-Passamaquoddy." In *Northeast*, ed. Bruce G. Trigger, 123–36. Vol. 15 of *Handbook of North American Indians*. Ed. William C. Sturtevant. Washington, DC: Smithsonian Inst.

Evans, Clifford. 1981. "Field Report of Frenchman's Island Project." *Archaeology In Newfoundland and Labrador 1980,* eds. J. Sproull Thomson and B. Ransom, Annual Report 1, 88–94. St John's: Historic Resources Division, Dept. of Culture, Recreation and Youth, Govt. of Newfoundland and Labrador.

– 1982. "Frenchman's Island Site (C1A1-1) Preliminary Field Report." *Archaeology in Newfoundland and Labrador 1981*, eds. J. Sproull Thomson and C. Thomson, Annual Report 2, 210–25. St John's: Historic Resources Division, Dept. of Culture, Recreation and Youth, Govt. of Newfoundland and Labrador.

Fardy, B.D. 1983. *Captain David Buchan in Newfoundland*. St John's: Harry Cuff Publ.

– 1985. *William Epps Cormack, Newfoundland Pioneer.* St John's: Creative Publ.

– 1988. *Demasduit, Native Newfoundlander.* St John's: Creative Publ.

Faucher de Saint Maurice, Narcisse-Henry-Edouard. 1888. *En route sept jours dans les Provinces Maritimes*. Quebec: Imprimerie Générale A. Coté et Cie.

Fay, C.R. 1956. *Life and Labour in Newfoundland*. Cambridge: W. Heffer and Sons.

– 1961. *Channel Islands and Newfoundland*. Cambridge: W. Heffer and Sons.

Feest, Christian F. 1978. "Nanticoke and Neighboring Tribes," "Virginia Algonquians," and "North Carolina Algonquians." In *Northeast*, ed. Bruce G. Trigger, 240–52, 253–70, 271–81. Vol. 15 of *Handbook of North American Indians*. Ed. William C. Sturtevant. Washington, DC: Smithsonian Inst.

Feest, Johanna E., and Christian F. Feest. 1978. "Ottawa." In *Northeast*, ed. Bruce G. Trigger, 772–87. Vol. 15 of *Handbook of North American Indians*. Ed. William C. Sturtevant. Washington, DC: Smithsonian Inst.

Fenton, William N. 1949. "An Elm Bark Canoe in the Peabody Museum of Salem." *The American Neptune* 9, no.3: 185–206.

– 1978. "Northern Iroquoian Culture Patterns." In *Northeast*, ed. Bruce G. Trigger, 296–321. Vol. 15 of *Handbook of North American Indians*. Ed. William C. Sturtevant. Washington, DC: Smithsonian Inst.

Fiedel, Stuart J. 1991. "Correlating Archaeology and Linguistics: The Algonquian Case." *Man in the Northeast* 41(1): 9–32.

Fisher, Robin. 1992. "Judging History: Reflections on the Reasons for Judgement in Delgamuukw v. BC" *BC Studies* 95: 43–54.

Fitzhugh, William W. 1972. *Environmental Archaeology and Cultural Systems in Hamilton Inlet, Labrador.* Smithsonian Contribution to Anthropology 16. Washington, DC: Smithsonian Inst.

– 1977. "Indian and Eskimo/Inuit Settlement History in Labrador: An Archaeological View." In *Our Footprints Are Everywhere: Inuit Land Use and Occupancy in Labrador*, ed. Carol Brice-Bennett, 1–41. Nain: Labrador Inuit Assoc.

– 1978. "Winter Cove 4 and the Point Revenge Occupation of the Central Labrador Coast." *Arctic Anthropology* 15, no.2: 146–74.

– 1980. "A Review of Paleo-Eskimo Culture History in Southern Quebec-Labrador and Newfoundland." *Études/Inuit/Studies* 4, nos.1–2: 21–31.

– 1985. "The Nulliak Pendants and Their Relation to Spiritual Traditions in Northeast Prehistory." *Arctic Anthropology* 22, no.2: 87–109.

Fitzhugh, William W., and Aron Crowell. 1988. *Crossroads of Continents, Cultures of Siberia and Alaska*. Washington, DC: Smithsonian Inst.

Forster, M.J.R. 1788. *Histoire des découvertes et des voyages faits dans Le Nord*. Vol. 1. Trans. M. Broussonet. Paris: Cuchet.

Foskett, Daphne. 1972. *A Dictionary of British Miniature Painters*. 2 vols. New York, Washington: Praeger.

Fraser, Allan M. 1962. "The Beothuks of Newfoundland." *Canadian Geographic Journal* 65, no.5: 156–9.

– "Shanawdithit, Last of the Beothuks." 1965. *The Atlantic Advocate* 56, no.3: 34–9.

Friederici, Georg. 1906. *Scalpieren und ähnliche Kriegsgebräuche in Amerika*. Braunschweig: Friedrich Vieweg und Sohn.

– *Die Schiffahrt der Indianer*. 1907. Stuttgart: Strecker und Schröder.

Ganong, William F. 1964. *Crucial Maps in the Early Cartography and Place Nomenclature of the Atlantic Coast of Canada*. Toronto: Univ. of Toronto Press.

Gatschet, Albert S. 1885. "The Beothuk Indians." *Proceedings of the American Philosophical Society* 22, no.120: 408–24.

– 1886. "The Beothuk Indians." *Proceedings of the American Philosophical Society* 23, no.121: 411–32.

– 1890. "The Beothuk Indians." *Proceedings of the American Philosophical Society* 28, no.132: 1–16.

Gazetteer of Canada. *Newfoundland and Labrador*. 1968. Ottawa: Canadian Permanent Committee on Geographical Names.

Gilbert, William. 1990. "Divers places: The Beothuk Indians and John Guy's Voyage into Trinity Bay in 1612." *Newfoundland Studies* 6, no.2: 147–67.

– 1992. "' … Great Good Done': Beothuk-European Relations in Trinity Bay 1612 to 1622." *Newfoundland Quarterly* 88, no.3: 2–10.

Gilbert, William, and Ken Reynolds. 1989. "A Report of an Archaeological Survey: The Come By Chance River and Dildo Pond." For the Dept. of Culture, Recreation and Youth, Government of Newfoundland and Labrador. Ts. Newfoundland Museum.

Goddard, Ives. 1967. "Notes on the Genetic Classification of the Algonquian Languages." *Contribution to Anthropology: Linguistics* 1. Bulletin 214, 7–12. Ottawa: National Museum of Canada.

– 1978. "Eastern Algonquian Languages," and "Delaware." In *Northeast*, ed. Bruce G. Trigger, 70–7, 213–39. Vol. 15 of *Handbook of North American Indians*. Ed. William C. Sturtevant. Washington, DC: Smithsonian Inst.

– 1979. "Comparative Algonquian." In *The languages of Native America, Historical and Comparative Assessments*, eds. Lyle Campbell and Marianne Mithun, 70–132. Austin and London: Univ. of Texas Press.

Gosse, Edmund. 1890. *The Life of Philip Henry Gosse F.R.S.* London: Kegan Paul, Trench, Truebner.

Graham, Edward. 1868. "Death of W.E. Cormack." *British Columbian*, 9 May.

Grant, William. 1967. *The Voyages by Samuel Champlain 1604–1618*. New York: Barnes and Noble.

Great Britain. Parliament. House of Commons. Committee on the State of the Trade to Newfoundland. *First, Second and Third Reports of the Committee appointed to enquire into the State of Trade to Newfoundland, 1793*. First Series Reports, House of Commons. Vol. 10. Miscell. 1785–1808, 392–503.

Greenberg, Joseph H. 1953. "Historical Linguistics and Unwritten Languages." In *Anthropology Today*, ed. A. L. Kroeber. Chicago: Univ. of Chicago Press.

Gursky, Karl-Heinz. 1964. "Bemerkungen zur Beothuk-sprache." *Abhandlungen der Völker-Kundlichen Arbeitsgemeinschaft* Heft 5.

Hacquebord, Louwrens, and Richard Vaughan, eds. 1987. *Between Greenland and America: Cross Cultural Contacts and the Environment in the Baffin Bay Area*. Groningen: Arctic Centre, Univ. of Groningen.

Hakluyt, Richard. 1582. *Diverse voyages touching the discouerie of America and the islands adiacent unto the same ...* London: Thomas Woodcocke. Reprint. New York: Barnes and Noble, 1967.

Hall, Richard Willmott. 1814. *Memoirs of Military Surgery and Campaigns of the French Armies*. From the French of D.J. Larrey, MD. 2 vols. Baltimore: Joseph Cushing.

Hallowell, A.F. 1926. "Bear Ceremonialism in the Northern Hemisphere." *American Anthropologist* 28, no.1: 1–175.

Handcock, W. Gordon. 1987. "The View from Mount Janus: John Cartwright's 1768 Exploits River Toponymy." *Newfoundland Quarterly* 85, no.1: 17–21.

Hardy, Christian, and Ingeborg Marshall. 1980. "A New Portrait of Mary March." *Newfoundland Quarterly* 76, no.1: 25–8.

Harp, Elmer, Jr. 1964. *The Cultural Affinities of the Newfoundland Dorset Eskimo*. Bulletin 200. Ottawa: National Museum of Canada.

– 1970. "Late Dorset Eskimo Art from Newfoundland." *Folk* 11–12: 109–24.

Harper, J. Russell. 1957. "Two Seventeenth-Century Copper-Kettle Burials." *Anthropologia* 4. Reprint. N.p.: K. Hopps, n.d., 11–36.

Harrisse, Henry. 1900. *Découverte et évolution cartographique de Terre-Neuve et des pays circonvoisins 1497–1501–1769*. Ed. H. Welter. London: Henry Stevens, Son and Stiles.

Hart, Simon. 1959. *The Prehistory of the New Netherland Company*. Amsterdam: City of Amsterdam Press.

Hatt, Gudmund. 1914. "Arctic Skin Clothing in Eurasia and America." Trans. from Danish. *Arctic Anthropology* 5, no.2: 3–132.

– 1916. *Moccasins and Their Relations to Arctic Footwear*. Memoirs of the American Anthropologist Association, Vol. 3. Reprint. New York: Kraus Rpt, 1964.

Hatton, J., and M. Harvey. 1883. *Newfoundland*. Boston: Doyle and Whittle.

Head, C. Grant. 1976. *Eighteenth Century Newfoundland*. Carleton Library No. 99. Ottawa: Carleton Univ. Press.

Hearne, Samuel. 1958. *A Journey from Prince of Wales's Fort in Hudson Bay to the Northern Ocean 1769–1772*. Ed. R. Glover. Toronto: Macmillan.

Heidenreich, Conrad E. 1978. "Huron." In *Northeast*, ed. Bruce G. Trigger, 368–88. Vol. 15 of *Handbook of North American Indians*. Ed. William C. Sturtevant. Washington, DC: Smithsonian Inst.

Helm, June. 1981. "Dogrib." In *Subarctic*, ed. June Helm, 291–309. Vol. 6 of *Handbook of North American Indians*. Ed. William C. Sturtevant, Washington, DC: Smithsonian Inst.

Helm, June, ed. *Subarctic*. Vol. 6 of *Handbook of North American Indians*, ed. William C. Sturtevant. 20 vols. Washington, DC: Smithsonian Inst.

Henriksen, Georg. 1973. *Hunters in the Barrens*. ISER Publ. 12. Toronto: Univ. Toronto Press.

Hewson, John. 1968. "The Etymology of 'Beothuk.' " *Newfoundland Quarterly* 66, no.3: 13–16.

– 1971. "Beothuk Consonant Correspondences." *International Journal of American Linguistics* 37, no.4: 244–9.

– 1978. *Beothuk Vocabularies*. St John's: Technical Papers of the Newfoundland Museum 2, 1978.

– 1981. "The Name *Presentic* and Other Ancient Micmac Toponyms." *Newfoundland Quarterly* 77, no.4: 11–14.

– 1982. "Beothuk and the Algonkian Northeast." *Languages in Newfoundland and Labrador*. 2d vers. Ed. Harold J. Paddock, 176–87. Ts. St John's: Dept. of Linguistics, Memorial Univ. of Newfoundland, and CNS.

Hiller, J.K. 1983–84. "The Newfoundland Seal fishery." *Bulletin of Canadian Studies* 7, no.2: 49–72.

Hind, H.Y. 1863. *Exploration in the Interior of the Labrador Peninsula*. 2 vols. London: Longman and Green, Longman, Roberts and Green. Reprint. New York: Kraus, 1973.

Hodge, F.W., ed. 1910. *Handbook of American Indians North of Mexico*. 2 vols. Bureau of American Ethology, Bulletin 30. Washington, DC: Smithsonian Inst.

Hoffman, Bernard G. 1955. "The Historical Ethnography of the Micmacs of the Sixteenth and Seventeenth Centuries." Ph.D. diss. Univ. of California.

– 1961. *Cabot to Cartier*. Toronto: Univ. of Toronto Press.

– 1963. "Account of a Voyage conducted in 1529 to the New World, Africa, Madagascar, and Sumatra, Translated from the Italian with Notes and Comments." *Ethnohistory* 10, no.1: 1–79.

Hoffman, W.J. 1891. "The Medewiwin or 'Grand Medicine Society' of the Ojibwa." *Seventh Annual Report of the Bureau of American Ethnology for the years 1885–1886*. 143–300. Smithsonian Institution. Washington, DC: Govt. Printing Office.

Honigman, John J. 1981. "West Main Cree." In *Subarctic*, ed. June Helm, 217–30. Vol. 6 of *Handbook of North American Indians*. Ed. William C. Sturtevant, Washington, DC: Smithsonian Inst.

Horwood, Harold. 1959. "The People Who Were Murdered for Fun." *MacLean's Magazine* 72, no.2 (10 October): 27, 36, 38, 40, 42–3.

– 1959. "The Story of the Beothucks." Five talks broadcast over CBN. Transcript in Library of Parliament, Ottawa.

– 1963. "Who were the Beothucks?" *Evening Telegram*, 30 January and 6 February.

Hosie, R.C. 1979. *Native Trees of Canada*. Don Mills: Fitzhenry and Whiteside.

Hosley, Edward H. 1981. "Environment and Culture in the Alaskan Plateau," and "Kolchan." In *Subarctic*, ed. June Helm, 533–45, 618–22. Vol. 6 of *Handbook of North American Indians*. Ed. William C. Sturtevant. Washington, DC: Smithsonian Inst.

Howley, J.P. N.d. "Reminiscences." Ed. G.M. Story, William J. Kirwin and Patrick O'Flaherty. Is to be published.

– 1893. "In Reference to Mary March – The 'Last of the Red Indians'." *Evening Telegram*, St John's, 7 June.

– 1915. *The Beothucks or Red Indians*. Cambridge: Cambridge Univ. Press.

Howley, Michael. 1903. "The Old French Graveyard." *Evening Telegram*, St John's, 23 June.

Humber, Alan George. 1969. "Index to J.P. Howley's *The Beothuks*." Ts. CNS.

Ingstad, Anne Stine. 1985. *The Norse Discovery of America*. 2 vols. Oslo: Norwegian Univ. Press.

Innes, Harold A. 1940. *The Codfisheries*. Toronto: Univ. of Toronto Press. Reprint. 1978.

Isasti, Lope de. 1850. *Compendio historical de la muy noble y muy leal provincia de Guipuzcoa*. San Sebastian: Presa Ramon Baroja.

Jenness, Diamond. 1929. "Notes on the Beothuk Indians of Newfoundland." *National Museum of Canada Dept. of Mines Annual Report for 1927. Bulletin 56*. 36–9.

– 1932. *The Indians of Canada*. National Museum of Canada Dept. of Mines. Bulletin 65. Ottawa: F.A. Acland.

– 1934. "The Vanished Red Indians of Newfoundland." *Canadian Geographic Journal* 8, no.1: 26–32.

– 1935. "The Ojibway Indians of Parry Island." *National Museum of Canada Dept. of Mines*, no.78. Ottawa: J.O. Patenande.

Jerkic, M., P. Horne, A. Aufderheide. 1995. "Biology and History: Studies of a Beothuk Mummy." Paper presented at the 2d International Congress on Mummy Studies, Feb. 6–9, 1995, Cartagena, Columbia.

Jochelson, Waldemar. 1906, 1907. "Past and Present Subterranean Dwellings of the Tribes of North Eastern Asia and North Western America." 2 vols. *Congrès International des Américanistes XVe Session*. Quebec.

– 1908. *The Koryak*. The Jesup North Pacific Expedition. Memoir of the American Museum of Natural History VI. Ed. Franz Boas. Reprint. New York: Brill, Leiden and G.E. Stechert, 1975.

Johnston, Angus A. 1960–61. *A History of the Catholic Church in Eastern Nova Scotia*. 2 vols. Antigonish, NS: St Francis Xavier Univ. Press.

Jonaitis, Aldona. 1978. "Land Otters and Shamans: Some Interpretations of Tlingit Charms." *American Indian Magazine* 4, no.1: 62–6.

Jones, A.W. 1982. "Assessment and Analysis of the Micmac Land Claim in Newfoundland." Ts. St John's: Govt. of Newfoundland and Labrador.

Jukes, J.B. 1842. *Excursions in and about Newfoundland during the Years 1839 and 1840*. 2 vols. London: J. Murray. Reprint. Toronto: Canadiana House, 1969.

– 1847. "Notice on the Aborigines of Newfoundland." *British Association for the Advancement of Science Report for 1846*, p. 114.

Kalm, Peter. 1770. *Peter Kalm's Travels in North America*. Trans. and ed. Adolph B. Benson. 2 vols. Reprint. New York: Dover, 1964.

Kennan, George. 1910. *Tent Life in Siberia*. New York: Knickerbocker Press.

Kennett, Brenda L. 1990. "Phillip's Garden East: An Examination of the Groswater Palaeo-Eskimo Phase." Master's thesis, Memorial University of Newfoundland, St John's.

King, J.C.H. 1982. *Thunderbird and Lightening*. London: British Museum.

Kirke, Henry. 1908. *The First English Conquest of Canada: With Some Accounts of the Earlier Settlements in Nova Scotia and Newfoundland*. 2d ed. London: S. Low Marston.

Kleivan, Helge. 1966. *The Eskimos of Northeast Labrador*. Oslo: Norsk Polar Inst.

Kleivan, Inge. 1984. "West Greenland before 1950." In *Arctic*, ed. David Damas, 595–621. Vol. 5 of *Handbook of North American Indians*. Ed. William C. Sturtevant. Washington, DC: Smithsonian Inst.

Kroeber, A.L. 1939. *Cultural and Natural Areas of Native North America*. Berkeley: Univ. of California Press. Reprint. New York: Kraus Rpt., 1963.

Kroeber, A.L., ed. 1953, *Anthropology Today*. Chicago: Univ. of Chicago Press.

Krol, Carol Frances. 1986. "Middle Dorset Settlement-Subsistence Patterns in Western Newfoundland: A View from Broom Point." Master's thesis, Memorial University of Newfoundland, St John's.

Kupp, J., and Simon Hart. 1976. "The Dutch in the Strait of Davis and Labrador during the Seventeenth and Eighteenth Centuries." *Man in the Northeast* 11, no.1 (Spring): 3–20.

Kuppermann, K.O. 1980. *Settling with the Indians*. Totowa, NJ: Rowman and Littlefield.

Laet, Ioannes de. 1625. *Nieuvve wereldt ofte beschryvinghe van West Indian; wt. veelderhande schriften*. Leyden: Druckerye van Isaac Elzevier.

– 1640. *L'histoire du Nouveau-Monde au description des Indes Occidentales*. Contenant dix Huit Livres, Leyde: Chez Bonaventure et Abraham Elzevier.

Lahey, R.J. 1977. "The Role of Religion in Lord Baltimore's Colonial Enterprise." *Maryland Historical Magazine* 72, no. 4: 492–511.

Lahontan, L.A. 1703. *New Voyage to North America*. 2 vols. Reprint. Chicago: McClury and Co., 1905.

Lane, Robert B. 1981. "Chilcotin." In *Subarctic*, ed. June Helm, 402–12. Vol. 6 of *Handbook of North American Indians*. Ed. William C. Sturtevant. Washington, DC: Smithsonian Inst.

Lane, Watson. 1976. "History of Glovertown." Ms. CNS.

Latham, Robert G. 1850. *Natural History of the Varieties of Man*. London: J. Van Voorst.

LeBlanc, Raymond Joseph. 1973. "The Wigwam Brook Site and the Historic Indians." Master's thesis, Memorial University of Newfoundland, St John's.

– 1984. *The Rat Indian Creek Site and the Late Prehistoric Period in the Interior Northern Yukon*. Ottawa: National Museum of Man, Mercury Series, Archaeological Survey of Canada, Paper No. 120.

LeClercq, Chrestien. 1910. *New Relations of Gaspesia – With Customs and Religion of the Gaspesian Indians*. Ed. William I. Ganong. Toronto: Champlain Society. Facs. ed. New York: Greenwood Press, 1968.

Lescarbot, Marc. 1609. *Nova Francia: A Description of Acadia*. Trans. P. Erondelle, London. Reprint, with an introduction by H.P. Biggar. New York and London: Harper and Bros., 1928.

– 1911. *History of New France*. 3 vols. Trans., notes, and app. by W.L. Grant. Toronto: Champlain Society. Facs. ed. New York: Greenwood Press, 1968.

Linnamae, Urve. 1971. "Preliminary Report of an Archaeological Survey of Placentia Bay, Newfoundland." Ts. Newfoundland Museum, St John's.

– 1975. *The Dorset Culture*. St John's: Technical Papers of the Newfoundland Museum 1.

Lloyd, T.G.B. 1875. "On the 'Beothucs,' a tribe of red Indians, supposed to be extinct, which formerly inhabited Newfoundland." *Royal Anthropological Institute of Great Britain and Ireland Journal* 4:21–39.

– 1876a. "A Further Account of the Beothucs of Newfoundland." *Royal Anthropological Institute of Great Britain and Ireland Journal* 5:222–30.

– 1876b. "On the Stone Implements of Newfoundland." *Royal Anthropological Institute of Great Britain and Ireland Journal* 5:233–48.

Locke, Don. 1972. "Three Beothuk Sites." *Newfoundland Quarterly* 69, no.2: 29–31.

– [1974]. *Beothuk Artifacts*. N.p.: n.p.

– 1975. "Historic and Prehistoric Sites: Indian Point Beothuk Historic Site, Wigwam Brook." Ts. CNS.

Loring, Stephen. 1983. "An Archaeological Survey of the Inner Bay Region between Nain and Davis Inlet, Labrador: A report of 1982 Field Work." In *Archaeology in Newfoundland and Labrador 1982*, eds. J. Sproull Thomson and C. Thomson, Annual Report 3, 32–56. St John's: Historic Resources Division, Dept. of Culture, Recreation and Youth, Govt. of Newfoundland and Labrador.

– 1985. "Archaeological Investigations into the Nature of the Late Prehistoric Indian Occupation in Labrador: A Report on the 1984 Field Season." In *Archaeology in Newfoundland and Labrador 1984*, eds. J. Sproull Thomson and C. Thomson, Annual Report 5, 122–53. St John's: Historic Resources Division, Dept. of Culture, Recreation and Youth, Govt. of Newfoundland and Labrador.

– 1988. "Keeping Things Whole: Nearly Two Thousand Years of Indian (Innu) Occupation in Northern Labrador." In *Boreal Forest and Sub-Arctic Archaeology*, ed. C.S. "Paddy" Reid, 157–71. London, Ontario: Occasional Publ. of the London Chapter, Ontario Archaeology Society No.6.

– 1989. "Tikkoatokak (HdCl-1): A Late Prehistoric Indian Site near Nain." In *Archaeology in Newfoundlandand and Labrador 1986*, eds. C. Thomson and J. Sproull Thomson, Annual Report 7, 52–69. St John's: Newfoundland Museum, Historic Resources Division, Dept. of Municipal and Provincial Affairs, Govt. of Newfoundland and Labrador.

– 1992. "Princes and Princesses of Ragged Fame; Innu Archaeology and Ethnohistory in Labrador." Ph.D. diss., Univ. of Massachusetts.

Lowie, Robert H., ed. 1936. *Essays in Anthropology in Honour of Alfred Louis Kroeber*. Berkely and Los Angeles: Univ. of California Press. Reprint. Freeport, NY: Books for Libraries Press, 1968.

Lurie, Nancy Oestreich. 1978. "Winnebago." In *Northeast*, ed. Bruce G. Trigger, 690–707. Vol. 15 of *Handbook of North American Indians*. Ed. William C. Sturtevant. Washington, DC: Smithsonian Inst.

Lysaght, A.M. 1971. *Joseph Banks in Newfoundland and Labrador*. Berkeley and Los Angeles: Univ. of California Press.

McCaffrey, Moira T. 1986. "La préhistoire des Îles de la Madeleine: bilan préliminaire." In *Les Micmacs et la mer*, ed. Charles A. Martijn, 98–162. Montreal: Recherches Amérindiennes au Québec.

McClellan, Catharine. 1981. "Tagish." In *Subarctic*, ed. June Helm, 481–92. Vol. 6 of *Handbook of North American Indians*. Ed. William C. Sturtevant. Washington, DC: Smithsonian Inst.

– "Tutchtone." In *Subarctic*, ed. June Helm, 493–505, Vol. 6. of Handbook of North American Indians. Washington, DC: Smithsonian Inst.

McClellan, Catharine, and Glenda Denninston. "Environment and Culture in the Cordillera." In *Subarctic*, ed. June Helm, 372–86. Vol. 6 of *Handbook of North American Indians*. Ed. William C. Sturtevant. Washington, DC: Smithsonian Inst.

MacDougall, Allen. 1891. "The Beothick Indians." *Transactions of the Canadian Institute* 2, no.3:98–102.

McGhee, Robert. 1974. "Late Dorset Art from Dundas Island, Arctic Canada." *Folk* 16–17: 133–45.

– 1978. *Canadian Arctic Prehistory*. National Museum of Man, National Museums of Canada. New York, London: Van Nostrand Reinhold.

– 1984a. "Contact between Native North Americans and the Medieval North: A Review of the Evidence." *American Antiquity* 49, no.1:4–26.

– 1984b. "Thule prehistory of Canada." In *Arctic*, ed. David Damas, 369–76. Vol. 5 of *Handbook of North American Indians*. Ed. William C. Sturtevant. Washington, DC: Smithsonian Inst.

McGhee, Robert, and James A. Tuck. 1975. *An Archaic Sequence from the Strait of Belle Isle, Labrador*. Ottawa: National Museum of Man, Mercury Series. Archaeological Survey of Canada, Paper No. 34.

McGregor, John. 1832. *British America*. 2 vols. Edinburgh: William Blackwood. London: T. Cadell. 2d ed. 1833.

"McGregor's British America." 1832. *Blackwood's Edinburgh Magazine* 31, no.6: 907–17.

McKennan, Robert A. 1981. "Tanana." In *Subarctic*, ed. June Helm, 562–76. Vol. 6 of *Handbook of North American Indians*. Ed.William C. Sturtevant. Washington, DC: Smithsonian Inst.

MacLean, Laurie. 1990a. "Inventory of Artifacts Obtained by Newfoundland Museum from Don Locke Jr Catalogued between 1 Dec. 1988 and 31 March 1989; 15 Jan. to 19 April, 1990." Ts. Newfoundland Museum, St John's.

– 1990b. "A 1989 Report on Archaeological Survey in Bonavista Bay." Ts. Newfoundland Museum, St John's.

– 1990c. "Beothuk Iron – Evidence for European trade?" *Newfoundland Studies* 6, no.2: 168–76.

– 1991. "Burnside Heritage Project: Archaeology Report for Summer 1990." Ts. Newfoundland Museum, St John's.

– 1993. "Burnside Heritage Project, Interim Report for 1992 Archaeological Field Season." Ts. Newfoundland Museum, St John's.

McLean, Ruari. 1972. *Victorian Book Design and Colour Printing*. Berkeley and Los Angeles: Univ. of California Press.

MacLeod, Donald. 1966. "Archaeological Field Trip to Newfoundland, 24 May to 3 June 1966 (DjAn-1)." Ts. 256. National Museum of Canada, Archaeological Survey.

McNutt, Frances August, trans. and ed. 1912. *De Orbe Novo. The Eight Decades of Peter Martyr D'Anghera*. 2 vols. London and New York: G.P. Putnam's Sons.

Macpherson, A.G., and J.B. Macpherson, eds. 1981. *The Natural Environment of Newfoundland Past and Present*. St John's: Department of Geography, Memorial University of Newfoundland.

Macpherson, David. 1805. *Annals of Commerce, Manufactures, Fisheries, Navigation, etc.* 4 vols. London and Edinburgh: Nichols and Son and Others.

Magnusson, Magnus, and Hermann Palsson. 1965. *The Vinland Sagas: The Norse Discovery of America*. Harmondsworth: Penguin Books. Reprint. 1976.

Mahoney, Shane P. 1980. "The Grey River Caribou Study, Newfoundland Wildlife Division."Ts. CNS.

Mailot, J., J.P. Simard, and S. Vincent. 1980. "On est toujours l'Esquimau de quelqu'un." *Études/Inuit/Studies* 4, nos.1–2:59–76.

Mannion, John J., ed. 1977. *The Peopling of Newfoundland*. ISER Publ. no.8. St John's: Memorial Univ. of Newfoundland.

Mansfield, A.W. 1964. *Seals of Arctic and Eastern Canada*. Bulletin 137. Ottawa: Fisheries Research Board of Canada.

Marshall, Ingeborg. 1973. "Report on the Survey of Beothuck Indian Burials in the Bay of Exploits, Notre Dame Bay." Ts. Newfoundland Museum, St John's.

– 1974a. "A New Collection of Beothuck Indian Decorated Bone Pieces." *Man in the Northeast*, no.8 (Spring):41–56.

– 1974b. "Report on the Field Trip to Notre Dame Bay, Newfoundland from 7 June to 7 July for the Newfoundland Museum." Ts. Newfoundland Museum, St John's.

– 1975. "Beothuk Carved Bone Pieces." Ts. In the author's possession.

– 1977a "An Unpublished Map Made by John Cartwright between 1768 and 1773 Showing Beothuck Indian Settlements and Artifacts and Allowing a New Population Estimate." *Ethnohistory* 24, no.3: 223–49.

– 1977b. "The miniature Portrait of Mary March." *Newfoundland Quarterly* 73, no.3: 4–7.

– 1978a. "Report on an Archaeological Survey, June/July 1978." Ts. Newfoundland Museum, St John's.

– 1978b. "The Significance of Beothuk Carved Bone Pendants." *Canadian Journal of Archaeology* 2:139–54.

– 1980. "Report on Beothuck Indian Sites on the Island of Newfoundland." Ts. Newfoundland Museum, St John's.

– 1981. "Disease as a Factor in the Demise of the Beothuk Indians." *Culture* 1, no.1: 71–7. Updated version in *Change and Continuity*, ed. Carol Wilton, 138–49. Toronto, Montreal: McGraw-Hill Ryerson, 1992.

– 1985. *Beothuk Bark Canoes: An Analysis and Comparative Study.* Ottawa: National Museum of Man, Mercury Series, Canadian Ethnology Service, Paper No. 102.

– 1986. "Methodist and Beothuk: Research in Methodist Archives." *Newfoundland Studies* 2, no.1: 18–28.

– 1988a. "Beothuk and Micmac: Re-examining Relationships." *Acadiensis* 17, no.2: 52–82.

– 1988b. "Newfoundland Beothuk Illustrated." *Man in the Northeast*, no.35 (Spring):47–70.

– 1989. *Reports and Letters by George Christopher Pulling, Relating to the Beothuk Indians of Newfoundland.* St John's: Breakwater Books.

– 1990. "Evidence for Two Beothuk Subsistence Economies." In *Papers of the Twenty-First Algonquian Conference*, ed. William Cowan, 216–26. Ottawa: Carleton Univ. Press.

Martijn, Charles A. 1980a. "La présence Inuit sur la Côte-Nord du Golfe St Laurent a l'époque historique." *Études/Inuit/Studies* 4, no.1–2: 105–25.

– 1980b. "The 'Esquimaux' in the Seventeenth and Eighteenth Century Cartography of the Gulf of St Lawrence: A Preliminary Discussion." *Études/Inuit/Studies* 4, no.1–2: 77–104.

– 1980c. "The Inuit of Southern Quebec-Labrador: A Rejoinder to J. Garth Taylor." *Études/Inuit/Studies* 4, no.1–2: 194–8.

– 1981. "Les armoiries de Terre-Neuve et l'iconographie Béothuk." *Recherches Amérindiennes au Québec* 11, no.4: 315–18.

– 1990a. "Innu (Montagnais) in Newfoundland." In *Papers of the Twenty-First Algonquian Conference*, ed. William Cowan, 227–46. Ottawa: Carleton Univ. Press.

– 1990b. "The Iroquoian Presence in the Estuary and Gulf of the Saint Lawrence River Valley: A Re-evaluation." *Man in the Northeast*, no.40 (Fall): 45–63.

Martijn, Charles A., ed. 1986. *Les Micmacs et la mer.* Montreal: Recherches Amérindiennes au Québec.

Martin, Calvin. 1978. *Keepers of the Game*. Berkeley and Los Angeles, London: Univ. of California Press.

Martin, R. Montgomery. 1837. *History of Nova Scotia*. London: Whittaker.

Mathiassen, Therkel. 1928. *Material culture of the Iglulik Eskimos*. Report of the Fifth Thule Expedition 1921–1924. Vol. 6, no. 1. Copenhagen: Gyldendalske Boghandel. Reprint. New York AMS Press, 1976.

Matthews, Keith. 1988. *Lectures on the History of Newfoundland 1500–1830*. St John's: Breakwater Books.

Mechling, W.H. 1914. *Malecite Tales*. Ottawa: Geological Survey of Canada, Memoir 49, Anthropological Series No.4.

Meldgaard, Morten. 1986. *The Greenland Caribou – Zoogeography, Taxonomy, and Population Dynamics*. Meddelelser om Groenland. Bioscience, monogr. 20.

Mercantile Journal, The. 1819. 27 May, 2; 3 June, 2; 19 August, 2.

Messurier, Le, W.H. 1916. "The Early Relations between Newfoundland and the Channel Islands." *Geographical Review* 2, no.6: 449–57.

Michelant, T., and A. Ramé. 1867. *Relation originale du voyage des Jacques Cartier au Canada en 1534*. Paris: Librairie Tross.

Millais, G.J. 1907. *Newfoundland and Its Untrodden Ways*. New York, London: Longmans, Green and Co.

Miller, Alfred J. 1973. *Braves and Buffalo, Plains Indian Life in 1837*. The Public Archives of Canada Series. Toronto: Univ. of Toronto Press.

Mission Field, The, a Monthly Record of the Proceedings of the Society for the Propagation of the Gospel, at Home and Abroad. 1856. Vol.1. London: Bell and Daldy, 186 Fleet Street.

Mooney, James. 1910. "Population." In *Handbook of American Indians North of Mexico*, ed. F.W. Hodge, vol. 2, 286–7. Bureau of American Ethnology, Bulletin 30. Washington, DC: Smithsonian Inst. Reprint. New York: Green Wood Press, 1969.

– 1928. *The Aboriginal Population of North America, North of Mexico*. Published posthumously by John R. Swanton. Smithson ian Miscellaneous Collections 80, no. 7. Washington, DC: Smithsonian Inst.

Moore, P.E. 1961. "No Longer Captain. A history of TB and Its Control amongst Canadian Indians." *Canadian Medical Association Journal* 84, no.18: 1012–16.

Moores, David. 1986. "Beothuck Memorial." *Newfoundland Herald*, St John's, 13 September.

Morandière, Charles Jolliot de la. 1962. *Histoire de la pêche Française de la morue dans l'Amérique septentrionale*. 3 vols. Généralités Paris: G.P. Maisonneuve et Larose.

Morice, Adrian G. 1905. *The History of the Northern Interior of British Columbia (Formerly New Caledonia) 1660–1880*. 3d ed. Toronto: William Briggs.

– 1907. "The Great Dene Race." *Anthropos* 2:1–34.

Morison, S.E. 1940. *Portuguese Voyages to America in the Fifteenth Century*. Cambridge, MA: Harvard Univ. Press.

– 1971. *The European Discovery of America: The Northern Voyages AD 1500–1600*. New York: Oxford Univ. Press.

Morris, Patrick. 1827. *Remarks on the State of Society, Religion, Morals and Education at Newfoundland*. London: A. Hancock.

Mullock, J.T. 1860. "Two Lectures on Newfoundland." New York: John Mullaly, Office of the Metropolitan Record.

Murray, Jean M., ed. 1968. *The Newfoundland Journal of Aaron Thomas*. Don Mills: Longmans Canada.

Nelson, Edward W. 1899. *The Eskimo about Bering Strait*. Annual Report of the Bureau of American Ethnology for the years 1896–1897, 18, no.1: 3–518. Smithsonian Institution, Reprint. New York: Johnson Rprt., 1971.

Newfoundland. 1858. "Abstract Census and Return of the Population etc. of Newfoundland, 1857." *Journal of the House of Assembly*. St John's: E.D. Shea.

Nietfeld, Patricia K.L. 1981. "Determinants of Aboriginal Micmac Political Structure." Ph.D. diss. University of Albuquerque, Albuquerque, New Mexico.

Noad, Joseph. 1859. *Lecture on the Aborigines of Newfoundland*. St John's: R.J. Parsons.

O'Callaghan, E.B., and B. Fernow. 1853–87. *Documents Related to the Colonial History of the State of New York*. 15 vols. Albany, NY: Weed, Parsons and Co.

Orchard, William C. 1984. *The Technique of Porcupine Quill Decoration among the North American Indians*. Ogden, Utah: Eagle's View Publ.

O'Reilly, James A., and William S. Grodinsky. 1982. "Consolidation of Historical Material Containing Specific References to the Use of Newfoundland by Micmacs prior to 1763 and Relating to the Land Claim Submitted by Ktaqamkuk Ilnui Saqimawoutie and the Conne River Indian Band Council." Ts. Govt. of Newfoundland.

Osborne, John W. 1972. *John Cartwright*. Cambridge: Cambridge Univ. Press.

Osgood, Cornelius. 1936. *Contributions to the Ethnography of the Kutchin*. Yale University Publications in Anthropology 14. Reprint. New Haven, CT: Human Relations Area File Press, 1970.

Packard, A.S. 1891. *The Labrador Coast: A Journal*. New York: N.D. Hodges.

Parsons, E.C. 1925. "Micmac Folklore." *Journal of American Folklore* 38, no.147: 55–133.

Parsons, Jacob. 1964. "The Origin and Growth of Newfoundland Methodism, 1765–1855." Master's thesis, Memorial University of Newfoundland, St John's.

Pastore, Ralph T. 1978. *Newfoundland Micmacs: A History of Their Traditional Life*. St John's: Newfoundland Historical Society Pamphlet No. 5.

– 1981. "A Survey of the Pilley's Island Region, Fall 1980; Preliminary Report." Ts. Newfoundland Museum, St John's.

– 1982. "Preliminary Report of a Survey of Eastern Notre Dame Bay." In *Archaeology in Newfoundland and Labrador 1981*, eds. J. Sproull Thomson and C. Thomson, Annual Report 2, 152–75. St John's: Historic Resources Division, Dept. of Culture, Recreation and Youth, Govt. of Newfoundland and Labrador.

– 1983. "A Preliminary Report on Investigations at Boyd's Cove – A Beothuk and Recent Indian Site in Notre Dame Bay, Newfoundland." In *Archaeology in Newfoundland and Labrador 1982*, eds. J. Sproull Thomson and C. Thomson, Annual Report 3, 133–60. St John's: Newfoundland Museum, Historic Resources Division, Govt. of Newfoundland and Labrador.

– 1984. "Excavation at Boyd's Cove, Notre Dame Bay – 1983." In *Archaeology in Newfoundland and Labrador 1983*, eds. J. Sproull Thomson and C. Thomson, Annual Report 4, 98–109. St John's: Historic Resources Division, Dept. of Culture, Recreation and Youth, Govt. of Newfoundland and Labrador.

– 1985. "Excavations at Boyd's Cove, 1984: A Preliminary Report." In *Archaeology in Newfoundland and Labrador 1984*, eds. J. Sproull Thomson and C. Thomson, Annual Report 5, 322–37. St John's: Historic Resources Division, Dept. of Culture, Recreation and Youth, Govt. of Newfoundland and Labrador.

– 1986a. "Excavations at Boyd's Cove: The 1985 Field Season, a Preliminary Report." In *Archaeology in Newfoundland and Labrador 1985*, eds. J. Sproull Thomson and C. Thomson, Annual Report 6, 218–32. St John's: Newfoundland Museum, Historic Resources Division, Dept. of Culture, Recreation and Youth, Govt. of Newfoundland and Labrador.

– 1986b. "The Spatial Distribution of Late Palaeo-Eskimo Sites on the Island of Newfoundland." *Paleo-Eskimo Cultures in Newfoundland, Labrador, and Ungava*. Reports in Archaeology No. 1, 125–34. St John's: Memorial Univ. of Newfoundland.

– 1987. "Fishermen, Furriers, and Beothuks: The Economy of Extinction." *Man in the Northeast* 33 (Spring):47–62.

– 1989a. "The Collapse of the Beothuk World." *Acadiensis* 19, no.1: 52–71.

– 1989b. "Report for Permit no. 86–16. Inspector Island (DiAq- 1)." In *Archaeology in Newfoundland and Labrador 1986*, eds. C. Thomson and J. Sproull Thomson, Annual Report 7, 260–9. St John's: Newfoundland Museum, Historic Resources Division, Dept. of Municipal and Provincial Affairs, Govt. of Newfoundland and Labrador.

– 1992. *Shanawdithit's People.* Atlantic Archaeology, St John's.

Patterson, George. 1892. "The Beothiks or Red Indians of Newfoundland." *Transactions of the Royal Society of Canada, 1891*. Sect.2:123–71.

– 1893. "Beothik Vocabularies. With a Few Notes on the Paper on the Beothiks in 'Transactions of Royal Society of Canada, 1891.'" *Transactions of the Royal Society of Canada, 1892*. Sect.2:19–26.

Payne, Brian. 1973. "An Analysis of Criminal and Civil Cases in the Ferryland and Placentia Court Records." Ts. Marit. Hist. Arch. Memorial Univ. of NF.

Pedley, Charles. 1863. *The History of Newfoundland from the Earliest Times to the Year 1860*. London: Longman, Roberts and Green.

Penney, Gerald. 1978. "An Archaeological Survey of the North Side of Trinity Bay from Cape Bonavista to the Isthmus of the Avalon." Ts. Newfoundland Museum, St John's.

– 1984a. "The Prehistory of the Southwest Coast of Newfoundland." Master's thesis, Memorial University of Newfoundland, St John's.

– 1984b. "The Historic Resources Cow Head/Spanish Room Oil Rig Repair Facility." Ts. Newfoundland Museum, St John's.

– 1985a. "Placentia Bay Environmental Impact Study Prepared for the Dept. of Development and Tourism." Ts. Newfoundland Museum, St John's.

– 1985b. "Micmac Project Report 1984, Spanish Room Survey 1984." In *Archaeology in Newfoundland and Labrador 1984*, eds. J. Sproull Thomson and C. Thomson, Annual Report 5, 338–43. St John's: Historic Resources Division, Dept. of Culture, Recreation and Youth, Govt. of Newfoundland and Labrador.

– 1986. "Results of Four Historic Resources Assessments in Newfoundland and Labrador." In *Archaeology in Newfoundland and Labrador 1985*, eds. J. Sproull Thomson and C. Thomson, Annual Report 6, 66–80. St John's: Newfoundland Museum, Historic Resources Division, Dept. of Culture, Recreation and Youth, Govt. of Newfoundland and Labrador.

– 1987a."Historic Resources Overview Assessment of the Proposed Hope Brook Station to Grand Bruit Station Distribution Line for Newfoundland-Labrador Hydro."Ts. Historic Resources Division, Government of Newfoundland and Labrador.

– 1987b. "Report on an Archaeological Survey of King George IV Lake." Ts. Historic Resources Division, Govt. of Newfoundland and Labrador.

– 1988. "An Archaeological Survey of Western Notre Dame Bay and Green Bay." Ts. Newfoundland Museum, St John's.

– 1989a. "Results of Six Historic Resources Overview Assessments in Newfoundland and Labrador – 1986." In *Archaeology in Newfoundland and Labrador 1986*, eds. C. Thomson and J. Sproull Thomson, Annual Report 7, 12–26. St John's: Newfoundland Museum, Historic Resources Division, Dept. of Municipal and Provincial Affairs, Govt. of Newfoundland and Labrador.

– 1989b. "Annual Report of Archaeological Activities 1989." Gerald Penney Assoc. St John's. Ts. Newfoundland Museum, St John's.

– 1994. "Preliminary Report Katalisk Archaeological Survey 1993." Ts. Historic Resources Division, Govt. of Newfoundland and Labrador.

Peters, Harold S., and Thomas D. Burleigh. 1951. *The Birds of Newfoundland*. St John's: Dept. of Natural Resources, Province of Newfoundland and Labrador.

Peyton, Amy Louise. 1987. *River Lords, Father and Son*. St John's: Jesperson Press.

– 1986. "Cormack Doesn't Deserve Credit." *Evening Telegram*, St John's, 12 February.

Pintal, Jean-Ives. 1989. "Contributions à la préhistoire reconte de Blanc Sablon." *Recherches Amérindiennes au Québec* 19, nos.2–3:33–44.

Podolinski Webber, Alika. 1980. *Hidden Patterns*. N.p., n.p. Copy in CNS, Memorial University of Newfoundland.

– 1984. *The Rod and the Circle*. N.p., n.p. Rev. ed. 1986. Copy in CNS, Memorial University of Newfoundland.

Powell, John W. 1891. "Indian linguistic families of America North of Mexico." *Seventh Annual Report of the Bureau of Ethnology for the years 1885–86*. 7–142. Smithsonian Institution. Washington, DC: Govt. Printing Office.

Poynter, F.N.L., ed. 1963. *The Journal of James Yonge 1647–1721, Plymouth Surgeon*. London: Longmans.

Preston, Richard J. 1981. "East Main Cree." In *Subarctic*, ed. June Helm, 196–207. Vol. 6 of *Handbook of North American Indians*. Ed. William C. Sturtevant. Washington, DC: Smithsonian Inst. Press.

Prowse, D.W. 1895. *A History of Newfoundland from the English, Colonial and Foreign Records*. London: Macmillan and Co. Facs. ed. Belleville, Ontario: Mika Studio, 1972.

Public Ledger, Tne. 1828. St John's, 15 January, 2 September.

Purchas, Samuel. 1905–07. *Hakluytus Posthumus or Purchas His Pilgrimes*. 20 vols. Glasgow: James MacLehose and Sons for the Hakluyt Society.

Quinn, Alison, and Raleigh Ashlin Skelton. 1965. *The Principal Navigations, Voyages and Discoveries of the English Nation*. 2 vols. London: Cambridge Univ. Press.

Quinn, David B. 1977. *North America from Earliest Discovery to First Settlements. The Norse Voyage to 1612*. New York, London: Harper and Row.

– 1979. *New American World*. 5 vols. New York: Arno Press.

– 1981. *Sources for the Ethnography of Northeastern North America to 1611*. Ottawa: National Museum of Man, Mercury Series, Canadian Ethnology Service, Paper No. 76.

Rand, Silas Tertius. 1894. *The Legends of the Micmacs*. Reprint. New York and London: Johnson Rpt., 1971.

Rasmussen, Knud J.V. 1929. *Intellectual Culture of the Iglulik Eskimos*. Report of the Fifth Thule Expedition 1921–24. Vol. 7. no. 1. Copenhagen: Gyldendalske Boghandel.

– 1931. *The Netsilik Eskimos*. Report of the Fifth Thule Expedition 1921–24. Vol. 8. no.1–2. Copenhagen: Gyldendalske Boghandel.

Raynauld, Francoy. 1974. "A Bibliography of the Beothuk Culture of Newfoundland." Ts. Museum of Man, Ottawa. Index no. 1467.3,III-A-10M.

– 1984. "Les pêcheurs et les colons Anglais n'ont pas exterminé les Béothuks de Terre-Neuve." *Recherches Amérindiennes au Québec* 14, no. 1: 45–59.

Reader, David. 1994. "Up the Creek." *Vis-à-Vis: Explorations in Anthropology* 5: 17–31.

"Red Indians of Newfoundland (The)." 1828. *The Kaleidoscope; or Literary and Scientific Mirror* (London), 26 February, 281.

Reid, C.S. "Paddy," ed. 1988. *Boreal Forest and Sub-Arctic Archaeology*. Occasional Publ. of the London Chapter 6. London, Ont.: Ontario Archaeology Society.

"Relict of a Red Indian." 1888. *Twillingate Sun*, Twillingate, 22 September.

Remmington, John, William Ellis and Samuel McDowell. 1809. "Extract of Letter from Messrs Rimmington, M'Dowell, and Ellis, to the Rev. Dr Coke." *Methodist Magazine* 33 (1810): 86.

Renouf, Miriam A.P. 1986. "1985 Excavations at Phillip's Garden and Pointe Riche, Port au Choix National Historic Park." In *Archaeology in Newfoundland and Labrador 1985*, eds. J. Sproull Thomson and C. Thomson, Annual Report 6, 159–95. St John's: Newfoundland Museum, Historic Resources Division, Dept. of Culture, Recreation and Youth, Govt. of Newfoundland and Labrador.

– 1987. *Archaeological Excavations at the Port au Choix National Historic Park: Report of 1986 Field Activities*. Prepared for Historic Resources Branch, Atlantic Region, Parks Canada. Halifax, NS: The Branch.

– 1991. "Archaeological Investigations at the Port au Choix National Historic Park; Report of the 1990 Field Season." Prepared for Archaeology, Atlantic Region, Canadian Parks Service, Halifax, NS. ts. CNS.

– 1992. "The 1991 Field Season, Port au Choix, National Historic Park, Report of Archaeological Excavations." Prepared for Archaeology, Atlantic Region, Parks Canada, Halifax NS.

– 1993. "The 1992 Field Season, Port au Choix, National Historic Park: Report of Archaeological Excavations." Prepared for Archaeology Atlantic Region, Parks Canada, Halifax, NS.

"Rev. John Clinch of Trinity's Vocabulary of the Language of the Native Indians …" 1888. *Harbour Grace Standard*, Harbour Grace, 2 May.

Reynolds, Barrie. 1978. "Beothuk." In *Northeast*, ed. Bruce G. Trigger, 101–08. Vol. 15 of *Handbook of North American Indians*. Ed. William C. Sturtevant. Washington, DC: Smithsonian Inst.

Ritzenthaler, Robert E. "The Building of a Chippewa Indian Birch-Bark Canoe." 1950. *Bulletin* (Public Museum of the City of Milwaukee), 19, no.2:53–99.

– 1978. "Southwestern Chippewa." In *Northeast*, ed. Bruce G. Trigger, 743–59. Vol. 15 of *Handbook of North American Indians*. Ed. William C. Sturtevant. Washington, DC: Smithsonian Inst.

Robbins, Douglas Taylor. 1982. "Preliminary Report on the Stock Cove Site (CkAl-3)." In *Archaeology in Newfoundland and Labrador 1981*, eds. J. Sproull Thomson and C. Thomson, Annual Report 2, 190–209. St John's: Historic Resources Division, Dept. of Culture, Recreation and Youth, Govt. of Newfoundland and Labrador.

– 1985. "Stock Cove, Trinity Bay: The Dorset Occupation of Newfoundland from a Southern Perspective." Master's thesis, Memorial University of Newfoundland, St John's.

– 1986. "'Newfoundland Dorset' Culture?" *Palaeo-Eskimo Cultures in Newfoundland, Labrador and Ungava*. Reports in Archaeology No. 1. 119–24. St John's: Memorial Univ. of Newfoundland.

– 1989. "Regards archéologiques sur les Béothuks de Terre- Neuve." *Recherches Amérindiennes au Québec*. 19, nos.2–3:21–32.

Robinson, Hercules. 1834 "Private Journal Kept on Board HMS 'Favorite,' 1820." *Royal Geographical Society Journal* 4:207–20.

Rogers, Edwards S. 1962. "Notes on Snowshoes among the Montagnais-Naskapi." In *Art and Archaeology Division 1961 Annual*, 57–66. Royal Ontario Museum. Toronto: Univ. of Toronto Press.

– 1963. *The Hunting Group-Hunting Territory Complex among the Mistassini Indians*. Ottawa; National Museum of Canada, Bulletin 195.

– 1967. *Material Culture of the Mistassini*. Ottawa: National Museum of Canada, Bulletin 218.

– 1978. "Southeastern Ojibwa." In *Northeast*, ed. Bruce G. Trigger, 760–71. Vol. 15 of *Handbook of North American Indians*. Ed. William C. Sturtevant. Washington, DC: Smithsonian Inst.

Rogers, Edward S., and Eleanor Leacock. 1981. "Montagnais-Naskapi." In *Subarctic*, ed. June Helm, 169–89. Vol. 6 of *Handbook of North American Indians*. Ed. William C. Sturtevant. Washington, DC: Smithsonian Inst.

Rogers, Edward S., and James G.E. Smith. 1981. "Environment and Culture in the Shield and Mackenzie Borderlands." In *Subarctic*, ed. June Helm, 130–45. Vol. 6 of *Handbook of North American Indians*. Ed. William C. Sturtevant. Washington, DC: Smithsonian Inst.

Rogers, Edward S., and J. Garth Taylor. 1981. "Northern Ojibwa." In *Subarctic*, ed. June Helm, 231–43. Vol. 6 of *Handbook of North American Indians*. Ed. William C. Sturtevant. Washington, DC: Smithsonian Inst.

Rowe, Frederick W. 1977. *Extinction: The Beothuks of Newfoundland*. Toronto: McGraw-Hill Ryerson.

Rowley-Conwy, Peter. 1990. "Settlement Pattern of the Beothuk Indians of Newfoundland: A View from Away." *Canadian Journal of Archaeology* 14, no.1: 13–32.

Royal Gazette, The. 1828. St John's, 21 October.

Rutherford, Douglas E., and William Gilbert. 1992. "An Archaeological Reconaissance of Dildo Arm and Collier Bay, Trinity Bay, Newfoundland." ts. Historic Resources Division, Govt. of Newfoundland and Labrador.

Ryan, D.W.S. 1948. "Relics of a Lost Race." *Atlantic Guardian* 5, no.7: 41–4.

Sagard-Théodat, Gabriel. 1939. *The Long Journey to the Country of the Huron (1632)*. Ed. George M. Wrong. Transl. H.H. Langton. Toronto: Champlain Society, Publication 25.

Salwen, Bert. 1978. "Indians of Southern New England and Long Island: Early Period." In *Northeast*, ed. Bruce G. Trigger, 160–76. Vol. 15 of *Handbook of North American Indians*. Ed. William C. Sturtevant. Washington DC: Smithsonian Inst.

Sanger, Chesley W. 1977. "The Evolution of Sealing and the Spread of Settlement in Northeastern Newfoundland." In *The Peopling of Newfoundland*, ed. John J. Mannion, 136–51. ISER Publ. no. 8. St John's: Memorial Univ. of Newfoundland.

Sapir, Edward. 1949. "Central and North American Languages." *Selected Writings of Edward Sapir*, ed. David G. Mandelbaum, 169–78. Berkeley and Los Angeles: Univ. of California Press.

Sauer, Carl O. 1968. *Northern Mists*. Berkeley and Los Angeles: Univ. of California Press.

Saunders, Douglas. 1988. "Government Indian Agencies in Canada." In *History of Indian-White Relations*, ed. Wilcombe Washburn, 276–83. Vol. 4 of *Handbook of North American Indians*. Ed. William C. Sturtevant. Washington, DC: Smithsonian Inst.

Saunders, Gary L. 1986. *Rattles and Steadies: Memoirs of a Gander Riverman*. St John's: Breakwater Books.

Schonback, Bengt, Birgitta Wallace, and Charles Lindsay. 1976. *Progress Report on Archaeological Fieldwork at L'Anse aux Meadows, June to October, 1975*. Ottawa: Parks Canada Research Bulletin no.33.

Schwarz, Fred A. 1984. "Little Passage Complex in Newfoundland, A Comparative Study of Assemblages." Honours thesis, Department of Anthropology, Memorial University of Newfoundland, St John's.

– 1992a. "Archaeological Investigation in the Newfoundland Interior." Ts. Newfoundland Museum, St John's.

– 1992b. "Archaeological Investigations in the Exploits Basin; Report on the 1992 Field Survey." Ts. Newfoundland Museum, St John's.

"Seals and Salmon: Reports Exaggerated." 1984. *Evening Telegram*, St John's, 3 July.

Seary, Edgar Ronald. 1971. *Place Names of the Avalon Peninsula of the Island of Newfoundland*. Toronto: Univ. of Toronto Press.

Select Committee on Aborigines. [1836] 1968. *Report from the Select Committee on Aborigines (British Settlements) together with Minutes of Evidence, 1836*. Series of British Parliamentary Papers. Vol.1. Anthropology, Aborigines. Dublin: Irish Univ. Press.

Service, Elman R. 1966. *The Hunters*. Englewood Cliffs, NJ: Prentice Hall.

Shevoroshkin, Vitaly. 1990. "The Mother Tongue." *The Sciences* 30, no.3: 20–7.

Simmons, William S. 1978. "Narragansett." In *Northeast*, ed. Bruce G. Trigger, 190–7. Vol. 15 of *Handbook of North American Indians*. Ed. William C. Sturtevant. Washington, DC: Smithsonian Inst.

Simpson, David N. 1984. "The Port au Port Peninsula Archaeology Project: A Preliminary Report." In *Archaeology in Newfoundland and Labrador 1983*, eds. J. Sproull Thomson and C. Thomson, Annual Report 4, 126–41. St John's: Historic Resources Division, Dept. of Culture, Recreation and Youth, Govt. of Newfoundland and Labrador.

– 1986. "Prehistoric Archaeology of the Port au Port Peninsula, Western Newfoundland." Master's thesis, Memorial University of Newfoundland, St John's.

"Sketches of Savage Life: Shaa-naan-dithit." 1836. *Fraser's Magazine for Town and Country* 13, no.75: 316–23.

Skinner, Alanson. 1911. *Notes on the Eastern Cree and Northern Saulteaux*. Anthropology Papers of the American Museum of Natural History, vol. 10, no. 1. New York.

Slobodin, Richard. 1981. "Kutchin." In *Subarctic*, ed. June Helm, 514–32. Vol. 6 of *Handbook of North American Indians*. Ed. William C. Sturtevant. Washington, DC: Smithsonian Inst.

Smallwood, J.R., eds. 1967. *The Book of Newfoundland*. 4 vols. St John's: Newfoundland Book Publisher.

Smith, Phillip E.L. 1986. "Beothuks and Methodists." *Acadiensis* 16, no.1: 118–35.

Smith, T. Watson. 1890. *History of the Methodist Church*. Halifax: S.F. Huestis.

Smith, Waldo E.L. 1961. *The Navy and its Chaplains in the Days of Sail*. Toronto: Ryerson Press.

Snow, Jeanne H. 1981. "Ingalic." In *Subarctic*, ed. June Helm, 602–17. Vol. 6 of *Handbook of North American Indians*. Ed. William C. Sturtevant. Washington, DC: Smithsonian Inst.

Speck, Frank G. 1919. "Functions of Wampum among the Eastern Algonkian." *Memoirs of the American Anthropological Association*. Vol. 6, 3–71. Reprint. New York: Kraus Rpt, 1964.

– 1922. *Beothuk and Micmac*. Indian Notes and Monographs. New York: Museum of the American Indian, Heye Foundation.

– 1926. "Culture Problems in northeastern North America." *American Philosophical Society Proceedings* 65:272–311.

– 1931. "Montagnais-Naskapi Bands and Early Eskimo Distribution in the Labrador Peninsula." *American Anthropology*, n.s. 33, no.4: 557–600.

– 1935. *Naskapi*. Norman, OK: Univ. of Oklahoma Press. Reprint. 1977.

– 1936. "Inland Eskimo Bands of Labrador." In *Essays in Anthropology in Honour of Alfred Louis Kroeber*, ed. Robert H. Lowie. 313–30. Berkeley and Los Angeles: Univ. of California Press. Reprint. Freeport, NY: Books for Libraries Press, 1968.

– 1937. *Montagnais Art in Birch Bark: A Circumpolar Trait*. Indian Notes and Monographs, vol. 11, 2. New York: Museum of the American Indian Heye Foundation.

– 1940. *Penobscot Man*. Philadelphia: Univ. of Pennsylvania Press.

Spindler, Louise S. 1978. "Menominee." In *Northeast*, ed. Bruce G. Trigger, 708–24. Vol. 15 of *Handbook of North American Indians*. Ed. William C. Sturtevant. Washington, DC: Smithsonian Inst.

Sproull Thomson, Jane. 1982. "Investigations at Red Indian Lake." In *Archaeology in Newfoundland and Labrador 1981*, eds. J. Sproull Thomson and C. Thomson, Annual Report 2, 174–89. St John's: Historic Resources Division, Dept. of Culture, Recreation and Youth, Govt. of Newfoundland and Labrador.

– 1984. "Shoewan and Guinyabutt: Beothuk Containers." *Newfoundland Quarterly* 80, no.1: 17–20.

Sproull Thomson, J., and C. Thomson, eds. 1982–86. *Archaeology in Newfoundland and Labrador.* Annual reports. St John's: Newfoundland Museum, Historic Resources Division, Govt. of Newfoundland and Labrador.

Stefansson, Viljalhmur. 1938. *The Three Voyages by Martin Frobisher*. 2 vols. London: Argonaut Press.

Steinbring, Jack H. 1981. "Saulteaux of Lake Winnipeg." In *Subarctic*, ed. June Helm, 244–55. Vol. 6 of *Handbook of North American Indians*. Ed. William C. Sturtevant. Washington, DC: Smithsonian Inst.

Stephen, L., and S. Lee, eds. 1921–22. *Dictionary of National Biography*. 22 vols. London: Oxford Univ. Press. Reprint. 1949–50.

Steward Julien H., and F.M. Setzler. 1938. "Function and Configuration in Archaeology." *American Antiquity* 4:4–10.

Story, George, W.J. Kirwin, and J.D.A. Widdowson, comps. 1982. *Dictionary of Newfoundland English*. Toronto: Univ. of Toronto Press.

Stroud, Harold. 1976. "A Brief History of Glovertown." Ms. CNS.

Sturtevant, William C. 1976. "First Visual Images." In *First Images of America*, ed. F. Chiapelli, 417–54. Berkeley, CA: Univ. of California Press.

– 1978. "Oklahoma Seneca-Cayuga." In *Northeast*, ed. Bruce G. Trigger, 537–43. Vol. 15 of *Handbook of North American Indians*. Ed. William C. Sturtevant. Washington, DC: Smithsonian Inst.

– 1980. "The First Inuit Depiction by Europeans." *Études/Inuit/Studies* 4, nos.1–2:47–9.

Sturtevant, William C., ed. *Handbook of North American Indians*. 20 vols. Washington, DC: Smithsonian Inst.

Such, Peter. 1973. *Riverrun*. Toronto, Vancouver: Clarke, Irwin.

Tanner, Adrian. 1979. *Bringing Home Animals*. ISER Publ. 23, St John's: Memorial Univ. of Newfoundland.

Tanner, Vaino. 1947. *Outlines of the Geography, Life and Customs of Newfoundland and Labrador*. 3d ed. Cambridge: Cambridge Univ. Press.

Taylor, J. Garth. 1964a. "An Archaeological Survey of Red Indian Lake and the Exploits River, Newfoundland." Ts. 687, National Museums of Canada, Archaeological Survey of Canada.

– 1964b. "Beothuk Archaeological Survey Notes (DfBa-1)." Ts. 744, National Museums of Canada, Archaeological Survey of Canada.

– 1980. "The Inuit of Southern Quebec-Labrador: Reviewing the Evidence."*Études/Inuit/Studies* 4, nos.1–2:185–94.

Taylor, V.R. 1985. *The Early Atlantic Salmon Fishery in Newfoundland and Labrador*. Canadian Special Publication of Fisheries and Aquatic Sciences 76. Ottawa: Dept. of Fisheries and Oceans.

Thevet, Andrevv. 1568. *The New Found World, or Antarctike, wherin is Contained Wonderful and Strange Things ...* English trans. London: Henrie Bynneman for Thomas Hacket.

Thompson, Fred F. 1961. *The French Shore Problem in Newfoundland: An Imperial Study*. Toronto: Univ. of Toronto Press.

Thompson, H.P. 1951. *Into All Lands. The History of the Society for the Propagation of the Gospel in Foreign Parts, 1701–1950*. London: Society for Promotion of Christian Knowledge.

Thompson, Judy. 1987. "No Little Variety of Ornament." In *The Spirit Sings; A Catalogued the Exhibition*, 133–68. Toronto: McClellan and Stewart and Glenbow Museum.

Thompson, Stith. 1932–36. *Motif-Index of Folk-Literature; A Classification of Narrative Elements in Folktales, Ballads, Myths, Fables, Mediaeval Romances, Exempla, Fabliaux, Jest-Books, and Local Legends*. 6 vols. Rev. ed. Bloomington: Indiana University Press, 1955–58.

Thomson, Callum. 1982. "An Archaeological Survey of the Exploits River from Red Indian Lake to Grand Falls, May 29 to June 19, 1982." Ts. Newfoundland Museum, St John's.

– 1983. "An Archaeological Survey of the Exploits River from Red Indian Lake to Grand Falls, May 29-June 19, 1982." In *Archaeology in Newfoundland and Labrador 1982*, eds. J. Sproull Thomson and C. Thomson, Annual Report 3, 161–75. St John's: Historic Resources Division, Dept. of Culture, Recreation and Youth, Govt. of Newfoundland and Labrador.

– 1989. "Terrestrial Archaeological Survey and Underwater Reconnaissance of Great Mosquito Cove, Bull Arm, Trinity Bay. A Summary of Heritage Resources Projects in Newfoundland and Labrador in 1989."Ts. Newfoundland Museum, St John's.

– 1990a. "Report of a Stage Two Terrestrial Archaeological Survey of Great Mosquito Cove, Trinity Bay, Newfoundland." Ts. LeDrew, Fudge, and Assoc., Halifax, and Newfoundland Museum, St John's.

– 1990b. "Report of the Stage Three Archaeological Salvage Excavation of CkAl-8 at Great Mosquito Cove, Bull Arm, Trinity Bay." Ts. LeDrew, Fudge and Assoc., Halifax, and Newfoundland Museum, St John's.

Thomson, Callum, and Jane Sproull Thomson, eds. 1989. *Archaeology in Newfoundland and Labrador*. Annual Report. St John's: Newfoundland Museum, Historic Resources Division, Govt. of Newfoundland and Labrador.

Thwaites, Reuben Gold, ed. 1896–1901. *The Jesuit Relations and Allied documents*. 73 vols. Cleveland, OH: Burroughs Bros. Reprint. New York: Pageant Book Co., 1959.

Tobey, Margaret L. 1981. "Carrier." In *Subarctic*, ed. June Helm, 413–32. Vol. 6 of *Handbook of American Indians*. Ed. William C. Sturtevant. Washington, DC: Smithsonian Inst.

Tocque, Philip. 1846. *Wandering Thoughts*. London: Thomas Richardson and Son.

– 1878. *Newfoundland as It Is in 1877*. Toronto: John B. Magurn.

– 1893. "The Last of the Aborigines. A Splendid Picture of Mary March Taken." *Evening Telegram*, St John's, 12 July.

Tompkins, Edward. 1986. *Newfoundland's Interior Explored*. St John's: Newfoundland Museum.

– 1978. "The League of the Iroquois: Its History, Politics, and Ritual." In *Northeast*, ed. Bruce G. Trigger, 418–41. Vol. 15 of *Handbook of North American Indians*. Ed. William C. Sturtevant. Washington, DC: Smithsonian Inst.

Townsend, Charles Wendell. 1911. *Captain Cartwright and his Labrador Journal*. Boston: D. Estes.

Townsend, Joan B. 1981. "Tanaina." In *Subarctic*, ed. June Helm, 623–40. Vol. 6 of *Handbook of North American Indians*. Ed. William C. Sturtevant. Washington, DC: Smithsonian Inst.

Trelease, A.W. 1960. *Indian Affairs in Colonial New York in the Seventeenth Century*. Ithaca: Cornell Univ. Press.

Trigger, Bruce G. 1978. "Early Iroquoian Contacts with Europeans." In *Northeast*, ed. Bruce G. Trigger 344–56. Vol. 15 of *Handbook of North American Indians*. Ed. William C. Sturtevant. Washington, DC: Smithsonian, Inst.

– 1985. *Natives and Newcomers: Canada's "Heroic Age" Reconsidered*. Montreal and Kingston: McGill-Queens Univ. Press.

Trigger, Bruce, ed. *Northeast*. Vol. 15 of *Handbook of North American Indians*, ed. William C. Sturtevant. 20 vols. Washington, DC: Smithsonian Inst.

Trudel, F. 1978. "The Inuit of Southern Labrador and the Development of French Sedentary Fisheries (1700–1760)." *Canadian Ethnology Society, Papers from The Fourth Annual Congress 1977*. Ottawa: National Museum of Man, Mercury Series, Canadian Ethnology Service, Paper No. 40, 99–121.

– 1980. "Les relations entre les Français et les Inuit au Labrador méridional, 1660–1760." *Études/Inuit/Studies* 4, nos.1–2:135–46.

Tuck, James A. 1976a. *Ancient People of Port au Choix*. ISER Publ. 17. St John's: Memorial Univ. of Newfoundland.

– 1976b. *Newfoundland and Labrador Prehistory*. Ottawa: National Museum of Man, National Museums of Canada.

– 1976c. "Lithic Artifacts from L'Anse aux Meadows, NF." Ts. National Historic Parks and Sites Branch, Parks Canada, Ottawa.

– 1978a. "Regional Cultural Development, 3000 to 300 BC." In *Northeast*, ed. Bruce G. Trigger, 28–43. Vol. 15 of *Handbook of North American Indians*. Ed. William C. Sturtevant. Washington, DC: Smithsonian Inst.

– 1978b. "Archaic Burial Ceremonialism in the 'Far Northeast.' " In *Essays in Northeastern Anthropology in Memory of Marian E. White*, eds. W.E. Engelbrecht and Donald K. Grayson, 67–77. Occasional Publications in Northeastern Anthropology 5. Rindge, NH: Franklin Pierce College.

– 1978c. "Excavations at Cow Head, Newfoundland: An Interim Report." *Études/Inuit/Studies* 2, no.1:138–41.

– 1980. "An Archaeological Survey of Terra Nova National Park. Prepared for Parks Canada Historic Properties." Ts. Newfoundland Museum, St John's.

– 1982. "Prehistoric Archaeology in Atlantic Canada since 1975." *Canadian Journal of Archaeology* 6: 201–18.

– 1983. "Excavations at Shambler's Cove – 1982: A Stage Three Impact Report." Ts. Newfoundland Museum, St John's.

– 1984a. *Maritime Provinces Prehistory*. Ottawa: National Museum of Man, National Museums of Canada.

– 1984b. "Historic Resources Evaluation of the Argentia Offshore Support Base Site." Ts. Argentia Development Corp., St John's, and Newfoundland Museum.

– 1985. "1984 Excavations at Red Bay, Labrador." In *Archaeology in Newfoundland and Labrador 1984*, eds. J. Sproull Thomson and C. Thomson, Annual Report 5, 224–47. St John's: Historic Resources Division, Dept. of Culture, Recreation and Youth, Govt. of Newfoundland and Labrador.

– 1987. "European-Native Contacts in the Strait of Belle Isle, Labrador." In *Between Greenland and America; Cross Cultural Contacts and the Environment in the Baffin Bay Area*, eds. Louwrens Hacquebord and Richard Vaughan, 61–74. Groningen: Arctic Centre, Univ. of Groningen.

– 1989a. "Excavations at Red Bay, Labrador – 1986." In *Archaeology in Newfoundland and Labrador 1986*, eds. C. Thomson and J. Sproull Thomson, Annual Report 7, 213–

37. St John's: Newfoundland Museum, Historic Resources Division, Dept. of Municipal and Provincial Affairs, Govt. of Newfoundland and Labrador.

– 1989b. "Excavations at Ferryland, Newfoundland – 1986." In *Archaeology in Newfoundland and Labrador 1986*, eds. C. Thomsom and J. Sproull Thomson, Annual Report 7, 296–307. St John's: Newfoundland Museum, Historic Resources Division, Dept. of Municipal and Provincial Affairs, Govt. of Newfoundland and Labrador.

– 1991. "The Beothuks." In *Micropaedia*, ed. Warren E. Preece, 116. Chicago: Encyclopaedia Britannica Educational Corp.

– 1992. "Some Speculations on Language and Prehistory in Newfoundland and Labrador." Paper presented at the Atlantic Canada Studies Conference, May, 1992, St John's, Newfoundland.

– 1993. "Archaeology at Ferryland, Newfoundland." *Newfoundland Studies* 9, no.2:194–310.

Tuck James A., and Ralph T. Pastore. 1985. "A Nice Place to Visit But ... Prehistoric Human Extinctions on the Island of Newfoundland." *Canadian Journal of Archaeology* 9, no.1: 69–79.

Tuck James A., and William Fitzhugh. 1986. "Palaeo-Eskimo Traditions of Newfoundland and Labrador: A Re-Appraisal." *Palaeo-Eskimo Cultures in Newfoundland, Labrador and Ungava*. Reports in Archaeology No. 1, 161–8. St John's: Memorial Univ. of Newfoundland.

Turner, Lucien M. 1894. *Ethnology of the Ungava District, Hudson Bay Territory. Indians and Eskimos in the Quebec-Labrador Peninsula*, ed. John Murdoch, 159–350. Eleventh Report of the Bureau of Ethnology for the year 1889–90. Washington, DC: Smithsonian Inst. Reprint. Quebec: Presses Coméditex, 1979.

Ubelaker, Douglas H. 1976. "The Sources and Methodology for Mooney's Estimates." In *The Native Population of the Americas in 1492*, ed. W.M. Denevan, 243–92. Madison, WI: Univ. of Wisconsin Press.

– 1988. "North American Indian Population Size, AD 1500 to 1985." *American Journal of Physical Anthropology* 77, no.3: 289–94.

Upton, L.F.S. 1977a. "The Extermination of the Beothucks of Newfoundland." *The Canadian Historical Review* 58, no.2: 133–53.

– 1977b. "A portrait by Shanawdithit." *The Newfoundland Quarterly* 72, no.2:44.

– 1978. "The Beothucks: Questions and Answers." *Acadiensis* 7 no.2: 150–5.

– 1979. *Micmac and Colonists, Micmac-White Relations in the Maritimes 1713–1867*. Vancouver: Univ. of British Columbia Press.

Wallace, Birgitta. 1977. *The 1976 Excavations at L'Anse aux Meadows, Newfoundland*. Ottawa: Parks Canada Research Bulletin no.67.

Wallis, Wilson D., and Ruth S. Wallis. 1955. *The Micmac Indians of Eastern Canada*. Minneapolis: Univ. of Minnesota Press.

Washburn, Wilcombe, ed. 1988. *History of Indian-White Relations*. Vol. 4 of *Handbook of North American Indians*. Ed. William C. Sturtevant. Washington, DC: Smithsonian Inst.

Washburne, Heluiz Chandler and Anauta. 1940. *Land of the Good Shadows*. New York: The John Day Co.

Webber, George. 1851. *"The Last of the Aborigines": A Poem Founded on Facts in Four Cantos*. St John's: Morning Post. Reprint. *Canadian Poetry* 2 (Spring/Summer 1978): 76–98.

Wetzel, Jerry, Pat Anderson, and Douglas Sanders. 1980. "Freedom to Live Our Own Way in Our Own Land." Ed. Peter J. Usher. Conne River: Ktaqamkuk Ilnui Saqimawoutie and the Conne River Indian Band Council.

Wherrett, G.J. 1977. *The Miracle of the Empty Beds. A History of TB in Canada*. Toronto: Univ. of Toronto Press.

Whitbourne, Capt. Richard. 1622. *A Discourse and Discovery of New-Found-Land*. London: Kingston.

White, Marian E. 1978. "Neutral and Wenro." In *Northeast*, ed. Bruce G. Trigger, 407–11. Vol. 15 of *Handbook of North American Indians*. Ed. William C. Sturtevant. Washington, DC: Smithsonian Inst.

Whitehead, Ruth Holmes. 1980. *Elitekey, Micmac Material Culture from 1600 AD to the Present*. Halifax: Nova Scotia Museum.

– 1984. "Everything They Make and Wear." In *12.000 Years of Maine Native History*, ed. Bruce J. Bourque. Augusta: Maine State Museum.

– 1987a. "I Have Lived Here since the World Began." In *The Spirit Sings*, 17–49. Toronto: McClelland and Stewart and Glenbow Museum.

– 1987b. "East Coast." In *The Spirit Sings; A Catalogue of the Exhibition*, 11–36. Toronto: McClelland and Stewart and Glenbow Museum.

– 1988. *Stories from the Six Worlds: Micmac Legends*. Halifax: Nimbus Publ.

– 1993. *Nova Scotia: The Protohistoric Period 1500–1630*. Halifax: Nova Scotia Museum Curatorial Report No.75.

Whitelaw, Marjory, ed. 1978. *The Dalhousie Journals*. N.p.: Oberon Press.

Wied, Maximilian zu, and Karl Bodmer. 1976. *People of the First Man*. New York: E.P. Dutton.

Williams, Alan F. 1987. *Father Baudoin's War: D'Iberville's Campaign in Acadia and Newfoundland, 1696, 1697*. Ed. Alan G. Macpherson. St John's: Dept. of Geography, Memorial Univ. of Newfoundland.

Williams, Griffith. 1765. *An Account of Newfoundland with the Nature of Its Trade, and Method of Carrying on the Fishery*. London, Temple Bar: Printed and sold by W. Owen.

Williamson, James Alexander. 1962. *The Cabot Voyages and Bristol Explorations under Henry VII*. Cambridge: Hakluyt Society Publications, 2d ser., vol. 120.

Wilson, Brian, and David Miller, eds. and trans. 1973. *English Stories from Herodotus*. London: Oxford Univ. Press.

Wilson, William. 1839. "Aborigines of Newfoundland." *Wesleyan Methodist Magazine* 62: 469–70.

– 1866. *Newfoundland and its Missionaries*. Halifax: Dakind Metcalf.

Wilton, Carol, ed. 1992. *Change and Continuity*. Toronto, Montreal: McGraw-Hill Ryerson.

Wintemberg, W.J. 1928. "The Discovery of Two Human Skeletons under the Indian Cliff between Bradore and Blanc Sablon, in 1888." Ts.: National Museums of Canada, Archaeological Survey of Canada.

– 1936. "Shell Beads of the Beothuk Indians." *Transactions of the Royal Society of Canada*, Sect. 2: 23–6.

Winter, Keith. 1975. *Shananditti – The Last of the Beothucks*. Vancouver: J.J. Douglas.

Wissler, Clark. 1915. "Costumes of the Plains Indians." *Anthropological Paper of the American Museum of Natural History* 17, no.2: 39–91.

Wix, Edward. 1836. *Six months of a Newfoundland Missionary's Journal, from February to August 1835*. London: Smith, Elder.

Wright, James W. 1972. *The Shield Archaic*. National Museum of Man Publication in Archaeology 3. Ottawa: National Museums of Canada.

Wroth, Lawrence C. 1970. *The Voyages of Giovannida Verrazzano, 1524–1528*. New Haven, CT: Yale Univ. Press.

Index

Note to readers: The abbreviations n, t, and f indicate note number(s), tables, and figures. Bold page references indicate that the main discussion of the subject is on those pages.

Index

Note to readers: The abbreviations n, t, and f indicate note number(s), tables, and figures. Bold page references indicate that the main discussion of the subject is on those pages.